VOLKSWAGEN

GOLF/JETTA/CABRIOLET
1990-99 REPAIR MANUAL

CHILTON'S

CEO	Rick Van Dalen
President	Dean F. Morgantini, S.A.E.
Vice President–Finance	Barry L. Beck
Vice President–Sales	Glenn D. Potere
Executive Editor	Kevin M. G. Maher, A.S.E.
Manager–Consumer Automotive	Richard Schwartz, A.S.E.
Manager–Professional Automotive	Richard J. Rivele
Manager–Marine/Recreation	James R. Marotta, A.S.E.
Production Specialist	Melinda Possinger
Project Managers	Tim Crain, A.S.E., Thomas A. Mellon, A.S.E., S.A.E., Eric Michael Mihalyi, A.S.E., S.T.S., S.A.E., Christine L. Sheeky, S.A.E., Richard T. Smith, Ron Webb
Schematics Editors	Christopher G. Ritchie, A.S.E., S.A.E., S.T.S., Stephanie A. Spunt
Editor	Paul T. DeSanto, A.S.E., S.A.E.

CHILTON *Automotive Books*

PUBLISHED BY **W. G. NICHOLS, INC.**

Manufactured in USA
© 2000 W. G. Nichols, Inc.
1025 Andrew Drive
West Chester, PA 19380
ISBN 0-8019-9122-6
Library of Congress Catalog Card No. 00-132516
2345678901 9876543210

www.chiltononline.com

Contents

Contents

See last page for information on additional titles

SAFETY NOTICE

Proper service and repair procedures are vital to the safe, reliable operation of all motor vehicles, as well as the personal safety of those performing repairs. This manual outlines procedures for servicing and repairing vehicles using safe, effective methods. The procedures contain ma NOTES, CAUTIONS and WARNINGS which should be followed, along with standard procedures to eliminate the possibility of personal injury o improper service which could damage the vehicle or compromise its safety.

It is important to note that repair procedures and techniques, tools and parts for servicing motor vehicles, as well as the skill and experience the individual performing the work vary widely. It is not possible to anticipate all of the conceivable ways or conditions under which vehicles m be serviced, or to provide cautions as to all possible hazards that may result. Standard and accepted safety precautions and equipment should used when handling toxic or flammable fluids, and safety goggles or other protection should be used during cutting, grinding, chiseling, pryin or any other process that can cause material removal or projectiles.

Some procedures require the use of tools specially designed for a specific purpose. Before substituting another tool or procedure, you must completely satisfied that neither your personal safety, nor the performance of the vehicle will be endangered.

Although information in this manual is based on industry sources and is complete as possible at the time of publication, the possibility exis that some car manufacturers made later changes which could not be included here. While striving for total accuracy, Nichols Publishing cannot assume responsibility for any errors, changes or omissions that may occur in the compilation of this data.

PART NUMBERS

Part numbers listed in this reference are not recommendations by Nichols Publishing for any product brand name. They are references that be used with interchange manuals and aftermarket supplier catalogs to locate each brand supplier's discrete part number.

SPECIAL TOOLS

Special tools are recommended by the vehicle manufacturer to perform their specific job. Use has been kept to a minimum, but where absolutely necessary, they are referred to in the text by the part number of the tool manufacturer. These tools can be purchased, under the appro priate part number, from your local dealer or regional distributor, or an equivalent tool can be purchased locally from a tool supplier or parts ou let. Before substituting any tool for the one recommended, read the SAFETY NOTICE at the top of this page.

ACKNOWLEDGMENTS

Nichols Publishing expresses appreciation to Volkswagen of America, Ltd. for their generous assistance.

Nichols Publishing would like to express thanks to all of the fine companies who participate in the production of our books:
- Hand tools supplied by Craftsman are used during all phases of our vehicle teardown and photography.
- Many of the fine specialty tools used in our procedures were provided courtesy of Lisle Corporation.
- Lincoln Automotive Products (1 Lincoln Way, St. Louis, MO 63120) has provided their industrial shop equipment, including jacks (engir transmission and floor), engine stands, fluid and lubrication tools, as well as shop presses.
- Rotary Lifts (1-800-640-5438 or www.Rotary-Lift.com), the largest automobile lift manufacturer in the world, offering the biggest variety surface and in-ground lifts available, has fulfilled our shop's lift needs.
- Much of our shop's electronic testing equipment was supplied by Universal Enterprises Inc. (UEI).
- Safety-Kleen Systems Inc. has provided parts cleaning stations and assistance with environmentally sound disposal of residual wastes.
- United Gilsonite Laboratories (UGL), manufacturer of Drylok® concrete floor paint, has provided materials and expertise for the coating a protection of our shop floor.

1

GENERAL INFORMATION AND MAINTENANCE

HOW TO USE THIS BOOK

Chilton's Total Car Care for Volkswagen Golf, Jetta, Fox, Cabrio, and Cabriolet is intended to help you learn more about your car and save you money on its upkeep and operation.

The first two sections of this manual are likely to be the most used, since they contain basic maintenance procedures and tune-up information. Later sections deal with the more complex systems of your car, and are covered to the extent that the average do-it-yourselfer can perform seemingly difficult operations with confidence.

A secondary purpose of this book is a reference for owners who want to understand their vehicle and/or their mechanics better. In this case, no tools at all are required.

This book will not explain such things as rebuilding a differential for the simple reason that the expertise required and the investment in special tools make this task uneconomical. It will, however, give you detailed instructions to help you change your own brake pads and shoes, replace spark plugs, and perform many more jobs that can save you money, give you personal satisfaction and help you avoid expensive problems.

Where To Begin

Before removing any bolts, read through the **entire** procedure. This will give you the overall view of what tools and supplies will be required. There is nothing more frustrating than having to walk to the bus stop on Monday morning because you were short one bolt on Sunday afternoon. So read ahead and plan ahead. Each operation should be approached logically and all procedures thoroughly understood before attempting any work.

All sections contain adjustments, maintenance, removal and installation procedures, and in some cases, repair or overhaul procedures. When repair is not considered practical, we tell you how to remove the part and then how to install the new or rebuilt replacement. In this way, you at least save labor costs. "Backyard" repair of some components is just not practical.

Avoiding Trouble

Many procedures in this book require you to "label and disconnect . . ." a group of lines, hoses or wires. Don't be lulled into thinking you can remember where everything goes—you won't. If you hook up vacuum or fuel lines incorrectly, the vehicle may run poorly, if at all. If you hook up electrical wiring incorrectly, you may instantly learn a very expensive lesson.

You don't need to know the official or engineering name for each hose or line. A piece of masking tape on the hose and a piece on its fitting will allow you to assign your own label such as the letter A or a short name. As long as you remember your own code, the lines can be reconnected by matching similar letters or names. Do remember that tape will dissolve in gasoline or other fluids; if a component is to be washed or cleaned, use another method of identification. A permanent felt-tipped marker or a metal scribe can be very handy for marking metal parts. Remove any tape or paper labels after assembly.

Maintenance Or Repair?

It's necessary to mention the difference between maintenance and repair. Maintenance includes routine inspections, adjustments, and replacement of parts which show signs of normal wear. Maintenance compensates for wear or deterioration. Repair implies that something has broken or is not working. A need for repair is often caused by lack of maintenance. Example: draining and refilling the automatic transmission fluid is maintenance recommended by the manufacturer at specific mileage intervals. Failure to do this can shorten the life of the transaxle, requiring very expensive repairs. While no maintenance program can prevent items from breaking or wearing out, a general rule can be stated: MAINTENANCE IS CHEAPER THAN REPAIR.

Two basic mechanic's rules should be mentioned here. First, whenever the left side of the vehicle or engine is referred to, it is meant to specify the driver's side. Conversely, the right side of the vehicle means the passenger's side. Second, screws and bolts are removed by turning counterclockwise, and tightened by turning clockwise unless specifically noted.

Safety is always the most important rule. Constantly be aware of the dangers involved in working on an automobile and take the proper precautions. See the information in this section regarding SERVICING YOUR VEHICLE SAFELY and the SAFETY NOTICE on the acknowledgment page.

Avoiding The Most Common Mistakes

♦ See Figure 1

Pay attention to the instructions provided. There are three common mistakes in mechanical work:

• Incorrect order of assembly, disassembly or adjustment. When taking something apart or putting it together, performing steps in the wrong order usually just costs you extra time; however, it CAN break something. Read the entire procedure before beginning disassembly. Perform everything in the order in which the instructions say you should, even if you can't immediately see a reason for it. When you're taking apart something that is very intricate, you might want to draw a picture of how it looks when assembled at one point in order to make sure you get everything back in its proper position.

• Overtorquing (or undertorquing). While it is more common for overtorquing to cause damage, undertorquing may allow a fastener to vibrate loose causing serious damage. Especially when dealing with aluminum parts, pay attention to torque specifications and utilize a torque wrench in assembly. If a torque figure is not available, remember that if you are using the right tool to perform the job, you will probably not have to strain yourself to get a fastener tight enough. The pitch of most threads is so slight that the tension you put on the wrench will be multiplied many times in actual force on what you are tightening. A good example of how critical torque is can be seen in the case of spark plug installation, especially where you are putting the plug into an aluminum cylinder head. Too little torque can fail to crush the gasket, causing leakage of combustion gases and consequent overheating of the plug and engine parts. Too much torque can damage the threads or distort the plug, changing the spark gap.

There are many commercial products available for ensuring that fasteners won't come loose, even if they are not torqued just right (a very common brand is Loctite®). If you're worried about getting something together tight enough to hold, but loose enough to avoid mechanical damage during assembly, one of these products might offer substantial insurance (as well as peace-of-mind). Before choosing a threadlocking compound, read the label on the package and make sure the product is compatible with the materials, fluids, etc. involved.

• Crossthreading. This occurs when a part such as a bolt is screwed into a nut or casting at the wrong angle and forced. Crossthreading is more likely to occur if access is difficult. It helps to clean and lubricate fasteners, then to start threading the bolt, spark plug, etc. with your fingers. If you encounter resistance, unscrew the part and start over again at a different angle until it can be inserted and turned several times without much effort. Keep in mind that many parts, especially spark plugs, have tapered threads, so that gentle turning will automatically bring the part you're threading to the proper angle. Don't put a wrench on the part until it's been tightened a couple of turns by hand. If you suddenly encounter resistance, and the part has not seated fully, don't force it. Pull it back out to make sure it's clean and threading properly.

Be sure to take your time and be patient, and always plan ahead. Allow yourself ample time to perform repairs and maintenance. You may find maintaining your car a satisfying and enjoyable experience.

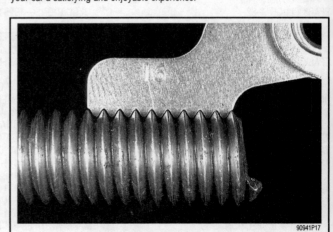

90941P17

Fig. 1 Use a thread pitch gauge to get an accurate measurement of a bolts threads if it needs to be replaced

TOOLS AND EQUIPMENT

▶ **See Figures 2 thru 16**

Naturally, without the proper tools and equipment it is impossible to properly service your vehicle. It would also be virtually impossible to catalog every tool that you would need to perform all of the operations in this book. Of course, It would be unwise for the amateur to rush out and buy an expensive set of tools on the theory that he/she may need one or more of them at some time.

The best approach is to proceed slowly, gathering a good quality set of those tools that are used most frequently. Don't be misled by the low cost of bargain tools. It is far better to spend a little more for better quality. Forged wrenches, 6 or 12-point sockets and fine tooth ratchets are by far preferable to their less expensive counterparts. As any good mechanic can tell you, there are few worse experiences than trying to work on a vehicle with bad tools. Your monetary savings will be far outweighed by frustration and mangled knuckles.

Begin accumulating those tools that are used most frequently: those associated with routine maintenance and tune-up. In addition to the normal assortment of screwdrivers and pliers, you should have the following tools:

• Wrenches/sockets and combination open end/box end wrenches in sizes from ⅛ –¾ in. or 3–19mm, as well as a ¹³⁄₁₆ in. or ⅝ in. spark plug socket (depending on plug type).

➡ **If possible, buy various length socket drive extensions. Universal-joint and wobble extensions can be extremely useful, but be careful when using them, as they can change the amount of torque applied to the socket.**

• Jackstands for support.
• Oil filter wrench.
• Spout or funnel for pouring fluids.

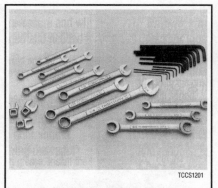
Fig. 2 All but the most basic procedures will require an assortment of ratchets and sockets

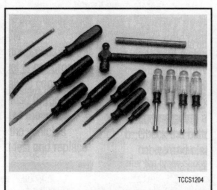
Fig. 3 In addition to ratchets, a good set of wrenches and hex keys will be necessary

Fig. 4 A hydraulic floor jack and a set of jackstands are essential for lifting and supporting the vehicle

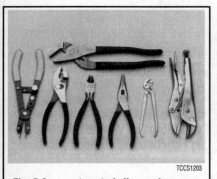
Fig. 5 An assortment of pliers, grippers and cutters will be handy for old rusted parts and stripped bolt heads

Fig. 6 Various drivers, chisels and prybars are great tools to have in your toolbox

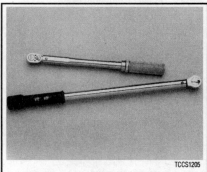
Fig. 7 Many repairs will require the use of a torque wrench to assure the components are properly fastened

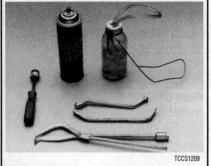
Fig. 8 Although not always necessary, using specialized brake tools will save time

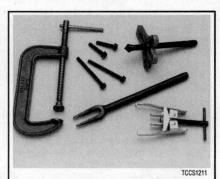
Fig. 9 A few inexpensive lubrication tools will make maintenance easier

Fig. 10 Various pullers, clamps and separator tools are needed for many larger, more complicated repairs

Fig. 11 A variety of tools and gauges should be used for spark plug gapping and installation

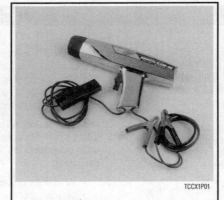

Fig. 12 Inductive type timing light

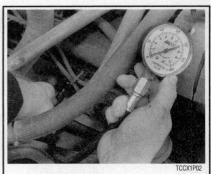

Fig. 13 A screw-in type compression gauge is recommended for compression testing

Fig. 14 A vacuum/pressure tester is necessary for many testing procedures

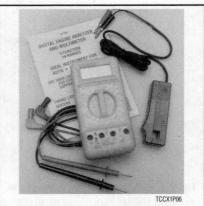

Fig. 15 Most modern automotive multimeters incorporate many helpful features

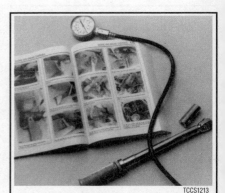

Fig. 16 Proper information is vital, so always have a Chilton Total Car Care manual handy

• Grease gun for chassis lubrication (unless your vehicle is not equipped with any grease fittings—for details, please refer to information on Fluids and Lubricants, later in this section).

• Hydrometer for checking the battery (unless equipped with a sealed, maintenance-free battery).

• A container for draining oil and other fluids.

• Rags for wiping up the inevitable mess.

In addition to the above items there are several others that are not absolutely necessary, but handy to have around. These include Oil Dry® (or an equivalent oil absorbent gravel—such as cat litter) and the usual supply of lubricants, antifreeze and fluids, although these can be purchased as needed. This is a basic list for routine maintenance, but only your personal needs and desire can accurately determine your list of tools.

After performing a few projects on the vehicle, you'll be amazed at the other tools and non-tools on your workbench. Some useful household items are: a large turkey baster or siphon, empty coffee cans and ice trays (to store parts), ball of twine, electrical tape for wiring, small rolls of colored tape for tagging lines or hoses, markers and pens, a note pad, golf tees (for plugging vacuum lines), metal coat hangers or a roll of mechanic's wire (to hold things out of the way), dental pick or similar long, pointed probe, a strong magnet, and a small mirror (to see into recesses and under manifolds).

A more advanced set of tools, suitable for tune-up work, can be drawn up easily. While the tools are slightly more sophisticated, they need not be outrageously expensive. There are several inexpensive tach/dwell meters on the market that are every bit as good for the average mechanic as a professional model. Just be sure that it goes to a least 1200–1500 rpm on the tach scale and that it works on 4, 6 and 8-cylinder engines. The key to these purchases is to make them with an eye towards adaptability and wide range. A basic list of tune-up tools could include:

• Tach/dwell meter.

• Spark plug wrench and gapping tool.

• Feeler gauges for valve adjustment.

• Timing light.

The choice of a timing light should be made carefully. A light which works on the DC current supplied by the vehicle's battery is the best choice; it should have a xenon tube for brightness. On any vehicle with an electronic ignition system, a timing light with an inductive pickup that clamps around the No. 1 spark plug cable is preferred.

In addition to these basic tools, there are several other tools and gauges you may find useful. These include:

• Compression gauge. The screw-in type is slower to use, but eliminates the possibility of a faulty reading due to escaping pressure.

• Manifold vacuum gauge.

• 12V test light.

• A combination volt/ohmmeter

• Induction Ammeter. This is used for determining whether or not there is current in a wire. These are handy for use if a wire is broken somewhere in a wiring harness.

As a final note, you will probably find a torque wrench necessary for all but the most basic work. The beam type models are perfectly adequate, although the newer click types (breakaway) are easier to use. The click type torque wrenches tend to be more expensive. Also keep in mind that all types of torque wrenches should be periodically checked and/or recalibrated. You will have to decide for yourself which better fits your pocketbook, and purpose.

Special Tools

Normally, the use of special factory tools is avoided for repair procedures, since these are not readily available for the do-it-yourself mechanic. When it is possible to perform the job with more commonly available tools, it will be pointed out, but occasionally, a special tool was designed to perform a specific function and should be used. Before substituting another tool, you should be convinced that neither your safety nor the performance of the vehicle will be compromised.

Special tools can usually be purchased from an automotive parts store or from your nearest Volkswagen dealer. In some cases special tools may be available directly from the tool manufacturer.

IN A SPORT THAT DEMANDS NERVES BE MADE OF STEEL, YOU CAN IMAGINE HOW TOUGH THE TOOLS HAVE TO BE.

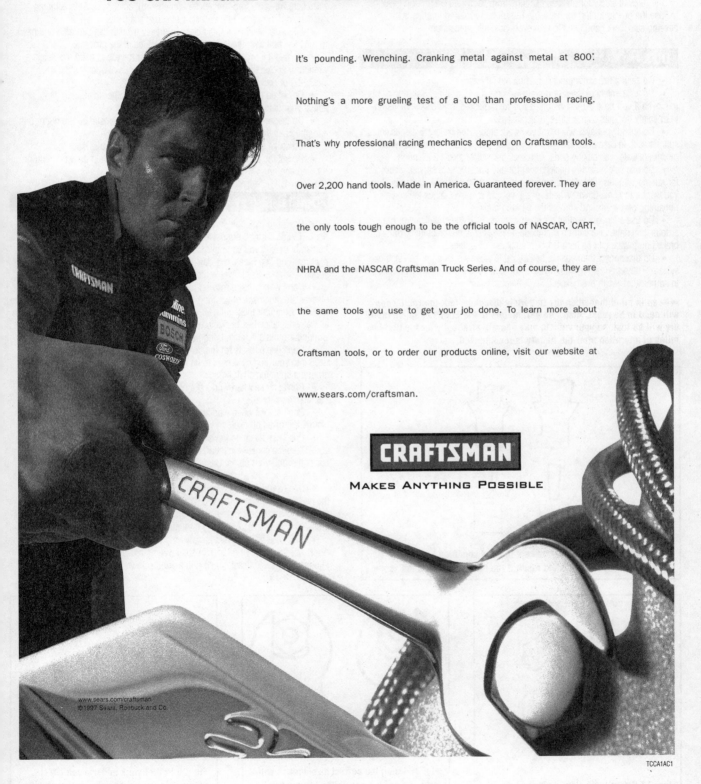

It's pounding. Wrenching. Cranking metal against metal at 800.

Nothing's a more grueling test of a tool than professional racing.

That's why professional racing mechanics depend on Craftsman tools.

Over 2,200 hand tools. Made in America. Guaranteed forever. They are

the only tools tough enough to be the official tools of NASCAR, CART,

NHRA and the NASCAR Craftsman Truck Series. And of course, they are

the same tools you use to get your job done. To learn more about

Craftsman tools, or to order our products online, visit our website at

www.sears.com/craftsman.

CRAFTSMAN

MAKES ANYTHING POSSIBLE

www.sears.com/craftsman
© 1997 Sears, Roebuck and Co.

TCCA1AC1

SERVICING YOUR VEHICLE SAFELY

♦ **See Figures 17, 18, 19 and 20**

It is virtually impossible to anticipate all of the hazards involved with automotive maintenance and service, but care and common sense will prevent most accidents.

The rules of safety for mechanics range from "don't smoke around gasoline," to "use the proper tool(s) for the job." The trick to avoiding injuries is to develop safe work habits and to take every possible precaution.

Do's

• Do keep a fire extinguisher and first aid kit handy.

• Do wear safety glasses or goggles when cutting, drilling, grinding or prying, even if you have 20–20 vision. If you wear glasses for the sake of vision, wear safety goggles over your regular glasses.

• Do shield your eyes whenever you work around the battery. Batteries contain sulfuric acid. In case of contact with the eyes or skin, flush the area with water or a mixture of water and baking soda, then seek immediate medical attention.

• Do use safety stands (jackstands) for any undervehicle service. Jacks are for raising vehicles; jackstands are for making sure the vehicle stays raised until you want it to come down. Whenever the vehicle is raised, block the wheels remaining on the ground and set the parking brake.

• Do use adequate ventilation when working with any chemicals or hazardous materials. Like carbon monoxide, the asbestos dust resulting from some brake lining wear can be hazardous in sufficient quantities.

• Do disconnect the negative battery cable when working on the electrical system. The secondary ignition system contains EXTREMELY HIGH VOLTAGE. In some cases it can even exceed 50,000 volts.

➡**Keep in mind that when the battery is disconnected, the radio code will need to be reset. Also, the parameters of the ECM's adaptive memory will be lost, so your vehicle may operate erratically for the first few miles of operation after the battery is reconnected.**

• Do follow manufacturer's directions whenever working with potentially hazardous materials. Most chemicals and fluids are poisonous if taken internally.

• Do properly maintain your tools. Loose hammerheads, mushroomed punches and chisels, frayed or poorly grounded electrical cords, excessively worn screwdrivers, spread wrenches (open end), cracked sockets, slipping ratchets, or faulty droplight sockets can cause accidents.

• Likewise, keep your tools clean; a greasy wrench can slip off a bolt head, ruining the bolt and often harming your knuckles in the process.

• Do use the proper size and type of tool for the job at hand. Do select a wrench or socket that fits the nut or bolt. The wrench or socket should sit straight, not cocked.

• Do, when possible, pull on a wrench handle rather than push on it, and adjust your stance to prevent a fall.

• Do be sure that adjustable wrenches are tightly closed on the nut or bolt and pulled so that the force is on the side of the fixed jaw.

• Do strike squarely with a hammer; avoid glancing blows.

• Do set the parking brake and block the drive wheels if the work requires a running engine.

Don'ts

• Don't run the engine in a garage or anywhere else without proper ventilation—EVER! Carbon monoxide is poisonous; it takes a long time to leave the human body and you can build up a deadly supply of it in your system by simply breathing in a little every day. You may not realize you are slowly poisoning yourself. Always use power vents, windows, fans and/or open the garage door.

• Don't work around moving parts while wearing loose clothing. Short sleeves are much safer than long, loose sleeves. Hard-toed shoes with neoprene soles protect your toes and give a better grip on slippery surfaces. Jewelry such as watches, fancy belt buckles, beads or body adornment of any kind is not safe working around a vehicle. Long hair should be tied back under a hat or cap.

• Don't use pockets for toolboxes. A fall or bump can drive a screwdriver deep into your body. Even a rag hanging from your back pocket can wrap around a spinning shaft or fan.

• Don't smoke when working around gasoline, cleaning solvent or other flammable material.

• Don't smoke when working around the battery. When the battery is being charged, it gives off explosive hydrogen gas.

• Don't use gasoline to wash your hands; there are excellent soaps available. Gasoline contains dangerous additives which can enter the body through a cut or through your pores. Gasoline also removes all the natural oils from the skin so that bone dry hands will suck up oil and grease.

• Don't service the air conditioning system unless you are equipped with the necessary tools and training. When liquid or compressed gas refrigerant is released to atmospheric pressure it will absorb heat from whatever it contacts. This will chill or freeze anything it touches.

• Don't use screwdrivers for anything other than driving screws! A screwdriver used as an prying tool can snap when you least expect it, causing injuries. At the very least, you'll ruin a good screwdriver.

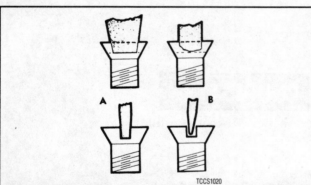

TCCS1020

Fig. 17 Screwdrivers should be kept in good condition to prevent injury or damage which could result if the blade slips from the screw

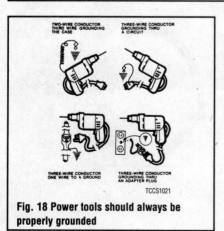

TCCS1021

Fig. 18 Power tools should always be properly grounded

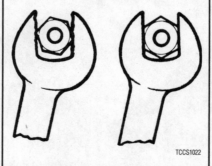

TCCS1022

Fig. 19 Using the correct size wrench will help prevent the possibility of rounding off a nut

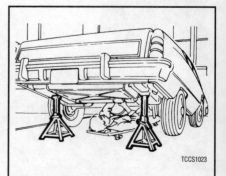

TCCS1023

Fig. 20 NEVER work under a vehicle unless it is supported using safety stands (jackstands)

• Don't use an emergency jack (that little ratchet, scissors, or pantograph jack supplied with the vehicle) for anything other than changing a flat! These jacks are only intended for emergency use out on the road; they are NOT designed as a maintenance tool. If you are serious about maintaining your vehicle yourself, invest in a hydraulic floor jack of at least a 1½ ton capacity, and at least two sturdy jackstands.

FASTENERS, MEASUREMENTS AND CONVERSIONS

Bolts, Nuts And Other Threaded Retainers

▶ **See Figures 21, 22, 23 and 24**

Although there are a great variety of fasteners found in the modern car or truck, the most commonly used retainer is the threaded fastener (nuts, bolts, screws, studs, etc.). Most threaded retainers may be reused, provided that they are not damaged in use or during the repair. Some retainers (such as stretch bolts or torque prevailing nuts) are designed to deform when tightened or in use and should not be reinstalled.

Whenever possible, we will note any special retainers which should be replaced during a procedure. But you should always inspect the condition of a retainer when it is removed and replace any that show signs of damage. Check all threads for rust or corrosion which can increase the torque necessary to achieve the desired clamp load for which that fastener was originally selected. Additionally, be sure that the driver surface of the fastener has not been compromised by rounding or other damage. In some cases a driver surface may become only partially rounded, allowing the driver to catch in only one direction. In many of these occurrences, a fastener may be installed and tightened, but the driver would not be able to grip and loosen the fastener again. (This could lead to frustration down the line should that component ever need to be disassembled again).

If you must replace a fastener, whether due to design or damage, you must ALWAYS be sure to use the proper replacement. In all cases, a retainer of the same design, material and strength should be used. Markings on the heads of

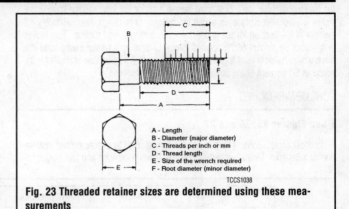

Fig. 23 Threaded retainer sizes are determined using these measurements

A - Length
B - Diameter (major diameter)
C - Threads per inch or mm
D - Thread length
E - Size of the wrench required
F - Root diameter (minor diameter)

TCCS1038

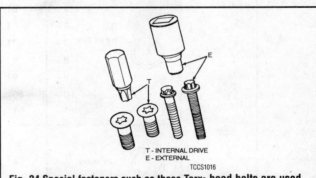

T - INTERNAL DRIVE
E - EXTERNAL

TCCS1016

Fig. 24 Special fasteners such as these Torx• head bolts are used by manufacturers to discourage people from working on vehicles without the proper tools

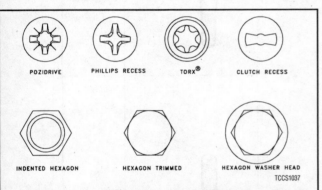

POZIDRIVE   PHILLIPS RECESS   TORX®   CLUTCH RECESS

INDENTED HEXAGON   HEXAGON TRIMMED   HEXAGON WASHER HEAD

TCCS1037

Fig. 21 Here are a few of the most common screw/bolt driver styles

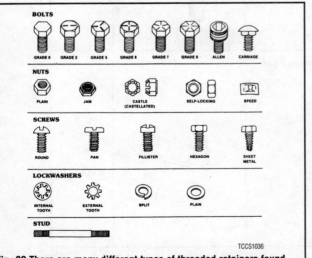

BOLTS
GRADE 0   GRADE 2   GRADE 5   GRADE 6   GRADE 7   GRADE 8   ALLEN   CARRIAGE

NUTS
PLAIN   JAM   CASTLE (CASTELLATED)   SELF-LOCKING   SPEED

SCREWS
ROUND   PAN   FILLISTER   HEXAGON   SHEET METAL

LOCKWASHERS
INTERNAL TOOTH   EXTERNAL TOOTH   SPLIT   PLAIN

STUD

TCCS1036

Fig. 22 There are many different types of threaded retainers found on vehicles

most bolts will help determine the proper strength of the fastener. The same material, thread and pitch must be selected to assure proper installation and safe operation of the vehicle afterwards.

Thread gauges are available to help measure a bolt or stud's thread. Most automotive and hardware stores keep gauges available to help you select the proper size. In a pinch, you can use another nut or bolt for a thread gauge. If the bolt you are replacing is not too badly damaged, you can select a match by finding another bolt which will thread in its place. If you find a nut which threads properly onto the damaged bolt, then use that nut to help select the replacement bolt. If however, the bolt you are replacing is so badly damaged (broken or drilled out) that its threads cannot be used as a gauge, you might start by looking for another bolt (from the same assembly or a similar location on your vehicle) which will thread into the damaged bolt's mounting. If so, the other bolt can be used to select a nut; the nut can then be used to select the replacement bolt.

In all cases, be absolutely sure you have selected the proper replacement. Don't be shy, you can always ask the store clerk for help.

✳✳ WARNING

Be aware that when you find a bolt with damaged threads, you may also find the nut or drilled hole it was threaded into has also been damaged. If this is the case, you may have to drill and tap the hole, replace the nut or otherwise repair the threads. NEVER try to force a replacement bolt to fit into the damaged threads.

Torque

Torque is defined as the measurement of resistance to turning or rotating. It tends to twist a body about an axis of rotation. A common example of this would be tightening a threaded retainer such as a nut, bolt or screw. Measuring torque is one of the most common ways to help assure that a threaded retainer has been properly fastened.

When tightening a threaded fastener, torque is applied in three distinct areas, the head, the bearing surface and the clamp load. About 50 percent of the measured torque is used in overcoming bearing friction. This is the friction between the bearing surface of the bolt head, screw head or nut face and the base material or washer (the surface on which the fastener is rotating). Approximately 40 percent of the applied torque is used in overcoming thread friction. This leaves only about 10 percent of the applied torque to develop a useful clamp load (the force which holds a joint together). This means that friction can account for as much as 90 percent of the applied torque on a fastener.

TORQUE WRENCHES

▶ See Figures 25, 26 and 27

In most applications, a torque wrench can be used to assure proper installation of a fastener. Torque wrenches come in various designs and most automo-

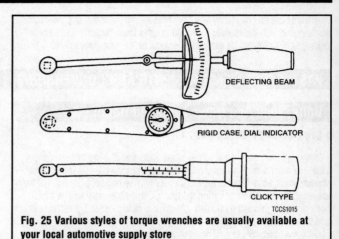

Fig. 25 Various styles of torque wrenches are usually available at your local automotive supply store

	Mark	Class		Mark	Class
Hexagon head bolt	Bolt head No. 4 4— 5— 6— 7— 8— 9— 10— 11—	4T 5T 6T 7T 8T 9T 10T 11T	Stud bolt	No mark	4T
	No mark	4T		Grooved	6T
Hexagon flange bolt w/ washer hexagon bolt	No mark	4T			
Hexagon head bolt	Two protruding lines	5T			
Hexagon flange bolt w/ washer hexagon bolt	Two protruding lines	6T	Welded bolt		4T
Hexagon head bolt	Three protruding lines	7T			
Hexagon head bolt	Four protruding lines	8T			

Fig. 26 Determining bolt strength of metric fasteners—NOTE: this is a typical bolt marking system, but there is not a worldwide standard

Class	Diameter mm	Pitch mm	Specified torque					
			Hexagon head bolt			Hexagon flange bolt		
			N·m	kgf·cm	ft·lbf	N·m	kgf·cm	ft·lbf
4T	6	1	5	55	48 in.·lbf	6	60	52 in.·lbf
	8	1.25	12.5	130	9	14	145	10
	10	1.25	26	260	19	29	290	21
	12	1.25	47	480	35	53	540	39
	14	1.5	74	760	55	84	850	61
	16	1.5	115	1,150	83	—	—	—
5T	6	1	6.5	65	56 in.·lbf	7.5	75	65 in.·lbf
	8	1.25	15.5	160	12	17.5	175	13
	10	1.25	32	330	24	36	360	26
	12	1.25	59	600	43	65	670	48
	14	1.5	91	930	67	100	1,050	76
	16	1.5	140	1,400	101	—	—	—
6T	6	1	8	80	69 in.·lbf	9	90	78 in.·lbf
	8	1.25	19	195	14	21	210	15
	10	1.25	39	400	29	44	440	32
	12	1.25	71	730	53	80	810	59
	14	1.5	110	1,100	80	125	1,250	90
	16	1.5	170	1,750	127	—	—	—
7T	6	1	10.5	110	8	12	120	9
	8	1.25	25	260	19	28	290	21
	10	1.25	52	530	38	58	590	43
	12	1.25	95	970	70	105	1,050	76
	14	1.5	145	1,500	108	165	1,700	123
	16	1.5	230	2,300	166	—	—	—
8T	8	1.25	29	300	22	33	330	24
	10	1.25	61	620	45	68	690	50
	12	1.25	110	1,100	80	120	1,250	90
9T	8	1.25	34	340	25	37	380	27
	10	1.25	70	710	51	78	790	57
	12	1.25	125	1,300	94	140	1,450	105
10T	8	1.25	38	390	28	42	430	31
	10	1.25	78	800	58	88	890	64
	12	1.25	140	1,450	105	155	1,600	116
11T	8	1.25	42	430	31	47	480	35
	10	1.25	87	890	64	97	990	72
	12	1.25	155	1,600	116	175	1,800	130

TCCS1241

Fig. 27 Typical bolt torque's for metric fasteners—WARNING: use only as a guide

tive supply stores will carry a variety to suit your needs. A torque wrench should be used any time we supply a specific torque value for a fastener. A torque wrench can also be used if you are following the general guidelines in the accompanying charts. Keep in mind that because there is no worldwide standardization of fasteners, the charts are a general guideline and should be used with caution. Again, the general rule of "if you are using the right tool for the job, you should not have to strain to tighten a fastener" applies here.

Beam Type

▶ See Figure 28

The beam type torque wrench is one of the most popular types. It consists of a pointer attached to the head that runs the length of the flexible beam (shaft) to

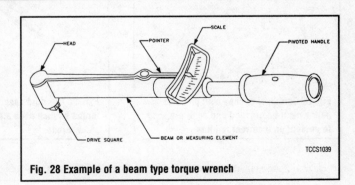

TCCS1039

Fig. 28 Example of a beam type torque wrench

a scale located near the handle. As the wrench is pulled, the beam bends and the pointer indicates the torque using the scale.

Click (Breakaway) Type

▶ See Figure 29

Another popular design of torque wrench is the click type. To use the click type wrench you pre-adjust it to a torque setting. Once the torque is reached, the wrench has a reflex signaling feature that causes a momentary breakaway of the torque wrench body, sending an impulse to the operator's hand.

Pivot Head Type

▶ See Figures 29 and 30

Some torque wrenches (usually of the click type) may be equipped with a pivot head which can allow it to be used in areas of limited access. BUT, it must be used properly. To hold a pivot head wrench, grasp the handle lightly, and as you pull on the handle, it should be floated on the pivot point. If the handle comes in contact with the yoke extension during the process of pulling, there is a very good chance the torque readings will be inaccurate because this could alter the wrench loading point. The design of the handle is usually such as to make it inconvenient to deliberately misuse the wrench.

➡ It should be mentioned that the use of any U-joint, wobble or extension will have an effect on the torque readings, no matter what type of wrench you are using. For the most accurate readings, install the socket directly on the wrench driver. If necessary, straight extensions (which hold a socket directly under the wrench driver) will have the least effect on the torque reading. Avoid any extension that alters the length of the wrench from the handle to the head/driving point (such as a crow's foot). U-joint or wobble extensions can greatly affect the readings; avoid their use at all times.

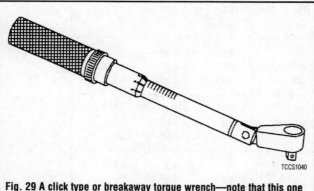

Fig. 29 A click type or breakaway torque wrench—note that this one has a pivoting head

Rigid Case (Direct Reading)

▶ See Figure 31

A rigid case or direct reading torque wrench is equipped with a dial indicator to show torque values. One advantage of these wrenches is that they can be held at any position on the wrench without affecting accuracy. These wrenches are often preferred because they tend to be compact, easy to read and have a great degree of accuracy.

TORQUE ANGLE METERS

▶ See Figure 32

Because the frictional characteristics of each fastener or threaded hole will vary, clamp loads which are based strictly on torque will vary as well. In most applications, this variance is not significant enough to cause worry. But, in certain applications, a manufacturer's engineers may determine that more precise clamp loads are necessary (such is the case with many aluminum cylinder heads). In these cases, a torque angle method of installation would be specified. When installing fasteners which are torque angle tightened, a predetermined seating torque and standard torque wrench are usually used first to remove any compliance from the joint. The fastener is then tightened the specified additional portion of a turn measured in degrees. A torque angle gauge (mechanical protractor) is used for these applications.

Standard And Metric Measurements

▶ See Figure 33

Throughout this manual, specifications are given to help you determine the condition of various components on your vehicle, or to assist you in their installation. Some of the most common measurements include length (in. or cm/mm), torque (ft. lbs., inch lbs. or Nm) and pressure (psi, in. Hg, kPa or mm Hg). In most cases, we strive to provide the proper measurement as determined by the manufacturer's engineers.

Though, in some cases, that value may not be conveniently measured with what is available in your toolbox. Luckily, many of the measuring devices which are available today will have two scales so the Standard or Metric measurements may easily be taken. If any of the various measuring tools which are available to you do not contain the same scale as listed in the specifications, use the accompanying conversion factors to determine the proper value.

The conversion factor chart is used by taking the given specification and multiplying it by the necessary conversion factor. For instance, looking at the first line, if you have a measurement in inches such as "free-play should be 2 in." but your ruler reads only in millimeters, multiply 2 in. by the conversion factor of 25.4 to get the metric equivalent of 50.8mm. Likewise, if the specification was given only in a Metric measurement, for example in Newton Meters (Nm), then look at the center column first. If the measurement is 100 Nm, multiply it by the conversion factor of 0.738 to get 73.8 ft. lbs.

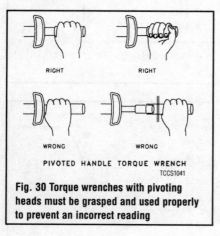

Fig. 30 Torque wrenches with pivoting heads must be grasped and used properly to prevent an incorrect reading

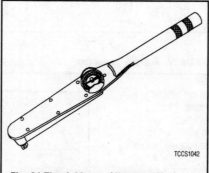

Fig. 31 The rigid case (direct reading) torque wrench uses a dial indicator to show torque

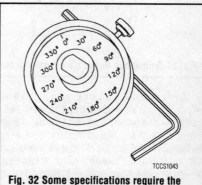

Fig. 32 Some specifications require the use of a torque angle meter (mechanical protractor)

CONVERSION FACTORS

LENGTH–DISTANCE

Inches (in.)	x 25.4	= Millimeters (mm)	x .0394	= Inches
Feet (ft.)	x .305	= Meters (m)	x 3.281	= Feet
Miles	x 1.609	= Kilometers (km)	x .0621	= Miles

VOLUME

Cubic Inches (in3)	x 16.387	= Cubic Centimeters	x .061	= in3
IMP Pints (IMP pt.)	x .568	= Liters (L)	x 1.76	= IMP pt.
IMP Quarts (IMP qt.)	x 1.137	= Liters (L)	x .88	= IMP qt.
IMP Gallons (IMP gal.)	x 4.546	= Liters (L)	x .22	= IMP gal.
IMP Quarts (IMP qt.)	x 1.201	= US Quarts (US qt.)	x .833	= IMP qt.
IMP Gallons (IMP gal.)	x 1.201	= US Gallons (US gal.)	x .833	= IMP gal.
Fl. Ounces	x 29.573	= Milliliters	x .034	= Ounces
US Pints (US pt.)	x .473	= Liters (L)	x 2.113	= Pints
US Quarts (US qt.)	x .946	= Liters (L)	x 1.057	= Quarts
US Gallons (US gal.)	x 3.785	= Liters (L)	x .264	= Gallons

MASS–WEIGHT

Ounces (oz.)	x 28.35	= Grams (g)	x .035	= Ounces
Pounds (lb.)	x .454	= Kilograms (kg)	x 2.205	= Pounds

PRESSURE

Pounds Per Sq. In. (psi)	x 6.895	= Kilopascals (kPa)	x .145	= psi
Inches of Mercury (Hg)	x .4912	= psi	x 2.036	= Hg
Inches of Mercury (Hg)	x 3.377	= Kilopascals (kPa)	x .2961	= Hg
Inches of Water (H_2O)	x .07355	= Inches of Mercury	x 13.783	= H_2O
Inches of Water (H_2O)	x .03613	= psi	x 27.684	= H_2O
Inches of Water (H_2O)	x .248	= Kilopascals (kPa)	x 4.026	= H_2O

TORQUE

Pounds–Force Inches (in–lb)	x .113	= Newton Meters (N·m)	x 8.85	= in–lb
Pounds–Force Feet (ft–lb)	x 1.356	= Newton Meters (N·m)	x .738	= ft–lb

VELOCITY

Miles Per Hour (MPH)	x 1.609	= Kilometers Per Hour (KPH)	x .621	= MPH

POWER

Horsepower (Hp)	x .745	= Kilowatts	x 1.34	= Horsepower

FUEL CONSUMPTION*

Miles Per Gallon IMP (MPG)	x .354	= Kilometers Per Liter (Km/L)		
Kilometers Per Liter (Km/L)	x 2.352	= IMP MPG		
Miles Per Gallon US (MPG)	x .425	= Kilometers Per Liter (Km/L)		
Kilometers Per Liter (Km/L)	x 2.352	= US MPG		

*It is common to covert from miles per gallon (mpg) to liters/100 kilometers (1/100 km), where mpg (IMP) x 1/100 km = 282 and mpg (US) x 1/100 km = 235.

TEMPERATURE

Degree Fahrenheit (°F)	= (°C x 1.8) + 32
Degree Celsius (°C)	= (°F – 32) x .56

TCCS1044

Fig. 33 Standard and metric conversion factors chart

SERIAL NUMBER IDENTIFICATION

Vehicle

▶ See Figure 34

All models have the standard 17 digit VIN plate on the left side of the dashboard, visible through the windshield. On Golf and Jetta, a second plate is on the top of the cowling behind the engine. On Cabriolet, the VIN also appears on the model identification plate in the luggage compartment.

The VIN number will show information on where the vehicle was manufactured, body style, engine type, passenger restraint system, vehicle model, model year, and the sequential serial number. This information can be helpful when locating parts or specifications.

➥Throughout this manual, certain procedures are covered by "platform" instead of model year. It is important to know which platform your particular vehicle is based upon, so you can refer to the correct procedure.

91221PB6

Fig. 34 The VIN tag is located at the lower left corner of the dashboard

VEHICLE IDENTIFICATION

Engine Code						Model Year	
Code	Liters	Cu. In. (cc)	Cyl.	Manufacturer		Code	Year
ME	1.6	97 (1588)	4	VW		L	1990
MF	1.6	97 (1588)	4	VW		M	1991
1V	1.6	97 (1588)	4	VW		N	1992
UM	1.8	109 (1780)	4	VW		P	1993
JN	1.8	109 (1780)	4	VW		R	1994
RV	1.8	109 (1781)	4	VW		S	1995
ACC	1.8	109 (1781)	4	VW		T	1996
PF	1.8	109 (1781)	4	VW		V	1997
2H	1.8	109 (1781)	4	VW		W	1998
AHU	1.9	116 (1896)	4	VW		X	1999
AAZ	1.9	116 (1896)	4	VW			
ABA	2.0	121 (1984)	4	VW			
9A	2.0	121 (1984)	4	VW			
AAA	2.8	170 (2792)	6	VW			

91221C01

Platform breakdown:
- 1990–1994 Cabriolet: A1 platform
- 1995–1999 Cabrio: A3 platform
- 1990–1992 Golf: A2 platform
- 1993–1999 Golf: A3 platform
- 1990–1992 Jetta: A2 platform
- 1993–1999 Jetta: A3 platform
- 1990–1994 Fox: Fox platform

Notice that the Cabriolet/Cabrio skips a platform generation. The A1 platform was a carryover from the 1984 and earlier Rabbits and Jetta's. In 1993, the A3 platform was introduced, which replaced the 1985–1992 A2 platform, while the Cabriolet remained an A1 platform. In 1995, the newly-designed A3-platformed Cabrio joined the Golf and Jetta.

Engine

▶ See Figures 35, 36, 37, 38 and 39

On 4-cylinder engines, the identification number is stamped into the block near the crankcase breather or upper coolant hose fitting. On VR6 engines, the

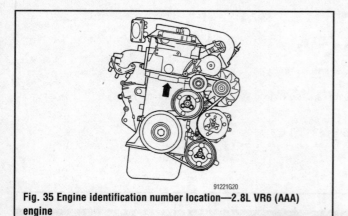

Fig. 35 Engine identification number location—2.8L VR6 (AAA) engine

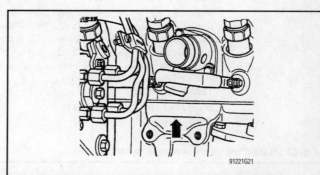

Fig. 36 Engine identification number location—diesel engines

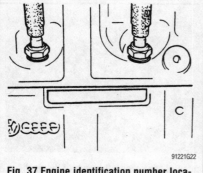

Fig. 37 Engine identification number location—gasoline engines

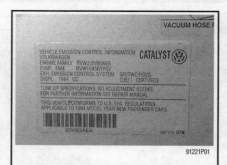

Fig. 38 The engine family can also be determined from the vehicles under hood emissions label

Fig. 39 A vacuum hose routing diagram can be located under the vehicles hood

ENGINE IDENTIFICATION AND SPECIFICATIONS

Year	Model	Engine ID/VIN	Engine Displacement Liters (cc)	No. of Cyl.	Engine Type	Fuel System Type	Net Horsepower @ rpm	Net Torque @ rpm (ft. lbs.)	Bore x Stroke (in.)	Compression Ratio	Oil Pressure @ rpm
1990	Jetta D (ECO)	1V	1.6 (1588)	4	SOHC	Bosch VE	59@4500	81@2400	3.01x3.40	23.0:1	28@2000
	Jetta D	ME	1.6 (1588)	4	SOHC	Bosch VE	52@4800	71@2500	3.01x3.40	23.0:1	28@2000
	Jetta TD	MF	1.6 (1588)	4	SOHC	Bosch VE	68@4500	98@2500	3.01x3.40	23.0:1	28@2000
	Jetta	RV	1.8 (1781)	4	SOHC	Digifant II ①	100@5400	107@3400	3.19x3.40	10.0:1	28@2000
	Jetta	PF	1.8 (1781)	4	SOHC	Digifant II ①	105@5400	110@2300	3.19x3.40	10.0:1	28@2000
	Jetta	9A	2.0 (1984)	4	DOHC	CIS-E/Motronic	134@5800	133@4400	3.25x3.65	10.8:1	28@2000
	Golf	RV	1.8 (1781)	4	SOHC	Digifant II ①	100@5400	107@3400	3.19x3.40	10.0:1	28@2000
	Golf	PF	1.8 (1781)	4	SOHC	Digifant II ①	105@5400	110@2300	3.19x3.40	10.0:1	28@2000
	Golf	9A	2.0 (1984)	4	DOHC	CIS-E	134@5800	133@4400	3.25x3.65	10.8:1	28@2000
	Cabriolet	2H	1.8 (1781)	4	SOHC	Digifant II ①	94@5400	100@3000	3.19x3.40	10.0:1	28@2000
	Cabriolet	UM	1.8 (1780)	4	SOHC	CIS	81@5500	93@3250	3.19x3.40	9.0:1	28@2000
	Fox	JN	1.8 (1780)	4	SOHC	CIS-E	81@5500	93@3250	3.19x3.40	9.0:1	28@2000
1991	Jetta D (ECO)	1V	1.6 (1588)	4	SOHC	Bosch VE	59@4500	81@2400	3.01x3.40	23.0:1	28@2000
	Jetta D	ME	1.6 (1588)	4	SOHC	Bosch VE	52@4800	71@2500	3.01x3.40	23.0:1	28@2000
	Jetta TD	MF	1.6 (1588)	4	SOHC	Bosch VE	68@4500	98@2500	3.01x3.40	23.0:1	28@2000
	Jetta	RV	1.8 (1781)	4	SOHC	Digifant II ①	100@5400	107@3400	3.19x3.40	10.0:1	28@2000
	Jetta	PF	1.8 (1781)	4	SOHC	Digifant II ①	105@5400	110@2300	3.19x3.40	10.0:1	28@2000
	Jetta	9A	2.0 (1984)	4	DOHC	CIS-E/Motronic	134@5800	133@4400	3.25x3.65	10.8:1	28@2000
	Golf	RV	1.8 (1781)	4	SOHC	Digifant II ①	100@5400	107@3400	3.19x3.40	10.0:1	28@2000
	GTI	PF	1.8 (1781)	4	SOHC	Digifant II ①	105@5400	110@2300	3.19x3.40	10.0:1	28@2000
	GTI	9A	2.0 (1984)	4	DOHC	Digifant II ①	134@5800	133@4400	3.25x3.65	10.8:1	28@2000
	Cabriolet	2H	1.8 (1781)	4	SOHC	Digifant II ①	94@5400	100@3000	3.19x3.40	10.0:1	28@2000
	Cabriolet	UM	1.8 (1780)	4	SOHC	CIS	81@5500	93@3250	3.19x3.40	9.0:1	28@2000
	Fox	JN	1.8 (1780)	4	SOHC	CIS-E	81@5500	93@3250	3.19x3.40	9.0:1	28@2000
1992	Jetta D (ECO)	1V	1.6 (1588)	4	SOHC	Bosch VE	59@4500	81@2400	3.01x3.40	23.0:1	28@2000
	Jetta D	ME	1.6 (1588)	4	SOHC	Bosch VE	52@4800	71@2500	3.01x3.40	23.0:1	28@2000
	Jetta TD	MF	1.6 (1588)	4	SOHC	Bosch VE	68@4500	98@2500	3.01x3.40	23.0:1	28@2000
	Jetta	RV	1.8 (1781)	4	SOHC	Digifant II ①	100@5400	107@3400	3.19x3.40	10.0:1	28@2000
	Jetta	PF	1.8 (1781)	4	SOHC	Digifant II ①	105@5400	110@2300	3.19x3.40	10.0:1	28@2000
	Jetta	9A	2.0 (1984)	4	DOHC	CIS-E/Motronic	134@5800	133@4400	3.25x3.65	10.8:1	28@2000
	Golf	RV	1.8 (1781)	4	SOHC	Digifant II ①	100@5400	107@3400	3.19x3.40	10.0:1	28@2000
	GTI	PF	1.8 (1781)	4	SOHC	Digifant II ①	105@5400	110@2300	3.19x3.40	10.0:1	28@2000
	GTI	9A	2.0 (1984)	4	DOHC	Digifant II ①	134@5800	133@4400	3.25x3.65	10.8:1	28@2000
	Cabriolet	2H	1.8 (1781)	4	SOHC	Digifant II ①	94@5400	100@3000	3.19x3.40	10.0:1	28@2000
	Fox	UM	1.8 (1780)	4	SOHC	CIS	81@5500	93@3250	3.19x3.40	9.0:1	28@2000
	Fox	JN	1.8 (1780)	4	SOHC	CIS-E	81@5500	93@3250	3.19x3.40	9.0:1	28@2000
1993	Jetta	AAZ	1.9 (1896)	4	SOHC	Bosch VE	75@4200	107@2500	3.13x3.76	22.5:1	29@2000
	Jetta	AHU	1.9 (1896)	4	SOHC	Bosch VE	90@4000	149@1900	3.13x3.76	19.5:1	29@2000
	Jetta	ACC	1.8 (1781)	4	SOHC	Mono-Motronic	90@5500	107@2500	3.19x3.40	9.0:1	29@2000
	Jetta	ABA	2.0 (1984)	4	SOHC	Motronic	115@5400	122@3200	3.25x3.65	10.4:1	29@2000
	Jetta	AAA	2.8 (2782)	6	SOHC	Motronic	172@5400	173@3200	3.56x3.19	10.0:1	29@2000
	Golf	AAZ	1.9 (1896)	4	SOHC	Bosch VE	75@4200	107@2500	3.13x3.76	22.5:1	29@2000
	Golf	AHU	1.9 (1896)	4	SOHC	Bosch VE	90@4000	149@1900	3.13x3.76	19.5:1	29@2000

91221C02

ENGINE IDENTIFICATION AND SPECIFICATIONS

Year	Model	Engine ID/VIN	Engine Displacement Liters (cc)	No. of Cyl.	Engine Type	Fuel System Type	Net Horsepower @ rpm	Net Torque @ rpm (ft. lbs.)	Bore x Stroke (in.)	Compression Ratio	Oil Pressure @ rpm
1993 cont'l	Golf	ACC	1.8 (1781)	4	SOHC	Mono-Motronic	90@5500	107@2500	3.19x3.40	9.0:1	29@2000
	Golf/GTI	ABA	2.0 (1984)	4	SOHC	Motronic	115@5400	122@3200	3.25x3.65	10.4:1	29@2000
	GTI	AAA	2.8 (2782)	6	DOHC	Motronic	172@5400	173@3000	3.56x3.40	10.0:1	29@2000
	Cabriolet	2H	1.8 (1781)	4	SOHC	Digifant II ①	94@5400	100@3000	3.19x3.40	10.0:1	28@2000
	Fox	JN	1.8 (1780)	4	SOHC	CIS-E	81@5500	93@3250	3.19x3.40	9.0:1	28@2000
1994	Jetta	AAZ	1.9 (1896)	4	SOHC	Bosch VE	75@4200	107@2500	3.13x3.76	22.5:1	29@2000
	Jetta	AHU	1.9 (1896)	4	SOHC	Bosch VE	90@4000	149@1900	3.13x3.76	19.5:1	29@2000
	Jetta	ACC	1.8 (1781)	4	SOHC	Mono-Motronic	90@5500	107@2500	3.19x3.40	9.0:1	29@2000
	Jetta	ABA	2.0 (1984)	4	SOHC	Motronic	115@5400	122@3200	3.25x3.65	10.4:1	29@2000
	Jetta	AAA	2.8 (2782)	6	SOHC	Motronic	172@5400	173@3200	3.56x3.19	10.0:1	29@2000
	Golf	AHU	1.9 (1896)	4	SOHC	Bosch VE	90@4000	149@1900	3.13x3.76	19.5:1	29@2000
	Golf	ACC	1.8 (1781)	4	SOHC	Mono-Motronic	90@5500	107@2500	3.19x3.40	9.0:1	29@2000
	Golf/GTI	ABA	2.0 (1984)	4	SOHC	Motronic	115@5400	122@3200	3.25x3.65	10.4:1	29@2000
	GTI	AAA	2.8 (2782)	6	DOHC	Motronic	172@5400	173@3000	3.56x3.40	10.0:1	29@2000
1995	Jetta	AAZ	1.9 (1896)	4	SOHC	Bosch VE	75@4200	107@2500	3.13x3.76	22.5:1	29@2000
	Jetta	AHU	1.9 (1896)	4	SOHC	Bosch VE	90@4000	149@1900	3.13x3.76	19.5:1	29@2000
	Jetta	ACC	1.8 (1781)	4	SOHC	Mono-Motronic	90@5500	107@2500	3.19x3.40	9.0:1	29@2000
	Jetta	ABA	2.0 (1984)	4	SOHC	Motronic	115@5400	122@3200	3.25x3.65	10.4:1	29@2000
	Jetta	AAA	2.8 (2782)	6	DOHC	Motronic	172@5400	173@3000	3.56x3.19	10.0:1	29@2000
	Golf	AHU	1.9 (1896)	4	SOHC	Bosch VE	90@4000	149@1900	3.13x3.76	19.5:1	29@2000
	Golf	ACC	1.8 (1781)	4	SOHC	Mono-Motronic	90@5500	107@2500	3.19x3.40	9.0:1	29@2000
	Golf/GTI	ABA	2.0 (1984)	4	SOHC	Motronic	115@5400	122@3200	3.25x3.65	10.4:1	29@2000
	GTI	AAA	2.8 (2782)	6	DOHC	Motronic	172@5400	173@3200	3.56x3.19	10.0:1	29@2000
1996	Jetta	AAZ	1.9 (1896)	4	SOHC	Bosch VE	75@4200	107@2500	3.13x3.76	22.5:1	29@2000
	Jetta	AHU	1.9 (1896)	4	SOHC	Bosch VE	90@4000	149@1900	3.13x3.76	19.5:1	29@2000
	Jetta	ACC	1.8 (1781)	4	SOHC	Mono-Motronic	90@5500	107@2500	3.19x3.40	9.0:1	29@2000
	Jetta	ABA	2.0 (1984)	4	SOHC	Motronic	115@5400	122@3200	3.25x3.65	10.4:1	29@2000
	Golf	AAZ	1.9 (1896)	4	SOHC	Bosch VE	75@4200	107@2500	3.13x3.76	22.5:1	29@2000
	Golf	AHU	1.9 (1896)	4	SOHC	Bosch VE	90@4000	149@1900	3.13x3.76	19.5:1	29@2000
	Golf	ACC	1.8 (1781)	4	SOHC	Mono-Motronic	90@5500	107@2500	3.19x3.40	9.0:1	29@2000
	Golf/GTI	ABA	2.0 (1984)	4	SOHC	Motronic	115@5400	122@3200	3.25x3.65	10.4:1	29@2000
	GTI	AAA	2.8 (2782)	6	DOHC	Motronic	172@5400	173@3200	3.56x3.19	10.0:1	29@2000
	Cabrio	ABA	2.0 (1984)	4	SOHC	Motronic	115@5400	122@3200	3.65x3.25	10.4:1	29@2000

91221C03

ENGINE IDENTIFICATION AND SPECIFICATIONS

Year	Model	Engine ID/VIN	Engine Displacement Liters (cc)	No. of Cyl.	Engine Type	Fuel System Type	Net Horsepower @ rpm	Net Torque @ rpm (ft. lbs.)	Bore x Stroke (in.)	Compression Ratio	Oil Pressure @ rpm
1997	Jetta	AAZ	1.9 (1896)	4	SOHC	Bosch VE	75@4200	107@2500	3.13x3.76	22.5:1	29@2000
	Jetta	AHU	1.9 (1896)	4	SOHC	Bosch VE	90@4000	149@1900	3.13x3.76	19.5:1	29@2000
	Jetta	ACC	1.8 (1781)	4	SOHC	Mono-Motronic	90@5500	107@2500	3.19x3.40	9.0:1	29@2000
	Jetta	ABA	2.0 (1984)	4	SOHC	Motronic	115@5400	122@3200	3.65x3.25	10.4:1	29@2000
	Jetta	AAA	2.8 (2782)	6	DOHC	Motronic	172@5400	173@3200	3.56x3.19	10.0:1	29@2000
	Golf	AAZ	1.9 (1896)	4	SOHC	Bosch VE	75@4200	107@2500	3.13x3.76	22.5:1	29@2000
	Golf	AHU	1.9 (1896)	4	SOHC	Bosch VE	90@4000	149@1900	3.13x3.76	19.5:1	29@2000
	Golf	ACC	1.8 (1781)	4	SOHC	Mono-Motronic	90@5500	107@2500	3.19x3.40	9.0:1	29@2000
	Golf/GTI	ABA	2.0 (1984)	4	SOHC	Motronic	115@5400	122@3200	3.65x3.25	10.4:1	29@2000
	GTI	AAA	2.8 (2782)	6	DOHC	Motronic	172@5400	173@3200	3.56x3.19	10.0:1	29@2000
	Cabrio	ABA	2.0 (1984)	4	SOHC	Motronic	115@5400	122@3200	3.65x3.25	10.4:1	29@2000
1998	Jetta	AAZ	1.9 (1896)	4	SOHC	Bosch VE	75@4200	107@2500	3.13x3.76	22.5:1	29@2000
	Jetta	AHU	1.9 (1896)	4	SOHC	Bosch VE	90@4000	149@1900	3.13x3.76	19.5:1	29@2000
	Jetta	ACC	1.8 (1781)	4	SOHC	Mono-Motronic	90@5500	107@2500	3.19x3.40	9.0:1	29@2000
	Jetta	ABA	2.0 (1984)	4	SOHC	Motronic	115@5400	122@3200	3.65x3.25	10.4:1	29@2000
	Jetta	AAA	2.8 (2782)	6	DOHC	Motronic	172@5400	173@3200	3.56x3.19	10.0:1	29@2000
	Golf	AAZ	1.9 (1896)	4	SOHC	Bosch VE	75@4200	107@2500	3.13x3.76	22.5:1	29@2000
	Golf	AHU	1.9 (1896)	4	SOHC	Bosch VE	90@4000	149@1900	3.13x3.76	19.5:1	29@2000
	Golf	ACC	1.8 (1781)	4	SOHC	Mono-Motronic	90@5500	107@2500	3.19x3.40	9.0:1	29@2000
	Golf/GTI	ABA	2.0 (1984)	4	SOHC	Motronic	115@5400	122@3200	3.65x3.25	10.4:1	29@2000
	GTI	AAA	2.8 (2782)	6	DOHC	Motronic	172@5400	173@3200	3.56x3.19	10.0:1	29@2000
	Cabrio	ABA	2.0 (1984)	4	SOHC	Motronic	115@5400	122@3200	3.65x3.25	10.4:1	29@2000
1999	Jetta	AAZ	1.9 (1896)	4	SOHC	Bosch VE	75@4200	107@2500	3.13x3.76	22.5:1	29@2000
	Jetta	AHU	1.9 (1896)	4	SOHC	Bosch VE	90@4000	149@1900	3.13x3.76	19.5:1	29@2000
	Jetta	ACC	1.8 (1781)	4	SOHC	Mono-Motronic	90@5500	107@2500	3.19x3.40	9.0:1	29@2000
	Jetta	ABA	2.0 (1984)	4	SOHC	Motronic	115@5400	122@3200	3.65x3.25	10.4:1	29@2000
	Jetta	AAA	2.8 (2782)	6	DOHC	Motronic	172@5400	173@3200	3.56x3.19	10.0:1	29@2000
	Golf	AAZ	1.9 (1896)	4	SOHC	Bosch VE	75@4200	107@2500	3.13x3.76	22.5:1	29@2000
	Golf	AHU	1.9 (1896)	4	SOHC	Bosch VE	90@4000	149@1900	3.13x3.76	19.5:1	29@2000
	Golf	ACC	1.8 (1781)	4	SOHC	Mono-Motronic	90@5500	107@2500	3.19x3.40	9.0:1	29@2000
	Golf/GTI	ABA	2.0 (1984)	4	SOHC	Motronic	115@5400	122@3200	3.65x3.25	10.4:1	29@2000
	GTI	AAA	2.8 (2782)	6	DOHC	Motronic	172@5400	173@3200	3.56x3.19	10.0:1	29@2000
	Cabrio	ABA	2.0 (1984)	4	SOHC	Motronic	115@5400	122@3200	3.65x3.25	10.4:1	29@2000

① California RV engine

91221C04

identification number is located directly above the crankshaft pulley, at the top of the cylinder block. The first two (or in the case of later engines, three) digits are the engine code and will be the most useful description of the engine when locating specifications or ordering parts.

Although Volkswagen engines share many components, the code indicates differences in engine management systems, emissions specifications, compression ratios, power ratings and other details. The engine code also appears in large type on the model identification label in the luggage compartment.

➡**As with the different vehicle platforms, sometimes headings and/or procedures in this manual are broken down by engine code. Make sure that you identify the engine in your vehicle, so you can refer to the appropriate procedure.**

Transaxle

▸ **See Figures 40 thru 45**

Volkswagen transaxles, whether manual or automatic, have two separate identification numbers stamped onto the case. The first sequence is the serial number, which indicates build date and gear ratios. The second number sequence (found on a different portion of the transaxle) identifies transaxle type, which can be one of five "families" of transaxle.

➡**As with the different vehicle platforms and engine codes, sometimes headings and/or procedures in this manual are broken down by transaxle code. Make sure that you identify the transaxle in your vehicle, so you can refer to the appropriate procedure.**

Automatic transaxle breakdown:
- A1 platform: 010 transaxle
- A2 platform: 010 transaxle
- A3 platform: 096 or 01M transaxle

Manual transaxle breakdown:
- A1 platform: 020 transaxle
- A2 platform: 020 transaxle
- A3 platform: 020 or 02A transaxle

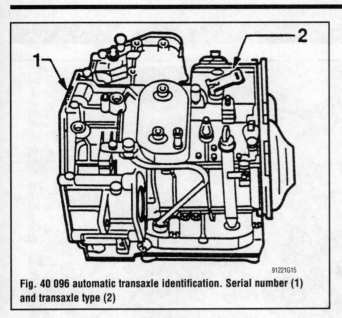

Fig. 40 096 automatic transaxle identification. Serial number (1) and transaxle type (2)

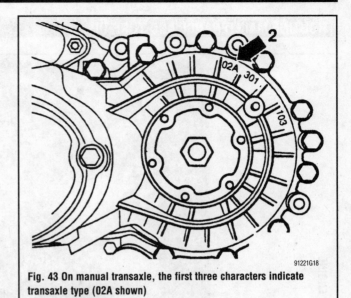

Fig. 43 On manual transaxle, the first three characters indicate transaxle type (02A shown)

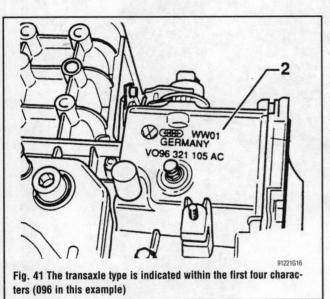

Fig. 41 The transaxle type is indicated within the first four characters (096 in this example)

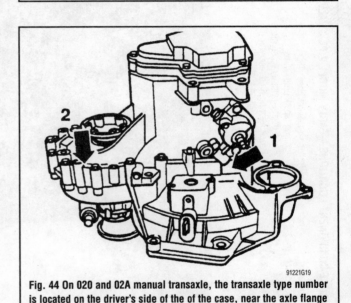

Fig. 44 On 020 and 02A manual transaxle, the transaxle type number is located on the driver's side of the of the case, near the axle flange

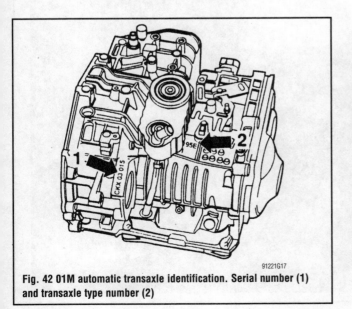

Fig. 42 01M automatic transaxle identification. Serial number (1) and transaxle type number (2)

Fig. 45 Typical VW transmission id tag

UNDERHOOD MAINTENANCE COMPONENT LOCATIONS—EARLY MODEL 2.0L 8 VALVE ENGINE

1. Air filter housing
2. Timing belt cover
3. Alternator belt
4. Oil level dipstick
5. Spark plugs
6. Oil filler cap
7. Distributor cap
8. Upper radiator hose
9. Ignition (spark plug) wires
10. Brake master cylinder reservoir
11. Power steering fluid reservoir
12. Coolant reservoir
13. Battery

91221PB7

UNDERHOOD MAINTENANCE COMPONENT LOCATIONS—LATE MODEL 2.0L 8 VALVE ENGINE

1. Washer solvent reservoir
2. Coolant recovery reservoir
3. Power steering fluid reservoir
4. Engine timing belt
5. Alternator belt
6. Engine cover
7. Engine oil dipstick
8. Throttle body
9. Engine oil filler cap
10. Brake fluid reservoir
11. Battery
12. Air filter housing

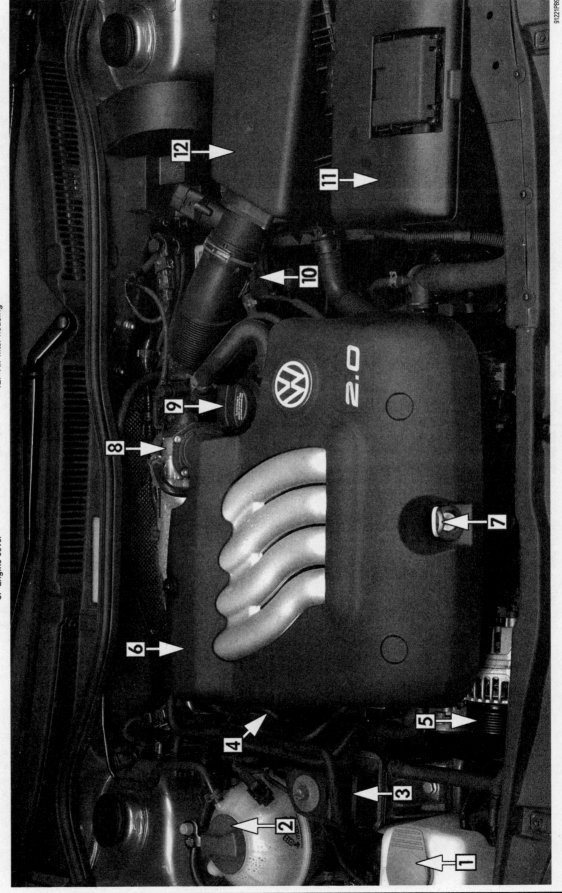

91221P89

UNDERHOOD MAINTENANCE COMPONENT LOCATIONS—2.0L 16 VALVE ENGINE

1. Air filter housing
2. Alternator belt
3. Timing belt cover
4. Engine oil filler cap
5. Spark plugs
6. Upper radiator hose
7. Engine oil dipstick
8. Engine oil filter
9. Radiator
10. Distributor rotor
11. Distributor cap
12. Brake master cylinder
13. Coolant reservoir
14. Ignition (spark plug) wires
15. Power steering fluid reservoir
16. Washer solvent reservoir
17. Battery

UNDERHOOD MAINTENANCE COMPONENT LOCATIONS—1.9L TURBO DIESEL INJECTED (TDI) ENGINE

1. Coolant reservoir
2. Washer solvent reservoir
3. Alternator belt
4. Timing belt cover
5. Oil filler cap
6. Engine oil dipstick hole
7. Positive Crankcase Ventilation (PCV) system
8. Radiator hose
9. Bypass hose
10. Battery
11. Air filter housing

UNDERHOOD MAINTENANCE COMPONENT LOCATIONS—2.8L VR6 ENGINE

1. Engine coolant reservoir
2. Power steering fluid reservoir
3. Washer solvent reservoir
4. Serpentine belt
5. Spark plugs
6. Engine oil dipstick
7. Engine oil filler cap
8. Ignition (spark plug) wires
9. Brake master cylinder and power booster
10. Air filter housing
11. Battery

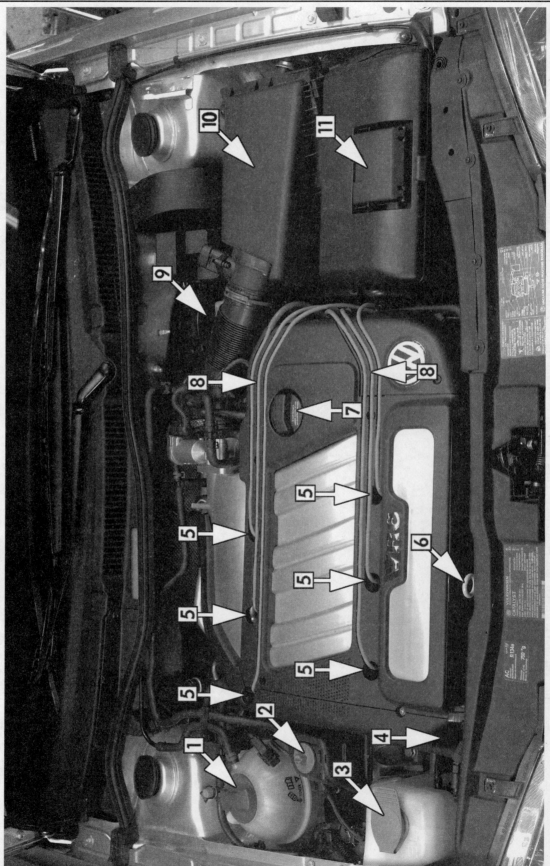

9121PC2

Proper maintenance and tune-up is the key to long and trouble-free vehicle life, and the work can yield its own rewards. Studies have shown that a properly tuned and maintained vehicle can achieve better gas mileage than an out-of-tune vehicle. As a conscientious owner and driver, set aside a Saturday morning, say once a month, to check or replace items which could cause major problems later. Keep your own personal log to jot down which services you performed, how much the parts cost you, the date, and the exact odometer reading at the time. Keep all receipts for such items as engine oil and filters, so that they may be referred to in case of related problems or to determine operating expenses. As a do-it-yourselfer, these receipts are the only proof you have that the required maintenance was performed. In the event of a warranty problem, these receipts will be invaluable.

The literature provided with your vehicle when it was originally delivered includes the factory recommended maintenance schedule. If you no longer have this literature, replacement copies are usually available from the dealer. A maintenance schedule is provided later in this section, in case you do not have the factory literature.

Air Cleaner

A restrictive, dirty air cleaner filter will cause a reduction in fuel economy and performance and an increase in emissions production. The air filter element should be replaced according to the maintenance interval chart in this section, or more often in dusty conditions.

REMOVAL & INSTALLATION

Fox

On CIS and CIS-E equipped models, the air cleaner element is mounted directly under the fuel distributor/air flow sensor assembly. When changing the filter element, the lower portion of the airbox stays in place and the distributor/sensor assembly is lifted up to access the element. It is not necessary to disconnect any fuel lines or wires, but use caution not to stretch the fuel lines and electrical connections.

On Digifant-equipped engines, the air cleaner element is contained within the airbox.

1. On models with CIS and CIS-E fuel injection, loosen the hose clamps to remove the rubber boot from the top of the air flow sensor.
2. On models with CIS and CIS-E fuel injection, loosen the clamp that secures the air boot to the throttle body, and slip the boot from the throttle body flange. This will make it easier to lift the upper portion of the airflow sensor/airbox assembly to retrieve the filter element.
3. Unsnap the cover retaining clips, starting with the hardest ones to reach. The last clip released will be difficult to unsnap, so it should be the easiest to reach.
4. Lift the cover enough to remove the air filter element. Be careful not to stretch the fuel lines and electrical connections.

➡**Any loose dirt, then examine the element. On CIS and CIS-E equipped engines, there may be fuel stains on the element. Dry stains are not a problem but if the element is wet with fuel, the fuel distributor is leaking. Section 5 describes how to pressure test the system. It should be noted that a small amount of oil on the filter element from the crankcase ventilation system is normal. If the filter element is excessively soaked with oil, inspect the crankcase ventilation system.**

To install:
5. Clean the inside of the air box and install the new element with the open pleats facing downward. Make sure the rubber seal fits properly into the groove in the airbox.
6. Lower the cover and secure the clips, starting with the least accessible clip.
7. On CIS and CIS-E equipped engines, install the air boot to both the throttle body and airflow sensor. When installing the boot, make sure the boot is fully seated all the way around the lip before tightening the clamp.

A1 Platform

All A1 platform Cabriolet models are equipped with Digifant fuel injection. The air cleaner element is contained within the airbox, located in the front portion of the engine compartment on the driver's side of the vehicle.

1. Unsnap the cover retaining clips around the perimeter of the airbox, starting with the hardest ones to reach. The last clip released will be difficult to unsnap, so it should be the easiest to reach.
2. Lift the upper portion of the air box from the vehicle, and set it aside.
3. Remove the air filter element.

To install:
4. Install the air filter element, with the open pleats facing downward.
5. Position the top half of the airbox, and snap the cover retaining clips, starting with the hardest ones to reach.

A2 Platform

♦ **See Figures 46 and 47**

1. On models CIS-E equipped engines, loosen the hose clamps to remove the rubber boot from the top of the air flow sensor.
2. On Digifant-equipped engines, loosen the clamp and remove the air duct from the air filter housing.
3. Unsnap the cover retaining clips, starting with the hardest ones to reach. The last clip released will be difficult to unsnap, so it should be the easiest to reach.
4. On Digifant-equipped engines, lift the cover off and remove the air filter element. If the air flow sensor is mounted to the cover, it's not necessary to disconnect the wires.
5. On CIS-E equipped engines, lift the fuel distributor/air flow sensor assembly enough to remove the filter element.
6. With the paper side down, drop the element just a few inches repeatedly on a flat surface to shake out any loose dirt, then examine the element. On CIS-E equipped engines, there may be fuel stains on the element. Dry stains are not a problem, but if the element is wet with fuel, the fuel distributor is leaking. Section 5 describes how to pressure test the system.

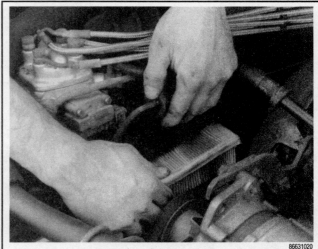

Fig. 46 On 2.0L 16v engines, the air cleaner element is located under the fuel distributor/airflow plate assembly

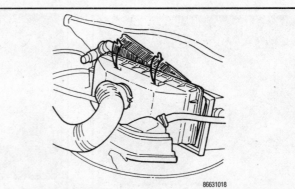

Fig. 47 On normally aspirated diesels, the air cleaner is mounted directly to the intake manifold

7. Wipe out the inside of the airbox and install the new element. Make sure the rubber seal fits properly into the groove in the lower portion of the airbox.

8. Replace the cover and secure the clips, starting with the least accessible clip.

9. When installing the boot on the CIS-E air flow sensor, make sure the boot is fully seated all the way around the lip before tightening the clamp.

A3 Platform

♦ **See Figures 48 thru 55**

On all A3 platform vehicles, the air cleaner element is located within the airbox, on the passenger side of the engine compartment. It is not necessary to disconnect any wiring or hoses from the airbox in order to remove the air cleaner element.

1. Starting with the clip that is most difficult to reach, disengage all of the clips that secure the upper portion of the airbox to the lower portion.

2. Lift the upper portion of the airbox, and remove the filter element. Be careful when lifting the upper portion of the element; excessive force may damage vacuum and electrical connections.

3. Using a clean rag, wipe any accumulated dirt and dust from the inside of the lower portion of the airbox.

To install:

4. Carefully install the new filter element into the lower portion of the airbox. Make sure to install it in the proper direction (open pleats face downward).

5. Starting with the clip that is the most difficult to reach, secure the clips around the perimeter of the airbox.

Fuel Filter

RELIEVING FUEL SYSTEM PRESSURE

♦ **See Figure 56**

All gasoline engines equipped with electric fuel pumps maintain fuel pressure even when the engine is not operating. Because of this, residual pressure may remain in the fuel system for several hours after the engine is shut down.

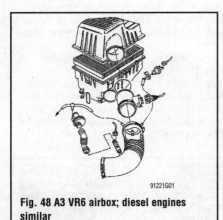

Fig. 48 A3 VR6 airbox; diesel engines similar

Fig. 49 Pull up on the bottom of the air cleaner housing clip to release it . . .

Fig. 50 . . . then unhook the clip from the notch on the upper air cleaner housing

Fig. 51 Remove all vacuum lines from the housing

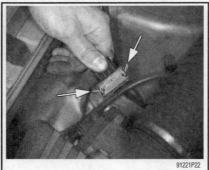

Fig. 52 Squeeze the arrowed clips to release the mass air flow sensor wiring harness

Fig. 53 Once all fasteners have been removed, lift off the air cleaner cover

Fig. 54 Remove the air cleaner

Fig. 55 If the filter is clogged with dirt, replace it

Fig. 56 Fuel filter location–1994 Jetta

To relieve the fuel system pressure on vehicles equipped with gasoline engines, perform the following:

1. Locate the fuel pump fuse, and remove it from the fuse panel.
2. Operate the engine until it runs out of fuel and stops.
3. Remove the fuel filler cap.
4. For safety purposes, disconnect the negative battery cable.

➡When the battery is disconnected, the radio security code will need to be reset. Be sure you obtain the security code (if the radio is equipped with a security system) before performing this procedure. Also, the engine management system's adaptive memory parameters may be lost; as a result, the vehicle may operate erratically for the first few miles after the battery is disconnected.

5. Proceed with the necessary fuel system component repairs. When finished, install the fuel pump fuse and connect the negative battery cable. Don't forget to install the fuel filler cap.

REMOVAL & INSTALLATION

Gasoline Engines

♦ See Figure 57

The fuel filter removes particulate matter from the fuel system which might clog the fuel distributor block or fuel injectors. All gasoline vehicles covered by this book are equipped with "lifetime" fuel filters. According to the manufacturer, unless the fuel system is damaged or contaminated, the filter is large enough to handle all normal fuel filtering requirements for the life of the engine. However, changing this filter more often than recommended can ease the load on the fuel pump, especially on higher mileage vehicles.

On gasoline engine-equipped vehicles, the fuel filter is under the car next to the fuel pump reservoir and looks like a large, metal container. Arrows point the direction of fuel flow through the filter. Banjo type fittings with copper gaskets connect the fuel lines to the filter. Always replace these gaskets any time the fittings are loosened.

✳✳✳ CAUTION

Never smoke when working around gasoline! Avoid all sources of sparks or ignition. Gasoline vapors are EXTREMELY volatile! This procedure will cause a small fuel spill. Make sure the work area is well ventilated, and observe appropriate fire safety precautions.

1. Relieve the fuel system pressure.
2. Raise and safely support the rear of the vehicle. Have a pan ready to catch the fuel that will run out of the reservoir.
3. Have a rag handy and wear safety glasses when loosening the fittings. The system will be under pressure and fuel will be sprayed.
4. Hold the filter with a 19mm or 22mm wrench and loosen the fittings with a 17mm wrench. Wrap the filter and wrenches with a rag to contain any pressurized fuel. Have the catch pan ready.

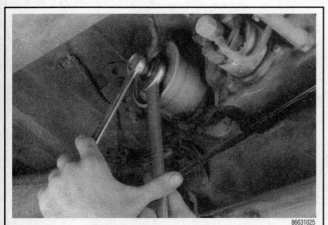

86631025

Fig. 57 Always use a back-up wrench to hold the fuel filter when loosening or tightening the fittings

➡Always use a back-up wrench to hold the filter, or the fuel lines may be damaged.

5. Disconnect the fuel lines, loosen the mounting bracket and remove the filter.
6. Install the new filter but do not tighten the mounting bracket yet.
7. Make sure all fittings and sealing surfaces are clean. Install the banjo bolts with new copper gaskets and torque to 14 ft. lbs. (20 Nm).

➡After replacing the fuel filter, it may take several attempts to start the engine. This is because the fuel pump needs to operate (while the engine is cranking) to pressurize the fuel system.

Diesel Engines

♦ See Figure 58

With diesel engines, absolute cleanliness is essential for the fuel system components. The injection pump of a diesel engine has extremely close tolerances; even small particles of dirt can seriously affect performance.

Changing the fuel filter on vehicles equipped with diesel engines is one of the most basic, yet critical forms of preventative maintenance. Replacement of the filter every 30,000 miles is recommended.

1. Open the fuel filler cap to relieve any pressure that may be in the tank.
2. Disconnect and plug the supply line and injection pump fuel lines from the filter.
3. Remove the clip from the control valve (located on top of the filter), then remove the valve, leaving the two lines connected. Position the valve and the lines off to the side.

➡The control valve is delicate, so be careful during removal and installation.

4. Loosen the mounting clamp nut/screw, then lift the filter assembly straight up. Discard the old filter.

To install:

5. Install the new filter onto the mounting clamp. If there are arrows indicating fuel flow direction, they point towards the front of the vehicle. Tighten the mounting nut/screw until the filter is secure.
6. Install new control valve O-ring seals (using fresh diesel fuel for lubrication) and install the control valve into the flange on the top of the filter. Secure the retaining clip.
7. Connect the fuel lines to the filter. Use new clamps if they are damaged.
8. Connect the negative battery cable, then start the engine. Accelerate the engine a few times (this will clear the air bubbles in the fuel system) and check for fuel leaks.
9. Don't forget to tighten the fuel filler cap.

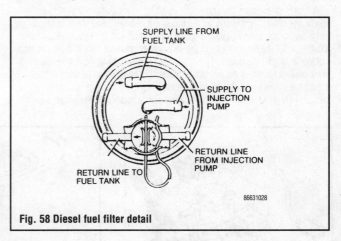

SUPPLY LINE FROM FUEL TANK

SUPPLY TO INJECTION PUMP

RETURN LINE FROM INJECTION PUMP

RETURN LINE TO FUEL TANK

86631028

Fig. 58 Diesel fuel filter detail

Fuel/Water Separator (Diesel Engines)

DRAINING WATER

Although diesel fuel and water do not readily mix, fuel does tend to entrap moisture from the air each time it is moved from one container to another. Eventually every diesel fuel system collects enough water to become a potential hazard. Fortunately, when it's allowed to settle out, the water will always drop to the bottom of the tank or filter housing. Some diesel fuel filters are equipped with a water drain; a bolt or petcock at the bottom of the housing.

Most 1990–92 diesel engine-equipped vehicles are equipped with a water separator, located in front of the fuel tank under the right side of the vehicle. The water seperator's purpose is to allow water to settle from the fuel right at the tank and to alert the driver when draining is required. When the water level in the separator reaches a certain point, a sensor turns on the glow plug indicator light on the dashboard, causing it to blink continuously. With the introduction of the A3 platform, the water separator was eliminated, and removing water from the fuel system is accomplished with a drain screw on the bottom of the fuel filter.

At The Water Separator

▶ See Figure 59

1. Raise and safely support the vehicle. Remove the fuel filler cap.
2. At the separator, connect a hose from the separator drain to a catch pan.
3. Open the drain valve (3 turns) and drain the separator until a steady stream of fuel flows from the separator, then close the valve. Don't forget to install the filler cap.

At The Filter

▶ See Figure 60

1. If the filter is equipped with a water drain at the bottom, place a suitable filter under the filter to catch the water and fuel.
2. Remove the retaining clip that secures the control valve (located on top of the filter), then remove the valve, leaving the two lines connected.
3. Loosen the drain screw, and allow any accumulated water to flow from the filter. When clear diesel fuel flows from the screw, tighten the screw securely.
4. Using a new O-ring, install the control valve, and secure the retaining clip.
5. Start the engine and accelerate a few times to clear any air in the system. Check for bubbles, which indicate an air leak in the system.

Crankcase Ventilation System

▶ See Figure 61

To send oil fumes and crankcase blow-by gasses back into the engine for burning, all engines are equipped with some type of crankcase breather control valve.

On early 8v engines, the crankcase ventilation system consists of a ventilation hose connecting a fitting on the top of the cylinder head cover to the airbox, and a secondary hose that attaching the intake manifold to the ventilation hose. A baffle under the hose fitting on the valve cover prevents excess oil vapor from making its way to the airbox. The small hose connecting to the intake manifold has a built-in restrictor orifice, which essentially creates a controlled vacuum leak to the intake manifold. When the throttle opening is small and manifold vacuum is high, crankcase oil fumes are drawn directly into the intake manifold.

When the throttle opening is large and manifold vacuum low, some of the oil fumes flow through the large hose to the airbox. 16v engines use this same system, except the ventilation hose attaches to a plastic baffle on the cylinder block, instead of the cylinder head cover.

Later model 8v engines are equipped with a equipped with diaphragm control valves, which take place of the previously described system. The diaphragm control valve is mounted to the cylinder head cover, and controls ventilation of the crankcase and cylinder head into the intake tract. The diaphragm control valve maintains a constant balance against manifold vacuum, keeping blow-by vapor flow at a constant percentage of the total intake air volume.

VR6 engines use a simple crankcase ventilation system, similar to the 4-cylinder engines. A single hose connects the cylinder head cover to the intake tract, ahead of the throttle body. A heater element is contained within the hose, which prevents the vapors from icing over in cold weather. As with the 4-cylinder engines, the cylinder head cover contains a metal mesh flame trap that contains any ignited vapors during the event of an engine backfire.

On all systems, there is no maintenance required other than to check for vacuum leaks and clogged hoses. When removing hoses for inspection, take note of the direction of the restriction valves. Replace any clogged or cracked hoses.

Evaporative Canister

SERVICING

▶ See Figures 62, 63 and 64

All vehicles with gasoline engines are equipped with some form of fuel vapor control device. The evaporative emission control system prevents the escape of raw fuel vapors (unburned hydrocarbons, or HC) into the atmosphere. On Volkswagens, a carbon (charcoal) canister is used to store fuel tank vapors that accumulate when the engine is not running. When the engine is running, the vapors in the canister are carried to the intake manifold by allowing fresh air into the bottom of the canister.

Other components of the system include a non-vented fuel filler cap, fuel tank expansion chamber and one or more check valves to prevent liquid fuel from entering the canister.

Early models use a vacuum-operated valve to vent the fuel vapors into the intake tract; later models use an electric valve actuated by the Electronic Control Module (ECM).

On all Fox models, the evaporative canister is located in the engine compartment, under the master cylinder. On all other models, the evaporative canister is located on the passenger side front wheel housing.

The evaporative control system does not require any service under normal conditions other than to check for leaks. Check the hoses visually for cracks, breaks, etc. Also check the seal on the gas tank filler cap. Replace the cap if the is split. If any hoses are in need of replacement, use only hoses marked EVAP, available from your local automotive supply store. If you suspect a problem with the purge valve or any other component, see Section 5 for information on testing the system.

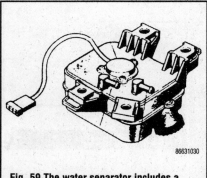

Fig. 59 The water separator includes a sensor that flashes the glow plug light when draining is required

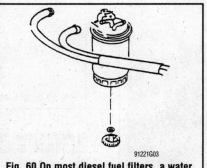

Fig. 60 On most diesel fuel filters, a water drain screw (bottom) is provided for bleeding any accumulated water from the fuel system

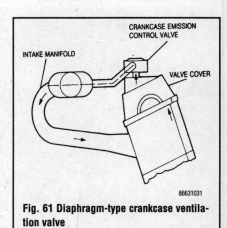

Fig. 61 Diaphragm-type crankcase ventilation valve

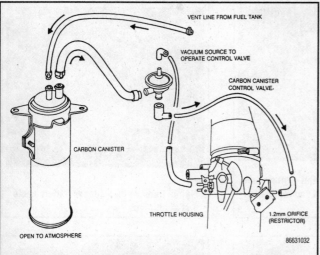

Fig. 62 Evaporative canister and purge valve used with Digifant engines

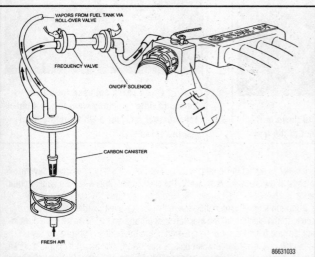

Fig. 63 Evaporative canister frequency valve and control valve system used 2.0L 16v engines

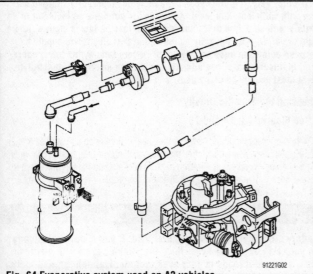

Fig. 64 Evaporative system used on A3 vehicles

Battery

PRECAUTIONS

Always use caution when working on or near the battery. Never allow a tool to bridge the gap between the negative and positive battery terminals. Also, be careful not to allow a tool to provide a ground between the positive cable/terminal and any metal component on the vehicle. Either of these conditions will cause a short circuit, leading to sparks and possible personal injury.

Do not smoke, have an open flame or create sparks near a battery; the gases contained in the battery are very explosive and, if ignited, could cause severe injury or death.

All batteries, regardless of type, should be carefully secured by a battery hold-down device. If this is not done, the battery terminals or casing may crack from stress applied to the battery during vehicle operation. A battery which is not secured may allow acid to leak out, making it discharge faster; such leaking corrosive acid can also eat away at components under the hood.

Always visually inspect the battery case for cracks, leakage and corrosion. A white corrosive substance on the battery case or on nearby components would indicate a leaking or cracked battery. If the battery is cracked, it should be replaced immediately.

➡Anytime the battery is disconnected, the radio security code will need to be reset. Be sure you obtain the security code (if the radio is equipped with a security system) before disconnecting the battery. Also, the engine management system's adaptive memory parameters may be lost; as a result, the vehicle may operate erratically for the first few miles after the battery is disconnected.

GENERAL MAINTENANCE

♦ **See Figures 65 thru 72**

A battery that is not sealed must be checked periodically for electrolyte level. You cannot add water to a sealed maintenance-free battery (though not all main-

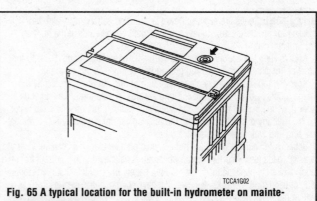

Fig. 65 A typical location for the built-in hydrometer on maintenance-free batteries

Fig. 66 The battery cover is held in place by several snaps

Fig. 67 The top flap of the battery cover must be removed to gain access to the posts

Fig. 68 Always have your anti-theft system or radio code handy before you remove the negative battery cable

Fig. 69 Remove the negative battery cable first at all times

Fig. 70 Once the negative is removed, loosen and remove the positive, and then the battery itself

Fig. 71 Remove the one hold down bolt and then slide the battery out of the tray

Fig. 72 If you car is not used for a long period of time, you may want to put a battery charger on it for a while before starting the vehicle

tenance-free batteries are sealed); however, a sealed battery must also be checked for proper electrolyte level, as indicated by the color of the built-in hydrometer "eye."

Always keep the battery cables and terminals free of corrosion. Refer to the removal, installation and cleaning procedures outlined in this section.

Keep the top of the battery clean, as a film of dirt can help completely discharge a battery that is not used for long periods. A solution of baking soda and water may be used for cleaning, but be careful to flush this off with clear water. DO NOT let any of the solution into the filler holes. Baking soda neutralizes battery acid and will de-activate a battery cell.

Batteries in vehicles which are not operated on a regular basis can fall victim to parasitic loads (small current drains which are constantly drawing current from the battery). Normal parasitic loads may drain a battery on a vehicle that is in storage and not used for 6–8 weeks. Vehicles that have additional accessories such as a cellular phone, an alarm system or other devices that increase parasitic load may discharge a battery sooner. If the vehicle is to be stored for 6–8 weeks in a secure area and the alarm system, if present, is not necessary, the negative battery cable should be disconnected at the onset of storage to protect the battery charge.

Remember that constantly discharging and recharging will shorten battery life. Take care not to allow a battery to be needlessly discharged.

BATTERY FLUID

Check the battery electrolyte level at least once a month, or more often in hot weather or during periods of extended vehicle operation. On non-sealed batteries, the level can be checked either through the case on translucent batteries or by removing the cell caps on opaque-cased types. The electrolyte level in each cell should be kept filled to the split ring inside each cell, or the line marked on the outside of the case.

If the level is low, add only distilled water through the opening until the level is correct. Each cell is separate from the others, so each must be checked and filled individually. Distilled water should be used, because the chemicals and minerals found in most drinking water are harmful to the battery and could significantly shorten its life.

If water is added in freezing weather, the vehicle should be driven several miles to allow the water to mix with the electrolyte. Otherwise, the battery could freeze.

Although some maintenance-free batteries have removable cell caps for access to the electrolyte, the electrolyte condition and level on all sealed maintenance-free batteries must be checked using the built-in hydrometer "eye." The exact type of eye varies between battery manufacturers, but most apply a sticker to the battery itself explaining the possible readings. When in doubt, refer to the battery manufacturer's instructions to interpret battery condition using the built-in hydrometer.

➡**Although the readings from built-in hydrometers found in sealed batteries may vary, a green eye usually indicates a properly charged battery with sufficient fluid level. A dark eye is normally an indicator of a battery with sufficient fluid, but one which may be low in charge. And a light or yellow eye is usually an indication that electrolyte supply has dropped below the necessary level for battery (and hydrometer) operation. In this last case, sealed batteries with an insufficient electrolyte level must usually be discarded.**

Checking the Specific Gravity

◢ **See Figures 73, 74 and 75**

A hydrometer is required to check the specific gravity on all batteries that are not maintenance-free. On batteries that are maintenance-free, the specific gravity is checked by observing the built-in hydrometer "eye" on the top of the battery case. Check with your battery's manufacturer for proper interpretation of its built-in hydrometer readings.

✳✳ CAUTION

Battery electrolyte contains sulfuric acid. If you should splash any on your skin or in your eyes, flush the affected area with plenty of clear water. If it lands in your eyes, get medical help immediately.

Fig. 73 On non-maintenance-free batteries, the fluid level can be checked through the case on translucent models; the cell caps must be removed on other models

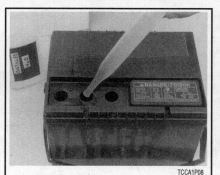

Fig. 74 If the fluid level is low, add only distilled water through the opening until the level is correct

Fig. 75 Check the specific gravity of the battery's electrolyte with a hydrometer

The fluid (sulfuric acid solution) contained in the battery cells will tell you many things about the condition of the battery. Because the cell plates must be kept submerged below the fluid level in order to operate, maintaining the fluid level is extremely important. And, because the specific gravity of the acid is an indication of electrical charge, testing the fluid can be an aid in determining if the battery must be replaced. A battery in a vehicle with a properly operating charging system should require little maintenance, but careful, periodic inspection should reveal problems before they leave you stranded.

As stated earlier, the specific gravity of a battery's electrolyte level can be used as an indication of battery charge. At least once a year, check the specific gravity of the battery. It should be between 1.20 and 1.26 on the gravity scale. Most auto supply stores carry a variety of inexpensive battery testing hydrometers. These can be used on any non-sealed battery to test the specific gravity in each cell.

The battery testing hydrometer has a squeeze bulb at one end and a nozzle at the other. Battery electrolyte is sucked into the hydrometer until the float is lifted from its seat. The specific gravity is then read by noting the position of the float.

If gravity is low in one or more cells, the battery should be slowly charged and checked again to see if the gravity has come up. Generally, if after charging, the specific gravity between any two cells varies more than 50 points (0.50), the battery should be replaced, as it can no longer produce sufficient voltage to guarantee proper operation.

CABLES

▶ **See Figures 76, 77, 78, 79 and 80**

Once a year (or as necessary), the battery terminals and the cable clamps should be cleaned. Loosen the clamps and remove the cables, negative cable first. On batteries with posts on top, the use of a puller specially made for this purpose is recommended. These are inexpensive and available in most auto parts stores. Side terminal battery cables are secured with a small bolt.

Clean the cable clamps and the battery terminal with a wire brush, until all corrosion, grease, etc., is removed and the metal is shiny. It is especially impor-

Fig. 76 Maintenance is performed with household items and with special tools like this post cleaner

Fig. 77 The underside of this special battery tool has a wire brush to clean post terminals

Fig. 78 Place the tool over the battery posts and twist to clean until the metal is shiny

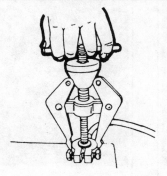

Fig. 79 A special tool is available to pull the clamp from the post

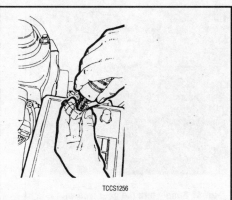

Fig. 80 The cable ends should be cleaned as well

tant to clean the inside of the clamp thoroughly (an old knife is useful here), since a small deposit of foreign material or oxidation there will prevent a sound electrical connection and inhibit either starting or charging. Special tools are available for cleaning these parts, one type for conventional top post batteries and another type for side terminal batteries. It is also a good idea to apply some dielectric grease to the terminal, as this will aid in the prevention of corrosion.

After the clamps and terminals are clean, reinstall the cables, negative cable last; DO NOT hammer the clamps onto battery posts. Tighten the clamps securely, but do not distort them. Give the clamps and terminals a thin external coating of grease after installation, to retard corrosion.

Check the cables at the same time that the terminals are cleaned. If the cable insulation is cracked or broken, or if the ends are frayed, the cable should be replaced with a new cable of the same length and gauge.

CHARGING

⁂ CAUTION

The chemical reaction which takes place in all batteries generates explosive hydrogen gas. A spark can cause the battery to explode and splash acid. To avoid serious personal injury, be sure there is proper ventilation and take appropriate fire safety precautions when connecting, disconnecting, or charging a battery and when using jumper cables.

A battery should be charged at a slow rate to keep the plates inside from getting too hot. However, if some maintenance-free batteries are allowed to discharge until they are almost "dead," they may have to be charged at a high rate to bring them back to "life." Always follow the charger manufacturer's instructions on charging the battery.

REPLACEMENT

When it becomes necessary to replace the battery, select one with an amperage rating equal to or greater than the battery originally installed. Deterioration

Fig. 81 Some tensioners may be of the gear type such as the one shown here

and just plain aging of the battery cables, starter motor, and associated wires makes the battery's job harder in successive years. The slow increase in electrical resistance over time makes it prudent to install a new battery with a greater capacity than the old.

Belts

INSPECTION

▶ **See Figures 81, 82 and 83**

As drive belts wear, they tend to stretch, or lengthen. As a belt stretches over time, the tension decreases, which causes the belt to slip on the pulleys. This slippage not only causes operating problems (erratic steering, high engine temperatures, and charging system problems), but can greatly accelerate wear and damage to the belts themselves. Excessive slippage can cause a drive belt to glaze, overheat, and eventually break. Regular inspection and adjustment of the accessory drive belts will prolong their life, and ensure proper operation of belt-driven components.

To thoroughly inspect accessory drive belts, it's advisable to remove the lower engine cover, and view the condition of the belts through the right front wheel housing. If necessary, raise and safely support the vehicle to allow access. Viewing the belts from the engine compartment is sometimes possible, but belt-driven components such as the power steering pump and air conditioner compressor are often out of view from the engine compartment.

Inspect the belts for signs of glazing or cracking. A glazed belt will be perfectly smooth from slippage, while a good belt will have a slight texture of fabric visible. Cracks will usually start at the inner edge of the belt and run outward. All worn or damaged drive belts should be replaced immediately. It is always best to replace all drive belts at one time, as a preventive maintenance measure, during this service operation.

CHECKING TENSION AND ADJUSTMENT

▶ **See Figure 84**

To check belt tension on V-belts, push in on the drive belt about midway between the crankshaft pulley and the driven component. If the belt is less than 39.4 in. (1m) long, it should deflect between 0.80–0.120 in. (2–5mm). For longer belts, it should deflect between 0.40–0.060 in. (10–15mm). Belt size is usually printed on the back side of the belt. If it can't be read, it's probably time to replace it.

To compensate for the natural stretching of the accessory drive belts, a means of adjustment is necessary to change the distance between the crankshaft pulley and the driven component. Volkswagen employs several methods to accomplish this task. The first, which is most common on late-model vehicles, is with the use of an automatic belt tensioner. Most engines with poly-ribbed belts, or serpentine belts, are fitted with automatic belt tensioners. These tensioners can be either arm-type or rotary type. The second method (most common with V-belts) involves the driven component being rotated on a pivot. A slotted bracket and or arm(s) are used to hold the component in place once the belt tension is set. Within this method, there are four variations. The most basic

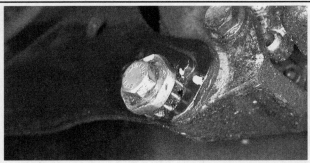

Fig. 82 Simply turn the gear type with a wrench to adjust

Fig. 83 Once the belt is loosened, slide it off the pulleys to remove it

Fig. 84 Adjust tension by loosening both the pivot bolt and the upper adjustment bolt

variation is a simple slotted bracket with a bolt. This requires pulling or pushing on the driven component to achieve the desired belt tension. Some diesel and Mono-motronic engines use a spring-loaded alternator bracket that sets the belt tension after the slotted bolt is loosened. Other models use a rack and pinion design on the slotted adjustment bracket. This allows for effortless belt adjustment, since the pinion gear can be turned with a wrench to make adjustments. The final variation of the slotted style adjustment design uses a long adjuster bolt that pushes or pulls the driven component once the slotted bolt is loosened.

Poly-Ribbed Belts

Most all Volkswagen engines equipped with poly-ribbed belts are equipped with automatic adjusters, and do not require adjustment. The spring action of the tensioner compensates for the stretching of the belt. However, on some 1.8L Mono-motronic (ACC) and 1.9L diesel (AAZ, AHU) engines, A "semi-automatic" belt tensioning system is employed. This procedure is for belt adjustment of these engines only.

1. Disconnect the negative battery cable.
2. Loosen the alternator pivot bolt, but do not remove it from the bracket.
3. Loosen, but do not remove the lower alternator bolt.
4. Push down on the alternator, and let it spring back up several times. If it does not spring freely, it may be necessary to further loosen the mounting bolts.
5. Reconnect the negative battery cable.
6. Start the engine, and allow it to idle for around 15 seconds.
7. Without leaning on the alternator, or touching the belt, tighten the alternator mounting bolts to 18 ft. lbs. (25 Nm).

➡When adjusting the driven components to set the drive belt tension, make absolutely sure all of the slotted bracket bolts are loosened before attempting to move the driven component. Attempting to rotate the pinion gear or push bolt without the slotted bolts loosened can cause damage to the fasteners, and in some cases, the component itself.

V-Belts

PLAIN SLOTTED BRACKETS

▶ See Figure 85

1. As a safety precaution, disconnect the negative battery cable.
2. Loosen the adjustment nut/bolt in the slotted bracket. Slightly loosen the pivot bolt.
3. Pull (don't pry) the component outward to increase tension. Push inward to reduce tension. Tighten the adjusting nut/bolt and the pivot bolt.
4. Recheck the drive belt tension, readjust if necessary.
5. Reconnect the negative battery cable.

SLOTTED BRACKETS WITH ADJUSTMENT BOLT

▶ See Figures 86 and 87

1. As a safety precaution, disconnect the negative battery cable.
2. Loosen the slotted bracket bolt(s), and slightly loosen the pivot bolt(s).
3. If equipped, loosen the locknut(s) on the adjustment bolt(s).
4. Turn the threaded adjustment bolt(s) as necessary to achieve the correct tension.
5. Tighten the pivot bolt(s) and the slotted bracket bolt(s) securely.
6. While holding adjustment bolt(s) in position, tighten the lock nut(s) if equipped.
7. Recheck the drive belt tension and readjust if necessary.
8. Reconnect the negative battery cable.

RACK AND PINION-TYPE SLOTTED BRACKETS

▶ See Figures 88 and 89

1. As a safety precaution, disconnect the negative battery cable.
2. Loosen the alternator pivot bolt, and the slotted bracket bolt, and the bracket mounting bolt.

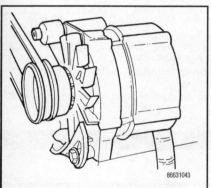

Fig. 85 Alternator mounting with slotted brackets

Fig. 86 Some components, like this air conditioner compressor, use a slotted bracket with an adjustment bolt. To adjust the tension, loosen the slotted bracket bolt . . .

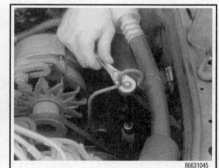

Fig. 87 . . . and turn the adjustment bolt as necessary to achieve the proper belt tension

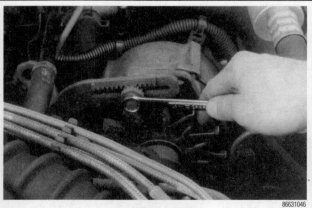

Fig. 88 Loosen the tension bolt (shown) and the alternator pivot bolt until the alternator swings freely under its own weight

Fig. 89 Adjust the V-belt by turning the nut on the tension bolt

3. Adjust the V-belt by turning the large nut (the pinion) nut while checking the belt deflection.

4. While holding the pinion nut steady, tighten the slotted bracket bolt to hold the adjustment setting.

5. Tighten the alternator pivot bolt, and the slotted bracket mounting bolt.

6. Recheck the drive belt tension and readjust if necessary.

7. Reconnect the negative battery cable.

Split Pulley (Fox only)

▶ See Figure 90

On Fox models, the air conditioner compressor drive belts are adjusted by varying the number of discs (shims) between the halves of the crankshaft pulley.

1. Remove the nuts/bolts securing the tensioner plate and crankshaft pulley halves.

2. Add or remove the amount of spacer discs between the pulley halves until the belt tension is correct.

➡If there are any shims left over, do not throw them away. Store the extra shims in front of the split pulley (behind the tensioner plate).

3. Secure the pulley halves. Torque the pulley nuts or bolts to 15 ft. lbs. (20 Nm).

REMOVAL & INSTALLATION

▶ See Figures 91, 92 and 93

If a belt must be replaced, the driven component must be loosened and moved to its extreme loosest position (usually by moving it toward the center of the motor). On models with automatic belt adjusters, refer to the illustrations for information on relieving belt tension. After removing the old belt, check the pulleys for dirt or built-up material which could affect belt contact. Carefully install the new belt, it may appear to be just a little too small to fit over the pulley flanges. Fit the belt over the largest pulley (usually the crankshaft pulley at the bottom center of the motor) first, then work on the smaller one(s). Gentle pressure in the direction of rotation is helpful. Some belts run around a third or idler pulley, which acts as an additional pivot in the belt's path. It may be possible to loosen the idler pulley as well as the main component, making your job much easier. Depending on which belt(s) you are changing, it may be necessary to loosen or remove other interfering belts to get at the one(s) you want.

When buying replacement belts, remember that the fit is critical according to the length of the belt, the width of the belt, the depth of the belt and the angle or profile of the V shape (always match up old belt with new belt if possible). The belt shape should exactly match the shape of the pulley; belts that are not an exact match can cause noise, slippage and premature failure.

After the new belt is installed, adjust it for proper tension. This is sometimes a three or four-handed job; you may find an assistant helpful. Make sure that all the bolts you loosened are retightened and that any other loosened belts have the correct tension. A new belt can be expected to stretch a bit after installation so be prepared to re-adjust your new belt.

➡After installing a new belt, run the engine for about 5 minutes and then recheck the belt tension.

Timing Belt

INSPECTION & ADJUSTMENT

All 4-cylinder Volkswagen engines use a toothed belt to drive the camshaft(s). This design is lightweight, and offers a low amount of parasitic drag on the crankshaft, which increases the output of the engine. Additionally, inspection and replacement of the belt is a relatively simple task, (as opposed to replacing a timing chain and sprockets) ensuring that the engine is operating at its peak efficiency.

The timing belt is a basic, yet critical engine component. If the belt were to break, the valvetrain can be seriously damaged. Frequent inspection, adjustment, and replacement of the timing belt and tensioning pulley is a must.

Volkswagen specifies a 15,000 mile (24,000 km) inspection/adjustment interval of the timing belt. For 1997–99 TDI engines, a 10,000 mile (16,000 km) inspection/adjustment interval is specified.

Volkswagen does not list a replacement interval for timing belts for gasoline engines, but do specify a 60,000 mile (96,000 km) interval for diesel engines. It is highly recommended on **all** 4-cylinder engines that the timing belt be replaced at this 60,000 mile interval.

Please refer to Section 3 for procedures on timing belt adjustment, removal and installation.

Hoses

INSPECTION

▶ See Figures 94, 95, 96, 97 and 98

Upper and lower radiator hoses, along with the heater hoses, should be checked for deterioration, leaks and loose hose clamps at least every 15,000 miles (24,000 km). It is also wise to check the hoses periodically in early spring

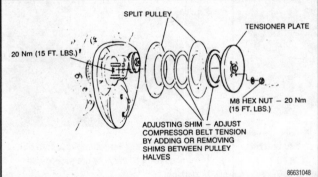

SPLIT PULLEY

TENSIONER PLATE

20 Nm (15 FT. LBS.)

M8 HEX NUT — 20 Nm (15 FT. LBS.)

ADJUSTING SHIM — ADJUST COMPRESSOR BELT TENSION BY ADDING OR REMOVING SHIMS BETWEEN PULLEY HALVES

86631048

Fig. 90 Belt adjusting shims on Fox models. Extra shims are stored behind the tensioner plate

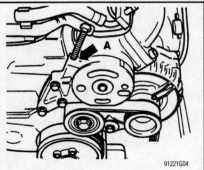

91221G04

Fig. 91 On VR6 engines, an M8 bolt can be temporarily installed in the belt tensioning mechanism to relieve belt tension

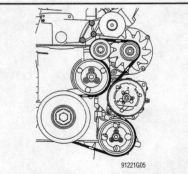

91221G05

Fig. 92 When removing ribbed belts, it's a good idea to mark the direction of the belt if it is to be reused

91221PB4

Fig. 93 Ribbed style serpentine belt

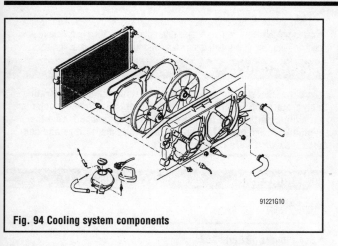

Fig. 94 Cooling system components

Fig. 95 The cracks developing along this hose are a result of age-related hardening

Fig. 96 A hose clamp that is too tight can cause older hoses to separate and tear on either side of the clamp

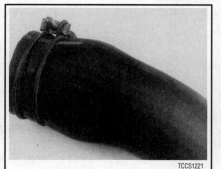

Fig. 97 A soft spongy hose (identifiable by the swollen section) will eventually burst and should be replaced

Fig. 98 Hoses are likely to deteriorate from the inside if the cooling system is not periodically flushed

and at the beginning of the fall or winter when you are performing other maintenance. A quick visual inspection could discover a weakened hose which can leave you stranded if it had remained un-repaired.

Whenever you are checking the hoses, make sure the engine and cooling system are cold. Visually inspect for cracking, rotting or collapsed hoses, and replace as necessary. Run your hand along the length of the hose. If a weak or swollen spot is noted when squeezing the hose wall, the hose should be replaced.

REMOVAL & INSTALLATION

▶ See Figures 99 and 100

1. Remove the radiator pressure cap.

✳✳ CAUTION

Never remove the pressure cap while the engine is running, or personal injury from scalding hot coolant or steam may result. If possible, wait until the engine has cooled to remove the pressure cap. If this is not possible, wrap a thick cloth around the pressure cap and turn it slowly to the stop. Step back while the pressure is released from the cooling system. When you are sure all the pressure has been released, use the cloth to turn and remove the cap.

2. Position a clean container under the radiator and/or engine draincock or plug, then open the drain and allow the cooling system to drain to an appropriate level. For some upper hoses, only a little coolant must be drained. To remove hoses positioned lower on the engine, such as a lower radiator hose, the entire cooling system must be emptied.

✳✳ CAUTION

When draining coolant, keep in mind that cats and dogs are attracted by ethylene glycol antifreeze, and are quite likely to drink any that is left in an uncovered container or in puddles on the

Fig. 99 Removing the hose clamp from the lower radiator hose

Fig. 100 Remove the clamp from the hose and then slide the hose off

ground. This will prove fatal in sufficient quantity. Always drain coolant into a resealable container. Coolant may be reused unless it is contaminated or several years old.

3. Loosen the hose clamps at each end of the hose requiring replacement. Clamps are usually either of the spring tension type (which require pliers to squeeze the tabs and loosen) or of the screw tension type (which require screw or hex drivers to loosen). Pull the clamps back on the hose away from the connection.

4. Twist, pull and slide the hose off the fitting, taking care not to damage the neck of the component from which the hose is being removed.

➡**If the hose is stuck at the connection, do not try to insert a screwdriver or other sharp tool under the hose end in an effort to free it, as the connection and/or hose may become damaged. Heater connections especially may be easily damaged by such a procedure. If the hose is to be replaced, use a single-edged razor blade to make a slice along the portion of the hose which is stuck on the connection, perpendicular to the end of the hose. Do not cut deep so as to prevent damaging the connection. The hose can then be peeled from the connection and discarded.**

5. Clean both hose mounting connections. Inspect the condition of the hose clamps and replace them, if necessary.

To install:

6. Dip the ends of the new hose into clean engine coolant to ease installation.

7. Slide the clamps over the replacement hose, then slide the hose ends over the connections into position.

8. Position and secure the clamps at least ¼ in. (6.35mm) from the ends of the hose. Make sure they are located beyond the raised bead of the connector.

9. Close the radiator or engine drains and properly refill the cooling system with the clean drained engine coolant or a suitable mixture of coolant and water.

➡**Volkswagen uses a special type of coolant in later model vehicles. It is recommended that the specified type of coolant only be used in the engine's cooling system, to prevent premature corrosion and deterioration of cooling system components. Refer to the Fluids And Lubricants heading within this section for more information.**

Fig. 101 CV-boots must be inspected periodically for damage

10. If available, install a pressure tester and check for leaks. If a pressure tester is not available, run the engine until normal operating temperature is reached (allowing the system to naturally pressurize), then check for leaks.

※※ **CAUTION**

If you are checking for leaks with the system at normal operating temperature, BE EXTREMELY CAREFUL not to touch any moving or hot engine parts. Once temperature has been reached, shut the engine OFF, and check for leaks around the hose fittings and connections which were removed earlier.

CV Joint Boots

INSPECTION

▸ **See Figures 101 and 102**

The CV (Constant Velocity) boots should be checked for damage each time the oil is changed and any other time the vehicle is raised for service. These boots keep water, grime, dirt and other damaging matter from entering the CV-joints. Any of these could cause early CV-joint failure which can be expensive to repair. Heavy grease thrown around the inside of the front wheel(s) and on the brake caliper/drum can be an indication of a torn boot. Thoroughly check the boots for missing clamps and tears. If the boot is damaged, it should be replaced immediately. Please refer to Section 7 for procedures.

Spark Plugs

▸ **See Figures 103 and 104**

A typical spark plug consists of a metal shell surrounding a ceramic insulator. A metal electrode extends downward through the center of the insulator and protrudes a small distance. Located at the end of the plug and attached to the side of the outer metal shell is the side electrode. The side electrode bends in at a 90 degree angle so that its tip is just past and parallel to the tip of the center electrode. The distance between these two electrodes (measured in thousandths of an inch or hundredths of a millimeter) is called the spark plug gap.

The spark plug does not produce a spark, but instead provides a gap across which the current can arc. The coil produces anywhere from 20,000 to 50,000 volts (depending on the type and application) which travels through the wires to the spark plugs. The current passes along the center electrode and jumps the gap to the side electrode, and in doing so, ignites the air/fuel mixture in the combustion chamber.

SPARK PLUG HEAT RANGE

▸ **See Figure 105**

Spark plug heat range is the ability of the plug to dissipate heat. The longer the insulator (or the farther it extends into the engine), the hotter the plug will operate; the shorter the insulator (the closer the electrode is to the block's cooling passages) the cooler it will operate. A plug that absorbs little heat and

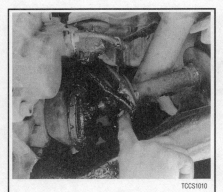

Fig. 102 A torn boot should be replaced immediately

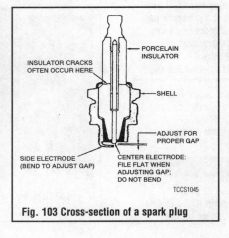

Fig. 103 Cross-section of a spark plug

INSULATOR CRACKS OFTEN OCCUR HERE

PORCELAIN INSULATOR

SHELL

ADJUST FOR PROPER GAP

SIDE ELECTRODE (BEND TO ADJUST GAP)

CENTER ELECTRODE: FILE FLAT WHEN ADJUSTING GAP; DO NOT BEND

Fig. 104 Close up of the electrode of a spark plug

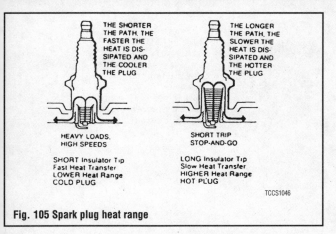

Fig. 105 Spark plug heat range

remains too cool will quickly accumulate deposits of oil and carbon since it is not hot enough to burn them off. This leads to plug fouling and consequently to misfiring. A plug that absorbs too much heat will have no deposits but, due to the excessive heat, the electrodes will burn away quickly and might possibly lead to preignition or other ignition problems. Preignition takes place when plug tips get so hot that they glow sufficiently to ignite the air/fuel mixture before the actual spark occurs. This early ignition will usually cause a pinging during low speeds and heavy loads.

The general rule of thumb for choosing the correct heat range when picking a spark plug is: if most of your driving is long distance, high speed travel, use a colder plug; if most of your driving is stop and go, use a hotter plug. Original equipment plugs are generally a good compromise between the 2 styles and most people never have the need to change their plugs from the factory-recommended heat range.

REMOVAL & INSTALLATION

♦ See Figure 106

A set of spark plugs usually requires replacement after about 20,000–30,000 miles (32,000–48,000 km), depending on your style of driving. In normal operation plug gap increases about 0.001 in. (0.025mm) for every 2500 miles (4000 km). As the gap increases, the plug's voltage requirement also increases. It requires a greater voltage to jump the wider gap and about two to three times as much voltage to fire the plug at high speeds than at idle. The improved air/fuel ratio control of modern fuel injection combined with the higher voltage output of modern ignition systems will often allow an engine to run significantly longer on a set of standard spark plugs, but keep in mind that efficiency will drop as the gap widens (along with fuel economy and power).

When you're removing spark plugs, work on one at a time. Don't start by removing the plug wires all at once, because, unless you number them, they may become mixed up. Take a minute before you begin and number the wires with tape.

1. Disconnect the negative battery cable, and if the vehicle has been run recently, allow the engine to thoroughly cool.

2. Carefully twist the spark plug wire boot to loosen it, then pull upward and remove the boot from the plug. Be sure to pull on the boot and not on the wire, otherwise the connector located inside the boot may become separated.

Fig. 106 A swivel socket may be needed to reach difficult plugs

➡On VR6 models, a special spark plug boot removal tool (usually supplied with the vehicle, attached to the hood prop rod) is required to remove the spark plug boots. Do NOT pull on the wires! They will be damaged.

3. Using compressed air, blow any water or debris from the spark plug well to assure that no harmful contaminants are allowed to enter the combustion chamber when the spark plug is removed. If compressed air is not available, use a rag or a brush to clean the area.

➡Remove the spark plugs when the engine is cold, if possible, to prevent damage to the threads. If removal of the plugs is difficult, apply a few drops of penetrating oil or silicone spray to the area around the base of the plug, and allow it a few minutes to work.

4. Using a spark plug socket that is equipped with a rubber insert to properly hold the plug, turn the spark plug counterclockwise to loosen and remove the spark plug from the bore.

✳✳ WARNING

Be sure not to use a flexible extension on the socket. Use of a flexible extension may allow a shear force to be applied to the plug. A shear force could break the plug off in the cylinder head, leading to costly and frustrating repairs.

To install:

5. Inspect the spark plug boot for tears or damage. If a damaged boot is found, the spark plug wire must be replaced.

6. Using a wire feeler gauge, check and adjust the spark plug gap. When using a gauge, the proper size should pass between the electrodes with a slight drag. The next larger size should not be able to pass while the next smaller size should pass freely.

7. Apply a light coating of anti-seize compound to the threads of the spark plug.

8. Carefully thread the plug into the bore by hand. If resistance is felt before the plug is almost completely threaded, back the plug out and begin threading again. In small, hard to reach areas, an old spark plug wire and boot could be used as a threading tool. The boot will hold the plug while you twist the end of the wire and the wire is supple enough to twist before it would allow the plug to crossthread.

✳✳ WARNING

Do not use the spark plug socket to thread the plugs. Always carefully thread the plug by hand or using an old plug wire to prevent the possibility of crossthreading and damaging the cylinder head bore.

9. Carefully tighten the spark plug. If the plug you are installing is equipped with a crush washer, seat the plug, then tighten about ¼ turn to crush the washer. If you are installing a tapered seat plug, tighten the plug to specifications provided by the vehicle or plug manufacturer.

10. Apply a small amount of silicone dielectric compound to the end of the spark plug lead or inside the spark plug boot to prevent sticking, then install the boot to the spark plug and push until it clicks into place. The click may be felt or heard, then gently pull back on the boot to assure proper contact.

INSPECTION & GAPPING

♦ See Figures 107, 108, 109, 110 and 111

Check the plugs for deposits and wear. If they are not going to be replaced, clean the plugs thoroughly. Remember that any kind of deposit will decrease the efficiency of the plug. Plugs can be cleaned on a spark plug cleaning machine, which can sometimes be found in service stations, or you can do an acceptable job of cleaning with a stiff brush. If the plugs are cleaned, the electrodes must be filed flat. Use an ignition points file, not an emery board or the like, which will leave deposits. The electrodes must be filed perfectly flat with sharp edges; rounded edges reduce the spark plug voltage by as much as 50%.

➡Do not use a metal brush to clean the electrode on platinum-type spark plugs.

Check spark plug gap before installation. The ground electrode (the L-shaped one connected to the body of the plug) must be parallel to the center electrode and the specified size wire gauge (please refer to the Tune-Up Specifications chart for details) must pass between the electrodes with a slight drag.

A normally worn spark plug should have light tan or gray deposits on the firing tip.

A carbon fouled plug, identified by soft, sooty, black deposits, may indicate an improperly tuned vehicle. Check the air cleaner, ignition components and engine control system.

This spark plug has been **left in the engine too long,** as evidenced by the extreme gap- Plugs with such an extreme gap can cause misfiring and stumbling accompanied by a noticeable lack of power.

An oil fouled spark plug indicates an engine with worn poston rings and/or bad valve seals allowing excessive oil to enter the chamber.

A physically damaged spark plug may be evidence of severe detonation in that cylinder. Watch that cylinder carefully between services, as a continued detonation will not only damage the plug, but could also damage the engine.

A bridged or almost bridged spark plug, identified by a build-up between the electrodes caused by excessive carbon or oil build-up on the plug.

TCCA1P40

Fig. 107 Inspect the spark plug to determine engine running conditions

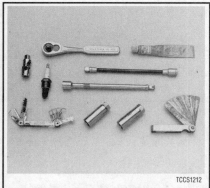

TCCS1212

Fig. 108 A variety of tools and gauges are needed for spark plug service

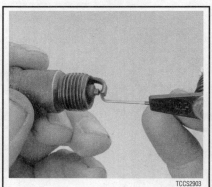

TCCS2903

Fig. 109 Checking the spark plug gap with a feeler gauge

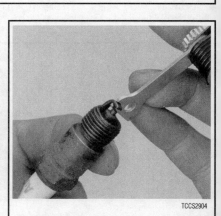

TCCS2904

Fig. 110 Adjusting the spark plug gap

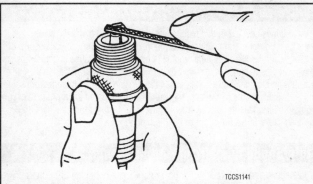

Fig. 111 If the standard plug is in good condition, the electrode may be filed flat—WARNING: do not file platinum plugs

Fig. 112 Number the plug wires before removal

➡**NEVER adjust the gap on a used platinum-type spark plugs.**

Always check the gap on new plugs as they are not always set correctly at the factory. Do not use a flat feeler gauge when measuring the gap on a used plug, because the reading may be inaccurate. A round-wire type gapping tool is the best way to check the gap. The correct gauge should pass through the electrode gap with a slight drag. If you're in doubt, try one size smaller and one larger. The smaller gauge should go through easily, while the larger one shouldn't go through at all. Wire gapping tools usually have a bending tool attached. Use that to adjust the side electrode until the proper distance is obtained. Absolutely never attempt to bend the center electrode. Also, be careful not to bend the side electrode too far or too often as it may weaken and break off within the engine, requiring removal of the cylinder head to retrieve it.

Spark Plug Wires

TESTING

At every tune-up/inspection, visually check the spark plug cables for burns cuts, or breaks in the insulation. Check the boots and the nipples on the distributor cap and/or coil. Replace any damaged wiring; cracked or shorted spark plug wires can short to ground, and cause a "miss" when the engine is running.

Every 50,000 miles (80,000 Km) or 60 months, the resistance of the wires should be checked with an ohmmeter. Wires with excessive resistance will cause misfiring, and may make the engine difficult to start in damp weather.

To check resistance, remove one wire from the engine, and measure the resistance from the spark plug connector to the distributor/coil pack connector. The resistance should be approximately 4600–7400 ohms. If the wire resistance is higher than 7400 ohms, the wire should be replaced. Coil wires (the wire that runs from the coil to the distributor) should have a resistance of 1200–2700 ohms.

Volkswagen uses a special type of spark plug wire connector that is unique; if the spark plug wires are in need of replacement, make sure to replace them with OEM-equivalent wires to ensure proper ignition system operation.

REMOVAL & INSTALLATION

▶ **See Figure 112**

If the wires are being replaced, remove one wire and match the length with the new wire. Install the new wire before removing the next old one. If the wires are to be reinstalled, remove them one at a time from the distributor cap before disconnecting them from the spark plugs. As each wire is removed from the distributor cap, mark the cylinder number on the boot and on the cap.

On some vehicles with the Motronic system, an ignition reference sensor is attached to the No. 4 plug wire. The ECU uses the input from this sensor when calculating the timing retard required to stop the engine knock.

Distributor Cap and Rotor

All vehicles covered by this manual with gasoline 4-cylinder engines use a standard distributor and rotor to supply spark to the engine. The VR6 engine

has a distributorless ignition system that combines the coil and distributor into a single solid state unit.

The distributor cap is fitted with a shield for radio interference suppression. Combined with the special suppressors on the spark plug wire terminals, any interference with radio reception is eliminated.

The rotor is pressed onto the distributor shaft, except for On 2.0L 16V (9A) engines which utilize a glued-on rotor to ensure precise spark control. The rotor must be destroyed for removal.

INSPECTION

To inspect the distributor cap, it is not necessary to remove the spark plug wires.
1. Disengage the two clips that secure the distributor cap to the rotor.
2. Lift the distributor cap (with the wires attached) away from the distributor. Some early models with metal suppression shields have a ground wire that is attached to the side of the distributor; make sure to unplug it before pulling the distributor cap away
3. Note the condition of the inside of the distributor cap. Check the metal terminals for burns, carbon build-up, pitting, cracking, etc. If the distributor cap is worn, it should be replaced to avoid driveability problems.
4. Next, check the condition of the rotor. On all engines except 2.0L 16V (9A), the rotor is pressed onto the distributor shaft. Pull straight up on the rotor to remove it from the distributor. Check for cracks on the sides of the rotor. As with the distributor cap, any excessive pitting, carbon build-up, etc. warrants rotor replacement.
5. When installing the distributor cap, make sure the tab at the base of the cap aligns with the notch on the distributor.

REMOVAL & INSTALLATION

1. Disengage the two clips that secure the distributor cap to the rotor.
2. Lift the distributor cap (with the wires attached) away from the distributor. Some early models with metal suppression shields have a ground wire that is attached to the side of the distributor; make sure to unplug it before pulling the distributor cap away from the distributor.
3. Using a paint marker or other means of identification, label each of the spark plug wires, and their relationship to the distributor cap. Make sure to mark the distributor cap itself, since the suppression shield is a separate component.
4. Once the relationship between the spark plug wires and the distributor cap are labeled, remove the wires from the cap. Make sure not to pull on the wires themselves, or they may be damaged.
5. Separate the suppression shield from the distributor cap.
6. Place the new distributor cap next to the old unit, using the alignment tab on the bottom of the distributor cap to orient them in the same direction. Copy the labels from the old distributor cap onto the new unit.
7. Install the suppression shield onto the new distributor cap.
8. Place a small amount of dielectric grease (usually supplied with the new distributor cap and rotor) on the tip of each wire connector. Using the labels on the wires and distributor cap, install the wires in the proper order.
9. To replace the rotor, simply pull straight up on the rotor to remove it from the distributor shaft. Align the tab inside the rotor with the groove on the distributor shaft, and push down until it is firmly seated. On 2.0L 16V (9A)

engines, the rotor is glued onto the distributor shaft. To remove the rotor, carefully break it up with pliers to avoid damage to the shaft. Do not hit it with a hammer! Be sure to remove all old adhesive and use the glue that comes with the new part to install the new rotor.

➡There are several different types of rotors, which appear similar, but have different resistance values. When replacing the distributor cap and rotor, make sure to obtain the correct parts for your particular vehicle.

10. Install the distributor cap onto the distributor, making sure the tab at the base of the cap aligns with the notch on the distributor.

11. Secure the clips that hold the cap onto the distributor. If the suppression shield is an older metal type, make sure to attach the ground wire.

Ignition Timing

Checking and adjusting the ignition timing are not a part of a normal maintenance schedule. The ignition system contains few moving parts, and does not require any type of adjustments to compensate for wear. Unless the timing belt has been changed, or the distributor has been removed from the engine, adjustment of the timing is not necessary. For more information on the ignition system, refer to Section 2.

Valve Lash

All engines covered in this manual are equipped with hydraulic cam followers, which do not require clearance adjustment. If a "ticking" noise is heard from the cylinder head while the engine is operating, the cause is usually air or small particles trapped within the cam followers themselves. This prevents oil pressure inside the follower, and causes the "ticking" sound. In some cases, an engine "flush" treatment can cure this annoying problem. If a hydraulic lifter (or multiple lifters) fails to quiet after an engine flush treatment, it may need to be replaced. Refer to Section 3 for more information.

Idle Speed and Mixture Adjustments

Idle speed and mixture adjustments are not a part of the manufacturer's maintenance schedule. On gasoline models, the idle speed and air/fuel mixture are controlled by the ECM, making routine adjustments unnecessary. Diesels (with the exception of the computer-controlled AHU TDI engine) use extremely precise mechanical components to regulate idle speed and air/fuel mixture, making routine adjustment unnecessary. If the engine is not in proper running order, a faulty sensor or other component is usually the cause. Refer to Section 4 for more information.

DIESEL ENGINE TUNE-UP SPECIFICATIONS

Year	Engine Code	Engine Displacement Liters (cc)	Valve Clearance Intake (in.)	Valve Clearance Exhaust (in.)	Injection Pump Static Timing (in.)	Injection Nozzle Pressure (psi) New	Injection Nozzle Pressure (psi) Used	Idle Speed (rpm)	Cranking Compression Pressure (psi)
1990	1V	1.6 (1588)	HYD	HYD	0.0393	2364	2030	800-850	493
	ME	1.6 (1588)	HYD	HYD	0.0354	1963	1706	800-850	493
	MF	1.6 (1588)	HYD	HYD	0.0393	2364	2030	800-850	493
1991	1V	1.6 (1588)	HYD	HYD	0.0393	2364	2030	800-850	493
	ME	1.6 (1588)	HYD	HYD	0.0354	1963	1706	800-850	493
	MF	1.6 (1588)	HYD	HYD	0.0393	2364	2030	800-850	493
1992	1V	1.6 (1588)	HYD	HYD	0.0393	2364	2030	800-850	493
	ME	1.6 (1588)	HYD	HYD	0.0354	1963	1706	800-850	493
	MF	1.6 (1588)	HYD	HYD	0.0393	2364	2030	800-850	493
1993	AAZ	1.9 (1896)	HYD	HYD	0.0315	2291	2030	870-930	493
	AHU	1.9 (1896)	HYD	HYD	N/A ①	2940	2499	870-930	493
1994	AAZ	1.9 (1896)	HYD	HYD	0.0315	2291	2030	870-930	493
	AHU	1.9 (1896)	HYD	HYD	N/A ①	2940	2499	870-930	493
1995	AAZ	1.9 (1896)	HYD	HYD	0.0315	2291	2030	870-930	493
	AHU	1.9 (1896)	HYD	HYD	N/A ①	2940	2499	870-930	493
1996	AAZ	1.9 (1896)	HYD	HYD	0.0315	2291	2030	870-930	493
	AHU	1.9 (1896)	HYD	HYD	N/A ①	2940	2499	870-930	493
1997	AAZ	1.9 (1896)	HYD	HYD	0.0315	2291	2030	870-930	493
	AHU	1.9 (1896)	HYD	HYD	N/A ①	2940	2499	870-930	493
1998	AAZ	1.9 (1896)	HYD	HYD	0.0315	2291	2030	870-930	493
	AHU	1.9 (1896)	HYD	HYD	N/A ①	2940	2499	870-930	493
1999	AAZ	1.9 (1896)	HYD	HYD	0.0315	2291	2030	870-930	493
	AHU	1.9 (1896)	HYD	HYD	N/A ①	2940	2499	870-930	493

HYD: Hydraulc Cam Followers, which are not adjustable.
① The injection timing is controlled by the ECU.

91221C06

GASOLINE ENGINE TUNE-UP SPECIFICATIONS

Year	Engine Code	Engine Displacement Liters (cc)	Spark Plug Gap (in.)	Ignition Timing (Deg) MT	Ignition Timing (Deg) AT	Fuel Pressure (psi)	Idle Speed (rpm) MT	Idle Speed (rpm) AT	Valve Clearance In.	Valve Clearance Ex.
1990	RV	1.8 (1781)	0.028	6 ②	6 ②	36	800-900	800-900	HYD	HYD
	9A	2.0 (1984)	0.032	6 ③	6 ③	88-96	800-900	800-900	HYD	HYD
	PF	1.8 (1781)	0.032	6 ②	6 ②	36	800-900	800-900	HYD	HYD
	2H	1.8 (1781)	0.032	6 ②	6 ②	36	850-1000	850-1000	HYD	HYD
	UM	1.8 (1781)	0.032	6 ②	6 ②	36	800-900	800-900	HYD	HYD
	JN	1.8 (1781)	0.032	6 ②	6 ②	36	800-900	800-900	HYD	HYD
1991	RV	1.8 (1781)	0.028	6 ②	6 ②	36	800-900	800-900	HYD	HYD
	9A	2.0 (1984)	0.032	6 ③	6 ③	88-96	800-900	800-900	HYD	HYD
	PF	1.8 (1781)	0.032	6 ②	6 ②	36	800-900	800-900	HYD	HYD
	2H	1.8 (1781)	0.032	6 ②	6 ②	36	850-1000	850-1000	HYD	HYD
	UM	1.8 (1781)	0.032	6 ②	6 ②	36	800-900	800-900	HYD	HYD
	JN	1.8 (1781)	0.032	6 ②	6 ②	36	800-900	800-900	HYD	HYD
1992	RV	1.8 (1781)	0.028	6 ②	6 ②	36	800-900	800-900	HYD	HYD
	9A	2.0 (1984)	0.032	6 ③	6 ③	88-96	800-900	800-900	HYD	HYD
	PF	1.8 (1781)	0.032	6 ②	6 ②	36	800-900	800-900	HYD	HYD
	2H	1.8 (1781)	0.032	6 ②	6 ②	36	850-1000	850-1000	HYD	HYD
	UM	1.8 (1781)	0.032	6 ②	6 ②	36	800-900	800-900	HYD	HYD
	JN	1.8 (1781)	0.032	6 ②	6 ②	36	800-900	800-900	HYD	HYD
1993	ACC	1.8 (1781)	0.031	6	6	11-17	770-1000 ⑥	770-1000 ⑥	HYD	HYD
	ABA	2.0 (1984)	0.024	12 ④	12 ④	36 ⑤	800-880 ⑥	800-880 ⑥	HYD	HYD
	2H	1.8 (1781)	0.032	6 ④	6 ④	36	850-1000	850-1000	HYD	HYD
	AAA	2.8 (2782)	0.028	6 ④	6 ④	58 ⑤	650-750 ⑥	650-750 ⑥	HYD	HYD
	UM	1.8 (1781)	0.032	6 ②	6 ②	36	800-900	800-900	HYD	HYD
	JN	1.8 (1781)	0.032	6 ②	6 ②	36	800-900	800-900	HYD	HYD
1994	ACC	1.8 (1781)	0.031	6	6	11-17	770-1000 ⑥	770-1000 ⑥	HYD	HYD
	ABA	2.0 (1984)	0.024	12 ④	12 ④	36 ⑤	800-880 ⑥	800-880 ⑥	HYD	HYD
	2H	1.8 (1781)	0.032	6 ④	6 ④	36	850-1000 ⑥	850-1000 ⑥	HYD	HYD
	AAA	2.8 (2782)	0.028	6 ④	6 ④	58 ⑤	650-750 ⑥	650-750 ⑥	HYD	HYD
	UM	1.8 (1781)	0.032	6 ②	6 ②	36	800-900	800-900	HYD	HYD
	JN	1.8 (1781)	0.032	6 ②	6 ②	36	800-900	800-900	HYD	HYD
1995	ACC	1.8 (1781)	0.031	6	6	11-17	770-1000 ⑥	770-1000 ⑥	HYD	HYD
	ABA	2.0 (1984)	0.024	12 ④	12 ④	36 ⑤	800-880 ⑥	800-880 ⑥	HYD	HYD
	AAA	2.8 (2782)	0.028	6 ④	6 ④	58 ⑤	650-750 ⑥	650-750 ⑥	HYD	HYD
1996	ACC	1.8 (1781)	0.031	6	6	11-17	770-1000 ⑥	770-1000 ⑥	HYD	HYD
	ABA	2.0 (1984)	0.024	12 ④	12 ④	36	800-880 ⑥	800-880 ⑥	HYD	HYD
	AAA	2.8 (2782)	0.028	6 ④	6 ④	58	650-750 ⑥	650-750 ⑥	HYD	HYD
1997	ACC	1.8 (1781)	0.031	6	6	11-17	770-1000 ⑥	770-1000 ⑥	HYD	HYD
	ABA	2.0 (1984)	0.024	12 ④	12 ④	36 ⑤	800-880 ⑥	800-880 ⑥	HYD	HYD
	AAA	2.8 (2782)	0.028	6 ④	6 ④	58 ⑤	650-750 ⑥	650-750 ⑥	HYD	HYD
1998	ACC	1.8 (1781)	0.031	6	6	11-17	770-1000 ⑥	770-1000 ⑥	HYD	HYD
	ABA	2.0 (1984)	0.024	12 ④	12 ④	36	800-880 ⑥	800-880 ⑥	HYD	HYD
	AAA	2.8 (2782)	0.028	6 ④	6 ④	58	650-750 ⑥	650-750 ⑥	HYD	HYD
1999	ACC	1.8 (1781)	0.031	6	6	11-17	770-1000 ⑥	770-1000 ⑥	HYD	HYD
	ABA	2.0 (1984)	0.024	12 ④	12 ④	36 ⑤	800-880 ⑥	800-880 ⑥	HYD	HYD
	AAA	2.8 (2782)	0.028	6 ④	6 ④	58 ⑤	650-750 ⑥	650-750 ⑥	HYD	HYD

HYD: Hydraulc Cam Followers, which are not adjustable.

① Fuel system pressure at idle.

② At 2250 rpm.

③ At idle speed.

④ For reference only. The ignition timing is controlled by the ECM and is not adjustable.

⑤ With the fuel pressure regulator vacuum line disconnected and the engine running.

⑥ For reference only. The idle speed is controlled by the ECM and is not adjustable.

Air Conditioning System

SYSTEM SERVICE & REPAIR

➡It is recommended that the A/C system be serviced by an EPA Section 609 certified automotive technician utilizing a refrigerant recovery/recycling machine.

The do-it-yourselfer should not service his/her own vehicle's A/C system for many reasons, including legal concerns, personal injury, environmental damage and cost. The following are some of the reasons why you may decide not to service your own vehicle's A/C system.

According to the U.S. Clean Air Act, it is a federal crime to service or repair (involving the refrigerant) a Motor Vehicle Air Conditioning (MVAC) system for money without being EPA certified. It is also illegal to vent R-12 and R-134a refrigerants into the atmosphere. Selling or distributing A/C system refrigerant (in a container which contains less than 20 pounds of refrigerant) to any person who is not EPA 609 certified is also not allowed by law.

State and/or local laws may be more strict than the federal regulations, so be sure to check with your state and/or local authorities for further information. For further federal information on the legality of servicing your A/C system, call the EPA Stratospheric Ozone Hotline.

➡Federal law dictates that a fine of up to $25,000 may be levied on people convicted of venting refrigerant into the atmosphere. Additionally, the EPA may pay up to $10,000 for information or services leading to a criminal conviction of the violation of these laws.

When servicing an A/C system you run the risk of handling or coming in contact with refrigerant, which may result in skin or eye irritation or frostbite. Although low in toxicity (due to chemical stability), inhalation of concentrated refrigerant fumes is dangerous and can result in death; cases of fatal cardiac arrhythmia have been reported in people accidentally subjected to high levels of refrigerant. Some early symptoms include loss of concentration and drowsiness.

➡Generally, the limit for exposure is lower for R-134a than it is for R-12. Exceptional care must be practiced when handling R-134a.

Also, refrigerants can decompose at high temperatures (near gas heaters or open flame), which may result in hydrofluoric acid, hydrochloric acid and phosgene (a fatal nerve gas).

R-12 refrigerant can damage the environment because it is a Chlorofluorocarbon (CFC), which has been proven to add to ozone layer depletion, leading to increasing levels of UV radiation. UV radiation has been linked with an increase in skin cancer, suppression of the human immune system, an increase in cataracts, damage to crops, damage to aquatic organisms, an increase in ground-level ozone, and increased global warming.

R-134a refrigerant is a greenhouse gas which, if allowed to vent into the atmosphere, will contribute to global warming (the Greenhouse Effect).

It is usually more economically feasible to have a certified MVAC automotive technician perform A/C system service on your vehicle. Some possible reasons for this are as follows:

• While it is illegal to service an A/C system without the proper equipment, the home mechanic would have to purchase an expensive refrigerant recovery/recycling machine to service his/her own vehicle.

• Since only a certified person may purchase refrigerant—according to the Clean Air Act, there are specific restrictions on selling or distributing A/C system refrigerant—it is legally impossible (unless certified) for the home mechanic to service his/her own vehicle. Procuring refrigerant in an illegal fashion exposes one to the risk of paying a $25,000 fine to the EPA.

R-12 Refrigerant Conversion

If your vehicle still uses R-12 refrigerant, one way to save A/C system costs down the road is to investigate the possibility of having your system converted to R-134a. The older R-12 systems can be easily converted to R-134a refrigerant by a certified automotive technician by installing a few new components and changing the system oil.

The cost of R-12 is steadily rising and will continue to increase, because it is no longer imported or manufactured in the United States. Therefore, it is often possible to have an R-12 system converted to R-134a and recharged for less than it would cost to just charge the system with R-12.

If you are interested in having your system converted, contact local automotive service stations for more details and information.

PREVENTIVE MAINTENANCE

♦ See Figures 113 thru 114

Although the A/C system should not be serviced by the do-it-yourselfer, preventive maintenance can be practiced and A/C system inspections can be performed to help maintain the efficiency of the vehicle's A/C system. For preventive maintenance, perform the following:

• The easiest and most important preventive maintenance for your A/C system is to be sure that it is used on a regular basis. Running the system for five minutes each month (no matter what the season) will help ensure that the seals and all internal components remain lubricated.

➡Some newer vehicles automatically operate the A/C system compressor whenever the windshield defroster is activated. When running, the compressor lubricates the A/C system components; therefore, the A/C system would not need to be operated each month.

• In order to prevent heater core freeze-up during A/C operation, it is necessary to maintain proper antifreeze protection. Use a hand-held coolant tester (hydrometer) to periodically check the condition of the antifreeze in your engine's cooling system.

➡Antifreeze should not be used longer than the manufacturer specifies.

• For efficient operation of an air conditioned vehicle's cooling system, the radiator cap should have a holding pressure which meets manufacturer's specifications. A cap which fails to hold these pressures should be replaced.

TCCS1233

Fig. 113 A coolant tester can be used to determine the freezing and boiling levels of the coolant in your vehicle

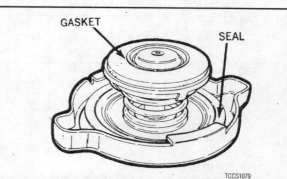

TCCS1079

Fig. 114 To ensure efficient cooling system operation, inspect the radiator cap gasket and seal

• Any obstruction of or damage to the condenser configuration will restrict air flow which is essential to its efficient operation. It is, therefore, a good rule to keep this unit clean and in proper physical shape.

➡**Bug screens which are mounted in front of the condenser (unless they are original equipment) are regarded as obstructions.**

• The condensation drain tube expels any water which accumulates on the bottom of the evaporator housing into the engine compartment. If this tube is obstructed, the air conditioning performance can be restricted and condensation buildup can spill over onto the vehicle's floor.

SYSTEM INSPECTION

▶ See Figure 115

Although the A/C system should not be serviced by the do-it-yourselfer, preventive maintenance can be practiced and A/C system inspections can be performed to help maintain the efficiency of the vehicle's A/C system. For A/C system inspection, perform the following:

The easiest and often most important check for the air conditioning system consists of a visual inspection of the system components. Visually inspect the air conditioning system for refrigerant leaks, damaged compressor clutch, abnormal compressor drive belt tension and/or condition, plugged evaporator drain tube, blocked condenser fins, disconnected or broken wires, blown fuses, corroded connections and poor insulation.

A refrigerant leak will usually appear as an oily residue at the leakage point in the system. The oily residue soon picks up dust or dirt particles from the surrounding air and appears greasy. Through time, this will build up and appear to be a heavy dirt impregnated grease.

For a thorough visual and operational inspection, check the following:
• Check the surface of the radiator and condenser for dirt, leaves or other material which might block air flow.
• Check for kinks in hoses and lines. Check the system for leaks.
• Make sure the drive belt is properly tensioned. When the air conditioning is operating, make sure the drive belt is free of noise or slippage.

• Make sure the blower motor operates at all appropriate positions, then check for distribution of the air from all outlets with the blower on **HIGH** or **MAX**.

➡**Keep in mind that under conditions of high humidity, air discharged from the A/C vents may not feel as cold as expected, even if the system is working properly. This is because vaporized moisture in humid air retains heat more effectively than dry air, thereby making humid air more difficult to cool.**

• Make sure the air passage selection lever is operating correctly. Start the engine and warm it to normal operating temperature, then make sure the temperature selection lever is operating correctly.

Windshield Wipers

ELEMENT (REFILL) CARE & REPLACEMENT

▶ See Figures 116 thru 125

For maximum effectiveness and longest element life, the windshield and wiper blades should be kept clean. Dirt, tree sap, road tar and so on will cause streaking, smearing and blade deterioration if left on the glass. It is advisable to wash the windshield carefully with a commercial glass cleaner at least once a month. Wipe off the rubber blades with the wet rag afterwards. Do not attempt to move wipers across the windshield by hand; damage to the motor and drive mechanism will result.

To inspect and/or replace the wiper blade elements, place the wiper switch in the **LOW** speed position and the ignition switch in the **ACC** position. When the wiper blades are approximately vertical on the windshield, turn the ignition switch to **OFF**.

Examine the wiper blade elements. If they are found to be cracked, broken or torn, they should be replaced immediately. Replacement intervals will vary with usage, although ozone deterioration usually limits element life to about one year. If the wiper pattern is smeared or streaked, or if the blade chatters across

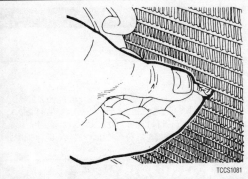

Fig. 115 Periodically remove any debris from the condenser and radiator fins

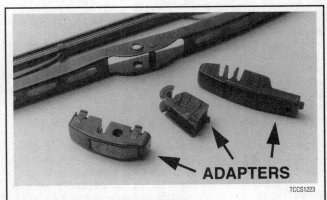

Fig. 116 Bosch® wiper blade and fit kit

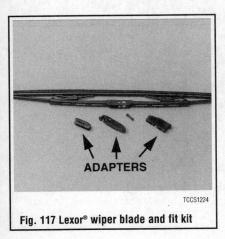

Fig. 117 Lexor® wiper blade and fit kit

Fig. 118 Pylon® wiper blade and adapter

Fig. 119 Trico® wiper blade and fit kit

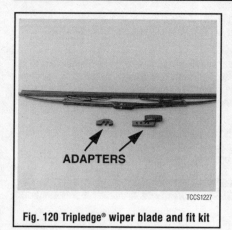

ADAPTERS

Fig. 120 Tripledge® wiper blade and fit kit

TCCS1227

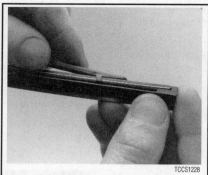

Fig. 121 To remove and install a Lexor® wiper blade refill, slip out the old insert and slide in a new one

TCCS1228

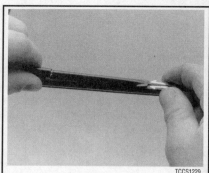

Fig. 122 On Pylon® inserts, the clip at the end has to be removed prior to sliding the insert off

TCCS1229

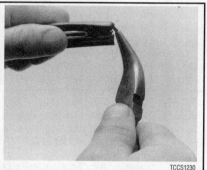

Fig. 123 On Trico® wiper blades, the tab at the end of the blade must be turned up . . .

TCCS1230

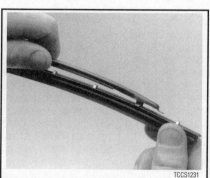

Fig. 124 . . . then the insert can be removed. After installing the replacement insert, bend the tab back

TCCS1231

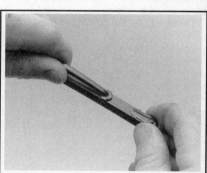

Fig. 125 The Tripledge® wiper blade insert is removed and installed using a securing clip

TCCS1232

the glass, the elements should be replaced. It is easiest and most sensible to replace the elements in pairs.

If your vehicle is equipped with aftermarket blades, there are several different types of refills and your vehicle might have any kind. Aftermarket blades and arms rarely use the exact same type blade or refill as the original equipment. Here are some typical aftermarket blades; not all may be available for your vehicle:

The Anco® type uses a release button that is pushed down to allow the refill to slide out of the yoke jaws. The new refill slides back into the frame and locks in place.

Some Trico® refills are removed by locating where the metal backing strip or the refill is wider. Insert a small screwdriver blade between the frame and metal backing strip. Press down to release the refill from the retaining tab.

Other types of Trico® refills have two metal tabs which are unlocked by squeezing them together. The rubber filler can then be withdrawn from the frame jaws. A new refill is installed by inserting the refill into the front frame jaws and sliding it rearward to engage the remaining frame jaws. There are usually four jaws; be certain when installing that the refill is engaged in all of them. At the end of its travel, the tabs will lock into place on the front jaws of the wiper blade frame.

Another type of refill is made from polycarbonate. The refill has a simple locking device at one end which flexes downward out of the groove into which the jaws of the holder fit, allowing easy release. By sliding the new refill through all the jaws and pushing through the slight resistance when it reaches the end of its travel, the refill will lock into position.

To replace the Tridon® refill, it is necessary to remove the wiper blade. This refill has a plastic backing strip with a notch about 1 in. (25mm) from the end. Hold the blade (frame) on a hard surface so that the frame is tightly bowed. Grip the tip of the backing strip and pull up while twisting counterclockwise. The backing strip will snap out of the retaining tab. Do this for the remaining tabs until the refill is free of the blade. The length of these refills is molded into the end and they should be replaced with identical types.

Regardless of the type of refill used, be sure to follow the part manufacturer's instructions closely. Make sure that all of the frame jaws are engaged as the refill is pushed into place and locked. If the metal blade holder and frame are allowed to touch the glass during wiper operation, the glass will be scratched.

Tires and Wheels

TIRE ROTATION

▶ **See Figures 126 and 127**

To equalize tire wear and increase the mileage you obtain from your tires, rotate them every 7500 miles. All Volkswagens are designed for radial tires. Radial tires should be rotated by moving the front tires to the rear and the rear tires to the front. Do not move them from side to side unless absolutely neces-

91221P47

Fig. 126 Break the lug bolts/nuts free while the vehicle is on the ground. Do not completely remove the lug bolts/nuts until the wheel is off the ground

Fig. 127 Once the vehicle is off the ground, remove the lugs

sary, or unless the tire is near the end of its life anyway. Radial tires tend to distort slightly and take a set in the direction of rotation. If a tire is moved from one side to the other and turns the opposite direction, the ride and handling will be affected and the tire may wear faster.

TIRE DESIGN

When buying new tires, they should always be replaced in sets of two or four. Always install the same type of tire on all four wheels. Mixing of different types (radial, bias-belted, fiberglass belted) can be hazardous because vehicle handling becomes inconsistent.

Conventional bias tires are constructed so that the cords run bead to bead at an angle. Alternate plies run at an opposite angle. This type of construction gives rigidity to both the tread and the side wall and is good for carrying heavy loads.

Bias belted tires are similar in construction to conventional bias ply tires. Belts run at an angle and also at a 90° angle to the bead, as in radial tires. Tread life is improved considerably over the conventional bias tire and the side wall remains fairly rigid.

On radial tires, instead of the cords and belts being at an angle of 90° to each other, they are all parallel and at an angle of 90° to the bead. The cords wrap directly across the carcass of the tire to make the shortest line from bead to bead. This gives the tread a great deal of rigidity and the side wall a great deal of flexibility. With this construction, it is easier for the tread to stay flat on the road when the car is turning and tire side loads are high. These tires also tend to be rounder and have less rolling resistance. Dry and wet road handling are greatly improved over bias or belted tires. This type of construction accounts for the characteristic bulge associated with radial tires because the side walls are relatively unsupported. This makes proper inflation pressure so important to tire life and performance.

TIRE STORAGE

Store the tires at the proper inflation pressure if they are mounted on wheels. Keep them in a cool dry place, laid on their sides. If the tires are stored in the garage or basement, do not let them stand on a concrete floor. Set them on strips of wood.

INFLATION PRESSURE

▶ See Figure 128

Tire inflation is the most ignored item of auto maintenance, and one of the most important. Buy a tire pressure gauge and keep it in the glovebox of your car. Service station air gauges are generally either not working or inaccurate and should not be relied upon. Also, using the same gauge all the time increases the accuracy of your pressure readings. The tire pressures recommended for your car are usually found on the left door post and in the owner's manual. If you are driving on replacement tires of a different type, follow the inflation recommendations of the tire manufacturer. Never exceed the maximum pressure shown on the tire sidewall. Always check tire pressure when the tires are cool because air pressure increases with heat. Readings can change as much as 4–6

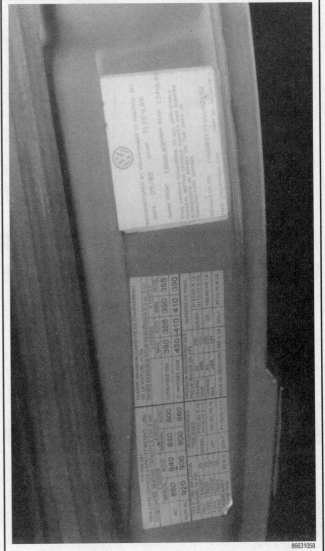

Fig. 128 Tire inflation pressure specifications can usually be found on the driver's side door post

psi depending on tire temperature. For every 10° rise (or drop) in tire temperature, there is a difference of 1 psi. This explains why tires loose pressure when the weather turns colder.

Excess heat generated while driving on an underinflated tire causes serious damage to the structure of the tire. For long highway drives, inflating the tires to within 3–4 psi (cold pressure) of the maximum allowed will increase fuel mileage and tire life.

TREAD DEPTH

▶ See Figures 129, 130 and 131

All tires have 7 built-in tread wear indicator bars that show up as 13mm (1/2 inch) wide smooth bands across the tire when 1.5mm (1/16 inch) of tread remains. The appearance of tread wear indicators means that the tires should be replaced. In fact, many states have laws prohibiting the use of tires with less than 1.5mm (1/16 inch) tread. You can check your own tread depth with an inexpensive gauge or by using a Lincoln head penny. Slip the Lincoln penny into several tread grooves. If you can see the top of Lincoln's head in 2 adjacent grooves, the tires have less than 1.5mm (1/16 inch) tread left and should be replaced. You can measure snow tires in the same manner by using the tails side of the Lincoln penny. If you can see the top of the Lincoln memorial, it's time to replace the snow tires.

Fig. 129 Most tires are made with built-in wear indicator bars; when the bars appear across the tread, the tire should be replaced

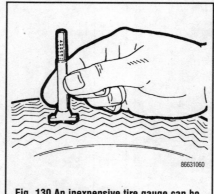

Fig. 130 An inexpensive tire gauge can be used to measure tread depth

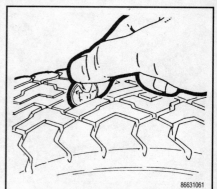

Fig. 131 A penny can be used to check tread depth as well

FLUIDS AND LUBRICANTS

Fluid Disposal

▶ See Figure 132

Used fluids such as engine oil, transmission fluid, antifreeze and brake fluid are hazardous wastes and must be disposed of properly. Before draining any fluids, consult with your local authorities; in many areas, waste oil, antifreeze, etc. is being accepted as a part of recycling programs. A number of service stations and auto parts stores are also accepting waste fluids for recycling.

Be sure of the recycling center's policies before draining any fluids, as many will not accept different fluids that have been mixed together.

Fuel Requirements

GASOLINE ENGINES

All vehicles sold in the U.S. with gasoline engines are designed to operate on lead-free fuel. The minimum octane ratings required by Volkswagen sometimes vary with where the vehicle was intended for sale and use (high altitude). Octane requirements are listed on the inside of the fuel filler door or on the door jamb. Use of leaded gasoline or certain additives will poison the catalytic converter and in some cases, possibly damage fuel injectors. Volkswagen recommends occasional use of Autobahn Gasoline Additive, VW part no. ZVW 246 001, for keeping injectors clean.

Fig. 132 Pour all fluids into suitable containers and take them to your local hazardous waste facility for proper disposal

DIESEL ENGINES

The Volkswagen diesel engine is designed to run on Diesel Fuel No. 2. Since diesel fuel is generally available, supply is not usually a problem, though it is wise to check in advance. Several diesel station guides are available from fuel companies and are normally sold at diesel fuel stations. Some U. S. States and Canadian provinces require purchasers of diesel fuel to obtain a special permit to buy diesel fuel. Check with your local VW dealer or fuel supplier for regulations in your area.

There is a difference between the refinement levels of Diesel fuel and home heating oil. While you may get away with running your diesel on home heating oil for a while, inevitably you will fill your tank with a batch of oil that will leave you stranded. Even though they don't mix, Diesel fuel tends to attract water. This is another reason to stick to mainstream suppliers when filling the tank. Also, never allow diesel fuel to come in contact with any rubber hoses or other parts. It attacks the rubber and causes it to become soft and unstable.

Engine Oil

ENGINE OIL RECOMMENDATIONS

Gasoline Engines

▶ See Figure 133

The SAE (Society of Automotive Engineers) grade number indicates the viscosity of the engine oil, and thus its ability to lubricate at a given temperature. The lower the SAE grade number, the lighter the oil. The lower the viscosity, the easier it is to crank the engine in cold weather. Oil viscosity's should be chosen from those oils recommended for the lowest anticipated temperatures during the oil change interval. Multi-viscosity oils (10W–30, 20W–50, etc.) offer the important advantage of being adaptable to temperature extremes. They allow easy starting at low temperatures, yet give good protection at high speeds and engine temperatures. This is a decided advantage in changeable climates or in long distance touring. The API (American Petroleum Institute) designation indicates the classification of engine oil for use under given operating conditions. Only oils designated for use Service SF or SG should be used. Oils of the SF or SG type perform a variety of functions inside the engine in addition to the basic function as a lubricant. Through a balanced system of metallic detergents and polymeric dispersants, the oil prevents the formation of high and low temperature deposits, and also keeps sludge and dirt particles in suspension. Acids, particularly sulfuric acid, as well as other by-products of combustion, are neutralized. Both the SAE grade number and the API designation can be found somewhere on the container.

➡ **Non-detergent or straight mineral oils must never be used.**

Oil must be selected with regard to the anticipated temperatures during the period before the next oil change. Using the chart, select the oil viscosity prior to the next oil change for the lowest expected temperature and you will be assured of easy cold starting and sufficient engine protection.

Fig. 133 Look for the API oil identification label when choosing your engine oil

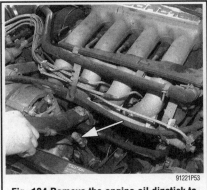

Fig. 134 Remove the engine oil dipstick to check the oil level

Fig. 135 Wipe the dipstick with a shop towel and then reinsert it into the tube

Diesel Engines

Engine oils should be selected from the accompanying chart. The SAE viscosity number should be chosen for the lowest anticipated temperature at which the engine will be required to start, not for the temperature at the time the oil is changed. Use only oils designated by the API (American Petroleum Institute) for service "CC" or "CD". The letters should appear somewhere on the oil can for example "SF/CC" or "SG/CD". This indicates that the oil provides protection from rust, corrosion and high temperature deposits in diesel engines in moderate to severe service.

CHECKING ENGINE OIL LEVEL

▶ **See Figures 134, 135, 136, 137 and 138**

Engine oil level should be checked weekly. Always check the oil with the car on level ground and after the engine has been shut off for about five minutes.

The oil dipstick is either located on the front side of engine or on the driver's side near the fuel pump.
1. Remove the dipstick and wipe it clean.
2. Reinsert the dipstick.
3. Remove the dipstick again. The oil level should be between the two marks. On the flat rod type dipstick, the level between the **MIN** and **MAX** marks is approximately 0.75L (0.79 quart).
4. Add oil through the capped opening on the top of the valve cover. Wipe up any spilled oil.

OIL & FILTER CHANGE

▶ **See Figures 139, 140, 141, 142 and 143**

Change the oil according to the maintenance interval chart in this Section. This interval is only for average driving. Change the oil and filter more fre-

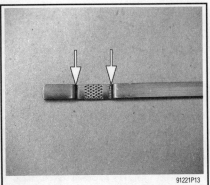

Fig. 136 The engine oil level should fall between the arrowed section of the stick

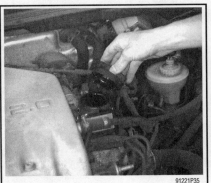

Fig. 137 Remove the oil filler cap by twisting it

Fig. 138 Use a funnel when adding oil to avoid any spills

Fig. 139 Remove the drain plug

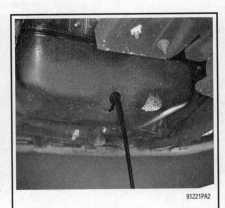

Fig. 140 Allow the oil to drain

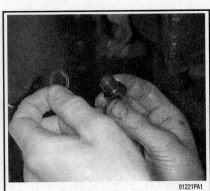

Fig. 141 Install a new washer on the oil drain plug

Fig. 142 Remove the used oil filter and install a new one

Fig. 143 Before installing a new oil filter, lightly coat the rubber gasket with clean oil

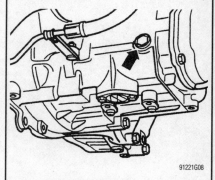

Fig. 144 Transaxle filler plug location— 02A transaxle

quently if your car is being used under dusty conditions or mostly stop and go city traffic, where acid and sludge buildup is a problem. When draining the oil, warm oil will flow easier and more contaminants will be removed. Dispose of use oil in accordance with state or local regulations.

1. Run the engine until it reaches the normal operating temperature.
2. Raise and safely support the front of the car on jack stands.
3. If equipped, remove the splash/sound shield from beneath the vehicle.
4. Slide a drain pan under the oil pan drain plug.
5. Loosen the drain plug with a socket or box wrench, and then remove it by hand. Push in lightly on the plug as you turn it out, so that no oil escapes until the plug is completely removed.
6. While the oil is draining, check the condition of the copper gasket on the plug. If it looks split or badly deformed, replace it to avoid an oil leak.
7. After the oil is drained, install the plug and torque it to 22 ft. lbs.
8. On 4 cylinder models, proceed as follows:

   a. Using a strap-type wrench, or other oil filter-removing tool of your choice, loosen the oil filter from its housing.

   b. Carefully lower the filter from its mounting, direct the filter into the oil pan and drain it before disposal.

   c. Clean the oil filter seating area with a clean rag.

   d. Lightly oil the rubber seal on the new filter and spin it on to the base. When the seal contacts the sealing surface, give it an additional ½ to ¾ turn. Tightening the filter more than this will not improve sealing, but just make it harder to remove the next time.

9. On VR6 models, proceed as follows:

   a. Remove the drain plug from the bottom of the oil filter housing, and drain the oil from the housing. Once the oil has drained from the filter housing, install the drain plug, using a new O-ring. Lightly lubricate the O-ring with clean engine oil before assembly. Tighten the drain plug to 89 inch lbs. (10 Nm).

   b. Using a large socket, unscrew the lower portion of the oil filter housing, and remove the oil filter element.

   c. Install the new oil filter element, using a new O-ring on the lower portion of the housing. Lightly lubricate the O-ring with clean engine oil before assembly. Tighten the lower housing to 22 ft. lbs. (30 Nm).

10. Refill the engine with the proper (amount and viscosity) of new oil. The empty containers can be used to return the used oil for recycling.
11. If equipped, install the splash/sound shield beneath the vehicle.
12. Lower the front of the car.
13. Run the engine and check for leaks.
14. If necessary, add oil (in small increments to avoid overfilling) as necessary to obtain a proper dipstick reading.

Manual Transaxle

FLUID RECOMMENDATIONS

Manual transaxle through 1992 use SAE 80W hypoid oil, API service GL-4, Mil-L-2105. 1993–99 transaxles are equipped from the manufacturer with SAE 75W90 synthetic oil. Volkswagen does not specify a maintenance interval for manual transaxle oil. If the transmission has been abused or used most of its life for towing, an oil change may be in order.

Even if you choose not to change the oil in your vehicle's manual transaxle, it is important to make sure the level is correct. A low oil level indicates leakage, and an over-full level may indicate excessive condensation/moisture in the oil.

LEVEL CHECK

▶ **See Figure 144**

1. Raise and safely support the front of the vehicle on jackstands.
2. Position a drain container under the oil filler plug.
3. Using a 17mm Allen wrench, remove the oil filler plug. If the transmission is over-full, allow the oil to drain from the filler plug opening until it stops.
4. Make sure the fluid level is even with the edge of the hole. If the level is low, add oil as required.
5. Install and tighten the plug.

DRAIN AND REFILL

1. Raise and safely support the front of the car on jackstands.
2. Slide drain pan under the transaxle.
3. Using a 17mm Allen wrench, remove the oil filler plug.
4. Using the same wrench, loosen the drain plug until it can be turned by hand.
5. While pushing in on the drain plug, turn it counterclockwise until it is free of the threads on the transaxle case. Then, quickly pull the drain plug away, and allow the oil to drain into the pan.

➡**A small amount of fine particles on the drain plug's magnet is considered normal. If large metal chunks may indicate problems with the internal components of the transaxle.**

6. When the oil has been completely drained, install the drain plug. Tighten to 18 ft. lbs.
7. Refill the gearbox (using the proper type and viscosity of gear oil) up to the level of the filler plug, until a small amount of oil drips from the threads.8. Install and tighten the filler plug to 18 ft. lbs.

Automatic Transaxle

FLUID RECOMMENDATIONS

Volkswagen transaxle are of a unique design; the differential is separated internally from the rest of the transaxle. Because of this unique design, different fluids are required for the transaxle gearset/torque converter and differential.

Dexron® ATF is used in the gearset/torque converter section of all 010 and 096 automatic transaxle. A3 platform vehicles equipped with 01M transaxle use a special synthetic ATF, available only from the manufacturer. Volkswagen recommends that the gearset/torque converter automatic transaxle fluid be replaced every 30,000 miles if you use your car for frequent trailer towing, mountain driving, or other severe service.

The differential section of all 010 automatic transaxle use 90W hypoid gear oil, API service GL-5, Mil-I–2105B. 096 automatic transaxle use SAE 75W90 synthetic gear oil. The 01M transaxle uses Volkswagen synthetic ATF to lubricate the differential.

Volkswagen does not specify a maintenance interval for changing the differential oil/fluid. However, periodic inspection of the level of the fluid (and the fluid itself) is recommended.

LEVEL CHECK

Gearset/Torque Converter Section

010 AND 096 TRANSAXLES

A1, A2, and A3 platform vehicles equipped with 010 and 096 "Phase I" transaxle use a standard dipstick to check the level of the gearset/torque converter fluid in the transaxle. On 096 transaxle, a special tool, VAG 1551, is used to measure the temperature of the fluid in the transaxle. The transaxle fluid can be checked with the fluid at 68 degrees Fahrenheit (20 degrees Celsius), or at 140 degrees Fahrenheit (60 degrees Celsius). Since Automatic Transaxle Fluid (ATF) expands according to temperature, it is recommended (but not necessary) that the VAG 1551 tool be used to measure the temperature of the transaxle fluid to ensure a proper reading.

➡ **With the engine at normal operating temperature, the temperature of the ATF is approximately 140 degrees Fahrenheit (60 degrees Celsius).**

✳✳ WARNING

DO NOT overfill an automatic transmission. Pressure is generated inside the case and over filling will cause fluid leaks.

In addition to the **MIN** and **MAX** marks on the dipstick, there is a **20°** mark at the very bottom of the dipstick. The difference between the **MIN** and **MAX** marks is 0.24 qts. When cold, fill the transaxle to the **20°** mark. Warm up the engine to normal operating temperature and check the level again. It should be between the MIN and MAX marks. If not, add fluid as required.

1. Make sure the engine and transaxle are warm. Drive the vehicle a few miles if necessary to bring the transaxle to normal operating temperature.
2. With the selector lever in **P**, remove the dipstick, wipe it clean, reinsert it, and withdraw it again.
3. The fluid level should be within the two marks. If the level is low, correct it by pouring Dexron® automatic transmission fluid (with an appropriate funnel) through the dipstick tube. Bear in mind that the difference between the two marks is less than one pint.

01M TRANSAXLES

A3 platform vehicles equipped with the 01M "Phase II" transaxle require special electronic tools to check and correct the fluid level. As a result, they are not equipped with a dipstick. Because of this, a procedure is not given. It is highly recommended that vehicles equipped with an 01M transaxle be taken to a qualified service facility for transaxle fluid service.

Differential Section

The manufacturer does not specify a maintenance interval for changing the differential oil/fluid. However, periodic inspection of the level of the fluid (and the fluid itself) is recommended. A high oil level indicates one of three conditions. First, the previous mechanic/owner may have accidentally overfilled the transaxle if the vehicle was not level. Secondly a high oil level (assuming the vehicle is level) can be caused by excessive condensation (water) in the differential. This may be a result of constant operation in wet areas, or high humidity. Moisture can condense inside of the transaxle in the same manner that a can of cold soda "sweats" when removed from a refrigerator. Lastly, a high oil condition may indicate that the internal seals that separate the differential section from the torque converter/gearset are possibly faulty, and ATF has contaminated the differential oil.

010 TRANSAXLES

1. Park the vehicle on a level surface.
2. Place a suitable drain receptacle underneath the rear of the transaxle.
3. Remove the filler plug on the passenger side of the transaxle, near the passenger side halfshaft flange.

➡ **Although access to the filler plug will be difficult with the vehicle on the ground, it is necessary to ensure an accurate reading. You may wish**

to raise and safely support the vehicle on jackstands in order to loosen the filler plug, then lower the vehicle to the ground making sure the vehicle is level before completely removing the filler plug.

4. Note the oil level; it should be even with the lower edge of the filler hole.
5. If the oil level is low, add oil (of the proper type and viscosity) as necessary to obtain the correct oil level.
6. Install the filler plug, and tighten it securely.

096 AND 01M TRANSAXLES

1. Park the vehicle on a level surface.
2. Locate the speedometer drive gear, (located near the right side driveshaft flange).
3. Unplug the connector from the gear, and unscrew the gear from the transaxle.
4. Using a clean, lint-free rag, wipe the end of the gear clean.
5. Screw the speedometer drive gear into the transaxle, until it is fully seated.
6. Remove the speedometer drive gear, and note the oil level. The oil level should not be above the MAX mark (flange) on the gear shaft. If the oil level is low, add oil (in small increments to avoid overfilling) through the speedometer gear hole in the transaxle.
7. Once the oil level is correct, install the speedometer drive gear, and secure the harness connector.

DRAIN AND REFILL

Gearset/Torque Converter Section

A3 platform vehicles equipped with the 01M "Phase II" transaxle require special electronic tools to check and correct the fluid level after the transaxle fluid. Because of this, no procedure is given. It is highly recommended that vehicles equipped with an 01M transaxle be taken to a qualified service facility for transaxle fluid service.

010 AND 096 TRANSAXLES ONLY

Since 010 and 096 transaxle do not have a drain plug, the only way to drain the automatic transaxle fluid is to remove the pan.

1. Raise and safely support the front of the vehicle.
2. Using a thick-bristled brush, clean any dirt and/or grease build-up from the area around the fluid pan.
3. Place drain receptacle (large enough to contain all of the transaxle fluid) under the transaxle.
4. Remove the two rear pan bolts, then loosen the two front pan bolts just enough to allow the fluid to drain.
5. Once the fluid ceased to drain from the pan, remove the remaining bolts and lower the pan.

➡ **There will be a small quantity of fluid in the pan. Lower the pan carefully to avoid spillage.**

6. Discard the old gasket and clean the pan with solvent. Make sure the gasket surface on the pan and the transaxle are clean, dry and free of all old gasket material.
7. Remove the bolts to remove the strainer and clean it. If the strainer is excessively dirty or damaged, it should be replaced.
   a. On 010 transaxle, torque the strainer bolts to 35 inch lbs. (4 Nm).
   b. On 096 transaxle, torque the strainer bolts to 71 inch lbs. (8 Nm).
8. Fit the gasket onto the pan. Usually the gasket does not require any type of sealing compound to form an effective seal. Sometimes a sealer is necessary to hold the gasket in place while installing the pan. Be sure to glue the gasket to the pan, not to the transaxle.
9. Fit the pan into place and start all the bolts.
   a. On 010 transaxle, torque the bolts (in a crisscross pattern) to 15 ft. lbs. (20 Nm).
   b. On 096 transaxle, torque the bolts (in a crisscross pattern) to 9 ft. lbs. (12 Nm).
10. Using a long-necked funnel, refill the transaxle with 3.2 quarts of fluid through the dipstick tube.
11. Lower the vehicle from the jackstands.
12. Run the engine to check for leaks and to check the level.
13. Add fluid as necessary to adjust the level. Do NOT overfill the transaxle!

Differential Section

Volkswagen does not specify a maintenance interval for changing the differential oil/fluid. Consequently, the manufacturer does not supply a drain plug for the differential section of 010, 096, and 01M transaxle. The oil/fluid can be removed from the differential housing with a suction-type oil changing tool (commonly available a boat supply facilities) placed inside of the check plug. Another method (although much more involved) of draining the oil/fluid is by removing the differential cover. This is less desirable, because access to the cover is limited.

Unless you believe that the differential oil is contaminated, changing the oil/fluid in the differential of the transaxle is not necessary. The manufacturer states that the differential is filled for the life of the transaxle, and that replacement of the fluid/oil is not necessary.

Cooling System

FLUID RECOMMENDATIONS

All Volkswagens are filled with a mixture of water and special phosphate-free antifreeze/coolant at the factory. This antifreeze/coolant has corrosion inhibitors that prevent frost, the formation of chalk and also raise the boiling point of the water. Later models (up to 1996) are filled at the factory with a special antifreeze/coolant, known as G11. From 1996 through 1999, a new type of antifreeze/coolant was used in all models, known as G12.

➡ **Standard antifreeze/coolant is bright green in color. The Volkswagen G11 coolant is blue, and the Volkswagen G12 coolant is pink. It is VERY important to identify which type of antifreeze/coolant your vehicle uses** if you intend adjust the level or replace it completely. The different types of coolant CANNOT be mixed together.

LEVEL CHECK

▶ **See Figures 145, 146, 147 and 148**

The coolant reservoir/expansion tank is translucent and if the reservoir is clean, it can be checked without removing the cap. The reservoir has **LOW** and **HIGH** level marks. The coolant must be between the two marks when the engine is cold, and slightly above the high mark at normal operating temperature. When removing the threaded pressure cap from the reservoir, loosen the cap slightly first. If the coolant begins to boil, tighten the cap again and wait for the engine to cool down.

✳✳ CAUTION

Never open, service or drain the cooling system when hot; serious burns can occur from the steam and hot coolant.

Some models are equipped with a coolant warning light on the dash that flashes until the coolant is filled to the normal level. Although this can be considered a convenience item, periodic inspection of the coolant level in the reservoir itself is highly recommended.

If the coolant level is mildly low, it can be adjusted to the proper level by adding distilled water until the coolant reaches the **MAX** mark on the reservoir. If the coolant level is extremely low, it is recommended that a ⁵⁰⁄₅₀ mixture of coolant (make sure to use the same type of coolant that is in the vehicle) and distilled water be used to adjust the level in the reservoir. In extremely cold climates, a ratio of 60 percent antifreeze/coolant and 40 percent distilled water can be used to prevent freezing.

Fig. 145 Coolant level marks on the expansion tank

Fig. 146 Unscrew the coolant reservoir cap to add fluid

Fig. 147 Add only the antifreeze that meets VW specifications

Fig. 148 Caution, it is easy to damage the plastic threads on the cap when installing it. If the cap does not feel like it is properly engaged with the threads, remove it and try threading it on the expansion tank again. DO NOT FORCE IT!

In large quantities, simply adding distilled water to the system can dilute the ratio of coolant and water, which reduces the cooling capabilities of the system, and in extreme cases, can cause freezing of the coolant if the vehicle is exposed to low temperatures. If the coolant freezes in the engine, the engine block can (and often times does) crack. To prevent the coolant mixture from freezing, avoid adding large quantities of distilled water to the system if it is low.

DRAIN & REFILL

All 4-Cylinder Engines

▶ **See Figure 149 and 150**

On 4-cylinder engines, the most thorough way to drain the coolant from the engine is by removing the thermostat. The thermostat on all 4-cylinder engines is located at the bottom of the water pump housing. The lower radiator hose attaches directly to the thermostat cover/elbow.

✳✳ CAUTION

Never attempt to drain the coolant from a hot engine. This is a messy job and there is no way to drain the coolant without getting it

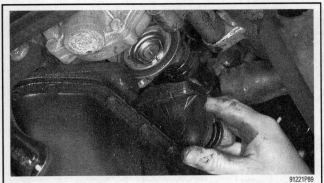

Fig. 149 Removing the thermostat from the bottom of the water pump

91221P89

Fig. 150 View of the thermostat in the housing

91221P88

on your hands. **Make sure the engine is thoroughly cooled before performing this procedure.**

1. Before raising the front of the vehicle, place the temperature control knob/slider to its warmest setting.
2. Raise and safely support the front of the vehicle on jackstands.
3. Some vehicles have a splash shield underneath the vehicle that may obstruct access to the thermostat cover/elbow. Remove the shield if necessary.
4. Place a large drain pan (large enough to contain the entire cooling system contents) under the water pump. Make sure the drain pan is clean, since the coolant should be reused unless it is dirty, or it does not pass a hydrometer test.
5. Using a 10mm socket and ratchet, loosen (but do not remove) the thermostat cover/elbow bolts. Coolant will start to flow from the elbow, so make sure the drain pan is positioned properly.
6. When the coolant stops flowing, remove the thermostat cover/elbow bolts, and set the cover/elbow aside. It's not necessary to disconnect the lower radiator hose. When removing the cover/elbow bolts, hold the cover/elbow in place; then, slowly lower the cover/elbow and hose. The thermostat may stick in place; be careful when removing it, as residual coolant may still be in the engine.
7. Once the thermostat is remove, remove the coolant reservoir cap to drain the rest of the coolant.

To install:

8. Clean and dry the thermostat housing and the rubber O-ring. Examine the O-ring for cracks or damage and replace as necessary.
9. Install the thermostat into the water pump housing on the engine, then fit the O-ring into place.
10. Install the thermostat housing and tighten the bolts evenly. Torque the bolts to 87 inch lbs. (10 Nm). Do not over torque these bolts or the housing may break.
11. If equipped, install the splash shield.
12. Lower the vehicle from the jackstands. Make sure the car is level.
13. Loosen the upper radiator hose and begin filling the system (with the proper mixture of coolant and distilled water) through the coolant reservoir. Loosening the upper hose will allow the air to escape and speed the process.

14. When the system will not take any more coolant, tighten the hose and start the engine. Watch for leaks, and add more coolant as required. Don't run the engine too long with the reservoir cap removed or it will boil over.

VR6 Engines Only

On VR6 engines, a drain plug is installed in the coolant pipe, which runs between the coolant pump and the thermostat housing.

1. Before raising the front of the vehicle, place the temperature control knob/slider to its warmest setting.
2. Raise and safely support the front of the vehicle on jackstands.
3. Some vehicles have a splash shield underneath the vehicle that may obstruct access to the coolant pipe. Remove the shield if necessary to allow adequate access to the coolant pipe.
4. Place a large drain pan (large enough to contain the entire cooling system contents) under the drain plug. Make sure the drain pan is clean, since the coolant should be reused unless it is dirty, or it does not pass a hydrometer test.
5. Loosen (but do not remove) the coolant drain plug. Push against the drain plug while unscrewing it by hand. When the drain plug is free of the threads, quickly remove it from the coolant pipe, and allow the coolant to drain from the vehicle.
6. While the coolant is draining, remove the coolant reservoir cap; this will allow thorough draining of the system.

To install:

7. Using a new O-ring on the drain plug, install the drain plug into the coolant pipe. Tighten the drain plug to 89 inch lbs. (10 Nm).
8. If equipped, install the splash shield.
9. Lower the vehicle from the jackstands. Make sure the car is level.
10. Using either the drained coolant, or a fresh mixture of the proper type of coolant and distilled water, slowly fill the cooling system through the coolant reservoir. If possible, loosen the upper hose; this will allow the air to escape and speed the process.
11. When the system will not take any more coolant, tighten the hose (if loosened) and start the engine. Watch for leaks, and add more coolant as required. Don't run the engine too long with the reservoir cap removed or it will boil over.

FLUSHING & CLEANING THE SYSTEM

On older vehicles equipped with standard coolant/antifreeze, the cooling system should be drained and refilled with new coolant at least every 30,000 miles or 24 months. If desired, a flush system designed specifically for aluminum cooling components should be used. Follow the instructions on the package.

On vehicles with G11 and G12 coolant/antifreeze, (blue and pink, respectively). Both G11 and G12 coolant is considered a "lifetime" coolant, the manufacturer does not recommend any special cooling system flushing or replacement.

Brake Master Cylinder

FLUID RECOMMENDATIONS

On all models covered by this manual, brake fluid that meets or exceeds DOT 4 specifications should be used in the brake system. Do NOT use DOT 5 fluid; the hydraulic system can be damaged.

LEVEL CHECK

▶ **See Figures 151, 152, 153 and 154**

The brake fluid reservoir is located on the left side of the engine compartment at the firewall. Fluid level can be checked visually without removing the cap on this translucent unit. Brake fluid level will decrease slowly as the brake pads wear thinner. If the level is close to the MIN line, check the brake pads and shoes for wear before adding brake fluid.

If the reservoir constantly needs refilling, chances are there is a leak in the system. The entire brake system should be thoroughly inspected for any signs of leakage.

Fig. 151 Master cylinder level marks

Fig. 152 Wipe around the cap of the master cylinder to remove any dirt

Fig. 153 Remove the cap

Fig. 154 Add brake fluid of at least DOT 3 specifications

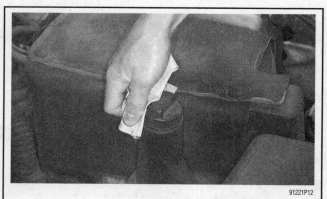

Fig. 155 Wipe the power steering reservoir cap before removing

Clutch Master Cylinder

FLUID RECOMMENDATIONS

On models equipped with a hydraulic clutch release mechanism, The hydraulic clutch uses fluid from the brake fluid reservoir.

Power Steering Pump

FLUID RECOMMENDATIONS

All vehicles covered by this manual use a special hydraulic fluid in the power steering system. This fluid (G 002 000) is available from Volkswagen dealers. The use of Dexron® Automatic Transmission Fluid (ATF) is not recommended.

LEVEL CHECK

▶ **See Figures 155, 156, 157 and 158**

On all vehicles except for A1 platform Cabriolet, the power steering fluid reservoir is located near the battery. On the A1 Cabriolet, the reservoir is located on the passenger side of the engine compartment, near the radiator.

The fluid level should be checked at regular intervals. With the engine running, the fluid level should be between the MAX and MIN marks on the outside of the reservoir, or on A3 platform vehicles, the MAX and MIN marks on the dipstick. If fluid is added, make sure the filler cap is secured.

Steering Gear

The rack and pinion steering gear is filled with lubricant and sealed at the factory. If you notice any leaks, the rack assembly must be repaired or replaced.

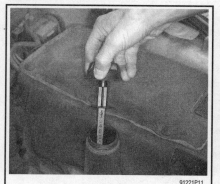

Fig. 156 Twist and remove to check the power steering fluid

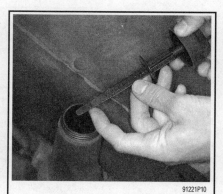

Fig. 157 The fluid must be up to the fill cold mark

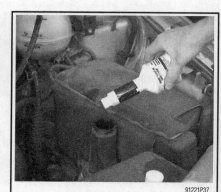

Fig. 158 Adding fluid to the power steering reservoir

Chassis Greasing

All vehicles covered by this manual do not require chassis greasing, and consequently, are not equipped with grease nipples.

Body Lubrication

Periodic lubrication will prevent squeaky, hard-to-open doors and lids. About every three months, pry the plastic caps off the door hinges and squirt in enough oil to fill the chambers. Press the plug back into the hinge after filling. Lightly oil the door check pivots. Finally, spray graphite lock lubricant onto your key and insert it into the door lock a few times.

Wheel Bearings

FRONT

On all vehicles covered by this manual, the front wheel bearings are sealed units, and lubrication is not required, or necessary.

REAR

On all vehicles covered by this manual, the rear wheel bearings are of the standard tapered-roller design. Periodic lubrication and adjustment is necessary to prevent premature bearing failure.

Removal, Packing, & Installation

1. Raise and safely support the vehicle, and remove the rear wheels.
2. On vehicles with rear drum brakes, insert a small pry tool through a wheel bolt hole and push up on the spring tensioned adjusting wedge to slacken the rear brake adjustment.
3. On vehicles with rear disc brakes, remove the two 8mm Allen bolts that secure the caliper to the axle. Hang the caliper from the spring with wire, do not let it hang by the hydraulic hose.
4. Pry off the grease cap, remove cotter pin, locking ring, axle nut and thrust washer. Carefully remove the bearing without dropping it.
5. Remove the brake drum or rotor and pry the bearing seal out of the hub. The seal will be destroyed, but be careful not to pry on the bearing.
6. Clean the bearings in solvent, and wipe the inside of the drum/rotor. Examine the bearings and inner races for discoloration, wear or damage.
7. Pack the bearings with new wheel bearing grease. Fill the inside of the drum/rotor with bearing grease also. Keep in mind that the grease not only lubricates the bearings, but also provides a means of cooling.
8. Place the freshly packed inside wheel bearing in the drum/rotor. Using a flat block of wood or other suitable tool, install the new axle seal onto the drum/rotor.

➡ **Do NOT attempt to drive the seal in place with a hammer, it will be damaged.**

9. Pack about 1 oz. of grease into the hub and fit the drum or disc onto the axle.
10. Pack the outer bearing with grease and fit the bearing, thrust washer and nut onto the axle. Adjust bearing pre-load and install the locking ring, cotter pin and grease cap.
11. Install the brake caliper, if removed.

Adjustment

1. Tighten the bearing nut while turning the drum or disc. Torque the nut to 87 inch lbs. (10 Nm) to seat the bearing, then loosen it again.
2. When tightening adjusting the nut again, move the thrust washer side to side with a screwdriver. The thrust washer must still be movable with light effort when adjustment is complete.
3. When installing the locking ring, keep trying different positions of the ring on the nut until the cotter pin goes into the hole. Don't turn the nut to align the locking ring with the hole in the axle. Use a new cotter pin.

JUMP STARTING A DEAD BATTERY

◆ **See Figure 159**

Whenever a vehicle is jump started, precautions must be followed in order to prevent the possibility of personal injury, as well as damage to vehicle electrical components. Remember that batteries contain a small amount of explosive hydrogen gas, which is a by-product of battery charging. Sparks should always be avoided when working around batteries, especially when attaching jumper cables. To minimize the possibility of accidental sparks, follow the procedure carefully.

❈❈ CAUTION

NEVER hook the batteries up in a series circuit or the entire electrical system will go up in smoke, including the starter!

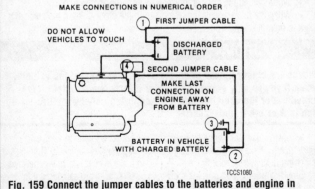

Fig. 159 Connect the jumper cables to the batteries and engine in the order shown

MAKE CONNECTIONS IN NUMERICAL ORDER
DO NOT ALLOW VEHICLES TO TOUCH
① FIRST JUMPER CABLE
DISCHARGED BATTERY
④ SECOND JUMPER CABLE
MAKE LAST CONNECTION ON ENGINE, AWAY FROM BATTERY
③
BATTERY IN VEHICLE WITH CHARGED BATTERY
②
TCCS1080

Jump Starting Precautions

- Be sure that both batteries are of the same voltage. Vehicles covered by this manual and most vehicles on the road today utilize a 12 volt charging system, so this should not be a problem.
- Be sure that both batteries are of the same polarity (have the same terminal, in most cases NEGATIVE grounded).
- Be sure that the vehicles are not touching or a short could occur.
- On serviceable batteries, be sure the vent cap holes are not obstructed.
- Do not smoke or allow sparks anywhere near the batteries.
- In cold weather, make sure the battery electrolyte is not frozen. This can occur more readily in a battery that has been in a state of discharge.
- Do not allow electrolyte to contact your skin or clothing. Electrolyte is a caustic acid, and can cause chemical burns to the skin.

Jump Starting Procedure

◆ **See Figures 160, 161, 162 and 163**

1. Make sure that the voltages of the 2 batteries are the same. Most batteries and charging systems are of the 12 volt variety.
2. Pull the jumping vehicle (with the good battery) into a position so the jumper cables can reach the dead battery and that vehicle's engine. Make sure that the vehicles do NOT touch.
3. Place the transmissions/transaxle of both vehicles in **Neutral** (MT) or **P** (AT), as applicable, then firmly set their parking brakes.

➡ **If necessary for safety reasons, the hazard lights on both vehicles may be operated throughout the entire procedure without significantly increasing the difficulty of jumping the dead battery.**

4. Turn all lights and accessories OFF on both vehicles. Make sure the ignition switches on both vehicles are turned to the **OFF** position.

Fig. 160 A fully charged battery has a voltage reading of 12.68 volts

Fig. 161 Connect the positive lead first

Fig. 162 Then attach the negative lead

Fig. 163 Only connect the positive cable to the battery on the vehicle with the dead battery. The negative must be attached to a know good ground like the engine block

5. Cover the battery cell caps with a rag, but do not cover the terminals.
6. Make sure the terminals on both batteries are clean and free of corrosion or proper electrical connection will be impeded. If necessary, clean the battery terminals before proceeding.
7. Identify the positive (+) and negative (-) terminals on both batteries.
8. Connect the first jumper cable to the positive (+) terminal of the dead battery, then connect the other end of that cable to the positive (+) terminal of the booster (good) battery.
9. Connect one end of the other jumper cable to the negative (-) terminal on the booster battery and the final cable clamp to an engine bolt head, alternative bracket or other solid, metallic point on the engine with the dead battery. Try to pick a ground on the engine that is positioned away from the battery in order to minimize the possibility of the 2 clamps touching should one loosen during the procedure. DO NOT connect this clamp to the negative (-) terminal of the bad battery.

✳✳ CAUTION

Be very careful to keep the jumper cables away from moving parts (cooling fan, belts, etc.) on both engines.

10. Check to make sure that the cables are routed away from any moving parts, then start the donor vehicle's engine. Run the engine at moderate speed for several minutes to allow the dead battery a chance to receive some initial charge.
11. With the donor vehicle's engine still running slightly above idle, try to start the vehicle with the dead battery. Crank the engine for no more than 10 seconds at a time and let the starter cool for at least 20 seconds between tries. If the vehicle does not start in 3 tries, it is likely that something else is also wrong or that the battery needs additional time to charge.
12. Once the vehicle is started, allow it to run at idle for a few seconds to make sure that it is operating properly.
13. Turn ON the headlights, heater blower and, if equipped, the rear defroster of both vehicles in order to reduce the severity of voltage spikes and subsequent risk of damage to the vehicles' electrical systems when the cables are disconnected. This step is especially important to any vehicle equipped with computer control modules (which includes the majority of vehicles covered in this manual).
14. Carefully disconnect the cables in the reverse order of connection. Start with the negative cable that is attached to the engine ground, then the negative cable on the donor battery. Disconnect the positive cable from the donor battery and finally, disconnect the positive cable from the formerly dead battery. Be careful when disconnecting the cables from the positive terminals not to allow the alligator clips to touch any metal on either vehicle or a short and sparks will occur.

JACKING

Your car is equipped with a single post, crank handle jack which fits the jacking points behind the front wheel and in front of the rear wheel. These are marked with triangular sections of the body stamping. Never use the tire changing jack for anything other than that. If you intend to use this book to perform your own maintenance, a good scissors or a small hydraulic jack and two sturdy jackstands would be a wise purchase. Always chock the wheels when changing a tire or working beneath the car. It cannot be overemphasized. **CLIMBING UNDER A CAR SUPPORTED BY JUST THE JACK IS EXTREMELY DANGEROUS!**

A jack can be safely placed just forward of or behind the same jacking points used by the tire changing jack. Place the jack on the rocker panel or on the seam, not inside the seam on the floor pan. Lift the car there and fit the jackstand at the normal jacking point.

Jacking Precautions

The following safety points cannot be overemphasized:
• Always block the opposite wheels or wheels to keep the vehicle from rolling off the jack.

• When raising the front of the vehicle, firmly apply the parking brake.
• When the drive wheels are to remain on the ground, leave the vehicle in park to help prevent it from rolling.

✳✳ CAUTION

Never use cinder blocks or stacks of wood to support the vehicle, even if you're only going to be under it for a few minutes. Never crawl under the vehicle when it is supported only by the tire-changing jack or other floor jack.

• Always use jackstands to support the vehicle when you are working underneath. Place the stands beneath the vehicle's jacking brackets. Before climbing underneath, rock the vehicle a bit to make sure it is firmly supported.

Small hydraulic (bottle jack), screw or scissors jacks are satisfactory for raising the vehicle. Drive-on trestles or ramps are also a handy and safe way to both raise and support the vehicle. Be careful though, some ramps may be too steep to drive your vehicle onto without scraping the front bottom panels. Never support on any suspension member (unless specifically instructed to do so by a repair manual).

• Never place the jack under the radiator, engine or transmission components, severe and extensive damage will result when he jack is raised. Additionally, never jack under the floorpan or bodywork.

Lift Points

REINFORCED FLOOR PAN

Front

♦ **See Figures 164, 165 and 166**

Lift the vehicle with a hydraulic floor jack by placing the jack pad on the reinforced floor pan just behind the front tire.

91221P58

Fig. 164 Lifting a VW Jetta by the reinforced floor pan

※ WARNING

Damage may occur if you lift the vehicle by the pinch weld, without using a grooved support block.

Rear

♦ **See Figures 167 and 168**

The rear of the vehicle can be lifted from the flat reinforced suspension pad just in front of the rear axle. A jackstand can also be placed under the rear of the car for support.

PINCH WELD

♦ **See Figures 169 and 170**

※ WARNING

The pinch weld is not very sturdy and will bend if the vehicle is improperly lifted by it.

1. Obtain a block of wood that is at least two inches wide by two inches tall by six inches long (2"x 2"x 6") .
2. Cut a groove the full length of the wooden block that is at least ⅜ inch (1 cm) wide and ½ inch (1.27 cm) deep.
3. Position the pinch weld in the support block.
4. Place a jack under the wooden block. This will prevent any damage to the vehicle's frame upon lifting.

91221P56

Fig. 165 A jackstand can also be positioned under the reinforced section of the floor pan to support the vehicle

91221P54

Fig. 166 The vehicle can be lifted via the front engine cradle and then supported with jackstands placed under the reinforced floor pans

91221P59

Fig. 167 The rear of the vehicle can be lifted from the flat reinforced suspension pad just in front of the rear axle

91221P62

Fig. 168 The arrowed area is where the jackstand and the emergency jack is to be placed

91221P50

Fig. 169 Wooden support block

91221P48

Fig. 170 Pinch weld properly supported in the wooden support block

MANUFACTURER RECOMMENDED MAINTENANCE INTERVALS

Component	Service	Every 7,500 Miles (12,000 Km)	Every 15,000 Miles (24,000 Km)	Every 30,000 Miles (48,000 Km)	Every 60,000 Miles (96,000 Km)	Every Two Years
Engine oil and filter	Replace	✓ ①				
Air cleaner	Replace			✓		✓
Diesel water separator	Drain	✓ ①				
Diesel fuel filter	Replace			✓		
Gasoline fuel filter	Replace					✓ ②
Spark plugs	Replace			✓		
Battery electrolyte level	Check		✓			
Wheels and tires	Rotate	✓				
Coolant level	Check		✓			
Coolant	Replace					
Power steering fluid level	Check		✓			
Automatic transaxle fluid level	Check		✓			
Automatic transaxle fluid	Replace			✓ ③		
Brake system hoses and connections	Check		✓			
Brake fluid level	Check		✓			
Brake fluid	Replace					✓
Brake pads and rotors	Check		✓			
Brake shoes and drums	Check		✓			
Drive belts	Check			✓		
Timing belt tension	Check		✓ ④			
Timing belt (4 cyl)	Replace				✓ ⑤	
CV joint boots	Check		✓			
Ball joints	Check			✓		
Hood Lock (Canada only)	Lubricate	✓				

① On 1997-99 models, the manufacturer recommends an interval of 10,000 miles.

② The manufacturer specifies the fuel filters on gasoline engines as "lifetime" units, and does not specify a maintenance interval. Although it is not necessary, Chilton recommends replacing the fuel filter every 2 years, regardless of the mileage of the vehicle.

③ The manufacturer does not specify an interval for normal operating conditons, although a severe use (towing, heavy traffic, continuous use in mountainous areas, etc.) interval of 30,000 miles is recommended.

④ An inspection/adjustment interval of 10,000 miles is specified for 1997-99 TDI engines

⑤ A replacement interval is not specified by the manufacturer. Because of the design of Volkswagen engines, Chilton recommends replacement of the timing belt every 60,000 miles.

91221C07

CAPACITIES

Year	Model	Engine ID/VIN	Engine Displacement Liters (cc)	Engine Crankcase with Filter (qts.)	Transmission 5-Spd (qts.)	Transmission Auto. (qts.)	Fuel Tank (gal.)	Cooling System (qts.)
1990	Jetta	1V	1.6 (1588)	4.8	2.0	3.2	14.5	7.3
	Jetta	ME	1.6 (1588)	4.8	2.0	3.2	14.5	7.3
	Jetta	MF	1.6 (1588)	4.8	2.0	3.2	14.5	7.3
	Jetta	RV	1.8 (1781)	4.3	2.0	3.2	14.5	7.3
	Jetta	PF	1.8 (1781)	4.3	2.0	3.2	14.5	7.3
	Jetta	9A	2.0 (1984)	4.3	2.0	3.2	14.5	7.3
	Golf	RV	1.8 (1781)	4.3	2.0	3.2	14.5	7.3
	GTI	PF	1.8 (1781)	4.3	2.0	3.2	14.5	7.3
	GTI 16V	9A	2.0 (1984)	4.3	2.0	3.2	14.5	7.3
	Cabriolet	2H	1.8 (1781)	4.3	2.0	3.2	13.8	7.3
	Fox	UM	1.8 (1780)	4.3	2.0	3.2	14.5	7.3
	Fox	JN	1.8 (1781)	4.3	2.0	3.2	14.5	7.3
1991	Jetta	1V	1.6 (1588)	4.8	2.0	3.2	14.5	7.3
	Jetta	ME	1.6 (1588)	4.8	2.0	3.2	14.5	7.3
	Jetta	MF	1.6 (1588)	4.8	2.0	3.2	14.5	7.3
	Jetta	RV	1.8 (1781)	4.3	2.0	3.2	14.5	7.3
	Jetta	PF	1.8 (1781)	4.3	2.0	3.2	14.5	7.3
	Jetta	9A	2.0 (1984)	4.3	2.0	3.2	14.5	7.3
	Golf	RV	1.8 (1781)	4.3	2.0	3.2	14.5	7.3
	GTI	PF	1.8 (1781)	4.3	2.0	3.2	14.5	7.3
	GTI 16V	9A	2.0 (1984)	4.3	2.0	3.2	14.5	7.3
	Cabriolet	2H	1.8 (1781)	4.3	2.0	3.2	13.8	7.3
	Fox	UM	1.8 (1780)	4.3	2.0	3.2	14.5	7.3
	Fox	JN	1.8 (1780)	4.3	2.0	3.2	14.5	7.3
1992	Jetta	1V	1.6 (1588)	4.8	2.0	3.2	14.5	7.3
	Jetta	ME	1.6 (1588)	4.8	2.0	3.2	14.5	7.3
	Jetta	MF	1.6 (1588)	4.8	2.0	3.2	14.5	7.3
	Jetta	RV	1.8 (1781)	4.3	2.0	3.2	14.5	7.3
	Jetta	PF	1.8 (1781)	4.3	2.0	3.2	14.5	7.3
	Jetta	9A	2.0 (1984)	4.3	2.0	3.2	14.5	7.3
	Golf	RV	1.8 (1781)	4.3	2.0	3.2	14.5	7.3
	GTI	PF	1.8 (1781)	4.3	2.0	3.2	14.5	7.3
	GTI 16V	9A	2.0 (1984)	4.3	2.0	3.2	14.5	7.3
	Cabriolet	2H	1.8 (1781)	4.3	2.0	3.2	13.8	7.3
	Fox	UM	1.8 (1780)	4.3	2.0	3.2	14.5	7.3
	Fox	JN	1.8 (1780)	4.3	2.0	3.2	14.5	7.3
1993	Jetta	ACC	1.8 (1781)	4.3	2.0	3.2	14.5	5.8
	Jetta	AAZ	1.9 (1896)	4.7	2.0	3.2	14.5	6.8
	Jetta	AHU	1.9 (1896)	4.7	2.0	3.2	14.5	6.8
	Jetta	ABA	2.0 (1984)	4.3	2.0	3.2	14.5	6.1
	Jetta	AAA	2.8 (2792)	5.8	2.1	3.2	14.5	10.6
	Golf	ACC	1.8 (1781)	4.3	2.0	3.2	14.5	5.8

91221C08

CAPACITIES

Year	Model	Engine ID/VIN	Engine Displacement Liters (cc)	Engine Crankcase with Filter (qts.)	Transmission 5-Spd (qts.)	Transmission Auto. (qts.)	Fuel Tank (gal.)	Cooling System (qts.)
1993 con't.	Golf	AAZ	1.9 (1896)	4.7	2.0	3.2	14.5	6.8
	Golf	AHU	1.9 (1896)	4.7	2.0	3.2	14.5	6.8
	Golf	ABA	2.0 (1984)	4.3	2.0	3.2	14.5	6.1
	GTI	ABA	2.0 (1984)	4.3	2.0	3.2	14.5	6.1
	GTI-VR6	AAA	2.8 (2792)	5.8	2.1	3.2	14.5	10.6
	Cabriolet	2H	1.8 (1781)	4.3	2.0	3.2	13.8	7.3
	Fox	UM	1.8 (1780)	4.3	2.0	3.2	14.5	7.3
	Fox	JN	1.8 (1780)	4.3	2.0	3.2	14.5	7.3
1994	Jetta	ACC	1.8 (1781)	4.3	2.0	3.2	14.5	5.8
	Jetta	AAZ	1.9 (1896)	4.7	2.0	3.2	14.5	6.8
	Jetta	AHU	1.9 (1896)	4.7	2.0	3.2	14.5	6.8
	Jetta	ABA	2.0 (1984)	4.3	2.0	3.2	14.5	6.1
	Jetta	AAA	2.8 (2792)	5.8	2.1	3.2	14.5	10.6
	Golf	ACC	1.8 (1781)	4.3	2.0	3.2	14.5	5.8
	Golf	AAZ	1.9 (1896)	4.7	2.0	3.2	14.5	6.8
	Golf	AHU	1.9 (1896)	4.7	2.0	3.2	14.5	6.8
	Golf	ABA	2.0 (1984)	4.3	2.0	3.2	14.5	6.1
	GTI	ABA	2.0 (1984)	4.3	2.0	3.2	14.5	6.1
	GTI-VR6	AAA	2.8 (2792)	5.8	2.1	3.2	14.5	10.6
	Cabriolet	2H	1.8 (1781)	4.3	2.0	3.2	13.8	7.3
	Fox	UM	1.8 (1780)	4.3	2.0	3.2	14.5	7.3
	Fox	JN	1.8 (1780)	4.3	2.0	3.2	14.5	7.3
1995	Jetta	ACC	1.8 (1781)	4.3	2.0	3.2	14.5	5.8
	Jetta	AAZ	1.9 (1896)	4.7	2.0	3.2	14.5	6.8
	Jetta	AHU	1.9 (1896)	4.7	2.0	3.2	14.5	6.8
	Jetta	ABA	2.0 (1984)	4.3	2.0	3.2	14.5	6.1
	Jetta	AAA	2.8 (2792)	5.8	2.1	3.2	14.5	10.6
	Golf	ACC	1.8 (1781)	4.3	2.0	3.2	14.5	5.8
	Golf	AAZ	1.9 (1896)	4.7	2.0	3.2	14.5	6.8
	Golf	AHU	1.9 (1896)	4.7	2.0	3.2	14.5	6.8
	Golf	ABA	2.0 (1984)	4.3	2.0	3.2	14.5	6.1
	GTI	ABA	2.0 (1984)	4.3	2.0	3.2	14.5	6.1
	GTI-VR6	AAA	2.8 (2792)	5.8	2.1	3.2	14.5	10.6
	Cabrio	ABA	2.0 (1984)	4.3	2.0	3.2	14.5	6.1
1996	Jetta	ACC	1.8 (1781)	4.3	2.0	3.2	14.5	5.8
	Jetta	AAZ	1.9 (1896)	4.7	2.0	3.2	14.5	6.8
	Jetta	AHU	1.9 (1896)	4.7	2.0	3.2	14.5	6.8
	Jetta	ABA	2.0 (1984)	4.3	2.0	3.2	14.5	6.1
	Jetta	AAA	2.8 (2792)	5.8	2.1	3.2	14.5	10.6
	Golf	ACC	1.8 (1781)	4.3	2.0	3.2	14.5	5.8
	Golf	AAZ	1.9 (1896)	4.7	2.0	3.2	14.5	6.8
	Golf	AHU	1.9 (1896)	4.7	2.0	3.2	14.5	6.8

91221C09

CAPACITIES

Year	Model	Engine ID/VIN	Engine Displacement Liters (cc)	Engine Crankcase with Filter (qts.)	Transmission (qts.)		Fuel Tank (gal.)	Cooling System (qts.)
					5-Spd	Auto.		
1996 con't.	Golf	ABA	2.0 (1984)	4.3	2.0	3.2	14.5	6.1
	GTI	ABA	2.0 (1984)	4.3	2.0	3.2	14.5	6.1
	GTI-VR6	AAA	2.8 (2792)	5.8	2.1	3.2	14.5	10.6
	Cabrio	ABA	2.0 (1984)	4.3	2.0	3.2	14.5	6.1
1997	Jetta	ACC	1.8 (1781)	4.3	2.0	3.2	14.5	5.8
	Jetta	AAZ	1.9 (1896)	4.7	2.0	3.2	14.5	6.8
	Jetta	AHU	1.9 (1896)	4.7	2.0	3.2	14.5	6.8
	Jetta	ABA	2.0 (1984)	4.3	2.0	3.2	14.5	6.1
	Jetta	AAA	2.8 (2792)	5.8	2.1	3.2	14.5	10.6
	Golf	ACC	1.8 (1781)	4.3	2.0	3.2	14.5	5.8
	Golf	AAZ	1.9 (1896)	4.7	2.0	3.2	14.5	6.8
	Golf	AHU	1.9 (1896)	4.7	2.0	3.2	14.5	6.8
	Golf	ABA	2.0 (1984)	4.3	2.0	3.2	14.5	6.1
	GTI	ABA	2.0 (1984)	4.3	2.0	3.2	14.5	6.1
	GTI-VR6	AAA	2.8 (2792)	5.8	2.1	3.2	14.5	10.6
	Cabrio	ABA	2.0 (1984)	4.3	2.0	3.2	14.5	6.1
1998	Jetta	ACC	1.8 (1781)	4.3	2.0	3.2	14.5	5.8
	Jetta	AAZ	1.9 (1896)	4.7	2.0	3.2	14.5	6.8
	Jetta	AHU	1.9 (1896)	4.7	2.0	3.2	14.5	6.8
	Jetta	ABA	2.0 (1984)	4.3	2.0	3.2	14.5	6.1
	Jetta	AAA	2.8 (2792)	5.8	2.1	3.2	14.5	10.6
	Golf	ACC	1.8 (1781)	4.3	2.0	3.2	14.5	5.8
	Golf	AAZ	1.9 (1896)	4.7	2.0	3.2	14.5	6.8
	Golf	AHU	1.9 (1896)	4.7	2.0	3.2	14.5	6.8
	Golf	ABA	2.0 (1984)	4.3	2.0	3.2	14.5	6.1
	GTI	ABA	2.0 (1984)	4.3	2.0	3.2	14.5	6.1
	GTI-VR6	AAA	2.8 (2792)	5.8	2.1	3.2	14.5	10.6
	Cabrio	ABA	2.0 (1984)	4.3	2.0	3.2	14.5	6.1
1999	Jetta	ACC	1.8 (1781)	4.3	2.0	3.2	14.5	5.8
	Jetta	AAZ	1.9 (1896)	4.7	2.0	3.2	14.5	6.8
	Jetta	AHU	1.9 (1896)	4.7	2.0	3.2	14.5	6.8
	Jetta	ABA	2.0 (1984)	4.3	2.0	3.2	14.5	6.1
	Jetta	AAA	2.8 (2792)	5.8	2.1	3.2	14.5	10.6
	Golf	ACC	1.8 (1781)	4.3	2.0	3.2	14.5	5.8
	Golf	AAZ	1.9 (1896)	4.7	2.0	3.2	14.5	6.8
	Golf	AHU	1.9 (1896)	4.7	2.0	3.2	14.5	6.8
	Golf	ABA	2.0 (1984)	4.3	2.0	3.2	14.5	6.1
	GTI	ABA	2.0 (1984)	4.3	2.0	3.2	14.5	6.1
	GTI-VR6	AAA	2.8 (2792)	5.8	2.1	3.2	14.5	10.6
	Cabrio	ABA	2.0 (1984)	4.3	2.0	3.2	14.5	6.1

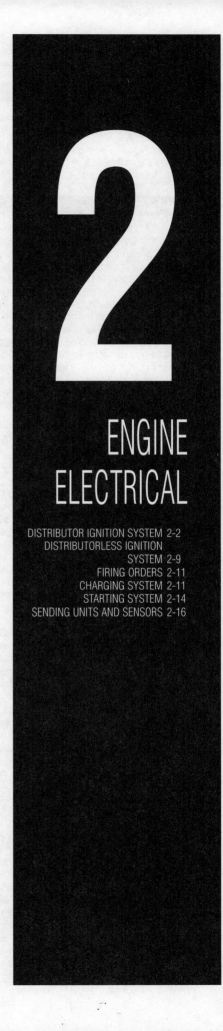

2

ENGINE ELECTRICAL

DISTRIBUTOR IGNITION SYSTEM

➡For information on understanding electricity and troubleshooting electrical circuits, please refer to Section 6 of this manual.

This heading covers 4-cylinder gasoline engines only. For information on the ignition system used on the 2.8L VR6 (AAA) engine, refer to the Distributorless Ignition System heading in this section.

General Information

Years ago, ignition systems consisted of a breaker-point distributor, with mechanical and manifold vacuum operated advance and retardation of the timing. Over time, the development of computerized fuel injection technology allowed the integration of electronically manipulated ignition control, which allows maximum efficiency and power from an internal combustion engine.

Volkswagen uses three different engine management systems on their gasoline engines: CIS-E-Motronic, Digifant, and Motronic. Although there are differences between the fuel management components on all three systems, the electronic ignition system is of the same basic design.

To allow the Electronic Control Module (ECM) to accurately control the ignition timing, various sensors are placed on the engine, and connected into the ECM to provide information regarding the operational state of the engine. These sensors allow variables such as engine coolant temperature, exhaust gas content, crankshaft position, throttle position, and air temperature to determine the amount of ignition timing advance or retardation the ECM can safely provide.

➡Because the ECM controls the advance and retardation of the ignition timing, the distributor is not equipped with any type of mechanical or vacuum operated advance mechanism.

Since the ECM can closely monitor the performance of the engine based on the sensor inputs, the ignition timing is continually adjusted to maintain peak horsepower. The main component responsible for this feature is the knock sensor. Because the ECM receives a continuous input from the knock sensor, the ignition timing can be advanced (meaning spark is created before each piston reaches top dead center) just below the threshold of detonation, providing peak performance from the engine.

The distributor ignition system is composed of the following components:
- **Electronic Control Module (ECM)**—The ECM is the "brain" of the ignition system. The ECM controls when the spark occurs, based on the input from the various sensors on the engine, which include the crankshaft and/or camshaft position sensor, the knock sensor, coolant temperature sensor, and the oxygen (02) sensor.
- **Distributor**—The distributor allows the high voltage from the ignition coil to be distributed to the spark plug in the proper order. The distributor also contains a Hall-type sensor, which is sometimes referred to as the camshaft position sensor. The information from this sensor, working together with the ignition control unit, allows the ECM to precisely calculate when to open the ground circuit of the primary ignition coil winding, which creates the high voltage necessary to create an electrical arc at the spark plugs.
- **Ignition Coil**—The ignition consists of a coil uses a mere 12 volts to generate over 25,000 volts to allow a "spark" (actually an electric arc) from the spark plugs. An ignition coil actually consists of two separate wire coils: Primary and Secondary. The primary coil is supplied with a 12 volt signal from the ignition switch. This current flow through the primary coil wiring creates a magnetic field. When the negative side of the primary coil wiring is opened, or "ungrounded" the magnetic field collapses, inducing a high voltage in the secondary coil winding. This high voltage travels through the coil wire to the distributor, through the spark plug wire, and finally, to the spark plug. Because the voltage is so powerful, the electricity actually "arcs" or jumps across the electrodes on the spark plug. This grounding and ungrounding of the primary coil wiring is controlled by the ignition control unit, or on later systems, the ECM. The Hall Sender (or crankshaft/camshaft position sensor) supplies the ignition control unit or ECM with a signal for proper coil operation.
- **Ignition Control Unit**—The ignition control unit is essentially a solid state switch that controls the ground circuit for the primary winding in the ignition coil. The ignition control unit works together with the Hall sensor in the distributor (or crankshaft position sensor) to control the ignition coil. On later systems, this component is integrated into the ECM, with a "power stage" mounted on the coil which essentially performs the same function.
- **Knock Sensor**—A knock sensor is a peizo-electric device that senses

detonation or pre-ignition from the engine block. When the engine begins to knock, the sensor produces a small amount of voltage; when detected by the ECM, the ignition timing is retarded slightly to prevent detonation.
- **Crankshaft/Camshaft Position Sensor**—This sensor determines the exact position of each piston in the engine. The information from the crankshaft/camshaft position sensor allows the ECM to precisely control when the ignition occurs. Typically, this sensor is located inside of the distributor itself. On later systems, this sensor is located on the engine block.

Diagnosis and Testing

Before beginning any diagnosis and testing procedures, visually inspect the components of the ignition system and engine control systems. Check for the following:
- Discharged battery
- Damaged or loose connections
- Damaged electrical insulation
- Poor coil and spark plug connections
- Ignition module connections
- Blown fuses
- Damaged vacuum hoses
- Damaged spark plugs

When attempting to search for ignition troubles, also keep in mind that various sensor inputs that the ECM employs to calculate timing may affect engine performance.

IGNITION SYSTEM PRECAUTIONS

Before proceeding with any type of ignition system testing, be sure to follow these important precautions:
- Make sure the ignition switch is **OFF** before connecting or disconnecting any wiring or test equipment.
- When cranking the engine without starting, as for a compression test, disconnect the power supply connector (+12V) from the coil to prevent it from receiving voltage. Other methods of disabling the ignition system are not recommended, and may result in electrical system damage.
- Always switch the multimeter to the appropriate measuring range BEFORE making the test connections. Use a high-impedance digital multimeter which is designed for testing computerized electrical components.
- DO NOT install a standard ignition coil in the system.
- DO NOT connect a condenser/suppressor or powered test light to the negative terminal (1) of the ignition coil.
- DO NOT connect any 12-volt test instruments to the positive terminal (15) of the ignition coil. The electronic control unit will be permanently damaged.
- DO NOT use a standard test light (electric bulb type) on electronic circuits. The high electrical consumption of these test lights can lead to electronic component damage.
- DO NOT connect a quick-charger to the battery for more than 1 minute, nor exceed 16.5 volts with the booster.

SECONDARY SPARK TEST

♦ See Figures 1, 2, 3 and 4

The best way to perform this procedure is to use a spark tester (available at most automotive parts stores). Three types of spark testers are commonly available. The Neon Bulb type is connected to the spark plug wire and flashes with each ignition pulse. The Air Gap type must be adjusted to the individual spark plug gap specified for the engine. The last type of spark plug tester looks like a spark plug with a grounding clip on the side, but there is no side electrode for the spark to jump to. The last two types of testers allows the user to not only detect the presence of spark, but also the intensity (orange/yellow is weak, blue is strong).

1. Disconnect a spark plug wire at the spark plug end.
2. Connect the plug wire to the spark tester and ground the tester to an appropriate location on the engine.
3. Crank the engine and check for spark at the tester.
4. If spark exists at the tester, the ignition system is functioning properly.

Fig. 1 This spark tester looks just like a spark plug, attach the clip to ground and crank the engine to check for spark

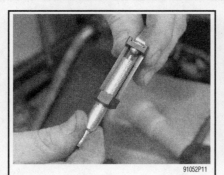

Fig. 2 This spark tester has an adjustable air-gap for measuring spark strength and testing different voltage ignition systems

Fig. 3 Attach the clip to ground and crank the engine to check for spark

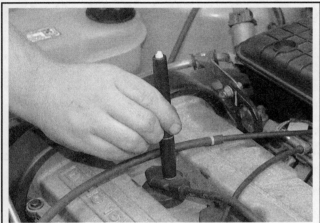

Fig. 4 This spark tester is the easiest to use—just place it on a plug wire so that the spark voltage is detected, and the bulb on the top will flash with each pulse

5. If spark does not exist at the spark plug wire, perform diagnosis of the ignition system using individual component diagnosis procedures.

CYLINDER DROP TEST

▶ **See Figures 5, 6 and 7**

The cylinder drop test is performed when an engine misfire is evident. This test helps determine which cylinder is not contributing the proper power. The easiest way to perform this test is to remove the plug wires one at a time from the cylinders with the engine running.

1. Place the transaxle in **P**, engage the emergency brake, and start the engine and let it idle.
2. Using a spark plug wire removing tool, preferably, the plier type, carefully remove the boot from one of the cylinders.

✳✳ WARNING

Make sure your body is free from touching any part of the car which is metal. The secondary voltage in the ignition system is high and although it cannot kill you, it will shock you and it does hurt.

3. The engine will sputter, run worse, and possibly nearly stall. If this happens reinstall the plug wire and move to the next cylinder. If the engine runs no differently, or the difference is minimal, shut the engine off and inspect the spark plug wire, spark plug, and if necessary, perform component diagnostics as covered in this section. Perform the test on all cylinders to verify the which cylinders are suspect.

Ignition Coil

TESTING

▶ **See Figures 8, 9 and 10**

This procedure is for testing the coil only. If the coil is functioning properly, (passes the test procedures given) and the ignition system still does not function, another component is probably faulty, or a problem may exist with the wiring harness.

➡**Although not necessary, it is often easier to remove the ignition coil for testing purposes.**

1. Make sure the ignition switch is **OFF** and disconnect all wiring from the coil. If necessary, mark the wires with tape or other means to ensure they are reconnected properly.

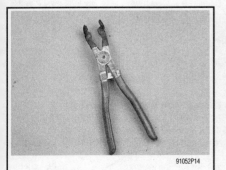

Fig. 5 These pliers are insulated and help protect the user from shock as well as the plug wires from being damaged

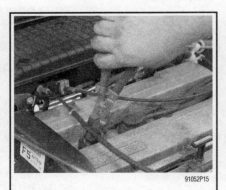

Fig. 6 To perform the cylinder drop test, remove one wire at a time and . . .

Fig. 7 . . . note the idle speed and idle characteristics of the engine. The cylinder(s) with the least drop is/are the non-contributing cylinder(s)

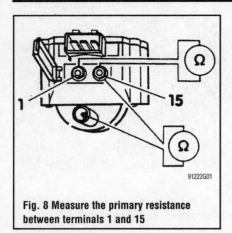

Fig. 8 Measure the primary resistance between terminals 1 and 15

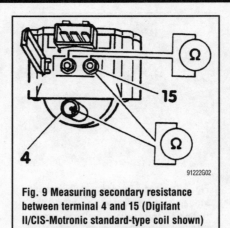

Fig. 9 Measuring secondary resistance between terminal 4 and 15 (Digifant II/CIS-Motronic standard-type coil shown)

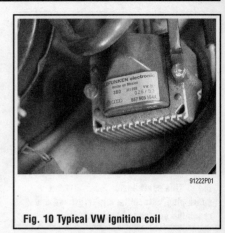

Fig. 10 Typical VW ignition coil

2. Using an ohmmeter, measure the primary circuit resistance across terminals **1** and **15**. The primary resistance should be as follows:
- CIS (FOX)–0.52–0.76 ohms
- CIS-E (FOX) –0.52–0.76 ohms
- CIS-Motronic–0.6–0.8 ohms
- Digifant I–0.5–0.7 ohms
- Digifant II–(green label)0.5–0.7 ohms
- Digifant II–(gray label)0.6–0.8 ohms
- Mono-Motronic–0.5–0.7 ohms
- Motronic–0.5–0.7 ohms

3. If the coil does not meet the specifications provided, it should be considered faulty, and should be replaced.

4. Next, measure the secondary circuit resistance across terminals **4** and **15**. The secondary resistance should be as follows:
- CIS (FOX)–2,400–3,500 ohms
- CIS-E (FOX)–2,400–3,500 ohms
- **CIS-Motronic**–6,500–8,500 ohms
- **Digifant I**–3,000–4,000 ohms
- **Digifant II**–(green label) 2,400–3,500 ohms
- **Digifant II**–(gray label) 6,900–8,500 ohms
- **Mono-Motronic**–3,000 to 4,000 ohms
- **Motronic**–3,000 to 4,000 ohms

5. If the coil does not meet the specifications provided, it should be considered faulty, and should be replaced.

6. If the coil meets the listed specifications, it can be considered to operating properly.

7. Make sure to replace the coil wires in the proper order when finished with testing.

REMOVAL & INSTALLATION

The ignition coil is mounted on the firewall, near the brake master cylinder/booster assembly.

1. Make sure the ignition switch is **OFF** and disconnect all wiring from the coil. If necessary, mark the wires with tape or other means to ensure they are reconnected properly.

2. Remove the plastic drain tray by removing the rubber seal (simply peel it off) and carefully lifting up on the lip. The drain tray is VERY fragile; use caution. It is only necessary to remove the forward edge of the drain tray to access the coil bracket fasteners.

3. Remove the fasteners that hold the ignition coil and mounting bracket to the firewall. Remove the coil from the vehicle.

To install:

4. Position the ignition coil and bracket to the firewall, and install the mounting fasteners.

5. Carefully work the lip of the plastic drain tray onto the edge of the firewall, and install the seal.

6. Plug in the coil wire, and the remaining connections to the ignition coil. Make sure the terminals are installed properly. The coil terminals are usually marked (+15 and -1) for proper connection.

Ignition Control Unit

TESTING

✳✳ WARNING

Testing the ignition control unit requires the use of a high impedance digital volt/ohm meter (DVOM) or LED test light. A standard analog voltmeter or incandescent light may cause damage to the unit.

CIS and CIS-E, FOX

VOLTAGE SUPPLY CHECK

1. Unplug the harness connector from the ignition control unit.

2. Using a digital voltmeter, connect the meter positive lead to terminal 4 and the negative lead to terminal 2 of the harness connector.

3. With the leads connected, turn the ignition switch **ON** and check for battery (12 volts) voltage.

4. If voltage does not exist, inspect the integrity of the wiring, and/or refer to the wiring diagrams in Section 6.

5. If 12 volts exists at the harness connector, proceed with the Component Check procedure.

COMPONENT CHECK

1. Unplug the harness connector from the Hall sender at the distributor.

2. Using a digital multimeter switched to the 20V range, connect the meter positive lead to terminal 15 and the negative lead to terminal 1 of the ignition coil.

3. Turn the ignition switch to the **ON** position. The meter must read a 2 volt minimum, then drop to 0 volts after 1–2 seconds.

4. If not, replace the Hall control unit and the ignition coil.

5. Using a jumper wire, briefly touch the center wire of the distributor harness connector to ground. Displayed voltage must rise briefly to at least 2 volts.

6. If not, replace the Hall control unit and the ignition coil.

Digifant II Systems Only

VOLTAGE SUPPLY CHECK

▶ See Figure 11

1. Unplug the harness connector from the ignition control unit.

2. Using a digital voltmeter, connect the meter positive lead to terminal 4 and the negative lead to terminal 2 of the harness connector.

3. With the leads connected, turn the ignition switch **ON** and check for battery (12 volts) voltage.

4. If voltage does not exist, inspect the integrity of the wiring, and/or refer to the wiring diagrams in Section 6.

5. If 12 volts exists at the harness connector, proceed with the component check procedure.

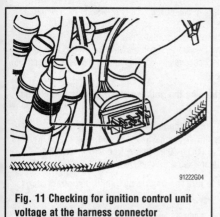

Fig. 11 Checking for ignition control unit voltage at the harness connector

91222G04

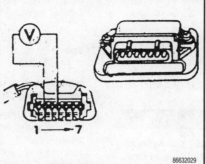

Fig. 12 Connect the meter positive lead to terminal 4 and the negative lead to terminal 2 of the control unit harness connector

86632029

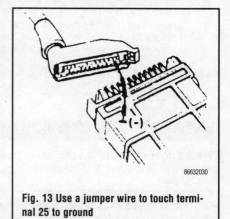

Fig. 13 Use a jumper wire to touch terminal 25 to ground

86632030

COMPONENT CHECK

▶ See Figures 12 and 13

Before testing, visually inspect all components of the system. Replace any noticeably damaged parts. Be sure to check the ignition coil and replace if it is leaking fluid.

1. Turn the ignition to the **OFF** position. Reconnect the control unit harness.
2. Unplug the harness connector from the Digifant control unit. Using a digital multimeter switched to the 20V range, connect the meter positive lead to terminal 15 and the negative lead to terminal 1 of the ignition coil. If necessary, unplug the wiring from ignition coil terminal 1, then reconnect it so that only the wire to the Hall control unit is engaged.
3. Turn the ignition switch to the **ON** position. The meter must read a 2 volt minimum, then drop to 0 volts after 1–2 seconds. If not, replace the Hall control unit.
4. Using a jumper wire, briefly touch terminal 25 of the Digifant control unit harness connector to ground. Displayed voltage must rise briefly to a 2 volt minimum.
5. Turn the ignition switch to the **OFF** position. Reconnect the control unit harness.

REMOVAL & INSTALLATION

FOX

The ignition control unit is located under the instrument panel on the passenger side of the vehicle, below the ECM.

1. Make sure the ignition key is in the **OFF** position.
2. Remove the rubber weather-strip seal from the firewall. Carefully pull the plastic drain tray from the cowling.
3. Unplug the connector from the ignition control unit.
4. Remove the screws securing the to the heat sink/bracket assembly.
5. Remove the ignition control unit control unit.

To install:

6. Clean the mating surface of the heat sink/bracket and the bottom of the ignition control unit. These surfaces must be free of any debris.
7. Spread an even coat of dielectric grease on the bottom of the ignition control unit (the bare metal side). The dielectric grease helps to make a better thermal connection between the ignition control unit and the heat sink.
8. Position the new ignition control unit on the heat sink/bracket, then tighten the screws until snug.
9. Engage the electrical connection.

Digifant II

The ignition control unit is located in the cowling above the firewall in the engine compartment.

1. Disconnect the negative battery cable.
2. Make sure the ignition key is in the **OFF** position.
3. Remove the rubber weather-strip seal from the firewall. Carefully pull the plastic drain tray from the cowling.
4. Unplug the connector from the ignition control unit.
5. Remove the screws securing the to the heat sink/bracket assembly.

6. Remove the ignition control unit control unit.

To install:

7. Clean the mating surface of the heat sink/bracket and the bottom of the ignition control unit. These surfaces must be free of any debris.
8. Spread an even coat of dielectric grease on the bottom of the ignition control unit (the bare metal side). The dielectric grease helps to make a better thermal connection between the ignition control unit and the heat sink.
9. Position the new ignition control unit on the heat sink/bracket, then tighten the screws until snug.
10. Engage the electrical connection.
11. Install the idle stabilizer or plastic cowling cover and weather-strip seal as applicable.
12. Connect the battery cable.

Power Stage

➡ On CIS-Motronic systems, the power stage is a separate component mounted near the ignition coil. On later systems, the power stage is integrated into the coil pack.

TESTING

▶ See Figure 14

Voltage Test

1. Make sure the ignition is in the **OFF** position.
2. Unplug the harness connector from the power stage.
3. Using a digital multimeter, connect the test leads to terminals 1 and 3.

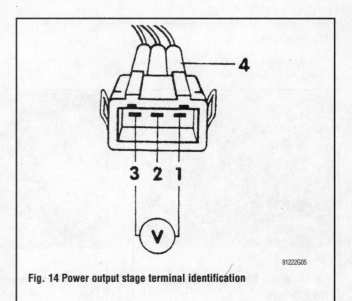

Fig. 14 Power output stage terminal identification

91222G05

4. Turn the ignition switch **ON** and check for battery voltage.

5. If battery voltage is not present, inspect the wiring for an open or other damage. Refer to Section 6 for wiring diagram information.

6. Plug the harness connector into the socket on the power stage.

Component Test

This test confirms that the ECM is sending an activation signal to the power stage for charging the ignition coil.

※ WARNING

This test requires the use of a LED test light. Do NOT use an incandescent test light; the current required to illuminate the lamp can damage the ECM.

➡**This test is dependant on the Hall sensor/camshaft sensor in the distributor functioning properly. Make sure it is operating properly before performing this procedure.**

1. Remove the fuel pump fuse to prevent the cylinders from filling with fuel while the engine is being cranked.

2. Remove the harness connector from the power stage.

3. Using an LED test light, connect the leads to terminal 2 and terminal 3.

4. Turn the ignition switch **ON** and crank the engine.

5. While the engine is cranking, the LED test light should flash. This indicates that a signal is being sent from the Hall sensor/camshaft position sensor to the power stage.

6. If the LED does not flash, and the Hall sensor/camshaft sensor in the distributor is functioning properly, replace the power stage. If replacement of the power stage does not allow the LED test light to flash, the ECM may be faulty.

7. Plug in the power stage connector.

8. Install the fuel pump fuse.

REMOVAL & INSTALLATION

1. Unplug the wiring harness connector from the power stage.

2. Remove the ignition coil.

3. Remove the power stage from the ignition coil.

To install:

4. Install the power stage to the ignition coil. Be careful not to overtighten the fasteners.

5. Install the ignition coil.

6. Plug the wiring harness connector into the socket on the power stage.

7. Install the connectors on the ignition coil.

Distributor

REMOVAL & INSTALLATION

♦ **See Figures 15 thru 30**

1. On vehicles with manual transaxle, remove the plastic plug on the transaxle bell housing to view the timing marks on the flywheel.

2. Remove the upper timing belt cover. This is necessary to view the camshaft timing marks.

3. Unsnap the clips and remove the distributor cap and suppressor shield. It is not necessary to remove the spark plug wires from the distributor cap; position the cap and the attached wires aside. Unplug the Hall sensor connector on the side of the distributor.

➡**Use caution when unplugging the hall sensor connector; the plastic socket is easily damaged.**

4. Using a breaker bar and an appropriate socket (usually 17mm) on the front crankshaft pulley bolt, turn the engine to Top Dead Center (TDC) on No. 1 piston. The No. 1 piston is at TDC on the compression stroke when the "0" mark on the flywheel and the marks on the camshaft align.

➡**Less effort is required to turn the engine by hand if the spark plugs are removed.**

5. Verify that the timing is correct by checking that the rotor aligns with the No. 1 spark plug wire terminal. The No. 1 cylinder is closest to the camshaft and crankshaft pulleys.

6. On most distributors, there is an alignment mark on the rim of the distributor housing that aligns with the rotor when the No. 1 cylinder is at TDC. If not, make a mark on the distributor housing with a scribe or paint marker.

7. Next, mark the relationship of the distributor base to the engine block (or on 9A engines, the cylinder head) with a scribe or paint marker.

8. On 8 valve engines, remove the single 13mm bolt, then lift off the hold-down flange. Slowly lift the distributor straight out of the engine.

➡**When the distributor is removed from the engine block, the rotor will turn slightly, this is due to the angled teeth on the distributor gear.**

9. On 16V engines, remove the two 10mm mounting bolts and pull the distributor straight out of the cylinder head. Note which holes the bolts came from to make sure the timing can be adjusted correctly.

To install:

10. If the engine has been disturbed (rotated) since the distributor has been removed, proceed as follows:

a. Using a breaker bar and an appropriate socket (usually 17mm) on the front crankshaft pulley bolt, turn the engine to Top Dead Center (TDC) on No. 1 piston. The No. 1 piston is at TDC on the compression stroke when the "0" mark on the flywheel and the marks on the camshaft align.

b. On 8v engines, use a long flat-bladed screwdriver to turn the oil pump drive slot. On all engines except for the ACC, align the drive slot so it is parallel to the engine's crankshaft. On ACC engines, align the oil pump drive slot so it aligns with the distributor hold-down bolt hole.

c. On 16V engines, verify the position of the slot in the camshaft by looking through the distributor mounting hole in the cylinder head. With the marks on the distributor and the cylinder head aligned, install the distributor in the cylinder head.

11. While aligning the rotor with the mark on the rim of the distributor, and the marks on the engine block/cylinder head and distributor base, carefully mount the distributor to the engine.

➡**On 8V engines, remember that the curved gear teeth will cause the rotor to twist slightly when the distributor is installed. It may take a few attempts for everything to align properly.**

Fig. 15 Remove the holding clips from the distributor cap

Fig. 16 A long prytool will be needed to remove the rear clip on the distributor cap

Fig. 17 Lift the cap away from the distributor

Fig. 18 Remove the rotor

Fig. 19 Remove the inner distributor dust cover

Fig. 20 If equipped, remove the dust cover from the hold down bolt

Fig. 21 Remove the distributor hold down bolt

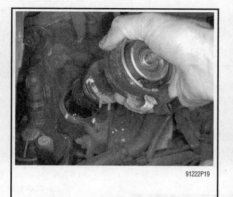

Fig. 22 Remove the distributor

Fig. 23 Distributor drive shaft alignment tab

Fig. 24 Distributor shaft and alignment slot

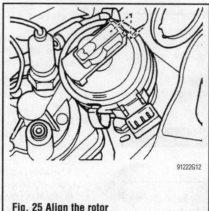

Fig. 25 Align the rotor

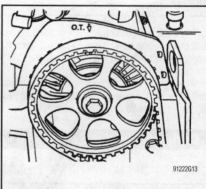

Fig. 26 Camshaft alignment–2.0L 16V (9A) engine

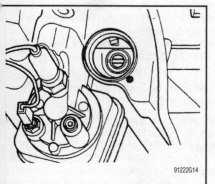

Fig. 27 Position the pump shaft parallel to the crankshaft

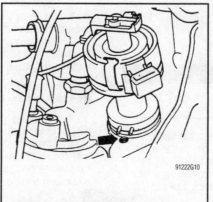

Fig. 28 Remove the distributor

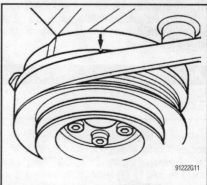

Fig. 29 An additional mark is located on the crankshaft damper/pulley

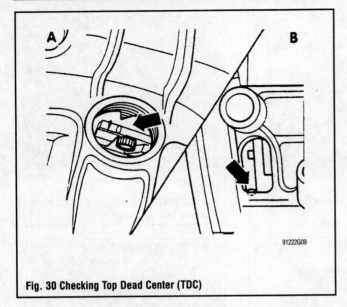

Fig. 30 Checking Top Dead Center (TDC)

12. Install the distributor hold-down bolt(s) and bracket (8V only) and secure the distributor. Tighten the bolt(s) so the distributor can be rotated with moderate force. On ABA engines with locating pins in the distributor, this is not necessary, because the timing cannot be adjusted.

13. Plug in the Hall sensor plug on the side of the distributor, and position the distributor cap on the distributor and secure the spring clips.

14. Install the upper timing belt cover.

15. Adjust the "base" timing as necessary.

Crankshaft Position Sensor

ABA ENGINE

The crankshaft position sensor, unique to the ABA engine, is located on the side of the engine block. A special toothed wheel mounted on the crankshaft works together with the sensor to provide the ECM with information regarding the position of the crankshaft.

Although the crankshaft position sensor is an essential input for the ECM to determine ignition timing, information on testing and removal and installation of the sensor is located in Section 4 of this manual.

Camshaft Position Sensor

DIGIFANT, MONO-MOTRONIC, AND CIS-MOTRONIC

The "camshaft" position sensor on these engines is actually a Hall-effect type sensor, which is located in the distributor. This sensor performs the same function as a crankshaft position sensor; providing a signal to the ECM regarding the position of the crankshaft.

Although the camshaft position sensor is an essential input for the ECM to determine ignition timing, information on testing the sensor is located in Section 4 of this manual.

Adjustments

FOX ONLY

Unless the timing belt has been changed, or the distributor has been removed from the engine, it is not necessary to adjust the ignition timing. On Digifant-equipped engines, the ignition timing is controlled by the ECM. The procedure listed for Digifant-equipped engines is only for establishing a "base" setting on which the computer retards and advances the timing, based on engine inputs from the engine's sensors.

CIS and CIS-E (Fox Only)

1. Start the engine and allow it to reach operating temperature. The engine is at operating temperature when the cooling fan on the radiator has cycled once.

2. Turn the engine **OFF**.

3. If the vehicle is not equipped with a tachometer, attach one to the engine according to the manufacturer's instructions.

4. Attach a timing light to the engine according to the manufacturer's instructions.

5. Switch all electrical accessories to the **OFF** position.

6. Start the engine, and verify the idle speed is within specifications.

➡**If the idle speed is not within specifications, the timing cannot be accurately adjusted.**

7. Aim the timing light at the check hole on the transaxle bell housing.

8. With the engine at idle, aim the timing light at the flywheel. The pointer in the timing check hole should point to the timing mark on the flywheel.

➡**Do not confuse the "0" mark with the ignition timing mark. The "0" mark indicates Top Dead Center (TDC).**

9. If the timing mark is not within specifications, turn the engine **OFF** and loosen the distributor hold-down bolt. Loosen the bolt enough to allow the distributor with moderate hand force. If the bolt is too loose, the distributor may spin when the engine is operating, which can cause an extreme variation in ignition timing, possibly stalling the engine.

10. Start the engine, and turn the distributor until the timing marks align. It may be necessary to adjust the idle speed once the timing marks are aligned.

11. Turn the engine **OFF** and tighten the distributor hold-down bolt.

12. Confirm the timing is correct by starting the engine again, and checking the timing marks.

13. Remove the timing light, and install the timing check hole plug, if equipped.

Digifant I and II (Fox only)

➡**On vehicles equipped with Digifant I, this procedure will generate a fault code, which is caused by disconnecting the coolant temperature sensor. Refer to Section 4 for information.**

1. Remove the plastic plug from the timing check hole with a 27mm Allen wrench. A 27mm bolt can be used, in conjunction with a 27mm socket to substitute for the Allen wrench. Although the plug has a cap, the entire plug must be removed to view the timing marks on the flywheel.

2. Connect a timing light to the engine according to the manufacturer's specifications. Make sure the wires do not contact any rotating parts (pulleys, radiator fan, etc.).

3. Start the engine, and allow it to reach operating temperature. The engine is at operating temperature when the radiator cooling fan has cycled once.

4. Raise the idle speed to 2200 rpm, and let it settle to idle. Perform this at least four times. This clears the ECM's memory and allows the high-idle and hot start function to be bypassed.

5. Disconnect the coolant temperature sensor on the cylinder head. Of the two sensors on the coolant pipe, the coolant temperature sensor is mounted underneath, and usually has a blue connector.

6. Raise the engine speed to 2000–2500 rpm, and aim the timing light at the flywheel. The pointer in the timing check hole should point to the timing mark on the flywheel.

➡**Do not confuse the "0" mark with the ignition timing mark. The "0" mark indicates Top Dead Center (TDC).**

7. If the timing is within specifications, turn the engine **OFF** and reconnect the coolant temperature sensor. Remove the timing light.

8. If the timing mark is not within specifications, loosen the distributor hold-down bolt. Loosen the bolt enough to allow the distributor with moderate hand force. If the bolt(s) are too loose, the distributor may spin when the engine is operating, which can cause an extreme variation in ignition timing, possibly stalling the engine.

9. with the engine speed between 2500–2500 rpm, and turn the distributor until the timing marks align.

10. Turn the engine **OFF** and tighten the distributor hold-down bolt. Make sure the timing was not changed when the distributor hold-down bolt was tightened.

11. Reconnect the coolant temperature sensor, and disconnect the timing light. If equipped, install the timing check hole plug.

12. Start the engine, accelerating to 3000 rpm at least three times. Verify that the idle speed is within specifications. Refer to the appropriate procedures in this section and Section 4 for more information.

Unless the timing belt has been changed, or the distributor has been removed from the engine, it is not necessary to adjust the ignition timing, as it is controlled by the ECM. The procedure listed is only for establishing a "base" setting, so the ECM can control the timing within preset parameters.

CIS-MOTRONIC AND MONO-MOTRONIC

1. On vehicles with a manual transaxle, remove the plastic plug from the timing check hole with a 27mm Allen wrench. A 27mm bolt can be used, in conjunction with a 27mm socket to substitute for the Allen wrench. Although the plug has a cap, the entire plug must be removed to view the ignition timing marks on the flywheel.

2. Connect a timing light to the engine according to the manufacturer's specifications. Typically, the timing light connects to the battery terminals, and the inductive pickup connects to the number one spark plug wire. Make sure the wires do not contact any rotating parts (pulleys, radiator fan, etc.).

3. Start the engine, and allow it to reach operating temperature. The engine is at operating temperature when the radiator cooling fan has cycled once.

➡**When viewing the timing marks, the radiator fan (or any other electrical component) should not be in operation.**

4. With the engine at idle, aim the timing light at the flywheel. The pointer in the timing check hole should point to the timing mark on the flywheel.

➡**Do not confuse the "0" mark with the ignition timing mark. The "0" mark indicates Top Dead Center (TDC).**

5. If the timing mark is not within specifications, turn the engine **OFF** and loosen the distributor hold-down bolt(s). Loosen the bolt(s) enough to allow the distributor with moderate hand force. If the bolt(s) are too loose, the distributor may spin when the engine is operating, which can cause an extreme variation in ignition timing, possibly stalling the engine.

6. Start the engine, and turn the distributor until the timing marks align. It may be necessary to adjust the idle speed once the timing marks are aligned.

7. Turn the engine **OFF** and tighten the distributor hold-down bolt(s).

8. Confirm the timing is correct by starting the engine again, and checking the timing marks.

9. Remove the timing light, and install the timing check hole plug, if equipped.

DIGIFANT I AND II

➡**On vehicles equipped with Digifant I, this procedure will generate a fault code, which is caused by disconnecting the coolant temperature sensor. Refer to Section 4 for information.**

1. Remove the plastic plug from the timing check hole with a 27mm Allen wrench. A 27mm bolt can be used, in conjunction with a 27mm socket to substitute for the Allen wrench. Although the plug has a cap, the entire plug must be removed to view the timing marks on the flywheel.

2. Connect a timing light to the engine according to the manufacturer's specifications. Make sure the wires do not contact any rotating parts (pulleys, radiator fan, etc.).

3. Start the engine, and allow it to reach operating temperature. The engine is at operating temperature when the radiator cooling fan has cycled once.

4. Raise the idle speed to 2200 rpm, and let it settle to idle. Perform this at least four times. This clears the ECM's memory and allows the high-idle and hot start function to be bypassed.

5. Disconnect the coolant temperature sensor on the cylinder head. Of the two sensors on the coolant pipe, the coolant temperature sensor is mounted closest to the cylinder head (the connector is typically blue).

6. Raise the engine speed to 2000–2500 rpm, and aim the timing light at the flywheel. The pointer in the timing check hole should point to the timing mark on the flywheel.

➡**Do not confuse the "0" mark with the ignition timing mark. The "0" mark indicates Top Dead Center (TDC).**

7. If the timing is within specifications, turn the engine **OFF** and reconnect the coolant temperature sensor. Remove the timing light.

8. If the timing mark is not within specifications, loosen the distributor hold-down bolt. Loosen the bolt enough to allow the distributor with moderate hand force. If the bolt(s) are too loose, the distributor may spin when the engine is operating, which can cause an extreme variation in ignition timing, possibly stalling the engine.

9. with the engine speed between 2500–2500 rpm, and turn the distributor until the timing marks align.

10. Turn the engine **OFF** and tighten the distributor hold-down bolt. Make sure the timing was not changed when the distributor hold-down bolt was tightened.

11. Reconnect the coolant temperature sensor, and disconnect the timing light. If equipped, install the timing check hole plug.

12. Start the engine, accelerating to 3000 rpm at least three times. Verify that the idle speed is within specifications. Refer to the appropriate procedures in this section and Section 4 for more information.

MOTRONIC

The ignition timing on all 1993–99 Motronic-equipped engines (ABA) is controlled by the ECM and is not adjustable. There are locating pins on the distributor base to ensure the distributor is installed in its proper location, so a "base" adjustment is not necessary.

DISTRIBUTORLESS IGNITION SYSTEM

➡**For information on understanding electricity and troubleshooting electrical circuits, please refer to Section 6 of this manual.**

General Information

The Distributorless Ignition System (DIS) is used on the 2.8L VR6 (AAA) engine exclusively. The DIS system eliminates any moving parts, providing a completely wear-free, solid state ignition system.

The Distributorless Ignition System does not use a conventional distributor. The heart of the system consists of a three separate ignition coils, which actually fire two cylinders simultaneously. These coils are controlled by the ECM, based on the inputs of the various sensors on the engine.

The Distributorless system uses a "waste spark" method of spark distribution. Companion cylinders are paired and the spark occurs simultaneously in the cylinder with the piston coming up on the compression stroke and in the companion cylinder with the piston coming up on the exhaust stroke.

The DIS system is composed of the following components:

• **Electronic Control Module (ECM)**—The ECM is the "brain" of the ignition system. The ECM controls when the spark occurs, based on the input from the various sensors on the engine, including the knock sensor, coolant temperature sensor, crankshaft position sensor, and the oxygen (02) sensor.

• **Ignition Coil Pack**—The ignition coil pack actually consists of three separate double-sided ignition coils. These coils operate in the same manner as a conventional coil.

• **Knock Sensor**—A knock sensor is a peizo-electric device that senses detonation or pre-ignition from the engine block. When the engine begins to knock, the sensor produces a small amount of voltage. This voltage is detected by the ECM, which typically retards the ignition timing slightly to prevent detonation. AAA engines use two sensors to detect detonation.

• **Crankshaft Position Sensor**—The crankshaft position sensor determines the exact position of each piston in the engine. The information from this sensor allows the ECM to precisely control when the ignition occurs. Typically, the crankshaft position sensor is located on the engine block. On some engines, this sensor is located inside of the distributor itself.

• **Camshaft Position Sensor**—The crankshaft position sensor performs the same function as the crankshaft position sensor; providing the ECM with information on the position of the engine. This sensor, located on the "intake" side of the engine block, near the flywheel, provides the ECM with the information necessary to precisely control when ignition occurs.

Diagnosis and Testing

Before beginning any diagnosis and testing procedures, visually inspect the components of the ignition system and engine control systems. Check for the following:
• Discharged battery
• Damaged or loose connections
• Damaged electrical insulation
• Poor coil and/or spark plug connections
• ECM connections
• Blown fuses
• Damaged spark plugs

When attempting to search for ignition troubles, also keep in mind that various sensor inputs which the ECM uses to calculate timing may affect engine performance.

IGNITION SYSTEM PRECAUTIONS

Before proceeding with any type of ignition system testing, be sure to follow these important precautions:
• Make sure the ignition switch is **OFF** before connecting or disconnecting any wiring or test equipment.
• When cranking the engine without starting, as for a compression test, disconnect the power supply connector (+12V) from the coil to prevent it from receiving voltage. Other methods of disabling the ignition system are not recommended, and may result in electrical system damage.
• Always switch the multimeter to the appropriate measuring range BEFORE making the test connections. Use a high-impedance digital multimeter which is designed for testing computerized electrical components.
• DO NOT install a standard ignition coil in the system.
• DO NOT connect a condenser/suppressor or powered test light to the negative terminal (1) of the ignition coil.
• DO NOT connect any 12-volt test instruments to the positive terminal (15) of the ignition coil. The electronic control unit will be permanently damaged.
• DO NOT use a standard test light (electric bulb type) on electronic circuits. The high electrical consumption of these test lights can lead to electronic component damage.
• DO NOT connect a quick-charger to the battery for more than 1 minute, nor exceed 16.5 volts with the booster.

SECONDARY SPARK TEST

Refer to testing under distributor ignition system in this section.

Ignition Coil Pack

TESTING

▸ **See Figure 31**

Voltage Supply Check

This test confirms the coil is receiving a voltage signal to charge the coils.
1. Remove the five-pin harness connector from the ignition coil pack.
2. Using a digital voltmeter, connect the negative lead to terminal 1 and the positive lead to terminal 5.
3. Turn the ignition switch **ON** but do not start the engine.
4. The voltmeter should read 10–12 volts.
5. If the voltmeter does not read 10–12 volts, check the integrity of the wiring, and supply voltage to the ECM.

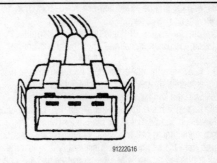

91222G16

Fig. 31 Ignition coil harness connector identification

6. Turn the ignition switch **OFF** and plug the five-pin harness connector into the coil pack.

Signal Check

This test confirms that the ECM is sending an activation signal to the coils for firing the spark plugs.

➡ **This test requires the use of a LED test light. Do NOT use an incandescent test light; the current required to illuminate the lamp can damage the ECM.**

1. Remove the fuel pump fuse to prevent the cylinders from filling with fuel while the engine is being cranked.
2. Remove the five-pin harness connector from the ignition coil pack.
3. Using an LED test light, connect the leads to terminal 2 and terminal 5.
4. Turn the ignition switch **ON** and crank the engine.
5. While the engine is cranking, the LED test light should flash. This indicates that a signal is being sent to the power stage inside the coil.
6. Turn the ignition switch **OFF** and reconnect the test leads to terminals 3 and 5.
7. Again, turn the ignition switch **ON** crank the engine. Verify that the LED flashes.
8. Turn the ignition switch **OFF** and reconnect the test leads to terminals 4 and 5.
9. Crank the engine with the ignition switch once again, and verify that the LED flashes.
10. If the LED does not flash, this indicates that a signal is not being sent to the coil. Causes include faulty wiring, or problems with the crankshaft position sensor and/or ECM. Refer to
11. Turn the ignition switch **OFF** and plug the five-pin harness connector into the coil pack.
12. Install the fuel pump fuse.

REMOVAL & INSTALLATION

1. Remove the five-pin harness connector from the ignition coil pack.
2. Using a paint marker or other means, mark each spark plug wire so they can be installed in their proper locations upon coil installation.
3. Once the spark plugs are marked, remove them from the coil pack. When removing the wires, make sure to pull on the boots, not the wires themselves, as they may be damaged.
4. Remove the four bolts that secure the coil pack to the cylinder head. Make sure to hold the coil pack when removing the bolts.
To install:
5. Clean the dielectric grease from the coil pack mounting surface on the cylinder head. If installing the old coil, make sure to clean the grease from the coil pack also.
6. Apply an even coat of dielectric grease to the coil pack mounting surface on the cylinder head.
7. Position the coil pack, and insert the mounting bolts. Finger-tighten the bolts to hold the coil pack in place.
8. Using a torque wrench, tighten the coil pack-to-cylinder head bolts to 7 ft. lbs. (10 Nm).

9. Place a small amount of dielectric grease on each spark plug wire terminal, and install the spark plug boots in the proper order. If a new coil pack is being is installed, note the marks on the old coil pack, using them as a guide to install the spark plug wires on the new coil pack.

10. Plug in the five-pin harness connector to the ignition coil pack.

Crankshaft Position Sensor

The crankshaft position sensor on the AAA engine is located on the "intake" side of the engine block, near the flywheel. This sensor provides a signal to the ECM regarding the position of the crankshaft.

Although the crankshaft position sensor is an essential input for the ECM to determine ignition timing, information on testing and removal and installation of the sensor is located in Section 4 of this manual.

Camshaft Position Sensor

The camshaft position sensor on the AAA engine is mounted on the side of the cylinder head, next to the coil pack. This sensor provides a signal to the ECM regarding the position of the camshaft.

Although the camshaft position sensor is an essential input for the ECM to determine ignition timing, information on testing the sensor is located in Section 4 of this manual.

Adjustments

There are no adjustable components on the DIS ignition system. If the ignition system is not functioning properly, it is possible a faulty component exists, failing to supply the ECM with the information necessary for proper ignition system operation.

FIRING ORDERS

▶ See Figure 32

➡ To avoid confusion, remove and tag the spark plug wires one at a time, for replacement.

If a distributor is not keyed for installation with only one orientation, it could have been removed previously and rewired. The resultant wiring would hold the correct firing order, but could change the relative placement of the plug towers in relation to the engine. For this reason it is imperative that you label all wires before disconnecting any of them. Also, before removal, compare the current wiring with the accompanying illustrations. If the current wiring does not match, make notes in your book to reflect how your engine is wired.

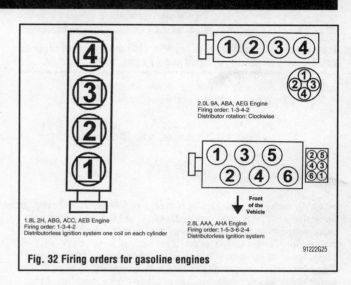

2.0L 9A, ABA, AEG Engine
Firing order: 1-3-4-2
Distributor rotation: Clockwise

Front of the Vehicle

1.8L 2H, ABG, ACC, AEB Engine
Firing order: 1-3-4-2
Distributorless ignition system one coil on each cylinder

2.8L AAA, AHA Engine
Firing order: 1-5-3-6-2-4
Distributorless ignition system

91222G25

Fig. 32 Firing orders for gasoline engines

CHARGING SYSTEM

General Information

The automobile charging system provides electrical power for operation of the vehicle's ignition and starting systems and all the electrical accessories. The battery serves as an electrical surge or storage tank, storing (in chemical form) the energy originally produced by the engine driven alternator. The system also provides a means of regulating generator output to protect the battery from being overcharged and to avoid excessive voltage to the accessories.

The storage battery is a chemical device incorporating parallel lead plates in a tank containing a sulfuric acid/water solution. Adjacent plates are slightly dissimilar, and the chemical reaction of the two dissimilar plates produces electrical energy when the battery is connected to a load such as the starter motor. The chemical reaction is reversible, so that when the generator is producing a voltage (electrical pressure) greater than that produced by the battery, electricity is forced into the battery, and the battery is returned to its fully charged state.

The vehicle's alternator is driven by a belt powered by the engine crankshaft. In an alternator, the field rotates while all the current produced passes only through the stator winding. The brushes bear against continuous slip rings rather than a commutator. This causes the current produced to periodically reverse the direction of its flow creating alternating current (AC). Diodes (electrical one-way switches) block the flow of current from traveling in the wrong direction. A series of diodes is wired together to permit the alternating flow of the stator to be converted to a pulsating, but unidirectional flow at the alternator output. The alternator's field is wired in series with the voltage regulator.

The regulator consists of several circuits. Each circuit has a core, or magnetic coil of wire, which operates a switch. Each switch is connected to ground through one or more resistors. The coil of wire responds directly to system voltage. When the voltage reaches the required level, the magnetic field created by the winding of wire closes the switch and inserts a resistance into the generator field circuit, thus reducing the output. The contacts of the switch cycle open and close many times each second to precisely control voltage.

Alternator Precautions

• Always disconnect the battery cables when removing or disconnecting the alternator.

• Disconnect the battery cables before using a fast charger. The charger has a tendency to force current "backwards" through the diodes and burn them out.

• Never disconnect the battery cables or alternator while the engine is running.

• Do not attempt to "polarize" an alternator.

• Never reverse battery connections. Do not connect the battery in series with another without disconnecting it from the charging system.

• When jump starting from another vehicle, try to avoid running the other car's engine. Do not allow alternators from two different charging systems to be running and connected with jumper cables.

• Do not ground the alternator output terminal.

• Disconnect the battery cables before using an electric arc welder on the car.

Alternator

TESTING

♦ See Figures 33 and 34

Voltage Test

1. Make sure the engine is **OFF**, and turn the headlights on for 15–20 seconds to remove any surface charge from the battery.
2. Using a Digital Volt/Ohm Meter (DVOM) set to volts DC, probe across the battery terminals.
3. Measure the battery voltage.
4. Write down the voltage reading and proceed to the next test.

No-Load Test

1. Connect a tachometer to the engine.

✳✳ CAUTION

Ensure that the transmission is in PARK and the emergency brake is set. Blocking a wheel is optional and an added safety measure.

2. Turn off all electrical loads (radio, blower motor, wipers, etc.)
3. Start the engine and increase engine speed to approximately 1500 rpm.
4. Measure the voltage reading at the battery with the engine holding a steady 1500 rpm. Voltage should have raised at least 0.5 volts, but no more than 2.5 volts.
5. If the voltage does not go up more than 0.5 volts, the alternator is not charging. If the voltage goes up more than 2.5 volts, the alternator is overcharging.

➡Usually under and overcharging is caused by a defective alternator, or its related parts (regulator), and replacement will fix the problem; however, faulty wiring and other problems can cause the charging system to malfunction. Further testing, which is not covered by this book, will reveal the exact component failure. Many automotive parts stores have alternator bench testers available for use by customers. An alternator bench test is the most definitive way to determine the condition of your alternator.

6. If the voltage is within specifications, proceed to the next test.

Load Test

1. With the engine running, turn on the blower motor and the high beams (or other electrical accessories to place a load on the charging system).
2. Increase and hold engine speed to 2000 rpm.
3. Measure the voltage reading at the battery.
4. The voltage should increase at least 0.5 volts from the voltage test. If

the voltage does not meet specifications, the charging system is malfunctioning.

➡Usually under and overcharging is caused by a defective alternator, or its related parts (regulator), and replacement will fix the problem; however, faulty wiring and other problems can cause the charging system to malfunction. Further testing, which is not covered by this book, will reveal the exact component failure. Many automotive parts stores have alternator bench testers available for use by customers. An alternator bench test is the most definitive way to determine the condition of your alternator.

REMOVAL & INSTALLATION

♦ See Figure 35

Before purchasing a replacement alternator, read the specification plate on the housing. The number 14V will appear to indicate maximum voltage rating. On the same line will be two more digits followed by the letter **A**. This is the maximum amperage output. Be sure to purchase an alternator with the same rating. The regulator can be replaced without removing the alternator.

Fox

1. Disconnect the negative battery cable.
2. Disconnect the wiring from the alternator. If necessary, mark the wires with tape or other means to ensure they are connected properly upon installation.
3. Loosen the alternator adjustment bolt, and remove the drive belt from the alternator.
4. Remove the alternator adjustment bolt, followed by the pivot bolt.
5. Carefully lift the alternator from the bracket.
To install:
6. Hold the alternator in position on the mounting bracket, and install the pivot bolt.
7. Install (but do not tighten) the alternator adjustment bolt.
8. Place the alternator drive belt on the pulley.
9. Adjust belt tension and tighten the mounting and adjustment bolts as necessary.
10. Connect the wiring to the alternator. If tape was used to identify the wires, make sure it is removed once the wires are connected.
11. Connect the negative battery cable.

All other vehicles

1. Disconnect the negative battery cable.
2. Disconnect the wiring from the alternator. If necessary, mark the wires with tape or other means to ensure they are connected properly upon installation.
3. Loosen the belt tension, and remove the drive belt from the alternator. On VR6 (AAA) engines only, remove the belt tensioner from the cylinder head.
4. Remove the alternator adjustment bolt, followed by the pivot bolts.

Fig. 33 Many VW alternators are similar to this BOSCH unit

Fig. 34 Remove the connections from the rear of the alternator

Fig. 35 Location of the alternator bolts on a 1994 Jetta 2.0L, 8 valve model

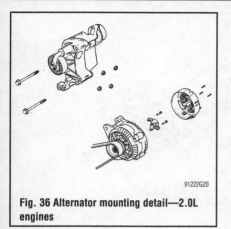

Fig. 36 Alternator mounting detail—2.0L engines

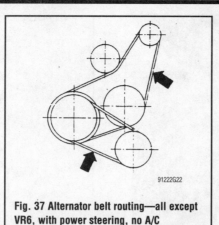

Fig. 37 Alternator belt routing—all except VR6, with power steering, no A/C

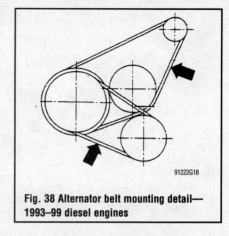

Fig. 38 Alternator belt mounting detail—1993–99 diesel engines

5. Carefully lift the alternator from the bracket.

To install:

6. Hold the alternator in position on the mounting bracket, and install the pivot bolt. On later engines with automatic belt tensioners, install the upper mounting bolt.

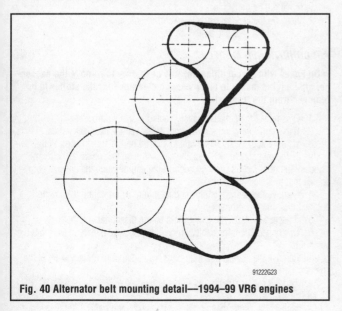

Fig. 39 Diesel engine belt alternator belt routing

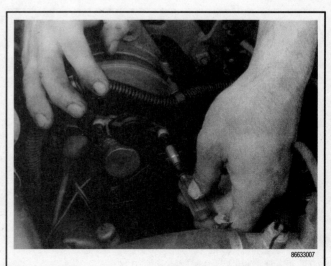

Fig. 40 Alternator belt mounting detail—1994–99 VR6 engines

7. Install (but do not tighten) the alternator adjustment bolt (earlier models only).

8. Place the alternator drive belt on the pulley.

9. Adjust belt tension and tighten the mounting and adjustment bolts as necessary.

10. Connect the wiring to the alternator. If tape was used to identify the wires, make sure it is removed once the wires are connected.

11. Connect the negative battery cable.

Voltage Regulator

REMOVAL & INSTALLATION

▶ See Figures 41, 42 and 43

The voltage regulator is attached to the rear of the alternator and includes the brushes. Since no adjustment can be performed on the regulator, it is serviced only by replacement.

1. If equipped, remove the cover on the back of the alternator.

2. It is not necessary to disconnect any wiring. Remove the mounting screws and remove the regulator.

3. Measure the free length of the brushes. If they are less than about 5mm (7/32 inches), the regulator must be replaced. New brushes are 13mm (½ inch) long.

4. Install the new regulator and tighten the screws.

5. If equipped, install the cover on the back of the alternator.

Fig. 41 To remove the voltage regulator, simply remove the two mounting screws . . .

Fig. 42 . . . and carefully remove it from the alternator

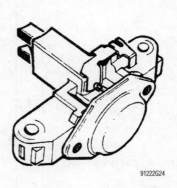

Fig. 43 Check the alternator's carbon brushes for wear

STARTING SYSTEM

General Information

The starting system includes the battery, starter motor, solenoid, ignition switch, circuit protection and wiring connecting the components. On automatic transaxle-equipped vehicles, an inhibitor switch located in the gear selector mechanism is included in the starting system to prevent the vehicle from being started with the vehicle in gear. On later vehicles with manual transaxle, an inhibitor switch is located on the clutch pedal. The clutch pedal must be depressed to start the vehicle.

When the ignition key is turned to the **START** position, current flows and energizes the starter's solenoid coil. The solenoid plunger and clutch shift lever are activated and the clutch pinion engages the ring gear on the flywheel. The switch contacts close and the starter cranks the engine until it starts.

To prevent damage caused by excessive starter armature rotation when the engine starts, the starter incorporates an over-running clutch in the pinion gear.

Starter

TESTING

Voltage Drop Test

➡The battery must be in good condition and fully charged prior to performing this test.

1. Disable the ignition system by unplugging the coil pack. Verify that the vehicle will not start.
2. Connect a voltmeter between the positive terminal of the battery and the starter **B+** circuit.
3. Turn the ignition key to the **START** position and note the voltage on the meter.
4. If voltage reads 0.5 volts or more, there is high resistance in the starter cables or the cable ground, repair as necessary. If the voltage reading is ok proceed to the next step.
5. Connect a voltmeter between the positive terminal of the battery and the starter **M** circuit.
6. Turn the ignition key to the **START** position and note the voltage on the meter.
7. If voltage reads 0.5 volts or more, there is high resistance in the starter. Repair or replace the starter as necessary.

➡Many automotive parts stores have starter bench testers available for use by customers. A starter bench test is the most definitive way to determine the condition of your starter.

REMOVAL & INSTALLATION

Fox

NON-AIR CONDITIONED MODELS

1. Disconnect the negative battery cable for safety purposes.
2. Raise and safely support the front of the vehicle with jackstands.
3. If necessary, label the small wires before disconnecting them.
4. Disconnect the large cable, which is the positive battery cable, from the solenoid.
5. Remove the starter mounting bolts, while supporting the weight of the starter.
6. Pull the starter straight out from the transaxle.
To install:
7. Inspect the starter bushing in the transaxle, and replace it if necessary.
8. Lightly lubricate the starter bushing with grease.
9. Place the starter into the transaxle, and tighten the starter mounting bolts to 18 ft. lbs. (25 Nm).
10. Reconnect the wiring to the starter. Do not overtighten the positive battery terminal nut on the starter solenoid.
11. Remove the jackstands, and lower the vehicle.
12. Connect the negative battery cable.

AIR CONDITIONED MODELS

➡On Foxes with air conditioning, it is necessary to remove the passenger side engine mount to allow enough clearance for the starter to be removed from the transaxle.

1. Disconnect the negative battery cable for safety purposes.
2. Raise and safely support the front of the vehicle with jackstands.
3. Using a floor jack, (with a block of wood on the chock) support the engine by the oil pan. Do NOT jack the car by the oil pan under any circumstances! The floor jack is ONLY to support the engine while the passenger side engine mount is being removed.
4. Remove the passenger side engine mount by unbolting it from the engine block and the subframe.
5. If necessary, label the small wires before disconnecting them.
6. Disconnect the large cable, which is the positive battery cable, from the solenoid.
7. Remove the starter mounting bolts, while supporting the weight of the starter.
8. Pull the starter straight out from the transaxle.
To install:
9. Inspect the starter bushing in the transaxle, and replace it if necessary.

10. Lightly lubricate the starter bushing with grease.

11. Place the starter into the transaxle, and tighten the starter mounting bolts to 18 ft. lbs. (25 Nm).

12. Reconnect the wiring to the starter. Do not overtighten the positive battery terminal nut on the starter solenoid.

13. Install the engine mount. Tighten the bracket-to-engine bolts to 26 ft. lbs. (35 Nm) and the engine mount-to-subframe nut to 30 ft. lbs. (40 Nm).

14. Remove the floor jack from the oil pan, and place it on the subframe. Raise the vehicle slightly to remove the jackstands, and lower the vehicle.

15. Connect the negative battery cable.

All others

♦ See Figures 44 thru 52

➥On A1 and A2 platform vehicles equipped with 010 automatic transaxle, access to the starter motor is limited. Although not necessary, it is recommended that the intake and exhaust manifolds be removed to access the starter.

1. For safety purposes, disconnect the battery ground cable.

2. Raise and safely support the front of the vehicle with jackstands.

3. For A3 vehicles, use a floor jack (with a block of wood on the chock) to support the engine by the oil pan. Do NOT jack the car by the oil pan under any circumstances! The floor jack is ONLY to support the engine while the starter is being removed. The bolts that secure the starter to the transaxle are also used to secure the front engine mount to the transaxle.

4. If necessary, label the small wires before disconnecting them.

5. Disconnect the large cable, which is the positive battery cable, from the solenoid.

6. On 010 transaxle-equipped vehicles, remove the bracket that secures the starter to the engine.

7. Remove the starter mounting bolts, while supporting the weight of the starter.

8. Pull the starter straight out from the transaxle.

To install:

➥On vehicles with a manual transaxle, there is a bushing where the starter shaft fits into the bell housing. If the shaft or bushing are worn or if the starter has been jamming, the bushing should be replaced. There is a special bushing removal tool available but a small inside bearing removal tool is usually sufficient.

9. Install the starter into the transaxle.

10. Tighten the starter mounting bolts as follows:

  a. All vehicles except 010 transaxle:
- M8 nut: 89 inch lbs. (10 Nm)
- M10 nut and bolt: 44 ft. lbs. (60 Nm)
- M12 bolt: 33 ft. lbs. (45 Nm)

  b. 010 transaxle only:
- Mounting flange bolt: 15 ft. lbs. (20 Nm)
- Mounting bracket bolt: 18 ft. lbs. (25 Nm)

11. Attach the electrical connections to the starter.

➥Be careful not to over tighten the battery cable connection. The metal is soft and the threads will strip easily.

12. Lower the vehicle from the jackstands.

13. Connect the negative battery cable.

SOLENOID OR RELAY REPLACEMENT

1. Remove the starter from the vehicle.

2. Remove the nut which secures the connector strip on the end of the solenoid.

3. Take out the two retaining screws on the mounting bracket and withdraw the solenoid after it has been unhooked from the operating lever.

4. Installation is the reverse of removal. In order to facilitate engagement of the lever, the pinion should be pulled out as far as possible when inserting the solenoid.

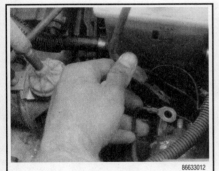

Fig. 44 After the negative battery cable is disconnected, remove the wire terminals from the starter solenoid

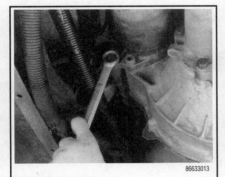

Fig. 45 Remove the lower starter mounting bolts . . .

Fig. 46 . . . followed by the upper bolt, then remove the starter from the transaxle housing

Fig. 47 Lower starter bolt locations—1994 2.0L, 8 valve

Fig. 48 Remove the upper starter bolts

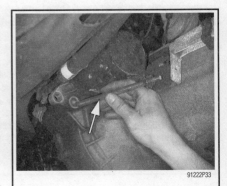

Fig. 49 Mark the location and length of each starter bolt

Fig. 50 Remove the starter

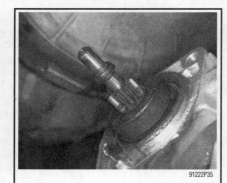

Fig. 51 Close up view of the starter drive gear

Fig. 52 When the solenoid is energized the starter drive is pushed out and meshes with the flywheel to crank the engine

SENDING UNITS AND SENSORS

➡This section describes the operating principles of sending units, warning lights and gauges. Sensors which provide information to the Electronic Control Module (ECM) are covered in Section 4 of this manual.

Instrument panels contain a number of indicating devices (gauges and warning lights). These devices are composed of two separate components. One is the sending unit, mounted on the engine or other remote part of the vehicle, and the other is the actual gauge or light in the instrument panel.

Several types of sending units exist, however most can be characterized as being either a pressure type or a resistance type. Pressure type sending units convert liquid pressure into an electrical signal which is sent to the gauge. Resistance type sending units are most often used to measure temperature and use variable resistance to control the current flow back to the indicating device. Both types of sending units are connected in series by a wire to the battery (through the ignition switch). When the ignition is turned **ON**, current flows from the battery through the indicating device and on to the sending unit.

Fuel Sending Unit

REMOVAL & INSTALLATION

1. The sending unit can be reached through the access panel under the rear seat.
2. Disconnect the wiring.
3. Unscrew the locking ring.
4. Lift the sending unit and transfer pump straight out.
5. Before installing the unit, check the condition of the O-ring, replace it if necessary.
6. Installation is the reverse of removal.

Coolant Temperature Gauge Sensor

▶ See Figure 53

The coolant temperature gauge sensor is a temperature-variable resistor, or thermistor. As coolant temperature increases, the resistance of the sensor decreases or decreases, depending on the type of sensor.

A1 and A2 platforms use a different type of circuit that A3 vehicles. On A1 and A2 vehicles, the circuit is a "resistance to ground" type. A3 vehicles use a "variable voltage" type, where a voltage is supplied to the sensor. Because of the circuitry design on A3 vehicles, testing of the coolant temperature gauge is limited.

TESTING

A1 and A2 Platform

1. Using the appropriate electrical testing equipment, ground the yellow/red wire on the coolant temperature sensor harness connector.

2. With the wire grounded, and the ignition switch in the **ON** position, the gauge in the instrument cluster should indicate that the vehicle is overheating.
3. If the gauge does not move, inspect the wiring that connects to the instrument cluster. If the wiring is intact, the gauge unit in the instrument cluster is faulty.

A3 Platform

4 CYLINDER ENGINES

➡Because the sensor on 4 cylinder A3 platform vehicles is combined with the coolant temperature sensor for the ECM, a Diagnostic Trouble Code (DTC) may be set, causing the engine light to illuminate. Refer to Section 4 for information on resetting the ECM.

On all 1993 and later engines, the coolant temperature gauge sensor is integrated into the coolant temperature sensor for the ECM. The combination 4-pin sensor is located on the coolant outlet on the side of the cylinder head. On 1993–95 vehicles, terminal 2 (ground) is brown, and terminal 4 (signal) is blue/white. On 1996–99 vehicles, terminal 2 (ground) is brown/green, and terminal 4 (signal) is red/yellow.

❊❊ WARNING

Use caution when identifying the coolant temperature sensor leads, as the signal for the ECM (terminal 3) is brown/green on 1993–95 vehicles and can easily be confused with terminal 2 on 1996–99 vehicles, which is also brown/green. If the test leads are incorrectly

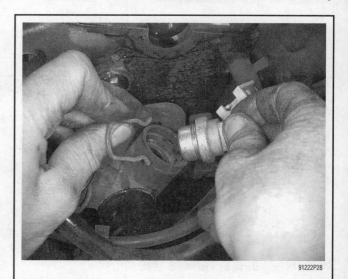

Fig. 53 Remove the coolant temperature sensor

connected when checking the coolant temperature gauge sensor, the ECM may be damaged.

1. With the ignition switch **OFF**, disconnect the harness connector from the sensor.

2. Using a multimeter, verify that terminal 2 is grounded.

3. If continuity does not exist between terminal 2 and ground, use the wiring diagrams in Section 6 to trace and repair any damaged wiring.

4. Set the multimeter to the DC voltage, and connect the test leads between terminal 4 and ground.

5. Turn the ignition switch **ON** and verify that voltage (approximately 5 volts) exists between terminals 4 and ground.

6. If voltage does not exist between terminal 4 and ground, use the wiring diagrams in Section 6 to trace and repair any damaged wiring.

7. If both terminals are in order, and the coolant temperature gauge does not work properly, check the function of the sensor as follows:

 a. Make sure the engine is **cold**.

 b. Set the multimeter to the resistance setting, and connect the test leads to terminals 2 and 4.

 c. Start the engine, and allow it to idle. As the engine warms, the resistance should change. This verifies that the sensor is changing resistance with coolant temperature, but does not guarantee that the sensor is working properly.

8. When finished with testing, turn the engine **OFF** and reconnect the sensor harness.

VR6 ENGINES ONLY

On VR6 (AAA) engines, the middle sensor (usually yellow in color) on the cooling elbow is the gauge sensor. As with the 4-cylinder engines, this 4-pin sensor is also a combination sensor, but the circuit is shared with the after-run coolant fan control.

On VR6 engines, the coolant temperature gauge sensor terminals are 2 (signal) which is blue/white, and terminal 4 (ground) which is brown. On 1996–99 vehicles, terminal 4 is identified by a brown/green wire.

➡Note that the polarity of sensor terminals 2 and 4 are the opposite of 4 cylinder engines.

1. With the ignition switch **OFF**, disconnect the harness connector from the sensor.

2. Using a multimeter, verify that terminal 4 is grounded.

3. If continuity does not exist between terminal 4 and ground, use the wiring diagrams in Section 6 to trace and repair any damaged wiring.

4. Set the multimeter to the DC voltage, and connect the test leads between terminal 2 and ground.

5. Turn the ignition switch **ON** and verify that voltage (approximately 5 volts) exists between terminals 2 and ground.

6. If voltage does not exist between terminal 2 and ground, use the wiring diagrams in Section 6 to trace and repair any damaged wiring.

7. If both terminals are in order, and the coolant temperature gauge does not work properly, check the function of the sensor as follows:

 a. Make sure the engine is **cold**.

 b. Set the multimeter to the resistance setting, and connect the test leads to terminals 2 and 4.

 c. Start the engine, and allow it to idle. As the engine warms, the resistance should change. This verifies that the sensor is changing resistance with coolant temperature, but does not guarantee that the sensor is working properly.

8. When finished with testing, turn the engine **OFF** and reconnect the sensor harness.

REMOVAL & INSTALLATION

1. Drain the coolant until it is just below the level of the sensor.

2. Disconnect the harness connector from the sensor.

3. Remove the sensor retaining clip, and pull the sensor straight out of the housing.

 To install:

4. Install a new O-ring on the sensor.

5. Using a small amount of fresh coolant, lightly lubricate the O-ring, and push the sensor in the housing.

6. While pushing inward on the sensor, install the retaining clip.

7. Plug in the harness connector to the sensor.

8. Refill the cooling system as necessary.

Coolant Level Sensor

The coolant level sensor, located in the coolant reservoir, sends a signal to the indicator light in the instrument cluster to warn the driver of a low coolant level.

TESTING

If the level of the coolant in the reservoir is full, and the indicator light in the instrument cluster is illuminated, proceed as follows:

1. With the key in the **ON** position, unplug the harness connector from the coolant reservoir.

2. Using a suitable jumper wire, connect the two terminals together.

3. With the key in the **ON** position, and the terminals bridged, the light in the instrument cluster should extinguish.

4. If the light extinguishes, replace the coolant level sensor.

5. If the light continues to illuminate, check the wiring circuit for broken terminals, blown fuses, cut wires, etc. Refer to

Oil Pressure Warning System Sensors

Volkswagen uses a two-sensor system to alert the driver of the vehicle of oil pressure status. These sensors both indicate a low oil pressure condition.

The Dynamic Oil Pressure Warning System consists of two oil pressure sensors, a warning light and buzzer, and an electronic control unit, mounted inside the instrument cluster.

The low pressure sensor is normally closed (causing the oil pressure light to flash) until the engine is started, and idling. At idle, the oil pressure is great enough to keep the switch open, preventing the light in the instrument cluster from flashing.

The high pressure sensor (normally open) operates in conjunction with electronic control unit. The electronic control unit receives reference signal from the tachometer when it reaches 2000–2500 rpm. If the high pressure switch is not closed before the engine reaches approximately 2500 rpm, the electronic control unit will illuminate the oil pressure light.

TESTING

☀☀ WARNING

If the oil pressure light in the instrument cluster is flashing while the engine is running, it should be assumed that an oil pressure problem exists. Before performing any electrical testing, the oil pressure should be checked with a mechanical gauge. If the mechanical oil pressure gauge indicates little or no oil pressure, the oil pump and pressure relief valve should be inspected and repaired/replaced as necessary. If the oil pressure is correct, proceed with electrical testing.

➡The switch pressure is usually inscribed on the switch itself.

If the oil pressure has been verified by a mechanical gauge, and the switches are functioning properly, the electronic control unit inside the instrument cluster is faulty, and should be replaced.

On all 8 valve engines up to 1992, and the 1.9L AAZ engine, the low pressure switch is located on the side of the cylinder head, and the high pressure switch is located on the oil filter housing. On VR6, 16 valve and 1993 and later 8 valve engines, (except for AAZ) both switches are located on the oil filter housing.

Low Pressure Switch

When the engine is not operating, the switch is grounded, which causes the oil pressure light in the instrument cluster to flash. When the engine is started, oil pressure rises, opening the circuit. The function of the circuit can be checked by using a test lead and grounding the pressure switch wire.

1. Start the engine, and disconnect the harness connector from the low pressure switch.
2. With the engine idling, check that the light in the instrument cluster flashes; if so, the circuit is functioning properly.
3. Using a test lead, ground the low pressure switch harness connector with the engine idling. The oil pressure warning lamp in the instrument cluster should extinguish.
4. If the instrument cluster warning lamp extinguishes, the switch is faulty.
5. If the instrument cluster warning lamp continues to flash while the harness connector is grounded, an open circuit exists between the harness connector and the instrument cluster. Refer to Sectiion 6 for more information.

High Pressure Switch

1. With the engine idling, disconnect the harness connector from the high pressure switch.
2. Raise the engine speed to 2500 rpm; the light should flash.
3. While holding the idle speed at 2500 rpm, ground the high pressure switch harness connector.
4. With the high pressure switch harness connector grounded, and the idle speed above 2500 rpm, the light should cease to flash. This indicates that the circuitry in the instrument panel is operating properly, and the switch is faulty.

REMOVAL & INSTALLATION

Removal of the switch is simply a matter of unscrewing it from the cylinder head/oil filter housing. When installing the switch, apply a light coating of thread sealer to prevent leakage. Tighten the switch to 18 ft. lbs. (25 Nm).

Electric Fan Switch

The electric fan switch, mounted in the radiator, supplies power to the fan (via relay) when the coolant reaches a certain temperature.

TESTING

Operation of the cooling fan is dependent on several factors, which include proper thermostat operation, A/C operation, and other switches, including the after-run thermoswitch. Before testing the radiator-mounted electric fan switch, verify that the cooling system is functioning properly, and that all electrical connections and wires are intact.

✳✳ CAUTION

Keep clear of the radiator fan blades. The fan can operate at any time.

1. Unplug the electrical harness connector from the radiator fan switch.
2. Using a suitable jumper wire, connect the red terminal on the harness connector to the red/white wire. The radiator fan should operate at low speed.
3. Using a suitable jumper wire, connect the red terminal on the harness connector to the red/black wire. The radiator fan should operate at high speed.
4. If the radiator fan operates properly at both speeds, the radiator fan switch is faulty and should be replaced.
5. If the radiator fan does not operate, check the radiator fan wiring circuit for broken terminals, blown fuses, cut wires, etc. Refer to Section for more information

REMOVAL & INSTALLATION

Fox

1. Raise and safely support the front of the vehicle on jackstands.
2. Remove the coolant reservoir cap to ensure there is no pressure in the cooling system.
3. Disconnect the harness connector from the sensor.

➡ **If the switch is being replaced, draining of the cooling system can be eliminated by having a new switch ready at the time of removal. A small amount of coolant will be lost, but refilling the system will not be necessary. Alternately, draining of the cooling system will be necessary for replacement of the fan switch.**

4. Place a drain receptacle underneath the switch.
5. Loosen the switch with a wrench until it can be turned by hand.
6. While pushing inward, unscrew the switch until the threads are free. Make sure to push inward on the switch with force; the pressure of the coolant will push outward. Keep a firm grip on the switch.
7. With the new switch (and new gasket placed on the switch) in your opposite hand, pull the old switch away from the radiator as quickly as possible while positioning the new switch in its place. Do this as fast as possible to prevent coolant from escaping from the radiator. Once positioned, screw the new switch into the radiator quickly to prevent coolant loss.
8. Tighten the switch to 18–26 ft. lbs. (25–35 Nm).
9. Plug the harness connector into the switch.
10. Lower the vehicle from the jackstands.
11. Adjust the level of the cooling system as necessary.

All Others

1. Raise and safely support the front of the vehicle on jackstands.
2. If applicable, remove the lower splash shield to access the switch.
3. Remove the coolant reservoir cap to ensure there is no pressure in the cooling system.
4. Disconnect the harness connector from the sensor.

➡ **If the switch is being replaced, draining of the cooling system can be eliminated by having a new switch ready at the time of removal. A small amount of coolant will be lost, but refilling the system will not be necessary. Alternately, complete draining of the cooling system will be necessary for replacement of the fan switch.**

5. Place a drain receptacle underneath the switch.
6. Loosen the switch with a wrench until it can be turned by hand.
7. While pushing inward, unscrew the switch until the threads are free. Make sure to push inward on the switch with force; the pressure of the coolant will push outward. Keep a firm grip on the switch.
8. With the new switch (and new gasket placed on the switch) in your opposite hand, pull the old switch away from the radiator as quickly as possible while positioning the new switch in its place. Do this as fast as possible to prevent coolant from escaping from the radiator. Once positioned, screw the new switch into the radiator quickly to prevent coolant loss.
9. Tighten the switch to 18–26 ft. lbs. (25–35 Nm).
10. Plug the harness connector into the switch.
11. As applicable, install the lower splash shield.
12. Lower the vehicle from the jackstands.
13. Adjust the level of the cooling system as necessary.

Troubleshooting Basic Starting System Problems

Problem	Cause	Solution
Starter motor rotates engine slowly	• Battery charge low or battery defective	• Charge or replace battery
	• Defective circuit between battery and starter motor	• Clean and tighten, or replace cables
	• Low load current	• Bench-test starter motor. Inspect for worn brushes and weak brush springs.
	• High load current	• Bench-test starter motor. Check engine for friction, drag or coolant in cylinders. Check ring gear-to-pinion gear clearance.
Starter motor will not rotate engine	• Battery charge low or battery defective	• Charge or replace battery
	• Faulty solenoid	• Check solenoid ground. Repair or replace as necessary.
	• Damaged drive pinion gear or ring gear	• Replace damaged gear(s)
	• Starter motor engagement weak	• Bench-test starter motor
	• Starter motor rotates slowly with high load current	• Inspect drive yoke pull-down and point gap, check for worn end bushings, check ring gear clearance
	• Engine seized	• Repair engine
Starter motor drive will not engage (solenoid known to be good)	• Defective contact point assembly	• Repair or replace contact point assembly
	• Inadequate contact point assembly ground	• Repair connection at ground screw
	• Defective hold-in coil	• Replace field winding assembly
Starter motor drive will not disengage	• Starter motor loose on flywheel housing	• Tighten mounting bolts
	• Worn drive end busing	• Replace bushing
	• Damaged ring gear teeth	• Replace ring gear or driveplate
	• Drive yoke return spring broken or missing	• Replace spring
Starter motor drive disengages prematurely	• Weak drive assembly thrust spring	• Replace drive mechanism
	• Hold-in coil defective	• Replace field winding assembly
Low load current	• Worn brushes	• Replace brushes
	• Weak brush springs	• Replace springs

TCCS2C01

Troubleshooting Basic Charging System Problems

Problem	Cause	Solution
Noisy alternator	• Loose mountings • Loose drive pulley • Worn bearings • Brush noise • Internal circuits shorted (High pitched whine)	• Tighten mounting bolts • Tighten pulley • Replace alternator • Replace alternator • Replace alternator
Squeal when starting engine or accelerating	• Glazed or loose belt	• Replace or adjust belt
Indicator light remains on or ammeter indicates discharge (engine running)	• Broken belt • Broken or disconnected wires • Internal alternator problems • Defective voltage regulator	• Install belt • Repair or connect wiring • Replace alternator • Replace voltage regulator/alternator
Car light bulbs continually burn out—battery needs water continually	• Alternator/regulator overcharging	• Replace voltage regulator/alternator
Car lights flare on acceleration	• Battery low • Internal alternator/regulator problems	• Charge or replace battery • Replace alternator/regulator
Low voltage output (alternator light flickers continually or ammeter needle wanders)	• Loose or worn belt • Dirty or corroded connections • Internal alternator/regulator problems	• Replace or adjust belt • Clean or replace connections • Replace alternator/regulator

TCCS2C02

3

ENGINE AND ENGINE OVERHAUL

ENGINE MECHANICAL

1.8L/2.0L GASOLINE ENGINE MECHANICAL SPECIFICATIONS

Description	English Specifications	Metric Specifications
General Information		
Engine type	4 cylinder in-line	
Displacement		
9A, ABA	121 cu. in.	1984cc
All others	109 cu. in.	1781cc
Bore		
9A, ABA	3.25 in.	82.5mm
All others	3.19 in.	81.0mm
Stroke		
9A, ABA	3.65 in.	92.8mm
All others	3.40 in.	86.4mm
Compression ratio		
ABA, PF, RV, 2H, and 9A engines	10.0:1	
ACC	9.0:1	
JN, UM, ABG engines	9.0:1	
Firing order	1-3-4-2	
Lubrication System		
Oil capacity	4.3 qts.	4.07L
Oil pump		
Gear backlash	0.002-0.008 in.	0.05-0.20mm
End play limit	0.006 in.	0.15mm
Pressure @ 2000 rpm (warm)	28-29 psi	1.90-1.97 BAR
Pistons		
Diameter		
1.8L engines		
Standard diameter	3.1884 in.	80.99mm
First oversize	3.1982 in.	81.24mm
Second oversize	3.2080 in.	81.49mm
Clearance-to-cylinder bore	0.00012-0.003 in.	0.03-0.08mm
2.0L engines		
Standard diameter	3.2474 in.	82.48mm
First oversize	3.2572 in.	82.73mm
Second oversize	3.2671 in.	82.98mm
Clearance-to-cylinder bore	0.00012-0.003 in.	0.03-0.08mm
Piston Pins		
Diameter		
1.8L engines	0.787 in.	20.0mm
2.0 8v (ABA) engines	0.827 in.	21.0mm
2.0 16v (9A) engines	N/A	
Length		
1.8L engines	2.280 in.	57.0mm
2.0 8v (ABA) engines	N/A	
2.0 16v (9A) engines	N/A	
Piston-to-pin clearance	Press fit	
Pin-to-rod clearance	N/A	

91223C01

1.8L/2.0L GASOLINE ENGINE MECHANICAL SPECIFICATIONS

Description	English Specifications	Metric Specifications
Piston Rings		
End gap		
1.8L engines except ACC		
Top compression	0.0118-0.0197 in.	0.30-0.45mm
Second compression	0.0118-0.0197 in.	0.30-0.45mm
Oil control	0.0098-0.0177 in.	0.25-0.45mm
2.0L and ACC 1.8L engines		
Top compression	0.0078-0.0157 in.	0.20-0.40mm
Second compression	0.0078-0.0157 in.	0.20-0.40mm
Oil control	0.0098-0.0197 in.	0.25-0.50mm
Groove clearance		
All engines except 2.0L 16v (9A)		
Top compression	0.0008-0.0020 in.	0.02-0.05mm
Second compression	0.0008-0.0020 in.	0.02-0.05mm
Oil control	0.0008-0.0020 in.	0.02-0.05mm
2.0L 16v (9A) only		
Top compression	0.0008-0.0028 in.	0.02-0.07mm
Second compression	0.0008-0.0028 in.	0.02-0.07mm
Oil control	0.0008-0.0024 in.	0.02-0.06mm
Crankshaft		
Main journal		
Diameter		
Standard diameter		
Nominal diameter	2.1260 in.	54.00mm
Tolerance	2.1243-2.1251 in.	53.958-53.976mm
1st undersize		
Nominal diameter	2.1161 in.	53.75mm
Tolerance	2.1145-2.1153 in.	53.708-53.728mm
2nd undersize		
Nominal diameter	2.1063 in.	53.50mm
Tolerance	2.1046-2.1054 in.	53.458-53.478mm
3rd undersize		
Nominal diameter	2.0965 in.	53.25mm
Tolerance	2.0948-2.0956 in.	53.208-53.228mm
Bearing clearance		
Radial		
New	0.0008-0.0024 in.	0.02-0.06mm
Wear limit	0.0067 in.	0.17mm
Axial (end play)		
New	0.0028-0.0067 in.	0.07-0.17mm
Wear limit	0.0098 in.	0.25mm
Rod bearing journal		
Diameter		
Standard diameter		
Nominal diameter	1.8812 in.	47.80mm
Tolerance	1.8802-1.8810 in.	47.758-47.778mm

91223C02

1.8L/2.0L GASOLINE ENGINE MECHANICAL SPECIFICATIONS

Description	English Specifications	Metric Specifications
Crankshaft (cont'd)		
1st undersize		
Nominal diameter	1.8720 in.	47.55mm
Tolerance	1.8704-1.8712 in.	47.508-47.528mm
2nd undersize		
Nominal diameter	1.8622 in.	47.30mm
Tolerance	1.8606-1.8613 in.	47.258-47.278mm
3rd undersize		
Nominal diameter	1.8523 in.	47.05mm
Tolerance	1.8507-1.8515 in.	47.008-47.028mm
Bearing clearance		
Radial		
New	0.0004-0.0024 in.	0.01-0.06mm
Limit	0.0047 in.	0.12mm
Axial (side)		
New	0.0020-0.0122 in.	0.05-0.31mm
Limit	0.0145 in.	0.37mm
Intermediate shaft		
Journal		
Diameter	N/A	N/A
Bearing clearance		
Radial		
New	N/A	N/A
Limit	N/A	N/A
Axial (side)		
New	N/A	N/A
Limit	0.0098 in.	0.25mm
Camshaft		
All engines except 16v (9A)		
Journal diameter		
Standard	1.0236 in.	26.00mm
Undersize	1.0138 in.	25.75mm
Bearing clearance	0.004 in.	0.1mm
Maximum run-out	0.0004 in.	0.01mm
End play	0.0059 in.	0.15mm
Lift	N/A	N/A
16v (9A) engine only		
Journal diameter		
Standard	N/A	N/A
Undersize	N/A	N/A
Bearing clearance	0.004 in.	0.1mm
Maximum run-out	N/A	N/A
End play	0.0059 in.	0.15mm
Lift	N/A	N/A

91223C03

1.8L/2.0L GASOLINE ENGINE MECHANICAL SPECIFICATIONS

Description	English Specifications	Metric Specifications
Valves		
UM, JN, and ABG engines		
Intake valves		
Stem diameter	0.3138 in.	7.97mm
Overall length	3.5827 in.	91.00mm
Face diameter	1.496 in.	38.0mm
Face angle	45°	
Stem-to-guide clearance	0.040 in.	1.0mm
Exhaust valves		
Stem diameter	0.3138 in.	7.97mm
Overall length	3.57498 in.	90.80mm
Face diameter	1.299 in.	33.0mm
Face angle	45°	
Stem-to-guide clearance	0.059 in.	1.3mm
2H, RV, and PF engines		
Intake valves		
Stem diameter	0.3138 in.	7.97mm
Overall length	3.5827 in.	91.00mm
Face diameter	1.575 in.	40.0mm
Face angle	45°	
Stem-to-guide clearance	0.040 in.	1.0mm
Exhaust valves		
Stem diameter	0.3138 in.	7.97mm
Overall length	3.57498 in.	90.80mm
Face diameter	1.299 in.	33.0mm
Face angle	45°	
Stem-to-guide clearance	0.059 in.	1.3mm
ABA engine only		
Intake valves		
Stem diameter	0.2744 in.	6.97mm
Overall length	3.6161 in.	91.85mm
Face diameter	1.5748 in.	40.0mm
Face angle	44.4°	
Stem-to-guide clearance	0.040 in.	1.0mm
Exhaust valves		
Stem diameter	0.2736 in.	6.95mm
Overall length	3.5886 in.	91.15mm
Face diameter	1.299 in.	33.0mm
Face angle	45.15°	
Stem-to-guide clearance	0.059 in.	1.3mm
9A engines only		
Intake valves		
Stem diameter	0.2744 in.	6.97mm
Overall length	3.761 in.	95.50mm
Face diameter	1.259 in.	32.0mm
Face angle	45°	

91223C04

1.8L/2.0L GASOLINE ENGINE MECHANICAL SPECIFICATIONS

Description	English Specifications	Metric Specifications
Valves (cont'd)		
Stem-to-guide clearance	0.040 in.	1.0mm
Exhaust valves		
Stem diameter	0.2732 in.	6.94mm
Overall length	3.866 in.	98.20mm
Face diameter	1.102 in.	28.0mm
Face angle	45°	45°
Stem-to-guide clearance	0.059 in.	1.3mm
Valve Seats		
UM, JN, and ABG engines		
Valve surface angle	45°	45°
Width		
Intake	0.079 in.	2.0mm
Exhaust	0.094 in.	2.4mm
Diameter		
Intake	1.465 in.	37.2mm
Exhaust	1.276 in.	32.4mm
2H, RV, and PF engines		
Valve surface angle	45°	45°
Width		
Intake	0.079 in.	2.0mm
Exhaust	0.094 in.	2.4mm
Diameter		
Intake	1.543 in.	39.2mm
Exhaust	1.276 in.	32.4mm
ABA engine only		
Valve surface angle		
Width		
Intake	0.079 in.	2.0mm
Exhaust	0.093 in.	2.4mm
Diameter		
Intake	1.406 in.	35.7mm
Exhaust	1.236 in.	31.4mm
9A engine only		
Valve surface angle	45°	45°
Width		
Intake	0.059-0.071 in.	1.5-1.8mm
Exhaust	0.071 in.	1.8mm
Diameter		
Intake	1.228 in.	31.2mm
Exhaust	1.087 in.	27.6mm
Cylinder Head		
Maximum warpage	0.004 in.	0.1mm
Minimum thickness		
8v	5.220 in.	132.6mm
16v	4.650 in.	118.1mm

91223C05

1.8L/2.0L GASOLINE ENGINE MECHANICAL SPECIFICATIONS

Description	English Specifications	Metric Specifications
Cylinder Block		
Maximum deck warpage	0.004 in.	0.01mm
Cylinder bore diameter		
1.8L engines		
Standard	3.1894 in.	81.01mm
1st oversize	3.1992 in.	81.26mm
2nd oversize	3.2091 in.	81.51mm
2.0L engines (8v & 16v)		
Standard	3.2484 in.	82.51mm
1st oversize	3.2583 in.	82.76mm
2nd oversize	3.2681 in.	83.01mm

91223C06

2.8L GASOLINE ENGINE MECHANICAL SPECIFICATIONS

Description	English Specifications	Metric Specifications
General Information		
Engine type	15 degree V6	
Displacement	170 cu. in.	2792cc
Bore	3.19 in.	81.0mm
Stroke	3.56 in.	90.3mm
Compression ratio	10.0:1	
Firing order	1-5-3-6-2-4	
Lubrication System		
Oil capacity	5.8 qts.	5.5L
Oil pump		
Gear backlash (max)	0.002-0.008 in.	0.05-0.20mm
Axial clearance	0.0039 in.	0.10mm
Pressure @ 2000 rpm (warm)	29 psi	1.97 BAR
Pistons		
Diameter		
Standard diameter	3.1884 in.	80.99mm
First oversize	3.2091 in.	81.48mm
Second oversize	3.2278 in.	81.99mm
Clearance-to-cylinder bore	0.0012-0.003 in.	0.03-0.08mm
Piston Pins		
Diameter	N/A	N/A
Length	N/A	N/A
Piston-to-pin clearance	Press fit	
Pin-to-rod clearance	N/A	N/A
Piston Rings		
End gap		
Top compression	0.0078-0.0157 in.	0.20-0.40mm
Second compression	0.0078-0.0157 in.	0.20-0.40mm
Oil control	0.0098-0.0196 in.	0.25-0.50mm
Groove clearance		
Top compression	0.0007-0.0027 in.	0.02-0.07mm
Second compression	0.0007-0.0027 in.	0.02-0.07mm
Oil control	0.0007-0.0024 in.	0.02-0.06mm
Crankshaft		
Main journal		
Diameter		
Nominal diameter	2.3622 in.	60.00mm
Tolerance	2.3606-2.1251 in.	59.958-59.978mm
Bearing clearance		
Radial		
New	0.0008-0.0024 in.	0.02-0.06mm
Wear limit	0.0039 in.	0.10mm
Axial (end play)		
New	0.0028-0.0091 in.	0.07-0.23mm
Wear limit	0.0118 in.	0.30mm

91223C07

2.8L GASOLINE ENGINE MECHANICAL SPECIFICATIONS

Description	English Specifications	Metric Specifications
Crankshaft (cont'd)		
Rod bearing journal		
Diameter		
Nominal diameter	2.1260 in.	54.00mm
Tolerance	2.1243-2.1251 in.	53.958-53.978mm
Bearing clearance		
Radial		
New	0.0004-0.0024 in.	0.01-0.06mm
Limit	0.0039 in.	0.10mm
Axial (side)		
New	0.0020-0.0122 in.	0.05-0.31mm
Limit	0.0157 in.	0.40mm
Camshaft		
Journal diameter	N/A	
Bearing clearance (wear limit)	0.004 in.	0.1mm
Maximum run-out	0.0004 in.	0.01mm
Axial Clearance (end play)	0.0059 in.	0.15mm
Lift	N/A	N/A
Valves		
Intake valves		
Stem diameter	0.2744 in.	6.97mm
Overall length	4.1713 in.	105.95mm
Face diameter	1.5354 in.	39.0mm
Face angle		45°
Stem-to-guide clearance	0.040 in.	1.0mm
Exhaust valves		
Stem diameter	0.2736 in.	6.95mm
Overall length	4.2106 in.	106.95mm
Face diameter	1.3465 in.	34.20mm
Face angle		45°
Stem-to-guide clearance	0.059 in.	1.3mm
Valve Seats		
Valve surface angle		45°
Width		
Intake	0.055-0.079 in.	1.4-2.0mm
Exhaust	0.079-0.098 in.	2.0-2.5mm
Diameter		
Intake	1.508 in.	38.3mm
Exhaust	1.319 in.	33.5mm
Cylinder Head		
Maximum warpage	0.004 in.	0.1mm
Minimum thickness	5.492 in.	139.5mm
Cylinder Block		
Maximum deck warpage	0.004 in.	0.01mm
Cylinder bore diameter		
Standard	3.1894 in.	81.01mm
1st oversize	3.2091 in.	81.51mm
2nd oversize	3.2287 in.	82.01mm

91223C08

1.6L/1.9L DIESEL ENGINE MECHANICAL SPECIFICATIONS

Description	English Specifications	Metric Specifications
General Information		
Engine type	4 cylinder in-line	
Displacement		
ME, MF, 1V	97 cu. in.	1588cc
AAZ,AHU	116 cu. in.	1896cc
Bore		
ME, MF, 1V	3.01 in.	76.5mm
AAZ,AHU	3.13 in.	79.5mm
Stroke		
ME, MF, 1V	3.40 in.	86.4mm
AAZ,AHU	3.76 in.	95.5mm
Compression ratio		
AAZ	22.5:1	
AHU	19.5:1	
ME, MF, 1V	23.0:1	
Firing order	1-3-4-2	
Lubrication System		
Oil capacity	4.8 qts.	4.5L
Oil pump		
Gear backlash	0.002-0.008 in.	0.05-0.20mm
End play limit	0.006 in.	0.15mm
Pressure @ 2000 rpm (warm)	29 psi	1.97 BAR
Pistons		
Diameter		
1.6L engines		
Standard diameter	3.0110 in.	76.48mm
First oversize	3.0209 in.	76.73mm
Second oversize	3.0307 in.	76.98mm
Third oversize	3.0504 in.	77.48mm
Clearance-to-cylinder bore	0.0012-0.003 in.	0.03-0.08mm
1.9L engines		
Standard diameter	3.1291 in.	79.48mm
First oversize ①	3.1390 in.	79.73mm
Second oversize	3.1488 in.	79.98mm
Clearance-to-cylinder bore	0.0012 in.	0.03mm
Piston height above block (at TDC)		
ME, MF, 1V and AAZ engines		
Use gasket with one notch	0.0260-0.0339 in.	0.66-0.86mm
Use gasket with two notches	0.0343-0.0354 in.	0.87-0.90mm
Use gasket with three notches	0.0358-0.402 in.	0.91-1.02mm
AHU engines		
Use gasket with one notch	0.0356-0.0394 in.	0.91-1.00mm
Use gasket with two notches	0.0398-0.0433 in.	1.01-1.10mm
Use gasket with three notches	0.0437-0.472 in.	1.11-1.20mm
Piston Pins		
Diameter		
1.6L engines	1.02 in.	26.0mm
1.9L engines	N/A	

91223C09

1.6L/1.9L DIESEL ENGINE MECHANICAL SPECIFICATIONS

Description	English Specifications	Metric Specifications
Piston Pins (cont'd)		
Length		
1.6L engines		N/A
1.9L engines		N/A
Piston-to-pin clearance		Press fit
Pin-to-rod clearance		N/A
Piston Rings		
End gap		
1.6L engines		
Top compression	0.0118-0.0197 in.	0.30-0.45mm
Second compression	0.0118-0.0197 in.	0.30-0.45mm
Oil control	0.0098-0.0177 in.	0.25-0.45mm
1.9L engines		
Top compression	0.0079-0.0157 in.	0.20-0.40mm
Second compression	0.0079-0.0157 in.	0.20-0.40mm
Oil control	0.0098-0.0197 in.	0.25-0.50mm
Groove clearance		
1.6L engines		
Top compression	0.0024-0.0035 in.	0.06-0.09mm
Second compression	0.0020-0.0031 in.	0.05-0.08mm
Oil control	0.0012-0.0024 in.	0.03-0.06mm
1.9L engines		
Top compression ②	0.0035-0.0047 in.	0.09-0.12mm
Second compression	0.0020-0.0031 in.	0.05-0.08mm
Oil control	0.0012-0.0024 in.	0.03-0.06mm
Crankshaft		
Main journal		
Diameter		
Standard diameter		
Nominal diameter	2.1260 in.	54.00mm
Tolerance	2.1243-2.1251 in. in.	53.958-53.978mm
1st undersize		
Nominal diameter	2.1161 in.	53.75mm
Tolerance	2.1145-2.1153mm in.	53.708-53.728mm
2nd undersize		
Nominal diameter	2.1063 in.	53.50mm
Tolerance	2.1046-2.1054 in.	53.458-53.478mm
3rd undersize		
Nominal diameter	2.0955 in.	53.25mm
Tolerance	2.0948-2.0956 in.	53.208-53.228mm
Bearing clearance		
Radial		
New	0.0012-0.0031 in.	0.03-0.08mm
Wear limit	0.0067 in.	0.17mm
Axial (end play)		
New	0.0028-0.0067 in.	0.07-0.17mm
Wear limit	0.0146 in.	0.37mm

91223C10

1.6L/1.9L DIESEL ENGINE MECHANICAL SPECIFICATIONS

Description	English Specifications	Metric Specifications
Crankshaft (cont'd)		
Rod bearing journal		
Diameter		
Standard diameter		
Nominal diameter	1.8819 in.	47.80mm
Tolerance	1.8802-1.8810 in.	47.758-47.778mm
1st undersize		
Nominal diameter	1.8720 in.	47.55mm
Tolerance	1.8704-1.8712 in.	47.508-47.528mm
2nd undersize		
Nominal diameter	1.8622 in.	47.30mm
Tolerance	1.8606-1.8613 in.	47.258-47.278mm
3rd undersize		
Nominal diameter	1.8524 in.	47.05mm
Tolerance	1.8507-1.8515 in.	47.008-47.028mm
Bearing clearance		
Radial		
New	0.0004-0.0024 in.	0.01-0.06mm
Limit	0.0031 in.	0.08mm
Axial (side)		
New	0.0020-0.0122 in.	0.05-0.31mm
Limit	0.0145 in.	0.37mm
Intermediate shaft		
Journal		
Diameter	N/A	N/A
Bearing clearance		
Radial		
New	N/A	N/A
Limit	N/A	N/A
Axial (side)		
New	N/A	N/A
Limit	0.0098 in.	0.26mm
Camshaft		
Journal diameter	N/A	N/A
Bearing clearance (max)	0.004 in.	0.1mm
Maximum run-out	0.0004 in.	0.01mm
End play	0.0059 in.	0.15mm
Lift	N/A	N/A
Valves		
ME, MF, 1V engines		
Intake valves		
Stem diameter	0.3138 in.	7.97mm
Overall length	3.740 in.	95.0mm
Face diameter	1.339 in.	34.0mm
Face angle	45°	
Stem-to-guide clearance	0.051 in.	1.3mm

91223C11

1.6L/1.9L DIESEL ENGINE MECHANICAL SPECIFICATIONS

Description	English Specifications	Metric Specifications
Valves (cont'd)		
Exhaust valves		
Stem diameter	0.3130 in.	7.95mm
Overall length	3.740 in.	95.0mm
Face diameter	1.220 in.	31.0mm
Face angle	45°	
Stem-to-guide clearance	0.051 in.	1.3mm
AAZ engine		
Intake valves		
Stem diameter	0.3138 in.	7.97mm
Overall length	3.740 in.	95.0mm
Face diameter	1.417 in.	36.0mm
Face angle	45°	
Stem-to-guide clearance	0.051 in.	1.3mm
Exhaust valves		
Stem diameter	0.3130 in.	7.95mm
Overall length	3.740 in.	95.0mm
Face diameter	1.220 in.	31.0mm
Face angle	45°	
Stem-to-guide clearance	0.051 in.	1.3mm
AHU engine		
Intake valves		
Stem diameter	0.3138 in.	7.97mm
Overall length	3.83 in.	96.85mm
Face diameter	1.415 in.	35.95mm
Face angle	45°	
Stem-to-guide clearance	0.059 in.	1.3mm
Exhaust valves		
Stem diameter	0.3138 in.	7.97mm
Overall length	3.83 in.	96.85mm
Face diameter	1.238 in.	31.45mm
Face angle	45°	
Stem-to-guide clearance	0.059 in.	1.3mm
Valve Seats		
ME, MF, 1V engines		
Valve surface angle	45°	
Width		
Intake	0.080 in.	2.0mm
Exhaust	0.094 in.	2.5mm
Diameter		
Intake	1.291 in.	32.8mm
Exhaust	1.197 in.	30.4mm
AAZ engine		
Valve surface angle	45°	
Width		
Intake	0.1063 in.	2.70mm
Exhaust	0.0807 in.	2.05mm
Diameter		
Intake	1.3701 in.	34.80mm
Exhaust	1.1968 in.	30.40mm

91223C12

1.6L/1.9L DIESEL ENGINE MECHANICAL SPECIFICATIONS

Description	English Specifications	Metric Specifications
Valve Seats (cont'd)		
AHU engine		
Valve surface angle	45°	
Width		
Intake	0.63 in.	1.6mm
Exhaust	1.06 in.	2.7mm
Diameter		
Intake	1.406 in.	35.7mm
Exhaust	1.236 in.	31.4mm
Cylinder Head		
Maximum warpage	0.004 in.	0.1mm
Minimum thickness	Cannot be machined	
Cylinder Block		
Maximum deck warpage	0.004 in.	0.01mm
Cylinder bore diameter		
1.6L engines		
Standard	3.0122 in.	76.51mm
1st oversize	3.0220 in.	76.76mm
2nd oversize	3.0319 in.	77.01mm
3rd oversize	3.0516 in.	77.51mm
1.9L engines		
Standard	3.1303 in.	79.51mm
1st oversize	3.1402 in.	79.76mm
2nd oversize	3.1500 in.	80.01mm

① AHU engines have a specification of 3.1385 in. (79.72mm)

② AHU engines have a specification of 0.0024–0.0047 in. (0.06–0.12mm)

91223C13

Description

GASOLINE (EXCEPT VR6)

The engine in all the models covered in this section are water cooled inline 4-cylinders with a cast iron block and an aluminum alloy cylinder head. The crankshaft is supported in five plain main bearings and the center bearing includes a 4-piece thrust bearing. The forged steel connecting rods are equipped with plain bearings at the big end and coated steel bushings at the small end. The full floating wrist pins are held in place in the pistons with circlips. The pistons are fitted with two compression rings and a 1-piece oil control ring. The oil pump is mounted below the crankshaft and driven by the intermediate shaft. The 16 valve 2.0 liter block has additional oil passages and spray nozzles for cooling the under side of the pistons. On 8 valve 1.8 liter engines, the oil pump drive shaft includes an extension that engages the drive lugs on the distributor.

The intermediate shaft and the camshaft are driven by a steel-reinforced toothed belt. The overhead camshaft acts directly on the valves through hydraulic lifters for quiet, maintenance free operation. The valves move in alloy guides that can be replaced when worn. The bearing surfaces for the camshafts and lifters are machined directly into the cylinder head and cannot be serviced.

On 16V engines, there are two overhead camshafts that operate 2 intake valves and 2 exhaust valves per cylinder. The exhaust camshaft is driven by the belt and the intake camshaft is driven by a chain connecting the two camshafts. The 4-valve per cylinder design allows a central spark plug location for a more controlled and symmetrical combustion. This allows a higher compression ratio for more power and cleaner combustion with the same fuel consumption. The intake and exhaust manifolds are on opposite sides of the cylinder head to improve the engine's ability to "breathe" over the entire rpm range.

VR6

Volkswagen's VR6 engine has a unique 15° V-angle between its cylinder banks. Traditional 60 or 90° engines require a great deal of engine compartment space. VW's compact VR6 was designed to enable it to fit into a chassis that was originally designed to accommodate a longitudinal inline 4 cylinder engine. The VR6 consists of a cast iron block with a one piece aluminum alloy cylinder head.

➡ **The engine was named the VR6 through the combination of two words. Vee (a reference to the configuration of the cylinders) and Reihenmotor (a German word for "inline"). Engineers were essentially referring to it as an inline V—6.**

DIESEL ENGINE

Aside from the obvious external features, there are several internal differences between the ECODiesel engine block and the standard 8 valve engine block it is based on. The cylinders have a smaller bore providing a total piston displacement of only 1.6 to 1.9 liters. There are also additional oil passages and spray nozzles for cooling the under side of the pistons. Even though this engine operates at a compression ratio of about 23:1, the special pistons are designed to do this using only two compression rings for reduced friction losses.

The cylinder head has spherical pre-combustion chambers made of steel set into the lower surface of the head. The fuel injector projects into the pre-chamber and combustion begins there almost at the very beginning of the injection cycle. The burning fuel/air mixture is given a swirl pattern by the chamber's shape. The swirl promotes more complete combustion as the process continues in the main combustion chamber. Using the swirl chamber has other advantages: it reduces the peak load which the force of combustion would normally exert on pistons, rods, bearings and crankshaft, enabling VW to use many standard components. Aside from the pre-chambers, the cylinder head is quite similar to the gasoline engine. The valve train is the same single overhead camshaft with hydraulic lifters

Engine

If the engine must be removed in order to service it, there are a few preliminary steps which must be executed first.
- Clear a place to work.
- Clean the engine compartment as well as the engine. This will help keep both you and your tools cleaner.
- Assume the vehicle will be out of order for quite some time.
- Label all hoses, wires, components, etc.
- Always plan ahead. Estimate the amount of needed time, tools, etc. Don't get cut short. This is a lengthy task.

REMOVAL AND INSTALLATION

The engine and transmission are removed as a unit and then disassembled. The removal of some front body work may be required.

Gasoline Engines

4CYL.

➡ **It is recommended that the hood be removed, to allow easier access to all areas of the engine, although it is not required.**

Always label all lines and hoses so they can be reconnected correctly.

➡ **On the 8 valve engines, special tools are required to remove and install the exhaust pipe to manifold spring clamps. These may be available at local parts retailers.**

✳ CAUTION

Fuel lines may be pressurized. Make sure the work area is well ventilated. Vapors can easily ignite.

1. Disconnect the battery cables and remove the battery.
2. If your vehicle is equipped with an anti-theft system, know your deactivation code before you remove any of the battery cables.
3. Relieve the fuel system pressure by completing the following:
   - Remove the fuel filler cap to relieve tank pressure.
   - Loosen the cold start injector line to relieve the fuel system pressure on CIS-E fuel injection systems.
   - On Digifant fuel injection, loosen the pressure test port fitting at the end of the fuel rail that supplies the injectors.
4. The air intake duct between the air cleaner and the throttle body must also be removed.
5. Detach the accelerator cable from the throttle and remove the cable housing from the bracket.
6. Set the heater temperature control to maximum.
7. Remove the radiator cap and place a pan under the thermostat housing and remove the thermostat flange to drain the coolant.
8. Remove the air conditioner compressor and the condenser without disconnecting the coolant lines and secure them out of the way.
9. Remove the upper radiator hose and disconnect the wiring from the radiator fan motor and switches. Remove the upper mounting brackets and lift out the radiator and fan as an assembly.
10. On Golf and Jetta, the front body section must be removed:
    - Detach the headlight electrical connectors and the hood release cable from the hood latch assembly.
    - Remove the lower valance and the front grille, and front apron.

11. Disconnect all electrical connections and vacuum lines, carefully labeling each one.

➡ **Don't forget ground connections that are screwed to the body.**

12. Remove the power steering pump and reservoir.

➡ **You may not have to disconnect the hydraulic lines and secure them out of the way.**

13. The entire fuel injection system can be removed as a unit if the vehicle is equipped with the CIS-E type.
    - Without disconnecting the lines, carefully pry the injectors from their holes and protect them with caps.

➡ **A little silicone spray can greatly ease the removal of the injectors.**

    - As you remove the cold start injector, tape all the injector lines together and set them aside.
    - Detach the wiring and the fuel supply line from the fuel distributor. Plug the fuel inlet to keep dirt out of the fuel distributor.
    - Disconnect the fuel return line from the pressure regulator.
    - Remove the bolts or clips required to change the air filter and lift the air flow sensor and fuel system out of the vehicle.

14. On engines with Digifant fuel injection, disconnect the fuel supply line from the pressure regulator and the fuel return line from the fuel rail. Disconnect the plug on the end of the injector wiring harness.
15. If equipped with an automatic transaxle, place the selector lever in the "PARK" position and disconnect the shifter cable at the transaxle. Remove the speedometer cable from the transaxle and plug the hole in the case.
16. On vehicles with a manual transaxle, remove the 2 rods with the plastic socket ends and unbolt the remaining linkage from the transaxle case as required. Disconnect the clutch cable, lift it from the case and set it aside.
17. Detach the wiring from the starter and the back-up light switch and disconnect the ground cable from the transaxle. Remove the speedometer cable from the transaxle and plug the hole in the case.
18. Raise and safely support the vehicle on jack stands.
19. Unbolt the halfshafts from the flanges and hang them from the body with wire.

✳ WARNING

DO NOT let the halfshafts hang by the outer CV joint or the joint may fall apart.

20. Unbolt the exhaust pipe from the manifold or remove the spring clamps holding the exhaust pipe to the manifold and lower the pipe.
21. If the exhaust pipe is secured to the manifold with spring clamps, use the proper tools and procedures for removal and installation.

✳ CAUTION

The springs are under heavy tension and can cause serious injury if mishandled.

22. To remove the spring clamps:
    - Push the pipe to one side to expand the opposite clamp. Insert a wedge into the expanded clamp.
    - Push the pipe to the other side and insert a wedge into the clamp.
    - Push the pipe the other way again to expand the clamp further. It should be possible to grab the wedge with locking pliers and pry the clamp off the pipe flange.
    - Leave the wedges in the clamps and put them in a box so they won't be disturbed and fly apart.
23. Attach a suitable chain sling to the lifting eyes.

➡ **On 16V engines, a rigid sling must be used. Remove the idle stabilizer valve and upper intake manifold and attach engine sling tool VW-2024A or equivalent, to the engine.**

24. Check to make sure everything is disconnected, then unbolt the mounts. Remove the starter first and the front mount with it.
25. Once all of the mounts have been unbolted, slightly lower the engine/transaxle assembly and tilt it towards the transaxle side.

26. Next, carefully lift the assembly from the vehicle. See Section 7 for information on separating the engine and transaxle.

To install:

➡️ See Section 7 for information on assembling the engine and transaxle. Make sure all mount brackets are securely bolted to the engine/transaxle. Fit the assembly into the engine bay and install the mounts, starting at the rear. Start all nuts and bolts that secure the mounts to the body but don't tighten them yet.

27. With all mounts installed and the engine safely in the vehicle, allow some slack in the lifting equipment. With the vehicle safely supported, shake the engine/transaxle as a unit to settle it in the mounts. Torque all mounting bolts, starting at the rear and working forward. Torque to 33 ft. lbs. (41 Nm) for 10mm bolts or 54 ft. lbs. (73 Nm) for 12mm bolts.

28. Install the starter and torque the bolts to 33 ft. lbs. (45 Nm).

29. Attach the halfshafts to the flanges and torque the bolts to 33 ft. lbs. (45 Nm).

30. Connect the exhaust pipe. On 16V engines, use new self locking nuts to secure the flange and torque the nuts to 30 ft. lbs. (40 Nm).

31. Attach the shift linkage and the clutch cable. Adjust the clutch and shift linkage as required.

32. Install the fuel system components and connect the lines.

33. On Golf and Jetta, install the front apron and connect the wiring.

34. Install the air conditioning compressor and/or power steering pump, if equipped. Install and adjust the drive belts.

35. Install the radiator, fan and heater hoses.

36. Use a new O-ring on the thermostat and torque the thermostat housing bolts to 7 ft. lbs. (10 Nm).

37. Connect all remaining wiring and vacuum hoses. Check carefully to make sure all components are correctly installed and connected.

38. Fill the cooling system. Check the adjustment of the accelerator cable.

VR-6

▶ See Figures 1 thru 6

➡️ The factory audio system is coded. Know your code before you remove the battery cables.

1. Disconnect the negative battery cable.
2. Drain the cooling system.
3. Remove the engine accessory drive belt.

➡️ General practice is to mark the accessory drive belt's rotation before removing the belt. This will aid in the installation of the belt.

4. Remove the spark plug connectors from the plugs, then remove the plug wire guides.

➡️ A special tool is required to remove the spark plug connectors from the plugs. A version of this tool is connected to the front hood support bar.

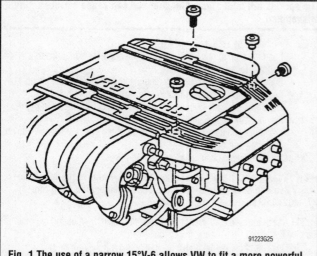

Fig. 1 The use of a narrow 15°V-6 allows VW to fit a more powerful engine (such as this VR6) where others cannot

5. Remove the round harness connector near the ignition coil on the rear of the cylinder head.

6. Remove the intake manifold cover.

7. Label and then disconnect all wires, hoses, and clips attached to the cylinder head.

8. Remove the air filter housing and intake air ducts. This only applies to vehicles with mass air flow sensors.

9. Disconnect the accelerator cable from the throttle.

10. Label then disconnect the fuel hoses from the cylinder head and position them out of the way.

11. Remove all necessary coolant hoses.

12. Detach the exhaust pipes from the manifolds.

13. Remove the drive axles.

14. Remove the radiator mounting bolts.

15. If the vehicle has A/C, remove all necessary components. This will require the skills of a certified technician to evacuate the refrigerant from the system.

Fig. 2 Installation of an engine hoist

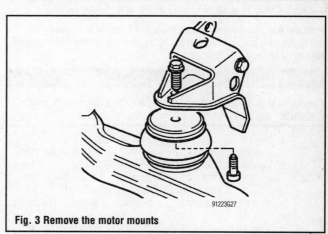

Fig. 3 Remove the motor mounts

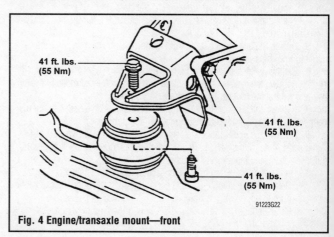

41 ft. lbs. (55 Nm)

41 ft. lbs. (55 Nm)

41 ft. lbs. (55 Nm)

Fig. 4 Engine/transaxle mount—front

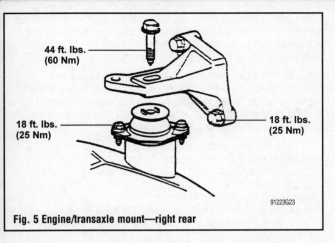

Fig. 5 Engine/transaxle mount—right rear

44 ft. lbs. (60 Nm)

18 ft. lbs. (25 Nm)

18 ft. lbs. (25 Nm)

91223G23

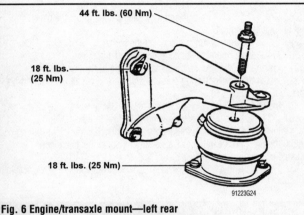

Fig. 6 Engine/transaxle mount—left rear

44 ft. lbs. (60 Nm)

18 ft. lbs. (25 Nm)

18 ft. lbs. (25 Nm)

91223G24

16. Detach the front body mounting bolts.
17. Remove all remaining electrical connectors, hoses, and brackets from the radiator assembly.
18. On vehicles with A/C, remove the radiator and the A/C condenser as a unit.
19. Unbolt and remove the power steering pump from its bracket and set it to the side.
20. Remove the electrical harness connectors from the transmission—automatic transmission equipped vehicles.
21. Detach the transmission cooler lines from the transmission—automatic transmission equipped vehicles.
22. Remove the clutch slave cylinder on manual transmission vehicles.
23. On automatic transmission equipped vehicles, place the selector lever in the park position.
24. Label the starter wiring from the starter. Then remove the wiring from the alternator.
25. Remove the intake air temperature sensor (IAT).
26. Install the engine hoist.
27. Remove the motor mounts.
28. Raise the engine and transmission from the vehicle.

To install:

➡See Section 7 for information on assembling the engine and transaxle. Make sure all mount brackets are securely bolted to the engine/transaxle. Fit the assembly into the engine bay and install the mounts, starting at the rear. Start all nuts and bolts that secure the mounts to the body but don't tighten them yet.

29. Properly torque all motor mount nuts and bolts. See included art for torque specs.
30. Using the engine hoist, lower the engine into the bay.
31. Install the front body assembly
32. Install all removed components, connectors, hoses, lines, etc.
33. The remainder of the installation process is the reverse of removal.

➡Tighten the drive axle flange bolts to 33 ft. lbs. (45 Nm) and the exhaust pipe to exhaust manifold to 30 ft. lbs. (40 Nm).

FOX

The engine is lifted from this vehicle without the transaxle attached.

1. Disconnect the battery ground cable and remove the battery.
2. Open the heater valve and the cap on the coolant expansion tank. Drain the coolant by removing the bottom hose. Disconnect the electrical connector from the radiator cooling fan.
3. Remove the radiator and fan as an assembly.
4. If equipped with air conditioning, remove the compressor and condenser and place them aside without disconnecting any refrigerant lines.
5. Detach and label all the electrical wires and vacuum lines connecting the engine to the body.
6. Much of the fuel system can be removed as a unit without disconnecting fuel lines. Remove the injectors from their holes and protect them with caps. Remove the cold start injector and warm-up regulator, if equipped. Disconnect the throttle cable and remove the air duct. Place these aside without disconnecting the fuel lines.
7. Disconnect the speedometer cable from the transaxle and plug the hole. Detach the clutch cable.
8. Loosen the charcoal filter clamp and move the filter to the rear of the engine compartment.
9. Remove the upper engine-to-transaxle bolts.
10. Remove the left and right engine mounting nuts.
11. Remove the front engine stop and the starter.
12. Remove the clutch cover and the 2 lower engine-to-transaxle bolts.
13. Disconnect the exhaust pipe from the manifold at the flange. Then remove the bolt from the exhaust pipe support and remove the exhaust pipe from the manifold.
14. Install transaxle support bar VW–758/1 or equivalent, with slight pre-load. This is to hold the transaxle in place while the engine is out.
15. Install sling US–1105, or equivalent, on the engine lifting eyes located on the left side of the cylinder head.
16. Lift the engine until its weight is taken off the engine mounts.
17. Adjust the support bar to contact the transaxle.
18. Separate the engine and transaxle.
19. Carefully lift the engine out of the engine compartment so as not to damage the transaxle main shaft, clutch and body.

To install:

20. Lubricate the clutch release bearing and transaxle main shaft splines with MOS₂grease or equivalent; do not lubricate the guide sleeve or the clutch release bearing.
21. Carefully guide the engine into the vehicle and attach to the transaxle while keeping weight off the motor mounts.
22. Remove the transaxle support bar and lower the engine onto the engine mounts.
23. The remainder of the installation is the reverse of the removal procedure. Torque the engine mounts and subframe bolts with the engine running at idle speed. This will minimize vibration.
24. Torque the following:
   • Cold start valve, the radiator mount bolts and the engine-to-transaxle cover plate bolts—7 ft. lbs. (10 Nm).
   • Engine-to-transaxle bolts—42 ft. lbs. (55 Nm).
   • Engine mount bolts—30 ft. lbs. (40 Nm).
   • Engine stop-to-body block and exhaust pipe support bolts—18 ft. lbs. (25 Nm).
   • Exhaust pipe-to-manifold bolts—22 ft. lbs. (30 Nm).
   • Starter bolts—18 ft. lbs. (25 Nm).

Diesel Engine

The engine and transmission are lifted from the vehicle as an assembly and separated afterwards. Some of the front body work must be removed but removing the hood is not necessary unless it interferes with the lifting equipment. Some components can be removed without disconnecting hydraulic or coolant hoses. Cover the front fenders so components can be hung over them. Before beginning the job, make sure you have some way of labeling the wires, lines and hoses so they can be reconnected correctly.

1. Remove the battery.
2. Turn the heater temperature control to maximum. Remove the radiator cap and the radiator hose at the thermostat housing and drain the cooling system. Remove the thermostat flange.
3. Disconnect the wiring from the radiator fan motor and the thermoswitch. Remove the upper radiator mounting brackets and lift the radiator and fan out of the vehicle.
4. Remove the fuel filter and base. Cap the fuel line connections to prevent leakage.
5. Detach the brake booster hose from the vacuum pump.
6. Remove the alternator wiring and then the unit.
7. Detach the wiring to the fuel shut-off solenoid, the glow plugs, the oil pressure switch and the coolant temperature sensor.
8. Disconnect the heater and the expansion tank hoses.
9. At the injection pump, disconnect the accelerator cable and the cold start cable.
10. Disconnect the fuel supply and the return lines from the injection pump. Plug the openings in the pump and cap the ends of the lines to prevent the entry of dirt into the system.
11. If equipped with air conditioning, the injection pump must be removed to remove the compressor. See Section 5 for instructions on removing the pump. To remove the compressor:
   - Remove the air conditioning belt tensioner, water pump pulley and drive belt.
   - Disconnect the wiring from the compressor and the pressure switches.
   - Remove the condenser and compressor together without disconnecting the coolant hoses.
   - Secure the compressor and condenser out of the way. Do not let them hang by the coolant hoses.
12. Remove the front body section as described:
   - Disconnect the headlight electrical connectors and the hood release cable from the hood latch assembly.
   - Remove the lower valance and the front grille.
   - Remove the front apron
13. If equipped with power steering, remove the pump without disconnecting the hydraulic hoses. Secure the pump out of the way, do not let it hang by the hoses.
14. Disconnect the wiring from the starter, back-up light switch and the transaxle mount ground wire.
15. If equipped with a manual transaxle, disconnect the clutch cable and shift linkage.
16. On vehicles with an automatic transaxle, place the selector lever in the P position and disconnect the shifter cable at the transaxle.
17. Remove the speedometer cable from the transaxle and plug the hole in the case.
18. If not already done, raise and safely support the vehicle on jack stands.
19. Unbolt the halfshafts from the flanges and hang them from the body with wire.

❋❋ WARNING

DO NOT let the halfshafts hang by the outer CV joint or the joint may fall apart.

➡**The exhaust pipe is secured to the manifold with spring clamps. Use the proper tools and procedures for removal and installation. The springs are under heavy tension and can cause serious injury if mishandled.**

20. To remove the exhaust pipe spring clamps:
   - Push the pipe to one side to expand the opposite clamp. Insert a wedge into the expanded clamp.
   - Push the pipe to the other side and insert a wedge into the clamp.
   - Push the pipe the other way again to expand the clamp further. It should be possible to grab the wedge with locking pliers and pry the clamp off the pipe flange.
21. Leave the wedges in the clamps and put them in a box so they won't be disturbed and fly apart.
22. Check carefully to make sure all necessary wiring, hoses and linkages have been disconnected. Attach a chain yoke and a hoist to the engine, then lift it slightly.

23. Unbolt the engine mounts, tilt the assembly down at the transaxle side and carefully lift the engine and transaxle out. See Section 7 for information on separating the engine and transaxle.

   To install:

➡**See Section 7 for information on assembling the engine and transaxle. Make sure all mount brackets are securely bolted to the engine/transaxle. Fit the assembly into the engine bay and install the mounts, starting at the rear. Start all nuts and bolts that secure the mounts to the body but don't tighten them yet.**

24. With all mounts installed and the engine safely in the vehicle, allow some slack in the lifting equipment. With the vehicle safely supported, shake the engine/transaxle as a unit to settle it in the mounts. Torque all mounting bolts, starting at the rear and working forward. Torque to 33 ft. lbs. (41 Nm) for 10mm bolts or 54 ft. lbs. (73 Nm) for 12mm bolts.
25. Install the starter and torque the bolts to 33 ft. lbs. (45 Nm).
26. Connect the halfshafts to the flanges and torque the bolts to 33 ft. lbs. (45 Nm).
27. Connect the exhaust pipe.
28. Connect the shift linkage and the clutch cable. Adjust the clutch and shift linkage as required.
29. Install the front apron and connect the wiring.
30. Install the air conditioner compressor and condenser.
31. Install the fuel injection pump as described in Section 5.
32. Install the power steering pump. Install and adjust all accessory drive belts.
33. Install the radiator, fan and heater hoses. Use a new O-ring on the thermostat and torque the thermostat housing bolts to 7 ft. lbs. (10 Nm).
34. Install the remaining components and connect all remaining wiring and vacuum hoses. Check carefully to make sure all components are correctly installed and connected.
35. Fill and bleed the cooling system. Check the adjustment of the accelerator cable.

Engine Mounts

ADJUSTMENT

If there is excessive engine vibration, an engine alignment procedure may cure the problem. Loosen all the bolts that go into the rubber mounts. Do not loosen engine or body mounting brackets. With the vehicle safely supported, shake the engine/transaxle as a unit to settle it in the mounts. Re-torque all mounting bolts, starting at the rear and working forward. If engine vibration is not reduced, check for torn rubber mounts. The mount at the timing belt end usually fails first.

Camshaft (Valve) Cover

REMOVAL & INSTALLATION

4 cyl.

◗ **See Figures 7, 8 and 9**

1. Remove the negative battery cable.

➡**If the VW you are working on has a theft deterrent system be sure to have the de-activation code before you remove any of the battery cables.**

2. On 2.0L engines, detach the air intake, then remove the intake manifold. Loosen the valve cover bolts
3. On 1.8L engines, remove the breather hose from the valve cover. Loosen and then remove all of the fasteners.
4. Remove the valve cover from the cylinder head.
5. Remove the valve cover gasket. Clean and prep the surface of the valve cover.
6. Clean the surface of the cylinder head.

Fig. 7 Location of valve cover bolts

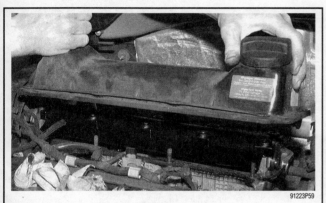

Fig. 8 Pull up on the valve cover to remove it

Fig. 9 Pull up the gasket at one corner of the valve cover and carefully work your finger around the perimeter.

To install:

7. Install a new gasket and then the valve cover.

➡**Always check to ensure that the valve cover gasket is properly seated on the head.**

8. The remainder of the procedure is the reverse of removal.

VR6

1. Remove the spark plug connectors.
2. Detach the intake manifold cover and the intake manifold.
3. Remove the Positive Crankcase Ventilation (PCV) breather valve.
4. Remove the air intake hose from the throttle housing.
5. Disconnect the throttle cable.
6. Remove the radiator cap.

✳✳ CAUTION

Never open the radiator cap when the engine is hot.

7. Clamp the coolant hose off at the throttle body.
8. Remove the oil dipstick guide tube.
9. Detach all necessary vacuum hoses and electrical connectors.
10. Remove the upper intake manifold. As a time saver leave the throttle housing connected to the intake during removal.
11. Remove the nuts along the perimeter of the cylinder head cover.
12. Lift off the cylinder head cover.
13. Remove the cylinder head cover gasket.
To install:
14. Installation is the reversal of removal. Remember to use a new gasket between the upper intake manifold and its lower portion. The cylinder head cover gasket is to be replaced if it is worn or damaged.

Thermostat

REMOVAL & INSTALLATION

4 Cyl. Models

▶ **See Figures 10, 11 and 12**

➡**On some models the thermostat is in the bottom of the water pump housing.**

1. Place a large drain pan under the vehicle to collect the coolant.
2. Remove the radiator cap and drain the cooling system.
3. Loosen one bolt at a time until coolant begins to flow.
4. Remove both bolts and remove the thermostat.
To install:
5. Install the new O-ring.
6. Torque the housing the bolts to 7 ft. lbs. (10 Nm).

Fig. 10 Remove the housing bolts

Fig. 11 Once all bolts have been remove, pull the thermostat housing away from the bottom of the water pump unit

Fig. 12 Note the position of the thermostat and gasket

VR-6

♦ **See Figure 13**

On 6 cylinder models, the thermostat is mounted in the housing. The thermostat housing is located on the rear of the cylinder head.

1. Drain the engine coolant.
2. Remove the mounting bolts from the flange.
3. Remove the flange and the thermostat.

To install:

4. Install the new thermostat and O—ring.
5. Install the thermostat housing.
6. Install and tighten the fasteners.
7. Fill the cooling system with approved antifreeze.

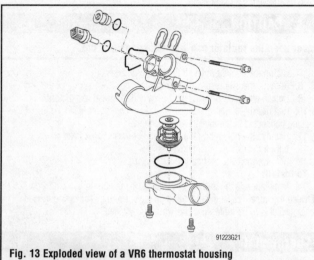

Fig. 13 Exploded view of a VR6 thermostat housing

91223G21

Fox

♦ **See Figures 14 thru 19**

1. The thermostat is in the bottom of the water pump housing and the lower radiator hose connects to the thermostat housing. Place a large drain pan under the thermostat housing. On some models, it will be necessary to position the power steering pump aside.
2. Remove the radiator cap and drain the cooling system.
3. Loosen one bolt at a time until coolant begins to flow. Allow this residual coolant to drain into a pan.
4. Remove both bolts, then remove the thermostat. It's not necessary to disconnect the radiator hose.
5. Discard the O-ring on the thermostat housing.

To install:

6. Place the thermostat into the water pump housing, then install the new O-ring. Install the housing and torque the bolts to 7 ft. lbs. (10 Nm).
7. Fill the cooling system. Start the engine and check for leaks.

Intake Manifold

REMOVAL & INSTALLATION

♦ **See Figures 20 thru 32**

1. Disconnect the negative battery cable.
2. Remove the engine cover as required.
3. Remove the air duct from the throttle body and disconnect the accelerator cable.
4. Label and disconnect the vacuum and coolant hoses as required.
5. Label and disconnect any remaining wiring as required.
6. Disconnect the fuel supply and return lines.
7. Disconnect any intake manifold support brackets.
8. If equipped, disconnect the EGR pipe.

Fig. 14 If necessary, remove the power steering pump

86633046

Fig. 15 Hang the pump with a wire and position it aside

86633047

Fig. 16 The thermostat housing is secured by two bolts

86633048

Fig. 17 Slowly pull the housing away from the engine. Stand back and allow any residual coolant to drain into a pan

86633049

Fig. 18 Pull the thermostat out of the water pump housing. Once again, stand back to allow any left over coolant to drain

86633050

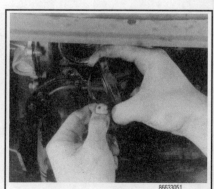

Fig. 19 Always replace the O-ring on the thermostat housing

86633051

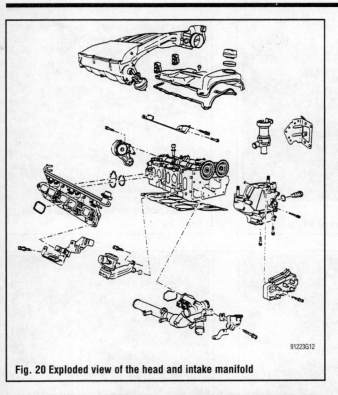

Fig. 20 Exploded view of the head and intake manifold

Fig. 23 Exploded view of the intake manifold mounting and related components—2.0L (ABA) engine

Fig. 21 Vacuum hose removal pliers such as these greatly speed up head removal

Fig. 24 2.0L, 8 valve upper intake manifold

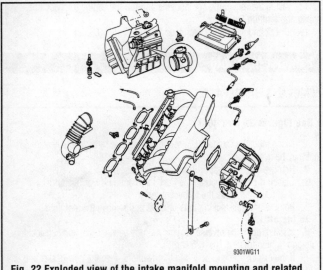

Fig. 22 Exploded view of the intake manifold mounting and related components—1.8L engine

Fig. 25 2.0L, 8 valve upper intake manifold bolt locations

Fig. 26 Lifting the upper intake manifold from its lower portion—2.0L, 8 valve engine

Fig. 27 Upper intake manifold gasket

Fig. 28 Location of the lower intake manifold bolts

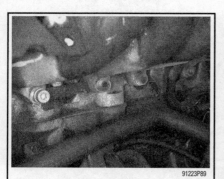

Fig. 29 There are a few intake manifold to cylinder head bolts that are hidden under the runners

Fig. 30 Once all bolts have been removed, remove the intake manifold

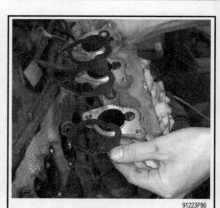

Fig. 31 Intake manifold to head gasket

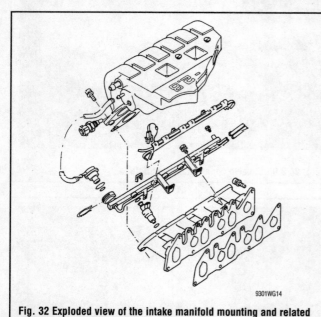

Fig. 32 Exploded view of the intake manifold mounting and related components—2.8L (AAA) engine

9. If equipped, remove the bolts to separate the upper intake manifold from the lower intake manifold.

10. Remove the bolts and remove the manifold from the cylinder head.

11. Place clean shop rags into the cylinder head openings to prevent dirt and debris from entering the engine.

To install:

12. Install the intake manifold(s) to the cylinder head with a new gasket(s). Tighten the bolts as follows:

- 1.8L and 2.8L (AHA) engines: 84 inch lbs. (10 Nm)
- 2.0L (ABA and AEG) engine upper and lower mounting bolts: 15 ft. lbs. (20 Nm)
- 2.8L (AAA) engine upper and lower mounting bolts: 18 ft. lbs. (25 Nm)

13. On 6-cylinder engines, if the fuel injectors were removed, examine the injector O-rings and replace as required. Install the injectors and rail.

14. Connect fuel system hoses or install the injectors now to protect the system.

15. Connect all vacuum hoses and wiring.

16. If equipped, connect the EGR pipe.

17. Connect and adjust the throttle cable as required.

18. Install the remaining components and run the engine to check idle speed and ignition timing.

19. Check and clear any Diagnostic Trouble Codes (DTCs).

Exhaust Manifold

REMOVAL & INSTALLATION

▶ See Figures 33 thru 46

1. Disconnect the Oxygen (O_2) sensor wiring and remove any heatshields that may be in the way.

2. Remove exhaust support brackets as necessary.

3. Detach the front exhaust pipe from the manifold or turbocharger.

4. If equipped, remove the turbocharger.

5. Remove the self-locking nuts or bolts and remove the manifold.

To install:

6. Installation is the reverse of removal. Use new gaskets and self-locking nuts and tighten to 18 ft. lbs. (25 Nm).

7. If the exhaust pipe is bolted to the manifold, install a new gasket and use new self-locking nuts. Tighten the nuts to 30 ft. lbs. (40 Nm).

8. Check and clear any Diagnostic Trouble Codes (DTCs).

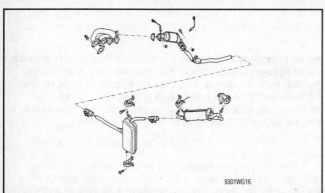

Fig. 33 Exploded view of the exhaust manifold mounting and related components—1.8L engine

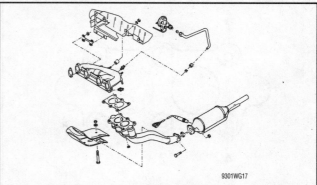

Fig. 34 Exploded view of the exhaust manifold mounting and related components—2.0L (ABA) engine

Fig. 35 Remove the emissions testing tube

Fig. 36 Heat shield bolt location

Fig. 37 Remove the exhaust manifold heat riser by sliding it towards the firewall and then pulling it up and out

Fig. 38 Once the exhaust manifold bolts have been removed, pull the manifold toward the fire wall and then out

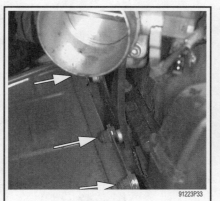

Fig. 39 It is advised that you replace the exhaust manifold gasket every time the manifold is removed. This will ensure a tight seal to the head

Fig. 40 View of exhaust manifold to down pipe gasket

Fig. 41 Exhaust manifold bolts are subject to extreme amounts of heat. This may lead them to break off upon removal. You may have to drill out the broken stud

Fig. 42 Always use two hands when using and easy out or screw extractor

Fig. 43 Slowly turn the screw extractor into the screw. The use of a penetrating oil is recommended

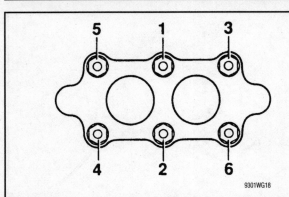

Fig. 44 Exhaust pipe-to-manifold torque sequence—2.0L (ABA) engine

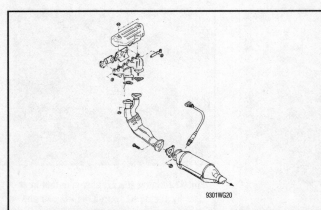

Fig. 45 Exploded view of the exhaust manifold mounting and related components—2.8L (AAA) engine

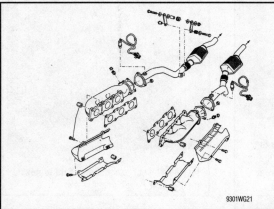

Fig. 46 Exploded view of the exhaust manifold mounting and related components—2.8L (AHA) engine

Turbocharger

REMOVAL & INSTALLATION

Turbochargers are subject to enormous amounts of heat and friction due to the speeds at which they operate. On some models the turbine shaft can rotate at speeds up to 70,000 rpm. Most turbo's are cooled and lubricated by a oil supply line from the vehicles engine that feeds the unit a fresh stream of filtered oil. There is also a return line back to the oil pan. The oil in this feed line is the life line of the turbocharger. Its like blood is to a human being, without it, the turbo will cease to operate. This is just another example of why it is important

that you change the oil at the manufacturers recommended intervals. If sludge formed in these lines and reduced the flow, the turbocharger unit would wear out very rapidly.

➡️**If the turbo charger is being replaced, the oil lines going to and from it must be removed and cleaned. If cleaning the lines is not enough, then they must be replaced. Also if the turbocharger is being replaced due to excessive exhaust smoke, there may still be some oil in the exhaust system once the new turbo has been installed. You may have to drive the vehicle for a few miles before this smoke clears.**

1. Disconnect the negative battery cable. If equipped with an automatic transaxle, remove the starter.
2. Remove the nuts to disconnect the exhaust outlet pipe from the turbocharger outlet. If it's necessary to separate the exhaust pipe from the outlet pipe, follow the procedure is described in exhaust manifold removal for gasoline engines before removing the outlet pipe.
3. Clean the oil supply fitting on the top of the turbocharger and remove the supply line and bracket.
4. Remove the inlet air duct.
5. Under the vehicle, remove the oil return line and the turbocharger mounting bracket.
6. Still underneath, remove the turbo-to-manifold bolts and lift the turbocharger out from the top. The exhaust manifold can be removed after removing the EGR valve.

To install:

7. If removed, install the exhaust manifold with a new gasket and torque the bolts to 18 ft. lbs. (25 Nm).
8. Use a new gasket and fit the turbocharger to the manifold. Coat the bolt threads with anti-seize and torque the turbocharger bolts to 33 ft. lbs. (45 Nm) and the bracket nuts to 18 ft. lbs. (25 Nm).
9. Use a new gasket and connect the oil return line. Torque the bolts to 22 ft. lbs. (30 Nm).
10. Use a new gasket and connect the outlet pipe. Torque the nuts to 18 ft. lbs. (25 Nm).
11. Connect the oil supply line, install the EGR valve.

Radiator and Fan Assembly

REMOVAL & INSTALLATION

▶ **See Figures 47 thru 60**

1. Disconnect the wiring from the cooling fan and remove the thermostat housing to drain the cooling system.
2. If the air conditioning coolant hose runs above the radiator, remove the shroud mounting bolts and move the fan and shroud assembly away from the radiator.
3. Disconnect the radiator hoses and the overflow hose.
4. Remove the upper brackets bolts and lift the radiator out. If the air conditioning hose does not interfere, the shroud and fan can be removed with the radiator.

To install:

5. Installation is the reverse of removal. After filling the cooling system, run the engine until the fan runs once and check the coolant level again.

Oil Cooler

REMOVAL & INSTALLATION

1. Remove the thermostat to drain the cooling system.
2. Remove the oil filter.
3. Disconnect the hoses from the cooler.
4. Remove the nut holding the cooler to the oil filter base and remove the cooler.

To install:

5. Installation is the reverse of removal. Connect the coolant hoses before tightening the nut.

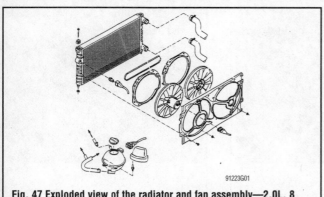

Fig. 47 Exploded view of the radiator and fan assembly—2.0L, 8 valve

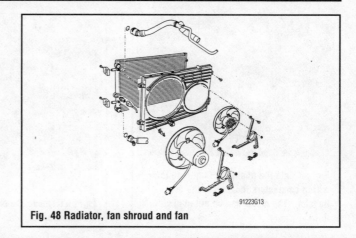

Fig. 48 Radiator, fan shroud and fan

Fig. 49 Detach all wiring harnesses necessary for radiator removal

Fig. 50 Use caution not to snap off any plastic wiring clips

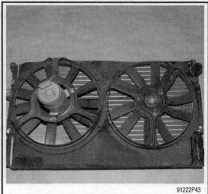

Fig. 51 The radiator fan assembly

Fig. 52 Remove the fasteners and then the fan assembly from the radiator

Fig. 53 The secondary fan is driven by a belt via the primary motor

Fig. 54 Remove the secondary fan rubber drive belt

Fig. 55 Detach the plastic retaining ring

Fig. 56 To remove the fan blades, detach the locking ring tab and then the center nut

Fig. 57 View of fan blade nut and locking tab

Fig. 58 Note the position of the fan motor wiring connectors location to the steel housing. The motor can be put in upside down

Fig. 59 Remove the electric fan motor mounting bolts

Fig. 60 Remove the radiator fan motor

Water Pump

REMOVAL & INSTALLATION

Gasoline 4 cyl.

▶ **See Figure 61**

➡ Complete failure of the water pump is not normally the case. Although after many miles coolant may begin to leak from the pump shaft. The pump must be replaced if it is leaking coolant.

1. Remove the expansion tank cap.

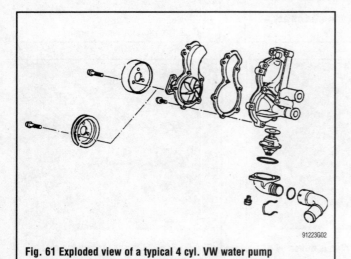

Fig. 61 Exploded view of a typical 4 cyl. VW water pump

☀☀ CAUTION

Do not remove the expansion tank cap if the engine is hot. Hot coolant can cause harm. Always allow the engine to cool before performing any work to the cooling system.

2. Set the heater control to the hot position.
3. Place a drain pan under the water pump.
4. Remove the attaching clip from the connector pipe that is going into the water pump.
5. Pull the connecting pipe from the water pump and allow the coolant to drain into the drain pan below.
6. Remove the negative battery cable.

➡ Always know the anti-theft code before disconnecting the negative battery cable.

1.9L (AAZ) Diesel Engine

▶ **See Figure 62**

On some Diesel engines, the belt tension is adjusted with shims between the outer and inner halves of the pulley. On others, the alternator swivels to adjust belt tension.

1. To drain the cooling system, remove the thermostat housing from under the water pump housing.
2. Raise and safely support the vehicle.
3. Working under the vehicle, loosen but don't remove the bolts holding the pulley to the water pump.
4. On vehicles with a movable alternator, loosen the alternator and remove the drive belt.
5. Remove the water pump pulley and remove the pump.
To install:
6. Installation is the reverse of removal. Be sure to clean the pump housing before installing the new gasket. Tighten the following:
   • Water pump-to-housing—7 ft. lbs. (10 Nm)
   • Water pump drive pulley—15 ft. lbs. (20 Nm)
   • Thermostat housing—7 ft. lbs. (10 Nm)
   • Alternator mounting bolts—18 ft. lbs. (25 Nm)

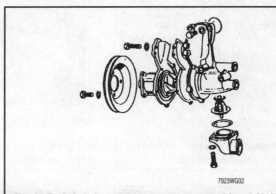

Fig. 62 Exploded view of the water pump assembly—1.9L (AAZ) engine

1.9L (AHH) Engine

▶ **See Figures 63 and 64**

1. Disconnect the negative battery cable.
2. Remove the engine cover and under cover.
3. Drain and recycle the engine coolant.
4. Position the lock carrier into the service position, as follows:
   a. Remove the front bumper.
   b. Tag and remove any wiring or connector that would inhibit locking the carrier.
   c. Remove the three quick-release screws on the front noise insulation panel.

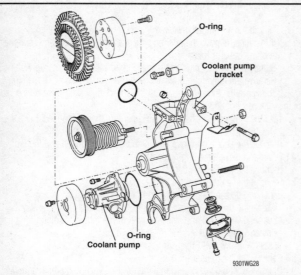

Fig. 63 Exploded view of the coolant pump, bracket and related components—1.9L (AHH) engine

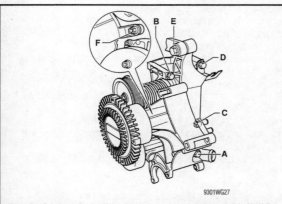

Fig. 64 Coolant pump bracket torque sequence—1.9L (AHH) engine

   d. Unbolt the air guide between the lock carrier and the air filter.

   e. If installed, remove the retaining clamps for the wiring harness at the left side of the radiator frame.

   f. Remove the No. 2 bolts and install Support tool 3369 or equivalent.

   g. Remove the remaining bolts and pull the lock carrier out to the stop.

   h. To secure the lock carrier, install the appropriate M6 bolts into the rear of the lock carrier and fender.

   5. Remove the accessory drive belt, fan clutch and belt pulleys.

   6. If necessary, remove the drive belt tensioner.

   7. Remove the coolant pump assembly bracket.

   8. Remove the coolant pump from the bracket.

   9. Clean all gasket and sealing surfaces.

To install:

   10. Using a new O-ring, install the coolant pump onto the bracket and tighten the mounting bolts to 7 ft. lbs. (10 Nm).

   11. Using a new gasket and O-ring, install the coolant pump bracket and tighten the mounting bolts in alphabetical sequence to 18 ft. lbs. (25 Nm).

   12. Tighten the coolant pump housing to the timing belt cover mounting bolt (F) to 7 ft. lbs. (10 Nm).

   13. If removed, install the drive belt tensioner.

   14. Install the belt pulleys, fan clutch and accessory drive belt.

   15. Return the lock carrier into the normal position.

   16. Fill the engine with coolant.

   17. Connect the negative battery cable.

   18. Start the vehicle and check for leaks.

   19. Install the engine cover and under cover.

   20. Check and clear any Diagnostic Trouble Codes (DTCs).

VR6

➡**To remove the coolant pump on VR6 engines you will need special engine lifting equipment.**

   1. Remove the negative battery cable.

➡**Always have the vehicle's antitheft code on hand before disconnecting the battery cable.**

   2. Drain the cooling system.

   3. Remove the air cleaner assembly.

   4. Loosen the coolant pump bolts once the accessory drive belt is loosened but still installed.

➡**It may be necessary to apply some pressure to the drive belt to keep the pulley from spinning.**

   5. Remove the drive belt from the pulleys once the direction of the belt has been marked.

   6. Separate the exhaust pipe from the catalytic converter.

   7. Unbolt and relocate the coolant reservoir out of your way.

   8. Raise the engine slightly.

   9. Remove the bolts from the right and left rear engine mounts.

   10. Remove the coolant pump mounting bolts.

   11. Raise the engine just enough that the water pump can be removed.

To install:

   12. Clean all surfaces of the pump and the mounting area before installing the pump.

   13. Align the engine on its mounts using the engine alignment procedure.

   14. The remainder of the procedure is the reverse of removal.

Cylinder Head

REMOVAL & INSTALLATION

◆ **See Figures 65, 66, 67 and 68**

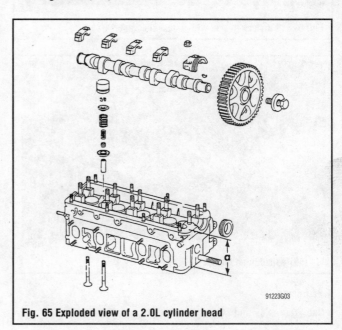

Fig. 65 Exploded view of a 2.0L cylinder head

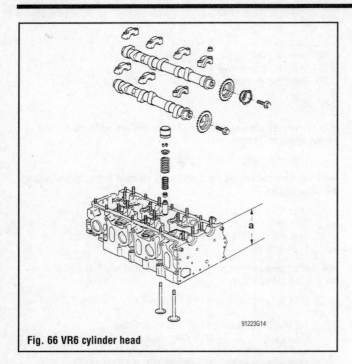

Fig. 66 VR6 cylinder head

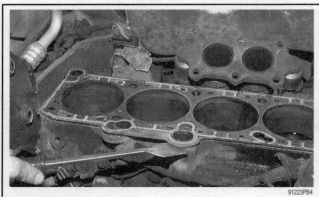

Fig. 67 Lift a stuck gasket with a gasket scraper

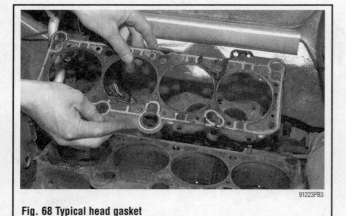

Fig. 68 Typical head gasket

1.8L Engine

▶ See Figures 69 and 70

1. Place the lock carrier into the service position as follows:
   a. Remove the front bumper.
   b. Tag and remove any wiring or connector that would inhibit locking the carrier.

   c. Remove the three quick-release screws on the front noise insulation panel.
   d. Unbolt the air guide between the lock carrier and the air filter.
   e. If installed, remove the retaining clamps for the wiring harness at the left side of the radiator frame.
   f. Remove the No. 2 bolts and install Support 3369 or equivalent.
   g. Remove the remaining bolts and pull the lock carrier out to the stop.
   h. To secure the lock carrier, install the appropriate M6 bolts into the rear of the lock carrier and fender.
2. Turn the ignition switch to the **OFF** position, then disconnect the negative battery cable.
3. Remove the accessory drive belt, then the engine driven cooling fan.
4. Drain and recycle the engine coolant.
5. Remove the intake manifold.
6. Remove the accessory drive belts.
7. Label and detach the following lines and electrical connectors:
   - Wastegate bypass regulator valve
   - Evaporative Emission (EVAP) canister purge regulator valve
   - Power outage stage
   - Mass Air Flow (MAF) sensor
8. Remove the air cleaner housing.
9. Detach the Engine Coolant Temperature (ECT) and the temperature II sensor harness connector.
10. Label and detach all connections from the cylinder head and position them aside.
11. Remove the crankcase breather line.
12. Disconnect the fuel supply and return lines.
13. Disconnect the oil supply line at the cylinder head.
14. Remove the exhaust manifold heat shield.
15. Unbolt the turbocharger from the exhaust manifold.
16. Disconnect the coolant hose to the heat exchanger at the rear of the cylinder head.
17. Remove the upper timing belt cover.
18. Turn the crankshaft, in the direction of rotation (clockwise), until the No. 1 cylinder is at Top Dead Center (TDC).
19. Using a T45 Torx® wrench, loosen the timing belt tensioner.
20. Push down on the tensioner, and remove the belt from the camshaft gear.
21. Remove the Torx® bolt and swing the tensioner assembly bracket forward.
22. Remove the valve cover.
23. Remove the cylinder head bolts in sequence, as shown.
24. Remove the cylinder head, then clean the gasket mating surfaces.
25. Clean and dry out the cylinder head bolt holes.

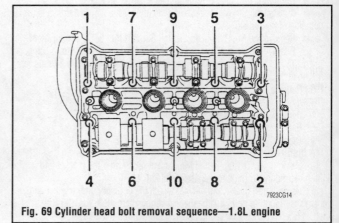

Fig. 69 Cylinder head bolt removal sequence—1.8L engine

To install:

✳✳ WARNING

Always replace the cylinder head bolts. Always replace self-locking nuts, bolts, gaskets and O-rings. Do not remove the new head gasket from the package until immediately before installing.

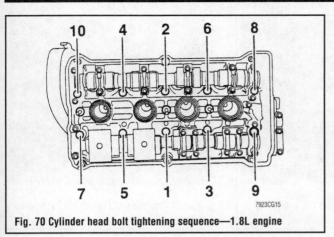

Fig. 70 Cylinder head bolt tightening sequence—1.8L engine

26. Before installing the cylinder head, be sure NO pistons are at TDC.

27. Loosen the turbocharger support bracket to reduce the likelihood of any tension while installing the cylinder head.

28. Install the head gasket with the part number visible from the intake side.

29. Install the cylinder head.

30. Install the new cylinder head bolts and tighten by hand.

31. Tighten the new cylinder head bolts in sequence in two steps:

   a. Tighten all of the bolts to 44 ft. lbs. (60 Nm).

   b. Tighten all of the bolts an additional ½ turn (180°).

➡It is not necessary to retighten the cylinder head bolts.

32. Using new gaskets, install the turbocharger to the exhaust manifold, coat the bolts with Hot Bolt Paste G 052 112 A3 (or equivalent), then tighten the mounting bolts to 26 ft. lbs. (35 Nm). Tighten the turbo support bracket mounting bolts to 33 ft. lbs. (40 Nm).

33. Install the valve cover.

34. Install the timing belt.

35. Install the accessory drive belts.

36. Install the exhaust manifold heat shield.

37. Connect the oil supply lines to the cylinder head and tighten the retaining straps to 15 ft. lbs. (20 Nm).

38. Install the crankcase breather.

39. Connect the fuel supply and return lines.

40. Attach any items removed during disassembly.

41. Connect the coolant temperature sensors, and install the air cleaner housing.

42. Fill the engine with coolant.

43. Connect the negative battery cable.

44. Fully close all power windows, operate all window switches for at least one second in the close direction to activate the one-touch opening/closing function

45. Check the oil level before starting the engine

46. Set the clock to the correct time.

➡Diagnostic Trouble Codes (DTCs) are stored when harness connectors are detached.

47. Read the DTCs and clear the fault codes.

48. Adjust the headlights.

2.0L

▶ See Figures 26, 27 and 71 thru 81

1. Disconnect the negative battery cable.

2. Open the radiator cap and drain the cooling system.

3. Disconnect the throttle cable. Label and disconnect all wiring and vacuum lines from the intake manifold.

4. Remove the upper intake manifold.

5. Disconnect the fuel supply and return lines.

6. Disconnect the radiator and heater hoses from the cylinder head.

7. Disconnect and label wiring for oil pressure and temperature sensors.

Fig. 71 Using rags or shop towels, plug the ports in the lower intake manifold to prevent foreign objects from entering

Fig. 72 Align the timing marks before removing any valve train components such as the timing belt

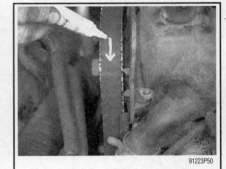

Fig. 73 It is always a good idea to mark the direction of the timing belt before removal

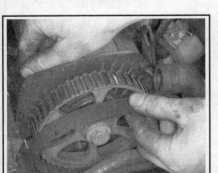

Fig. 74 Remove the timing belt once the tensioner has been released

Fig. 75 The head bolts are located in the sill below the arrow. Caution, many VW models use head bolts with a TORX® head. Use only the proper size tool when removing these bolts

Fig. 76 A long breaker bar is needed to attain enough leverage to break the head bolts free

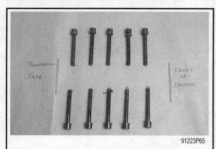

Fig. 77 Once all of the head bolts have been loosened in the proper sequence, remove them and place them in their equivalent position on a marked piece of paper or cardboard

Fig. 78 Pull the head from the vehicle as shown

Fig. 79 Remove and inspect the hydraulic lifters

Fig. 80 The head can be cleaned once it is removed using a parts washer such as this one from Safety Kleen®. If not accessible, your local machine shop should supply such services

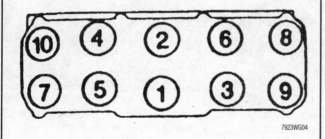

Fig. 81 Tighten the cylinder head bolts in the sequence shown— 2.0L (ABA) engine

8. Remove the distributor cap and wires.
9. Disconnect the exhaust pipe from the exhaust manifold.
10. If equipped, remove the EGR pipe from the exhaust manifold.
11. Remove the accessory drive belts and any accessory that is bolted to the head.
12. Remove the cylinder head cover, timing belt cover and belt.
13. Loosen the cylinder head bolts in the reverse of the tightening sequence.
14. Remove the bolts and lift the head straight off.

To install:

15. Before reinstalling the head, check the flatness of the head and block in both width and length, then diagonally from each corner.
16. Install the new cylinder head gasket with the word TOP or OPEN facing upward; do not use any sealing compound.

17. To align the cylinder head, install Guide Pins from tool 3070, or equivalent, into the holes for cylinder head bolts 8 and 10.
18. Install the cylinder head.
19. Install the cylinder head bolts, except 8 and 10, by hand.
20. Remove the Guide Pins using tool 3070 or equivalent, then install head bolts 8 and 10.
21. Tighten the head bolts in sequence in the following steps:
    a. With a torque wrench: 30 ft. lbs. (40 Nm).
    b. With a torque wrench: 44 ft. lbs. (60 Nm).
    c. With a standard wrench: ¼ turn (90°).
    d. With a standard wrench: an additional ¼ turn (90°).
22. Install the camshaft drive belt and adjust the tension.
23. Connect the exhaust pipe to the manifold. Use new gaskets and self-locking nuts and tighten to 18 ft. lbs. (25 Nm).
24. Connect the EGR pipe, if equipped.
25. Connect wiring to the oil pressure and temperature sensors.
26. Install the ignition system components.
27. Connect the radiator and heater hoses.
28. Connect the throttle cable and all wiring and vacuum lines.
29. Install the thermostat with a new O-ring. Tighten the housing bolts to 7 ft. lbs. (10 Nm). Refill the cooling system.
30. Install the accessory drive belts and adjust the tension.
31. Install the upper intake manifold.
32. Connect all wiring and vacuum lines disconnected from the intake manifold. Connect the throttle cable.
33. Connect the fuel supply and return lines.
34. Install the battery, if removed. Connect the negative and positive battery cables.
35. Refill and bleed the cooling system.
36. When everything has been properly installed and connected, be sure to change the oil and filter before starting the engine.

2.8L VR6

♦ See Figure 82

This procedure requires special tool 3268 or equivalent. This is a setting tool that holds the camshafts in the correct position for installing the timing chains. Before removing the cylinder head, be sure new bolts are available. The cylinder head bolts are made to stretch and cannot be used again.

1. Disconnect the battery cables and remove the battery.
2. Disconnect the wiring and vacuum lines as required to remove the air cleaner, Mass Air Flow (MAF) sensor and duct.
3. Open the radiator cap and remove the drain plug from the coolant pipe below the intake manifold to drain the cooling system.
4. Remove the engine trim cover. Remove the distributor cap, ignition wires and wire guide as an assembly.
5. Disconnect the throttle cable. Label and disconnect the wiring and vacuum lines from the intake manifold and remove the upper manifold.
6. The injectors and fuel rail assembly may be left on the manifold. Disconnect the fuel supply and return lines and the wiring connector for the injectors.
7. Disconnect the radiator and heater hoses.
8. Thread a long 8 x 10mm bolt into the accessory drive belt tensioner to release the tension. Move the tensioner only as required to remove the belt.

9. Remove the alternator and the belt tensioner.

10. Remove the heatshield and the bolts to disconnect the 2 piece exhaust manifold from the engine. Note the position of the gaskets.

11. Remove the distributor and the timing chain tensioner bolt from the timing chain cover.

12. Remove the cylinder head cover, upper timing chain cover and the retaining plate.

13. If possible, rotate the crankshaft to TDC of No. 1 piston. Clean the oil off the chain and sprockets and mark the direction of rotation for assembly.

14. Hold the camshafts at the flats with a 24mm wrench and remove the bolts to remove the sprockets and chain. Note the position of the distributor drive on the short camshaft.

✳✳ WARNING

Do not use the setting tool to hold the camshafts when removing or installing the sprocket bolts. The camshafts and the tool will be damaged.

15. Carefully check to be sure all necessary wires, hoses and brackets and components have been removed.

16. Loosen the cylinder head bolts in the reverse of the torque sequence. Remove and discard the bolts.

17. Remove the cylinder head.

To install:

18. Carefully clean the old gasket material from the head and the block. Before reinstalling the head, check the flatness of the head and block in both width and length, then diagonally from each corner. Maximum allowable distortion is 0.004 in. (0.1mm).

19. If the new head gasket already has sealant in the small holes at the timing chain end, remove the sealant. Apply a silicone sealer to the timing chain end and install the gasket onto the block with the word TOP or OPEN facing up.

20. Fit the cylinder head over the locating dowels and set the head onto the engine. Install new bolts and hand-tighten them. Do not attempt to re-use the old bolts.

21. Tighten the bolts in sequence as described in the following steps:
   a. Tighten all bolts to 30 ft. lbs. (40 Nm).
   b. Tighten all bolts to 44 ft. lbs. (60 Nm).
   c. Tighten all bolts an additional ¼ turn (90°).
   d. Tighten all bolts an additional ¼ turn (90°).

22. Be sure the crankshaft is at TDC on No. 1 piston. Install the setting tool to lock the camshafts in place, then install the timing chain and sprockets. Be sure they are positioned to rotate in the original direction.

23. Hold the camshaft with a 24mm wrench and install the sprocket bolt. Be sure the distributor drive is correctly positioned and tighten the bolts to 74 ft. lbs. (100 Nm).

24. Install the tensioner shoe and temporarily install the upper timing chain cover. Install the tensioner bolt and remove the setting tool. Rotate the crankshaft 4 full turns and stop at TDC of No. 1 piston. The setting tool should fit into the camshafts.

25. Remove the tensioner bolt and upper timing chain cover again. Apply new sealant as required, install the cover and tighten the bolts to 82 inch lbs. (10 Nm). Install the tensioner bolt and tighten to 15 ft. lbs. (20 Nm).

26. Install the cylinder head cover.

27. Use new gaskets and install the intake and exhaust manifolds. Tighten the nuts and bolts to 18 ft. lbs. (25 Nm).

28. Install the alternator belt and adjust tension.

29. Install the accessory drive belt and adjust tension.

30. Connect the radiator and heater hoses.

31. Install the injectors, fuel rail assembly and manifold. Connect the fuel supply and return lines. Connect the wiring connector for the injectors.

32. Install the upper manifold. Tighten the manifold bolts to 18 ft. lbs. (25 Nm).

33. Connect the wiring and vacuum lines disconnected from the intake manifold. Connect the throttle cable.

34. Install the distributor cap, ignition wires and wire guide as an assembly. Install the engine trim cover.

35. Disconnect the battery cables and remove the battery.

36. Refill and bleed the cooling system.

37. When everything has been properly installed and connected, be sure to change the oil and filter before starting the engine.

Oil Pan

REMOVAL & INSTALLATION

▶ **See Figures 83 thru 88**

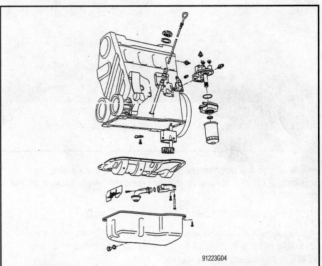

Fig. 83 Exploded view of the oil pan and the components of the oiling system—4 cyl engines

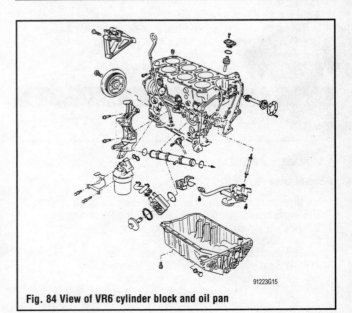

Fig. 84 View of VR6 cylinder block and oil pan

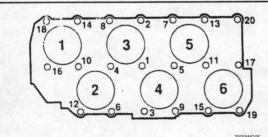

Fig. 82 Be sure to tighten the cylinder head bolts in the sequence shown—2.8L (AAA) engine

Fig. 85 The bolts at the flywheel side of the engine may be difficult to access

Fig. 86 Once all the bolts have been removed, lower the oil pan

Fig. 87 Due to extreme heat and pressure, the oil pan gasket may stick to the block and the pan. Do not pry on the pan or between the gasket and the block or the windage tray may bend

Fig. 88 The oil pump must be removed before you remove the oil windage tray

Fig. 89 A hex key is required to remove the oil pump pickup bolts

➥The oil pan can be removed with the engine in the vehicle. On some vehicles, it may be necessary to lower the subframe to service the oil pan.

1. Raise and safely support the vehicle and drain the oil.

➥On some VW 4 cyl. engines, it may be difficult to access the pan mounting bolts at the flywheel side of the engine. VW special tool #3185 or equivalent may be needed.

2. Loosen and remove the bolts retaining the oil pan.
3. Lower the pan from the engine.

To install:

4. Be sure the gasket surface is flat and install the pan with a new gasket.
5. Tighten the retaining bolts in a crisscross pattern as follows:
   • 2.0L (ABA) engine: 15 ft. lbs. (20 Nm)
   • 1.8L (AEB) and 2.8L (AAA) engine: 11 ft. lbs. (15 Nm)
6. Refill the engine with oil. Start the engine and check for leaks.

Oil Pump

REMOVAL & INSTALLATION

1.8L, 2.0L, and 2.8L Engines

▶ See Figures 89 thru 97

1. Raise and safely support the vehicle and remove the oil pan.
2. Remove the mounting bolts and lower the pump from the engine.
3. Install the oil pump in the reverse order of removal.
4. Observe the following values:
   • Oil pump bottom cover bolts—7 ft. lbs. (10 Nm)
   • Oil pump suction foot bolts—7 ft. lbs. (10 Nm)
   • Oil pump retaining bolts—18 ft. lbs. (25 Nm)

Fig. 90 Once the bolts have been removed, pull the oil pump pickup tube down and toward you. You may have to gently rock the tube to free it from the pump

Fig. 91 A ratchet and a socket can be used to speed the removal of the oil pump bolts

Fig. 92 As always, note the location and length of each bolt upon removal

Fig. 93 Remove the lower pump housing to inspect the gears

Fig. 94 A gear driven pump produces pressure by compressing the oil with the teeth of the gears as they spin

Fig. 95 Look for chips or teeth missing

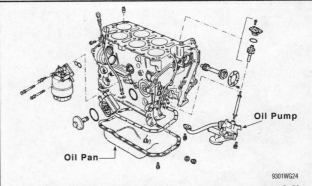

Fig. 97 Exploded view of the lubrication system components—2.8L (AAA) engine

Crankshaft Damper

REMOVAL & INSTALLATION

♦ **See Figures 98, 99 and 100**

1. Remove the negative battery cable.
2. Detach the wheel well splash shield if it interferes with damper removal.
3. Remove any engine accessory drive belts that are driven by the damper
4. Remove the crankshaft damper bolt(s).
5. Remove the crankshaft damper.

To install:

6. Installation is the reverse of removal.

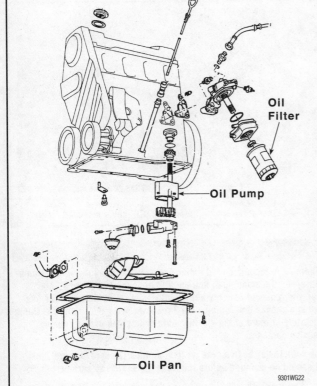

Fig. 96 Exploded view of the lubrication system components—1.8L engine, 2.0L (ABA) engine similar

Fig. 98 Hex keys may be required to remove the damper bolts

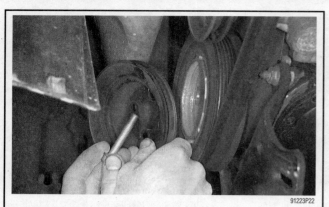

Fig. 99 Once loose, pull the bolts from the damper

Fig. 100 Remove the damper by sliding it off the crankshaft

Timing Belt Cover

REMOVAL & INSTALLATION

▶ **See Figures 101 thru 104**

1. Remove the accessory drive belts.
2. To remove the crankshaft accessory drive pulley, hold the center crankshaft sprocket bolt with a socket and loosen the pulley bolts.
3. The cover is now accessible. It comes off in 2 pieces, remove the upper half first. Take note of any special spacers or other hardware.

To install:

4. Installation is the reverse of removal.

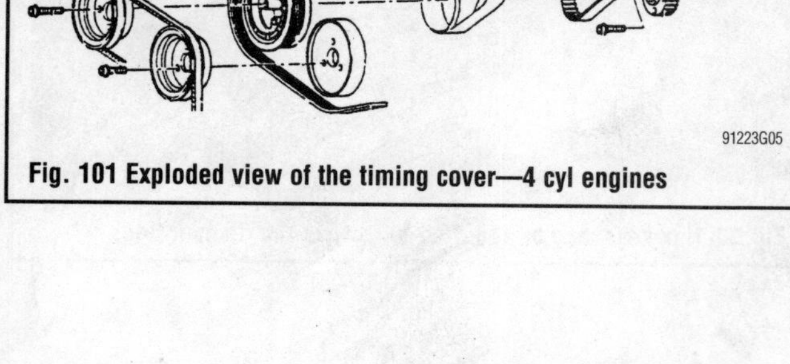

Fig. 101 Exploded view of the timing cover—4 cyl engines

Fig. 102 Remove the timing cover bolts

Fig. 103 Carefully pull the cover away from the belt

Fig. 104 View of the timing belt on a 2.0L—cover removed

Timing Belt

➡There is no recommended timing belt service interval from the manufacturer. We recommended that the belt be inspected every 30,000 miles and replaced at every 60,000 mile interval. If the belt stretches there is a chance that it may jump a tooth throwing the timing off. If this occurs one or more of the pistons could contact the valves causing extensive damage.

If the vehicle has been stored for long periods (2 years or more), the belt should be changed before returning the vehicle to service.

REMOVAL & INSTALLATION

➡ **Do not turn the engine or camshaft with the timing belt removed. The pistons will contact the valves and cause internal engine damage.**

Gasoline Engines

▶ **See Figures 105 thru 110 and 74**

1. Disconnect the negative battery cable and remove the accessory drive belts, crankshaft pulley and the timing belt cover(s).

2. Temporarily reinstall the crankshaft pulley bolt and turn the crankshaft to TDC of No. 1 piston. The mark on the camshaft sprocket should be aligned with the mark on the inner timing belt cover or the edge of the cylinder head.

3. With the distributor cap removed, the rotor should be pointing toward the No. 1 mark on the rim of the distributor housing. On 8 valve engines, the notch on the crankshaft pulley should align with the dot on the intermediate shaft sprocket.

4. Loosen the locknut on the tensioner pulley and turn the tensioner counterclockwise to relieve the tension on the timing belt.

5. Slide the timing belt from the sprockets.

To install:

6. Check the alignment of the timing marks. On 16 valve engines, the mark on the tooth should align with the mark on the rear belt cover.

7. Install the new timing belt and tension the belt so it can be twisted 90° at the middle of it's longest section, between the camshaft and intermediate sprockets.

8. Recheck the alignment of the timing marks and, if correct, turn the engine 2 full revolutions to return to TDC of No. 1 piston. Recheck belt tension and timing marks. Readjust as required. Torque the tensioner nut to 33 ft. lbs. (45 Nm).

9. Install the belt cover and accessory drive belts.

10. If the belt is too tight, there will be a growling noise that rises and falls with engine speed.

Diesel Engines

Some special tools are required. A flat bar, VW tool no. 2065A, is used to secure the camshaft in position. A pin, VW tool no. 2064, is used to fix the pump position while the timing belt is removed. The camshaft and pump work against spring pressure and will move out of position when the timing belt is removed. It is not difficult to find substitutes but do not remove the timing belt without these tools.

➡ **Do not turn the engine or camshaft with the timing belt removed. The pistons will contact the valves and cause internal engine damage.**

1. Disconnect the negative battery cable and remove the accessory drive belts, crankshaft pulley and the timing belt cover(s). Remove the camshaft cover and rubber plug at the back end of the camshaft.

2. Temporarily reinstall the crankshaft pulley bolt and turn the crankshaft to TDC of No. 1 piston. The mark on the camshaft sprocket should be aligned with the mark on the inner timing belt cover or the edge of the cylinder head.

3. With the engine at TDC, insert the bar into the slot at the back of the camshaft. The bar rests on the cylinder head to will hold the camshaft in position.

4. Insert the pin into the injection pump drive sprocket to hold the pump in position.

5. Loosen the locknut on the tensioner pulley and turn the tensioner counterclockwise to relieve the tension on the timing belt. Slide the timing belt from the sprockets.

To install:

6. Install the new timing belt and adjust the tension so the belt can be twisted 45 degrees at a point between the camshaft and pump sprockets. Torque the tensioner nut to 33 ft. (45 Nm).

7. Remove the holding tools.

8. Turn the engine 2 full revolutions to return to TDC of No. 1 piston. Recheck belt tension and timing mark alignment, readjust as required.

9. Install the belt cover and accessory drive belts.

10. If the belt is too tight, there will be a growling noise that rises and falls with engine speed.

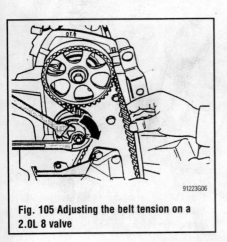

Fig. 105 Adjusting the belt tension on a 2.0L 8 valve

Fig. 106 Remove the timing belt cover

Fig. 107 Align the timing marks

Fig. 108 Locate the tensioner

Fig. 109 Loosen the tensioner bolt

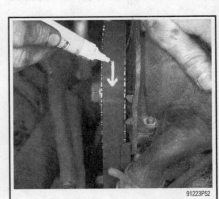

Fig. 110 Mark the belt's direction of rotation

Timing Sprockets

REMOVAL & INSTALLATION

▶ See Figure 111

➥The 12 point crankshaft sprocket bolt is meant to be used one time only and must be replaced when removed.

1. Remove the timing belt covers and the timing belt. The crankshaft sprocket should slide off easily when the center bolt is removed. Don't lose the Woodruff key.
2. Remove the cylinder head cover.
3. Use a wrench to hold the camshaft on the flat section and remove the sprocket retaining bolt.

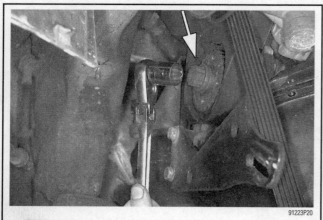

Fig. 111 View of the 12 point crankshaft sprocket

4. Gently pry or tap the sprocket off the shaft with a soft mallet. If the sprocket will not easily slide off the shaft, use a gear puller.

✳✳ WARNING

Do not hammer on the sprocket or damage to the sprocket or bearings could occur.

On 16 valve engines, make sure the camshaft sprockets are installed so that the curved portion of the sprocket key faces the surface of the engine block. If the sprocket is installed incorrectly, the timing will be advanced and cause the valves to hit the pistons.

5. Installation is the reverse of removal. On crankshaft sprocket bolts, oil the threads before installing the bolt. Torque the bolts as follows:
   - Camshaft sprocket on 8 valve gasoline engines—59 ft. lbs. (80 Nm).
   - Camshaft sprocket on 16 valve engines—48 ft. lbs. (65 Nm).
   - Camshaft sprocket on diesel engines—33 ft. lbs. (45 Nm)
   - Crankshaft sprocket 6 sided bolt—137 ft. lbs. (180 Nm).
   - Crankshaft sprocket 12 sided bolt—66 ft. lbs. (90 Nm) plus ½ turn.
   - Install the timing belt, check valve timing, adjust the belt tension, and install the covers.

Camshaft, Bearings and Lifters

REMOVAL & INSTALLATION

8 Valve Engine

▶ See Figures 112 thru 120

1. Disconnect the negative battery cable. Remove the timing belt cover(s), the timing belt, cylinder head cover and the camshaft sprocket.
2. Number the bearing caps from front to back. If the cap does not already have one, scribe an arrow pointing towards the front of the engine. The caps are

Fig. 112 Remove the nuts and washers noting their exact position

Fig. 113 Notice that some of the camshaft bearing caps have an integral nut/washer assembly

Fig. 114 Lift the bearing caps straight off the studs. Do not rock the caps side to side or the studs may bend

Fig. 115 Inspect the camshaft bearing caps for wear

Fig. 116 Lift the camshaft straight up once all the caps have been freed

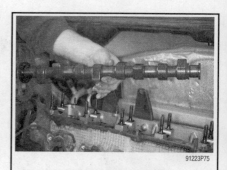

Fig. 117 After all the caps have been removed and placed in their correct position on a marked sheet of paper, remove the camshaft

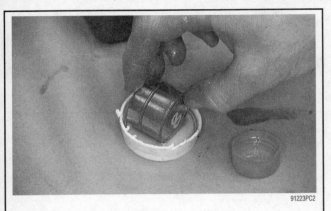

Fig. 118 Lubricate the hydraulic lifter. . .

Fig. 119 . . . then install it into the cylinder head

Fig. 120 Lifters reinstalled in the head in their correct positions

offset and must be installed correctly. Factory numbers on the caps are not always on the same side.

3. Remove the front and rear bearing caps. Loosen the remaining bearing cap nuts a little at a time to avoid bending the camshaft. Start from the outside caps near the ends of the head and work toward the center.

4. Remove the bearing caps and the camshaft.

To install:

5. Install a new oil seal and end plug in the cylinder head. Lubricate the camshaft bearing journals and lobes and set the camshaft in place.

6. Install the bearing caps in the correct position with the arrow pointing towards the front of the engine. Tighten the cap nuts diagonally and in several steps until they are torqued to 15 ft. lbs. (20 Nm). Do not over torque. Camshaft shaft endplay should be about 0.006 inches (0.15mm).

7. Install the drive sprocket and timing belt. Wait at least ½ an hour after installing camshaft shaft before starting the engine to allow the lifters to leak down.

16v Engines

1. Remove the timing belt cover.
2. Remove the upper intake manifold and cylinder head cover.
3. Turn the engine to TDC on cylinder No. 1, then slacken and remove the timing belt and camshaft sprocket.
4. With a felt marker only, matchmark the timing chain to the camshafts for reinstallation.
5. Remove the camshaft chain.
6. On the intake camshaft, remove bearing caps No. 5 and 7 and the chain end cap. Then loosen bearing caps No. 6 and 8 alternately and diagonally.
7. On the exhaust camshaft, remove bearing caps No. 1 and 3 and the end caps. Then loosen bearing caps No. 2 and 4 alternately and diagonally.
8. Remove the remaining bearing cap bolts and remove the camshafts.

To install:

9. Lubricate the camshaft bearing journals and lobes and set the camshafts in place. Install the camshaft drive chain so the marks on the chain sprockets are matched at the base of the cylinder head, directly across from each other.

➡ **When installing the bearing caps, make sure the notch points towards the intake side of the head.**

10. On the intake camshaft, install and torque bearing caps No. 6 and 8 alternately and diagonally to 11 ft. lbs. (15 Nm).
11. Install and torque the remaining intake camshaft bearing caps.
12. On the exhaust camshaft, torque bearing caps No. 2 and 4 alternately and diagonally to 11 ft. lbs. (15 Nm).
13. Install and torque the remaining exhaust camshaft bearing caps. Camshaft shaft end play on both camshafts should be about 0.006 inches (0.15mm).
14. Install the drive sprocket and timing belt.
15. Install remaining parts in reverse order of removal. Wait at least ½ hour after installing camshaft shafts before starting the engine to allow the hydraulic lifters to leak down.

INSPECTION

Degrease the camshaft using a safe solvent. Visually inspect the cam lobes and bearing journals for excessive wear. If a lobe is questionable or a bearing journal scored, the camshaft should be replaced. Check the lobes and journals with a micrometer. Measure the lobes from nose to heel. If all intake or all exhaust lobes do not measure the same, replace the camshaft. If the lobes and journals appear intact, place the front and rear journals in V-blocks. Position a dial indicator on the center journal and rotate the camshaft. If deviation exceeds 0.01mm (0.0004 inches) replace the camshaft.

Intermediate Shaft

REMOVAL & INSTALLATION

1. Remove timing belt cover(s), timing belt and intermediate shaft drive sprocket.
2. On 8 valve gasoline engines, remove distributor.
3. Remove the mounting flange retaining bolts. Reinstall sprocket bolt and remove the flange and shaft by pulling on the sprocket bolt.
4. Remove flange from the intermediate shaft and install new oil seal.

To install:

5. Install in reverse order of removal. Lubricate the oil seal lips. When installing the mounting flange, be sure to align the oil return hole at the bottom. Tighten the flange mounting bolts to 18 ft. lbs. (25 Nm).

Rear Main Seal

REMOVAL & INSTALLATION

▶ **See Figure 121**

The rear main oil seal is located in a housing on the rear of the cylinder block. To replace the seal on all vehicles it is necessary to remove the transaxle and flywheel.

Fig. 121 Typical VW rear main seal

1. Remove the transaxle and flywheel.
2. On 6-cylinder engines, pry the old seal out of the support ring.
3. On 4-cylinder engines, remove the oil seal with the mounting flange as a complete unit.

To install:

4. On 6-cylinder engines, oil the new seal and press it into place using tool VW-2003/2A, or equivalent, to start the seal and tool VW-2003/1, or equivalent, to seat the seal. Be careful not to damage the seal or score the crankshaft.

5. On 4-cylinder engines, install a new mounting flange with seal using a new gasket. Tighten the mounting flange bolts to 7 ft. lbs. (10 Nm).
6. Install the flywheel and transaxle.

Flywheel/Flexplate

REMOVAL & INSTALLATION

➡**The flywheel bolts are stretch bolts and cannot be used again once they have been removed. Make sure new bolts are on hand before removing the flywheel.**

1. On automatic transaxles, mark the flywheel so it can be installed with the same face towards the transaxle.
2. The flywheel bolts are secured with a thread locking compound and will be difficult to remove. Use VW tool 558 or an equivalent locking tool to hold the flywheel from turning.
3. Remove the bolts and remove the flywheel. Clean the thread locking compound out of the bolt holes in the crankshaft with a tap.
4. Before installing the automatic transaxle flywheel:
   - Temporarily install the flywheel with only 2 bolts.
   - Use a depth caliper to measure the distance between the outer face of the ring gear and the cylinder block.
   - The distance must be 1.20–1.28 inches (30.6–32mm). Remove the flywheel and change the shims as required.
   - Install the flywheel and apply a thread locking compound to the bolts. Torque the bolts in the sequence shown to 22 ft. lbs. (30 Nm). After tightening all the bolts, tighten them an additional ¼ turn in the same sequence.

EXHAUST SYSTEM

Inspection

◆ **See Figures 122 thru 129**

➡**Safety glasses should be worn at all times when working on or near the exhaust system. Older exhaust systems will almost always be covered with loose rust particles which will shower you when disturbed. These particles are more than a nuisance and could injure your eye.**

✳✳ CAUTION

DO NOT perform exhaust repairs or inspection with the engine or exhaust hot. Allow the system to cool completely before attempting any work. Exhaust systems are noted for sharp edges, flaking metal and rusted bolts. Gloves and eye protection are required. A healthy supply of penetrating oil and rags is highly recommended.

Your vehicle must be raised and supported safely to inspect the exhaust system properly. By placing 4 safety stands under the vehicle for support should provide enough room for you to slide under the vehicle and inspect the system completely. Start the inspection at the exhaust manifold or turbocharger pipe where the header pipe is attached and work your way to the back of the vehicle. On dual exhaust systems, remember to inspect both sides of the vehicle. Check the complete exhaust system for open seams, holes loose connections, or other deterioration which could permit exhaust fumes to seep into the passenger compartment. Inspect all mounting brackets and hangers for deterioration, some models may have rubber O-rings that can be overstretched and non-supportive. These components will need to be replaced if found. It has always been a practice to use a pointed tool to poke up into the exhaust system where the deterioration spots are to see whether or not they crumble. Some models may have heat shield covering certain parts of the exhaust system , it will be necessary to remove these shields to have the exhaust visible for inspection also.

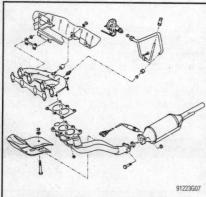

Fig. 122 Exploded view of a typical VW exhaust system

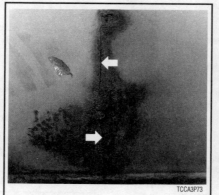

Fig. 123 Cracks in the muffler are a guaranteed leak

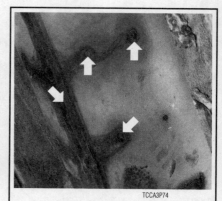

Fig. 124 Check the muffler for rotted spot welds and seams

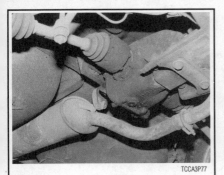

Fig. 125 Make sure the exhaust components are not contacting the body or suspension

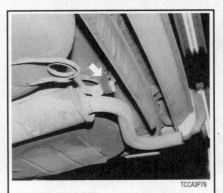

Fig. 126 Check for overstretched or torn exhaust hangers

Fig. 127 Example of a badly deteriorated exhaust pipe

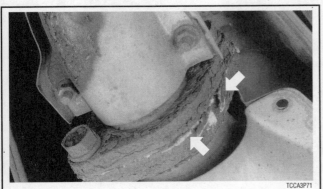

Fig. 128 Inspect flanges for gaskets that have deteriorated and need replacement

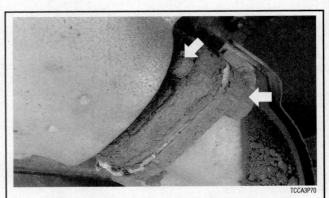

Fig. 130 Nuts and bolts will be extremely difficult to remove when deteriorated with rust

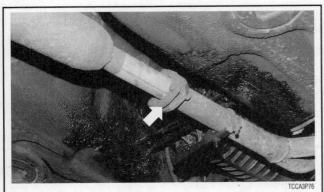

Fig. 129 Some systems, like this one, use large O-rings (doughnuts) in between the flanges

REPLACEMENT

▶ See Figure 130

There are basically two types of exhaust systems. One is the flange type where the component ends are attached with bolts and a gasket in-between. The other exhaust system is the slip joint type. These components slip into one another using clamps to retain them together.

✳✳ CAUTION

Allow the exhaust system to cool sufficiently before spraying a solvent exhaust fasteners. Some solvents are highly flammable and could ignite when sprayed on hot exhaust components.

Before removing any component of the exhaust system, ALWAYS squirt a liquid rust dissolving agent onto the fasteners for ease of removal. A lot of knuckle

skin will be saved by following this rule. It may even be wise to spray the fasteners and allow them to sit overnight.

Flange Type

▶ See Figures 131 and 132

✳✳ CAUTION

Do NOT perform exhaust repairs or inspection with the engine or exhaust hot. Allow the system to cool completely before attempting any work. Exhaust systems are noted for sharp edges, flaking metal and rusted bolts. Gloves and eye protection are required. A healthy supply of penetrating oil and rags is highly recommended. Never spray liquid rust dissolving agent onto a hot exhaust component.

Fig. 131 Example of a flange type exhaust system joint

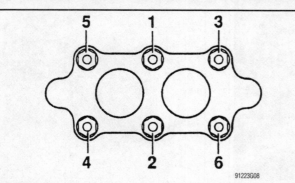

Fig. 132 When reinstalling a flange type exhaust connection such as this one, always follow a torque sequence that starts in the middle and works its way out

Before removing any component on a flange type system, ALWAYS squirt a liquid rust dissolving agent onto the fasteners for ease of removal. Start by unbolting the exhaust piece at both ends (if required). When unbolting the headpipe from the manifold, make sure that the bolts are free before trying to remove them. if you snap a stud in the exhaust manifold, the stud will have to be removed with a bolt extractor, which often means removal of the manifold itself. Next, disconnect the component from the mounting; slight twisting and turning may be required to remove the component completely from the vehicle. You may need to tap on the component with a rubber mallet to loosen the component. If all else fails, use a hacksaw to separate the parts. An oxy-acetylene cutting torch may be faster but the sparks are DANGEROUS near the fuel tank, and at the very least, accidents could happen, resulting in damage to the undercar parts, not to mention yourself.

Slip Joint Type

◆ See Figure 133

Before removing any component on the slip joint type exhaust system, ALWAYS squirt a liquid rust dissolving agent onto the fasteners for ease of removal. Start by unbolting the exhaust piece at both ends (if required). When unbolting the headpipe from the manifold, make sure that the bolts are free before trying to remove them. if you snap a stud in the exhaust manifold, the stud will have to be removed with a bolt extractor, which often means removal of the manifold itself. Next, remove the mounting U-bolts from around the exhaust pipe you are extracting from the vehicle. Don't be surprised if the U-bolts break while removing the nuts. Loosen the exhaust pipe from any mounting brackets retaining it to the floor pan and separate the components.

Fig. 133 Example of a common slip joint type system

ENGINE RECONDITIONING

Determining Engine Condition

Anything that generates heat and/or friction will eventually burn or wear out (for example, a light bulb generates heat, therefore its life span is limited). With this in mind, a running engine generates tremendous amounts of both; friction is encountered by the moving and rotating parts inside the engine and heat is created by friction and combustion of the fuel. However, the engine has systems designed to help reduce the effects of heat and friction and provide added longevity. The oiling system reduces the amount of friction encountered by the moving parts inside the engine, while the cooling system reduces heat created by friction and combustion. If either system is not maintained, a break-down will be inevitable. Therefore, you can see how regular maintenance can affect the service life of your vehicle. If you do not drain, flush and refill your cooling system at the proper intervals, deposits will begin to accumulate in the radiator, thereby reducing the amount of heat it can extract from the coolant. The same applies to your oil and filter; if it is not changed often enough it becomes laden with contaminates and is unable to properly lubricate the engine. This increases friction and wear.

There are a number of methods for evaluating the condition of your engine. A compression test can reveal the condition of your pistons, piston rings, cylinder bores, head gasket(s), valves and valve seats. An oil pressure test can warn you of possible engine bearing, or oil pump failures. Excessive oil consumption, evidence of oil in the engine air intake area and/or bluish smoke from the tailpipe may indicate worn piston rings, worn valve guides and/or valve seals. As a general rule, an engine that uses no more than one quart of oil every 1000 miles is in good condition. Engines that use one quart of oil or more in less than 1000 miles should first be checked for oil leaks. If any oil leaks are present, have them fixed before determining how much oil is consumed by the engine, especially if blue smoke is not visible at the tailpipe.

COMPRESSION TEST

A noticeable lack of engine power, excessive oil consumption and/or poor fuel mileage measured over an extended period are all indicators of internal engine wear. Worn piston rings, scored or worn cylinder bores, blown head gas-

kets, sticking or burnt valves, and worn valve seats are all possible culprits. A check of each cylinder's compression will help locate the problem.

Gasoline Engines

◆ See Figure 134

➡A screw-in type compression gauge is more accurate than the type you simply hold against the spark plug hole.

Although it takes slightly longer to use, it's worth the effort to obtain a more accurate reading.

1. Make sure that the proper amount and viscosity of engine oil is in the crankcase, then ensure the battery is fully charged.
2. Warm-up the engine to normal operating temperature, then shut the engine OFF.
3. Disable the ignition system.

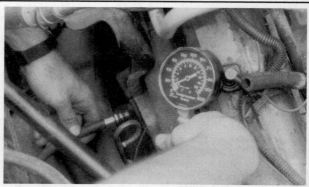

Fig. 134 A screw-in type compression gauge is more accurate and easier to use without an assistant

4. Label and disconnect all of the spark plug wires from the plugs.

5. Thoroughly clean the cylinder head area around the spark plug ports, then remove the spark plugs.

6. Set the throttle plate to the fully open (wide-open throttle) position. You can block the accelerator linkage open for this, or you can have an assistant fully depress the accelerator pedal.

7. Install a screw-in type compression gauge into the No. 1 spark plug hole until the fitting is snug.

❊❊ WARNING

Be careful not to crossthread the spark plug hole.

8. According to the tool manufacturer's instructions, connect a remote starting switch to the starting circuit.

9. With the ignition switch in the **OFF** position, use the remote starting switch to crank the engine through at least five compression strokes (approximately 5 seconds of cranking) and record the highest reading on the gauge.

10. Repeat the test on each cylinder, cranking the engine approximately the same number of compression strokes and/or time as the first.

11. Compare the highest readings from each cylinder to that of the others. The indicated compression pressures are considered within specifications if the lowest reading cylinder is within 75 percent of the pressure recorded for the highest reading cylinder. For example, if your highest reading cylinder pressure was 150 psi (1034 kPa), then 75 percent of that would be 113 psi (779 kPa). So the lowest reading cylinder should be no less than 113 psi (779 kPa).

12. If a cylinder exhibits an unusually low compression reading, pour a tablespoon of clean engine oil into the cylinder through the spark plug hole and repeat the compression test. If the compression rises after adding oil, it means that the cylinder's piston rings and/or cylinder bore are damaged or worn. If the pressure remains low, the valves may not be seating properly (a valve job is needed), or the head gasket may be blown near that cylinder. If compression in any two adjacent cylinders is low, and if the addition of oil doesn't help raise compression, there is leakage past the head gasket. Oil and coolant in the combustion chamber, combined with blue or constant white smoke from the tailpipe, are symptoms of this problem. However, don't be alarmed by the normal white smoke emitted from the tailpipe during engine warm-up or from cold weather driving. There may be evidence of water droplets on the engine dipstick and/or oil droplets in the cooling system if a head gasket is blown.

Diesel Engines

Checking cylinder compression on diesel engines is basically the same procedure as on gasoline engines except for the following:

1. A special compression gauge adapter suitable for diesel engines (because these engines have much greater compression pressures) must be used.

2. Remove the injector tubes and remove the injectors from each cylinder.

❊❊ WARNING

Do not forget to remove the washer underneath each injector. Otherwise, it may get lost when the engine is cranked.

3. When fitting the compression gauge adapter to the cylinder head, make sure the bleeder of the gauge (if equipped) is closed.

4. When reinstalling the injector assemblies, install new washers underneath each injector.

OIL PRESSURE TEST

Check for proper oil pressure at the sending unit passage with an externally mounted mechanical oil pressure gauge (as opposed to relying on a factory installed dash-mounted gauge). A tachometer may also be needed, as some specifications may require running the engine at a specific rpm.

1. With the engine cold, locate and remove the oil pressure sending unit.

2. Following the manufacturer's instructions, connect a mechanical oil pressure gauge and, if necessary, a tachometer to the engine.

3. Start the engine and allow it to idle.

4. Check the oil pressure reading when cold and record the number. You may need to run the engine at a specified rpm, so check the specifications.

5. Run the engine until normal operating temperature is reached (upper radiator hose will feel warm).

6. Check the oil pressure reading again with the engine hot and record the number. Turn the engine **OFF**.

7. Compare your hot oil pressure reading to that given in the chart. If the reading is low, check the cold pressure reading against the chart. If the cold pressure is well above the specification, and the hot reading was lower than the specification, you may have the wrong viscosity oil in the engine. Change the oil, making sure to use the proper grade and quantity, then repeat the test.

Low oil pressure readings could be attributed to internal component wear, pump related problems, a low oil level, or oil viscosity that is too low. High oil pressure readings could be caused by an overfilled crankcase, too high of an oil viscosity or a faulty pressure relief valve.

Buy or Rebuild?

Now that you have determined that your engine is worn out, you must make some decisions. The question of whether or not an engine is worth rebuilding is largely a subjective matter and one of personal worth. Is the engine a popular one, or is it an obsolete model? Are parts available? Will it get acceptable gas mileage once it is rebuilt? Is the car it's being put into worth keeping? Would it be less expensive to buy a new engine, have your engine rebuilt by a pro, rebuild it yourself or buy a used engine from a salvage yard? Or would it be simpler and less expensive to buy another car? If you have considered all these matters and more, and have still decided to rebuild the engine, then it is time to decide how you will rebuild it.

➡**The editors at Chilton feel that most engine machining should be performed by a professional machine shop. Don't think of it as wasting money, rather, as an assurance that the job has been done right the first time. There are many expensive and specialized tools required to perform such tasks as boring and honing an engine block or having a valve job done on a cylinder head. Even inspecting the parts requires expensive micrometers and gauges to properly measure wear and clearances. Also, a machine shop can deliver to you clean, and ready to assemble parts, saving you time and aggravation. Your maximum savings will come from performing the removal, disassembly, assembly and installation of the engine and purchasing or renting only the tools required to perform the above tasks. Depending on the particular circumstances, you may save 40 to 60 percent of the cost doing these yourself.**

A complete rebuild or overhaul of an engine involves replacing all of the moving parts (pistons, rods, crankshaft, camshaft, etc.) with new ones and machining the non-moving wearing surfaces of the block and heads. Unfortunately, this may not be cost effective. For instance, your crankshaft may have been damaged or worn, but it can be machined undersize for a minimal fee.

So, as you can see, you can replace everything inside the engine, but, it is wiser to replace only those parts which are really needed, and, if possible, repair the more expensive ones. Later in this section, we will break the engine down into its two main components: the cylinder head and the engine block. We will discuss each component, and the recommended parts to replace during a rebuild on each.

Engine Overhaul Tips

Most engine overhaul procedures are fairly standard. In addition to specific parts replacement procedures and specifications for your individual engine, this section is also a guide to acceptable rebuilding procedures. Examples of standard rebuilding practice are given and should be used along with specific details concerning your particular engine.

Competent and accurate machine shop services will ensure maximum performance, reliability and engine life. In most instances it is more profitable for the do-it-yourself mechanic to remove, clean and inspect the component, buy the necessary parts and deliver these to a shop for actual machine work.

Much of the assembly work (crankshaft, bearings, piston rods, and other components) is well within the scope of the do-it-yourself mechanic's tools and abilities. You will have to decide for yourself the depth of involvement you desire in an engine repair or rebuild.

TOOLS

The tools required for an engine overhaul or parts replacement will depend on the depth of your involvement. With a few exceptions, they will be the tools

found in a mechanic's tool kit (see Section 1 of this manual). More in-depth work will require some or all of the following:
- A dial indicator (reading in thousandths) mounted on a universal base
- Micrometers and telescope gauges
- Jaw and screw-type puller
- Scraper
- Valve spring compressor
- Ring groove cleaner
- Piston ring expander and compressor
- Ridge reamer
- Cylinder hone or glaze breaker
- Plastigage®
- Engine stand

The use of most of these tools is illustrated in this section. Many can be rented for a one-time use from a local parts jobber or tool supply house specializing in automotive work.

Occasionally, the use of special tools is called for. See the information on Special Tools and the Safety Notice in the front of this book before substituting another tool.

OVERHAUL TIPS

Aluminum has become extremely popular for use in engines, due to its low weight. Observe the following precautions when handling aluminum parts:
- Never hot tank aluminum parts (the caustic hot tank solution will eat the aluminum.
- Remove all aluminum parts (identification tag, etc.) from engine parts prior to the tanking.
- Always coat threads lightly with engine oil or anti-seize compounds before installation, to prevent seizure.
- Never overtighten bolts or spark plugs especially in aluminum threads.

When assembling the engine, any parts that will be exposed to frictional contact must be prelubed to provide lubrication at initial start-up. Any product specifically formulated for this purpose can be used, but engine oil is not recommended as a prelube in most cases.

When semi-permanent (locked, but removable) installation of bolts or nuts is desired, threads should be cleaned and coated with Loctite® or another similar, commercial non-hardening sealant.

CLEANING

▶ **See Figures 135, 136, 137 and 138**

Before the engine and its components are inspected, they must be thoroughly cleaned. You will need to remove any engine varnish, oil sludge and/or carbon deposits from all of the components to insure an accurate inspection. A crack in the engine block or cylinder head can easily become overlooked if hidden by a layer of sludge or carbon.

Most of the cleaning process can be carried out with common hand tools and readily available solvents or solutions. Carbon deposits can be chipped away using a hammer and a hard wooden chisel. Old gasket material and varnish or sludge can usually be removed using a scraper and/or cleaning solvent.

Extremely stubborn deposits may require the use of a power drill with a wire brush. If using a wire brush, use extreme care around any critical machined surfaces (such as the gasket surfaces, bearing saddles, cylinder bores, etc.). USE OF A WIRE BRUSH IS NOT RECOMMENDED ON ANY ALUMINUM COMPONENTS. Always follow any safety recommendations given by the manufacturer of the tool and/or solvent. You should always wear eye protection during any cleaning process involving scraping, chipping or spraying of solvents.

An alternative to the mess and hassle of cleaning the parts yourself is to drop them off at a local garage or machine shop. They will, more than likely, have the necessary equipment to properly clean all of the parts for a nominal fee.

❊❊ CAUTION

Always wear eye protection during any cleaning process involving scraping, chipping or spraying of solvents.

Remove any oil galley plugs, freeze plugs and/or pressed-in bearings and carefully wash and degrease all of the engine components including the fasteners and bolts. Small parts such as the valves, springs, etc., should be placed in a metal basket and allowed to soak. Use pipe cleaner type brushes, and clean all passageways in the components. Use a ring expander and remove the rings from the pistons. Clean the piston ring grooves with a special tool or a piece of broken ring. Scrape the carbon off of the top of the piston. You should never use a wire brush on the pistons. After preparing all of the piston assemblies in this manner, wash and degrease them again.

❊❊ WARNING

Use extreme care when cleaning around the cylinder head valve seats. A mistake or slip may cost you a new seat.

When cleaning the cylinder head, remove carbon from the combustion chamber with the valves installed. This will avoid damaging the valve seats.

TCCS3132

Fig. 135 Use a gasket scraper to remove the old gasket material from the mating surfaces

TCCS3211

Fig. 136 Use a ring expander tool to remove the piston rings

TCCS3208

Fig. 137 Clean the piston ring grooves using a ring groove cleaner tool, or . . .

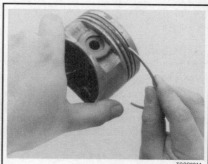

TCCS3911

Fig. 138 . . . use a piece of an old ring to clean the grooves. Be careful, the ring can be quite sharp

REPAIRING DAMAGED THREADS

▶ **See Figures 139 thru 146**

Several methods of repairing damaged threads are available. Heli-Coil® (shown here), Keenserts® and Microdot® are among the most widely used. All involve basically the same principle—drilling out stripped threads, tapping the hole and installing a prewound insert—making welding, plugging and oversize fasteners unnecessary.

Two types of thread repair inserts are usually supplied: a standard type for most inch coarse, inch fine, metric course and metric fine thread sizes and a spark lug type to fit most spark plug port sizes. Consult the individual tool manufacturer's catalog to determine exact applications. Typical thread repair kits will contain a selection of prewound threaded inserts, a tap (corresponding to the outside diameter threads of the insert) and an installation tool. Spark plug inserts usually differ because they require a tap equipped with pilot threads and a combined reamer/tap section. Most manufacturers also supply blister-packed thread repair inserts separately in addition to a master kit containing a variety of taps and inserts plus installation tools.

Before attempting to repair a threaded hole, remove any snapped, broken or damaged bolts or studs. Penetrating oil can be used to free frozen threads. The offending item can usually be removed with locking pliers or using a screw/stud extractor. After the hole is clear, the thread can be repaired, as shown in the series of accompanying illustrations and in the kit manufacturer's instructions.

Engine Preparation

To properly rebuild an engine, you must first remove it from the vehicle, then disassemble and diagnose it. Ideally you should place your engine on an engine stand. This affords you the best access to the engine components. Follow the manufacturer's directions for using the stand with your particular engine. Remove the flywheel or flexplate before installing the engine to the stand.

Fig. 139 Use a penetrating lubricant to help remove a bolt that has snapped off

Fig. 140 Using a screw extractor to remove a snapped exhaust manifold stud—1994 2.0L, 8 valve exhaust manifold

Fig. 141 The screw extractor did the job this time. Sometimes a technician must use other methods to remove a stuck bolt

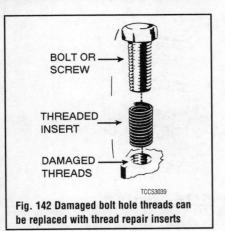
Fig. 142 Damaged bolt hole threads can be replaced with thread repair inserts

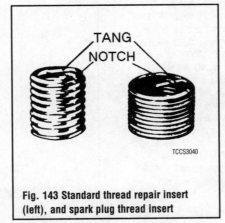
Fig. 143 Standard thread repair insert (left), and spark plug thread insert

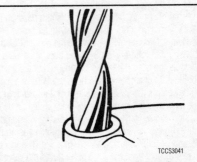
Fig. 144 Drill out the damaged threads with the specified size bit. Be sure to drill completely through the hole or to the bottom of a blind hole

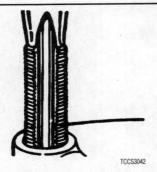
Fig. 145 Using the kit, tap the hole in order to receive the thread insert. Keep the tap well oiled and back it out frequently to avoid clogging the threads

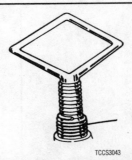
Fig. 146 Screw the insert onto the installer tool until the tang engages the slot. Thread the insert into the hole until it is ¼–½ turn below the top surface, then remove the tool and break off the tang using a punch

Now that you have the engine on a stand, and assuming that you have drained the oil and coolant from the engine, it's time to strip it of all but the necessary components. Before you start disassembling the engine, you may want to take a moment to draw some pictures, or fabricate some labels or containers to mark the locations of various components and the bolts and/or studs which fasten them. Modern day engines use a lot of little brackets and clips which hold wiring harnesses and such, and these holders are often mounted on studs and/or bolts that can be easily mixed up. The manufacturer spent a lot of time and money designing your vehicle, and they wouldn't have wasted any of it by haphazardly placing brackets, clips or fasteners on the vehicle. If it's present when you disassemble it, put it back when you assemble, you will regret not remembering that little bracket which holds a wire harness out of the path of a rotating part.

You should begin by unbolting any accessories still attached to the engine, such as the water pump, power steering pump, alternator, etc. Then, unfasten any manifolds (intake or exhaust) which were not removed during the engine removal procedure. Finally, remove any covers remaining on the engine such as the rocker arm, front or timing cover and oil pan. Some front covers may require the vibration damper and/or crank pulley to be removed beforehand. The idea is to reduce the engine to the bare necessities (cylinder head(s), valve train, engine block, crankshaft, pistons and connecting rods), plus any other 'in block' components such as oil pumps, balance shafts and auxiliary shafts.

Finally, remove the cylinder head(s) from the engine block and carefully place on a bench. Disassembly instructions for each component follow later in this section.

Cylinder Head

There are two basic types of cylinder heads used on today's automobiles: the Overhead Valve (OHV) and the Overhead Camshaft (OHC). The latter can also be broken down into two subgroups: the Single Overhead Camshaft (SOHC) and the Dual Overhead Camshaft (DOHC). Generally, if there is only a single camshaft on a head, it is just referred to as an OHC head. Also, an engine with an OHV cylinder head is also known as a pushrod engine.

Most cylinder heads these days are made of an aluminum alloy due to its light weight, durability and heat transfer qualities. However, cast iron was the material of choice in the past, and is still used on many vehicles today. Whether made from aluminum or iron, all cylinder heads have valves and seats. Some use two valves per cylinder, while the more hi-tech engines will utilize a multi-valve configuration using 3, 4 and even 5 valves per cylinder. When the valve contacts the seat, it does so on precision machined surfaces, which seals the combustion chamber. All cylinder heads have a valve guide for each valve. The guide centers the valve to the seat and allows it to move up and down within it. The clearance between the valve and guide can be critical. Too much clearance and the engine may consume oil, lose vacuum and/or damage the seat. Too little, and the valve can stick in the guide causing the engine to run poorly if at all, and possibly causing severe damage. The last component all cylinder heads have are valve springs. The spring holds the valve against its seat. It also returns the valve to this position when the valve has been opened by the valve train or camshaft. The spring is fastened to the valve by a retainer and valve locks (sometimes called keepers). Aluminum heads will also have a valve

spring shim to keep the spring from wearing away the aluminum.

An ideal method of rebuilding the cylinder head would involve replacing all of the valves, guides, seats, springs, etc. with new ones. However, depending on how the engine was maintained, often this is not necessary. A major cause of valve, guide and seat wear is an improperly tuned engine. An engine that is running too rich, will often wash the lubricating oil out of the guide with gasoline, causing it to wear rapidly. Conversely, an engine which is running too lean will place higher combustion temperatures on the valves and seats allowing them to wear or even burn. Springs fall victim to the driving habits of the individual. A driver who often runs the engine rpm to the redline will wear out or break the springs faster then one that stays well below it. Unfortunately, mileage takes it toll on all of the parts. Generally, the valves, guides, springs and seats in a cylinder head can be machined and re-used, saving you money. However, if a valve is burnt, it may be wise to replace all of the valves, since they were all operating in the same environment. The same goes for any other component on the cylinder head. Think of it as an insurance policy against future problems related to that component.

Unfortunately, the only way to find out which components need replacing, is to disassemble and carefully check each piece. After the cylinder head(s) are disassembled, thoroughly clean all of the components.

DISASSEMBLY

♦ See Figures 147, 148, 149 and 150

Whether it is a single or dual overhead camshaft cylinder head, the disassembly procedure is relatively unchanged. One aspect to pay attention to is careful labeling of the parts on the dual camshaft cylinder head. There will be an

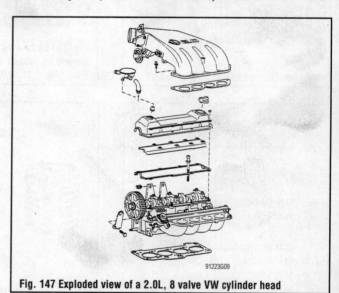

Fig. 147 Exploded view of a 2.0L, 8 valve VW cylinder head

Fig. 148 Exploded view of a valve, seal, spring, retainer and locks from an OHC cylinder head

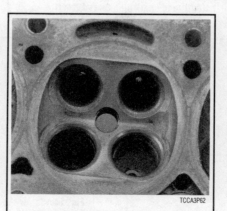

Fig. 149 Example of a multi-valve cylinder head. Note how it has 2 intake and 2 exhaust valve ports

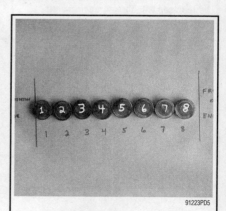

Fig. 150 Always number and label the position of each cylinder head part. This will ensure proper installation

intake camshaft and followers as well as an exhaust camshaft and followers and they must be labeled as such. In some cases, the components are identical and could easily be installed incorrectly. DO NOT MIX THEM UP! Determining which is which is very simple; the intake camshaft and components are on the same side of the head as was the intake manifold. Conversely, the exhaust camshaft and components are on the same side of the head as was the exhaust manifold.

Cup Type Camshaft Followers

▶ **See Figures 151, 152 and 153**

Most cylinder heads with cup type camshaft followers will have the valve spring, retainer and locks recessed within the follower's bore. You will need a C-clamp style valve spring compressor tool, an OHC spring removal tool (or equivalent) and a small magnet to disassemble the head.

1. If not already removed, remove the camshaft(s) and/or followers. Mark their positions for assembly.
2. Position the cylinder head to allow use of a C-clamp style valve spring compressor tool.

➡**It is preferred to position the cylinder head gasket surface facing you with the valve springs facing the opposite direction and the head laying horizontal.**

3. With the OHC spring removal adapter tool positioned inside of the follower bore, compress the valve spring using the C-clamp style valve spring compressor.
4. Remove the valve locks. A small magnetic tool or screwdriver will aid in removal.
5. Release the compressor tool and remove the spring assembly.
6. Withdraw the valve from the cylinder head.
7. If equipped, remove the valve seal.

Fig. 151 C-clamp type spring compressor and an OHC spring removal tool (center) for cup type followers

Fig. 152 Most cup type follower cylinder heads retain the camshaft using bolt-on bearing caps

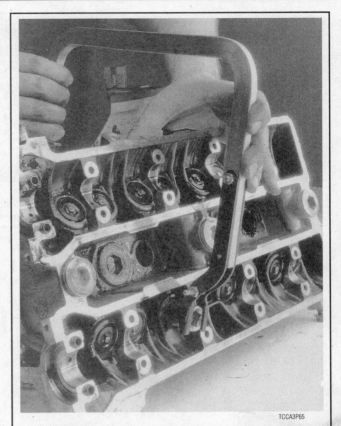

Fig. 153 Position the OHC spring tool in the follower bore, then compress the spring with a C-clamp type tool

➡**Special valve seal removal tools are available. Regular or needlenose type pliers, if used with care, will work just as well. If using ordinary pliers, be sure not to damage the follower bore. The follower and its bore are machined to close tolerances and any damage to the bore will effect this relationship.**

8. If equipped, remove the valve spring shim. A small magnetic tool or screwdriver will aid in removal.
9. Repeat Steps 3 through 8 until all of the valves have been removed.

Valves

▶ **See Figures 154, 155, 156, 157 and 158**

The first thing to inspect are the valve heads. Look closely at the head, margin and face for any cracks, excessive wear or burning. The margin is the best place to look for burning. It should have a squared edge with an even width all

Fig. 154 Close up of two valves seated in the cylinder head

Fig. 155 View: the top of the two valves installed on an 8 valve cylinder head

Fig. 156 Looking through the intake port of an 8 valve cylinder head

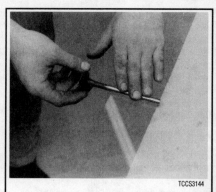

Fig. 157 Valve stems may be rolled on a flat surface to check for bends

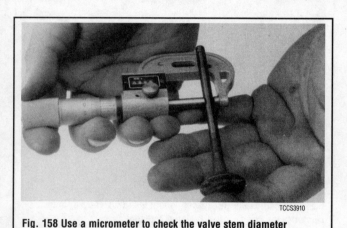

Fig. 158 Use a micrometer to check the valve stem diameter

around the diameter. When a valve burns, the margin will look melted and the edges rounded. Also inspect the valve head for any signs of tulipping. This will show as a lifting of the edges or dishing in the center of the head and will usually not occur to all of the valves. All of the heads should look the same, any that seem dished more than others are probably bad. Next, inspect the valve lock grooves and valve tips. Check for any burrs around the lock grooves, especially if you had to file them to remove the valve. Valve tips should appear flat, although slight rounding with high mileage engines is normal. Slightly worn valve tips will need to be machined flat. Last, measure the valve stem diameter with the micrometer. Measure the area that rides within the guide, especially towards the tip where most of the wear occurs. Take several measurements along its length and compare them to each other. Wear should be even along the length with little to no taper. If no minimum diameter is given in the specifications, then the stem should not read more than 0.001 in. (0.025mm) below the unworn area of the valve stem. Any valves that fail these inspections should be replaced.

Springs, Retainers and Valve Locks

♦ See Figures 159 and 160

The first thing to check is the most obvious, broken springs. Next check the free length and squareness of each spring. If applicable, insure to distinguish between intake and exhaust springs. Use a ruler and/or carpenter's square to measure the length. A carpenter's square should be used to check the springs for squareness. If a spring pressure test gauge is available, check each springs rating and compare to the specifications chart. Check the readings against the specifications given. Any springs that fail these inspections should be replaced.

The spring retainers rarely need replacing, however they should still be checked as a precaution. Inspect the spring mating surface and the valve lock retention area for any signs of excessive wear. Also check for any signs of cracking. Replace any retainers that are questionable.

Valve locks should be inspected for excessive wear on the outside contact area as well as on the inner notched surface. Any locks which appear worn or broken and its respective valve should be replaced.

Cylinder Head

There are several things to check on the cylinder head: valve guides, seats, cylinder head surface flatness, cracks and physical damage.

VALVE GUIDES

♦ See Figure 161

Now that you know the valves are good, you can use them to check the guides, although a new valve, if available, is preferred. Before you measure anything, look at the guides carefully and inspect them for any cracks, chips or breakage. Also if the guide is a removable style (as in most aluminum heads), check them for any looseness or evidence of movement. All of the guides should appear to be at the same height from the spring seat. If any seem lower (or higher) from another, the guide has moved. Mount a dial indicator onto the spring side of the cylinder head. Lightly oil the valve stem and insert it into the cylinder head. Position the dial indicator against the valve stem near the tip and

Fig. 159 Use a caliper to check the valve spring free-length

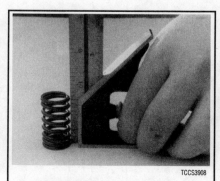

Fig. 160 Check the valve spring for squareness on a flat surface; a carpenter's square can be used

Fig. 161 A dial gauge may be used to check valve stem-to-guide clearance; read the gauge while moving the valve stem

zero the gauge. Grasp the valve stem and wiggle towards and away from the dial indicator and observe the readings. Mount the dial indicator 90 degrees from the initial point and zero the gauge and again take a reading. Compare the two readings for a out of round condition. Check the readings against the specifications given. An Inside Diameter (I.D.) gauge designed for valve guides will give you an accurate valve guide bore measurement. If the I.D. gauge is used, compare the readings with the specifications given. Any guides that fail these inspections should be replaced or machined.

VALVE SEATS

A visual inspection of the valve seats should show a slightly worn and pitted surface where the valve face contacts the seat. Inspect the seat carefully for severe pitting or cracks. Also, a seat that is badly worn will be recessed into the cylinder head. A severely worn or recessed seat may need to be replaced. All cracked seats must be replaced. A seat concentricity gauge, if available, should be used to check the seat run-out. If run-out exceeds specifications the seat must be machined (if no specification is given use 0.002 in. or 0.051mm).

CYLINDER HEAD SURFACE FLATNESS

▶ See Figures 162 and 163

After you have cleaned the gasket surface of the cylinder head of any old gasket material, check the head for flatness.

Place a straightedge across the gasket surface. Using feeler gauges, determine the clearance at the center of the straightedge and across the cylinder head at several points. Check along the centerline and diagonally on the head surface. If the warpage exceeds 0.003 in. (0.076mm) within a 6.0 in. (15.2cm) span, or 0.006 in. (0.152mm) over the total length of the head, the cylinder

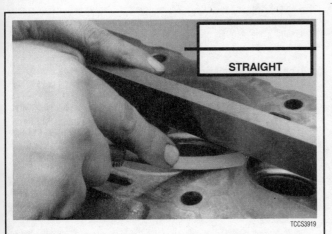

TCCS3919

Fig. 162 Check the head for flatness across the center of the head surface using a straightedge and feeler gauge

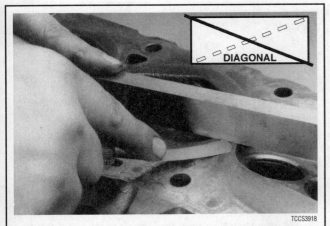

TCCS3918

Fig. 163 Checks should also be made along both diagonals of the head surface

head must be resurfaced. After resurfacing the heads of a V-type engine, the intake manifold flange surface should be checked, and if necessary, milled proportionally to allow for the change in its mounting position.

CRACKS AND PHYSICAL DAMAGE

Generally, cracks are limited to the combustion chamber, however, it is not uncommon for the head to crack in a spark plug hole, port, outside of the head or in the valve spring/rocker arm area. The first area to inspect is always the hottest: the exhaust seat/port area.

A visual inspection should be performed, but just because you don't see a crack does not mean it is not there. Some more reliable methods for inspecting for cracks include Magnaflux®, a magnetic process or Zyglo®, a dye penetrant. Magnaflux® is used only on ferrous metal (cast iron) heads. Zyglo® uses a spray on fluorescent mixture along with a black light to reveal the cracks. It is strongly recommended to have your cylinder head checked professionally for cracks, especially if the engine was known to have overheated and/or leaked or consumed coolant. Contact a local shop for availability and pricing of these services.

Physical damage is usually very evident. For example, a broken mounting ear from dropping the head or a bent or broken stud and/or bolt. All of these defects should be fixed or, if unrepairable, the head should be replaced.

Camshaft and Followers

Inspect the camshaft(s) and followers as described earlier in this section.

REFINISHING & REPAIRING

Many of the procedures given for refinishing and repairing the cylinder head components must be performed by a machine shop. Certain steps, if the inspected part is not worn, can be performed yourself inexpensively. However, you spent a lot of time and effort so far, why risk trying to save a couple bucks if you might have to do it all over again?

Valves

Any valves that were not replaced should be refaced and the tips ground flat. Unless you have access to a valve grinding machine, this should be done by a machine shop. If the valves are in extremely good condition, as well as the valve seats and guides, they may be lapped in without performing machine work.

It is a recommended practice to lap the valves even after machine work has been performed and/or new valves have been purchased. This insures a positive seal between the valve and seat.

LAPPING THE VALVES

➡ Before lapping the valves to the seats, read the rest of the cylinder head section to insure that any related parts are in acceptable enough condition to continue.

➡ Before any valve seat machining and/or lapping can be performed, the guides must be within factory recommended specifications.

1. Invert the cylinder head.
2. Lightly lubricate the valve stems and insert them into the cylinder head in their numbered order.
3. Raise the valve from the seat and apply a small amount of fine lapping compound to the seat.
4. Moisten the suction head of a hand-lapping tool and attach it to the head of the valve.
5. Rotate the tool between the palms of both hands, changing the position of the valve on the valve seat and lifting the tool often to prevent grooving.
6. Lap the valve until a smooth, polished circle is evident on the valve and seat.
7. Remove the tool and the valve. Wipe away all traces of the grinding compound and store the valve to maintain its lapped location.

✳✳ WARNING

Do not get the valves out of order after they have been lapped. They must be put back with the same valve seat with which they were lapped.

Springs, Retainers and Valve Locks

There is no repair or refinishing possible with the springs, retainers and valve locks. If they are found to be worn or defective, they must be replaced with new (or known good) parts.

Cylinder Head

Most refinishing procedures dealing with the cylinder head must be performed by a machine shop. Read the sections below and review your inspection data to determine whether or not machining is necessary.

VALVE GUIDE

➡️If any machining or replacements are made to the valve guides, the seats must be machined.

Unless the valve guides need machining or replacing, the only service to perform is to thoroughly clean them of any dirt or oil residue.

There are only two types of valve guides used on automobile engines: the replaceable-type (all aluminum heads) and the cast-in integral-type (most cast iron heads). There are four recommended methods for repairing worn guides.
- Knurling
- Inserts
- Reaming oversize
- Replacing

Knurling is a process in which metal is displaced and raised, thereby reducing clearance, giving a true center, and providing oil control. It is the least expensive way of repairing the valve guides. However, it is not necessarily the best, and in some cases, a knurled valve guide will not stand up for more than a short time. It requires a special knurlizer and precision reaming tools to obtain proper clearances. It would not be cost effective to purchase these tools, unless you plan on rebuilding several of the same cylinder head.

Installing a guide insert involves machining the guide to accept a bronze insert. One style is the coil-type which is installed into a threaded guide. Another is the thin-walled insert where the guide is reamed oversize to accept a split-sleeve insert. After the insert is installed, a special tool is then run through the guide to expand the insert, locking it to the guide. The insert is then reamed to the standard size for proper valve clearance.

Reaming for oversize valves restores normal clearances and provides a true valve seat. Most cast-in type guides can be reamed to accept an valve with an oversize stem. The cost factor for this can become quite high as you will need to purchase the reamer and new, oversize stem valves for all guides which were reamed. Oversizes are generally 0.003 to 0.030 in. (0.076 to 0.762mm), with 0.015 in. (0.381mm) being the most common.

To replace cast-in type valve guides, they must be drilled out, then reamed to accept replacement guides. This must be done on a fixture which will allow centering and leveling off of the original valve seat or guide, otherwise a serious guide-to-seat misalignment may occur making it impossible to properly machine the seat.

Replaceable-type guides are pressed into the cylinder head. A hammer and a stepped drift or punch may be used to install and remove the guides. Before removing the guides, measure the protrusion on the spring side of the head and record it for installation. Use the stepped drift to hammer out the old guide from the combustion chamber side of the head. When installing, determine whether or not the guide also seals a water jacket in the head, and if it does, use the recommended sealing agent. If there is no water jacket, grease the valve guide and its bore. Use the stepped drift, and hammer the new guide into the cylinder head from the spring side of the cylinder head. A stack of washers the same thickness as the measured protrusion may help the installation process.

VALVE SEATS

➡️Before any valve seat machining can be performed, the guides must be within factory recommended specifications.

➡️If any machining or replacements were made to the valve guides, the seats must be machined.

If the seats are in good condition, the valves can be lapped to the seats, and the cylinder head assembled. See the valves section for instructions on lapping.

If the valve seats are worn, cracked or damaged, they must be serviced by a machine shop. The valve seat must be perfectly centered to the valve guide, which requires very accurate machining.

CYLINDER HEAD SURFACE

If the cylinder head is warped, it must be machined flat. If the warpage is extremely severe, the head may need to be replaced. In some instances, it may be possible to straighten a warped head enough to allow machining. In either case, contact a professional machine shop for service.

➡️Any OHC cylinder head that shows excessive warpage should have the camshaft bearing journals align bored after the cylinder head has been resurfaced.

✳✳ WARNING

Failure to align bore the camshaft bearing journals could result in severe engine damage including but not limited to: valve and piston damage, connecting rod damage, camshaft and/or crankshaft breakage.

CRACKS AND PHYSICAL DAMAGE

Certain cracks can be repaired in both cast iron and aluminum heads. For cast iron, a tapered threaded insert is installed along the length of the crack. Aluminum can also use the tapered inserts, however welding is the preferred method. Some physical damage can be repaired through brazing or welding. Contact a machine shop to get expert advice for your particular dilemma.

ASSEMBLY

◆ See Figure 164

The first step for any assembly job is to have a clean area in which to work. Next, thoroughly clean all of the parts and components that are to be assembled. Finally, place all of the components onto a suitable work space and, if necessary, arrange the parts to their respective positions.

Cup Type Camshaft Followers

To install the springs, retainers and valve locks on heads which have these components recessed into the camshaft follower's bore, you will need a small screwdriver-type tool, some clean white grease and a lot of patience. You will also need the C-clamp style spring compressor and the OHC tool used to disassemble the head.

1. Lightly lubricate the valve stems and insert all of the valves into the cylinder head. If possible, maintain their original locations.
2. If equipped, install any valve spring shims which were removed.
3. If equipped, install the new valve seals, keeping the following in mind:
   - If the valve seal presses over the guide, lightly lubricate the outer guide surfaces.
   - If the seal is an O-ring type, it is installed just after compressing the spring but before the valve locks.
4. Place the valve spring and retainer over the stem.

TCCA3P64

Fig. 164 Once assembled, check the valve clearance and correct as needed

5. Position the spring compressor and the OHC tool, then compress the spring.

6. Using a small screwdriver as a spatula, fill the valve stem side of the lock with white grease. Use the excess grease on the screwdriver to fasten the lock to the driver.

7. Carefully install the valve lock, which is stuck to the end of the screwdriver, to the valve stem then press on it with the screwdriver until the grease squeezes out. The valve lock should now be stuck to the stem.

8. Repeat Steps 6 and 7 for the remaining valve lock.

9. Relieve the spring pressure slowly and insure that neither valve lock becomes dislodged by the retainer.

10. Remove the spring compressor tool.

11. Repeat Steps 2 through 10 until all of the springs have been installed.

12. Install the followers, camshaft(s) and any other components that were removed for disassembly.

Rocker Arm Type Camshaft Followers

1. Lightly lubricate the valve stems and insert all of the valves into the cylinder head. If possible, maintain their original locations.

2. If equipped, install any valve spring shims which were removed.

3. If equipped, install the new valve seals, keeping the following in mind:
- If the valve seal presses over the guide, lightly lubricate the outer guide surfaces.
- If the seal is an O-ring type, it is installed just after compressing the spring but before the valve locks.

4. Place the valve spring and retainer over the stem.

5. Position the spring compressor tool and compress the spring.

6. Assemble the valve locks to the stem.

7. Relieve the spring pressure slowly and insure that neither valve lock becomes dislodged by the retainer.

8. Remove the spring compressor tool.

9. Repeat Steps 2 through 8 until all of the springs have been installed.

10. Install the camshaft(s), rockers, shafts and any other components that were removed for disassembly.

Engine Block

GENERAL INFORMATION

▶ See Figures 165 and 166

A thorough overhaul or rebuild of an engine block would include replacing the pistons, rings, bearings, timing belt/chain assembly and oil pump. For OHV engines also include a new camshaft and lifters. The block would then have the cylinders bored and honed oversize (or if using removable cylinder sleeves, new sleeves installed) and the crankshaft would be cut undersize to provide new wearing surfaces and perfect clearances. However, your particular engine may not have everything worn out. What if only the piston rings have worn out and

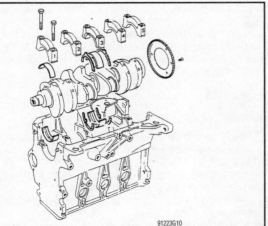

Fig. 165 Exploded view of a 2.0L engine crankshaft, block, and bearings

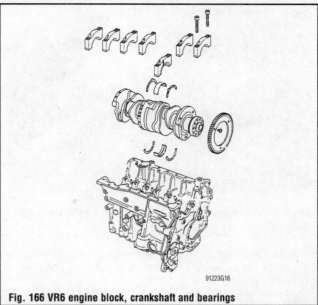

Fig. 166 VR6 engine block, crankshaft and bearings

the clearances on everything else are still within factory specifications? Well, you could just replace the rings and put it back together, but this would be a very rare example. Chances are, if one component in your engine is worn, other components are sure to follow, and soon. At the very least, you should always replace the rings, bearings and oil pump. This is what is commonly called a "freshen up".

Cylinder Ridge Removal

Because the top piston ring does not travel to the very top of the cylinder, a ridge is built up between the end of the travel and the top of the cylinder bore.

Pushing the piston and connecting rod assembly past the ridge can be difficult, and damage to the piston ring lands could occur. If the ridge is not removed before installing a new piston or not removed at all, piston ring breakage and piston damage may occur.

➡It is always recommended that you remove any cylinder ridges before removing the piston and connecting rod assemblies. If you know that new pistons are going to be installed and the engine block will be bored oversize, you may be able to forego this step. However, some ridges may actually prevent the assemblies from being removed, necessitating its removal.

There are several different types of ridge reamers on the market, none of which are inexpensive. Unless a great deal of engine rebuilding is anticipated, borrow or rent a reamer.

1. Turn the crankshaft until the piston is at the bottom of its travel.

2. Cover the head of the piston with a rag.

3. Follow the tool manufacturers instructions and cut away the ridge, exercising extreme care to avoid cutting too deeply.

4. Remove the ridge reamer, the rag and as many of the cuttings as possible. Continue until all of the cylinder ridges have been removed.

DISASSEMBLY

▶ See Figures 167 and 168

The engine disassembly instructions following assume that you have the engine mounted on an engine stand. If not, it is easiest to disassemble the engine on a bench or the floor with it resting on the bell housing or transmission mounting surface. You must be able to access the connecting rod fasteners and turn the crankshaft during disassembly. Also, all engine covers (timing, front, side, oil pan, whatever) should have already been removed. Engines which are seized or locked up may not be able to be completely disassembled, and a core (salvage yard) engine should be purchased.

If not done during the cylinder head removal, remove the timing chain/belt and/or gear/sprocket assembly. Remove the oil pick-up and pump assembly

Fig. 167 Place rubber hose over the connecting rod studs to protect the crankshaft and cylinder bores from damage

and, if necessary, the pump drive. If equipped, remove any balance or auxiliary shafts. If necessary, remove the cylinder ridge from the top of the bore. See the cylinder ridge removal procedure earlier in this section.

Rotate the engine over so that the crankshaft is exposed. Use a number punch or scribe and mark each connecting rod with its respective cylinder number. The cylinder closest to the front of the engine is always number 1. However, depending on the engine placement, the front of the engine could either be the flywheel or damper/pulley end. Generally the front of the engine faces the front

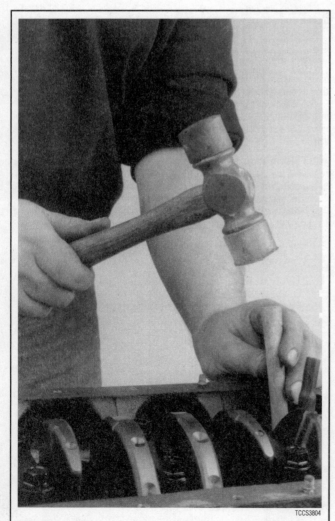

Fig. 168 Carefully tap the piston out of the bore using a wooden dowel

of the vehicle. Use a number punch or scribe and also mark the main bearing caps from front to rear with the front most cap being number 1 (if there are five caps, mark them 1 through 5, front to rear).

✳✳ WARNING

Take special care when pushing the connecting rod up from the crankshaft because the sharp threads of the rod bolts/studs will score the crankshaft journal. Insure that special plastic caps are installed over them, or cut two pieces of rubber hose to do the same.

Again, rotate the engine, this time to position the number one cylinder bore (head surface) up. Turn the crankshaft until the number one piston is at the bottom of its travel, this should allow the maximum access to its connecting rod. Remove the number one connecting rods fasteners and cap and place two lengths of rubber hose over the rod bolts/studs to protect the crankshaft from damage. Using a sturdy wooden dowel and a hammer, push the connecting rod up about 1 in. (25mm) from the crankshaft and remove the upper bearing insert. Continue pushing or tapping the connecting rod up until the piston rings are out of the cylinder bore. Remove the piston and rod by hand, put the upper half of the bearing insert back into the rod, install the cap with its bearing insert installed, and hand-tighten the cap fasteners. If the parts are kept in order in this manner, they will not get lost and you will be able to tell which bearings came form what cylinder if any problems are discovered and diagnosis is necessary. Remove all the other piston assemblies in the same manner. On V-style engines, remove all of the pistons from one bank, then reposition the engine with the other cylinder bank head surface up, and remove that banks piston assemblies.

The only remaining component in the engine block should now be the crankshaft. Loosen the main bearing caps evenly until the fasteners can be turned by hand, then remove them and the caps. Remove the crankshaft from the engine block. Thoroughly clean all of the components.

INSPECTION

Now that the engine block and all of its components are clean, it's time to inspect them for wear and/or damage. To accurately inspect them, you will need some specialized tools:

- Two or three separate micrometers to measure the pistons and crankshaft journals
- A dial indicator
- Telescoping gauges for the cylinder bores
- A rod alignment fixture to check for bent connecting rods

If you do not have access to the proper tools, you may want to bring the components to a shop that does.

Generally, you shouldn't expect cracks in the engine block or its components unless it was known to leak, consume or mix engine fluids, it was severely overheated, or there was evidence of bad bearings and/or crankshaft damage. A visual inspection should be performed on all of the components, but just because you don't see a crack does not mean it is not there. Some more reliable methods for inspecting for cracks include Magnaflux®, a magnetic process or Zyglo®, a dye penetrant. Magnaflux® is used only on ferrous metal (cast iron). Zyglo® uses a spray on fluorescent mixture along with a black light to reveal the cracks. It is strongly recommended to have your engine block checked professionally for cracks, especially if the engine was known to have overheated and/or leaked or consumed coolant. Contact a local shop for availability and pricing of these services.

Engine Block

ENGINE BLOCK BEARING ALIGNMENT

Remove the main bearing caps and, if still installed, the main bearing inserts. Inspect all of the main bearing saddles and caps for damage, burrs or high spots. If damage is found, and it is caused from a spun main bearing, the block will need to be align-bored or, if severe enough, replacement. Any burrs or high spots should be carefully removed with a metal file.

Place a straightedge on the bearing saddles, in the engine block, along the centerline of the crankshaft. If any clearance exists between the straightedge and the saddles, the block must be align-bored.

Align-boring consists of machining the main bearing saddles and caps by means of a flycutter that runs through the bearing saddles.

DECK FLATNESS

▶ See Figure 169

The top of the engine block where the cylinder head mounts is called the deck. Insure that the deck surface is clean of dirt, carbon deposits and old gasket material. Place a straightedge across the surface of the deck along its centerline and, using feeler gauges, check the clearance along several points. Repeat the checking procedure with the straightedge placed along both diagonals of the deck surface. If the reading exceeds 0.003 in. (0.076mm) within a 6.0 in. (15.2cm) span, or 0.006 in. (0.152mm) over the total length of the deck, it must be machined.

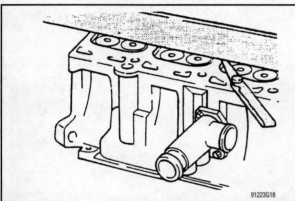

Fig. 169 Measuring deck flatness with a straight edge and a feeler gauge

CYLINDER BORES

▶ See Figure 170

The cylinder bores house the pistons and are slightly larger than the pistons themselves. A common piston-to-bore clearance is 0.0015–0.0025 in. (0.0381mm–0.0635mm). Inspect and measure the cylinder bores. The bore should be checked for out-of-roundness, taper and size. The results of this inspection will determine whether the cylinder can be used in its existing size and condition, or a rebore to the next oversize is required (or in the case of removable sleeves, have replacements installed).

The amount of cylinder wall wear is always greater at the top of the cylinder than at the bottom. This wear is known as taper. Any cylinder that has a taper of 0.0012 in. (0.305mm) or more, must be rebored. Measurements are taken at a number of positions in each cylinder: at the top, middle and bottom and at two points at each position; that is, at a point 90 degrees from the crankshaft centerline, as well as a point parallel to the crankshaft centerline. The measurements

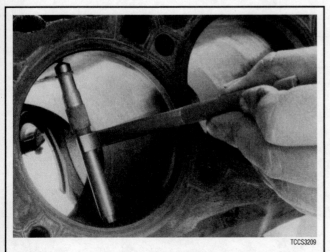

Fig. 170 Use a telescoping gauge to measure the cylinder bore diameter—take several readings within the same bore

are made with either a special dial indicator or a telescopic gauge and micrometer. If the necessary precision tools to check the bore are not available, take the block to a machine shop and have them mike it. Also if you don't have the tools to check the cylinder bores, chances are you will not have the necessary devices to check the pistons, connecting rods and crankshaft. Take these components with you and save yourself an extra trip.

For our procedures, we will use a telescopic gauge and a micrometer. You will need one of each, with a measuring range which covers your cylinder bore size.

1. Position the telescopic gauge in the cylinder bore, loosen the gauges lock and allow it to expand.

➡ **Your first two readings will be at the top of the cylinder bore, then proceed to the middle and finally the bottom, making a total of six measurements.**

2. Hold the gauge square in the bore, 90 degrees from the crankshaft centerline, and gently tighten the lock. Tilt the gauge back to remove it from the bore.

3. Measure the gauge with the micrometer and record the reading.

4. Again, hold the gauge square in the bore, this time parallel to the crankshaft centerline, and gently tighten the lock. Again, you will tilt the gauge back to remove it from the bore.

5. Measure the gauge with the micrometer and record this reading. The difference between these two readings is the out-of-round measurement of the cylinder.

6. Repeat steps 1 through 5, each time going to the next lower position, until you reach the bottom of the cylinder. Then go to the next cylinder, and continue until all of the cylinders have been measured.

The difference between these measurements will tell you all about the wear in your cylinders. The measurements which were taken 90 degrees from the crankshaft centerline will always reflect the most wear. That is because at this position is where the engine power presses the piston against the cylinder bore the hardest. This is known as thrust wear. Take your top, 90 degree measurement and compare it to your bottom, 90 degree measurement. The difference between them is the taper. When you measure your pistons, you will compare these readings to your piston sizes and determine piston-to-wall clearance.

Crankshaft

Inspect the crankshaft for visible signs of wear or damage. All of the journals should be perfectly round and smooth. Slight scores are normal for a used crankshaft, but you should hardly feel them with your fingernail. When measuring the crankshaft with a micrometer, you will take readings at the front and rear of each journal, then turn the micrometer 90 degrees and take two more readings, front and rear. The difference between the front-to-rear readings is the journal taper and the first-to-90 degree reading is the out-of-round measurement. Generally, there should be no taper or out-of-roundness found, however, up to 0.0005 in. (0.0127mm) for either can be overlooked. Also, the readings should fall within the factory specifications for journal diameters.

If the crankshaft journals fall within specifications, it is recommended that it be polished before being returned to service. Polishing the crankshaft insures that any minor burrs or high spots are smoothed, thereby reducing the chance of scoring the new bearings.

Pistons and Connecting Rods

PISTONS

▶ See Figures 171 thru 184

The piston should be visually inspected for any signs of cracking or burning (caused by hot spots or detonation), and scuffing or excessive wear on the skirts. The wrist pin attaches the piston to the connecting rod. The piston should move freely on the wrist pin, both sliding and pivoting. Grasp the connecting rod securely, or mount it in a vise, and try to rock the piston back and forth along the centerline of the wrist pin. There should not be any excessive play evident between the piston and the pin. If there are C-clips retaining the pin in the piston then you have wrist pin bushings in the rods. There should not be any excessive play between the wrist pin and the rod bushing. Normal clearance for the wrist pin is approx. 0.001–0.002 in. (0.025mm–0.051mm).

Use a micrometer and measure the diameter of the piston, perpendicular to the wrist pin, on the skirt. Compare the reading to its original cylinder measure-

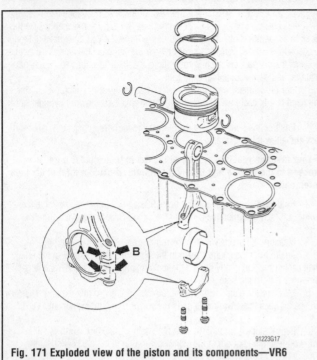

Fig. 171 Exploded view of the piston and its components—VR6 engine

Fig. 172 Place rubber caps over the connecting rod studs before you push the piston up and out of the block

Fig. 173 Removing the piston from the block

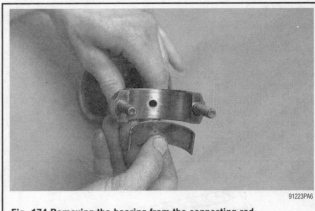

Fig. 174 Removing the bearing from the connecting rod

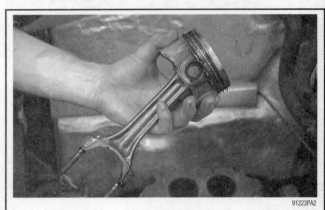

Fig. 175 Visually inspect the piston for cracking

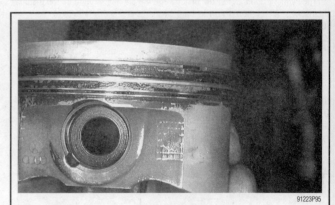

Fig. 176 Also check for any signs of wear

Fig. 177 Removing the ring from the piston

Fig. 178 Measure the piston's outer diameter, perpendicular to the wrist pin, with a micrometer

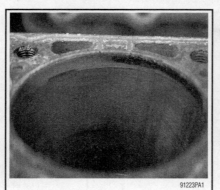

Fig. 179 Notice the ring of carbon at the top to the cylinder

Fig. 180 A ridge reamer can be used to remove any residual carbon stuck at the top of the cylinders. This will ease piston removal

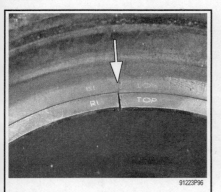

Fig. 181 Fit the piston ring into the cylinder as shown

Fig. 182 Use a feeler gauge to measure end gap

Fig. 183 Soak the piston and rings in oil before re-installing them into the engine

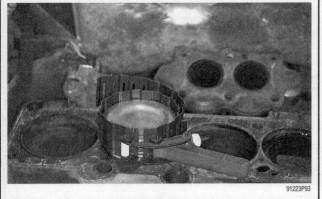

Fig. 184 A piston ring installer is needed to reinsert the piston

ment obtained earlier. The difference between the two readings is the piston-to-wall clearance. If the clearance is within specifications, the piston may be used as is. If the piston is out of specification, but the bore is not, you will need a new piston. If both are out of specification, you will need the cylinder rebored and oversize pistons installed. Generally if two or more pistons/bores are out of specification, it is best to rebore the entire block and purchase a complete set of oversize pistons.

CONNECTING ROD

You should have the connecting rod checked for straightness at a machine shop. If the connecting rod is bent, it will unevenly wear the bearing and piston, as well as place greater stress on these components. Any bent or twisted connecting rods must be replaced. If the rods are straight and the wrist pin clearance is within specifications, then only the bearing end of the rod need be checked. Place the connecting rod into a vice, with the bearing inserts in place, install the cap to the rod and torque the fasteners to specifications. Use a tele-

scoping gauge and carefully measure the inside diameter of the bearings. Compare this reading to the rods original crankshaft journal diameter measurement. The difference is the oil clearance. If the oil clearance is not within specifications, install new bearings in the rod and take another measurement. If the clearance is still out of specifications, and the crankshaft is not, the rod will need to be reconditioned by a machine shop.

➡You can also use Plastigage® to check the bearing clearances. The assembling section has complete instructions on its use.

Camshaft

Inspect the camshaft and lifters/followers as described earlier in this section.

Bearings

All of the engine bearings should be visually inspected for wear and/or damage. The bearing should look evenly worn all around with no deep scores or pits. If the bearing is severely worn, scored, pitted or heat blued, then the bearing, and the components that use it, should be brought to a machine shop for inspection. Full-circle bearings (used on most camshafts, auxiliary shafts, balance shafts, etc.) require specialized tools for removal and installation, and should be brought to a machine shop for service.

Oil Pump

◆ See Figure 185

➡The oil pump is responsible for providing constant lubrication to the whole engine and so it is recommended that a new oil pump be installed when rebuilding the engine.

Completely disassemble the oil pump and thoroughly clean all of the components. Inspect the oil pump gears and housing for wear and/or damage. Insure that the pressure relief valve operates properly and there is no binding or sticking due to varnish or debris. If all of the parts are in proper working condition, lubricate the gears and relief valve, and assemble the pump.

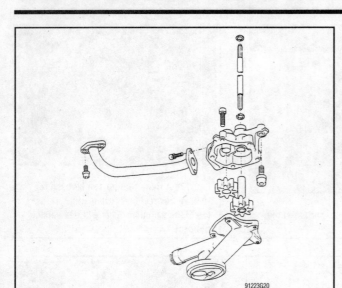

Fig. 185 Exploded view of a typical VW oil pump

REFINISHING

♦ See Figure 186

Almost all engine block refinishing must be performed by a machine shop. If the cylinders are not to be rebored, then the cylinder glaze can be removed with a ball hone. When removing cylinder glaze with a ball hone, use a light or penetrating type oil to lubricate the hone. Do not allow the hone to run dry as this may cause excessive scoring of the cylinder bores and wear on the hone. If new pistons are required, they will need to be installed to the connecting rods. This should be performed by a machine shop as the pistons must be installed in the correct relationship to the rod or engine damage can occur.

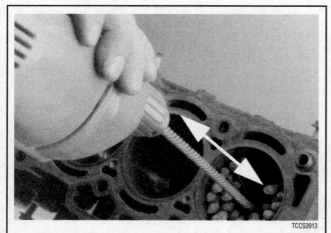

Fig. 186 Use a ball type cylinder hone to remove any glaze and provide a new surface for seating the piston rings

Pistons and Connecting Rods

♦ See Figure 187

Only pistons with the wrist pin retained by C-clips are serviceable by the home-mechanic. Press fit pistons require special presses and/or heaters to remove/install the connecting rod and should only be performed by a machine shop.

All pistons will have a mark indicating the direction to the front of the engine and the must be installed into the engine in that manner. Usually it is a notch or arrow on the top of the piston, or it may be the letter F cast or stamped into the piston.

Fig. 187 Most pistons are marked to indicate positioning in the engine (usually a mark means the side facing the front)

ASSEMBLY

Before you begin assembling the engine, first give yourself a clean, dirt free work area. Next, clean every engine component again. The key to a good assembly is cleanliness.

Mount the engine block into the engine stand and wash it one last time using water and detergent (dishwashing detergent works well). While washing it, scrub the cylinder bores with a soft bristle brush and thoroughly clean all of the oil passages. Completely dry the engine and spray the entire assembly down with an anti-rust solution such as WD-40® or similar product. Take a clean lint-free rag and wipe up any excess anti-rust solution from the bores, bearing saddles, etc. Repeat the final cleaning process on the crankshaft. Replace any freeze or oil galley plugs which were removed during disassembly.

Crankshaft

♦ See Figures 188, 189, 190, 191 and 192

1. Remove the main bearing inserts from the block and bearing caps.
2. If the crankshaft main bearing journals have been refinished to a definite undersize, install the correct undersize bearing. Be sure that the bearing inserts and bearing bores are clean. Foreign material under inserts will distort bearing and cause failure.
3. Place the upper main bearing inserts in bores with tang in slot.

➡The oil holes in the bearing inserts must be aligned with the oil holes in the cylinder block.

4. Install the lower main bearing inserts in bearing caps.
5. Clean the mating surfaces of block and rear main bearing cap.
6. Carefully lower the crankshaft into place. Be careful not to damage bearing surfaces.
7. Check the clearance of each main bearing by using the following procedure:

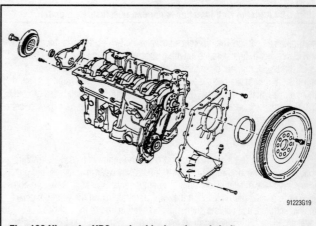

Fig. 188 View of a VR6 engine block and crankshaft

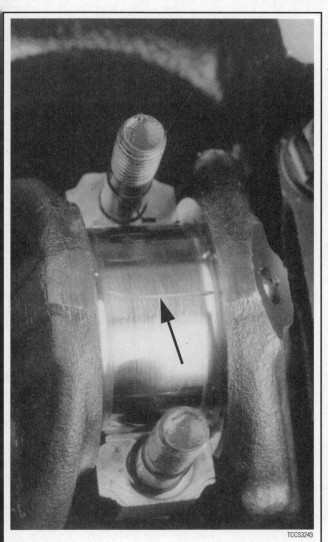

Fig. 189 Apply a strip of gauging material to the bearing journal, then install and torque the cap

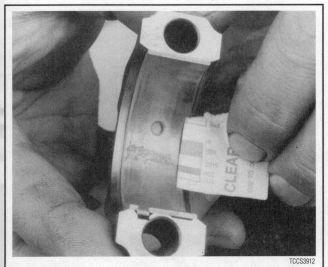

Fig. 190 After the cap is removed again, use the scale supplied with the gauging material to check the clearance

Fig. 191 A dial gauge may be used to check crankshaft end-play

a. Place a piece of Plastigage® or its equivalent, on bearing surface across full width of bearing cap and about ¼ in. off center.

b. Install cap and tighten bolts to specifications. Do not turn crankshaft while Plastigage® is in place.

c. Remove the cap. Using the supplied Plastigage® scale, check width of Plastigage® at widest point to get maximum clearance. Difference between readings is taper of journal.

d. If clearance exceeds specified limits, try a 0.001 in. or 0.002 in. under-size bearing in combination with the standard bearing. Bearing clearance must be within specified limits. If standard and 0.002 in. undersize bearing does not bring clearance within desired limits, refinish crankshaft journal, then install undersize bearings.

8. Install the rear main seal.

9. After the bearings have been fitted, apply a light coat of engine oil to the journals and bearings. Install the rear main bearing cap. Install all bearing caps except the thrust bearing cap. Be sure that main bearing caps are installed in original locations. Tighten the bearing cap bolts to specifications.

10. Install the thrust bearing cap with bolts finger-tight.

11. Pry the crankshaft forward against the thrust surface of upper half of bearing.

12. Hold the crankshaft forward and pry the thrust bearing cap to the rear. This aligns the thrust surfaces of both halves of the bearing.

13. Retain the forward pressure on the crankshaft. Tighten the cap bolts to specifications.

14. Measure the crankshaft end-play as follows:

a. Mount a dial gauge to the engine block and position the tip of the gauge to read from the crankshaft end.

Fig. 192 Carefully pry the crankshaft back and forth while reading the dial gauge for end-play

b. Carefully pry the crankshaft toward the rear of the engine and hold it there while you zero the gauge.

c. Carefully pry the crankshaft toward the front of the engine and read the gauge.

d. Confirm that the reading is within specifications. If not, install a new thrust bearing and repeat the procedure. If the reading is still out of specifications with a new bearing, have a machine shop inspect the thrust surfaces of the crankshaft, and if possible, repair it.

15. Rotate the crankshaft so as to position the first rod journal to the bottom of its stroke.

Pistons and Connecting Rods

▶ See Figures 193, 194, 195 and 196

1. Before installing the piston/connecting rod assembly, oil the pistons, piston rings and the cylinder walls with light engine oil. Install connecting rod bolt protectors or rubber hose onto the connecting rod bolts/studs. Also perform the following:

a. Select the proper ring set for the size cylinder bore.

b. Position the ring in the bore in which it is going to be used.

c. Push the ring down into the bore area where normal ring wear is not encountered.

d. Use the head of the piston to position the ring in the bore so that the ring is square with the cylinder wall. Use caution to avoid damage to the ring or cylinder bore.

e. Measure the gap between the ends of the ring with a feeler gauge. Ring gap in a worn cylinder is normally greater than specification. If the ring gap is greater than the specified limits, try an oversize ring set.

f. Check the ring side clearance of the compression rings with a feeler gauge inserted between the ring and its lower land according to specification. The gauge should slide freely around the entire ring circumference without binding. Any wear that occurs will form a step at the inner portion of the lower land. If the lower lands have high steps, the piston should be replaced.

2. Unless new pistons are installed, be sure to install the pistons in the cylinders from which they were removed. The numbers on the connecting rod and bearing cap must be on the same side when installed in the cylinder bore. If a connecting rod is ever transposed from one engine or cylinder to another, new bearings should be fitted and the connecting rod should be numbered to correspond with the new cylinder number. The notch on the piston head goes toward the front of the engine.

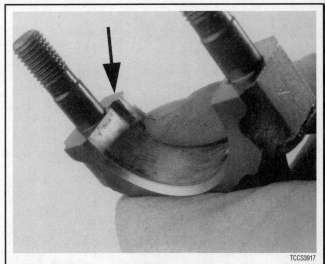

Fig. 194 The notch on the side of the bearing cap matches the tang on the bearing insert

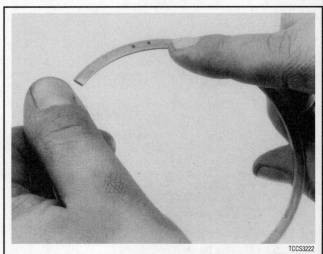

Fig. 195 Most rings are marked to show which side of the ring should face up when installed to the piston

Fig. 193 Checking the piston ring-to-ring groove side clearance using the ring and a feeler gauge

Fig. 196 Install the piston and rod assembly into the block using a ring compressor and the handle of a hammer

3. Install all of the rod bearing inserts into the rods and caps.

4. Install the rings to the pistons. Install the oil control ring first, then the second compression ring and finally the top compression ring. Use a piston ring expander tool to aid in installation and to help reduce the chance of breakage.

5. Make sure the ring gaps are properly spaced around the circumference of the piston. Fit a piston ring compressor around the piston and slide the piston and connecting rod assembly down into the cylinder bore, pushing it in with the wooden hammer handle. Push the piston down until it is only slightly below the top of the cylinder bore. Guide the connecting rod onto the crankshaft bearing journal carefully, to avoid damaging the crankshaft.

6. Check the bearing clearance of all the rod bearings, fitting them to the crankshaft bearing journals. Follow the procedure in the crankshaft installation above.

7. After the bearings have been fitted, apply a light coating of assembly oil to the journals and bearings.

8. Turn the crankshaft until the appropriate bearing journal is at the bottom of its stroke, then push the piston assembly all the way down until the connecting rod bearing seats on the crankshaft journal. Be careful not to allow the bearing cap screws to strike the crankshaft bearing journals and damage them.

9. After the piston and connecting rod assemblies have been installed, check the connecting rod side clearance on each crankshaft journal.

10. Prime and install the oil pump and the oil pump intake tube.

11. Install the auxiliary/balance shaft(s)/assembly(ies).

Cylinder Head(S)

1. Install the cylinder head(s) using new gaskets.
2. Install the timing sprockets/gears and the belt/chain assemblies.

Engine Covers and Components

Install the timing cover(s) and oil pan. Refer to your notes and drawings made prior to disassembly and install all of the components that were removed. Install the engine into the vehicle.

Engine Start-up and Break-in

STARTING THE ENGINE

Now that the engine is installed and every wire and hose is properly connected, go back and double check that all coolant and vacuum hoses are connected. Check that your oil drain plug is installed and properly tightened. If not already done, install a new oil filter onto the engine. Fill the crankcase with the proper amount and grade of engine oil. Fill the cooling system with a 50/50 mixture of coolant/water.

1. Connect the vehicle battery.
2. Start the engine. Keep your eye on your oil pressure indicator; if it does not indicate oil pressure within 10 seconds of starting, turn the vehicle off.

✳✳ WARNING

Damage to the engine can result if it is allowed to run with no oil pressure. Check the engine oil level to make sure that it is full. Check for any leaks and if found, repair the leaks before continuing. If there is still no indication of oil pressure, you may need to prime the system.

3. Confirm that there are no fluid leaks (oil or other).
4. Allow the engine to reach normal operating temperature (the upper radiator hose will be hot to the touch).
5. At this point you can perform any necessary checks or adjustments, such as checking the ignition timing.
6. Install any remaining components or body panels which were removed.

BREAKING IT IN

Make the first miles on the new engine, easy ones. Vary the speed but do not accelerate hard. Most importantly, do not lug the engine, and avoid sustained high speeds until at least 100 miles. Check the engine oil and coolant levels frequently. Expect the engine to use a little oil until the rings seat. Change the oil and filter at 500 miles, 1500 miles, then every 3000 miles past that.

KEEP IT MAINTAINED

Now that you have just gone through all of that hard work, keep yourself from doing it all over again by thoroughly maintaining it. Not that you may not have maintained it before, heck you could have had one to two hundred thousand miles on it before doing this. However, you may have bought the vehicle used, and the previous owner did not keep up on maintenance. Which is why you just went through all of that hard work. See?

TORQUE SPECIFICATIONS

Components	English	Metric
Starter Torque		
10mm bolts	33 ft. lbs.	41 Nm
12mm bolts	54 ft. lbs.	73 Nm
Halfshafts to the flanges	33 ft. lbs.	45 Nm
Exhaust pipe, 16V engine	30 ft. lbs.	40 Nm
Thermostat housing bolts	7 ft. lbs.	10 Nm
Drive axle flange bolts	33 ft. lbs	45 Nm
Exhaust pipe to exhaust manifold	30 ft. lbs	40 Nm
Fox		
Radiator mount bolts	7 ft. lbs.	10 Nm
Engine-to-transaxle cover plate bolts	7 ft. lbs.	10 Nm
Engine-to-transaxle bolts	42 ft. lbs.	55 Nm
Engine mount bolts	30 ft. lbs.	40 Nm
Engine stop-to-body block	18 ft. lbs.	25 Nm
Exhaust pipe support bolts	18 ft. lbs.	25 Nm
Exhaust pipe-to-manifold bolts	22 ft. lbs.	30 Nm
Starter bolts	18 ft. lbs.	25 Nm
Diesel Engine		
Camshaft sprocket	33 ft. lbs.	45 Nm
Motor Mounts		
10mm bolts	33 ft. lbs.	41 Nm
12mm bolts	54 ft. lbs.	73 Nm
Starter	33 ft. lbs.	45 Nm
Halfshafts to the flanges	33 ft. lbs.	45 Nm
Thermostat housing bolts	7 ft. lbs.	10 Nm
Intake Manifold		
1.8L and 2.8L (AHA) engines:	84 inch lbs.	10 Nm
2.0L (ABA and AEG) engine upper and lower bolts:	15 ft. lbs.	20 Nm
2.8L (AAA) engine upper and lower bolts:	18 ft. lbs.	25 Nm
Exhaust Manifold	18 ft. lbs.	25 Nm
Exhaust pipe to the manifold	30 ft. lbs.	40 Nm
Turbocharger		
Turbocharger bolts	33 ft. lbs.	45 Nm
Bracket nuts	18 ft. lbs.	25 Nm
Oil return line	22 ft. lbs.	30 Nm
Exhaust manifold		
Bolts	18 ft. lbs.	25 Nm
Nuts	18 ft. lbs.	25 Nm
Tensioner nut	33 ft. lbs.	45 Nm
Water Pump		
Gasoline 4 cyl.		
1.9L (AAZ) Engine		
Water pump-to-housing	7 ft. lbs.	10 Nm
Water pump drive pulley	15 ft. lbs.	20 Nm
Thermostat housing	7 ft. lbs.	10 Nm
Alternator mounting bolts	18 ft. lbs.	25 Nm
1.9L (AHH) Engine		
Water pump-to-housing	7 ft. lbs.	10 Nm
water pump bracket	18 ft. lbs.	25 Nm

TORQUE SPECIFICATIONS

Components	English	Metric
Cylinder Head		
1.8L Engine		
Head bolts		
Step 1	44 ft. lbs.	60 Nm
Step 2	Tighten bolts additional 180 degrees	
2.0L Engine		
Head bolts		
Step 1	30 ft. lbs.	40 Nm
Step 2	44 ft. lbs.	60 Nm
Step 3	Turn head bolts 90 degrees	
Step 4	Turn head bolts an additional 90 degrees	
2.8L VR6		
Step 1	30 ft. lbs.	40 Nm
Step 2	44 ft. lbs.	60 Nm
Step 3	Turn head bolts 90 degrees	
Step 4	Turn head bolts an additional 90 degrees	
Camshaft sprocket bolt	74 ft. lbs.	100 Nm
Tensioner bolt		
Upper timing chain cover	82 inch lbs.	10 Nm
Intake manifold	18 ft. lbs.	25 Nm
Exhaust manifold	18 ft. lbs.	25 Nm
Upper manifold	18 ft. lbs.	25 Nm
Oil Pan		
2.0L (ABA) engine	15 ft. lbs.	20 Nm
1.8L (AEB) and 2.8L (AAA) engines:	11 ft. lbs.	15 Nm
Oil Pump		
Oil pump bottom cover bolts	7 ft. lbs.	10 Nm
Oil pump suction foot bolts	7 ft. lbs.	10 Nm
Oil pump retaining bolts	18 ft. lbs.	25 Nm
Crankshaft Damper		
Tensioner nut	33 ft. lbs.	45 Nm
Timing Sprockets		
Camshaft sprocket on 8 valve gasoline engines	59 ft. lbs.	80 Nm
Camshaft sprocket on 16V engines	48 ft. lbs.	65 Nm
Crankshaft sprocket 6 sided bolt	137 ft. lbs.	180 Nm
Crankshaft sprocket 12 sided bolt	66 ft. lbs. plus 180 °	90 Nm plus 180 °
Camshaft, Bearings and Lifters		
8 Valve Engine		
Bearing cap nuts	15 ft. lbs.	20 Nm
16v Engines		
Intake camshaft		
Bearing caps No. 6 and 8	11 ft. lbs.	15 Nm
Exhaust camshaft		
Bearing caps No. 2 and 4	11 ft. lbs.	15 Nm
Rear Main Seal		
Mounting flange with seal	7 ft. lbs.	10 Nm
Flywheel/Flexplate		
Flywheel bolts		
Step 1	22 ft. lbs.	30 Nm
Step 2	Tighten 90 degrees	

91223C15

USING A VACUUM GAUGE

White needle = steady needle   *Dark needle = drifting needle*

The vacuum gauge is one of the most useful and easy-to-use diagnostic tools. It is inexpensive, easy to hook up, and provides valuable information about the condition of your engine.

Indication: Normal engine in good condition

Gauge reading: Steady, from 17–22 in./Hg.

Indication: Sticking valve or ignition miss

Gauge reading: Needle fluctuates from 15–20 in./Hg. at idle

Indication: Late ignition or valve timing, low compression, stuck throttle valve, leaking carburetor or manifold gasket.

Gauge reading: Low (15–20 in./Hg.) but steady

Indication: Improper carburetor adjustment, or minor intake leak at carburetor or manifold

NOTE: Bad fuel injector O-rings may also cause this reading.

Gauge reading: Drifting needle

Indication: Weak valve springs, worn valve stem guides, or leaky cylinder head gasket (vibrating excessively at all speeds).

NOTE: A plugged catalytic converter may also cause this reading.

Gauge reading: Needle fluctuates as engine speed increases

Indication: Burnt valve or improper valve clearance. The needle will drop when the defective valve operates.

Gauge reading: Steady needle, but drops regularly

Indication: Choked muffler or obstruction in system. Speed up the engine. Choked muffler will exhibit a slow drop of vacuum to zero.

Gauge reading: Gradual drop in reading at idle

Indication: Worn valve guides

Gauge reading: Needle vibrates excessively at idle, but steadies as engine speed increases

TCCS3C01

Troubleshooting Engine Mechanical Problems

Problem	Cause	Solution
External oil leaks	• Cylinder head cover RTV sealant broken or improperly seated	• Replace sealant; inspect cylinder head cover sealant flange and cylinder head sealant surface for distortion and cracks
	• Oil filler cap leaking or missing	• Replace cap
	• Oil filter gasket broken or improperly seated	• Replace oil filter
	• Oil pan side gasket broken, improperly seated or opening in RTV sealant	• Replace gasket or repair opening in sealant; inspect oil pan gasket flange for distortion
	• Oil pan front oil seal broken or improperly seated	• Replace seal; inspect timing case cover and oil pan seal flange for distortion
	• Oil pan rear oil seal broken or improperly seated	• Replace seal; inspect oil pan rear oil seal flange; inspect rear main bearing cap for cracks, plugged oil return channels, or distortion in seal groove
	• Timing case cover oil seal broken or improperly seated	• Replace seal
	• Excess oil pressure because of restricted PCV valve	• Replace PCV valve
	• Oil pan drain plug loose or has stripped threads	• Repair as necessary and tighten
	• Rear oil gallery plug loose	• Use appropriate sealant on gallery plug and tighten
	• Rear camshaft plug loose or improperly seated	• Seat camshaft plug or replace and seal, as necessary
Excessive oil consumption	• Oil level too high	• Drain oil to specified level
	• Oil with wrong viscosity being used	• Replace with specified oil
	• PCV valve stuck closed	• Replace PCV valve
	• Valve stem oil deflectors (or seals) are damaged, missing, or incorrect type	• Replace valve stem oil deflectors
	• Valve stems or valve guides worn	• Measure stem-to-guide clearance and repair as necessary
	• Poorly fitted or missing valve cover baffles	• Replace valve cover
	• Piston rings broken or missing	• Replace broken or missing rings
	• Scuffed piston	• Replace piston
	• Incorrect piston ring gap	• Measure ring gap, repair as necessary
	• Piston rings sticking or excessively loose in grooves	• Measure ring side clearance, repair as necessary
	• Compression rings installed upside down	• Repair as necessary
	• Cylinder walls worn, scored, or glazed	• Repair as necessary

TCCS3C02

Troubleshooting Engine Mechanical Problems

Problem	Cause	Solution
Excessive oil consumption (cont.)	• Piston ring gaps not properly staggered	• Repair as necessary
	• Excessive main or connecting rod bearing clearance	• Measure bearing clearance, repair as necessary
No oil pressure	• Low oil level	• Add oil to correct level
	• Oil pressure gauge, warning lamp or sending unit inaccurate	• Replace oil pressure gauge or warning lamp
	• Oil pump malfunction	• Replace oil pump
	• Oil pressure relief valve sticking	• Remove and inspect oil pressure relief valve assembly
	• Oil passages on pressure side of pump obstructed	• Inspect oil passages for obstruction
	• Oil pickup screen or tube obstructed	• Inspect oil pickup for obstruction
	• Loose oil inlet tube	• Tighten or seal inlet tube
Low oil pressure	• Low oil level	• Add oil to correct level
	• Inaccurate gauge, warning lamp or sending unit	• Replace oil pressure gauge or warning lamp
	• Oil excessively thin because of dilution, poor quality, or improper grade	• Drain and refill crankcase with recommended oil
	• Excessive oil temperature	• Correct cause of overheating engine
	• Oil pressure relief spring weak or sticking	• Remove and inspect oil pressure relief valve assembly
	• Oil inlet tube and screen assembly has restriction or air leak	• Remove and inspect oil inlet tube and screen assembly. (Fill inlet tube with lacquer thinner to locate leaks.)
	• Excessive oil pump clearance	• Measure clearances
	• Excessive main, rod, or camshaft bearing clearance	• Measure bearing clearances, repair as necessary
High oil pressure	• Improper oil viscosity	• Drain and refill crankcase with correct viscosity oil
	• Oil pressure gauge or sending unit inaccurate	• Replace oil pressure gauge
	• Oil pressure relief valve sticking closed	• Remove and inspect oil pressure relief valve assembly
Main bearing noise	• Insufficient oil supply	• Inspect for low oil level and low oil pressure
	• Main bearing clearance excessive	• Measure main bearing clearance, repair as necessary
	• Bearing insert missing	• Replace missing insert
	• Crankshaft end-play excessive	• Measure end-play, repair as necessary
	• Improperly tightened main bearing cap bolts	• Tighten bolts with specified torque
	• Loose flywheel or drive plate	• Tighten flywheel or drive plate attaching bolts
	• Loose or damaged vibration damper	• Repair as necessary

Troubleshooting Engine Mechanical Problems

Problem	Cause	Solution
Connecting rod bearing noise	• Insufficient oil supply	• Inspect for low oil level and low oil pressure
	• Carbon build-up on piston	• Remove carbon from piston crown
	• Bearing clearance excessive or bearing missing	• Measure clearance, repair as necessary
	• Crankshaft connecting rod journal out-of-round	• Measure journal dimensions, repair or replace as necessary
	• Misaligned connecting rod or cap	• Repair as necessary
	• Connecting rod bolts tightened improperly	• Tighten bolts with specified torque
Piston noise	• Piston-to-cylinder wall clearance excessive (scuffed piston)	• Measure clearance and examine piston
	• Cylinder walls excessively tapered or out-of-round	• Measure cylinder wall dimensions, rebore cylinder
	• Piston ring broken	• Replace all rings on piston
	• Loose or seized piston pin	• Measure piston-to-pin clearance, repair as necessary
	• Connecting rods misaligned	• Measure rod alignment, straighten or replace
	• Piston ring side clearance excessively loose or tight	• Measure ring side clearance, repair as necessary
	• Carbon build-up on piston is excessive	• Remove carbon from piston
Valve actuating component noise	• Insufficient oil supply	• Check for: (a) Low oil level (b) Low oil pressure (c) Wrong hydraulic tappets (d) Restricted oil gallery (e) Excessive tappet to bore clearance
	• Rocker arms or pivots worn	• Replace worn rocker arms or pivots
	• Foreign objects or chips in hydraulic tappets	• Clean tappets
	• Excessive tappet leak-down	• Replace valve tappet
	• Tappet face worn	• Replace tappet; inspect corresponding cam lobe for wear
	• Broken or cocked valve springs	• Properly seat cocked springs; replace broken springs
	• Stem-to-guide clearance excessive	• Measure stem-to-guide clearance, repair as required
	• Valve bent	• Replace valve
	• Loose rocker arms	• Check and repair as necessary
	• Valve seat runout excessive	• Regrind valve seat/valves
	• Missing valve lock	• Install valve lock
	• Excessive engine oil	• Correct oil level

TCCS3C04

Troubleshooting Engine Performance

Problem	Cause	Solution
Hard starting (engine cranks normally)	• Faulty engine control system component	• Repair or replace as necessary
	• Faulty fuel pump	• Replace fuel pump
	• Faulty fuel system component	• Repair or replace as necessary
	• Faulty ignition coil	• Test and replace as necessary
	• Improper spark plug gap	• Adjust gap
	• Incorrect ignition timing	• Adjust timing
	• Incorrect valve timing	• Check valve timing; repair as necessary
Rough idle or stalling	• Incorrect curb or fast idle speed	• Adjust curb or fast idle speed (If possible)
	• Incorrect ignition timing	• Adjust timing to specification
	• Improper feedback system operation	• Refer to Chapter 4
	• Faulty EGR valve operation	• Test EGR system and replace as necessary
	• Faulty PCV valve air flow	• Test PCV valve and replace as necessary
	• Faulty TAC vacuum motor or valve	• Repair as necessary
	• Air leak into manifold vacuum	• Inspect manifold vacuum connections and repair as necessary
	• Faulty distributor rotor or cap	• Replace rotor or cap (Distributor systems only)
	• Improperly seated valves	• Test cylinder compression, repair as necessary
	• Incorrect ignition wiring	• Inspect wiring and correct as necessary
	• Faulty ignition coil	• Test coil and replace as necessary
	• Restricted air vent or idle passages	• Clean passages
	• Restricted air cleaner	• Clean or replace air cleaner filter element
Faulty low-speed operation	• Restricted idle air vents and passages	• Clean air vents and passages
	• Restricted air cleaner	• Clean or replace air cleaner filter element
	• Faulty spark plugs	• Clean or replace spark plugs
	• Dirty, corroded, or loose ignition secondary circuit wire connections	• Clean or tighten secondary circuit wire connections
	• Improper feedback system operation	• Refer to Chapter 4
	• Faulty ignition coil high voltage wire	• Replace ignition coil high voltage wire (Distributor systems only)
	• Faulty distributor cap	• Replace cap (Distributor systems only)
Faulty acceleration	• Incorrect ignition timing	• Adjust timing
	• Faulty fuel system component	• Repair or replace as necessary
	• Faulty spark plug(s)	• Clean or replace spark plug(s)
	• Improperly seated valves	• Test cylinder compression, repair as necessary
	• Faulty ignition coil	• Test coil and replace as necessary

Troubleshooting Engine Performance

Problem	Cause	Solution
Faulty acceleration (cont.)	• Improper feedback system operation	• Refer to Chapter 4
Faulty high speed operation	• Incorrect ignition timing • Faulty advance mechanism	• Adjust timing (if possible) • Check advance mechanism and repair as necessary (Distributor systems only)
	• Low fuel pump volume • Wrong spark plug air gap or wrong plug	• Replace fuel pump • Adjust air gap or install correct plug
	• Partially restricted exhaust manifold, exhaust pipe, catalytic converter, muffler, or tailpipe	• Eliminate restriction
	• Restricted vacuum passages • Restricted air cleaner	• Clean passages • Cleaner or replace filter element as necessary
	• Faulty distributor rotor or cap	• Replace rotor or cap (Distributor systems only)
	• Faulty ignition coil • Improperly seated valve(s)	• Test coil and replace as necessary • Test cylinder compression, repair as necessary
	• Faulty valve spring(s)	• Inspect and test valve spring tension, replace as necessary
	• Incorrect valve timing	• Check valve timing and repair as necessary
	• Intake manifold restricted	• Remove restriction or replace manifold
	• Worn distributor shaft	• Replace shaft (Distributor systems only)
	• Improper feedback system operation	• Refer to Chapter 4
Misfire at all speeds	• Faulty spark plug(s) • Faulty spark plug wire(s) • Faulty distributor cap or rotor	• Clean or relace spark plug(s) • Replace as necessary • Replace cap or rotor (Distributor systems only)
	• Faulty ignition coil • Primary ignition circuit shorted or open intermittently • Improperly seated valve(s)	• Test coil and replace as necessary • Troubleshoot primary circuit and repair as necessary • Test cylinder compression, repair as necessary
	• Faulty hydraulic tappet(s) • Improper feedback system operation • Faulty valve spring(s)	• Clean or replace tappet(s) • Refer to Chapter 4 • Inspect and test valve spring tension, repair as necessary
	• Worn camshaft lobes • Air leak into manifold	• Replace camshaft • Check manifold vacuum and repair as necessary
	• Fuel pump volume or pressure low • Blown cylinder head gasket • Intake or exhaust manifold passage(s) restricted	• Replace fuel pump • Replace gasket • Pass chain through passage(s) and repair as necessary
Power not up to normal	• Incorrect ignition timing • Faulty distributor rotor	• Adjust timing • Replace rotor (Distributor systems only)

TCCS3C06

Troubleshooting Engine Performance

Problem	Cause	Solution
Power not up to normal (cont.)	• Incorrect spark plug gap	• Adjust gap
	• Faulty fuel pump	• Replace fuel pump
	• Faulty fuel pump	• Replace fuel pump
	• Incorrect valve timing	• Check valve timing and repair as necessary
	• Faulty ignition coil	• Test coil and replace as necessary
	• Faulty ignition wires	• Test wires and replace as necessary
	• Improperly seated valves	• Test cylinder compression and repair as necessary
	• Blown cylinder head gasket	• Replace gasket
	• Leaking piston rings	• Test compression and repair as necessary
	• Improper feedback system operation	• Refer to Chapter 4
Intake backfire	• Improper ignition timing	• Adjust timing
	• Defective EGR component	• Repair as necessary
	• Defective TAC vacuum motor or valve	• Repair as necessary
Exhaust backfire	• Air leak into manifold vacuum	• Check manifold vacuum and repair as necessary
	• Faulty air injection diverter valve	• Test diverter valve and replace as necessary
	• Exhaust leak	• Locate and eliminate leak
Ping or spark knock	• Incorrect ignition timing	• Adjust timing
	• Distributor advance malfunction	• Inspect advance mechanism and repair as necessary (Distributor systems only)
	• Excessive combustion chamber deposits	• Remove with combustion chamber cleaner
	• Air leak into manifold vacuum	• Check manifold vacuum and repair as necessary
	• Excessively high compression	• Test compression and repair as necessary
	• Fuel octane rating excessively low	• Try alternate fuel source
	• Sharp edges in combustion chamber	• Grind smooth
	• EGR valve not functioning properly	• Test EGR system and replace as necessary
Surging (at cruising to top speeds)	• Low fuel pump pressure or volume	• Replace fuel pump
	• Improper PCV valve air flow	• Test PCV valve and replace as necessary
	• Air leak into manifold vacuum	• Check manifold vacuum and repair as necessary
	• Incorrect spark advance	• Test and replace as necessary
	• Restricted fuel filter	• Replace fuel filter
	• Restricted air cleaner	• Clean or replace air cleaner filter element
	• EGR valve not functioning properly	• Test EGR system and replace as necessary
	• Improper feedback system operation	• Refer to Chapter 4

TCCS3C07

Troubleshooting the Serpentine Drive Belt

Problem	Cause	Solution
Tension sheeting fabric failure (woven fabric on outside circumference of belt has cracked or separated from body of belt)	• Grooved or backside idler pulley diameters are less than minimum recommended • Tension sheeting contacting (rubbing) stationary object • Excessive heat causing woven fabric to age • Tension sheeting splice has fractured	• Replace pulley(s) not conforming to specification • Correct rubbing condition • Replace belt • Replace belt
Noise (objectional squeal, squeak, or rumble is heard or felt while drive belt is in operation)	• Belt slippage • Bearing noise • Belt misalignment • Belt-to-pulley mismatch • Driven component inducing vibration • System resonant frequency inducing vibration	• Adjust belt • Locate and repair • Align belt/pulley(s) • Install correct belt • Locate defective driven component and repair • Vary belt tension within specifications. Replace belt.
Rib chunking (one or more ribs has separated from belt body)	• Foreign objects imbedded in pulley grooves • Installation damage • Drive loads in excess of design specifications • Insufficient internal belt adhesion	• Remove foreign objects from pulley grooves • Replace belt • Adjust belt tension • Replace belt
Rib or belt wear (belt ribs contact bottom of pulley grooves)	• Pulley(s) misaligned • Mismatch of belt and pulley groove widths • Abrasive environment • Rusted pulley(s) • Sharp or jagged pulley groove tips • Rubber deteriorated	• Align pulley(s) • Replace belt • Replace belt • Clean rust from pulley(s) • Replace pulley • Replace belt
Longitudinal belt cracking (cracks between two ribs)	• Belt has mistracked from pulley groove • Pulley groove tip has worn away rubber-to-tensile member	• Replace belt • Replace belt
Belt slips	• Belt slipping because of insufficient tension • Belt or pulley subjected to substance (belt dressing, oil, ethylene glycol) that has reduced friction • Driven component bearing failure • Belt glazed and hardened from heat and excessive slippage	• Adjust tension • Replace belt and clean pulleys • Replace faulty component bearing • Replace belt
"Groove jumping" (belt does not maintain correct position on pulley, or turns over and/or runs off pulleys)	• Insufficient belt tension • Pulley(s) not within design tolerance • Foreign object(s) in grooves	• Adjust belt tension • Replace pulley(s) • Remove foreign objects from grooves

TCCS3C09

Troubleshooting the Serpentine Drive Belt

Problem	Cause	Solution
"Groove jumping" (belt does not maintain correct position on pulley, or turns over and/or runs off pulleys)	• Excessive belt speed • Pulley misalignment • Belt-to-pulley profile mismatched • Belt cordline is distorted	• Avoid excessive engine acceleration • Align pulley(s) • Install correct belt • Replace belt
Belt broken (Note: identify and correct problem before replacement belt is installed)	• Excessive tension • Tensile members damaged during belt installation • Belt turnover • Severe pulley misalignment • Bracket, pulley, or bearing failure	• Replace belt and adjust tension to specification • Replace belt • Replace belt • Align pulley(s) • Replace defective component and belt
Cord edge failure (tensile member exposed at edges of belt or separated from belt body)	• Excessive tension • Drive pulley misalignment • Belt contacting stationary object • Pulley irregularities • Improper pulley construction • Insufficient adhesion between tensile member and rubber matrix	• Adjust belt tension • Align pulley • Correct as necessary • Replace pulley • Replace pulley • Replace belt and adjust tension to specifications
Sporadic rib cracking (multiple cracks in belt ribs at random intervals)	• Ribbed pulley(s) diameter less than minimum specification • Backside bend flat pulley(s) diameter less than minimum • Excessive heat condition causing rubber to harden • Excessive belt thickness • Belt overcured • Excessive tension	• Replace pulley(s) • Replace pulley(s) • Correct heat condition as necessary • Replace belt • Replace belt • Adjust belt tension

TCCS3C10

Troubleshooting the Cooling System

Problem	Cause	Solution
High temperature gauge indication—overheating	• Coolant level low • Improper fan operation • Radiator hose(s) collapsed • Radiator airflow blocked • Faulty pressure cap • Ignition timing incorrect • Air trapped in cooling system • Heavy traffic driving • Incorrect cooling system component(s) installed • Faulty thermostat • Water pump shaft broken or impeller loose • Radiator tubes clogged • Cooling system clogged • Casting flash in cooling passages • Brakes dragging • Excessive engine friction • Antifreeze concentration over 68% • Missing air seals • Faulty gauge or sending unit • Loss of coolant flow caused by leakage or foaming • Viscous fan drive failed	• Replenish coolant • Repair or replace as necessary • Replace hose(s) • Remove restriction (bug screen, fog lamps, etc.) • Replace pressure cap • Adjust ignition timing • Purge air • Operate at fast idle in neutral intermittently to cool engine • Install proper component(s) • Replace thermostat • Replace water pump • Flush radiator • Flush system • Repair or replace as necessary. Flash may be visible by removing cooling system components or removing core plugs. • Repair brakes • Repair engine • Lower antifreeze concentration percentage • Replace air seals • Repair or replace faulty component • Repair or replace leaking component, replace coolant • Replace unit
Low temperature indication—undercooling	• Thermostat stuck open • Faulty gauge or sending unit	• Replace thermostat • Repair or replace faulty component
Coolant loss—boilover	• Overfilled cooling system • Quick shutdown after hard (hot) run • Air in system resulting in occasional "burping" of coolant • Insufficient antifreeze allowing coolant boiling point to be too low • Antifreeze deteriorated because of age or contamination • Leaks due to loose hose clamps, loose nuts, bolts, drain plugs, faulty hoses, or defective radiator	• Reduce coolant level to proper specification • Allow engine to run at fast idle prior to shutdown • Purge system • Add antifreeze to raise boiling point • Replace coolant • Pressure test system to locate source of leak(s) then repair as necessary

TCCS3C11

Troubleshooting the Cooling System

Problem	Cause	Solution
Coolant loss—boilover	• Faulty head gasket • Cracked head, manifold, or block • Faulty radiator cap	• Replace head gasket • Replace as necessary • Replace cap
Coolant entry into crankcase or cylinder(s)	• Faulty head gasket • Crack in head, manifold or block	• Replace head gasket • Replace as necessary
Coolant recovery system inoperative	• Coolant level low • Leak in system • Pressure cap not tight or seal missing, or leaking • Pressure cap defective • Overflow tube clogged or leaking • Recovery bottle vent restricted	• Replenish coolant to FULL mark • Pressure test to isolate leak and repair as necessary • Repair as necessary • Replace cap • Repair as necessary • Remove restriction
Noise	• Fan contacting shroud • Loose water pump impeller • Glazed fan belt • Loose fan belt • Rough surface on drive pulley • Water pump bearing worn • Belt alignment	• Reposition shroud and inspect engine mounts (on electric fans inspect assembly) • Replace pump • Apply silicone or replace belt • Adjust fan belt tension • Replace pulley • Remove belt to isolate. Replace pump. • Check pulley alignment. Repair as necessary.
No coolant flow through heater core	• Restricted return inlet in water pump • Heater hose collapsed or restricted • Restricted heater core • Restricted outlet in thermostat housing • Intake manifold bypass hole in cylinder head restricted • Faulty heater control valve • Intake manifold coolant passage restricted	• Remove restriction • Remove restriction or replace hose • Remove restriction or replace core • Remove flash or restriction • Remove restriction • Replace valve • Remove restriction or replace intake manifold

NOTE: *Immediately after shutdown, the engine enters a condition known as heat soak. This is caused by the cooling system being inoperative while engine temperature is still high. If coolant temperature rises above boiling point, expansion and pressure may push some coolant out of the radiator overflow tube. If this does not occur frequently it is considered normal.*

TCCS3C12

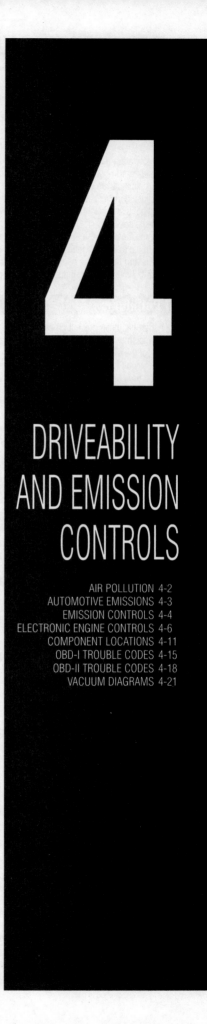

4

DRIVEABILITY AND EMISSION CONTROLS

AIR POLLUTION

The earth's atmosphere, at or near sea level, consists approximately of 78 percent nitrogen, 21 percent oxygen and 1 percent other gases. If it were possible to remain in this state, 100 percent clean air would result. However, many varied sources allow other gases and particulates to mix with the clean air, causing our atmosphere to become unclean or polluted.

Some of these pollutants are visible while others are invisible, with each having the capability of causing distress to the eyes, ears, throat, skin and respiratory system. Should these pollutants become concentrated in a specific area and under certain conditions, death could result due to the displacement or chemical change of the oxygen content in the air. These pollutants can also cause great damage to the environment and to the many man made objects that are exposed to the elements.

To better understand the causes of air pollution, the pollutants can be categorized into 3 separate types, natural, industrial and automotive.

Natural Pollutants

Natural pollution has been present on earth since before man appeared and continues to be a factor when discussing air pollution, although it causes only a small percentage of the overall pollution problem. It is the direct result of decaying organic matter, wind born smoke and particulates from such natural events as plain and forest fires (ignited by heat or lightning), volcanic ash, sand and dust which can spread over a large area of the countryside.

Such a phenomenon of natural pollution has been seen in the form of volcanic eruptions, with the resulting plume of smoke, steam and volcanic ash blotting out the sun's rays as it spreads and rises higher into the atmosphere. As it travels into the atmosphere the upper air currents catch and carry the smoke and ash, while condensing the steam back into water vapor. As the water vapor, smoke and ash travel on their journey, the smoke dissipates into the atmosphere while the ash and moisture settle back to earth in a trail hundreds of miles long. In some cases, lives are lost and millions of dollars of property damage result.

Industrial Pollutants

Industrial pollution is caused primarily by industrial processes, the burning of coal, oil and natural gas, which in turn produce smoke and fumes. Because the burning fuels contain large amounts of sulfur, the principal ingredients of smoke and fumes are sulfur dioxide and particulate matter. This type of pollutant occurs most severely during still, damp and cool weather, such as at night. Even in its less severe form, this pollutant is not confined to just cities. Because of air movements, the pollutants move for miles over the surrounding countryside, leaving in its path a barren and unhealthy environment for all living things.

Working with Federal, State and Local mandated regulations and by carefully monitoring emissions, big business has greatly reduced the amount of pollutant introduced from its industrial sources, striving to obtain an acceptable level. Because of the mandated industrial emission clean up, many land areas and streams in and around the cities that were formerly barren of vegetation and life, have now begun to move back in the direction of nature's intended balance.

Automotive Pollutants

The third major source of air pollution is automotive emissions. The emissions from the internal combustion engines were not an appreciable problem years ago because of the small number of registered vehicles and the nation's small highway system. However, during the early 1950's, the trend of the American people was to move from the cities to the surrounding suburbs. This caused an immediate problem in transportation because the majority of suburbs were not afforded mass transit conveniences. This lack of transportation created an attractive market for the automobile manufacturers, which resulted in a dramatic increase in the number of vehicles produced and sold, along with a marked increase in highway construction between cities and the suburbs. Multi-vehicle families emerged with a growing 'emphasis placed on an individual vehicle per family member. As the increase in vehicle ownership and usage occurred, so did pollutant levels in and around the cities, as suburbanites drove daily to their businesses and employment, returning at the end of the day to their homes in the suburbs.

It was noted that a smoke and fog type haze was being formed and at times, remained in suspension over the cities, taking time to dissipate. At first this "smog," derived from the words "smoke" and "fog," was thought to result from industrial pollution but it was determined that automobile emissions shared the blame. It was discovered that when normal automobile emissions were exposed to sunlight for a period of time, complex chemical reactions would take place.

It is now known that smog is a photo chemical layer which develops when certain oxides of nitrogen (NOx) and unburned hydrocarbons (HC) from automobile emissions are exposed to sunlight. Pollution was more severe when smog would become stagnant over an area in which a warm layer of air settled over the top of the cooler air mass, trapping and holding the cooler mass at ground level. The trapped cooler air would keep the emissions from being dispersed and diluted through normal air flows. This type of air stagnation was given the name "Temperature Inversion."

TEMPERATURE INVERSION

In normal weather situations, surface air is warmed by heat radiating from the earth's surface and the sun's rays. This causes it to rise upward, into the atmosphere. Upon rising it will cool through a convection type heat exchange with the cooler upper air. As warm air rises, the surface pollutants are carried upward and dissipated into the atmosphere.

When a temperature inversion occurs, we find the higher air is no longer cooler, but is warmer than the surface air, causing the cooler surface air to become trapped. This warm air blanket can extend from above ground level to a few hundred or even a few thousand feet into the air. As the surface air is trapped, so are the pollutants, causing a severe smog condition. Should this stagnant air mass extend to a few thousand feet high, enough air movement with the inversion takes place to allow the smog layer to rise above ground level but the pollutants still cannot dissipate. This inversion can remain for days over an area, with the smog level only rising or lowering from ground level to a few hundred feet high. Meanwhile, the pollutant levels increase, causing eye irritation, respiratory problems, reduced visibility, plant damage and in some cases, even disease.

This inversion phenomenon was first noted in the Los Angeles, California area. The city lies in terrain resembling a basin and with certain weather conditions, a cold air mass is held in the basin while a warmer air mass covers it like a lid.

Because this type of condition was first documented as prevalent in the Los Angeles area, this type of trapped pollution was named Los Angeles Smog, although it occurs in other areas where a large concentration of automobiles are used and the air remains stagnant for any length of time.

HEAT TRANSFER

Consider the internal combustion engine as a machine in which raw materials must be placed so a finished product comes out. As in any machine operation, a certain amount of wasted material is formed. When we relate this to the internal combustion engine, we find that through the input of air and fuel, we obtain power during the combustion process to drive the vehicle. The by-product or waste of this power is, in part, heat and exhaust gases with which we must dispose.

The heat from the combustion process can rise to over 4000°F (2204°C). The dissipation of this heat is controlled by a ram air effect, the use of cooling fans to cause air flow and a liquid coolant solution surrounding the combustion area to transfer the heat of combustion through the cylinder walls and into the coolant. The coolant is then directed to a thin-finned, multi-tubed radiator, from which the excess heat is transferred to the atmosphere by 1 of the 3 heat transfer methods, conduction, convection or radiation.

The cooling of the combustion area is an important part in the control of exhaust emissions. To understand the behavior of the combustion and transfer of its heat, consider the air/fuel charge. It is ignited and the flame front burns progressively across the combustion chamber until the burning charge reaches the cylinder walls. Some of the fuel in contact with the walls is not hot enough to burn, thereby snuffing out or quenching the combustion process. This leaves unburned fuel in the combustion chamber. This unburned fuel is then forced out of the cylinder and into the exhaust system, along with the exhaust gases.

Many attempts have been made to minimize the amount of unburned fuel in the combustion chambers due to quenching, by increasing the coolant temperature and lessening the contact area of the coolant around the combustion area. However, design limitations within the combustion chambers prevent the complete burning of the air/fuel charge, so a certain amount of the unburned fuel is still expelled into the exhaust system, regardless of modifications to the engine.

AUTOMOTIVE EMISSIONS

Before emission controls were mandated on internal combustion engines, other sources of engine pollutants were discovered along with the exhaust emissions. It was determined that engine combustion exhaust produced approximately 60 percent of the total emission pollutants, fuel evaporation from the fuel tank and carburetor vents produced 20 percent, with the final 20 percent being produced through the crankcase as a by-product of the combustion process.

Exhaust Gases

The exhaust gases emitted into the atmosphere are a combination of burned and unburned fuel. To understand the exhaust emission and its composition, we must review some basic chemistry. When the air/fuel mixture is introduced into the engine, we are mixing air, composed of nitrogen (78 percent), oxygen (21 percent) and other gases (1 percent) with the fuel, which is 100 percent hydrocarbons (HC), in a semi-controlled ratio. As the combustion process is accomplished, power is produced to move the vehicle while the heat of combustion is transferred to the cooling system. The exhaust gases are then composed of nitrogen, a diatomic gas (N_2), the same as was introduced in the engine, carbon dioxide (CO_2), the same gas that is used in beverage carbonation, and water vapor (H_2O). The nitrogen (N_2), for the most part, passes through the engine unchanged, while the oxygen (O_2) reacts (burns) with the hydrocarbons (HC) and produces the carbon dioxide (CO_2) and the water vapors (H_2O). If this chemical process would be the only process to take place, the exhaust emissions would be harmless. However, during the combustion process, other compounds are formed which are considered dangerous. These pollutants are hydrocarbons (HC), carbon monoxide (CO), oxides of nitrogen (NOx) oxides of sulfur (SOx) and engine particulates.

HYDROCARBONS

Hydrocarbons (HC) are essentially fuel which was not burned during the combustion process or which has escaped into the atmosphere through fuel evaporation. The main sources of incomplete combustion are rich air/fuel mixtures, low engine temperatures and improper spark timing. The main sources of hydrocarbon emission through fuel evaporation on most vehicles used to be the vehicle's fuel tank and carburetor float bowl.

To reduce combustion hydrocarbon emission, engine modifications were made to minimize dead space and surface area in the combustion chamber. In addition, the air/fuel mixture was made more lean through the improved control which feedback carburetion and fuel injection offers and by the addition of external controls to aid in further combustion of the hydrocarbons outside the engine. Two such methods were the addition of air injection systems, to inject fresh air into the exhaust manifolds and the installation of catalytic converters, units that are able to burn traces of hydrocarbons without affecting the internal combustion process or fuel economy.

To control hydrocarbon emissions through fuel evaporation, modifications were made to the fuel tank to allow storage of the fuel vapors during periods of engine shut-down. Modifications were also made to the air intake system so that at specific times during engine operation, these vapors may be purged and burned by blending them with the air/fuel mixture.

CARBON MONOXIDE

Carbon monoxide is formed when not enough oxygen is present during the combustion process to convert carbon (C) to carbon dioxide (CO_2). An increase in the carbon monoxide (CO) emission is normally accompanied by an increase in the hydrocarbon (HC) emission because of the lack of oxygen to completely burn all of the fuel mixture.

Carbon monoxide (CO) also increases the rate at which the photo chemical smog is formed by speeding up the conversion of nitric oxide (NO) to nitrogen dioxide (NO_2). To accomplish this, carbon monoxide (CO) combines with oxygen (O_2) and nitric oxide (NO) to produce carbon dioxide (CO_2) and nitrogen dioxide (NO_2). ($CO + O_2 + NO = CO_2 + NO_2$).

The dangers of carbon monoxide, which is an odorless and colorless toxic gas are many. When carbon monoxide is inhaled into the lungs and passed into the blood stream, oxygen is replaced by the carbon monoxide in the red blood cells, causing a reduction in the amount of oxygen supplied to the many parts of the body. This lack of oxygen causes headaches, lack of coordination, reduced mental alertness and, should the carbon monoxide concentration be high enough, death could result.

NITROGEN

Normally, nitrogen is an inert gas. When heated to approximately 2500°F (1371°C) through the combustion process, this gas becomes active and causes an increase in the nitric oxide (NO) emission.

Oxides of nitrogen (NOx) are composed of approximately 97–98 percent nitric oxide (NO). Nitric oxide is a colorless gas but when it is passed into the atmosphere, it combines with oxygen and forms nitrogen dioxide (NO_2). The nitrogen dioxide then combines with chemically active hydrocarbons (HC) and when in the presence of sunlight, causes the formation of photo-chemical smog.

Ozone

To further complicate matters, some of the nitrogen dioxide (NO_2) is broken apart by the sunlight to form nitric oxide and oxygen. (NO_2+ sunlight = NO + O). This single atom of oxygen then combines with diatomic (meaning 2 atoms) oxygen (O_2) to form ozone (O_3). Ozone is one of the smells associated with smog. It has a pungent and offensive odor, irritates the eyes and lung tissues, affects the growth of plant life and causes rapid deterioration of rubber products. Ozone can be formed by sunlight as well as electrical discharge into the air.

The most common discharge area on the automobile engine is the secondary ignition electrical system, especially when inferior quality spark plug cables are used. As the surge of high voltage is routed through the secondary cable, the circuit builds up an electrical field around the wire, which acts upon the oxygen in the surrounding air to form the ozone. The faint glow along the cable with the engine running that may be visible on a dark night, is called the "corona discharge." It is the result of the electrical field passing from a high along the cable, to a low in the surrounding air, which forms the ozone gas. The combination of corona and ozone has been a major cause of cable deterioration. Recently, different and better quality insulating materials have lengthened the life of the electrical cables.

Although ozone at ground level can be harmful, ozone is beneficial to the earth's inhabitants. By having a concentrated ozone layer called the "ozonosphere," between 10 and 20 miles (16–32 km) up in the atmosphere, much of the ultra violet radiation from the sun's rays are absorbed and screened. If this ozone layer were not present, much of the earth's surface would be burned, dried and unfit for human life.

OXIDES OF SULFUR

Oxides of sulfur (SOx) were initially ignored in the exhaust system emissions, since the sulfur content of gasoline as a fuel is less than $\frac{1}{10}$ of 1 percent. Because of this small amount, it was felt that it contributed very little to the overall pollution problem. However, because of the difficulty in solving the sulfur emissions in industrial pollution and the introduction of catalytic converters to automobile exhaust systems, a change was mandated. The automobile exhaust system, when equipped with a catalytic converter, changes the sulfur dioxide (SO_2) into sulfur trioxide (SO_3).

When this combines with water vapors (H_2O), a sulfuric acid mist (H_2SO_4) is formed and is a very difficult pollutant to handle since it is extremely corrosive. This sulfuric acid mist that is formed, is the same mist that rises from the vents of an automobile battery when an active chemical reaction takes place within the battery cells.

When a large concentration of vehicles equipped with catalytic converters are operating in an area, this acid mist may rise and be distributed over a large ground area causing land, plant, crop, paint and building damage.

PARTICULATE MATTER

A certain amount of particulate matter is present in the burning of any fuel, with carbon constituting the largest percentage of the particulates. In gasoline, the remaining particulates are the burned remains of the various other compounds used in its manufacture. When a gasoline engine is in good internal condition, the particulate emissions are low but as the engine wears internally, the particulate emissions increase. By visually inspecting the tail pipe emissions, a determination can be made as to where an engine defect may exist. An engine with light gray or blue smoke emitting from the tail pipe normally indicates an increase in the oil consumption through burning due to internal engine wear. Black smoke would indicate a defective fuel delivery system, causing the engine to operate in a rich mode. Regardless of the color of the smoke, the internal part of the engine or the fuel delivery system should be repaired to prevent excess particulate emissions.

Diesel and turbine engines emit a darkened plume of smoke from the exhaust system because of the type of fuel used. Emission control regulations are mandated for this type of emission and more stringent measures are being used to prevent excess emission of the particulate matter. Electronic components are being introduced to control the injection of the fuel at precisely the proper time of piston travel, to achieve the optimum in fuel ignition and fuel usage. Other particulate after-burning components are being tested to achieve a cleaner emission.

Good grades of engine lubricating oils should be used, which meet the manufacturer's specification. Cut-rate oils can contribute to the particulate emission problem because of their low flash or ignition temperature point. Such oils burn prematurely during the combustion process causing emission of particulate matter.

The cooling system is an important factor in the reduction of particulate matter. The optimum combustion will occur, with the cooling system operating at a temperature specified by the manufacturer. The cooling system must be maintained in the same manner as the engine oiling system, as each system is required to perform properly in order for the engine to operate efficiently for a long time.

Crankcase Emissions

Crankcase emissions are made up of water, acids, unburned fuel, oil fumes and particulates. These emissions are classified as hydrocarbons (HC) and are formed by the small amount of unburned, compressed air/fuel mixture entering the crankcase from the combustion area (between the cylinder walls and piston rings) during the compression and power strokes. The head of the compression and combustion help to form the remaining crankcase emissions.

Since the first engines, crankcase emissions were allowed into the atmosphere through a road draft tube, mounted on the lower side of the engine block. Fresh air came in through an open oil filler cap or breather. The air passed through the crankcase mixing with blow-by gases. The motion of the vehicle and the air blowing past the open end of the road draft tube caused a low pressure area (vacuum) at the end of the tube. Crankcase emissions were simply drawn out of the road draft tube into the air.

To control the crankcase emission, the road draft tube was deleted. A hose and/or tubing was routed from the crankcase to the intake manifold so the blow-by emission could be burned with the air/fuel mixture. However, it was found

that intake manifold vacuum, used to draw the crankcase emissions into the manifold, would vary in strength at the wrong time and not allow the proper emission flow. A regulating valve was needed to control the flow of air through the crankcase.

Testing, showed the removal of the blow-by gases from the crankcase as quickly as possible, was most important to the longevity of the engine. Should large accumulations of blow-by gases remain and condense, dilution of the engine oil would occur to form water, soots, resins, acids and lead salts, resulting in the formation of sludge and varnishes. This condensation of the blow-by gases occurs more frequently on vehicles used in numerous starting and stopping conditions, excessive idling and when the engine is not allowed to attain normal operating temperature through short runs.

Evaporative Emissions

Gasoline fuel is a major source of pollution, before and after it is burned in the automobile engine. From the time the fuel is refined, stored, pumped and transported, again stored until it is pumped into the fuel tank of the vehicle, the gasoline gives off unburned hydrocarbons (HC) into the atmosphere. Through the redesign of storage areas and venting systems, the pollution factor was diminished, but not eliminated, from the refinery standpoint. However, the automobile still remained the primary source of vaporized, unburned hydrocarbon (HC) emissions.

Fuel pumped from an underground storage tank is cool but when exposed to a warmer ambient temperature, will expand. Before controls were mandated, an owner might fill the fuel tank with fuel from an underground storage tank and park the vehicle for some time in warm area, such as a parking lot. As the fuel would warm, it would expand and should no provisions or area be provided for the expansion, the fuel would spill out of the filler neck and onto the ground, causing hydrocarbon (HC) pollution and creating a severe fire hazard. To correct this condition, the vehicle manufacturers added overflow plumbing and/or gasoline tanks with built in expansion areas or domes.

However, this did not control the fuel vapor emission from the fuel tank. It was determined that most of the fuel evaporation occurred when the vehicle was stationary and the engine not operating. Most vehicles carry 5–25 gallons (19–95 liters) of gasoline. Should a large concentration of vehicles be parked in one area, such as a large parking lot, excessive fuel vapor emissions would take place, increasing as the temperature increases.

To prevent the vapor emission from escaping into the atmosphere, the fuel systems were designed to trap the vapors while the vehicle is stationary, by sealing the system from the atmosphere. A storage system is used to collect and hold the fuel vapors from the carburetor (if equipped) and the fuel tank when the engine is not operating. When the engine is started, the storage system is then purged of the fuel vapors, which are drawn into the engine and burned with the air/fuel mixture.

EMISSION CONTROLS

The emission control system begins at the air intake and ends at the tailpipe. The emission control system includes various sub-systems such as the positive crankcase ventilation system, evaporative emission control system, the exhaust gas recalculation system and exhaust catalyst, as well as the electronic controls that govern the fuel and ignition system. These components are combined to control engine operation for maximum engine efficiency and minimal exhaust emissions.

Positive Crankcase Ventilation System

OPERATION

▶ **See Figures 1 and 2**

The system consists of a tube from the air filter housing to the rocker/camshaft cover and a second tube from the rocker/camshaft cover to the intake manifold. Under normal operating conditions, clean air flows from the air filter into the rocker/camshaft cover where it mixes with crankcase oil vapors. These vapors are drawn through the PCV valve and into the intake manifold to be burned with the air/fuel mixture. The flow to the intake manifold is metered

by the PCV valve. When manifold vacuum is high, the valve is pulled closed and flow is restricted to maintain a smooth idle. If crankcase pressure is very high, vapors can flow directly into the air filter housing.

A plugged PCV system will cause oil leaks or a build up of sludge in the engine. An air filter coated with engine oil indicates excessive crankcase pressure. A leaking valve or hose might cause rough or high idle, engine stalling and/or Powertrain Control Module (PCM) trouble codes.

COMPONENT TESTING

1. Visually inspect the PCV valve hose, the fresh air supply hose and their attaching nipples or grommets for splits, cuts, damage, clogging, or restrictions. Repair or replace, as necessary.
2. If the hoses pass inspection, start the engine and allow it to warm until normal operating temperature is reached.
3. Remove the PCV valve from the rocker arm cover, but leave it connected to the hose. With the engine at idle, feel the end of the valve for manifold vacuum. If there is no vacuum, check for a plugged or leaking hose, PCV valve or manifold port. Replace a plugged or damaged hose.
4. Stop the engine and remove the PCV valve. It should rattle when shaken. If the valve does not rattle or it is plugged, replace the valve.

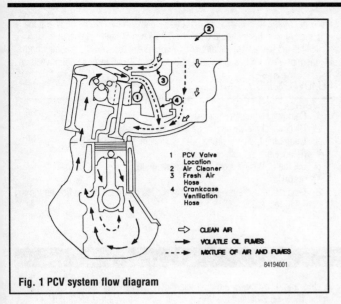

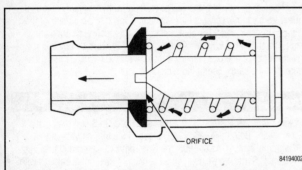

1   PCV Valve Location
2   Air Cleaner
3   Fresh Air Hose
4   Crankcase Ventilation Hose

⇨   CLEAN AIR
→   VOLATILE OIL FUMES
- - - ►   MIXTURE OF AIR AND FUMES

84194001

Fig. 1 PCV system flow diagram

ORIFICE

84194002

Fig. 2 Cutaway view of the PCV valve, allowing the flow of mixed air into the intake manifold

REMOVAL & INSTALLATION

PCV valve removal and installation is covered in Section 1. Refer to Section 1 for any maintenance regarding the PCV system.

Evaporative Emission Controls

OPERATION

This system prevents the escape of raw fuel vapors (unburned hydrocarbons, or HC) into the atmosphere. When the engine is not running, fuel vapors that build up in the tank flow through a hose to a carbon canister located in the inner fender below the air cleaner. When the engine is running, the vapors in the canister are carried to the intake manifold and burned in the engine.

On vehicles with a Digifant engine management system, the evaporative emission system is completely vacuum operated. The canister is purged of fuel vapors when a vacuum actuated valve is opened and fresh air is drawn into the open bottom of the canister. Vacuum for the valve is generated only at partial throttle openings. The purge air flows to the intake manifold through an orifice that limits the flow. These two features avoid radical air/fuel mixture changes when the canister is purged.

On vehicles with CIS-E fuel injection, the carbon canister is isolated from the intake manifold by a solenoid valve and a frequency valve. The solenoid valve is **ON** (open) whenever the engine is running. The frequency valve is cycled open and closed by the Motronic control unit to control flow rate depending on coolant temperature and engine speed/load conditions.

On both systems, the vacuum line to the canister connects to the vacuum vent valve. This valve is mounted near the fuel filler and allows vapors to flow to the canister but will close if the vehicle turns over to prevent a liquid fuel leak.

The system does not require any service under normal conditions other than

to check for leaks. Check the hoses visually for cracks and check the seal on the gas tank filler cap. Replace the cap if the seal is split. If any hoses are in need of replacement, use only hoses marked EVAP, available from your local automotive supply store. If there is a strong smell of raw fuel from under the hood when the engine is not running, test the purge control valve.

COMPONENT TESTING

Motronic System

1. With the engine OFF, disconnect the hoses from both valves and connect a clean length of hose. It should be possible to blow through the frequency valve (normally open) but not the solenoid valve (normally closed).
2. With the engine coolant less than 140°F (60°C), disconnect the purge hose from the canister to the frequency valve. With the engine at idle, there should be no vacuum.
3. As the engine warms to operating temperature, the solenoid valve should be **ON** and open. The frequency valve should begin to cycle **ON** and **OFF**>, open and closed. There will be strong vacuum for about 30 seconds, then little or no vacuum for about 60 seconds.
4. If the system does not perform as described, pull back the connector boots so a voltmeter or test light can be connected with the wiring still connected to the valves. If voltage appears at the intervals described, 1 or both of the valves is faulty. If there is no voltage, the wiring or the engine control unit may be faulty.

Digifant System

1. Disconnect the top hose from the valve and connect a hand vacuum pump to the small port on top of the valve.
2. Disconnect the hose from the carbon canister to the control valve and run the engine at idle to provide vacuum to the bottom port.
3. Place a finger over the open port of the valve. When there is vacuum at the bottom port, you should not feel any vacuum at the open port.
4. Draw a vacuum on the small top port. The valve should open and you should feel vacuum at the open port.

Exhaust Gas Recalculation System

OPERATION

▶ **See Figure 3**

Vehicles sold in some parts of the U.S. with Motronic fuel injection are equipped with an EGR valve. To reduce oxides of nitrogen (NOx) emissions, metered amounts of exhaust gases are added to the air/fuel mixture to lower combustion temperatures during combustion. The vacuum operated EGR valve controls the volume of exhaust gas flow into the intake manifold. Vacuum for

91224P22

Fig. 3 This tube is used by trained professional mechanics with the proper equipment to monitor the exhaust gases before they enter the catalytic converter

the valve is controlled by coolant temperature and supplied through a vacuum amplifier. The EGR valve is closed when the engine is cold or at idle or full throttle. The valve is partially open just above idle and fully open at mid throttle settings.

COMPONENT TESTING

1. While idling the engine, connect a hand vacuum pump to the EGR valve and draw a vacuum. The engine should idle rough or even stall. This indicates the valve is opening and closing fully.

2. Reconnect the vacuum hose to the EGR valve, disconnect the vacuum supply hose at the thermoswitch and connect the hand pump. Draw a vacuum to make sure the thermoswitch operates. If the engine is cold, the idle should not change. If the coolant temperature is above about 120°F (49°C), the thermoswitch should open and allow vacuum to the EGR valve.

3. To test the vacuum amplifier, connect a tee fitting and vacuum gauge or mercury column to the amplifier input hose, between the throttle body and the amplifier. At idle, there should be about 0.3 inches (7.6mm) Hg vacuum.

4. Tee the gauge into the amplifier output hose, between the amplifier and the thermoswitch. At idle there should be about 1.9–3.5 inches (Hg) of vacuum.

REMOVAL & INSTALLATION

1. Remove the negative battery cable.
2. Disconnect the vacuum hose from the EGR valve.
3. Unbolt the EGR line fitting on the opposite side of the valve.
4. Remove the two retaining bolts.
5. Lift the EGR valve from the intake manifold.
To install:
6. Installation is the reverse of removal. Use new gaskets and tighten the bolts to 7 ft. lbs. (10 Nm).

ELECTRONIC ENGINE CONTROLS

Digifant System

The Digifant system is all electronic, using electric injectors at a low injection pressure. All injectors are operated by the Electronic Control Unit (ECU) so injector timing and duration can be closely controlled for reduced emissions and improved fuel mileage. During deceleration above a specific rpm, the injectors are shut off to save fuel and reduce emissions. The air flow sensor uses an air vane that moves a potentiometer to signal its position to the ECU. The electric idle stabilizer a motorized rotary valve that controls the amount of air allowed to bypass the throttle plate. Very precise control is maintained over a wide range of idle loads and engine temperatures. The ECU has the ability to store fault codes but codes and other self diagnostic functions can only be read with the VAG 1551 tester. Procedures described here are for testing without the VAG 1551.

Mono-motronic

The mono-motronic system is used on the ACC engine. It integrates the ignition and fuel system together. This system has a built in diagnostic function that detects and stores codes. Fuel is controlled through the use of various sensors that relay information to the Electronic Control Unit (ECU). Through a constant monitoring of such parameters as the oxygen content of the exhaust, camshaft position and throttle position the fuel management system can maintain the correct air fuel ratio under all engine operating conditions. The ECM has the ability to control components such as the intake manifold heater, fuel injectors, ignition coil, and Evaporative Canister Purge Regulator Valve (EVAP).

Motronic System

The CIS-E Motronic system used on the 16 valve engines is yet another version of the CIS-E fuel injection system. The system uses mechanical injectors, a fuel distributor, fuel pump and air flow sensor that are similar to those on earlier systems. Most of the electronic system controls are also the same. The major difference that the Electronic Control Unit (ECU) now controls the ignition system as well as fuel injection. The new ECU is equipped with an adaptive learning program which allows it to learn and remember the normal operating range of the mixture control output signal. This gives the system the capability to compensate for changes in altitude, slight vacuum leaks or other changes due to things such as engine wear. Cold engine drivability and emissions are improved. The new ECU also is capable of cold start enrichment without the use of a thermo-time switch.

The fuel injector pressure is higher for better fuel atomization and residual pressure. The threads on the new injectors are different so they cannot be interchanged with older units. Some other components such as sensors are similar to those used on the Digifant engine management system. Some of the testing procedures are the same but the parts are not necessarily interchangeable.

Motronic 2.9

The motronic 2.9 engine management system was designed by the Robert Bosch• Corporation. This system combines the ignition and fuel systems together and incorporates a built in diagnostic system. The motronic 2.9 system on the 1993–95 2.0L and the VR6 is of the adaptive type that can adjust the fuel air ratio as needed. No adjustments can be made. Fuel metering is controlled via the input from various sensors such as engine speed and the mass of the incoming air. On this system, the camshaft position sensor relays the number one firing position to the Electronic Control Unit (ECU). Throttle position is measured through the use of a position sensor. A heated oxygen sensor is used to measure the amount oxygen in the exhaust stream.

Motronic 5.9

This version of VW's engine management system is On Board Diagnostic II (OBD II) compliant. Both the 1996–99 2.0 liter and the VR6 engines are equipped with this system. As of 1995, the Government mandated that all vehicles sold in the U.S. must have an engine operating system that complies with OBD II standards. Several changes were made to the Motronic system that enabled it to meet the necessary requirements. One change between this system and the Motronic 2.9 is that there are two Heated Oxygen Sensors (HO2S) on this type system, one pre-catalyst (before the catalytic converter) and one post catalyst (after the catalytic converter).

Electronic Control Unit (ECU)

OPERATION

Motronic System

This unit is located above the firewall in the engine compartment. The ECU is supplied with an internal voltage regulator and operates at 8 volts to prevent control fluctuations when vehicle accessories are switched on. The ECU accepts the various input signals and calculates optimum fuel injection and ignition output control signals. The main output devices are the differential pressure regulator, ignition coil and the idle air stabilizer valve. The maximum engine speed is limited by the ECU through the differential pressure regulator. Above the tachometer "red line", the lower chamber pressure is increased relative to the system pressure and the fuel supply to the injectors is interrupted.

The ECU is equipped with an adaptive learning program that learns the normal operating point of the air/fuel mixture. This information comes from the oxygen sensor and is only read when the charcoal canister frequency valve is in the OFF cycle. As the engine wears or is driven differently or with changes in altitude, control signals that the ECU considers "normal" are modified to account for the deviations.

Digifant

The ECU controls all fuel injection, idle speed and ignition functions and also acts as a rev limiter. Above the maximum rpm rating, the ECU will intermittently shut off the fuel injectors to prevent over-revving the engine. If an input or output device fault is detected and it is serious enough to cause engine control problems, the ECU will switch into a "limp home" mode and the engine will be operated at a pre-set condition. The ECU is mounted in the tray above the fire wall.

Diesel and Turbo Diesel Injected (TDI) models

This fuel injection system is very similar to the Motronic system. It uses various sensors to monitor and adjust combustion as necessary. Sensors send inputs to the computer, based on preset programs adjustments are made, and the performance and emissions are controlled to obtain optimum levels.

REMOVAL & INSTALLATION

1. Disconnect the negative battery cable.
2. Detach all wiring harnesses from the Electronic Control Module (ECU).

➡ **Use caution when detaching the wiring harnesses from the ECU, old plastic harnesses are very fragile and may break upon removal if too much force is exerted.**

3. Remove the mounting fasteners from the ECU.
4. Ground yourself at all times when handling the ECU. Ground straps are sold at most electronic stores and make a wise investment if you plan to do work on sensitive components such as the engine computer.
5. Remove the ECU.

To install:

6. Installation is the reverse of removal.

Oxygen Sensor

OPERATION

▶ **See Figures 4 and 5**

The oxygen (O2) sensor is a device which produces an electrical voltage when exposed to the oxygen present in the exhaust gases. The sensor is mounted in the exhaust system, usually in the manifold or a boss located on the down pipe before the catalyst. The oxygen sensors used on many VW models are electrically heated internally for faster switching when the engine is started cold. The oxygen sensor produces a voltage within 0 and 1 volt. When there is a large amount of oxygen present (lean mixture), the sensor produces a low voltage (less than 0.4v). When there is a lesser amount present (rich mixture) it produces a higher voltage (0.6–1.0v). The stoichiometric or correct fuel to air ratio will read between 0.4 and 0.6v. By monitoring the oxygen content and converting it to electrical voltage, the sensor acts as a rich-lean switch. The voltage is transmitted to the ECU.

Fig. 5 Use an oxygen sensor socket or an open end wrench to remove the sensor

TESTING

▶ **See Figure 6**

1. To test the oxygen sensor, do not disconnect the wiring harness but insert a back-probe or other devise such as a paper clip into the rear of the wiring harness at terminal # 4 on 1990–99 VW's. This wire is the signal wire.
2. Using a Digital Volt Ohm Meter (DVOM) measure the oxygen sensors output by connecting the positive lead of the DVOM to the #4 terminal and the negative lead to a good ground.
3. Make sure all testing equipment is clear of any moving parts and then start the vehicle.
4. Within a few minutes the oxygen sensor should begin producing voltage. At idle this reading should be between 0.3 and 1.0 volts. The reading should fluctuate!
5. If the oxygen sensor output is out of range, you will have to test the sensors heating element. This can be accomplished by turning the engine off and disconnecting the four (4) pin harness.
6. Perform a test for battery voltage at terminals one (1) and two (2) of the connector. This once again must be performed with the engine running. The resistance should be approximately 2 ohms.
7. If the oxygen sensor signal is not as specified, replace the sensor.

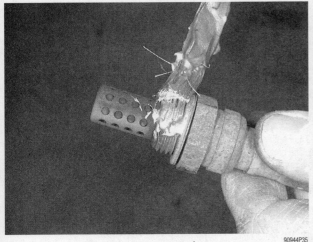

Fig. 4 Apply an antisieze compound to the threads of the oxygen sensor before reinstalling it

Fig. 6 A portable, hand-held, oscilloscope can be purchased through professional tool suppliers and makes a great diagnostic tool

REMOVAL & INSTALLATION

1. Disconnect the negative battery cable and place it away from the battery's post.
2. Detach the oxygen sensor electrical wiring harness.
3. Using a oxygen sensor socket (sold at most parts warehouses) of a closed end wrench of comparable size, loosen the sensor from the exhaust.
4. Remove the oxygen sensor from the exhaust.
To install:
The sensor is threaded into the catalytic converter or the exhaust pipe with an anti-seize compound on the threads.
5. To install simply thread the sensor into the exhaust and tighten.

➡**When replacing it, be careful not to get anti-seize in the slots of the outer shield. Tighten to 37 ft. lbs. (50 Nm).**

Idle Stabilizer Valve

The idle speed is controlled electronically on vehicles equipped with the Mono-Motronic fuel control system. This system also controls the idle speed by adjusting the engine timing. The Electronic Control Unit (ECU) monitors all engine loads and adjusts the idle speed accordingly.

OPERATION

◢ **See Figure 7**

Motronic

The idle stabilizer is a motorized rotary valve that is operated by the ECU to control the amount of air that bypasses the throttle. This design allows very precise control of idle speed regardless of engine temperature or load. The valve is spring loaded towards the minimum opening position. The voltage that holds the valve open is applied in variable length pulses called a duty cycle. The duty cycle ranges from 5–95 percent. Because of this design, there is no idle speed adjustment.

Digifont

The idle stabilizer is a linear motor solenoid valve that is operated by the ECU. The linear motion moves a plunger to control an opening in the valve which controls the amount of air that bypasses the throttle. This design allows very precise control of idle speed regardless of engine temperature or load. The voltage supplied to the valve can't really be measured because it is not constant. To test the duty cycle of the valve in operation, a special adapter is required that allows connecting a multi-meter that reads milliamps while the wiring is connected to the valve.

Fig. 7 Typical VW idle stabilizer valve.

91224P20

TESTING

➡**On vehicles with high mileage on them, carbon deposits may form on the throttle plates and restrict air flow. This will affect the operation of the IAC system.**

Motronic

1. With the valve installed, turn the ignition switch **ON** but do not start the engine. It should be possible to hear or feel the valve hum and/or vibrate.
2. Turn the ignition switch **OFF**. Unplug the connector from the idle stabilizer valve and connect an ohmmeter across the valve terminals. There should be 7–11 ohms resistance. Resistance may be higher on a warm engine.
3. Disable the ignition system so the engine will not start. Connect a voltmeter or an LED test lamp between terminal 1 of the connector and ground. When the starter is operated, there should be voltage at terminal 1.
4. Remove the valve and check for visual signs of scoring or binding on the rotating portion. Do not lubricate the valve. If it is receiving voltage but does not operate, it must be replaced.

Digifont

1. With the ignition **ON** but the engine not running, the valve should vibrate to the touch. If not, make sure the idle switch on the throttle body is working properly and that the throttle is fully closed.
2. If there is no vibration at the valve, turn the ignition **OFF** and unplug the connector. Use an ohmmeter to check the resistance across the terminals on the valve. There should be about 2–10 ohms resistance.
3. Connect the adapter so a multi-meter can be connected. With the engine at operating temperature and idling, the current to the valve should fluctuate from 390–460 milliamps. With the blue temperature sensor wiring disconnected, the current should be steady.
4. If the current is not correct, remove the valve and check for visual signs of sticking. Do not lubricate the valve. If no other problem is found, check the continuity of the wiring between the valve and the ECU with the ignition **OFF**.
5. If the idle stabilizer valve seems to work properly but engine idle is out of specification, check for a vacuum leak, a faulty coolant temperature sensor or some other problem with the engine control system.

Coolant Temperature Sensor

DESCRIPTION

Monotronic System

The Engine Coolant Temperature (ECT) sensor is mounted in the water outlet on the back side of the head. If you vehicle still has a original VW part it will be black in color with a four terminal connector. This device signals the engine management system with the current coolant temperature, the ECU takes this information and uses it to control other such circuits as the idle speed, knock control system, oxygen sensor circuit, exhaust gas recalculation, and fuel tank venting. It is also important to note that if at any time ECU does not receive a signal from the ECT it will substitute a value of 176°F (80°C).

VR6

The Engine Coolant Temperature sensor is mounted in the thermostat housing. The body of the sensor will be blue and the sensor will be blue and have two terminals if it is an original factory VW part.

Digifont

There are two coolant temperature sensors mounted in the upper radiator hose-to-engine flange. The black connector is for the gauge on the instrument panel. The blue connector is for the ECU.

There is also an air temperature sensor at the inlet end of the air flow sensor. Both temperature sensors operate with the same resistance values.

TESTING

Motronic

1. Unplug the sensor connector and use an ohmmeter to check sensor resistance:
- 55°F (13°C)—3000–3800 ohms
- 65°F (18°C)—2200–3000 ohms
- 75°F (24°C)—1800–2500 ohms
- 85°F (29°C)—1500–2100 ohms
- 150°F (65°C)—400–550 ohms
- 200°F (93°C)—200–270 ohms

Digifont

1. Unplug the sensor connector and use an ohmmeter to check sensor resistance:
- 1.55°F (13°C)—3000–3800 ohms
- 2.65°F (18°C)—2200–3000 ohms
- 3.75°F (24°C)—1800–2500 ohms
- 85°F (29°C)—1500–2100 ohms
- 150°F (65°C)—400–550 ohms
- 200°F (93°C)—200–270 ohms

Air Flow Sensor

OPERATION

◆ See Figures 8, 9 and 10

Motronic

The fuel distributor is mounted on top of a mechanical air flow sensor. Under the air duct boot is a venturi with a plate in the narrowest part of the bore. As the throttle opens and air flow increases, the plate is pushed farther up in the bore. This lifts a piston that uncovers slots in the fuel distributor to allow more fuel to the upper chamber.

The vertical position of the plate is measured with a potentiometer. A voltage is supplied to the position sensor and the portion of the signal returned to the ECU indicates the height of the sensor plate in the bore.

Digifont

This unit converts air flow to a voltage signal. Air enters and moves a spring-loaded vane which moves a potentiometer. The potentiometer modulates a voltage sent from the ECU and the return signal represents the mass of air flowing to the intake manifold. Air temperature is also measured and

Fig. 9 View of the mass air flow sensor's heated air metering device

reported to the ECU. The air/fuel mixture adjustment is also in this unit, which is an adjusting screw that allows a certain amount of air to bypass the vane and enter the engine unmeasured. More unmeasured air means a leaner mixture.

TESTING

Motronic

1. Remove the rubber boot from the top of the air flow sensor and lift the plate with pliers or a magnet. DO NOT loosen the bolt. The plate should move up smoothly with some resistance and should drop when released. The plate rests on a spring which allows it to move down if the engine backfires.

2. To test the position sensor, make sure the ignition switch is **OFF** and unplug the connector. Check the resistance between terminals 1 and 2; it should be more than 4000 ohms. Check the resistance between terminals 2 and 3; it should be less than 1000 ohms.

3. With the ohmmeter connected to terminals 2 and 3, move the plate up and down. The resistance should change smoothly to more than 4000 ohms at full travel.

4. Turn the ignition switch **ON**. Connect a voltmeter between terminals 1 and 3 of the wiring connector. There should be 4.5–5.5 volts from the ECU.

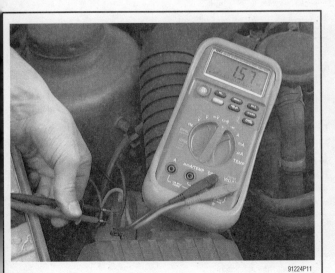

Fig. 8 Testing the mass air flow meter

Fig. 10 Mass air flow meter mounted in the air box

Digifont

1. With the ignition **OFF**, unplug the sensor connector and measure the resistance across the end terminals of the sensor. These are for the air temperature sensor. At 60 °F (15oC), there should be about 3000 ohms. At 80 °F (27 °C), there should be about 1900 ohms.

2. The resistance between terminals 3 and 4 should be 500–1000 ohms when the flap is in the rest position.

3. Connect the ohmmeter between the center terminals 2 and 3 and move the vane inside the sensor. The resistance should change smoothly and linearly as the vane is moved. There is a strong return spring on the flap but is should move smoothly with no binding.

Throttle Position Switches

OPERATION

▶ **See Figure 11**

There are 2 switches on the throttle body, one above and one below. The lower switch signals the ECU when the throttle is at idle and the upper switch signals full throttle. This information is used to calculate fuel shut-off and ignition timing during deceleration, idle stabilizer valve operation and full throttle enrichment. If there is a problem with any of these functions, check these switches first.

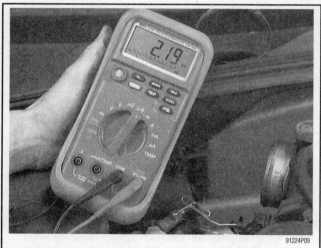
Fig. 11 Using a multimeter to test the throttle position sensor

TESTING

1. Locate the switches on the throttle body and unplug the connector.
2. Connect an ohmmeter to the idle switch and make sure it is closed when the throttle is against the stop. Open the throttle, position a 0.024 inch (0.60mm) feeler gauge against the stop and let the throttle close on the gauge. The switch must remain open. DO NOT adjust the throttle stop screw.
3. Connect the ohmmeter to the full throttle switch. Open the throttle all the way to the stop and make sure the switch closes. The switch should open when the throttle is allowed to close 10 degrees from the stop.
4. Turn the ignition switch **ON** and use a voltmeter to check for 5 volts at each switch connector. This signal comes directly from the ECU.

Intake Air Temperature Sensor (IAT)

OPERATION

▶ **See Figures 12 and 13**

IAT sensor is located on the rear upper intake manifold of the 2.8 VR6 engine. On the 2.0L engine this sensor can be found by the right center of the engine compartment.

Fig. 12 Connect the probes of a digital multimeter to the intake air temperature sensor

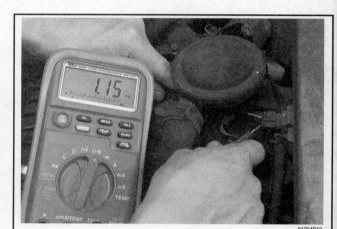
Fig. 13 Checking the resistance of the IAT sensor

The Intake Air Temperature (IAT) sensor determines the air temperature inside the intake manifold. Resistance changes in response to the ambient air temperature. The sensor has a negative temperature coefficient. As the temperature of the sensor rises the resistance across the sensor decreases. This provides a signal to the PCM indicating the temperature of the incoming air charge. This sensor helps the PCM to determine spark timing and air/fuel ratio. Information from this sensor is added to the pressure sensor information to calculate the air mass being sent to the cylinders.

TESTING

1. Turn the ignition switch **OFF**.
2. Disconnect the wiring harness from the IAT sensor.
3. Measure the resistance between the sensor terminals.
4. If the resistance is not within specification, the IAT may be faulty.
5. Connect the wiring harness to the sensor.

REMOVAL & INSTALLATION

➡**The IAT sensor is part of the wiring harness connector for the fuel injector. You may not be able to purchase it separately at a local auto parts store. To date, VW offers the part only as a unit.**

The IAT sensor is located in the side of the intake manifold.
1. Remove the negative battery cable.
2. Remove the wiring harness from the sensor.
3. Unscrew the sensor.
To install:
4. Install the new sensor.
5. Attach the wiring harness to the sensor.
6. Install the negative cable.

COMPONENT LOCATIONS

ELECTRONIC ENGINE CONTROL AND EMISSIONS COMPONENT LOCATIONS—EARLY MODEL 2.0L 8 VALVE ENGINE

1. Throttle position sensor
2. PCV system
3. Intake air temperature sensor
4. Heat riser hose
5. Vacuum hose
6. Oxygen sensor
7. Exhaust gas test port
8. Idle air control motor
9. Coolant temperature sensor

ELECTRONIC ENGINE CONTROL AND EMISSIONS COMPONENT LOCATIONS—LATE MODEL 2.0L 8 VALVE ENGINE

1. Oxygen sensor connector
2. Catalytic converter
3. Idle air control motor
4. Throttle valve
5. Manifold vacuum port
6. Throttle position sensor
7. PCV system
8. Vacuum hose

ELECTRONIC ENGINE CONTROL AND EMISSIONS COMPONENT LOCATIONS—2.0L 16 VALVE ENGINE

1. Oxygen sensor wiring harness
2. Intake air temperature sensor
3. Exhaust gas test port
4. Throttle switch harness connector
5. Ported vacuum hose
6. Cold start valve
7. Charcoal canister solenoid valves
8. Fuel pressure regulator
9. Heated air intake control door
10. Knock sensor
11. Cold start injector

ELECTRONIC ENGINE CONTROL AND EMISSIONS COMPONENT LOCATIONS—2.8L VR6 ENGINE

1. Oxygen sensor wiring harness connector
2. Catalytic converter
3. Idle air control motor
4. Manifold vacuum port
5. PCV system vacuum hose
6. Emissions catalyst information label
7. Vacuum hose routing label

OBD-I TROUBLE CODES

General Information

CIS-E FUEL INJECTION

▶ **See Figures 14 and 15**

The CIS-E Motronic system is the latest development of the electronically controlled mechanical Continuous Injection System (CIS). This system uses injectors, fuel pump and air flow sensor that are similar to those on earlier systems. The fuel distributor is equipped with an electronically controlled differential pressure regulator. This is operated by the ECU to control the fuel pressure in the lower chamber of the fuel distributor, which controls air/fuel mixture.

The ECU is now equipped with an adaptive learning program which allows it to learn and remember the normal operating range of the mixture control output signal. This gives the system the capability to compensate for changes in altitude, slight vacuum leaks or other changes due to things such as engine wear. Cold engine driveability and emissions are improved. The new ECU also is capable of cold start enrichment without the use of a thermo-time switch. The Fox still uses the thermo-time switch on CIS equipped vehicles.

The fuel injector pressure has been increased for better fuel atomization and residual pressure. The threads on the new injectors are different so they cannot be interchanged with older units. Some of the other components used on the CIS-E system are similar to those used on the fully electronic engine management systems. Some of the testing procedures are the same but the parts are not necessarily interchangeable.

MOTRONIC AND MOTRONIC 2.9 MULTIPORT FUEL INJECTION (MFI) SYSTEMS

Motronic and Motronic 2.9 systems are developments of the electronically controlled Multiport Fuel Injection (MFI) system. The two systems are almost identical. The engine control module (ECM) monitors engine intake air quantity using the Mass Air Flow (MAF) sensor. This is a true mass air measurement system. Using input from the MAE and other sensors, the ECM can calculate the length of time the injectors should be opened, and also controls the ignition system timing.

The ECM is equipped with an adaptive learning program which allows it to learn and remember the normal operating range of the mixture control output signal. This allows the system to compensate for changes in altitude, slight vacuum leaks or other changes due to other things such as engine wear. Cold engine driveability and emissions are improved.

The ECM is also equipped with a fault memory. If the sensor signal or output solenoid feedback signal is outside preprogrammed parameters, the ECM will

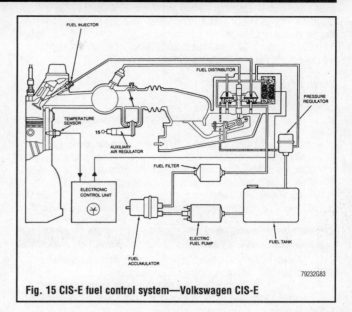

Fig. 15 CIS-E fuel control system—Volkswagen CIS-E

store a fault code representing the fault and sensor involved. The ECM will also illuminate the Malfunction Indicator Lamp (MIL) to inform the vehicle operator that the vehicle requires service.

MONO-MOTRONIC THROTTLE BODY FUEL INJECTION (TBI) SYSTEM

The Mono-Motronic system is development of the electronically controlled Throttle Body Fuel Injection (TBI) system. Based on outputs from the Throttle Position (TP), Engine Coolant Temperature (ECT) and Intake Air Temperature/Fuel Injector Temperature (IAT/FIT) sensors, the Engine Control Module (ECM) can infer intake air flow by air temperature and throttle position. This is a speed-density type control system. The ECM calculates the length of time the injector(s) should be opened, and with input from other sensors, also controls ignition timing.

The ECM is equipped with an adaptive learning program which allows it to learn and remember the normal operating range of the mixture control output signal. This allows the system to compensate for changes in altitude, slight vacuum leaks or other changes due to other things such as engine wear. Cold engine driveability and emissions are improved. The ECM is also equipped with a fault memory. If the sensor signal or output solenoid feedback signal is outside preprogrammed parameters, the ECM will store a fault code representing the fault and sensor involved. The ECM will also illuminate the Malfunction Indicator Lamp (MIL) to inform the vehicle operator that the vehicle requires service.

DIGIFANT MULTIPORT FUEL INJECTION (MFI) SYSTEM

The Digifant Motronic system is development of the electronically controlled Multiport Fuel Injection (MFI) system. This system is quite similar on all models, but there is one significant difference among the three engines, intake air flow is measured using one of two systems. The 1.8L NA engine is equipped with a Vane Air Flow (VAF) sensor. This is a true mass air measurement system. The 1.8L SC and 2.5L NA engines use a Manifold Absolute Pressure (MAP) sensor.

Along with output from the Intake Air Temperature (IAT) sensor, the ECM can infer intake air flow by air temperature and pressure. This is a speed-density type control system. Using either measurement system, the ECM calculates the length of time the injectors should be opened, and with input from other sensors, also controls ignition timing.

The ECM is equipped with an adaptive learning program which allows it to learn and remember the normal operating range of the mixture control output signal. This allows the system to compensate for changes in altitude, slight vacuum leaks or other changes due to other things such as engine wear. Cold engine driveability and emissions are improved.

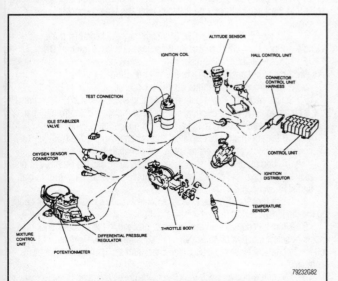

Fig. 14 CIS-E fuel system components—Volkswagen CIS-E

The ECM is also equipped with a fault memory. If the sensor signal or output solenoid feedback signal is outside preprogrammed parameters, the ECM will store a fault code representing the fault and sensor involved. The ECM will also illuminate the Malfunction Indicator Lamp (MIL) to inform the vehicle operator that the vehicle requires service. Some vehicles equipped with both the Digifant Motronic system and California specification emissions equipment also have the capability of flashing diagnostic codes.

Service Precautions

• Do not disconnect the battery or the control unit before reading the fault codes. On the Motronic system, fault code memory is erased when power is interrupted.
• Make sure the ignition switch is **OFF** before disconnecting any wiring.
• Before removing or installing a control unit, disconnect the negative battery cable. The unit receives power through the main connector at all times and will be permanently damaged if improperly powered up or down.
• Keep all parts and harnesses dry during service. Protect the control unit and all solid-state components from rough handling or extremes of temperature.

Reading Codes

Only California vehicles with the Digifant II and Digifant I systems were equipped with the capability of flashing diagnostic codes.

On the Digifant II system codes were viewed through a combination rocker switch/indicator light. The following California vehicles were equipped with the Digifant II system:

1990 Golf, Jetta and GTI with 2.0L 16 valve engine
1990 Cabriolet with engine code 2H

On the Digifant I system a jumper cable would have to be connected and then the codes would flash from the CHECK engine light on the dash. The following California vehicles were equipped with the Digifant I system:

1990–93 Fox—Digifant I
1991–93 Cabriolet—Digifant I

On all other systems, codes can only be retrieved with the use of a special diagnostic tester, the VAG 1551. This tester is available at car dealerships. The VAG 1551 tester can be used on all vehicles that have code capability.

➡**Some diagnostic codes may be retrieved by connecting special jumper cable 357 971 514E or an equivalent to the check connectors. Others for the most part are going to require the use of a special VAG 1551 tester and adapter to retrieve any remaining codes.**

DIGIFANT II SYSTEM—ROCKER SWITCH METHOD

California models are the only vehicles equipped with the On-Board Diagnostic (OBD) lamp. On these models codes may be accessed by 2 methods. The first is the use of a combination rocker switch/lamp located on the instrument panel. The second is used by the dealers, they use a special tool called the VAG 1551.

An indicator light labeled CHECK is located in a rocker switch on the instrument panel. Each time the engine is started, the indicator light will flash once to inform the operator the bulb is working.

The light will come on and stay on if a fault develops in the engine management system. It will also display diagnostic codes to assist in trouble diagnosis.

A diagnostic code consists of 4 groups of flashes. There is a 2.5 second pause (light OFF), between each group of flashes.

The indicator light will come on for two and half seconds prior to displaying a fault code when the diagnostic procedure has been activated. The fault code will continue repeating while the ignition is **ON**.

If the fault is not repaired the indicator light will come on and stay on when the ignition is turned **ON** to signify the fault still exists.

The following California vehicles were equipped with the Digifant II system:
1990 Golf, Jetta and GTI with 2.0L 16 valve engine
1990 Cabriolet with engine code 2H

Prior to checking for codes, drive the vehicle for 10 minutes or more.

1. Turn the ignition to the **ON** position, do not start the engine.
2. Press and hold down the rocker switch for 4–6 seconds then release the switch. The CHECK indicator lamp will begin flashing a diagnostic code.
3. Press and hold down the rocker switch again for 4–6 seconds then release it. The indicator lamp will flash the next diagnostic code and continue until all codes have been displayed.

When all diagnostic codes have been displayed, the indicator lamp will flash a series of 2.5 second flashes ON and 2.5 seconds OFF. This is an 'End Of Fault Sequence' code. If there are no faults stored in the control unit memory, the indicator lamp will flash Code 4444.

➡**Occasionally the control unit will sense various deviations or changes in the air/fuel mixture. Because of the sensitivity of this system a fault code may set without any apparent problem showing up. This is a normal function with systems of this type.**

DIGIFANT I SYSTEM—JUMPER CABLE METHOD

California models are the only vehicles equipped with the On-Board Diagnostic (OBD) lamp. On these models codes may be access by 2 methods. The first is the use of a special jumper cable connected to the diagnostic connector. The second is used by the dealers, they use a special tool called the VAG 1551.

The following California vehicles were equipped with the Digifant I system:

• 1990–93 Fox—Digifant I
• 1991–93 Cabriolet—Digifant I

1. Verify that all the fuses and grounds in the engine compartment are good.
2. Turn the ignition key **ON**.
3. Connect jumper cable 357 971 514E or equivalent to the connectors located in the center console. The black end of jumper wire connects to the black diagnostic connector in the console. The white end of the jumper wire connects to white diagnostic connector in the console.
4. Connect the jumper wire for about S seconds. When the OBD light begins flashing, remove the jumper wire.
5. Count the flashes of the light to get codes, each separate flash, in one code, will be have a short interval in between. Each interval between codes will be about 2.5 seconds. Count flashes until either Code 4444 or 0000 appears. To end this procedure turn the ignition switch **OFF**.
6. Output checks can not be performed without a diagnostic tester.

DIGIFANT I SYSTEM—WITH DIAGNOSTIC TESTER

This method is used by the Dealers and requires the use of the special tester VAG 1551. The following vehicles can only be accessed using this tester:

• 1991–92 Golf, Jetta—Digifant I system
• All CIS-E Motronic and Motronic systems

1. Make sure ignition switch is **OFF** and that all fuses are good. Make sure all grounds in engine compartment are good, especially those for the battery and control module.
2. Make sure the air conditioning system is OFF.
3. Connect the VAG 1551 diagnostic tester using VAG 1551/1 Adapter cable or equivalent. The diagnostic connectors are located in the center console, under the shifter. The shifter knob and console cover must be removed to access diagnostic connectors. Connect diagnostic connector 1 (black) to the black connector on the scan tool. Connect diagnostic connector 2 (white) to the white connector on the scan tool. The blue connector is not required.
4. Turn the ignition switch **ON**; now start the vehicle and let it idle. If vehicle will not start, crank engine for 6 seconds and leave ignition **ON**.
5. Turn the tester ON and make sure it is receiving power. The screen will display 2 menu options; Rapid Data Transfer and Blink Code Output.
6. If you choose to use mode 02, Blink Code Output, skip to Step 10.
7. Select mode 01, Rapid Data Transfer, and address word 01. Now press the 0 button to enter your selection. The tester will display a control unit part number, the system it controls and an application (country) code.
    a. If the information is displayed and is correct, press the (run) key to continue. The display 'Select function XX' will appear.
    b. If 'Control unit does not answer' is displayed, use the Help key to display a list of possible causes. When the problem is repaired, return to step 1 and start over again.
8. When function 02 is selected, the control module will report fault codes to the diagnostic tester.
9. When all codes have been reported, proceed to the Output Check diagnosis or select function 06 to exit the fault code memory without erasing the codes. Repair and erase the faults, then check and see if all faults have been corrected.
10. The following steps will retrieve engine codes by using Blink Code Output.

11. To operate the VAG 1551 tester in Blink Code Output, select menu option # 2. An asterisk will appear and flash the codes, which the tester will count and report on the screen as

numbers. If Code 4444 or 0000 is displayed, no faults are found in memory.

➡**On vehicles that use 4444 for no codes present, the 0000 will stand for output ended.**

12. If the engine is not running, some codes may be displayed. These can be ignored if the engine was intentionally stalled, but should be investigated if the engine will not start.

13. Press the (run) key to advance to the next code. Read through entire code list before starting repairs.

14. When the 0000 (output ended) code is displayed, pressing the (run) key again will proceed to another control module. If no other control modules are to be tested, the following display will appear: Blink Code Output is ended. To stop the program without erasing the codes, turn the ignition key **OFF** and press the clear C button once.

15. Repair and erase the faults, then check to see if all faults have been corrected.

Output Check Diagnosis

Only the Motronic system is equipped with this program. It allows testing most of the engine output devices without running the engine. The program cannot be run without the VAG 1551 Diagnostic Tester or equivalent. During the test, four output devices are activated in the following order:

- Differential pressure regulator
- Carbon canister frequency valve
- Idle stabilizer valve
- Cold start valve

Testing the differential pressure regulator requires a multi-meter that will read milliamps. The other items can be checked with a voltmeter, test light or by listening and feeling for valve activation. The cold start valve is activated for a limited time to avoid flooding the engine.

1. Connect the diagnostic tester, turn the ignition switch **ON** and confirm that the tester will communicate with the control unit. See the procedure for retrieving fault codes.

2. Select Rapid Data Transfer and Function 03. When the test is started by pressing the Q button (enter), the first output signal is generated.

3. Each time the Run button is pressed, the tester will send an output signal to the next device on the list.

4. When the last item has been tested, select Function 06 to exit the program. To repeat the test, turn the ignition switch **OFF** and **ON** again.

➡**Leave the ignition OFF for approximately 20 seconds, before selecting Output Check diagnosis again.**

Clearing Codes

WITHOUT DIAGNOSTIC TESTER

1. To erase codes, wait until Code 4444 or 0000 is displayed.
2. Turn ignition switch **OFF** and connect jumper wire to diagnostic connectors again.
3. Turn the ignition switch **ON** and leave connectors jumpered for about 5 seconds, When Code 4444 or 0000 appears the codes will be erased.
4. Turn the ignition switch **OFF** and remove jumper wire.

WITH DIAGNOSTIC TESTER

For both engine and automatic transaxle, after all fault codes have been retrieved, select Function 05 and press the Q button to enter the selection. The memory will be erased only if all fault codes have been retrieved. Test drive the vehicle for at least 10 minutes, including at least 1 full throttle application above 3000 rpm. Check the fault code memory again to make sure all faults have been repaired.

Diagnostic Trouble Codes

➡**The 5 digit code groups are used with a diagnostic tester. The 4 digit code groups are the flashing codes.**

00000 or 4444 No faults in memory
00281 or 1231 Vehicle Speed Sensor (VSS) signal is missing
00282 or 1232 Throttle actuator solenoid or wiring harness
00513 or 2111 Engine RPM sensor signal is missing
00514 or 2112 Ignition reference sensor signal is missing
00515 or 2113 Hall sender signal is missing
00516 or 2121 Idle switch has open short in circuit
00517 or 2123 Full throttle switch
00518 or 2212 Throttle position sensor
00519 or 2222 Manifold absolute pressure (MAP) sensor
00520 or 2232 Air flow sensor signal is missing
00521 or 2242 CO potentiometer
00522 or 2312 Engine coolant temperature (ECT) sensor
00523 or 2322 Intake air temperature (IAT) sensor
00524 or 2142 Knock sensor 1 signal is missing
00525 or 2342 Oxygen sensor signal missing
00527 or 2412 Intake air temperature (IAT) sensor has open/short in circuit
00532 or 2234 Supply voltage is too high
00533 or 2231 Idle speed regulation out of limit
00535 or Both 2141/2142 Knock sensor or control program
00537 or 2341 Oxygen sensor signal out of limit
00540 or 2144 Knock sensor 2 signal is missing
00543 or 2214 RPM exceeds maximum limit
00545 or 2314 Engine/Transmission electrical connection
00549 or 2314 Fuel consumption signal
00552 or 2323 Air flow sensor signal missing
00553 or 2324 Mass Air Flow (MAE) sensor signal is out of range
00558 or NA Adaptive mixture control lean (Fuel injector leak, EVAP purge system)
00559 or NA Adaptive mixture control rich (vacuum leak)
00560 or 2411 EGR temperature sensor circuit
00561 or 2413 Mixture adaptation limits are out of range
00585 or 2411 EGR temperature sensor circuit (2.8L AAA engine only)
00586 EGR controlling system, EGR valve is sticking or false signals
00587 Adjustment limit mixture regulator is lean
00609 Ignition output 1 circuit
00624 A/C compressor engagement circuit has mechanical or electrical malfunction
00640 or 3434 Heated Oxygen sensor relay has open/short circuit
01025—Malfunction indicator lamp (MIL) circuit
01242 or 4332 Output stages in engine control module (ECM)
01247 or 4343 EVAP frequency valve 1 has open/short in circuit
01249 or 4411 Fuel injector #1 circuit has open/short
01250 or 4412 Fuel injector #2 circuit has open/short
01251 or 4413 Fuel injector #3 circuit has open/short
01252 or 4414 Fuel injector #4 circuit has open/short
01253 or 4421 Fuel injector #5 circuit has open/short
01254 or 4422 Fuel injector #6 circuit has open/short
01257 or 4431 Idle Air Control (IAC) valve has open/short in circuit or a mechanical malfunction
01259 or 4433 Fuel pump relay is faulty or short circuited
01265 or 4312 EGR frequency valve has open/short in circuit
65535 or 1111 Engine Control Module (ECM) is defective
0000 End of output
NA Not Available

OBD-II TROUBLE CODES

General Information

Beginning in 1996 the U.S. government required a second generation diagnostic system, also know as On Board Diagnostic II (OBDII) on all vehicles sold in the United States. This Diagnostic Trouble Code (DTC) information is accessible to technicians without using the manufacturers scan tool. The manufacturers VAG 1551 VW scan can be used in generic mode to retrieve the trouble codes. While the VAG 1551 is not the only code retrieval device that can be used it is the only one discussed in this book. For information on other models, check with you local aftermarket parts supplier.

Diagnostic Connector

LOCATION

♦ See Figure 16

The diagnostic connector is located on the dashboard, below the climate controls, hidden behind a cover plate.

Reading Codes

Reading the control module memory is one of the first steps in OBD II system diagnostics. This step should be initially performed to determine the general nature of the fault. Subsequent readings will determine if the fault has been cleared.

Reading codes can be performed by any of the methods below:
- Read the control module memory with the Generic Scan Tool (GST)
- Read the control module memory with the Vag 1550 tester

To read the fault codes, connect the scan tool or tester according to the manufacturer's instructions. Follow the manufacturer's specified procedure for reading the codes.

Clearing Codes

Control module reset procedures are a very important part of OBD II System diagnostics. This step should be done at the end of any fault code repair and at the end of any drive-ability repair.

Clearing codes can be performed by any of the methods below:
- Clear the control module memory with the Generic Scan Tool (GST)
- Clear the control module memory with the vehicle manufacturer's specific tester
- Turn the ignition **OFF** and remove the negative battery cable for at least 1 minute.

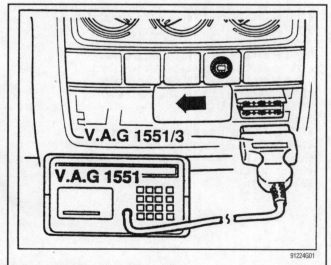

Fig. 16 Location of diagnostic connector

Removing the negative battery cable may cause other systems in the vehicle to loose their memory. Prior to removing the cable, ensure you have the proper reset codes for radios and alarms.

➡**The MIL will may also be de-activated for some codes if the vehicle completes 3 consecutive trips without a fault detected with vehicle conditions similar to those present during the fault.**

Diagnostic Trouble Codes

P0102 Mass or Volume Air Flow Circuit Low Input
P0103 Mass or Volume Air Flow Circuit High Input
P0107 Manifold Absolute Pressure or Barometric Pressure Low Input
P0108 Manifold Absolute Pressure or Barometric Pressure High Input
P0112 Intake Air Temperature Circuit Low Input
P0113 Intake Air Temperature Circuit High Input
P0116 Engine Coolant Temperature Circuit Range/Performance
P0117 Engine Coolant Temperature Circuit Low Input
P0118 Engine Coolant Temperature Circuit High Input
P0120 Throttle Position Sensor "A" Circuit Malfunction
P0121 Throttle/Pedal Position Sensor "A" Circuit Range/Performance
P0122 Throttle/Pedal Position Sensor "A" Circuit Low Input
P0123 Throttle/Pedal Position Sensor "A" Circuit High Input
P0125 Insufficient Coolant Temperature For Closed Loop Fuel Control
P0130 Oxygen Sensor (O_2S) Circuit, Bank #1-Sensor #1 Malfunction
P0131 Oxygen Sensor (O_2S) Circuit, Bank #1-Sensor #1 Low Voltage
P0132 Oxygen Sensor (O_2S) Circuit, Bank #1-Sensor #1 High Voltage
P0133 Oxygen Sensor (O_2S) Circuit, Bank #1-Sensor #1 Slow Response
P0134 Oxygen Sensor (O_2S) Circuit, Bank #1-Sensor #1 No Activity Detected
P0135 Oxygen Sensor (O_2S) Heater Circuit, Bank #1-Sensor #1 Malfunction
P0136 Oxygen Sensor (O_2S) Circuit, Bank #1-Sensor #2 Malfunction
P0137 Oxygen Sensor (O_2S) Circuit, Bank #1-Sensor #2 Low Voltage
P0138 Oxygen Sensor (O_2S) Circuit, Bank #1-Sensor #2 High Voltage
P0140 Oxygen Sensor (O_2S) Circuit, Bank #1-Sensor #2 No Activity Detected
P0141 Oxygen Sensor (O_2S) Heater Circuit, Bank #1-Sensor #2 Malfunction
P0150 Oxygen Sensor (O_2S) Circuit, Bank #2-Sensor #1 Malfunction
P0151 Oxygen Sensor (O_2S) Circuit, Bank #2-Sensor #1 Low Voltage
P0152 Oxygen Sensor (O_2S) Circuit, Bank #2-Sensor #1 High Voltage
P0153 Oxygen Sensor (O_2S) Circuit, Bank #2-Sensor #1 Slow Response
P0154 Oxygen Sensor (O_2S) Circuit, Bank #2-Sensor #1 No Activity Detected
P0156 Oxygen Sensor (O_2S) Circuit, Bank #2-Sensor #2 Malfunction
P0157 Oxygen Sensor (O_2S) Circuit, Bank #2-Sensor #2 Low Voltage
P0158 Oxygen Sensor (O_2S) Circuit, Bank #2-Sensor #2 High Voltage
P0160 Oxygen Sensor (O_2S) Circuit, Bank #2-Sensor #2 No Activity Detected
P0171 System Too Lean, Bank #1
P0172 System Too Rich, Bank #1
P0300 Random Multiple Misfire Detected
P0301 Cylinder #1 Misfire Detected
P0302 Cylinder #2 Misfire Detected
P0303 Cylinder #3 Misfire Detected
P0304 Cylinder #4 Misfire Detected
P0305 Cylinder #5 Misfire Detected
P0306 Cylinder #6 Misfire Detected
P0321 Ignition Distributor Engine Speed Input Circuit Range/Performance
P0322 Ignition /Distributor Engine Speed Input Circuit No Signal
P0327 Knock sensor #1 Circuit Low Input
P0328 Knock Sensor #1 Circuit, High Input
P0332 Knock sensor #2 Circuit Low Input
P0333 Knock Sensor #2 Circuit, High Input
P0341 Camshaft Position Sensor Circuit Range/Performance
P0411 Secondary Air Injection System Incorrect Flow Detected
P0422 Main Catalyst Efficiency Below Threshold (Bank #1)
P0422 Main Catalyst, Bank I Efficiency Below Threshold
P0440 Evaporative Emission Control System Malfunction
P0441 EVAP Emission Control System Incorrect Purge Flow

P0442 EVAP Emission Control System (Small Leak) Leak Detected
P0455 EVAP Emission Control System (Gross Leak) Leak Detected
P0501 Vehicle Speed Sensor Range/Performance
P0506 Idle Control System RPM Lower Than Expected
P0507 Idle Control System RPM Higher Than Expected
P0510 Closed Throttle Position Switch Malfunction
P0560 System Voltage Malfunction
P0562 System Voltage Low Voltage
P0563 System Voltage High Voltage
P0601 Internal Contr. Module Memory Check Sum Error
P0604 Internal Contr. Module Random Access Memory (RAM) Error
P0605 Internal Control Module Read Only Memory (ROM) Error
P0707 Transmission Range Sensor Circuit Low Input
P0708 Transmission Range Sensor Circuit High Input
P0715 Input Turbine Speed Sensor Circuit Malfunction
P0722 Output Speed Sensor Circuit No Signal
P0725 Engine Speed Input Circuit Malfunction
P0748 Pressure Control Solenoid Electrical
P0753 Shift Solenoid "A" Electrical
P0758 Shift Solenoid "B" Electrical
P0763 Shift Solenoid "C" Electrical
P0768 Shift Solenoid "D" Electrical
P0773 Shift Solenoid "E" Electrical
P1102 Oxygen Sensor Heating Circuit, Bank #1-Sensor #1 Short to B+
P1105 Oxygen Sensor Heating Circuit, Bank #1-Sensor #2 Short to B+
P1107 Oxygen Sensor Heating Circuit, Bank #2-Sensor #1 Short to B+
P1110 Oxygen Sensor Heating Circuit, Bank #2-Sensor #2 Short to B+
P1127 Long Term Fuel Trim Multiplicative, Bank #1 System Too Rich
P1128 Long Term Fuel Trim Multiplicative, Bank #1 System Too Lean
P1129 Long Term Fuel Trim Multiplicative, Bank #2 System too Rich
P1130 Long Term Fuel Trim Multiplicative, Bank #2 System too Lean
P1136 Long Term Fuel Trim Additive, Bank #1 System Too Lean
P1137 Long Term Fuel Trim Additive, Bank #1 System Too Rich
P1138 Long Term Fuel Trim Additive Fuel, Bank #1 System too Lean
P1139 Long Term Fuel Trim Additive Fuel, Bank #1 System too Rich
P1141 Load Calculation Cross Check Range/Performance
P1176 Oxygen Correction Behind Catalyst, B1 Limit Attained
P1177 Oxygen Correction Behind Catalyst. 82 Limit Attained
P1196 Oxygen Sensor (O_2S) Heater Circuit, Bank #1-Sensor #1 Electrical Malfunction
P1197 Oxygen Sensor (O_2S) Heater Circuit, Bank #2-Sensor #1 Electrical Malfunction
P1198 Oxygen Sensor (O_2S) Heater Circuit, Bank #1-Sensor #2 Electrical Malfunction
P1198 Oxygen Sensor (O_2S) Heater Circuit, Bank #1-Sensor #2 Electrical Malfunction
P1199 Oxygen Sensor (O_2S) Heater Circuit, Bank #2-Sensor #2 Electrical Malfunction
P1201 Cylinder #1, Fuel Injection Circuit Electrical Malfunction
P1202 Cylinder #2, Fuel Injection Circuit Electrical Malfunction
P1203 Cylinder #3, Fuel Injection Circuit Electrical Malfunction
P1204 Cylinder #4, Fuel Injection Circuit Electrical Malfunction
P1205 Cylinder #5, Fuel Injection Circuit Electrical Malfunction
P1206 Cylinder #6, Fuel Injection Circuit Electrical Malfunction
P1207 Cylinder #7, Fuel Injection Circuit Electrical Malfunction
P1208 Cylinder #8, Fuel Injection Circuit Electrical Malfunction
P1213 Cylinder #1-Fuel Injection Circuit Short to B+
P1214 Cylinder #2-Fuel Injection Circuit Short to B+
P1215 Cylinder #3 Fuel Injection Circuit Short to B+
P1216 Cylinder #4 Fuel Injection Circuit Short to B+
P1217 Cylinder #5 Fuel Injection Circuit Short to B+
P1218 Cylinder #6 Fuel Injection Circuit Short to B+
P1219 Cylinder #7, Fuel Injection Circuit Short to B+
P1219 Cylinder #8, Fuel Injection Circuit Short to B+
P1225 Cylinder #1 Fuel Injection Circuit Short to Ground
P1226 Cylinder #2 Fuel Injection Circuit Short to Ground
P1227 Cylinder #3 Fuel Injection Circuit Short to Ground
P1228 Cylinder #4 Fuel Injection Circuit Short to Ground
P1229 Cylinder #5 Fuel Injection Circuit Short to Ground
P1230 Cylinder #6 Fuel Injection Circuit Short to Ground
P1237 Cylinder #1 Fuel Injection Circuit Open Circuit

P1238 Cylinder #2 Fuel Injection Circuit Open Circuit
P1239 Cylinder #3 Fuel Injection Circuit Open Circuit
P1240 Cylinder #4 Fuel Injection Circuit Open Circuit
P1241 Cylinder #5 Fuel Injection Circuit Open Circuit
P1242 Cylinder #6 Fuel Injection Circuit Open Circuit
P1250 Fuel Level Too Low
P1280 Fuel Injection Air Control Valve Circuit Flow too Low
P1283 Fuel Injection Air Control Valve Circuit Electrical Malfunction
P1325 Cylinder #1 Knock Control Limit Attained
P1326 Cylinder #2 Knock Control Limit Attained
P1327 Cylinder #3 Knock Control Limit Attained
P1328 Cylinder #4 Knock Control Limit Attained
P1329 Cylinder #5 Knock Control Limit Attained
P1330 Cylinder #6 Knock Control Limit Attained
P1331 Cylinder #7, Knock Control Limit Attained
P1332 Cylinder #8, Knock Control Limit Attained
P1337 Camshaft Position Sensor, Bank #1 Short to Ground
P1338 Camshaft Position Sensor, Bank #1 Open Circuit/Short to B+
P1340 Boost Pressure Control Valve Short to B+
P1386 Internal Control Module Knock Control Circuit Error
P1391 Camshaft Position Sensor, Bank #2 Short to Ground
P1392 Camshaft Position Sensor, Bank #2 Open Circuit/Short to B+
P1410 Tank Ventilation Valve Circuit Short to B+
P1420 Secondary Air Injection Module Short To B+
P1421 Secondary Air Injection Module Short To Ground
P1422 Secondary Air Injection Valve Circuit Short to B+
P1425 Tank Vent Valve Short To Ground
P1426 Tank Vent Valve Open
P1432 Secondary Air Injection Valve Open
P1433 Secondary Air Injection System Pump Relay Circuit Open
P1434 Secondary Air Injection System Pump Relay Circuit Short to B+
P1435 Secondary Air Injection System Pump Relay Circuit Short to Ground
P1436 Secondary Air Injection System Pump Relay Circuit Electrical Malfunction
P1450 Secondary Air Injection System Circuit Short To B+
P1451 Secondary Air Injection System Circuit Short To Ground
P1452 Secondary Air Injection System Open Circuit
P1471 EVAP Emission Control LDP Circuit Short to B+
P1472 EVAP Emission Control LDP Circuit Short to Ground
P1473 EVAP Emission Control LDP Circuit Open Circuit
P1475 EVAP Emission Control LDP Circuit Malfunction/Signal Circuit Open
P1476 EVAP Emission Control LDP Circuit Malfunction/Insufficient Vacuum
P1477 EVAP Emission Control LDP Circuit Malfunction
P1500 Fuel Pump Relay Circuit Electrical Malfunction
P1501 Fuel Pump Relay Circuit Short to Ground
P1502 Fuel Pump Relay Circuit Short to B+
P1505 Closed Throttle Position Switch Does Not Close/Open Circuit
P1506 Closed Throttle Position Switch Does Not Open/Short to Ground
P1507 Idle System Learned Value Lower Limit Attained
P1508 Idle System Learned Value Upper Limit Attained
P1512 Intake Manifold Changeover Valve Circuit, Short to B+
P1515 Intake Manifold Changeover Valve Circuit, Short to Ground
P1516 Intake Manifold Changeover Valve Circuit, Open
P1519 Intake Camshaft Control, Bank #1 Malfunction
P1522 Intake Camshaft Control, Bank #2 Malfunction
P1543 Throttle Actuation Potentiometer Signal Too Low
P1544 Throttle Actuation Potentiometer Signal Too High
P1545 Throttle Position Control Malfunction
P1547 Boost Pressure Control Valve Short to Ground
P1548 Boost Pressure Control Valve Open
P1555 Charge Pressure Upper Limit Exceeded
P1556 Charge Pressure Negative Deviation
P1557 Charge Pressure Positive Deviation
P1558 Throttle Actuator Electrical Malfunction
P1559 Idle Speed Control Throttle Position Adaptation Malfunction
P1560 Maximum Engine Speed Exceeded
P1564 Idle Speed Control, Throttle Position Low Voltage During Adaptation
P1580 Throttle Actuator (B1) Malfunction
P1582 Idle Adaptation At Limit
P1602 Power Supply (B+) Terminal 30 Low Voltage
P1606 Rough Road Spec Engine Torque ABS-ECU Electrical Malfunction

P1611 MIL Call-up Circuit/Transmission Control Module Short to Ground
P1612 Electronic Control Module Incorrect Coding
P1613 MIL Call-up Circuit Open/Short to B+
P1624 MIL Request Signal Active
P1625 CAN-Bus Implausible Message from Transmission Control
P1626 CAN-Bus Missing Message from Transmission Control
P1640 Internal Control Module (EEPROM) Error
P1681 Control Unit Programming not Finished
P1690 Malfunction Indicator Light Malfunction
P1693 Malfunction Indicator Light Short to B+
P1778 Solenoid EV7 Electrical Malfunction
P1780 Engine Intervention Readable

OBD II TROUBLE CODE EQUIVALENTS

16486 Mass or Volume Air Flow Circuit Low Input
16487 Mass or Volume Air Flow Circuit High Input
16491 Manifold Absolute Pressure or Barometric Pressure Low Input
16492 Manifold Absolute Pressure or Barometric Pressure High Input
16496 Intake Air Temperature Circuit Low Input
16497 Intake Air Temperature Circuit High Input
16500 Engine Coolant Temperature Circuit Range/Performance
16501 Engine Coolant Temperature Circuit Low Input
16502 Oxygen Engine Coolant Temperature Circuit High Input
16504 Throttle Position Sensor "A" Circuit Malfunction
16505 Throttle/Pedal Position Sensor "A" Circuit Range/Performance
16506 Throttle/Pedal Position Sensor "A" Circuit Low Input
16507 Throttle/Pedal Position Sensor "A" Circuit High Input
16509 Insufficient Coolant Temperature For Closed Loop Fuel Control
16514 Oxygen Sensor (O_2S) Circuit, Bank #1-Sensor #1 Malfunction
16515 Oxygen Sensor (O_2S) Circuit, Bank #1-Sensor #1 Low Voltage
16516 Oxygen Sensor (O_2S) Circuit, Bank #1-Sensor #1 High Voltage
16517 Oxygen Sensor (O_2S) Circuit, Bank #1-Sensor #1 Slow Response
16518 Oxygen Sensor (O_2S) Circuit, Bank #1-Sensor #1 No Activity Detected
16519 Oxygen Sensor (O_2S) Heater Circuit, Bank #1-Sensor #1 Malfunction
16520 Oxygen Sensor (O_2S) Circuit, Bank #1-Sensor #2 Malfunction
16521 Oxygen Sensor (O_2S) Circuit, Bank #1-Sensor #2 Low Voltage
16522 Oxygen Sensor (O_2S) Circuit, Bank #1-Sensor #2 High Voltage
16524 Oxygen Sensor (O_2S) Circuit, Bank #1-Sensor #2 No Activity Detected
16525 Oxygen Sensor (O_2S) Heater Circuit, Bank #1-Sensor #2 Malfunction
16534 Oxygen Sensor (O_2S) Circuit, Bank #2-Sensor #1 Malfunction
16535 Oxygen Sensor (O_2S) Circuit, Bank #2-Sensor #1 Low Voltage
16536 Oxygen Sensor (O_2S) Circuit, Bank #2-Sensor #1 High Voltage
16537 Oxygen Sensor (O_2S) Circuit, Bank #2-Sensor #1 Slow Response
16538 Oxygen Sensor (O_2S) Circuit, Bank #2-Sensor #1 No Activity Detected
16540 Oxygen Sensor (O_2S) Circuit, Bank #2-Sensor #2 Malfunction
16541 Oxygen Sensor (O_2S) Circuit, Bank #2-Sensor #2 Low Voltage
16542 Oxygen Sensor (O_2S) Circuit, Bank #2-Sensor #2 High Voltage
16544 Oxygen Sensor (O_2S) Circuit, Bank #2-Sensor #2 No Activity Detected
16555 Oxygen System Too Lean, Bank #1
16556 Oxygen System Too Rich, Bank #1
16684 Random Multiple Misfire Detected
16685 Cylinder #1 Misfire Detected
16686 Cylinder #2 Misfire Detected
16687 Cylinder #3 Misfire Detected
16688 Cylinder #4 Misfire Detected
16689 Cylinder #5 Misfire Detected
16690 Cylinder #6 Misfire Detected
16705 Ignition Distributor Engine Speed Input Circuit Range/Performance
16706 Ignition /Distributor Engine Speed Input Circuit No Signal
16711 Knock Sensor #1 Circuit Low Input
16712 Knock Sensor #1 Circuit, High Input
16716 Knock Sensor #2 Circuit Low Input
16717 Knock Sensor #2 Circuit, High Input
16725 Camshaft Position Sensor Circuit Range/Performance
16795 Secondary Air Injection System Incorrect Flow Detected
16806 Main Catalyst Efficiency Below Threshold (Bank #1)

16824 Evaporative Emission Control System Malfunction
16825 EVAP Emission Control System Incorrect Purge Flow
16826 EVAP Emission Control System (Small Leak) Leak Detected
16839 EVAP Emission Control System (Gross Leak) Leak Detected
16885 Vehicle Speed Sensor Range/Performance
16890 Idle Control System RPM Lower Than Expected
16891 Idle Control System RPM Higher Than Expected
16894 Closed Throttle Position Switch Malfunction
16944 System Voltage Malfunction
16946 System Voltage Low Voltage
16947 System Voltage High Voltage
16985 Internal Control Module Memory Check Sum Error
16988 Internal Control Module Random Access Memory (RAM) Error
16989 Internal Control Module Read Only Memory (ROM) Error
17091 Transmission Range Sensor Circuit Low Input
17092 Transmission Range Sensor Circuit High Input
17099 Input Turbine Speed Sensor Circuit Malfunction
17106 Output Speed Sensor Circuit No Signal
17109 Engine Speed Input Circuit Malfunction
17132 Pressure Control Solenoid Electrical
17137 Shift Solenoid "A" Electrical
17142 Shift Solenoid "B" Electrical
17147 Shift Solenoid "C" Electrical
17152 Shift Solenoid "D" Electrical
17157 Shift Solenoid "E" Electrical
16684 Random/Multiple Cylinder Misfire Detected
16685 Cylinder #1 Misfire Detected
16686 Cylinder #2 Misfire Detected
17510 Oxygen Sensor Heating Circuit, Bank #1-Sensor #1 Short to B+
17513 Oxygen Sensor Heating Circuit, Bank #1-Sensor #2 Short to B+
17515 Oxygen Sensor Heating Circuit, Bank #2-Sensor #1 Short to B+
17518 Oxygen Sensor Heating Circuit, Bank #2-Sensor #2 Short to B+
17535 Long Term Fuel Trim Multiplicative, Bank #1 System Too Rich
17536 Long Term Fuel Trim Multiplicative, Bank #1 System Too Lean
17537 Long Term Fuel Trim Multiplicative, Bank #2 System too Rich
17538 Long Term Fuel Trim Multiplicative, Bank #2 System too Lean
17544 Long Term Fuel Trim Additive, Bank #1 System Too Lean
17545 Long Term Fuel Trim Additive, Bank #1 System Too Rich
17546 Long Term Fuel Trim Additive Fuel, Bank #1 System too Lean
17547 Long Term Fuel Trim Additive Fuel, Bank #1 System too Rich
17549 Load Calculation Cross Check Range/Performance
17584 Oxygen Correction Behind Catalyst, B1 Limit Attained
17585 Oxygen Correction Behind Catalyst, B2 Limit Attained
17604 Oxygen Sensor (O_2S) Heater Circuit, Bank #1-Sensor #1 Electrical Malfunction
17605 Oxygen Sensor (O_2S) Heater Circuit, Bank #2-Sensor #1 Electrical Malfunction
17606 Oxygen Sensor (O_2S) Heater Circuit, Bank #1-Sensor #2 Electrical Malfunction
17607 Oxygen Sensor (O_2S) Heater Circuit, Bank #2-Sensor #2 Electrical Malfunction
17609 Cylinder #1, Fuel Injection Circuit Electrical Malfunction
17610 Cylinder #2, Fuel Injection Circuit Electrical Malfunction
17611 Cylinder #3, Fuel Injection Circuit Electrical Malfunction
17612 Cylinder #4, Fuel Injection Circuit Electrical Malfunction
17613 Cylinder #5, Fuel Injection Circuit Electrical Malfunction
17614 Cylinder #6, Fuel Injection Circuit Electrical Malfunction
17615 Cylinder #7, Fuel Injection Circuit Electrical Malfunction
17616 Cylinder #8, Fuel Injection Circuit Electrical Malfunction
17621 Cylinder #1-Fuel Injection Circuit Short to B+
17622 Cylinder #2-Fuel Injection Circuit Short to B+
17623 Cylinder #3 Fuel Injection Circuit Short to B+
17624 Cylinder #4 Fuel Injection Circuit Short to B+
17625 Cylinder #5 Fuel Injection Circuit Short to B+
17626 Cylinder #6 Fuel Injection Circuit Short to B+
17627 Cylinder #7, Fuel Injection Circuit Short to B+
17628 Cylinder #8, Fuel Injection Circuit Short to B+
17633 Cylinder #1 Fuel Injection Circuit Short to Ground
17634 Cylinder #2 Fuel Injection Circuit Short to Ground
17635 Cylinder #3 Fuel Injection Circuit Short to Ground
17636 Cylinder #4 Fuel Injection Circuit Short to Ground

17637 Cylinder #5 Fuel Injection Circuit Short to Ground
17638 Cylinder #6 Fuel Injection Circuit Short to Ground
17645 Cylinder #I Fuel Injection Circuit Open Circuit
17646 Cylinder #2 Fuel Injection Circuit Open Circuit
17647 Cylinder #3 Fuel Injection Circuit Open Circuit
17648 Cylinder #4 Fuel Injection Circuit Open Circuit
17649 Cylinder #5 Fuel Injection Circuit Open Circuit
17650 Cylinder #6 Fuel Injection Circuit Open Circuit
17658 Fuel Level Too Low
17688 Fuel Injection Air Control Valve Circuit Flow too Low
17691 Fuel Injection Air Control Valve Circuit Electrical Malfunction
17733 Cylinder #I Knock Control Limit Attained
17734 Cylinder #2 Knock Control Limit Attained
17735 Cylinder #3 Knock Control Limit Attained
17736 Cylinder #4 Knock Control Limit Attained
17737 Cylinder #5 Knock Control Limit Attained
17738 Cylinder #6 Knock Control Limit Attained
17739 Cylinder #7 Knock Control Limit Attained
17740 Cylinder #8 Knock Control Limit Attained
17745 Camshaft Position Sensor, Bank #1 Short to Ground
17746 Camshaft Position Sensor, Bank #1 Open Circuit/Short to B+
17954 Boost Pressure Control Valve Short to B+
17794 Internal Control Module Knock Control Circuit Error
17799 Camshaft Position Sensor, Bank #2 Short to Ground
17800 Camshaft Position Sensor, Bank #2 Open Circuit/Short to B+
17818 Tank Ventilation Valve Circuit Short to B+
17828 Secondary Air Injection Module Short To B+
17829 Secondary Air Injection Module Short To Ground
17829 Secondary Air Injection Valve Circuit Short to Ground
17830 Secondary Air Injection Valve Circuit Short to B+
17833 Tank Vent Valve Short To Ground
17834 Tank Vent Valve Open
17840 Secondary Air Injection Valve Open
17841 Secondary Air Injection System Pump Relay Circuit Open
17842 Secondary Air Injection System Pump Relay Circuit Short to B+
17843 Secondary Air Injection System Pump Relay Circuit Short to Ground
17844 Secondary Air Injection System Pump Relay Circuit Electrical Malfunction
17858 Secondary Air Injection System Circuit Short To B+
17859 Secondary Air Injection System Circuit Short To Ground
17860 Secondary Air Injection System Open Circuit
17879 EVAP Emission Control LDP Circuit Short to B+
17880 EVAP Emission Control LDP Circuit Short to Ground

17881 EVAP Emission Control LDP Circuit Open Circuit
17883 EVAP Emission Control LDP Circuit Malfunction/Signal Circuit Open
17884 EVAP Emission Control LDP Circuit Malfunction/Insufficient Vacuum
17885 EVAP Emission Control LDP Circuit Malfunction
17908 Fuel Pump Relay Circuit Electrical Malfunction
17909 Fuel Pump Relay Circuit Short to Ground
17910 Fuel Pump Relay Circuit Short to B+
17913 Closed Throttle Position Switch Does Not Close/Open Circuit
17914 Closed Throttle Position Switch Does Not Open/Short to Ground
17915 Idle System Learned Value Lower Limit Attained
17916 Idle System Learned Value Upper Limit Attained
17920 Intake Manifold Changeover Valve Circuit, Short to B+
17923 Intake Manifold Changeover Valve Circuit, Short to Ground
17924 Intake Manifold Changeover Valve Circuit, Open
17927 Intake Camshaft Control, Bank #2 Malfunction
17951 Throttle Actuation Potentiometer Signal Too Low
17952 Throttle Actuation Potentiometer Signal Too High
17953 Throttle Position Control Malfunction
17955 Boost Pressure Control Valve Short to Ground
17956 Boost Pressure Control Valve Open
17963 Charge Pressure Upper Limit Exceeded
17964 Charge Pressure Negative Deviation
17965 Charge Pressure Positive Deviation
17966 Throttle Actuator Electrical Malfunction
17967 Idle Speed Control Throttle Position Adaptation Malfunction
17968 Maximum Engine Speed Exceeded
17972 Idle Speed Control, Throttle Position Low Voltage During Adaptation
17988 Throttle Actuator (B1) Malfunction
17990 Idle Adaptation At Limit
18010 Power Supply (B+) Terminal 30 Low Voltage
18014 Rough Road Spec Engine Torque ABS-ECU Electrical Malfunction
18019 MIL Call-up Circuit/Transmission Control Module Short to Ground
18020 Electronic Control Module Incorrect Coding
18021 MIL Call-up Circuit Open/Short to B+
18032 MIL Request Signal Active
18033 CAN-Bus Implausible Message from Transmission Control
18034 CAN-Bus Missing Message from Transmission Control
18048 Internal Control Module (EEPROM) Error
18089 Control Unit Programming not Finished
18098 Malfunction Indicator Light Malfunction
18101 Malfunction Indicator Light Short to B+
18186 Solenoid EV7 Electrical Malfunction
18188 Engine Intervention Readable

VACUUM DIAGRAMS

Following are vacuum diagrams for most of the engine and emissions package combinations covered by this manual. Because vacuum circuits will vary based on various engine and vehicle options, always refer first to the vehicle emission control information label, if present. Should the label be missing, or should vehicle be equipped with a different engine from the vehicle's original equipment, refer to the diagrams below for the same or similar configuration.

If you wish to obtain a replacement emissions label, most manufacturers make the labels available for purchase. The labels can usually be ordered from a local dealer.

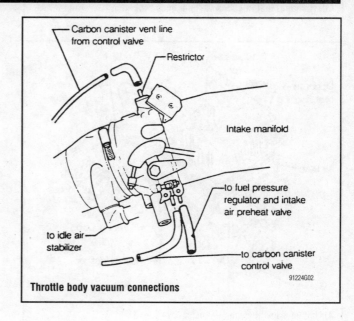

Throttle body vacuum connections

91224G02

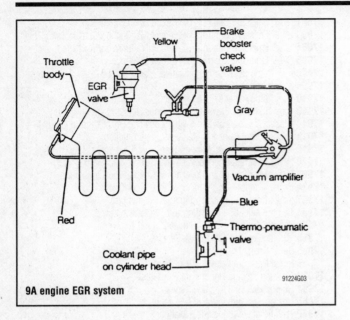

9A engine EGR system

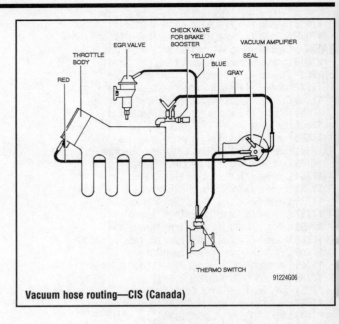

Vacuum hose routing—CIS (Canada)

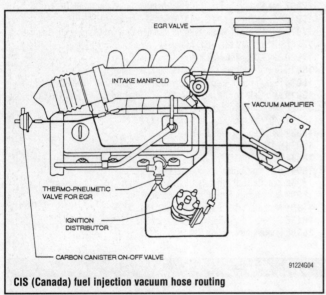

CIS (Canada) fuel injection vacuum hose routing

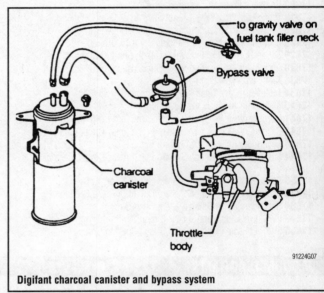

Digifant charcoal canister and bypass system

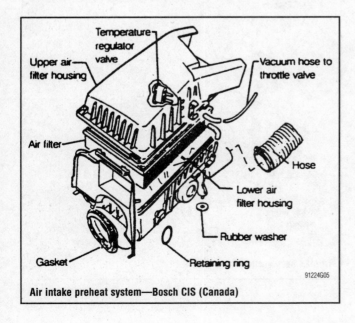

Air intake preheat system—Bosch CIS (Canada)

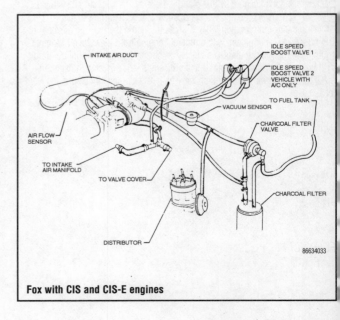

Fox with CIS and CIS-E engines

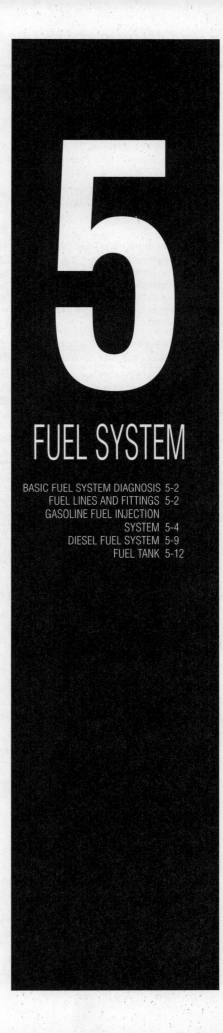

5

FUEL SYSTEM

BASIC FUEL SYSTEM DIAGNOSIS

When there is a problem starting or driving a vehicle, two of the most important checks involve the ignition and the fuel systems. The questions most mechanics attempt to answer first, "is there spark?" and "is there fuel?" will often lead to solving most basic problems. For ignition system diagnosis and testing, please refer to the information on engine electrical components and ignition systems found earlier in this manual. If the ignition system checks out (there is spark), then you must determine if the fuel system is operating properly (is there fuel?).

FUEL LINES AND FITTINGS

♦ See Figure 1

➡Quick-connect (push type) fuel line fittings must be disconnected using proper procedure or the fitting may be damaged. There are two types of retainers used on the push connect fittings. Line sizes of ⅜ and ⁵⁄₁₆ in. diameter use a hairpin clip retainer. The ¼ in. diameter line connectors use a duck-bill clip retainer. In addition, some engines use spring-lock connections, secured by a garter spring, which require special tools for removal.

☀ CAUTION

Observe all applicable safety precautions when working around fuel. Whenever servicing the fuel system, always work in a well ventilated area. Do not allow fuel spray or vapors to come in contact with a spark or open flame. Keep a dry chemical fire extinguisher near the work area. Always keep fuel in a container specifically designed for fuel storage; also, always properly seal fuel containers to avoid the possibility of fire or explosion.

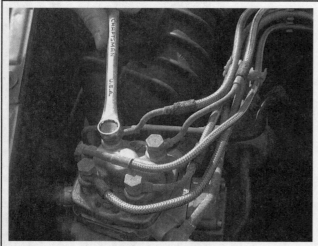

Fig. 1 Always relieve the fuel pressure before opening any lines

Clamped Fittings

REMOVAL & INSTALLATION

♦ See Figures 2 and 3

The conventional clamped fitting is used when a flexible hose is installed over a fitting and clamped in place. This type of fuel fitting is found in a variety of locations and sizes throughout the vehicle, such as the fuel filler neck and Evaporative Canister hoses. The flexible fuel hose is installed over a fitting with a clamp to secure the hose to the fitting. The clamp is either spring loaded and released using a pliers, or mechanically tightened, requiring a screwdriver or related tool to loosen or tighten.

To remove a clamped type fitting:

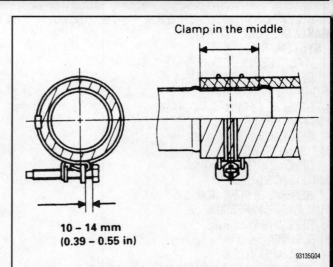

**10 – 14 mm
(0.39 – 0.55 in)**

Fig. 2 The mechanically tightened clamp should be centered on the fitting and properly secured. Use care to not overtighten

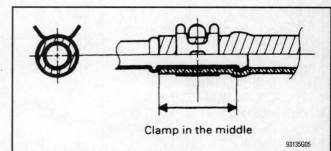

Fig. 3 The spring-loaded clamp is released by using flat-nosed pliers to squeeze the tabs together and slide the clamp off the clamped portion of the fitting

1. Release the clamp's tension and slide the clamp off the section of hose that is attached to the fitting.
2. Carefully slide the hose off the fitting.
To install:
3. Carefully slide the hose over the fitting.
4. Center the clamp over the middle of the section of hose covering the fitting.
5. Release the clamp or tighten as necessary.

Compression Fittings

REMOVAL & INSTALLATION

♦ See Figures 4, 5, 6, 7 and 8

The compression fitting has a flared metal tube or a compression fitting that is surrounded by a threaded flare nut. Because the tube is flared or has a compression fitting installed, the threaded flare nut cannot be removed from the line and is considered part of the assembly.

Fig. 4 An example of an internally threaded flare nut on this fuel line. Note the use of a flare nut wrench loosen the nut while the component is held with another wrench

Fig. 5 The open-end wrench on the left compared to a flare nut wrench on the right. The slot allows the flare nut wrench to clear the line, yet will grip the flare nut on all 6 sides

Fig. 6 An externally threaded flare nut is used on both fuel lines and hydraulic brake lines. A flare nut wrench is shown loosening the flare nut on a hydraulic brake line fitting

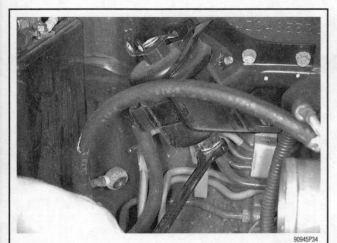

Fig. 7 The fuel inlet line on a firewall mounted fuel filter is a compression fitting. The flare nut has external threads and is threaded into the bottom of the fuel filter

Compression fittings are most often used when a pressure line attaches to an assembly, much like the fluid lines found at the brake master cylinder or on the inlet fuel line for the firewall mounted fuel filter.

The compression fitting does not have a gasket or seal, rather it uses the threaded flare nut to seal the flared end of the line or a compression fitting on the line to the assembly. The flared end of the fuel line or the compression fitting is sealed between the component and the flare nut.

A compression fitting is most often found where the fluid in the line is under considerable pressure.

The flare nut is one of two types:

• An internally threaded flare nut: This type of fitting uses a compression fitting on the line and the nut threads onto a threaded fitting.

To disconnect a fuel line using a compression fitting:

1. Hold the component that the flare nut is threaded onto securely, and using a flare nut type wrench, loosen the flare nut.

To install:

2. Installation is the reverse of the removal procedure.

Banjo Bolt Fittings

REMOVAL & INSTALLATION

▶ See Figures 9 and 10

The banjo bolt fitting has a hollow bolt that is installed through a round hollowed out chamber with a hose fitting incorporated onto the chamber. The hol-

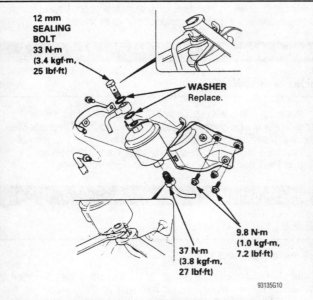

```
12 mm
SEALING
BOLT
33 N·m
(3.4 kgf·m,
25 lbf·ft)

WASHER
Replace.

9.8 N·m
(1.0 kgf·m,
7.2 lbf·ft)

37 N·m
(3.8 kgf·m,
27 lbf·ft)

93135G10
```

Fig. 8 An exploded view of the firewall mounted fuel filter and mounting bracket. The filter outlet (Top) uses a banjo bolt fitting, the inlet (Bottom) is a compression fitting

Fig. 9 The outlet line of on a firewall mounted fuel filter uses a banjo bolt type fitting. Always use new sealing washers when reinstalling the banjo bolt

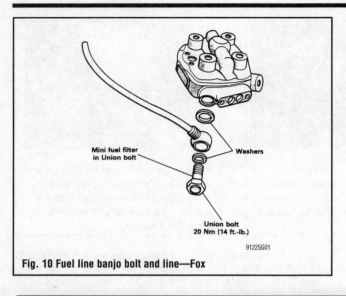

Fig. 10 Fuel line banjo bolt and line—Fox

lowed out chamber and hose fitting resemble the shape of a banjo, hence the name banjo bolt. The banjo bolt uses a sealing washer on each side of the hollowed chamber that should be replaced during reassembly.

Banjo bolt fittings are used where the fluid in the fluid lines is under pressure.

To remove a banjo bolt type of fitting:

1. Secure the component the banjo bolt is threaded into and loosen the banjo bolt using a boxed end wrench if room permits.

To install:

2. Using new sealing washer on either side of the banjo fitting, install the banjo bolt and carefully tighten to specification. The sealing washers should be slightly "crushed" between the banjo bolt the banjo fitting and the component.

GASOLINE FUEL INJECTION SYSTEM

Digifant Fuel Injection System

GENERAL DESCRIPTION

▶ **See Figure 11**

The Digifant system is all electronic, using electric injectors at a relatively low injection pressure. All injectors are operated by the Electronic Control Unit (ECU) so injector opening timing and duration can be closely controlled for reduced emissions and improved fuel mileage. During deceleration above about 1500 rpm, the injectors are shut off to save fuel and reduce emissions. The system uses an air vane and potentiometer type air flow sensor and an inlet air temperature sensor to calculate air flow into the engine. An idle stabilizer valve is used to control idle speed. This is a motorized rotary valve that controls the amount of air allowed to bypass the throttle plate.

The fuel pump is mounted in a reservoir under the vehicle along with the filter. The reservoir holds about 1 liter of fuel and is supplied by a small transfer pump in the fuel tank. The transfer pump is part of the fuel gauge sending unit assembly but it can be replaced separately.

The electric fuel injectors are secured in place by the fuel rail, which also houses the wiring. All injectors are wired together in parallel and are operated at the same time. Power is supplied to all injectors any time the ECU is receiving an rpm signal.

Other components in the Digifant system include the oxygen sensor, a coolant temperature sensor, a throttle position switch, the idle air stabilizer valve, the fuel system pressure regulator and the ignition system. The function and testing of fuel system items is described in Section 4, Electronic Engine Controls.

Most of the following procedures will produce fuel vapors. Make sure there is proper ventilation and take the appropriate fire safety precautions.

Mono-Motronic

GENERAL INFORMATION

This Bosch system was used on the ACC (1.8L) engine. Fuel is metered into the engine by monitoring engine speed and throttle position. The Engine Management System meters this fuel by firing the fuel injectors at a varying rate. Fuel volume is controlled by the duration of time the injector is left on. This "Injector Dwell Time" is usually measured in milliseconds of time.

CIS-E Motronic

GENERAL INFORMATION

▶ **See Figures 12 and 13**

The CIS-E Motronic system used on the 16V engine is a highly developed and electronically controlled version of the original Bosch Continuous Injection System (CIS). The main components are the fuel distributor, mechanical injectors and a fuel pump.

The fuel pump is mounted in a reservoir under the vehicle, along with the filter and fuel accumulator. The reservoir holds about 1 liter of fuel and is supplied by a small transfer pump in the fuel tank. The transfer pump is part of the fuel gauge sending unit assembly but it can be replaced separately.

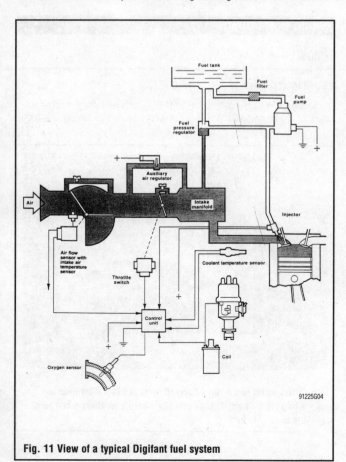

Fig. 11 View of a typical Digifant fuel system

The fuel distributor used in the Motronic system is very different from that used in earlier CIS systems. The unit is made of aluminum and is slightly smaller. It is still divided into an upper and a lower chamber but the pressure difference between chambers is not constant. A differential pressure regulator mounted on the side controls the pressure in the lower chamber which ultimately controls the fuel flow to the injectors. Control plunger movement controls the amount of fuel supplied to the upper chamber. When the engine is not running, the control plunger rests on an O-ring and there is some free-play between the plunger and air flow sensor arm. If the fuel distributor is replaced, the plunger free-play must be adjusted.

The fuel distributor is mounted on the mechanical air mass sensor. As air flows into the air cleaner and up through the sensor assembly, the air pushes the sensor plate up, which lifts up the fuel distributor plunger. When the engine is not running, the arm that the plate is bolted to rests on a spring. This allows some opposite movement of the plate if the engine back fires. There is no service procedure that requires disassembly of the air flow sensor. If the plate is removed, a special tool is required to center the plate in the bore.

The fuel injectors are purely mechanical and open at 54–70 psi (3.7–4.8 BAR) fuel line pressure. All injectors are open when the engine is running, injecting fuel to the intake ports continuously. They are mounted into plastic inserts that are threaded into the intake manifold. An O-ring is used to hold the injector in place and at the same time to seal the insert. Injectors can be

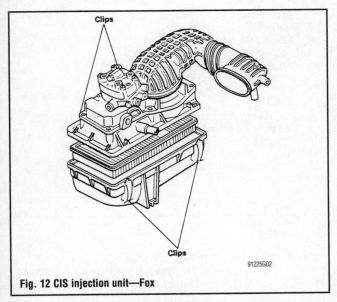

Fig. 12 CIS injection unit—Fox

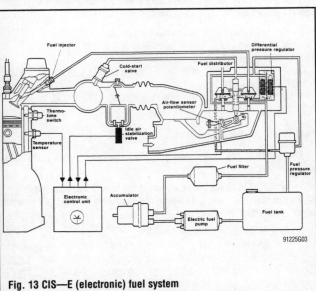

Fig. 13 CIS—E (electronic) fuel system

removed from the insert without disconnecting the fuel line. The cold start injector is mounted at the flywheel end of the intake manifold. It is a simple solenoid valve with a spray nozzle tip. During starter operation, the control unit operates this injector when engine depending on coolant temperature is below 86°F (30°C).

Other components in the Motronic system include the oxygen sensor, a coolant temperature sensor, a position sensor in the air flow sensor, two throttle position switches, the idle air stabilizer valve, and the fuel system pressure regulator. The function and testing of all these items is described in Section 4, Electronic Engine Controls.

✳✳ CAUTION

Never smoke when working around gasoline! Avoid all sources of sparks or ignition. Gasoline vapors are EXTREMELY volatile!

➡**Most of the following procedures will produce fuel vapors. Make sure there is proper ventilation and take the appropriate fire safety precautions.**

Motronic 2.9

GENERAL DESCRIPTION

This type fuel system complies with OBD 1 standards and was used on both the 2.0L and the 2.8L. Fuel is metered via engine speed and the mass of the air entering the intake manifold. The Engine Management System meters this fuel by firing the fuel injectors at a varying rate. Fuel volume is controlled by the duration of time the injector is left on. This "Injector Dwell Time" is usually measured in milliseconds of time.

Motronic 5.9

GENERAL DESCRIPTION

This fuel injection system was derived from the original Bosch Motronic Engine Management System that was first used on early nineties VW's. Fuel metering is derived from engine speed as well as load. The Engine Management System meters this fuel by sequentially firing the fuel injectors at a varying rate. Fuel volume is controlled by the duration of time the injector is left on. This "Injector Dwell Time" is usually measured in milliseconds of time.

Fuel System Pressure

RELIEVING PRESSURE

◆ See Figure 14

✳✳ CAUTION

Observe all applicable safety precautions when working around fuel. Whenever servicing the fuel system, always work in a well ventilated area. Do not allow fuel spray or vapors to come in contact with a spark or open flame. Keep a dry chemical fire extinguisher near the work area. Always keep fuel in a container specifically designed for fuel storage; also, always properly seal fuel containers to avoid the possibility of fire or explosion.

The fuel injection system operates under high pressure. This makes it necessary to first relieve the system of pressure before servicing. The pressurized fuel, when released, may ignite or cause personal injury.

1. Disconnect the power to the fuel pump by removing the relay or the fuel pump fuse. Check the list on the fuse box lid to be sure. The fuse can be removed to stop the fuel pump from running. With the engine operating at idle, wait until the engine stalls from fuel starvation.

2. Switch the ignition **OFF** and remove the negative battery cable.

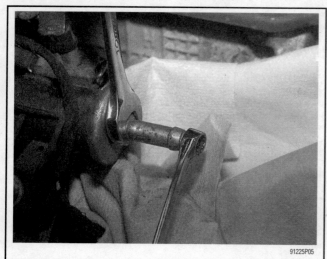

Fig. 14 Relieving the fuel system pressure on a 2.0L, 8 valve engine in a 1994 Jetta

3. Carefully loosen the fuel line on the control pressure regulator or component to be serviced.

4. Wrap a clean rag around the connection, while loosening, to catch any fuel.

5. After service is complete, discard the fuel soaked rag in the proper manner and reconnect the negative battery cable, relay or fuses.

Fuel Pump

DESCRIPTION

On a Digifant fuel system, the fuel pump is mounted in a reservoir under the rear of the vehicle. The fuel filter is also in this area. The reservoir holds one liter of fuel and is supplied by a small transfer pump in the tank. The transfer pump can be replaced separately even though they are installed and removed as a unit.

The Motronic system uses two fuel pumps. The first is a small transfer pump to get the fuel out of the tank and the second boosts the fuel pressure to the necessary amount. The transfer pump is located inside the tank and the main pressure pump can be found under the vehicle. This transfer pump is located under the rear seat and is part of the fuel gauge sending unit. The main fuel pump can be found in the reservoir in front of the rear axle beam. There is a check valve inside this pump to maintain pressure in the lines, especially on hot days, to avoid vapor lock. The fuel filter is mounted to the side of the reservoir. This filter has no specified replacement interval and should be good for the entire service life of the vehicle. Whenever the ignition key is in the on position, the pump should run for at least two (2) seconds to pressurize the fuel lines. If the Engine Control Unit (ECM) does not see a signal from the Hall Effect sensor in the distributor it will shut the pump off. If a Hall Effect signal is present, the pump will continue to run as long as a signal is detected. It is this Hall Effect signal that signals the ECM that the engine is rotating therefore indicating that fuel is needed. The pump is operated via a relay that is controlled by the ECM. This relay is located in the vehicles fuse panel. The main contacts of the relay can be jumped to run the pump during testing.

REMOVAL & INSTALLATION

➡**On CIS systems the main fuel pump is located under the vehicle in front of the rear axle or in front of the tank on the right side.**

1990–92 Cabriolet, Golf, Jetta and Fox

TRANSFER PUMP

1. Remove the rear seat and the access cover.
2. Disconnect the wiring and hoses and unscrew the lock ring.

3. Carefully lift out the pump and gauge sending unit assembly.
4. When installing the assembly, use a new seal.

MAIN PUMP

1. Disconnect the negative battery cable.
2. Relieve the fuel system pressure.
3. Raise and safely support the rear or right side of the vehicle on jack stands.
4. Disconnect the wiring from the pump. Clean any dirt away from the fuel line fitting.
5. Use locking pliers to pinch off the fuel line from the transfer pump to the main pump. If the fuel line is metal, remove the rear seat and access panel and disconnect the line at the transfer pump.
6. Place a pan under the pump and disconnect the fuel line fitting from the pump.
7. Remove the retaining ring screws and slide the pump out of the reservoir.
To install:
8. Moisten the pump O-ring with a little fuel and slide it into the reservoir. Install the retaining ring screws.
9. When connecting the fittings, use new copper washers and tighten the fittings to 15 ft. lbs. (20 Nm).

1993–99 Cabrio, Golf, and Jetta

1. Remove the negative battery cable.
2. Raise and safely support the vehicle.
3. Relieve the fuel system pressure.
4. Remove the rear seat and the access cover.
5. Disconnect the wiring and hoses.
6. Remove the fuel lines from the pump.
7. On 1993–99 Golf, Jetta and Cabrio vehicles, unscrew the fuel pump retaining ring.
8. On all other models, remove the mounting bolts and the fuel pump.
9. Carefully lift out the pump and gauge sending unit assembly.
10. Empty the fuel pump into an approved container.
To install:
11. Installation is the reverse of removal. Be sure to use new sealing rings and/or gaskets.

TESTING

Fuel Pump Test

The fuel pump runs only when the engine is running or is being started. Therefore the fuel pump relay must be jumped. This will enable the pump to run constantly so that an accurate test can be performed.

➡**If the pump does not run, make sure it has a good ground and is getting the necessary 12 volts from the battery.**

1. Remove the fuel pump relay from the fuse box.
2. With the ignition off, bridge the number 87 terminal of the relay to the positive post of the battery using a jumper wire.
3. If the pump runs only when the jumper wire is attached, check the wiring going to the fuel pump.
4. Once you are sure that the wiring to the pump is not at fault, the Electronic Control Module (ECM) may be bad.

Fuel Pump Electrical Circuit

1. To begin testing the fuel pump electrical circuit first check that the battery is at a full state of charge.

➡**Do not forget to check the condition of the fuse in the box, if it is blown the fuel pump will not receive the necessary electricity it needs to operate correctly.**

2. Remove the access panel from the fuel pump.
3. Turn the key to the on position and have a helper listen for the pump to begin running. If the system is operating correctly, the pump should run for a short period and then shut off. If the pump does not run, continue on to the following steps.
4. Remove the fuel pump relay and operate the pump as shown in the fuel

pump test. If the pump runs after performing the fuel pump test, proceed to the next diagnostic step in this procedure.

5. Pull the jumper cable from the relay and then while the ignition switch is off, connect an Digital Volt Ohm Meter (DVOM) to the #3 terminal and the # 85 terminal on the relay. Turn the key on, there should be a momentary ground signal. If a ground is present at terminal # 85, the relay is faulty. If no ground is detected, check the wiring at the engine control module. If no faults can be found in the wiring the Electronic Control Unit (ECU) is the cause.

Throttle Body

REMOVAL & INSTALLATION

1. Detach the negative battery cable.
2. Disconnect the air intake duct and place it off to the side of the throttle valve housing.
3. Remove the throttle position sensor wiring harness.
4. Detach the accelerator cable from the housing of the throttle valve.
5. On the VR-6 engine, remove the expansion tank filler cap. Clamp off any coolant hoses that connect to the throttle body and then remove them.
6. On four (4) cylinder models, detach the Evaporative Emissions (EVAP) vent hose from its port on the throttle body.
7. Remove all attaching bolts that hold the throttle body to the intake manifold.
8. Remove the throttle body.
To install:
9. Use a new gasket any time the throttle body has been removed from the intake manifold. If this gasket were to leak, an unmetered air source would enter the engine thus creating a lean condition in the cylinders.
10. If you are replacing the throttle body housing, remember to transfer all sensors to the new unit before installing it back on the intake manifold.
11. The remainder of the installation procedure is the reverse of removal.

Fuel Injector(s)

REMOVAL & INSTALLATION

⬥ **See Figures 15, 16, 17, 18 and 19**

1. Relieve the fuel system pressure.
2. On CIS-E Motronic systems pull the injectors straight out of the intake manifold using a tool designed specifically for the job. Fuel injector removal tools are sold at most automotive suppliers or at your local VW dealer.

➡ **Use a spray lubricant to ease the removal of any stuck injectors.**

3. Now hold the fitting with a line wrench and unscrew the injector.

➡ **If it is difficult to remove the injectors from their lines, use a penetrant to aid in the process.**

4. The injectors can now be removed from the lines if desired.
To install:
5. Install the fuel injectors on the lines.
6. Lubricate the injector O-rings with a spray lubricant or gasoline.
7. Install the injectors.

TESTING

⬥ **See Figures 20 and 21**

1. Unplug the connector at the end of the fuel rail.
2. Connect a Digital Volt Ohm Meter (DVOM) to the terminals and measure the resistance
3. If the resistance is high, remove the wiring from each injector and recheck each individually.
4. The resistance should be between 14–18 ohms.
5. If the injectors are not within specification, replace them with new ones.

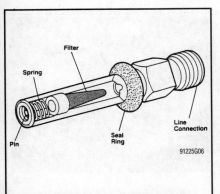

Fig. 15 Inner view of a mechanical fuel injector

Fig. 16 Pull the fuel injector wiring harness from the injector

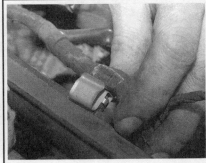

Fig. 17 Observe the location of the injector wiring harness spring clips

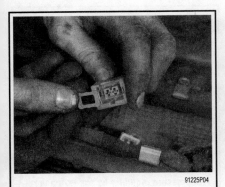

Fig. 18 Close up of injector wiring harness

Fig. 19 Notice the arch in the injector wiring harness connector. It will only slide over the injector in one direction

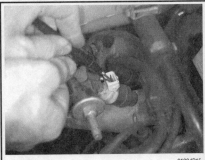

Fig. 20 To test the injectors probe the two prongs at the rear of each injector with the leads of a multimeter . . .

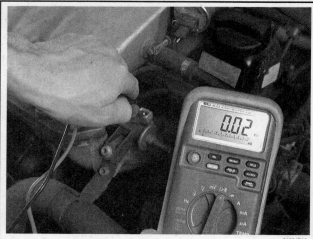

Fig. 21 . . . set the meter to the ohms scale and check the resistance of each injector. A shorted injector will show zero ohms

Fuel Rail

REMOVAL & INSTALLATION

▶ See Figures 22, 23, 24 and 25

1. Remove the negative battery cable.
2. On 2.0L engines, remove the upper intake manifold to gain access to the fuel rail.
3. Detach the injector wiring harness connectors.

4. Relieve the fuel system pressure.
5. Detach the vacuum hose from the pressure regulator.
6. Loosen the clamps and remove the fuel supply hose.
7. Detach the fuel return hose.
8. Remove the fuel rail retaining bolts.
9. Remove the fuel rail and the injectors as an assembly away from the intake manifold.

To install:

10. The procedure for the installation of the fuel rail and the injectors is the reverse of the removal procedure.

➡**Always replace the fuel injector O-rings with new ones every time the injectors have been removed. Check that all vacuum hoses and electrical connections have been made. Always check for fuel leaks immediately after the engine has been started.**

11. Tighten the fuel rail bolts to 84 inch lbs. (10 Nm) on 2.0L engines.

Fuel Pressure Regulator

REMOVAL & INSTALLATION

▶ See Figures 26 and 27

1990–92 Cabriolet, Fox, Golf, and Jetta

1. Relieve the fuel system pressure.
2. Detach all electrical connectors and or wiring harnesses leading to the regulator.
3. On CIS-E fuel systems, remove the vacuum lines.
4. Remove the fasteners that secure the regulator to the fuel rail.

➡**Always clean any dirt away from the fuel line fittings before loosening them.**

Fig. 22 Remove the ignition wire holder to gain access to the fuel rail on 2.0L 8 valve engines

Fig. 23 Hex keys are needed to remove the fuel rail retaining bolts

Fig. 24 Note the position and length of each fuel rail retaining bolt

Fig. 25 Lift the fuel rail away from the injectors

Fig. 26 Removing the retaining clip from the fuel pressure regulator–2.0L 8 valve engine

Fig. 27 Remove the rubber hoses from the fuel pressure regulator by squeezing the clips with a pair of needle nose pliers–2.0L 8 valve engine

5. Remove the fuel pressure regulator.

To install:

6. Installation is the reverse of removal.

1993–99 Cabrio, Golf and Jetta

1. Remove the negative battery cable.
2. Remove the vacuum hose from the regulator.
3. Remove the retaining clip from the fuel pressure regulator.
4. Cover the fuel pressure regulator with a shop towel and remove it from the fuel rail.

To install:

5. Installation is the reverse of removal.

Differential Pressure Regulator

REMOVAL & INSTALLATION

➡ **The differential pressure regulator is located on the CIS-E injection system only.**

1. Disconnect the wiring.
2. Clean any dirt away from the fuel line fitting and remove the fitting.
3. Remove the 2 screws to remove the regulator. The screws are made of non-magnetic material. If the screws must be replaced, make sure they are non-magnetic.

To install:

4. Installation is the reverse of removal.

DIESEL FUEL SYSTEM

Description

◆ **See Figure 28**

Starting in the 1991 model year, Volkswagen introduced the ECO Diesel engine in the Jetta. This is a standard diesel engine with a turbo charger and a catalytic converter. The turbo charger provides only about 6 psi boost but about a 40 percent increase in air flowing through the engine. This provides a modest power increase, but the objective is to greatly improve the engine's emissions performance. Since the system is designed for improved emissions rather than power, there is no fuel enrichment device on the injection pump. The Turbo Diesel Injected (TDI) engine was later introduced. It provided far greater performance with slightly less fuel economy than the ECO Diesel.

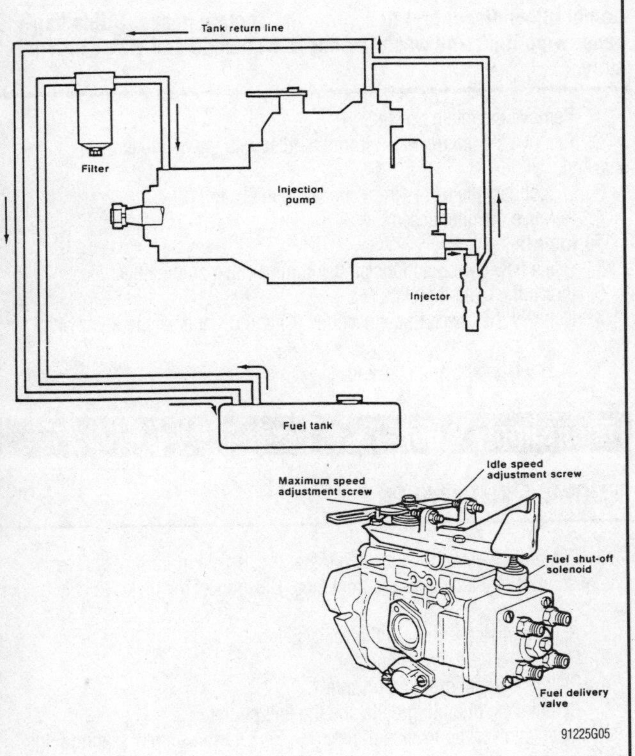

The speed of a diesel engine is controlled by the amount of fuel that is sprayed into the cylinders. There is no throttle plate, therefore no vacuum in the intake plenum. A diesel engine is stopped by cutting off its fuel supply.

Clean, dry diesel fuel is the key to a well running engine. Any dirt in the fuel system can get caught in the fuel rail and injectors and inhibit the quantity of fuel sprayed into the engine. Any reduction in the flow and or pressure of the fuel system can greatly reduce the performance of a diesel engine.

Relieving Fuel System Pressure

RELIEVING

◆ **See Figure 14**

The fuel injection system operates under high pressure. This makes it necessary to first relieve the system of pressure before servicing. The pressurized fuel, when released, may ignite or cause personal injury.

1. Disconnect the power to the fuel pump by removing the relay or the fuel pump fuse. Check the list on the fuse box lid to be sure. The fuse can be removed to stop the fuel pump from running. With the engine operating at idle, wait until the engine stalls from fuel starvation.
2. Switch the ignition **OFF** and remove the negative battery cable.
3. Carefully loosen the fuel line on the control pressure regulator or component to be serviced.
4. Wrap a clean rag around the connection, while loosening, to catch any fuel.
5. After service is complete, discard the fuel soaked rag in the proper manner and reconnect the negative battery cable, relay or fuses.

Fuel System Service Precautions

Although Diesel fuel is not as flammable as gasoline, whenever working on or around Diesel fuel or the fuel delivery system heed the following precautions:

• Do not allow fuel spray or fuel vapors to come into contact with a heating element or open flame. Do not smoke while working on the fuel system.

• Always disconnect the negative battery cable unless the repair or test procedure requires that battery voltage be applied.

• Always relieve the fuel system pressure prior to disconnecting any fitting or fuel line connection.

• To control fuel spray when relieving system pressure, place a shop towel around the fitting prior to loosening to catch the spray. Ensure that all fuel spillage is quickly wiped up and that all fuel soaked rags are deposited into a proper fire safety container.

• Always keep a dry chemical (Class B) fire extinguisher near the work area.

• Always use a back-up wrench when loosening and tightening fuel line fittings.

• Do not re-use fuel system gaskets and O-rings, replace with new ones. Do not substitute fuel hose where fuel pipe is installed.

Tank return line

Filter

Injection pump

Injector

Fuel tank

Maximum speed adjustment screw

Idle speed adjustment screw

Fuel shut-off solenoid

Fuel delivery valve

91225G05

Fig. 28 VW diesel fuel system

Injection Lines

REMOVAL & INSTALLATION

1. The lines should be removed as a set. Loosen the fittings at each injector.
2. Use a back-up wrench to loosen the lines from the injection pump.
3. Remove the lines as a set, and cap the injectors and pump fittings immediately.

To install:

4. Make sure the flares on the lines are not split or flattened. If so, the line should be replaced. They can be purchased or made up separately but are usually replaced as a set.
5. Fit the lines into place and start all the nuts. Use a back-up wrench and tighten the line nuts at the pump to 18 ft. lbs. (25 Nm). Do not over tighten the nuts or the flares will split and the line will leak.
6. Tighten the nuts at the nozzle end to 18 ft. lbs. (25 Nm).

Injectors

REMOVAL & INSTALLATION

1. Relieve the fuel system pressure.
2. Remove the fuel pipe by unscrewing the union nuts.
3. Remove the fuel pipes at the pump and at the injectors.
4. Remove the fuel injection lines as an assembly.
5. Unscrew the injector from the cylinder head.

To install:

➡**Replace the heat shields at each injector hole every time a new injector is installed.**

6. Screw the new injector into the cylinder head and tighten it.
7. Install the fuel line assembly.

TESTING

A smoky black soot from the exhaust system, engine misfire, excessive blue smoke during startup, and or loss of power could be signs of injection system malfunction.

Idle Speed

ADJUSTMENT

▶ **See Figure 29**

Diesel engines have both an idle speed and a maximum speed adjustment. The maximum speed adjustment is a high idle speed that prevents the engine from over-revving when the control lever is in the full speed position but there is no load on the engine. No increase in power is available through this adjustment. The control lever idle stop screw is no longer used for idle speed adjustment. The idle speed boost linkage includes an adjustment for basic idle speed.

1. If the vehicle has no tachometer, connect a suitable Diesel engine tachometer as per the manufacturer's instructions.
2. Run the engine to normal operating temperature.
3. Be sure the manual cold start/idle speed boost knob is pushed in all the way.
4. Turn the linkage cap nut to adjust idle speed to 820–880 rpm, at a point where there is the least vibration.
5. Advance the control lever to full speed. The high idle speed is 5300–5400 rpm. Adjust as needed and secure the locknut with sealer.

Fuel Filter/Water Separator

DRAINING WATER

Although Diesel fuel and water do not readily mix, fuel does tend to entrap moisture from the air each time it is moved from one container to another. Eventually every Diesel fuel system collects enough water to become a potential hazard. Fortunately, when it's allowed to settle out, the water will always drop to the bottom of the tank or filter housing. Some Diesel fuel filters are equipped with a water drain; a bolt or petcock at the bottom of the housing.

At The Water Separator

1. Raise and safely support the vehicle. Remove the fuel filler cap.
2. At the separator, connect a hose from the separator drain to a catch pan.
3. Open the drain valve (3 turns) and drain the separator until a steady stream of fuel flows from the separator, then close the valve.

➡**Don't forget to install the filler cap.**

At The Filter

1. If the filter is equipped with a water drain at the bottom, place a pan under the drain to catch the water and fuel.
2. If equipped, loosen the vent bolt on the filter base. If there is no vent, loosen the return line at the pump (the line not connected to the filter).
3. Loosen the bolt or valve. When fuel flows in a clean stream, close the drain and tighten the vent or return line.

REMOVAL & INSTALLATION

▶ **See Figure 30**

✳✳ WARNING

Do not allow diesel fuel to contact the coolant hoses. If this happens, wipe it off and wash the hoses with soap and water immediately.

1. Remove the retaining clips (5).
2. Remove the control valve from the filter with the fuel lines attached.
3. Disconnect the hoses from connections (1) and (2).
4. Remove the filter assembly.

To install:

5. Use a new O-ring and install the control valve on the filter.
6. Install the retaining clips (5).
7. Connect the hoses to connections (1) and (2) and secure them with clamps.
8. Start the engine and check for leaks.

Fuel Supply Pump

REMOVAL & INSTALLATION

1. The main fuel pump is located under the vehicle in front of the rear axle or in front of the tank on the right side. Disconnect the negative battery cable.
2. Raise and safely support the vehicle.
3. Detach the electrical connector.
4. Relieve the fuel system pressure.
5. Remove the mounting bolts and the fuel pump.
6. Installation is the reverse of removal. Be sure to use new sealing rings and/or gaskets.

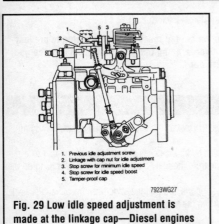

Fig. 29 Low idle speed adjustment is made at the linkage cap—Diesel engines

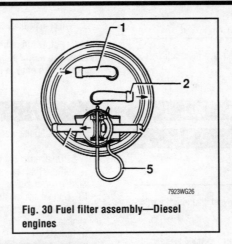

Fig. 30 Fuel filter assembly—Diesel engines

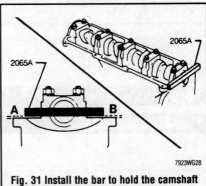

Fig. 31 Install the bar to hold the camshaft in position during Diesel injection pump service

Diesel Injection Pump

REMOVAL & INSTALLATION

♦ See Figure 31

➡Special tools are required for injection pump installation. Do not remove the pump without these tools on hand.

1. Disconnect the negative battery cable and remove the air cleaner, cylinder head cover and timing belt cover.
2. Turn the engine to TDC of No. 1 cylinder and insert a setting bar into the slot on the rear of the camshaft, VW tool 2065A or equivalent, to hold the camshaft in place. Remove the timing belt. Be careful to not turn the engine while the belt is removed.
3. Loosen the pump drive sprocket nut but don't remove it yet. Install a puller on the sprocket and apply moderate tension.
4. Rap the puller bolt with light hammer taps until the sprocket jumps off the tapered shaft, then remove the puller and sprocket. Be careful not to lose the Woodruff key.
5. Hold the pump fittings with a wrench and using a line wrench, remove the injection lines from the pump. Cap the pump fittings to keep dirt out. It may be easier to remove the lines from the injectors also and set them aside as an assembly. Cap the injector fittings to keep dirt out.
6. Disconnect the control cables, fuel solenoid wire and fuel supply and return lines.
7. Remove the pump mounting bolts and lift the pump from the vehicle.
To install:
8. When reinstalling, align the marks on the top of the mounting flange and the pump and tighten the mounting bolts to 18 ft. lbs. (25 Nm).
9. Install the Woodruff key and sprocket and tighten the nut to 33 ft. lbs. (45 Nm).
10. When reinstalling the supply and return lines, be sure the fitting marked OUT is used for the return line. This fitting has an orifice and must be in the correct place. Use new gaskets.
11. Turn the pump sprocket so the mark aligns with the mark on the side of the mounting flange and insert a pin through the hole in the sprocket to hold it in place.
12. Install the camshaft drive sprocket and belt and set the belt tension. Tension the drive belt by turning the tensioner pulley clockwise until the belt can be flexed ½ in. (13mm) between the camshaft and the pump sprockets. Remove the pin.
13. Remove the camshaft holding bar. Turn the engine through 2 full turns, return to TDC of the No. 1 cylinder and recheck the belt tension and camshaft timing.
14. Reinstall the injection lines, wiring and control cables. Tighten the line nuts to 18 ft. lbs. (25 Nm).

INJECTION TIMING

1. Turn the engine to TDC of No. 1 cylinder.

2. Make sure the pump control lever is fully against the low idle stop. If equipped with a manual cold start knob, make sure the knob is all the way in against the stop.
3. Remove the center plug on the pump head and install the adapter tool VW–2066 or equivalent, and a dial indicator. Preload the dial indicator to 2.5mm.
4. Slowly turn the engine counterclockwise until the dial gauge stops moving, then zero the dial indicator. This is the bottom of the pump stroke.
5. Turn the engine clockwise until the TDC mark on the flywheel aligns with the pointer on the bell housing.
6. The dial indicator should read 0.95–1.05mm (0.0374–0.0413 inches).
7. If adjustment is required, remove the timing belt cover and loosen the pump mounting bolts without turning the engine.
8. Turn the pump body to make the dial indicator read 1.00mm (0.0394 inches).
9. Tighten the mounting bolts to 18 ft. lbs. (25 Nm) and turn the engine backwards about 1 turn. Turn the engine forwards to TDC of No. 1 cylinder and recheck the dial indicator.
10. When the correct setting is reached on the dial indicator, reinstall the belt cover and the center plug on the pump. Use a new copper gasket.

Glow Plugs

DIAGNOSIS & TESTING

1. Disconnect the engine temperature sensor.
2. Connect a test light between No. 4 cylinder glow plug and ground. The glow plugs are connected by a flat, coated busbar, located near the bottom of the cylinder head.
3. Turn the ignition key **ON**; the test light should light, then go out after 8–30 seconds.
4. If there is no voltage, go to Step 7.
5. To test each plug individually, disconnect the wire and remove the busbar from the glow plugs.
6. Connect an ohmmeter to each glow plug connection or use a test light. Each plug must have continuity to ground. The engine will probably start with one defective glow plug, but it will make a lot of smoke.
7. To test the glow plug control system, remove the glow plug relay from the bottom right socket of the main fuse/relay panel.
8. With the ignition switch **OFF**, there should be 12 volts at terminal 30 on the socket in the panel. Terminal 85 should have continuity to ground.
9. Disconnect the stop solenoid wire from the pump so the engine will not start. With the ignition switch **ON**, there should be 12 volts at terminal 86. When the starter is operated with the ignition switch, there should be 12 volts at terminal 50.
10. Install the relay and disconnect and ground the temperature sensor wire. Connect a voltmeter or test light to the glow plug busbar.
11. With the stop solenoid wire still disconnected, operate the starter with the ignition switch. There should be power to the glow plugs.
12. If all voltages at the socket are correct but there is not power to the glow plugs, the relay is faulty and must be replaced.

REMOVAL & INSTALLATION

1. Remove the busbar connecting the glow plugs and determine which plugs need replacement.
2. Remove the defective plugs.

FUEL TANK

Fuel Tank Assembly

REMOVAL & INSTALLATION

Always ground yourself to the vehicle's chassis to prevent sparks while working on or around the fuel tank.
1. Disconnect the negative battery cable.
2. Remove the access panel under the rear seat or in the luggage compartment.
3. Disconnect the gauge sending unit wiring and hoses.
4. Raise and safely support the vehicle.
5. Drain the fuel tank into an approved container.
6. On Cabriolet models, remove the right rear inner fender and disconnect the breather hose from the filler. Remove, but do not disconnect the gravity valve.
7. Detach the fuel pump bracket from the body.
8. Lower the pump enough to disconnect the fuel hoses from the tank.

3. When installing new plugs, tighten to 22 ft. lbs. (30 Nm).

➡**Diesel glow plugs have an air gap much like a spark plug to prevent overheating of the plug. Over-torquing the glow plug will close the gap and cause the plug to burn out.**

9. On Cabriolet models, the rear axle must be dropped out of the way as follows:
   a. Disconnect the brake hydraulic hoses at both sides of the rear axle.
   b. Detach the rear axle from the body on both sides and let it hang on the parking brake cables.
10. Unhook the muffler supports and pull the large hose from the filler neck.
11. Support the tank, loosen the straps and carefully lower the tank out of the vehicle.
To install:
12. If a new tank is being installed, glue new foam strips to the tank in the same location as the old ones.
13. Position the tank and secure it with the straps.
14. Connect the wiring and hoses to the sending unit.
15. Attach the fuel pump bracket to the body.
16. On Cabriolet models, install the rear axle, connect the hydraulic lines and bleed the brakes.
17. Install the access panel once all electrical connections have been made.
18. Connect the negative battery cable.
19. Fill the tank with fuel and check for leaks.

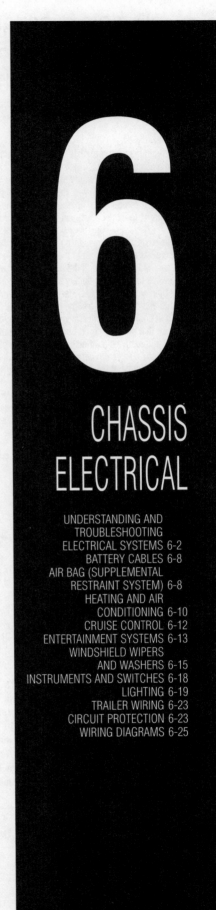

6

CHASSIS ELECTRICAL

UNDERSTANDING AND TROUBLESHOOTING ELECTRICAL SYSTEMS

Basic Electrical Theory

▶ See Figure 1

For any 12 volt, negative ground, electrical system to operate, the electricity must travel in a complete circuit. This simply means that current (power) from the positive (+) terminal of the battery must eventually return to the negative (-) terminal of the battery. Along the way, this current will travel through wires, fuses, switches and components. If, for any reason, the flow of current through the circuit is interrupted, the component fed by that circuit will cease to function properly.

Perhaps the easiest way to visualize a circuit is to think of connecting a light bulb (with two wires attached to it) to the battery—one wire attached to the negative (-) terminal of the battery and the other wire to the positive (+) terminal. With the two wires touching the battery terminals, the circuit would be complete and the light bulb would illuminate. Electricity would follow a path from the battery to the bulb and back to the battery. It's easy to see that with longer wires on our light bulb, it could be mounted anywhere. Further, one wire could be fitted with a switch so that the light could be turned on and off.

The normal automotive circuit differs from this simple example in two ways. First, instead of having a return wire from the bulb to the battery, the current travels through the frame of the vehicle. Since the negative (-) battery cable is attached to the frame (made of electrically conductive metal), the frame of the vehicle can serve as a ground wire to complete the circuit. Secondly, most automotive circuits contain multiple components which receive power from a single circuit. This lessens the amount of wire needed to power components on the vehicle.

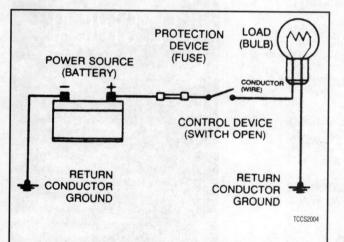

Fig. 1 This example illustrates a simple circuit. When the switch is closed, power from the positive (+) battery terminal flows through the fuse and the switch, and then to the light bulb. The light illuminates and the circuit is completed through the ground wire back to the negative (-) battery terminal. In reality, the two ground points shown in the illustration are attached to the metal frame of the vehicle, which completes the circuit back to the battery

HOW DOES ELECTRICITY WORK: THE WATER ANALOGY

Electricity is the flow of electrons—the subatomic particles that constitute the outer shell of an atom. Electrons spin in an orbit around the center core of an atom. The center core is comprised of protons (positive charge) and neutrons (neutral charge). Electrons have a negative charge and balance out the positive charge of the protons. When an outside force causes the number of electrons to unbalance the charge of the protons, the electrons will split off the atom and look for another atom to balance out. If this imbalance is kept up, electrons will continue to move and an electrical flow will exist.

Many people have been taught electrical theory using an analogy with water. In a comparison with water flowing through a pipe, the electrons would be the water and the wire is the pipe.

The flow of electricity can be measured much like the flow of water through a pipe. The unit of measurement used is amperes, frequently abbreviated as amps (a). You can compare amperage to the volume of water flowing through a pipe. When connected to a circuit, an ammeter will measure the actual amount of current flowing through the circuit. When relatively few electrons flow through a circuit, the amperage is low. When many electrons flow, the amperage is high.

Water pressure is measured in units such as pounds per square inch (psi); The electrical pressure is measured in units called volts (v). When a voltmeter is connected to a circuit, it is measuring the electrical pressure.

The actual flow of electricity depends not only on voltage and amperage, but also on the resistance of the circuit. The higher the resistance, the higher the force necessary to push the current through the circuit. The standard unit for measuring resistance is an ohm. Resistance in a circuit varies depending on the amount and type of components used in the circuit. The main factors which determine resistance are:

• Material—some materials have more resistance than others. Those with high resistance are said to be insulators. Rubber materials (or rubber-like plastics) are some of the most common insulators used in vehicles as they have a very high resistance to electricity. Very low resistance materials are said to be conductors. Copper wire is among the best conductors. Silver is actually a superior conductor to copper and is used in some relay contacts, but its high cost prohibits its use as common wiring. Most automotive wiring is made of copper.

• Size—the larger the wire size being used, the less resistance the wire will have. This is why components which use large amounts of electricity usually have large wires supplying current to them.

• Length—for a given thickness of wire, the longer the wire, the greater the resistance. The shorter the wire, the less the resistance. When determining the proper wire for a circuit, both size and length must be considered to design a circuit that can handle the current needs of the component.

• Temperature—with many materials, the higher the temperature, the greater the resistance (positive temperature coefficient). Some materials exhibit the opposite trait of lower resistance with higher temperatures (negative temperature coefficient). These principles are used in many of the sensors on the engine.

OHM'S LAW

There is a direct relationship between current, voltage and resistance. The relationship between current, voltage and resistance can be summed up by a statement known as Ohm's law.

Voltage (E) is equal to amperage (I) times resistance (R) $E=I \times R$

Other forms of the formula are $R=E/I$ and $I=E/R$

In each of these formulas, E is the voltage in volts, I is the current in amps and R is the resistance in ohms. The basic point to remember is that as the resistance of a circuit goes up, the amount of current that flows in the circuit will go down, if voltage remains the same.

The amount of work that the electricity can perform is expressed as power. The unit of power is the watt (w). The relationship between power, voltage and current is expressed as:

Power (w) is equal to amperage (I) times voltage (E): $W=I \times E$

This is only true for direct current (DC) circuits; The alternating current formula is a tad different, but since the electrical circuits in most vehicles are DC type, we need not get into AC circuit theory.

Electrical Components

POWER SOURCE

Power is supplied to the vehicle by two devices: The battery and the alternator. The battery supplies electrical power during starting or during periods when the current demand of the vehicle's electrical system exceeds the output capacity of the alternator. The alternator supplies electrical current when the engine is running. Just not does the alternator supply the current needs of the vehicle, but it recharges the battery.

The Battery

In most modern vehicles, the battery is a lead/acid electrochemical device consisting of six 2 volt subsections (cells) connected in series, so that the unit is capable of producing approximately 12 volts of electrical pressure. Each subsection consists of a series of positive and negative plates held a short distance apart in a solution of sulfuric acid and water.

The two types of plates are of dissimilar metals. This sets up a chemical reaction, and it is this reaction which produces current flow from the battery when its positive and negative terminals are connected to an electrical load. The power removed from the battery is replaced by the alternator, restoring the battery to its original chemical state.

The Alternator

On some vehicles there isn't an alternator, but a generator. The difference is that an alternator supplies alternating current which is then changed to direct current for use on the vehicle, while a generator produces direct current. Alternators tend to be more efficient and that is why they are used.

Alternators and generators are devices that consist of coils of wires wound together making big electromagnets. One group of coils spins within another set and the interaction of the magnetic fields causes a current to flow. This current is then drawn off the coils and fed into the vehicles electrical system.

GROUND

Two types of grounds are used in automotive electric circuits. Direct ground components are grounded to the frame through their mounting points. All other components use some sort of ground wire which is attached to the frame or chassis of the vehicle. The electrical current runs through the chassis of the vehicle and returns to the battery through the ground (-) cable; if you look, you'll see that the battery ground cable connects between the battery and the frame or chassis of the vehicle.

→**It should be noted that a good percentage of electrical problems can be traced to bad grounds.**

PROTECTIVE DEVICES

▶ **See Figure 2**

It is possible for large surges of current to pass through the electrical system of your vehicle. If this surge of current were to reach the load in the circuit, the surge could burn it out or severely damage it. It can also overload the wiring, causing the harness to get hot and melt the insulation. To prevent this, fuses, circuit breakers and/or fusible links are connected into the supply wires of the electrical system. These items are nothing more than a built-in weak spot in the system. When an abnormal amount of current flows through the system, these protective devices work as follows to protect the circuit:

• Fuse—when an excessive electrical current passes through a fuse, the fuse "blows" (the conductor melts) and opens the circuit, preventing the passage of current.

• Circuit Breaker—a circuit breaker is basically a self-repairing fuse. It will open the circuit in the same fashion as a fuse, but when the surge subsides, the circuit breaker can be reset and does not need replacement.

• Fusible Link—a fusible link (fuse link or main link) is a short length of special, high temperature insulated wire that acts as a fuse. When an excessive electrical current passes through a fusible link, the thin gauge wire inside the link melts, creating an intentional open to protect the circuit. To repair the circuit, the link must be replaced. Some newer type fusible links are housed in plug-in modules, which are simply replaced like a fuse, while older type fusible links must be cut and spliced if they melt. Since this link is very early in the electrical path, it's the first place to look if nothing on the vehicle works, yet the battery seems to be charged and is properly connected.

✼✼ CAUTION

Always replace fuses, circuit breakers and fusible links with identically rated components. Under no circumstances should a component of higher or lower amperage rating be substituted.

SWITCHES & RELAYS

▶ **See Figures 3, 4 and 5**

Switches are used in electrical circuits to control the passage of current. The most common use is to open and close circuits between the battery and the various electric devices in the system. Switches are rated according to the amount of amperage they can handle. If a sufficient amperage rated switch is not used in a circuit, the switch could overload and cause damage.

Some electrical components which require a large amount of current to operate use a special switch called a relay. Since these circuits carry a large amount of current, the thickness of the wire in the circuit is also greater. If this large wire were connected from the load to the control switch, the switch would have to carry the high amperage load and the fairing or dash would be twice as large to accommodate the increased size of the wiring harness. To prevent these problems, a relay is used.

Relays are composed of a coil and a set of contacts. When the coil has a current passed though it, a magnetic field is formed and this field causes the contacts to move together, completing the circuit. Most relays are normally open, preventing current from passing through the circuit, but they can take any electrical form depending on the job they are intended to do. Relays can be considered "remote control switches." They allow a smaller current to operate devices that require higher amperages. When a small current operates the coil, a larger current is allowed to pass by the contacts. Some common circuits which may

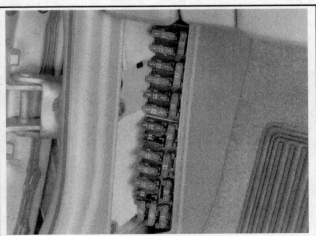

Fig. 2 Most vehicles use one or more fuse panels. This one is located on the driver's side kick panel

TCCA6P01

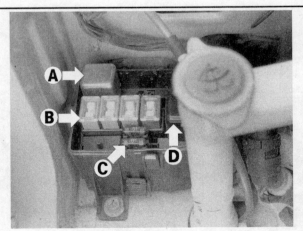

A. Relay   C. Fuse
B. Fusible link   D. Flasher

TCCA6P02

Fig. 3 The underhood fuse and relay panel usually contains fuses, relays, flashers and fusible links

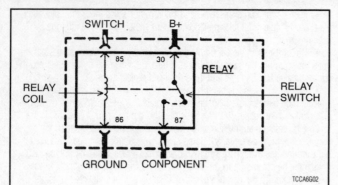

TCCA6G02

Fig. 4 Relays are composed of a coil and a switch. These two components are linked together so that when one operates, the other operates at the same time. The large wires in the circuit are connected from the battery to one side of the relay switch (B+) and from the opposite side of the relay switch to the load (component). Smaller wires are connected from the relay coil to the control switch for the circuit and from the opposite side of the relay coil to ground

use relays are the horn, headlights, starter, electric fuel pump and other high draw circuits.

LOAD

Every electrical circuit must include a "load" (something to use the electricity coming from the source). Without this load, the battery would attempt to deliver its entire power supply from one pole to another. This is called a "short circuit." All this electricity would take a short cut to ground and cause a great amount of damage to other components in the circuit by developing a tremendous amount of heat. This condition could develop sufficient heat to melt the insulation on all the surrounding wires and reduce a multiple wire cable to a lump of plastic and copper.

WIRING & HARNESSES

The average vehicle contains meters and meters of wiring, with hundreds of individual connections. To protect the many wires from damage and to keep them from becoming a confusing tangle, they are organized into bundles, enclosed in plastic or taped together and called wiring harnesses. Different harnesses serve different parts of the vehicle. Individual wires are color coded to help trace them through a harness where sections are hidden from view.

Automotive wiring or circuit conductors can be either single strand wire, multi-strand wire or printed circuitry. Single strand wire has a solid metal core and is usually used inside such components as alternators, motors, relays and other devices. Multi-strand wire has a core made of many small strands of wire twisted together into a single conductor. Most of the wiring in an automotive electrical system is made up of multi-strand wire, either as a single conductor or grouped together in a harness. All wiring is color coded on the insulator,

either as a solid color or as a colored wire with an identification stripe. A printed circuit is a thin film of copper or other conductor that is printed on an insulator backing. Occasionally, a printed circuit is sandwiched between two sheets of plastic for more protection and flexibility. A complete printed circuit, consisting of conductors, insulating material and connectors for lamps or other components is called a printed circuit board. Printed circuitry is used in place of individual wires or harnesses in places where space is limited, such as behind instrument panels.

Since automotive electrical systems are very sensitive to changes in resistance, the selection of properly sized wires is critical when systems are repaired. A loose or corroded connection or a replacement wire that is too small for the circuit will add extra resistance and an additional voltage drop to the circuit.

The wire gauge number is an expression of the cross-section area of the conductor. Vehicles from countries that use the metric system will typically describe the wire size as its cross-sectional area in square millimeters. In this method, the larger the wire, the greater the number. Another common system for expressing wire size is the American Wire Gauge (AWG) system. As gauge number increases, area decreases and the wire becomes smaller. An 18 gauge wire is smaller than a 4 gauge wire. A wire with a higher gauge number will carry less current than a wire with a lower gauge number. Gauge wire size refers to the size of the strands of the conductor, not the size of the complete wire with insulator. It is possible, therefore, to have two wires of the same gauge with different diameters because one may have thicker insulation than the other.

It is essential to understand how a circuit works before trying to figure out why it doesn't. An electrical schematic shows the electrical current paths when a circuit is operating properly. Schematics break the entire electrical system down into individual circuits. In a schematic, usually no attempt is made to represent wiring and components as they physically appear on the vehicle; switches and other components are shown as simply as possible. Face views of harness connectors show the cavity or terminal locations in all multi-pin connectors to help locate test points.

CONNECTORS

▶ **See Figures 6 and 7**

Three types of connectors are commonly used in automotive applications—weatherproof, molded and hard shell.

- Weatherproof—these connectors are most commonly used where the connector is exposed to the elements. Terminals are protected against moisture and dirt by sealing rings which provide a weathertight seal. All repairs require the use of a special terminal and the tool required to service it. Unlike standard blade type terminals, these weatherproof terminals cannot be straightened once they are bent. Make certain that the connectors are properly seated and all of the sealing rings are in place when connecting leads.
- Molded—these connectors require complete replacement of the connector if found to be defective. This means splicing a new connector assembly into the harness. All splices should be soldered to insure proper contact. Use care when probing the connections or replacing terminals in them, as it is possible to create a short circuit between opposite terminals. If this happens to the wrong terminal pair, it is possible to damage certain components. Always use jumper wires between connectors for circuit checking and NEVER probe through weatherproof seals.

90946P19

Fig. 5 Close up of the hundreds of bell wire windings found within an average relay

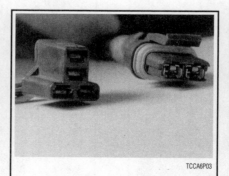

TCCA6P03

Fig. 6 Hard shell (left) and weatherproof (right) connectors have replaceable terminals

TCCA6P04

Fig. 7 Weatherproof connectors are most commonly used in the engine compartment or where the connector is exposed to the elements

• Hard Shell—unlike molded connectors, the terminal contacts in hard-shell connectors can be replaced. Replacement usually involves the use of a special terminal removal tool that depresses the locking tangs (barbs) on the connector terminal and allows the connector to be removed from the rear of the shell. The connector shell should be replaced if it shows any evidence of burning, melting, cracks, or breaks. Replace individual terminals that are burnt, corroded, distorted or loose.

Test Equipment

Pinpointing the exact cause of trouble in an electrical circuit is most times accomplished by the use of special test equipment. The following describes different types of commonly used test equipment and briefly explains how to use them in diagnosis. In addition to the information covered below, the tool manufacturer's instructions booklet (provided with the tester) should be read and clearly understood before attempting any test procedures.

JUMPER WIRES

▶ See Figure 8

✳✳ CAUTION

Never use jumper wires made from a thinner gauge wire than the circuit being tested. If the jumper wire is of too small a gauge, it may overheat and possibly melt. Never use jumpers to bypass high resistance loads in a circuit. Bypassing resistances, in effect, creates a short circuit. This may, in turn, cause damage and fire. Jumper wires should only be used to bypass lengths of wire or to simulate switches.

Jumper wires are simple, yet extremely valuable, pieces of test equipment. They are basically test wires which are used to bypass sections of a circuit. Although jumper wires can be purchased, they are usually fabricated from lengths of standard automotive wire and whatever type of connector (alligator clip, spade connector or pin connector) that is required for the particular application being tested. In cramped, hard-to-reach areas, it is advisable to have insulated boots over the jumper wire terminals in order to prevent accidental grounding. It is also advisable to include a standard automotive fuse in any jumper wire. This is commonly referred to as a "fused jumper". By inserting an in-line fuse holder between a set of test leads, a fused jumper wire can be used for bypassing open circuits. Use a 5 amp fuse to provide protection against voltage spikes.

Jumper wires are used primarily to locate open electrical circuits, on either the ground (-) side of the circuit or on the power (+) side. If an electrical component fails to operate, connect the jumper wire between the component and a good ground. If the component operates only with the jumper installed, the

ground circuit is open. If the ground circuit is good, but the component does not operate, the circuit between the power feed and component may be open. By moving the jumper wire successively back from the component toward the power source, you can isolate the area of the circuit where the open is located. When the component stops functioning, or the power is cut off, the open is in the segment of wire between the jumper and the point previously tested.

You can sometimes connect the jumper wire directly from the battery to the "hot" terminal of the component, but first make sure the component uses 12 volts in operation. Some electrical components, such as fuel injectors or sensors, are designed to operate on about 4 to 5 volts, and running 12 volts directly to these components will cause damage.

TEST LIGHTS

▶ See Figure 9

The test light is used to check circuits and components while electrical current is flowing through them. It is used for voltage and ground tests. To use a 12 volt test light, connect the ground clip to a good ground and probe wherever necessary with the pick. The test light will illuminate when voltage is detected. This does not necessarily mean that 12 volts (or any particular amount of voltage) is present; it only means that some voltage is present. It is advisable before using the test light to touch its ground clip and probe across the battery posts or terminals to make sure the light is operating properly.

✳✳ WARNING

Do not use a test light to probe electronic ignition, spark plug or coil wires. Never use a pick-type test light to probe wiring on computer controlled systems unless specifically instructed to do so. Any wire insulation that is pierced by the test light probe should be taped and sealed with silicone after testing.

Like the jumper wire, the 12 volt test light is used to isolate opens in circuits. But, whereas the jumper wire is used to bypass the open to operate the load, the 12 volt test light is used to locate the presence of voltage in a circuit. If the test light illuminates, there is power up to that point in the circuit; if the test light does not illuminate, there is an open circuit (no power). Move the test light in successive steps back toward the power source until the light in the handle illuminates. The open is between the probe and a point which was previously probed.

The self-powered test light is similar in design to the 12 volt test light, but contains a 1.5 volt penlight battery in the handle. It is most often used in place of a multimeter to check for open or short circuits when power is isolated from the circuit (continuity test).

The battery in a self-powered test light does not provide much current. A weak battery may not provide enough power to illuminate the test light even when a complete circuit is made (especially if there is high resistance in the cir-

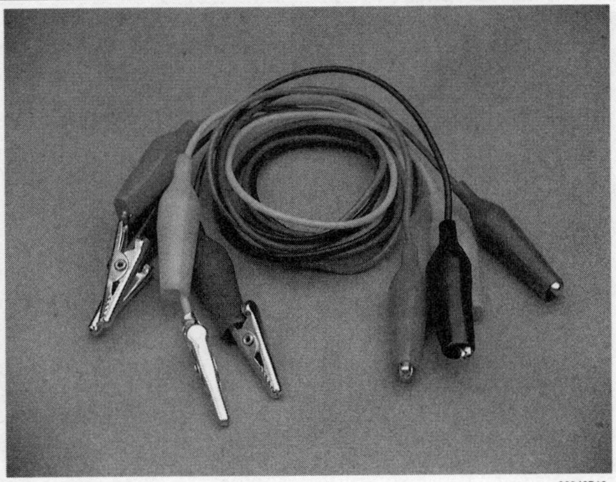

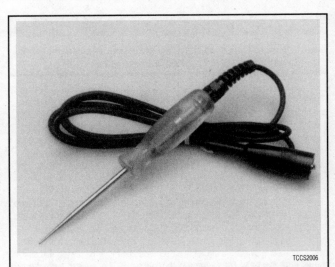

90946P10

Fig. 8 Jumper wires are simple, yet extremely valuable, pieces of test equipment

TCCS2006

Fig. 9 A 12 volt test light is used to detect the presence of voltage in a circuit

cuit). Always make sure that the test battery is strong. To check the battery, briefly touch the ground clip to the probe; if the light glows brightly, the battery is strong enough for testing.

➡**A self-powered test light should not be used on any computer controlled system or component. The small amount of electricity transmitted by the test light is enough to damage many electronic automotive components.**

MULTIMETERS

Multimeters are an extremely useful tool for troubleshooting electrical problems. They can be purchased in either analog or digital form and have a price range to suit any budget. A multimeter is a voltmeter, ammeter and ohmmeter (along with other features) combined into one instrument. It is often used when testing solid state circuits because of its high input impedance (usually 10 megaohms or more). A brief description of the multimeter main test functions follows:

• Voltmeter—the voltmeter is used to measure voltage at any point in a circuit, or to measure the voltage drop across any part of a circuit. Voltmeters usually have various scales and a selector switch to allow the reading of different voltage ranges. The voltmeter has a positive and a negative lead. To avoid damage to the meter, always connect the negative lead to the negative (-) side of the circuit (to ground or nearest the ground side of the circuit) and connect the positive lead to the positive (+) side of the circuit (to the power source or the nearest power source). Note that the negative voltmeter lead will always be black and that the positive voltmeter will always be some color other than black (usually red).

• Ohmmeter—the ohmmeter is designed to read resistance (measured in ohms) in a circuit or component. Most ohmmeters will have a selector switch which permits the measurement of different ranges of resistance (usually the selector switch allows the multiplication of the meter reading by 10, 100, 1,000 and 10,000). Some ohmmeters are "auto-ranging" which means the meter itself will determine which scale to use. Since the meters are powered by an internal battery, the ohmmeter can be used like a self-powered test light. When the ohmmeter is connected, current from the ohmmeter flows through the circuit or component being tested. Since the ohmmeter's internal resistance and voltage are known values, the amount of current flow through the meter depends on the resistance of the circuit or component being tested. The ohmmeter can also be used to perform a continuity test for suspected open circuits. In using the meter for making continuity checks, do not be concerned with the actual resistance readings. Zero resistance, or any ohm reading, indicates continuity in the circuit. Infinite resistance indicates an opening in the circuit. A high resistance reading where there should be none indicates a problem in the circuit. Checks for short circuits are made in the same manner as checks for open circuits, except that the circuit must be isolated from both power and normal ground. Infinite resistance indicates no continuity, while zero resistance indicates a dead short.

✳✳ WARNING

Never use an ohmmeter to check the resistance of a component or wire while there is voltage applied to the circuit.

• Ammeter—an ammeter measures the amount of current flowing through a circuit in units called amperes or amps. At normal operating voltage, most circuits have a characteristic amount of amperes, called "current draw" which can be measured using an ammeter. By referring to a specified current draw rating, then measuring the amperes and comparing the two values, one can determine what is happening within the circuit to aid in diagnosis. An open circuit, for example, will not allow any current to flow, so the ammeter reading will be zero. A damaged component or circuit will have an increased current draw, so the reading will be high. The ammeter is always connected in series with the circuit being tested. All of the current that normally flows through the circuit must also flow through the ammeter; if there is any other path for the current to follow, the ammeter reading will not be accurate. The ammeter itself has very little resistance to current flow and, therefore, will not affect the circuit, but it will measure current draw only when the circuit is closed and electricity is flowing. Excessive current draw can blow fuses and drain the battery, while a reduced current draw can cause motors to run slowly, lights to dim and other components to not operate properly.

Troubleshooting Electrical Systems

When diagnosing a specific problem, organized troubleshooting is a must. The complexity of a modern automotive vehicle demands that you approach any problem in a logical, organized manner. There are certain troubleshooting techniques, however, which are standard.

• Establish when the problem occurs. Does the problem appear only under certain conditions? Were there any noises, odors or other unusual symptoms? Isolate the problem area. To do this, make some simple tests and observations, then eliminate the systems that are working properly. Check for obvious problems, such as broken wires and loose or dirty connections. Always check the obvious before assuming something complicated is the cause.

• Test for problems systematically to determine the cause once the problem area is isolated. Are all the components functioning properly? Is there power going to electrical switches and motors. Performing careful, systematic checks will often turn up most causes on the first inspection, without wasting time checking components that have little or no relationship to the problem.

• Test all repairs after the work is done to make sure that the problem is fixed. Some causes can be traced to more than one component, so a careful verification of repair work is important in order to pick up additional malfunctions that may cause a problem to reappear or a different problem to arise. A blown fuse, for example, is a simple problem that may require more than another fuse to repair. If you don't look for a problem that caused a fuse to blow, a shorted wire (for example) may go undetected.

Experience has shown that most problems tend to be the result of a fairly simple and obvious cause, such as loose or corroded connectors, bad grounds or damaged wire insulation which causes a short. This makes careful visual inspection of components during testing essential to quick and accurate troubleshooting.

Testing

OPEN CIRCUITS

◆ **See Figure 10**

This test already assumes the existence of an open in the circuit and it is used to help locate the open portion.

1. Isolate the circuit from power and ground.
2. Connect the self-powered test light or ohmmeter ground clip to the ground side of the circuit and probe sections of the circuit sequentially.
3. If the light is out or there is infinite resistance, the open is between the probe and the circuit ground.
4. If the light is on or the meter shows continuity, the open is between the probe and the end of the circuit toward the power source.

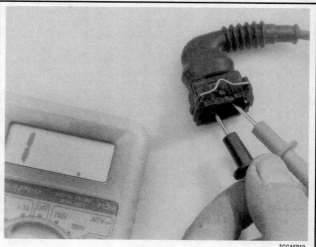

TCCA6P10

Fig. 10 The infinite reading on this multimeter indicates that the circuit is open

SHORT CIRCUITS

➡**Never use a self-powered test light to perform checks for opens or shorts when power is applied to the circuit under test. The test light can be damaged by outside power.**

1. Isolate the circuit from power and ground.

2. Connect the self-powered test light or ohmmeter ground clip to a good ground and probe any easy-to-reach point in the circuit.

3. If the light comes on or there is continuity, there is a short somewhere in the circuit.

4. To isolate the short, probe a test point at either end of the isolated circuit (the light should be on or the meter should indicate continuity).

5. Leave the test light probe engaged and sequentially open connectors or switches, remove parts, etc. until the light goes out or continuity is broken.

6. When the light goes out, the short is between the last two circuit components which were opened.

VOLTAGE

This test determines voltage available from the battery and should be the first step in any electrical troubleshooting procedure after visual inspection. Many electrical problems, especially on computer controlled systems, can be caused by a low state of charge in the battery. Excessive corrosion at the battery cable terminals can cause poor contact that will prevent proper charging and full battery current flow.

1. Set the voltmeter selector switch to the 20V position.

2. Connect the multimeter negative lead to the battery's negative (-) post or terminal and the positive lead to the battery's positive (+) post or terminal.

3. Turn the ignition switch **ON** to provide a load.

4. A well charged battery should register over 12 volts. If the meter reads below 11.5 volts, the battery power may be insufficient to operate the electrical system properly.

VOLTAGE DROP

▶ **See Figure 11**

When current flows through a load, the voltage beyond the load drops. This voltage drop is due to the resistance created by the load and also by small resistances created by corrosion at the connectors and damaged insulation on the wires. The maximum allowable voltage drop under load is critical, especially if there is more than one load in the circuit, since all voltage drops are cumulative.

1. Set the voltmeter selector switch to the 20 volt position.

2. Connect the multimeter negative lead to a good ground.

3. Operate the circuit and check the voltage prior to the first component (load).

4. There should be little or no voltage drop in the circuit prior to the first component. If a voltage drop exists, the wire or connectors in the circuit are suspect.

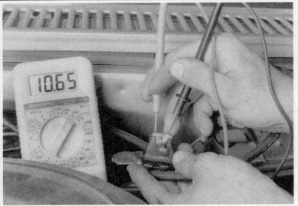

TCCA6P07

Fig. 11 This voltage drop test revealed high resistance (low voltage) in the circuit

5. While operating the first component in the circuit, probe the ground side of the component with the positive meter lead and observe the voltage readings. A small voltage drop should be noticed. This voltage drop is caused by the resistance of the component.

6. Repeat the test for each component (load) down the circuit.

7. If a large voltage drop is noticed, the preceding component, wire or connector is suspect.

RESISTANCE

▶ **See Figures 12 and 13**

✵✵ WARNING

Never use an ohmmeter with power applied to the circuit. The ohmmeter is designed to operate on its own power supply. The normal 12 volt electrical system voltage could damage the meter!

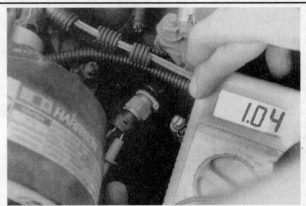

TCCA6P08

Fig. 12 Checking the resistance of a coolant temperature sensor with an ohmmeter. Reading is 1.04 kilohms

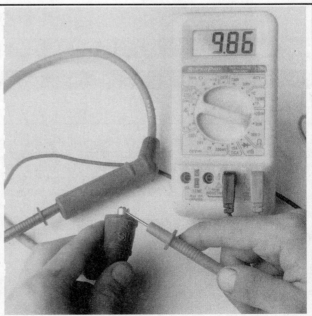

TCCA6P09

Fig. 13 Spark plug wires can be checked for excessive resistance using an ohmmeter

1. Isolate the circuit from the vehicle's power source.
2. Ensure that the ignition key is **OFF** when disconnecting any components or the battery.
3. Where necessary, also isolate at least one side of the circuit to be checked, in order to avoid reading parallel resistances. Parallel circuit resistances will always give a lower reading than the actual resistance of either of the branches.
4. Connect the meter leads to both sides of the circuit (wire or component) and read the actual measured ohms on the meter scale. Make sure the selector switch is set to the proper ohm scale for the circuit being tested, to avoid misreading the ohmmeter test value.

Wire and Connector Repair

Almost anyone can replace damaged wires, as long as the proper tools and parts are available. Wire and terminals are available to fit almost any need. Even the specialized weatherproof, molded and hard shell connectors are now available from aftermarket suppliers.

Be sure the ends of all the wires are fitted with the proper terminal hardware and connectors. Wrapping a wire around a stud is never a permanent solution and will only cause trouble later. Replace wires one at a time to avoid confusion. Always route wires exactly the same as the factory.

➡**If connector repair is necessary, only attempt it if you have the proper tools. Weatherproof and hard shell connectors require special tools to release the pins inside the connector. Attempting to repair these connectors with conventional hand tools will damage them.**

BATTERY CABLES

Disconnecting the Cables

◆ **See Figure 14**

When working on any electrical component on the vehicle, it is always a good idea to disconnect the negative (-) battery cable. This will prevent potential damage to many sensitive electrical components such as the Engine Control Unit (ECU), radio, alternator, etc.

➡**Any time you disengage the battery cables, it is recommended that you disconnect the negative (-) battery cable first. This will prevent your accidentally grounding the positive (+) terminal to the body of the vehicle when disconnecting it, thereby preventing damage to the above mentioned components.**

Before you disconnect the cable(s), first turn the ignition to the **OFF** position. This will prevent a draw on the battery which could cause arcing (electricity trying to ground itself to the body of a vehicle, just like a spark plug jumping the gap) and, of course, damaging some components such as the alternator diodes.

When the battery cable(s) are reconnected (negative cable last), be sure to check that your lights, windshield wipers and other electrically operated safety components are all working correctly. If your vehicle contains an Electronically Tuned Radio (ETR), don't forget to also reset your radio stations. Ditto for the clock.

91221P79

Fig. 14 Always remove the negative battery cable first

AIR BAG (SUPPLEMENTAL RESTRAINT SYSTEM)

General Information

SERVICE PRECAUTIONS

The Air Bag system or Supplemental Restraint System (SRS) is designed to provide additional protection for front seat occupants when used in conjunction with a seat belt. The system is an electronically controlled, mechanically operated system. The system contains two basic subsytems: the air bag module(s) (the actual air bag(s) themselves), and the electrical system. The system consists of:

- The crash sensors
- The safing sensor
- The air bag module(s)
- The diagnostic monitor
- The instrument cluster indicator
- The sliding contacts (clock spring assembly)

The system is operates as follows: The system remains out of sight until activated in an accident that is determined to be the equivalent of hitting a parked car of the same size and weight with the vehicle receiving severe front end damage. This determination is made by crash and safing sensors mounted on the vehicle which when an sufficient impact occurs, close their contacts completing the electrical circuit and inflating the air bags. When not activated the system is monitored by the air bag diagnostic monitor and system readiness is indicated by the lamp located on the instrument cluster. Any fault detected by the diagnostic monitor will illuminate the lamp and store a Diagnostic Trouble Code (DTC).

Whenever working around, or on, the air bag supplemental restraint system, ALWAYS adhere to the following warnings and cautions.

- Always wear safety glasses when servicing an air bag vehicle and when handling an air bag module.
- Carry a live air bag module with the bag and trim cover facing away from your body, so that an accidental deployment of the air bag will have a small chance of personal injury.
- Place an air bag module on a table or other flat surface with the bag and trim cover pointing up.
- Wear gloves, a dust mask and safety glasses whenever handling a deployed air bag module. The air bag surface may contain traces of sodium hydroxide, a by-product of the gas that inflates the air bag and which can cause skin irritation.
- Ensure to wash your hands with mild soap and water after handling a deployed air bag.
- All air bag modules with discolored or damaged cover trim must be replaced, not repainted.
- All component replacement and wiring service must be made with the negative and positive battery cables disconnected from the battery for a minimum of one minute prior to attempting service or replacement.
- NEVER probe the air bag electrical terminals. Doing so could result in air bag deployment, which can cause serious physical injury.

- If the vehicle is involved in a fender-bender which results in a damaged front bumper or grille, have the air bag sensors inspected by a qualified automotive technician to ensure that they were not damaged.
- If at any time, the air bag light indicates that the computer has noted a problem, have your vehicle's SRS serviced immediately by a qualified automotive technician. A faulty SRS can cause severe physical injury or death.

DISARMING THE SYSTEM

❊❊ CAUTION

The air bag system must be disarmed before performing service around air bag components or wiring. Failure to do so may cause accidental deployment of the air bag, resulting in unnecessary repairs and/or personal injury.

The back-up power supply for the air bag is in the control unit. It will drain down by itself after the battery is disconnected but this takes about 20 minutes. Do not use a computer memory saver device. It will keep the back-up power supply charged. If it is necessary to remove the steering wheel, disconnect the negative battery cable and wait at least 20 minutes for the power supply to discharge. To remove the air bag unit, remove the Torx® screws on either side of the back of the steering wheel. The screws must be replaced when removed. Tilt the unit down and disconnect the wire. Place the air bag unit face up where it will not be disturbed and do not place anything on top of it.

1. Position the vehicle with the front wheels in a straight ahead position.
2. Disconnect the negative battery cable.
3. Disconnect the positive battery cable.
4. Wait at least twenty (20) minutes for the air bag back-up power supply to drain before continuing.
5. Proceed with the repair.

ARMING THE SYSTEM

1. Connect the positive battery cable.
2. Stand outside the vehicle and carefully turn the ignition to the **RUN** position. Be sure that no part of your body is in front of the air bag module on the steering wheel, to prevent injury in case of an accidental air bag deployment.
3. Connect the negative battery cable.

❊❊ CAUTION

Ensure that no one is inside the vehicle upon installation of the negative battery cable.

4. Ensure the air bag indicator light turns off after approximately 6 seconds. If the light does not illuminate at all, does not turn off, or starts to flash, have the system tested by a qualified automotive technician. If the light does turn off after 6 seconds and does not flash, the SRS is working properly.

System Service

❊❊ CAUTION

Some vehicles are equipped with an air bag system. The system must be disabled before performing service on or around air bag system components, steering column, instrument panel components, wiring and sensors. Failure to follow safety and disabling procedures could result in accidental air bag deployment, possible personal injury and unnecessary SRS system repairs.

Air Bag Module(s)

The air bag module(s) are located in the steering wheel and the passenger side of the instrument panel, if equipped with a passenger side air bag. The modules are molded to fit into their designated areas, the driver's side is located in the center of the steering wheel. The passenger side module is molded to fit into the instrument panel and is located above the glove box, it is generally unnoticeable until deflated.

The module contain four parts: an inflator, a bag, a container, and the cover. The purpose of the inflator is to generate the gas needed to fill the air bag, it consists of a high strength steel casing containing a propellant that is activated by an igniter. The igniter is fired by the electrical signal received when the safing sensor closes. When the igniter is fired, the propellant discharge is ignited and fills the bag. As the bag fills, invisible "split seams" in the cover tear open allowing the bag to inflate and cushion the forward motion of the occupant and protect against serious injury.

Crash Sensors

The crash sensors are located in the front of the vehicle on either side of the front radiator support. In the event of a head-on impact (or at least a ¾ frontal impact, the sensing mass inside the sensor breaks away from the bias magnet. The sensor mass rolls along a cylinder toward two electrical contacts, if the deceleration is sufficient, the sensing mass will bridge the contacts and complete the primary deployment circuit to the air bag module.

The mounting and orientation of the sensors is vital to system operation. The sensors should be inspected by a qualified individual after any impact where the sensors could have been damaged. If any structural damage is evident, the area must be repaired to its original condition, otherwise the sensor orientation could be compromised. If the sensor(s) have received damage, they must be replaced.

Safing Sensor

The safing sensor is located behind the kick panel on the passenger side, below the instrument panel. The safing sensor operates identical to the crash sensor, except for the calibration. This is accomplished using a slightly weaker bias magnet. If the safing sensor contacts close simultaneously with the crash sensor, the air bag(s) will be deployed.

The safing sensor is essentially a safety for the air bag system. It protects the bag(s) from deploying due to an electrical short. The safing sensor is used to verify the force of a collision and complete the air bag(s) deployment. The sensor is located inside the passenger compartment so that a forceful enough impact could be detected, and a false signal from the crash sensor would not deploy the air bag(s) at an inappropriate time.

Air Bag Indicator

The air bag indicator is located on the instrument cluster and illuminates when activated by the diagnostic monitor. The indicator illuminates when the key is placed in the ignition and turned to **RUN**, this is the bulb prove-out. The indicator will stay illuminated after the vehicle is started while the diagnostic monitor checks the system for faults, if no faults are detected, the indicator will go out after about 6 seconds. If the indicator does not go out after 6 seconds, a fault has been detected in the system, a DTC will be flashed using the indicator.

Sliding Contact

The clock spring assembly is located in the steering column, behind the steering wheel. The function of the clock spring assembly is to keep the electrical connection intact while the steering wheel is rotated while the driver is turning the wheel to steer the vehicle.

HEATING AND AIR CONDITIONING

Blower Motor

REMOVAL & INSTALLATION

Cabriolet

The blower motor and series resistor are reached from under the hood, just in front of the windshield.

1. Disconnect the negative battery cable.
2. Remove the clips and gasket holding the water deflector in place and remove the deflector.
3. To remove the plastic cover that is now visible. Some vehicles have fasteners which are accessed from both under the hood and under the dash. If after removing all screws, bolts or clips visible from above, the cover still won't lift off, check under the dash for more screws.
4. On vehicles with air conditioning, disconnect the linkage for the air distribution flaps. Remove the remaining plastic cover.
5. The blower and series resistor are now accessible. Remove the screws and the motor.
6. Installation is the reverse of removal. Be sure the seal around the motor is properly reinstalled.

Fox

1. Disconnect the negative battery cable.
2. Remove the front cover sealing gasket.
3. Remove the water deflector.
4. Loosen the fresh air housing cover retaining clips, then remove the front fresh air housing cover.
5. If equipped with air conditioning, undo the lock and disconnect the air distribution flap levers.
6. Remove the rear fresh air housing cover.
7. If equipped with air conditioning, label and disconnect the vacuum servo motor hoses and hoses from the grommets in the lower portion of the fresh air housing covers.
8. Remove the thermal resistor and thermal circuit breaker from the support.
9. Loosen the blower motor mounting screw and disconnect the blower wiring connectors.
10. Remove the lower fresh air covers.
11. Maneuver the fan and motor towards the front of the car, then remove it from the fresh air (blower) housing.

To install:

12. Install the fan and motor assembly into the fresh air (blower) housing.
13. Install the lower fresh air covers.
14. Connect the blower wiring and install the blower motor mounting screw.
15. Attach the thermal circuit breaker and thermal resistor to the support.
16. Connect the hoses to the lower fresh air housing covers and connect the vacuum servo motor hoses.
17. Install the rear fresh air housing cover.
18. If equipped with air conditioning, connect the air distribution flap levers and engage the lock.
19. Install the front fresh air housing cover and lock the retaining clips.
20. Install the water deflector.
21. Connect the negative battery cable and check the blower operation at all speeds.

1990–93 Golf and Jetta

The blower motor is located behind the glove box and it may be easier to remove the glove box to gain access to the motor. The series resistor is mounted on the motor.

1. Disconnect the wires at the blower motor.
2. At the blower motor flange near the cowl, disengage the retaining lug; pull down on the lug.
3. Turn the motor assembly clockwise to release it from it's mount, then remove it from the plenum.

4. The resistor can be checked by connecting an ohmmeter to terminal A and terminals 1 and 2. At terminal 1, resistance should be about 3.3 ohms. At terminal 2, resistance should be about 0.8 ohms.
5. Installation is the reverse of removal.

1994–99 Golf, Jetta and Cabrio

1. Remove the negative battery cable.
2. Detach the connector from the wiring leading to the blower motor.
3. Remove the five attaching screws from the blower motor.
4. To remove the blower motor, pull it downward.
5. Installation is the reverse of removal.

Heater Core

REMOVAL & INSTALLATION

Cabriolet

It is necessary to remove the instrument panel and to discharge the air conditioning system. Have a MVAC certified tech recover the A/C system refrigerant.

1. Disconnect the battery cable.
2. Remove the steering wheel. Tilt the shelf downward, remove the screws and remove the shelf.
3. From the driver's side, remove the instrument panel cover-to-instrument panel screws, pry out the clips and pull the cover downward.
4. Remove the shift knob and pull the boot out of the console.
5. From the driver's side, remove the instrument panel cover-to-instrument panel screws, pry out the clips and pull the cover downward.
6. From the passenger's side, remove the shelf-to-instrument panel screws and the shelf. Pry out the lower instrument panel cover-to-instrument panel clips and pull the cover from the guides.
7. At the console, remove the screws and pull the lower part of the console rearward.
8. From the heater/fresh air control, remove the knobs and trim.
9. From the upper part of the console, remove the screws and pull the upper part of the console out slightly. Detach the electrical connectors from the console and remove the upper console pan.
10. At the upper part of the instrument cluster, remove the instrument cluster trim screws and the trim. Remove the instrument cluster (center) screw and tip the cluster forward. Pull off the vacuum hose and multi-point connector from the instrument cluster. Disconnect the speedometer cable from the instrument cluster.
11. From the instrument panel, push the switch forward (out of the panel), pull the air ducts from the side vents.
12. Detach the electrical connectors from the ashtray housing and the wiring harness from the instrument panel.
13. Open the glove box and remove the screws from the center, left and right sides.
14. Pull out the heater/fresh air control, pry off the E-clip and disconnect the flap cable. Remove the control.
15. Remove the instrument panel-to-chassis screws and clips. Remove the instrument panel from the vehicle.
16. Drain the cooling system.
17. Disconnect the hoses from the heater core.
18. Discharge the air conditioning system into freon recovery equipment.
19. Detach the vacuum connectors from the fresh air box.
20. Disconnect the cables as required from the evaporator housing. Remove the retaining bolts, the heater core hoses, the evaporator inlet and outlet hoses and cap or plug the openings immediately.
21. Remove the heater assembly from the vehicle. Remove the screw and lift the heater core out of the housing.
22. Install the heater core into the housing and fit the housing into the vehicle. Connect the heater hoses and the air conditioner lines.
23. Position the instrument panel into the vehicle and install the screws and clips.

24. Install the heater/fresh air control, connect the flap control and the E-clip.
25. Install the glove box and secure with the screws.
26. Connect the wiring harness to the instrument panel.
27. Connect the speedometer cable, vacuum hose and multi-point connector to the instrument cluster. Install the instrument cluster and trim.
28. Install the upper console pan and connect the electrical connectors.
29. Install the heater controls, knobs and trim.
30. At the passenger's side, install the instrument panel cover and the shelf.
31. At the driver's side, install the instrument panel cover.
32. Install the shelf and tilt it upward. Install the steering wheel.
33. Have a MVAC certified tech evacuate and recharge the A/C system.

Fox

1. Disconnect the negative battery cable.
2. Drain the engine coolant.
3. Disconnect the heater inlet hoses at the firewall.
4. Inside the vehicle, remove the center console side panels. Disconnect the temperature control cables at the heater case.
5. Remove the left and right air distribution ducts.
6. In the engine compartment, remove the cowl cover and remove the air distribution housing cover.
7. Inside the vehicle, remove the lower housing retaining clips and remove the housing.

➡On vehicles equipped with A/C the heater box also contains the A/C system evaporator mounted in the lower housing cover. When removing the lower cover on these models lay the cover and evaporated aside WITHOUT disconnecting the refrigerant lines.

8. Remove the bolts retaining the heater case and remove the case.
9. Remove the clips holding the case together and split the case, the heater core can now be removed.
To install:
10. Insert the heater core into the case, then reassemble it.
11. Install the case into the vehicle. Attach the lower heater case cover to the heater case. Install the air distribution ducts and the control cables.
12. Install the center console side panels. Reconnect the heater inlet hoses. Install the air distribution housing cover and the cowl.
13. Fill the cooling system to the proper level.

1990–92 Golf and Jetta

It is necessary to remove the instrument panel and to discharge the air conditioning system. Have a MVAC certified tech recover the A/C system refrigerant.
1. Disconnect the negative battery cable.
2. Drain the cooling system and disconnect the heater hoses from the firewall.
3. Properly discharge the air conditioning system using freon recovery equipment.
4. Remove the gear shift knob and boot and remove the center console.
5. Remove the steering wheel.
6. Remove the knee bar from below the dashboard.
7. Remove the steering column support bracket and lower the column.
8. Pull the knobs off the heater controls and remove the control assembly and the radio.
9. Remove the headlight switch and switch blanks to gain access to the screws. Remove the instrument cluster and trim panel around the cluster.
10. Remove the glove compartment.
11. At the firewall, remove the plastic tray and remove the 2 nuts holding the top of the dashboard.
12. Remove the main fuse panel and disconnect the plugs at the back. Disconnect the ground wires.
13. Disconnect any remaining wiring from the dashboard and remove the 4 last screws; 1 at each end and 1 at each end of the instrument cluster area. Remove the dashboard.
14. Disconnect the ducts and remove the heater housing. Remove the screws and slide the heater core out of the housing.
To install:
15. Install the heater core and make sure the housing seals and gaskets are in good condition. Replace as necessary.
16. With the heater housing properly installed, install the dashboard and connect the wiring. Install the steering column bracket bolts.

17. Install the fuse panel and connect the wiring.
18. Install the glove compartment, shift boot and knob and steering wheel.
19. Have a MVAC certified tech evacuate and recharge the A/C system.

1993–99 Golf, Jetta, and Cabrio

➡**The recovery of the air conditioning system refrigerant must be performed before the heater core can be removed. Have a MVAC certified tech recover the A/C system refrigerant.**

1. Drain the engine coolant.
2. Remove the instrument panel.
3. Detach the support bracket.
4. From the engine compartment, label and remove all hoses and necessary wiring.
5. Remove and plug all A/C lines.
6. Remove the heater box which contains the evaporator.
7. Unclip the heater core box.
8. Remove the heater core.
9. Installation is the reverse of removal. Always make sure all seals are installed properly during the installation process.
10. Seal all seams of the heater box with RTV.
11. Have a MVAC certified tech evacuate and recharge the A/C system.

Air Conditioning Components

▸ **See Figure 15**

Repair or service of air conditioning components is not covered by this manual, because of the risk of personal injury or death, and because of the legal ramifications of servicing these components without the proper EPA certification and experience. Cost, personal injury or death, environmental damage, and legal considerations (such as the fact that it is a federal crime to vent refrigerant into the atmosphere), dictate that the A/C components on your vehicle should be serviced only by a Motor Vehicle Air Conditioning (MVAC) trained, and EPA certified automotive technician.

➡**If your vehicle's A/C system uses R-12 refrigerant and is in need of recharging, the A/C system can be converted over to R-134a refrigerant (less environmentally harmful and expensive). Refer to Section 1 for additional information on R-12 to R-134a conversions, and for additional considerations dealing with your vehicle's A/C system.**

Control Cables

REMOVAL & INSTALLATION

1. Disconnect the negative battery cable.
2. Remove the bezel in order to gain access to the control head.

Fig. 15 Location of the air conditioning compressor–1994 2.0L, 8 valve

91222P27

3. Remove the screws that fasten the control head to the instrument panel. Remove the control panel and disconnect the blower switch wiring.

4. Pry the cable clips free and disconnect the cables from the control levers to remove the control head.

5. Release the clips to disconnect the cables from the heater. Take note of the cable routing.

To install:

6. Fit the cables into place but don't install the retaining clips yet.

7. Connect the self-adjusting clip to the door crank and secure the cable.

8. Connect the upper end of the cable to the control head.

9. Place the temperature lever on the coolest side of its travel. Allowing the self-adjusting clip to slide on the cable, rotate the door counterclockwise by hand until it stops.

10. Cycle the lever back and forth a few times to make sure the cable moves freely.

ADJUSTMENT

1. Move the temperature control lever to the full cold position.

2. With the control cable attached to the air mix door link, pull the cable housing out and push the inner cable in the opposite direction.

Fig. 16 Removing the control panel face plate

Fig. 17 Location of the control panel retaining screws

3. Secure the cable in this position with the retaining clamp.

4. Operate the temperature control lever and check freedom of movement at full stroke range.

Control Panel

REMOVAL & INSTALLATION

▶ **See Figures 16 and 17**

1. Pull the control knobs out to remove them.

2. Carefully pry out the control panel off the dashboard.

3. Remove the screws and pull the control head out far enough to disconnect the vacuum lines and control cable.

4. Installation is the reverse of removal.

CRUISE CONTROL

Control Switch

REMOVAL & INSTALLATION

1990–92 Cabriolet, Fox, Golf, and Jetta

1. Disconnect the negative battery cable.

2. Remove the horn pad.

➡ **On Cabriolet, disarm the air bag system and remove the air bag unit.**

3. Mark the position of the steering wheel to the shaft and remove the wheel.

4. Remove the combination switch retaining screws. Carefully remove the switch from the steering column.

5. Remove the screws retaining the cruise control switch to combination switch and remove the cruise control switch.

To install:

6. Assemble the cruise control switch to the combination switch.

7. Install the combination switch and connect the wiring.

8. Align the marks made for the steering wheel-to-column position and install the steering wheel. Tighten the nut to 30 ft. lbs. (40 Nm).

9. Install the horn pad. On Cabriolet, install the air bag unit and make sure no one is in the vehicle when connecting the battery.

1993–99 Cabrio, Golf and Jetta

1. Disconnect the negative battery cable.

2. Position the steering wheel straight ahead.

3. If equipped with an airbag, see the proper removal procedure earlier in this chapter.

4. Remove the steering wheel trim screws.

5. Detach the switch assembly from the steering column by removing the fasteners.

6. Pull the assembly off the steering column and detach the connectors from the backs of the switches.

7. Remove the switch assembly

8. Installation is the reverse of removal.

Speed Sensor

REMOVAL & INSTALLATION

1. Disconnect the negative battery cable.

2. Remove the instrument cluster assembly.

3. From behind the cluster, detach the harness connector at the speedometer.

4. Unscrew the sensor from the instrument cluster and remove it.

To install:

5. Position the sensor in place and screw it in securely.

6. Connect the wiring to the sensor and instruments and install the instrument cluster.

7. Connect the negative battery cable. Road test the vehicle and check the cruise control operation.

Control Unit

REMOVAL & INSTALLATION

1. Disconnect the negative battery cable.

2. On models with the 16V engine, the control unit is in the center console. On all other models, the control unit is under the right side of the dashboard.

3. Detach the electrical connector from the control unit.

4. Remove the bracket retaining screw and remove the control unit.

To install:

5. Plug in the electrical connector to the control unit.

6. Secure the control unit in place with the retaining screw.

7. Connect the negative battery cable. Road test the vehicle and check the cruise control operation.

ENTERTAINMENT SYSTEMS

Radio Receiver/Amplifier/Tape Player/CD Player

REMOVAL & INSTALLATION

1990–92 Models

1. On vehicles with a theft protected radio, obtain the security code.

2. Insert two removal pins into the sides of the face plate.

3. Push the tools away from each other to release the spring clips and pull the radio out far enough to unplug the wiring in the back.

To install:

4. Connect the wiring and push the radio part way into the slot.

5. Enter the security code before pushing it in all the way.

1993–97 Models

▶ See Figures 18 thru 23

1. Remove the negative battery cable.

2. Insert the radio removal clip tools into the radio head unit. A VW radio removal tool is available at your local dealer or local auto parts supplier.

3. Pull the radio removal clips outward and pull the unit from the dash.

4. Detach all connectors.

5. Remove the radio antenna.

6. Remove the radio from the dashboard.

Vacuum Servo

REMOVAL & INSTALLATION

1. Remove the air cleaner were applicable.

2. Disconnect the rod and the vacuum line from the servo.

3. Remove the nuts and remove the actuator from the engine.

4. Installation is the reverse of removal.

Connecting Rod

ADJUSTMENT

1. Disconnect the connecting rod from the throttle lever ball socket.

2. Make sure the throttle is fully closed against the stop screw.

3. Adjust the length of the rod to fit exactly between the servo and the throttle, then turn the ball socket out one more turn to lengthen the rod.

4. Make sure the idle speed is correct and check the throttle for smooth movement.

98–99 Models

1. Disconnect the negative battery cable.

2. Insert the radio removal tool into the slots on the sides of the radio.

3. Push the removal tools all the way in until they click and lock in.

4. Now pull the radio out of the dashboard.

5. Remove all wiring from the rear of the radio. Do not forget to remove the radio antenna lead.

6. Remove the tools from the slots in the sides of the radio.

7. Installation is the reverse of removal.

ENTERING SECURITY CODE

Most vehicles are equipped with Heidelberg V or VI radios that are equipped with a theft protection program. When the battery has been is disconnected or if the radio has been removed, the radio will lock-up electronically and cannot be operated until the security code is entered. On the Heidelberg V, if the proper code is not entered in six attempts, the radio will lock-up permanently and cannot be repaired. On the Heidelberg VI, two incorrect attempts will lock the radio for about 1 hour.

The Heidelberg V may have a code assigned at the factory or a personal code created by the owner. The Hiedelberg VI has a code assigned at the factory and entered by the dealer during pre-delivery inspection. New radios come with the code printed on a sticker but not entered into memory. All codes are 4 digits. To code the radio:

91226P67

Fig. 18 The removal of most VW radios require a special tool. Two strong paper clips may work if the tool is unavailable

91226P71

Fig. 19 Observe how the tool disengages the spring clip

91226P72

Fig. 20 Once the radio has been disengaged from the dash, pull the unit out

Fig. 21 To remove the radio antenna simply twist slightly while pulling

Fig. 22 The tab on the back of the unit slides into the . . .

Fig. 23 . . . slotted radio brace at the rear of the dash

Heidelberg V

1. Turn the radio **ON**. The radio should display the word SAF. DO NOT attempt to eject a cassette with the radio in this mode.

2. Push the AM/FM and SCAN buttons at the same time and hold them until the display changes, then release them immediately. The number 1000 will appear for about 3 seconds, then the display will go blank. Release the buttons then.

➡️**If the buttons are held too long, the radio will interpret this as an attempt to enter an incorrect code.**

3. Use the first four station selector buttons to enter the code. The first digit of the code is always 1. Each time the other buttons are pushed, the number in that position will change.

4. When the code appears correctly in the display, push the AM/FM and SCAN buttons at the same time. When the radio plays and displays a frequency, release the buttons.

Fig. 24 Use a wooden paint scraper under a suitable pry tool to prevent any scratches along the trim of the dashboard

5. If the code was entered incorrectly three times, momentarily disconnect the battery and try again. If the code is entered incorrectly three more times, the radio cannot be coded and cannot be repaired.

Heidelberg VI

1. Turn the radio **ON**. The radio should display the word SAF. DO NOT attempt to eject a cassette with the radio in this mode.

2. Push the AM/FM and SCAN buttons at the same time and hold them until the display changes, then release them immediately. The number 1000 will appear and remain in the display.

➡️**If the buttons are held too long, the radio will interpret this as an attempt to enter an incorrect code.**

3. Use the first four station selector buttons to enter the code. Each time a button is pushed, the number in that position will change.

4. When the code appears correctly in the display, push the AM/FM and SCAN buttons at the same time. When SAF appears in the display, release the buttons. The radio should play and display a frequency.

5. If the code was entered incorrectly two times, leave the radio **ON** for one hour and try again. This can be repeated as often as required.

Speakers

REMOVAL & INSTALLATION

Dash mounted

▶ **See Figures 24, 25, 26 and 27**

Dash mounted speakers can be accessed after removing the appropriate trim panel. These panels are usually retained by screws and clips. Be sure you have removed all of the attaching screws before prying the panel from the dash. Do not use excessive force on the panel as this will only lead to damage.

Fig. 25 Depress the speakers' connectors using a small pry tool that has a blunt edge

Fig. 26 Pull the speaker from the dash

Fig. 27 Detach the wiring from the speaker

Once the panel has been removed, loosen the speaker attaching bolts/screws, then pull the speaker from the dash and unplug the electrical connection.

Door and panel mounted

▶ **See Figures 28 thru 34**

1. Disconnect the negative battery cable.
2. Remove any necessary paneling to gain access to the speaker.
3. Remove the protective mesh grill if applicable.
4. Unfasten the speaker mounting screws.
5. Pull the speaker partially up, then detach the electrical connector.
6. Remove the speaker from the vehicle.

To install:

7. Install in the reverse order of removal.

Rear Speakers

Removing the rear speakers involves basically the same procedure as the front speakers. Remove the appropriate trim panel, then remove the speaker. The rear speakers on some models can be accessed from inside the trunk.

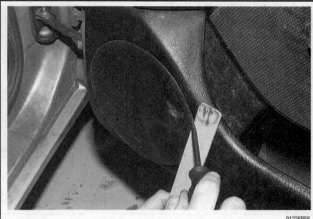

Fig. 28 Use a wooden scraper to protect the integrity of the door panel when prying the speaker cover out

Fig. 29 Remove the speaker cover from the door's kick panel

Fig. 30 Using a Phillips screw driver, remove the screws from the door speaker

Fig. 31 Note the length of each door speaker screw and its location

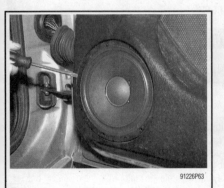

Fig. 32 If the speaker is stuck in the door, carefully pry it out

Fig. 33 Pull the speaker from the door by the edges only. Do not touch the poly-coated paper cone with your fingers. Doing so can cause speaker driver damage

Fig. 34 Remove the wiring harness. Do not disturb the voice coils below the harness

WINDSHIELD WIPERS AND WASHERS

Wiper Arm

REMOVAL & INSTALLATION

▶ **See Figures 35, 36, 37, 38 and 39**

1. Flip the cap up and pull it up to remove it.
2. Remove the nut to remove the arm.

3. When installing the arm, measure the distance between the center of the wiper blade and the base of the windshield: Golf and Jetta—2.375 in. (60mm) from the base of the windshield, Cabriolet—1.375 in. (35mm) on the driver's side and 2.5 in. (65mm) on the passenger side.
4. Tighten the nut to 5 ft. lbs. (7 Nm). Do not over tighten this nut or the linkage will bind.
5. Install the cap.

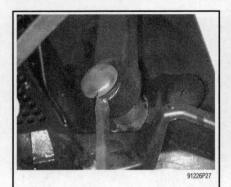

Fig. 35 Remove the cap from the wiper arm

Fig. 36 Remove the nut from the wiper arm

Fig. 37 Matchmark the wiper arm's position to the stud

Fig. 38 A battery cable puller can be used to remove the arm from the splines

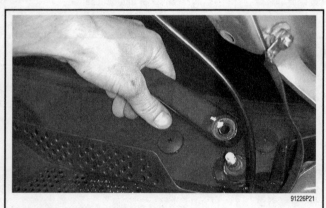

Fig. 39 Lift the arm from the splines

Rear Wiper Arm

REMOVAL & INSTALLATION

1. Flip the cap up and pull it up to remove it.
2. Remove the nut to remove the arm.
3. When installing the arm, the end of the wiper blade should be 0.375 in. (10mm) from the base of the window.
4. Tighten the nut to 5 ft. lbs. (7 Nm). Do not over tighten this nut or the linkage will bind.
5. Install the cap.

Windshield Wiper Motor

REMOVAL & INSTALLATION

▶ See Figures 40 thru 48

When removing the wiper motor, leave the mounting frame in place. If possible, do not remove the wiper drive crank from the motor shaft.

1. Disconnect the negative battery cable and remove the water shield at the base of the windshield.
2. Disconnect the relay rods from the wiper motor.
3. Note the position of the crank arm on the shaft. When the motor is in the parked position, the arm should be about 4 degrees up from horizontal.
4. Disconnect the wiring and remove the bolts to remove the motor from the frame.

To install:

5. Temporarily connect the wiring and run the motor. When the wiper switch is turned **OFF**, the motor will stop in the parked position.
6. Install the motor and connect the linkage.
7. Run the motor again and make sure the arms and blades are properly positioned when the motor stops.

Rear Window Wiper Motor

REMOVAL & INSTALLATION

Golf and GTI

1. Remove the inside trim panel from the hatch.
2. Disconnect the relay rod from the drive crank on the motor.
3. Remove the 3 bolts securing the motor bracket to the body and move the assembly so the wiring can be disconnected.
4. Remove the assembly and separate the motor from the mounting bracket.
5. Installation is the reverse of removal. Before connecting the relay rod, run the motor for about 1 minute and turn the switch **OFF**. When the motor stops at the park position, install the relay rod and make sure the wiper arm is in the correct position.

Wiper Linkage

REMOVAL & INSTALLATION

▶ See Figures 47 and 48

1. Remove the wiper arms and the motor.
2. Remove the relay rods.
3. Remove the nut that secures the wiper shaft to the body and push it out of the frame.
4. Installation is the reverse of removal.

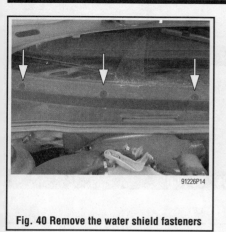

Fig. 40 Remove the water shield fasteners

Fig. 41 Using a suitable pry tool, lift up the base of the clip while turning the head

Fig. 42 View of water shield retaining clip

Fig. 43 Removal of the water shield weather stripping

Fig. 44 Pull away the water shield

Fig. 45 Remove any dirt and debris from under the water shield at this time

Fig. 46 Detach the wiper motor wiring harness

Fig. 47 Removing the wiper motor and linkage assembly

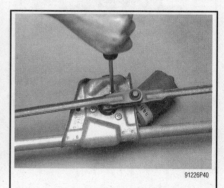

Fig. 48 Remove the screws from the wiper motor assembly

Windshield Washer Pump and Fluid Reservoir

REMOVAL & INSTALLATION

The reservoir is held in place with a single nut that can be reached with a long extension and socket. It may be easier to remove the nut and lift the reservoir out to disconnect the pump wiring and hose. The pump is held in place with a grommet and can be easily pulled out.

Rear Window Washer Pump and Fluid Reservoir

REMOVAL & INSTALLATION

The reservoir is behind the trim panel in the right side of the luggage compartment. Remove the 2 screws and pull the reservoir out to disconnect the wiring and hose. The pump is held to the reservoir with a grommet.

INSTRUMENTS AND SWITCHES

Instrument Cluster

REMOVAL & INSTALLATION

▶ **See Figures 49, 50, 51, 52 and 53**

1. Disconnect the negative battery cable. This job is easier with the steering wheel removed.

2. To disconnect the speedometer cable, reach behind the panel from below and squeeze the tabs of the plastic cable clip. Pull the cable out. On 1993–99 Golf and Jetta models you will have to pull the instrument cluster out of the dash to access the wiring harnesses.

3. Remove the radio and the heater control knobs.

4. The switches are held in place with spring clips or barbs. Carefully pry the switches out of the dashboard and disconnect the wiring.

5. Remove the screws to remove the instrument trim panel.

6. Remove the screws and lay the instrument cluster down on the steering column. Disconnect the wiring and remove the cluster.

To install:

7. Connect the wiring and fit the lower edge of the instrument cluster into place.

8. Lift the cluster into place and install the screws.

9. Install the trim panel and all the switches.

10. Before installing the radio, connect the battery and make sure all switches and instruments work properly.

11. Install the radio and heater controls. Enter the radio security code.

Gauges

REMOVAL & INSTALLATION

▶ **See Figure 54**

The gauges cannot be removed from the instrument cluster. Only the cluster housing can be removed.

Windshield Wiper Switch

REMOVAL & INSTALLATION

Golf and Jetta

1. Disarm the air bag system and remove the steering wheel as described in the beginning of this Section.

2. Remove the horn pad from the steering wheel.

3. Make sure the front wheels are straight ahead and remove the nut and the steering wheel.

4. Remove the steering column covers and disconnect the wiring to the switches.

5. Remove the screws to remove the turn signal switch and the windshield wiper switch.

6. Installation is the reverse of removal. Tighten the steering wheel nut to 30 ft. lbs. (40 Nm).

Fig. 49 Remove the instrument cluster trim panel

Fig. 50 Remove the fasteners at each side of the instrument cluster

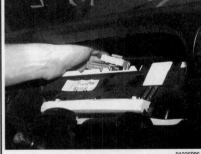

Fig. 51 Reach behind the instrument cluster and remove the wiring harness

Fig. 52 Turn and then remove the unit

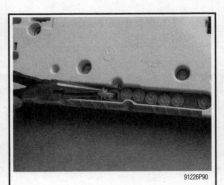

Fig. 53 Instrument cluster bulb removal

Fig. 54 View of the instrument cluster with the housing removed

Fox

1. Disarm the air bag system and remove the steering wheel as described in the beginning of this Section.
2. Disconnect the negative battery cable.
3. Pull off the steering wheel cover/horn pad.
4. Remove the steering wheel lock nut and spacer.
5. Using a steering wheel puller, remove the steering wheel.
6. Remove the retaining screws, then remove the combination turn signal/headlight switch.
7. Remove the windshield wiper/washer switch from the steering column.

To install:

8. Install the windshield wiper/washer switch onto the steering column.
9. Install the combination turn signal/headlight switch.
10. Install the steering wheel, lock nut and spacer. Tighten the nut to 30 ft. lbs. (40 Nm).
11. Install the steering wheel cover.
12. Connect the battery cable.

Cabriolet

1. Disarm the air bag system and remove the steering wheel as described in the beginning of this Section.
2. The air bag connects to the spiral spring behind the steering wheel. Note how the wheel fits into the spring assembly.
3. Remove the 3 Phillips head screws to remove the spiral spring.
4. Remove the steering column covers and disconnect the wiring to the switches.
5. Remove the screws to remove the turn signal switch and the windshield wiper switch.

LIGHTING

Headlights

REMOVAL & INSTALLATION

Cabriolet

1. Disconnect the negative battery cable.
2. Remove the grille. If equipped with dual headlights, loosen the grille for access, then disengage the driving lamp harness and remove the grille completely.
3. Remove the 2 retaining screws which secure the outer grille trim, then remove the trim piece.
4. Unplug the connector from the back of the headlight.
5. Remove the 3 retainer ring screws and remove the light.
6. Installation is the reverse of the removal procedure.

To install:

6. Install the wiper and turn signal switches and connect the wiring. Install the column covers.
7. Install the spiral spring. If the spring was turned while removed, it must be returned to its center position. Turn the spring all the way in one direction, then turn it back 4 full turns.
8. Install the spiral spring.
9. Install the steering wheel, making sure it fits into the spiral spring. Tighten the nut to 30 ft. lbs. (40 Nm).
10. If the battery was connected while the air bag unit was removed, disconnect the battery and wait at least 20 minutes for the back-up power supply to discharge before installing the air bag unit.
11. With the battery disconnected, install the air bag unit with new Torx® screws and tighten them to 7 ft. lbs. (10 Nm).
12. Make sure no one is in the vehicle when connecting the battery. Turn the ignition switch **ON** and make sure the warning light on the instrument panel stays **ON** for 5–8 seconds, then turns **OFF**.

Headlight Switch

REMOVAL & INSTALLATION

1. Disconnect the negative battery cable.
2. The headlight switch is held in place with spring clips or plastic barbs. The switch can be removed by carefully prying it out of the instrument panel. On Golf and Jetta, pry the top and bottom of the switch. On Cabriolet, pry the left and right sides.
3. Disconnect the wiring and remove the switch.
4. Installation is the reverse of removal.

Golf and Jetta

▶ **See Figures 55 thru 60**

1. Pull the connector off the bulb at the back of the headlight.
2. Push down on the clip to disengage it.
3. Pull the headlight bulb out of the housing. If it is difficult to remove, gently rock it up and down.
4. Be careful not to touch the glass part of the bulb. Any oil or dirt even from clean hands will cause a hot spot on the glass during operation and the bulb will break.
5. To ease installation, spray some silicone lubricant on your finger and rub it onto the rubber O-ring. Do not spray directly on the O-ring because it will also get on the bulb.
6. Install the bulb, snap the clip into place and connect the wiring.

Fig. 55 Using a suitable pry tool lift the locking tabs up

Fig. 56 Pull the wiring harness from the light

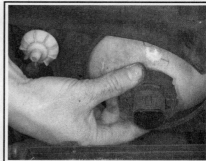

Fig. 57 You must twist the locking collar to remove it from the bulb

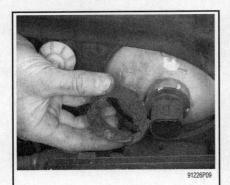

Fig. 58 Locking collar removed from the bulb

Fig. 59 Pull the bulb from the lens assembly

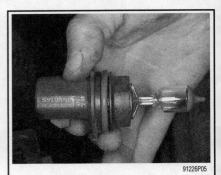

Fig. 60 Do not touch the glass part of the bulb. Oil from you skin will cause premature bulb failure

Fox

1. Disconnect the negative battery cable.
2. Remove the two clips from the top of the headlight frame using a small prytool.
3. Remove the headlight frame.
4. Remove the four screws at each corner of the headlight.
5. Gently pull the headlamp from the support and unplug the connector from the back of the sealed beam.
6. Install in the reverse order.

AIMING THE HEADLIGHTS

▶ **See Figures 61, 62 and 63**

The headlights must be properly aimed to provide the best, safest road illumination. The lights should be checked for proper aim and adjusted as necessary. Certain state and local authorities have requirements for headlight aiming; these should be checked before adjustment is made.

✳✳ CAUTION

About once a year, when the headlights are replaced or any time front end work is performed on your vehicle, the headlight should be accurately aimed by a reputable repair shop using the proper equipment. Headlights not properly aimed can make it virtually impossible to see and may blind other drivers on the road, possibly causing an accident. Note that the following procedure is a temporary fix, until you can take your vehicle to a repair shop for a proper adjustment.

Headlight adjustment may be temporarily made using a wall, as described below, or on the rear of another vehicle. When adjusted, the lights should not glare in oncoming car or truck windshields, nor should they illuminate the passenger compartment of vehicles driving in front of you. These adjustments are rough and should always be fine-tuned by a repair shop which is equipped with headlight aiming tools. Improper adjustments may be both dangerous and illegal.

For most of the vehicles covered by this manual, horizontal and vertical aiming of each sealed beam unit is provided by two adjusting screws which move the retaining ring and adjusting plate against the tension of a coil spring. There is no adjustment for focus; this is done during headlight manufacturing.

➡**Because the composite headlight assembly is bolted into position, no adjustment should be necessary or possible. Some applications, however, may be bolted to an adjuster plate or may be retained by adjusting screws. If so, follow this procedure when adjusting the lights, BUT always have the adjustment checked by a reputable shop.**

Before removing the headlight bulb or disturbing the headlamp in any way, note the current settings in order to ease headlight adjustment upon reassembly. If the high or low beam setting of the old lamp still works, this can be done using the wall of a garage or a building:

1. Park the vehicle on a level surface, with the fuel tank about ½ full and with the vehicle empty of all extra cargo (unless normally carried). The vehicle should be facing a wall which is no less than 6 feet (1.8m) high and 12 feet (3.7m) wide. The front of the vehicle should be about 25 feet from the wall.
2. If aiming is to be performed outdoors, it is advisable to wait until dusk in order to properly see the headlight beams on the wall. If done in a garage, darken the area around the wall as much as possible by closing shades or hanging cloth over the windows.
3. Turn the headlights **ON** and mark the wall at the center of each light's low beam, then switch on the brights and mark the center of each light's high beam. A short length of masking tape which is visible from the front of the vehicle may be used. Although marking all four positions is advisable, marking one position from each light should be sufficient.
4. If neither beam on one side is working, and if another like-sized vehicle is available, park the second one in the exact spot where the vehicle was and

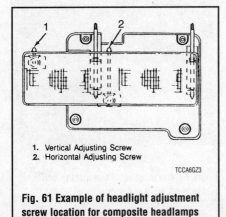

1. Vertical Adjusting Screw
2. Horizontal Adjusting Screw

Fig. 61 Example of headlight adjustment screw location for composite headlamps

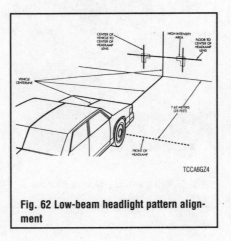

Fig. 62 Low-beam headlight pattern alignment

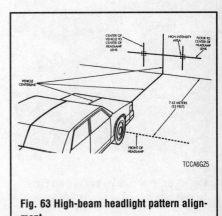

Fig. 63 High-beam headlight pattern alignment

mark the beams using the same-side light. Then switch the vehicles so the one to be aimed is back in the original spot. It must be parked no closer to or farther away from the wall than the second vehicle.

5. Perform any necessary repairs, but make sure the vehicle is not moved, or is returned to the exact spot from which the lights were marked. Turn the headlights **ON** and adjust the beams to match the marks on the wall.

6. Have the headlight adjustment checked as soon as possible by a reputable repair shop.

Signal and Marker Lights

REMOVAL & INSTALLATION

1990–92 Golf, Jetta and Cabriolet

FRONT

On the front turn signal and side marker lights, the bulb can be removed after removing the lens. Inspect the condition of the lens seal and replace if required before installing the new bulb. Front turn signals bulbs are No.1034, side marker lights are bulb No.194.

REAR

The rear light bulbs can be reached from inside the luggage compartment. On Jetta and Cabriolet, the entire light bulb panel can be removed by squeezing the clips. On Golf and GTI, squeeze the spring clips and turn to remove the socket.

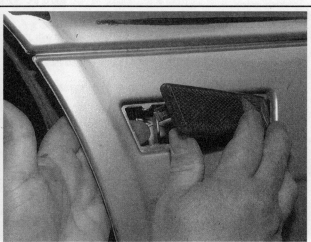

Fig. 64 Removing the side marker lens

Fox

FRONT AND REAR

To remove the front marker lights, open the hood, then pull the rubber cap covering the bulb holder. Squeeze the lug on the bulb holder (if equipped), then remove it from the lens assembly. Press the bulb into the holder slightly, then turn it left and take it out.

For the turn signal bulbs, remove the screws securing the lens, then pull it out of the bumper. Push the bulb in slightly, then turn it and take it out.

1993–99 Cabrio, Golf and Jetta

FRONT TURN SIGNAL AND PARKING LIGHTS

▶ See Figures 64, 65, 66 and 67

1. Disconnect the turn signal bulb socket from the rear of the lens by rotating the socket ¼ of a turn, then pulling the socket rearward until the bulb clears the housing. Lift the socket/harness for access.
2. Remove the bulb from the socket/harness.
3. Installation is the reverse of removal.

SIDE MARKER LIGHT

▶ See Figure 64

1. Disconnect the negative battery cable.
2. Remove the retaining screws, then carefully pull the lamp out of the front fascia.
3. Twist the lamp socket ¼ turn counterclockwise, then withdraw it from the lens.
4. Remove the bulb.
5. Installation is the reverse of removal.

REAR TURN SIGNAL, BRAKE AND PARKING LIGHTS

1. Disconnect the negative battery cable.
2. Remove the trim panel fasteners, then carefully remove the trim panel.
3. Remove the 2 retaining screws from the side of the lamp assembly, then pull the lamp assembly straight back and out of the opening.
4. Tilt the assembly downward for access to the sockets, then twist and remove the socket(s) from the lamp assembly. Replace the bulb(s), as necessary.
5. Installation is the reverse of removal.

HIGH-MOUNT BRAKE LIGHT

1. Disconnect the negative battery cable.

➡ **You may have to open the trunk/hatch for access to the lamps.**

2. Locate the bulbs at the rear underside of the trunk lid. Remove the bulb(s) by twisting, then pulling straight out.
3. Installation is the reverse of removal.

DOME LIGHT

1. Disconnect the negative battery cable.
2. Remove the bulb from its retaining clip contacts. If the bulb has tapered ends, gently depress the spring clip/metal contact and disengage the light bulb, then pull it free of the two metal contacts.

Fig. 65 Using a plastic pry tool, remove the reflector assembly

Fig. 66 Always use caution around lens assemblies. Age and weather have caused these plastics to become very brittle

Fig. 67 Typical location of VW front marker bulb and lens

To install:

3. Before installing the light bulb into the metal contacts, ensure that all electrical conducting surfaces are free of corrosion or dirt.

4. Insert the bulb into the holder. If the contacts have small holes, be sure that the tapered ends of the bulb are situated in them.

5. To ensure that the replacement bulb functions properly, activate the applicable switch to illuminate the bulb which was just replaced. If the replacement light bulb does not illuminate, either it is faulty or there is a problem in the bulb circuit or switch. Correct as necessary.

6. Install the cover until its retaining tabs are properly engaged.

7. Connect the negative battery cable.

CARGO OR PASSENGER AREA LAMPS

1. Disconnect the negative battery cable.
2. Remove the bulb from its electrical connector.
3. Installation is the reverse of removal.

LICENSE PLATE LIGHTS

1. Disconnect the negative battery cable.
2. Remove the license plate light lens.
3. Remove the bulb from its electrical connector.
4. Installation is the reverse of removal.

Fog/Driving Lights

REMOVAL & INSTALLATION

1. Disconnect the negative battery cable.
2. Remove the lens from the housing.
3. Unplug the wiring connectors from the lamp.
4. Remove the retainer clip, then remove the bulb from the housing.
5. Installation is the reverse of removal.

INSTALLING AFTERMARKET AUXILIARY LIGHTS

➡ **Before installing any aftermarket light, make sure it is legal for road use. Most acceptable lights will have a DOT approval number. Also check your local and regional inspection regulations. In certain areas, aftermarket lights must be installed in a particular manner or they may not be legal for inspection.**

1. Disconnect the negative battery cable.

2. Unpack the contents of the light kit purchased. Place the contents in an open space where you can easily retrieve a piece if needed.

3. Choose a location for the lights. If you are installing fog lights, below the bumper and apart from each other is desirable. Most fog lights are mounted below or very close to the headlights. If you are installing driving lights, above the bumper and close together is desirable. Most driving lights are mounted between the headlights.

4. Drill the needed hole(s) to mount the light. Install the light, and secure using the supplied retainer nut and washer. Tighten the light mounting hardware, but not the light adjustment nut or bolt.

5. Install the relay that came with the light kit in the engine compartment, in a rigid area, such as a fender. Always install the relay with the terminals facing down. This will prevent water from entering the relay assembly.

6. Using the wire supplied, locate the ground terminal on the relay, and connect a length of wire from this terminal to a good ground source. You can drill a hole and screw this wire to an inside piece of metal; just scrape the paint away from the hole to ensure a good connection.

7. Locate the light terminal on the relay; and attach a length of wire between this terminal and the fog/driving lamps.

8. Locate the ignition terminal on the relay, and connect a length of wire between this terminal and the light switch.

9. Find a suitable mounting location for the light switch and install. Some examples of mounting areas are a location close to the main light switch, auxiliary light position in the dash panel, if equipped, or in the center of the dash panel.

10. Depending on local and regional regulations, the other end of the switch can be connected to a constant power source such as the battery, an ignition opening in the fuse panel, or a parking or headlight wire.

11. Locate the power terminal on the relay, and connect a wire with an in-line fuse of at least 10 amperes between the terminal and the battery.

12. With all the wires connected and tied up neatly, connect the negative battery cable.

13. Turn the lights ON and adjust the light pattern, if necessary.

LIGHT BULB SPECIFICATIONS

Bulb	Industry Number
Turn Signal - Front	7528
Turn Signal - Rear	7506
Side Marker - Front	2821
Side Marker - Rear	2821
Tail Lamp	7506, 7528, 1157
Headlamp	9003 Cabrio, 9004 all except Cabrio
Fog	H3-55W
High Mount Stop	2825
Cornering	7506
Back-up	7506
License Plate	2825
Map	6411
Dome	6411
Step / Coutesy	6418
Trunk	6418

91226C01

AIMING

1. Park the vehicle on level ground, so it is perpendicular to and, facing a flat wall about 25 ft. (7.6m) away.
2. Remove any stone shields, if equipped, and switch ON the lights.
3. Loosen the mounting hardware of the lights so you can aim them as follows:

a. The horizontal distance between the light beams on the wall should be the same as between the lights themselves.

b. The vertical height of the light beams above the ground should be 4 in. (10cm) less than the distance between the ground and the center of the lamp lenses for fog lights. For driving lights, the vertical height should be even with the distance between the ground and the center of the lamp.

4. Tighten the mounting hardware.
5. Test to make sure the lights work correctly, and the light pattern is even.

TRAILER WIRING

Wiring the vehicle for towing is fairly easy. There are a number of good wiring kits available and these should be used, rather than trying to design your own.

All trailers will need brake lights and turn signals as well as tail lights and side marker lights. Most areas require extra marker lights for overwide trailers. Also, most areas have recently required back-up lights for trailers, and most trailer manufacturers have been building trailers with back-up lights for several years.

Some trailers may have electric brakes. Add to this number an accessories wire, to operate trailer internal equipment or to charge the trailer's battery, and you can have as many as seven wires in the harness.

Determine the equipment on your trailer and buy the wiring kit necessary. The kit will contain all the wires needed, plus a plug adapter set which includes the female plug, mounted on the bumper or hitch, and the male plug, wired into, or plugged into the trailer harness.

When installing the kit, follow the manufacturer's instructions. The color coding of the wires is usually standard throughout the industry. One point to note: some domestic vehicles, and most imported vehicles, have separate turn signals. On most domestic vehicles, the brake lights and rear turn signals operate with the same bulb. For those vehicles without separate turn signals, you can purchase an isolation unit so that the brake lights won't blink whenever the turn signals are operated.

One, final point, the best kits are those with a spring loaded cover on the vehicle mounted socket. This cover prevents dirt and moisture from corroding the terminals. Never let the vehicle socket hang loosely; always mount it securely to the bumper or hitch.

CIRCUIT PROTECTION

Fuses

REPLACEMENT

▶ See Figure 68

Fuses are located either in the engine compartment or passenger compartment fuse and relay panels. If a fuse blows, a single component or single circuit will not function properly.

1. Remove the fuse or relay box cover.
2. Inspect the fuses to determine which is faulty.
3. Unplug and discard the fuse.
4. Inspect the box terminals and clean if corroded. If any terminals are damaged, replace the terminals.
5. Plug in a new fuse of the same amperage rating.

✳✳ WARNING

Never exceed the amperage rating of a blown fuse. If the replacement fuse also blows, check for a problem in the circuit.

6. Check for proper operation of the affected component or circuit.

Fig. 68 Typical VW fuse box

91226PA2

Maxi-Fuses (Fusible Links)

Maxi-fuses are located in the engine compartment relay box. If a maxi-fuse blows, an entire circuit or several circuits will not function properly.

REPLACEMENT

1. Remove the fuse and relay box cover.
2. Inspect the fusible links to determine which is faulty.
3. Unplug and discard the fusible link.
4. Inspect the box terminals and clean if corroded. If any terminals are damaged, replace the terminals.
5. Plug in a new fusible link of the same amperage rating.

✳✳ WARNING

Never exceed the amperage rating of a blown maxi-fuse. If the replacement fuse also blows, check for a problem in the circuit(s).

6. Check for proper operation of the affected circuit(s).

Circuit Breakers

RESETTING AND/OR REPLACEMENT

Circuit breakers are located inside the fuse panel. They are automatically reset when the problem corrects itself, is repaired, or the circuit cools down to allow operation again.

Fusible Link

The fuse link is a short length of wire, integral with the engine compartment wiring harness and should not be confused with standard wire. The fusible link wire gauge is smaller than the circuit which it protects. Under no circumstances should a fuse link replacement repair be made using a length of standard wire cut from bulk stock or from another wiring harness.

Fusible link wire is covered with a special thick, non-flammable insulation. An overload condition causes the insulation to blister. If the overall condition continues, the wire will melt. To check a fusible link, look for blistering insulation. If the insulation is okay, pull gently on the wire. If the fusible link stretches, the wire has melted.

Fusible links are often identified by the color coding of the insulation. Refer to the accompanying illustration for wire link size and color.

Flashers

REPLACEMENT

Turn Signal Flasher

1. Disconnect the negative battery cable.
2. Remove the upper and lower steering column shrouds.
3. Pull the flasher from the back of the multi-function switch.
To install:
4. Install a new flasher in the multi-function switch.

5. Install the column shrouds.
6. Connect the negative battery cable.

Hazard Warning Flasher

1. Disconnect the negative battery cable.
2. Remove the knee bolster panel from the underside of the driver's side of the instrument panel.
3. Grasp and pull the flasher from the connector located near the top of the steering column.
To install:
4. Install a new flasher in the connector.
5. Install the knee bolster panel.
6. Connect the negative battery cable.

FUSE SPECIFICATIONS

Circuit	Amperage Rating
Low beam-left	10
Low beam-right	10
Instruments and liscense plate	10
Rear window wiper / washer	15
ABS	15
Windshield wiper / washer	20
Fresh air fan	30
Right-tail and side marker	10
Left-tail and side marker	10
Rear window defroster / heated mirrors	20
Fog lights	15
High beam - left	10
High beam - right	10
Horn	10
Back-up lights	15
Engine electronics	10
Warning/indicator lights	10
Power roof	10
Turn signals	10
Fuel pump	20
Radiator fan/Air conditioning	30
Brake lights	10
Dome and luggage compartment lights	15
Clock	15
Radio	10
ABS hydraulic pump relay	30
ABS main relay	30
A/C	30
Power windows	20
Cruise control	5
Cigarette lighter	15
Glow Plugs	50

FUSE COLOR CODES

Light brown	5 ampere
Red	10 ampere
Blue	15 ampere
Yellow	20 ampere
Green	30 ampere

91226C02

WIRING DIAGRAMS

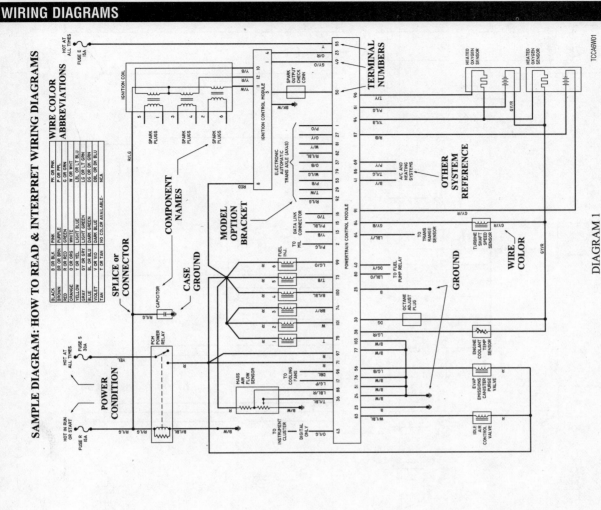

SAMPLE DIAGRAM: HOW TO READ & INTERPRET WIRING DIAGRAMS

DIAGRAM 1

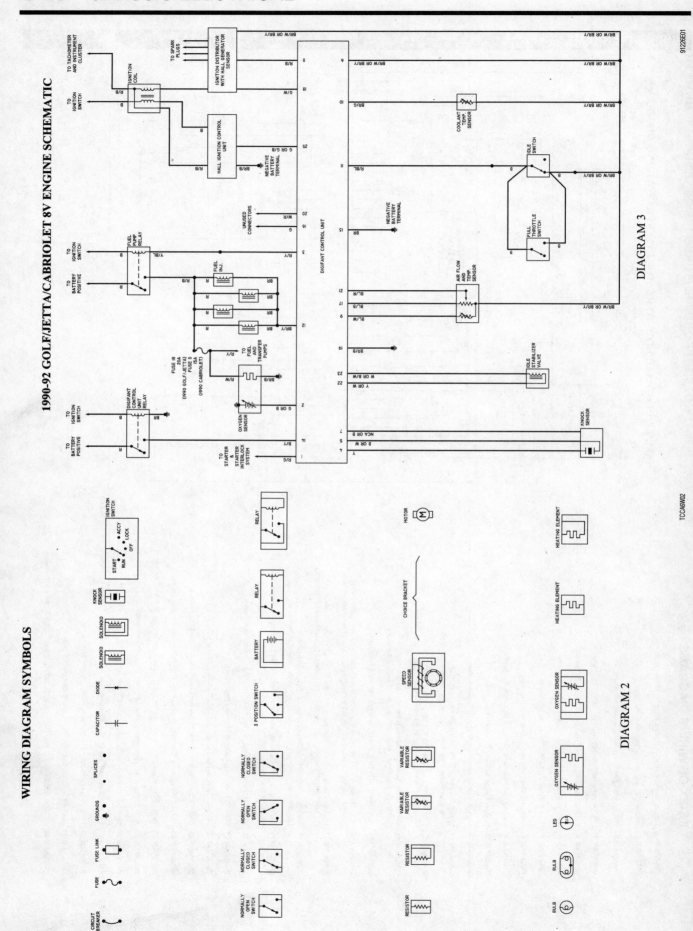

WIRING DIAGRAM SYMBOLS

1990-92 GOLF/JETTA/CABRIOLET 8V ENGINE SCHEMATIC

DIAGRAM 2

DIAGRAM 3

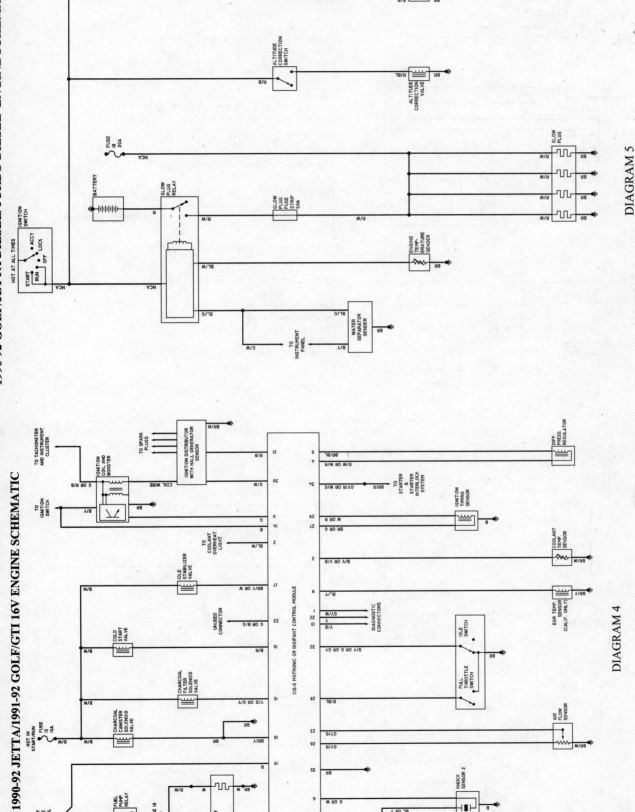

1990-92 GOLF/JETTA DIESEL/TURBO DIESEL ENGINE SCHEMATIC

DIAGRAM 5

1990-92 JETTA/1991-92 GOLF/GTI 16V ENGINE SCHEMATIC

DIAGRAM 4

1993-94 GOLF III/JETTA III 2.0L ENGINE SCHEMATIC

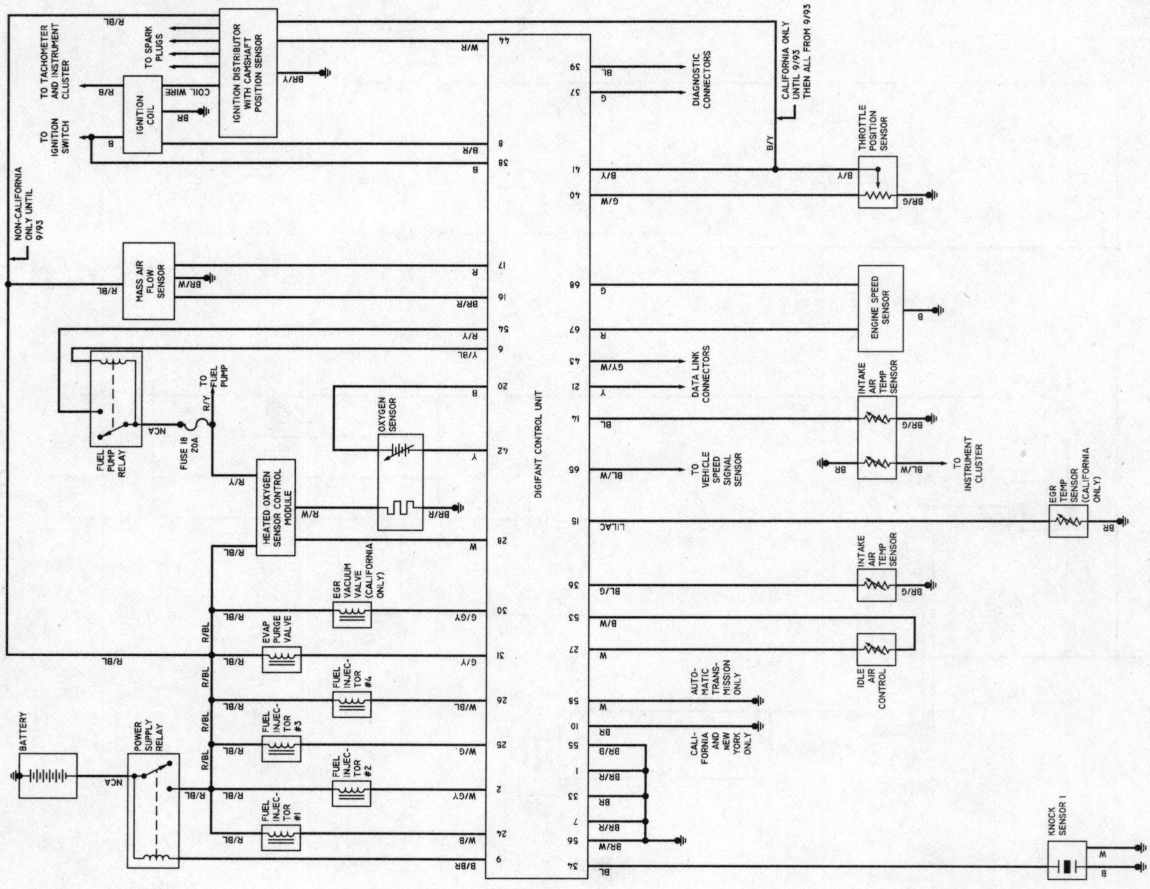

DIAGRAM 7

1991-92 GOLF GL/GTI 8V (CALIFORNIA) ENGINE SCHEMATIC

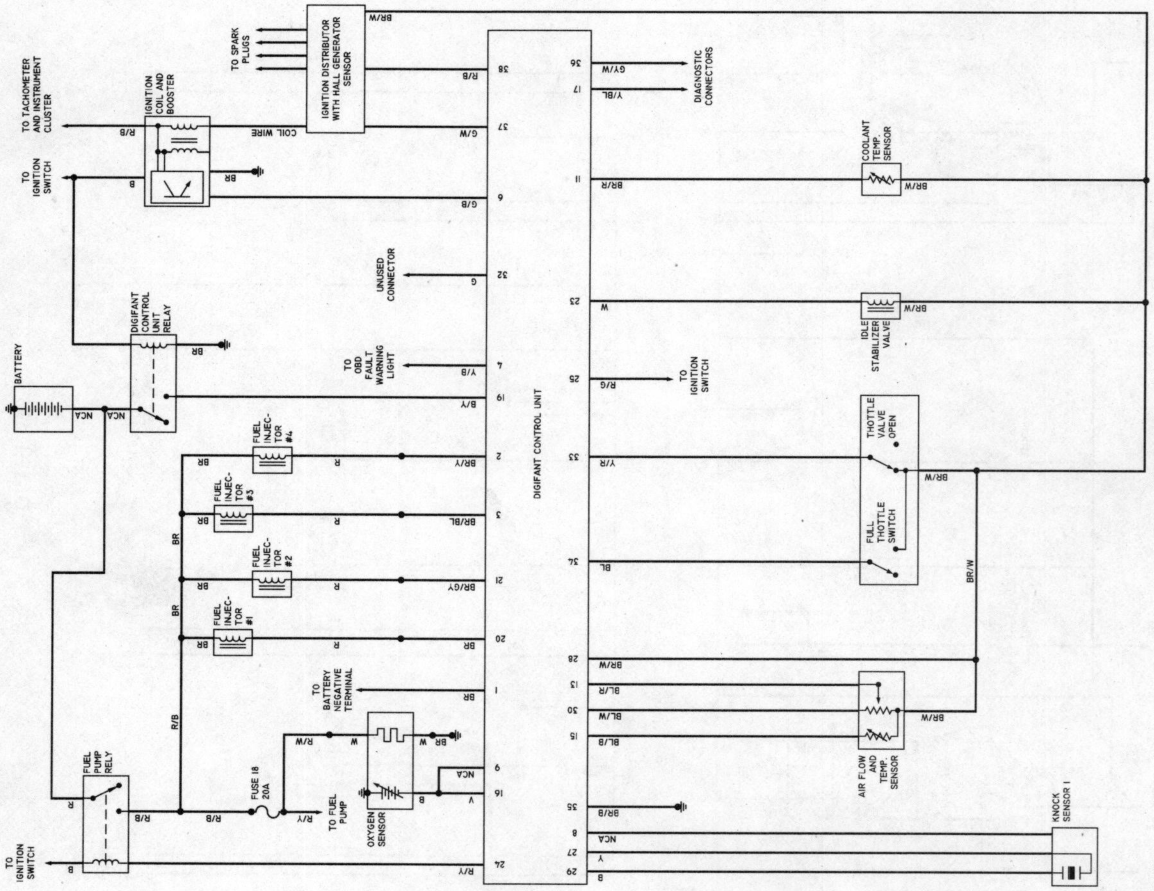

DIAGRAM 6

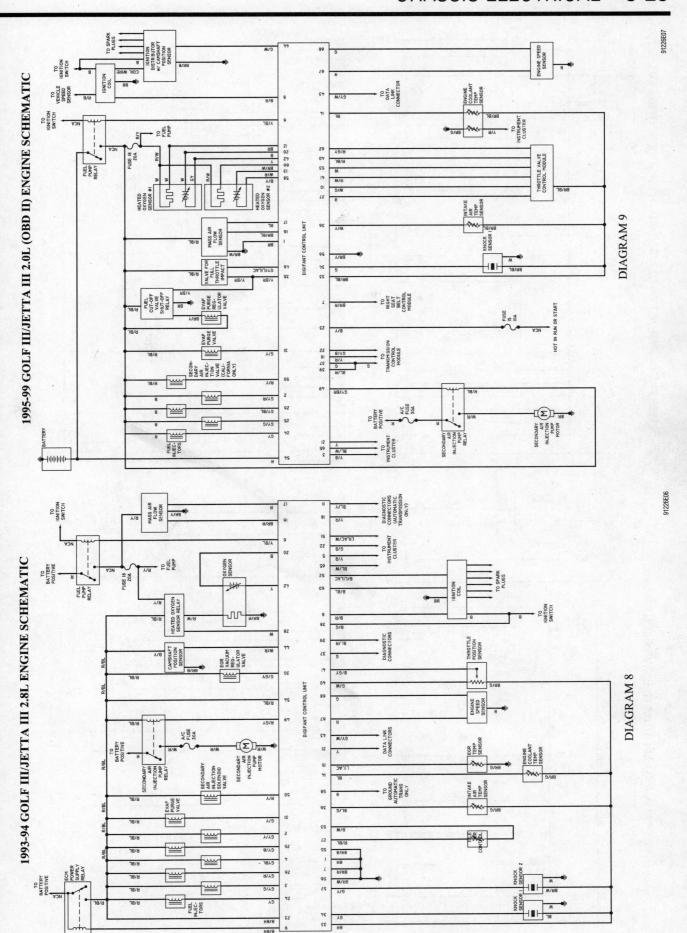

1995-99 GOLF III/JETTA III 2.0L (OBD II) ENGINE SCHEMATIC

DIAGRAM 9

1993-94 GOLF III/JETTA III 2.8L ENGINE SCHEMATIC

DIAGRAM 8

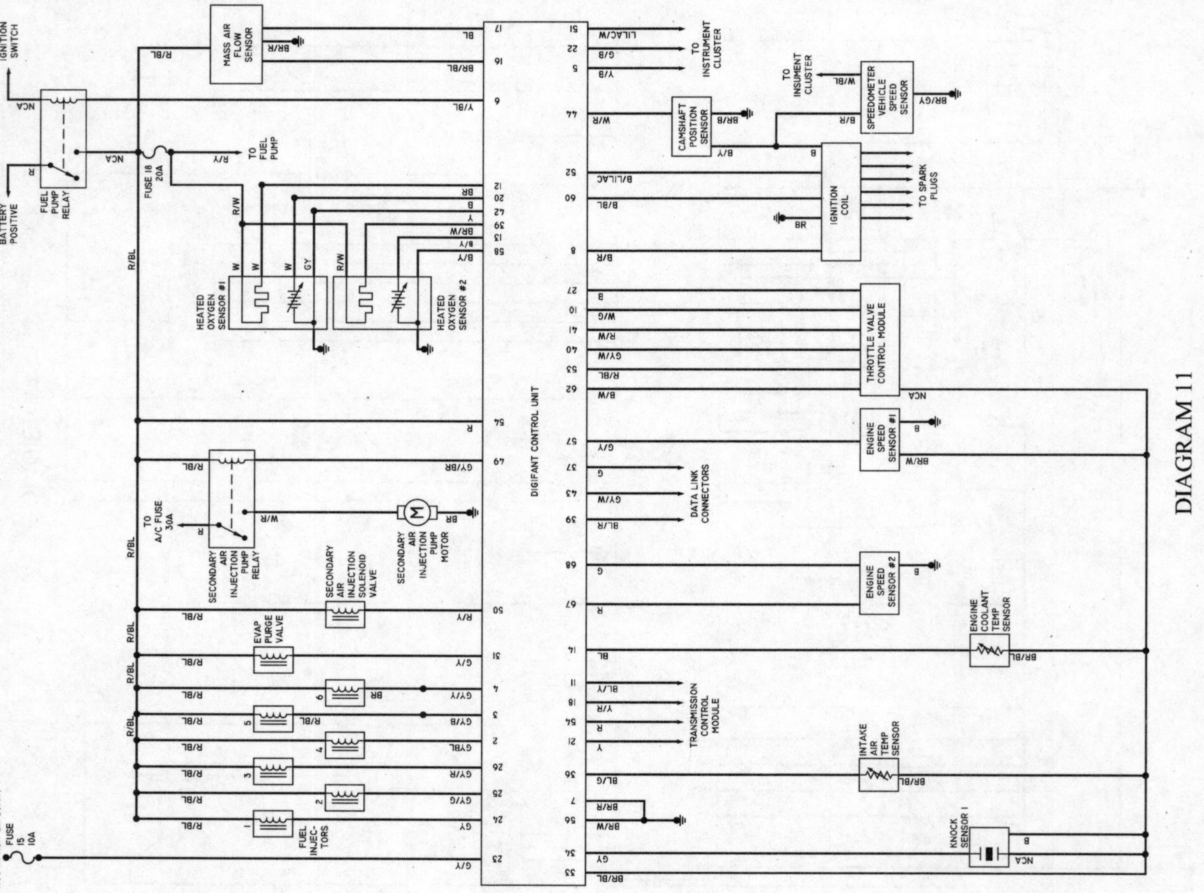

1995-99 GOLF III/JETTA III 2.8L (OBD II) ENGINE SCHEMATIC

DIAGRAM 11

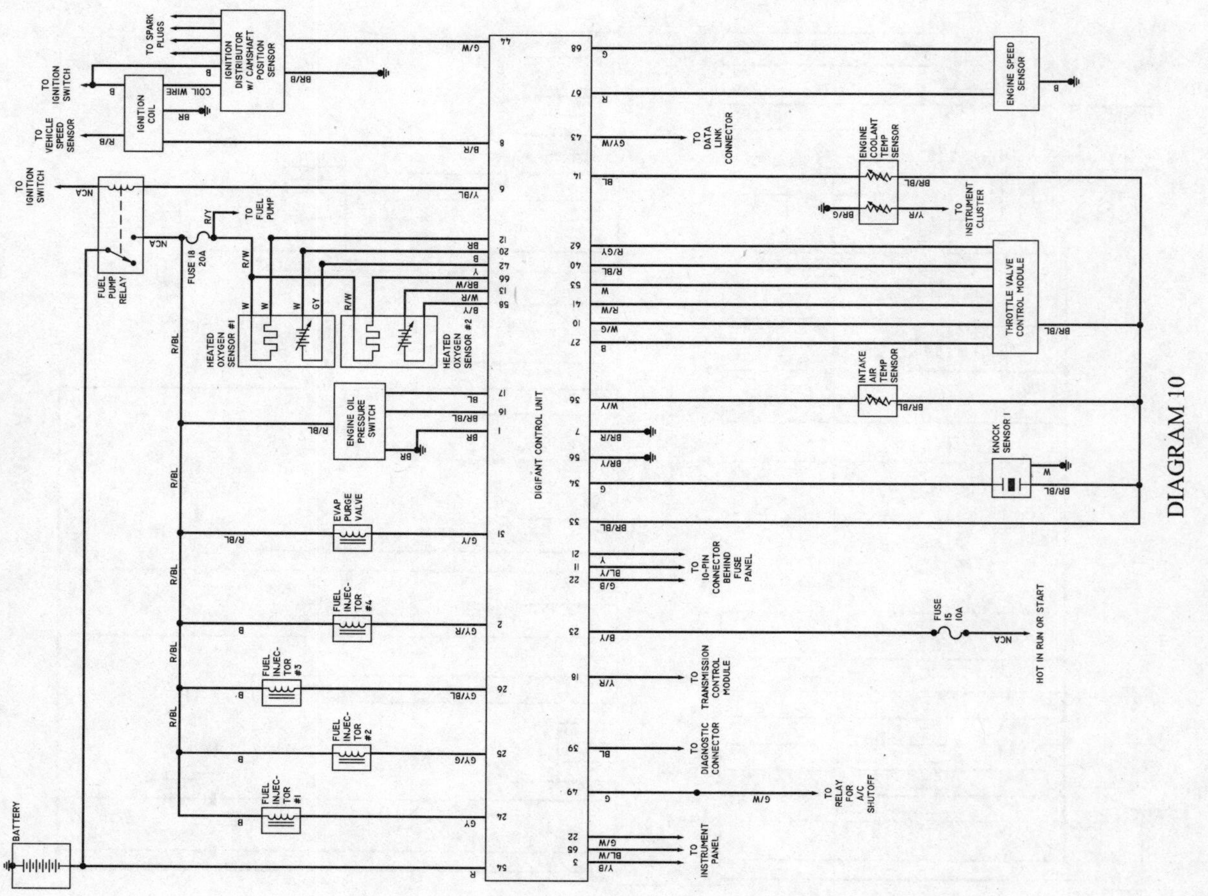

1995-99 CABRIO 2.0L (OBD II) ENGINE SCHEMATIC

DIAGRAM 10

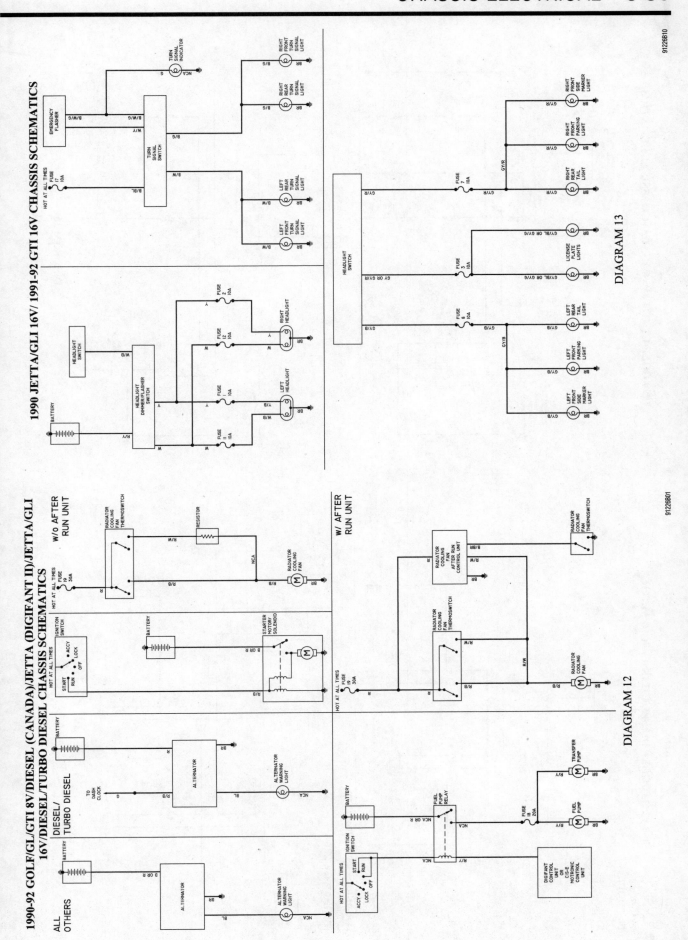

1990 JETTA/GLI 16V/ 1991-92 GTI 16V CHASSIS SCHEMATICS

DIAGRAM 13

1990-92 GOLF/GL/GTI 8V/DIESEL (CANADA)/JETTA (DIGIFANT II)/JETTA/GLI 16V/DIESEL/TURBO DIESEL CHASSIS SCHEMATICS

DIAGRAM 12

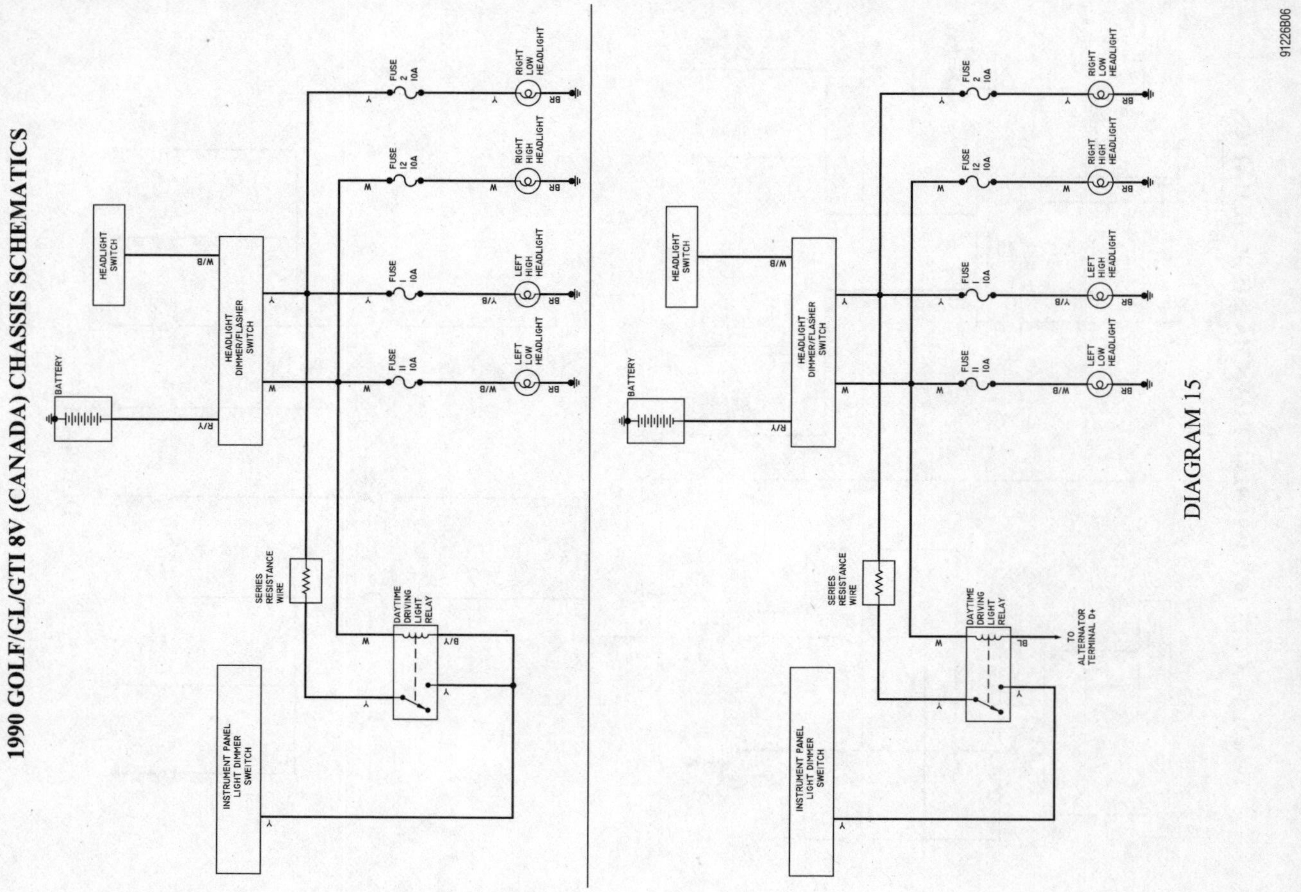
1990 GOLF/GL/GTI 8V (CANADA) CHASSIS SCHEMATICS
BATTERY
HEADLIGHT SWITCH
HEADLIGHT DIMMER/FLASHER SWITCH
FUSE 2 10A
FUSE 12 10A
FUSE 1 10A
FUSE 11 10A
RIGHT LOW HEADLIGHT
RIGHT HIGH HEADLIGHT
LEFT HIGH HEADLIGHT
LEFT LOW HEADLIGHT
SERIES RESISTANCE WIRE
DAYTIME DRIVING LIGHT RELAY
INSTRUMENT PANEL LIGHT DIMMER SWITCH
TO ALTERNATOR TERMINAL D+
DIAGRAM 15
91226B06

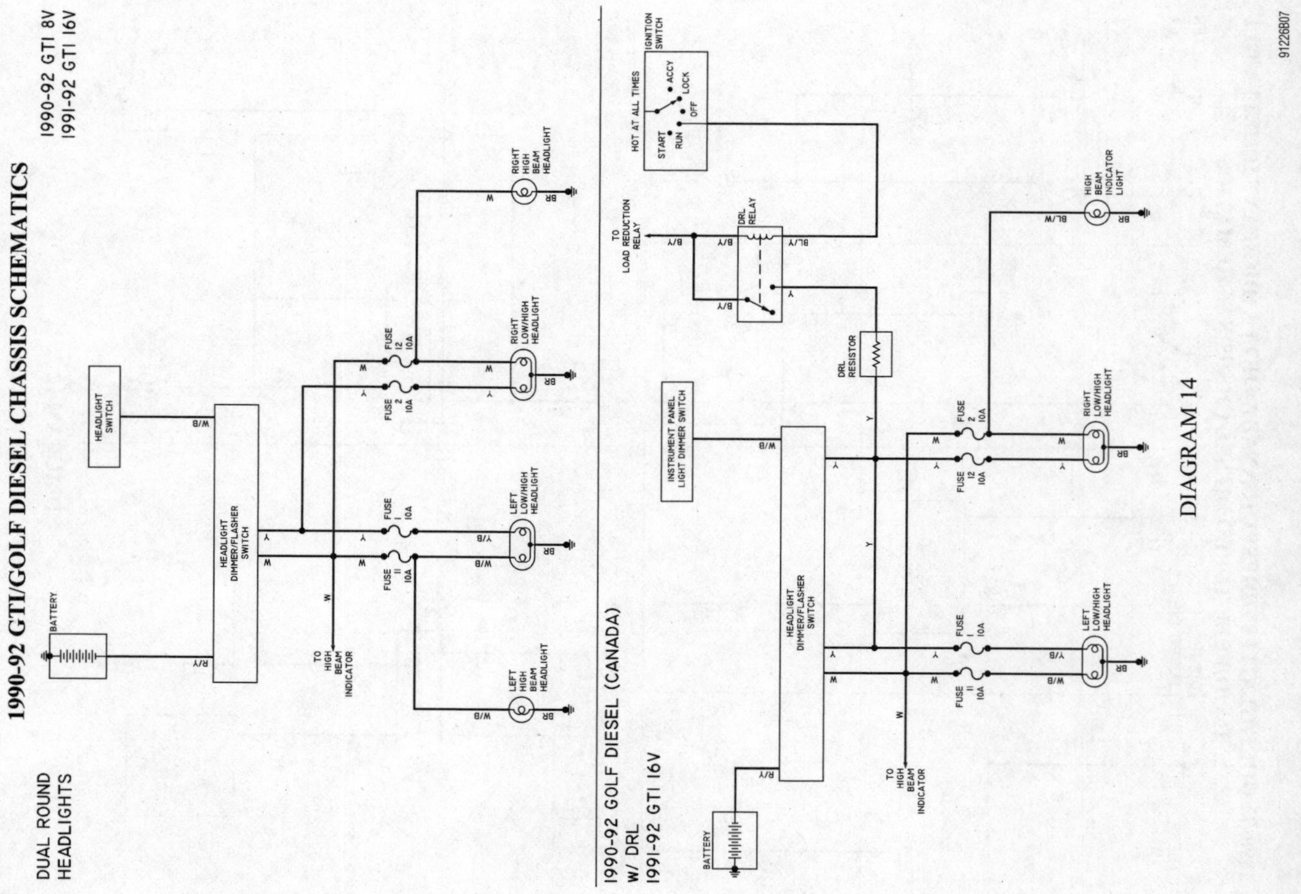
1990-92 GTI/GOLF DIESEL CHASSIS SCHEMATICS
1990-92 GTI 8V
1991-92 GTI 16V
DUAL ROUND HEADLIGHTS
BATTERY
HEADLIGHT SWITCH
HEADLIGHT DIMMER/FLASHER SWITCH
TO HIGH BEAM INDICATOR
LEFT HIGH BEAM HEADLIGHT
LEFT LOW/HIGH HEADLIGHT
RIGHT LOW/HIGH HEADLIGHT
RIGHT HIGH BEAM HEADLIGHT
1990-92 GOLF DIESEL (CANADA)
W/ DRL
1991-92 GTI 16V
IGNITION SWITCH
HOT AT ALL TIMES
START RUN ACCY LOCK OFF
TO LOAD REDUCTION RELAY
DRL RELAY
DRL RESISTOR
INSTRUMENT PANEL LIGHT DIMMER SWITCH
HIGH BEAM INDICATOR LIGHT
DIAGRAM 14
91226B07

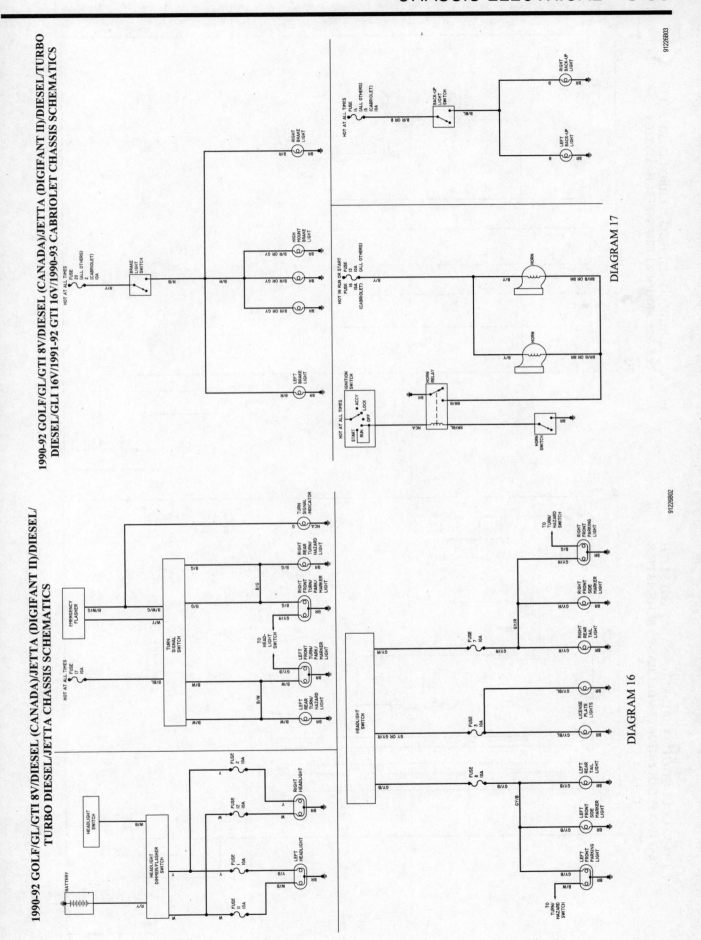

1990-92 GOLF/GL/GTI 8V/DIESEL (CANADA)/JETTA (DIGIFANT II)/DIESEL/TURBO DIESEL/GLI 16V/1991-92 GTI 16V/1990-93 CABRIOLET CHASSIS SCHEMATICS

DIAGRAM 17

1990-92 GOLF/GL/GTI 8V/DIESEL (CANADA)/JETTA (DIGIFANT II)/DIESEL/ TURBO DIESEL/JETTA CHASSIS SCHEMATICS

DIAGRAM 16

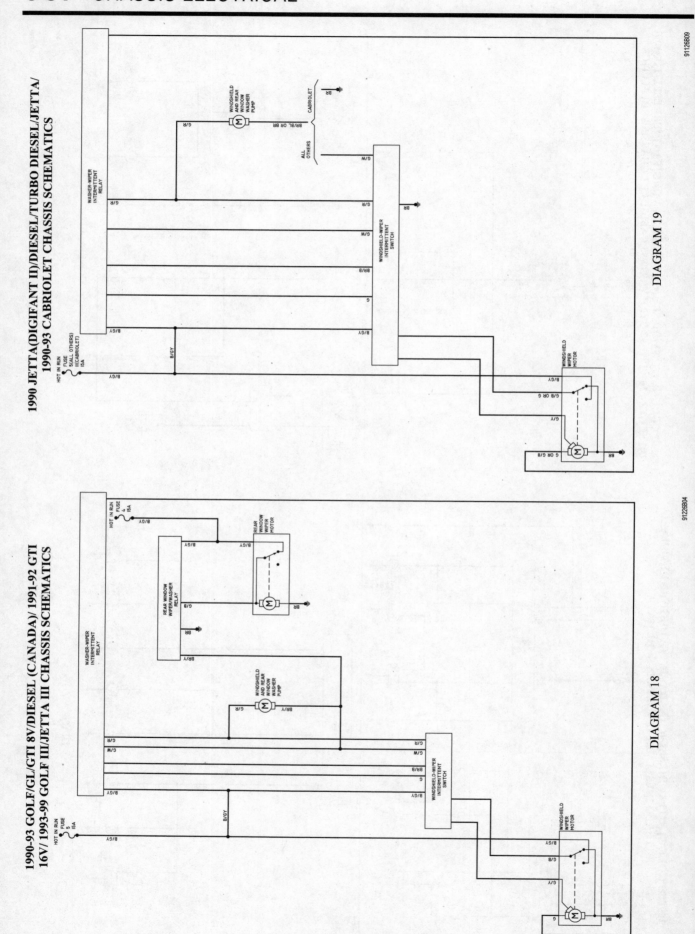

1990 JETTA(DIGIFANT II)/DIESEL/TURBO DIESEL/JETTA/
1990-93 CABRIOLET CHASSIS SCHEMATICS

DIAGRAM 19

1990-93 GOLF/GL/GTI 8V/DIESEL (CANADA)/ 1991-92 GTI
16V/ 1993-99 GOLF III/JETTA III CHASSIS SCHEMATICS

DIAGRAM 18

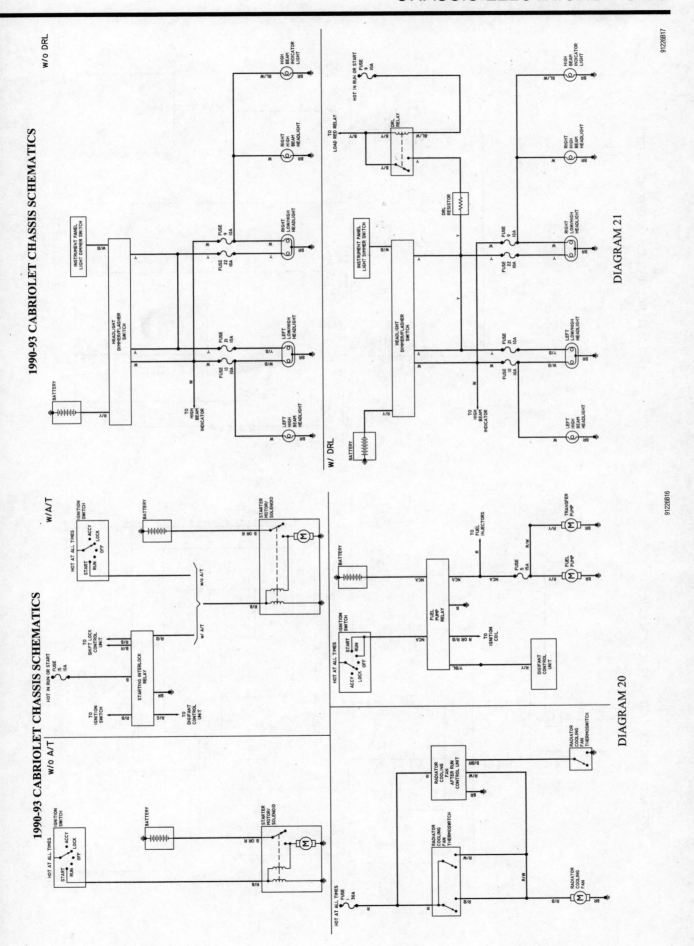

1990-93 CABRIOLET CHASSIS SCHEMATICS

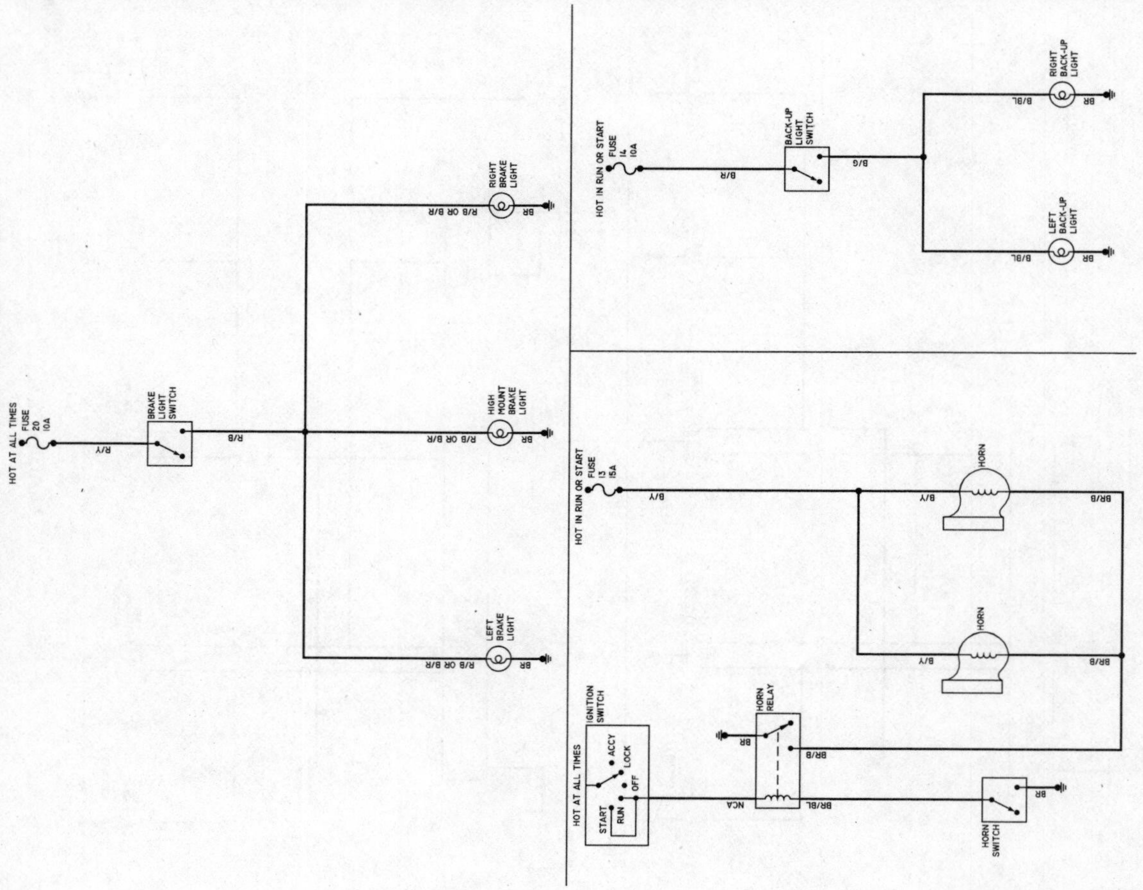

DIAGRAM 23

91226B20

1990-93 CABRIOLET CHASSIS SCHEMATICS

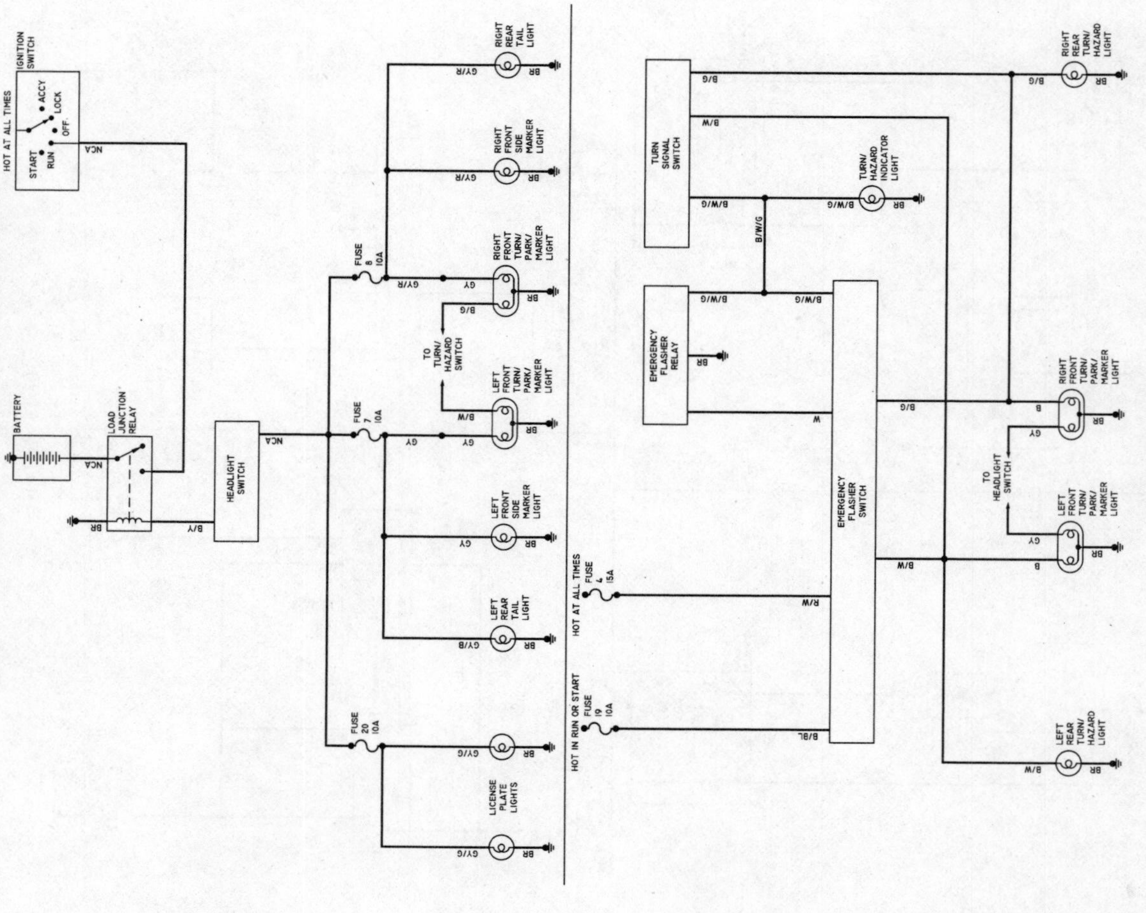

DIAGRAM 22

91226B11

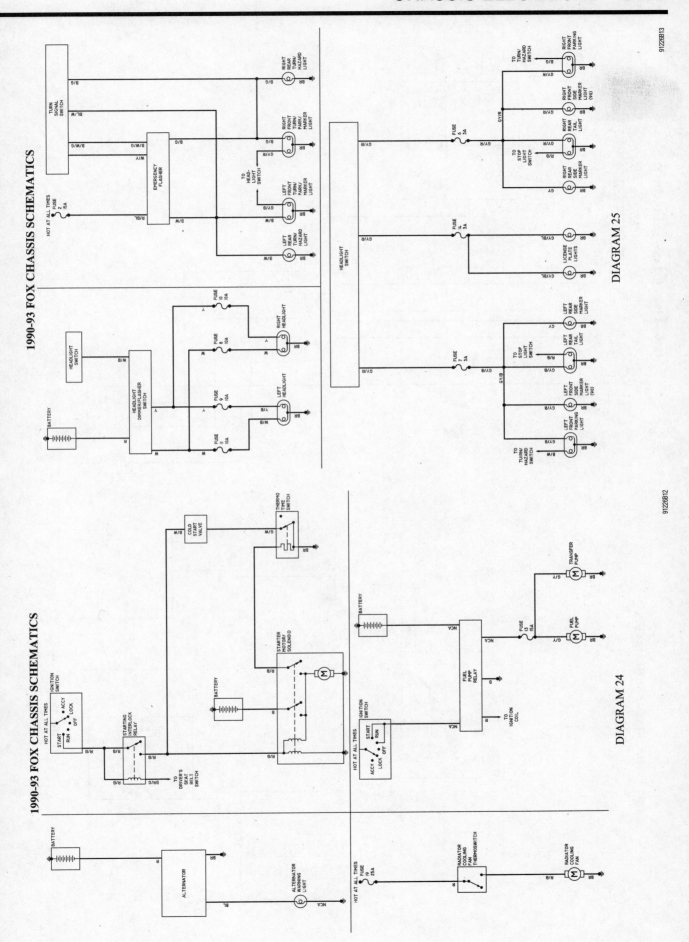

1990-93 FOX CHASSIS SCHEMATICS

DIAGRAM 25

1990-93 FOX CHASSIS SCHEMATICS

DIAGRAM 24

1990-93 FOX CHASSIS SCHEMATICS

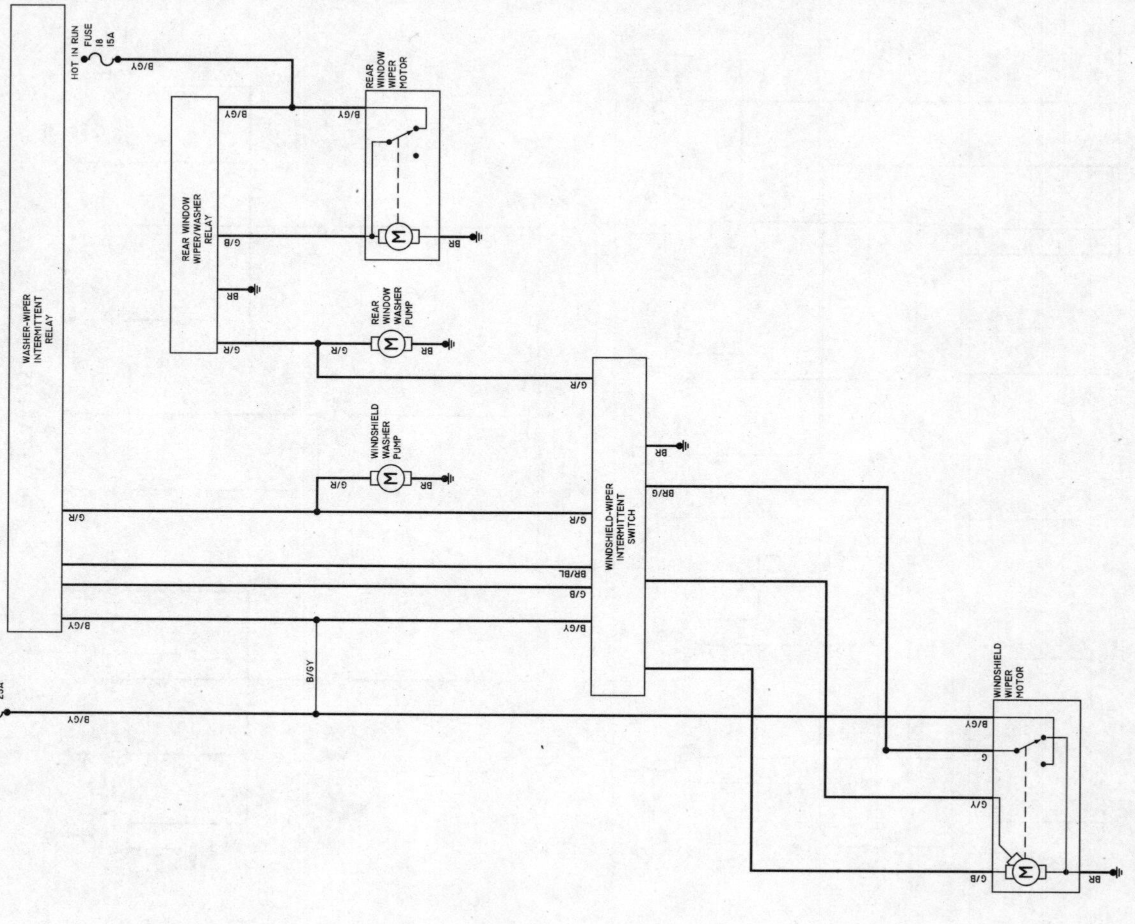

DIAGRAM 27

1990-93 FOX CHASSIS SCHEMATICS

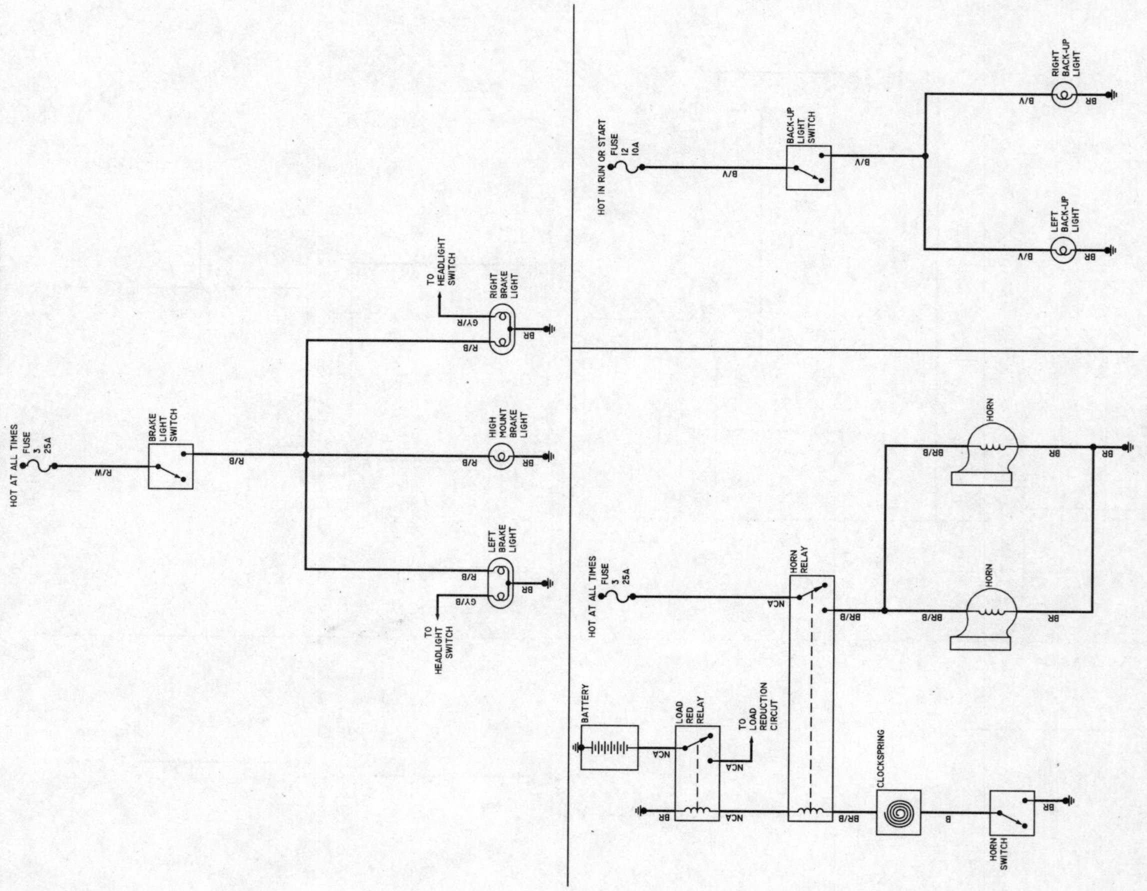

DIAGRAM 26

w/o DRL

91226B22

1993-99 GOLF III/JETTA III CHASSIS SCHEMATICS

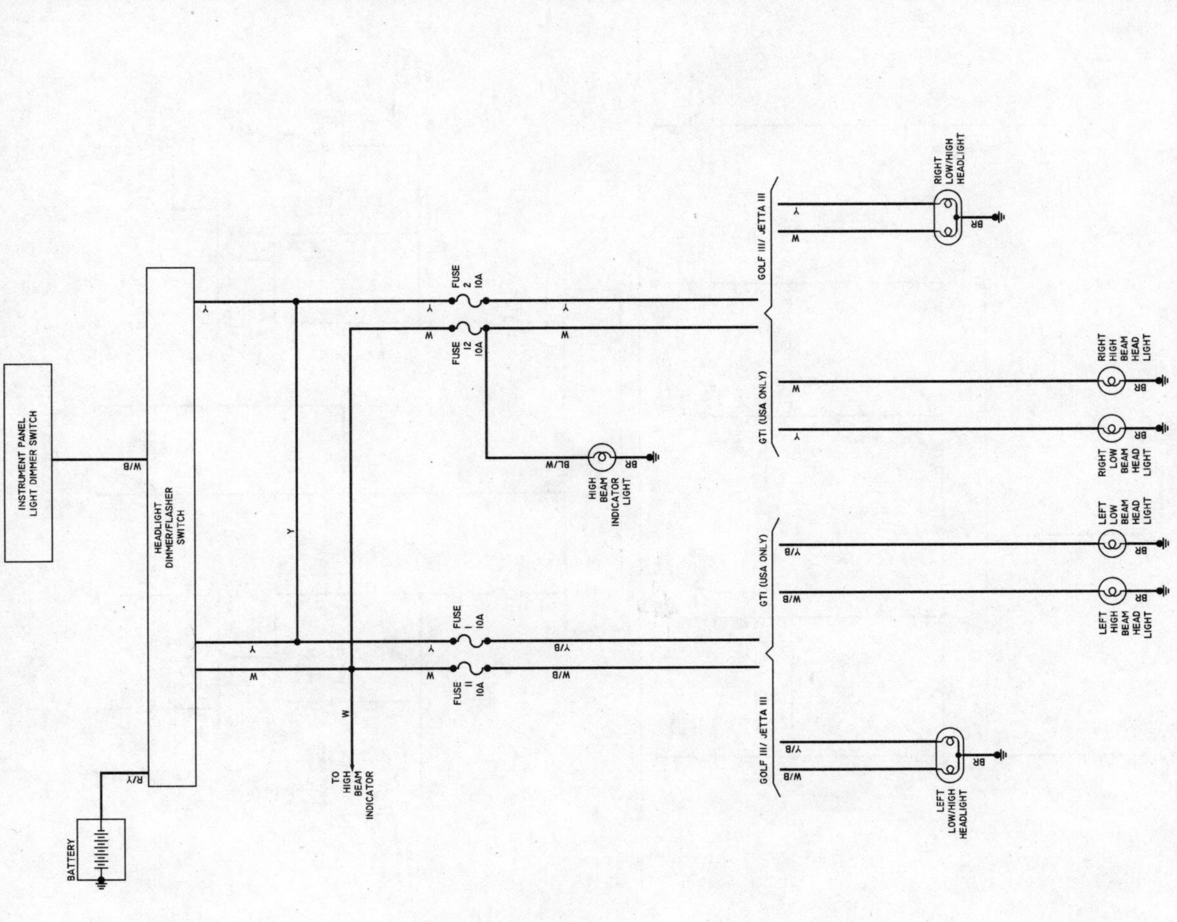

INSTRUMENT PANEL
LIGHT DIMMER SWITCH

HEADLIGHT
DIMMER/FLASHER
SWITCH

BATTERY

FUSE 2 10A

FUSE 12 10A

HIGH BEAM INDICATOR LIGHT

FUSE 11 10A

FUSE 1 10A

TO HIGH BEAM INDICATOR

GOLF III/ JETTA III

GTI (USA ONLY)

GTI (USA ONLY)

GOLF III/ JETTA III

RIGHT LOW/HIGH HEADLIGHT

RIGHT HIGH BEAM HEAD LIGHT

RIGHT LOW BEAM HEAD LIGHT

LEFT LOW BEAM HEAD LIGHT

LEFT HIGH BEAM HEAD LIGHT

LEFT LOW/HIGH HEADLIGHT

DIAGRAM 29

91226B18

1993-99 GOLF III/JETTA III CHASSIS SCHEMATICS

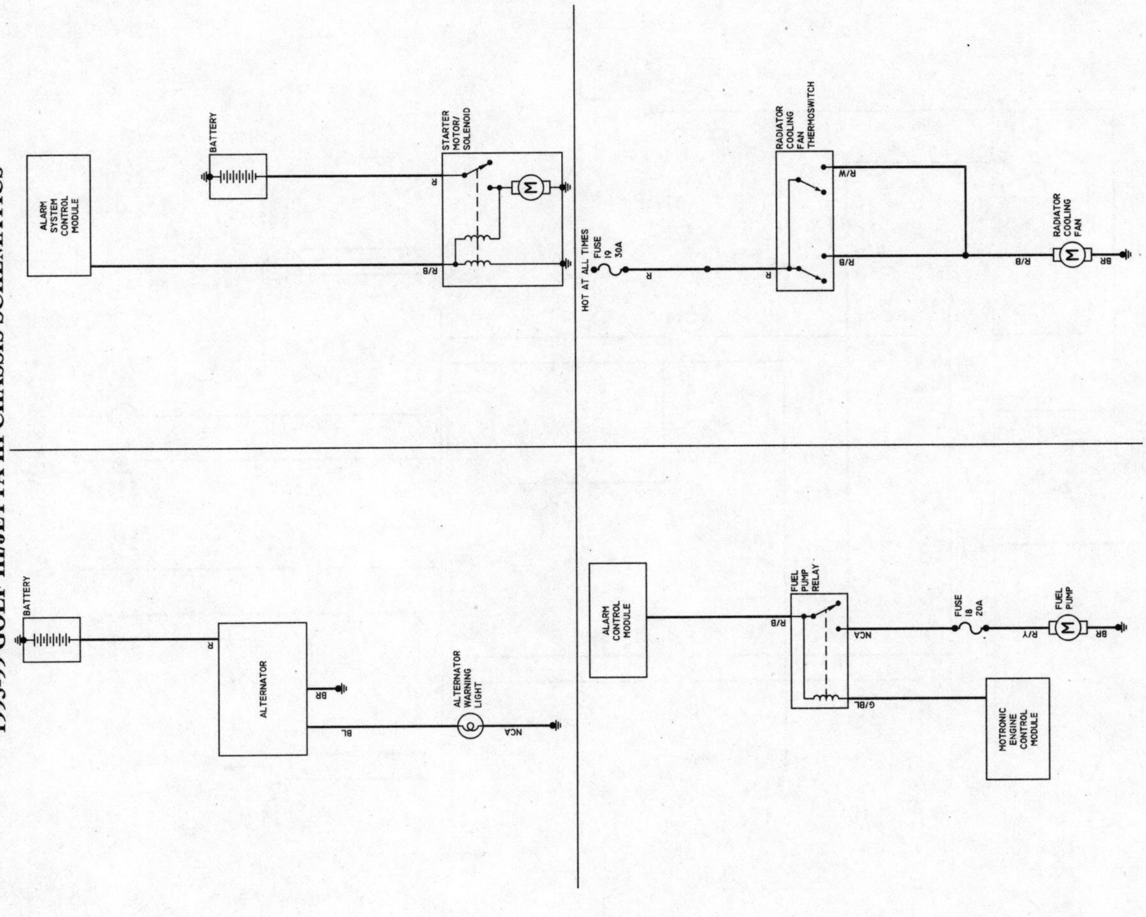

ALARM SYSTEM CONTROL MODULE

BATTERY

STARTER MOTOR/ SOLENOID

HOT AT ALL TIMES

FUSE 19 30A

RADIATOR COOLING FAN THERMOSWITCH

RADIATOR COOLING FAN

BATTERY

ALTERNATOR

ALTERNATOR WARNING LIGHT

ALARM CONTROL MODULE

FUEL PUMP RELAY

FUSE 18 20A

FUEL PUMP

MOTRONIC ENGINE CONTROL MODULE

DIAGRAM 28

91226B19

1993-99 GOLF III/JETTA III CHASSIS SCHEMATICS

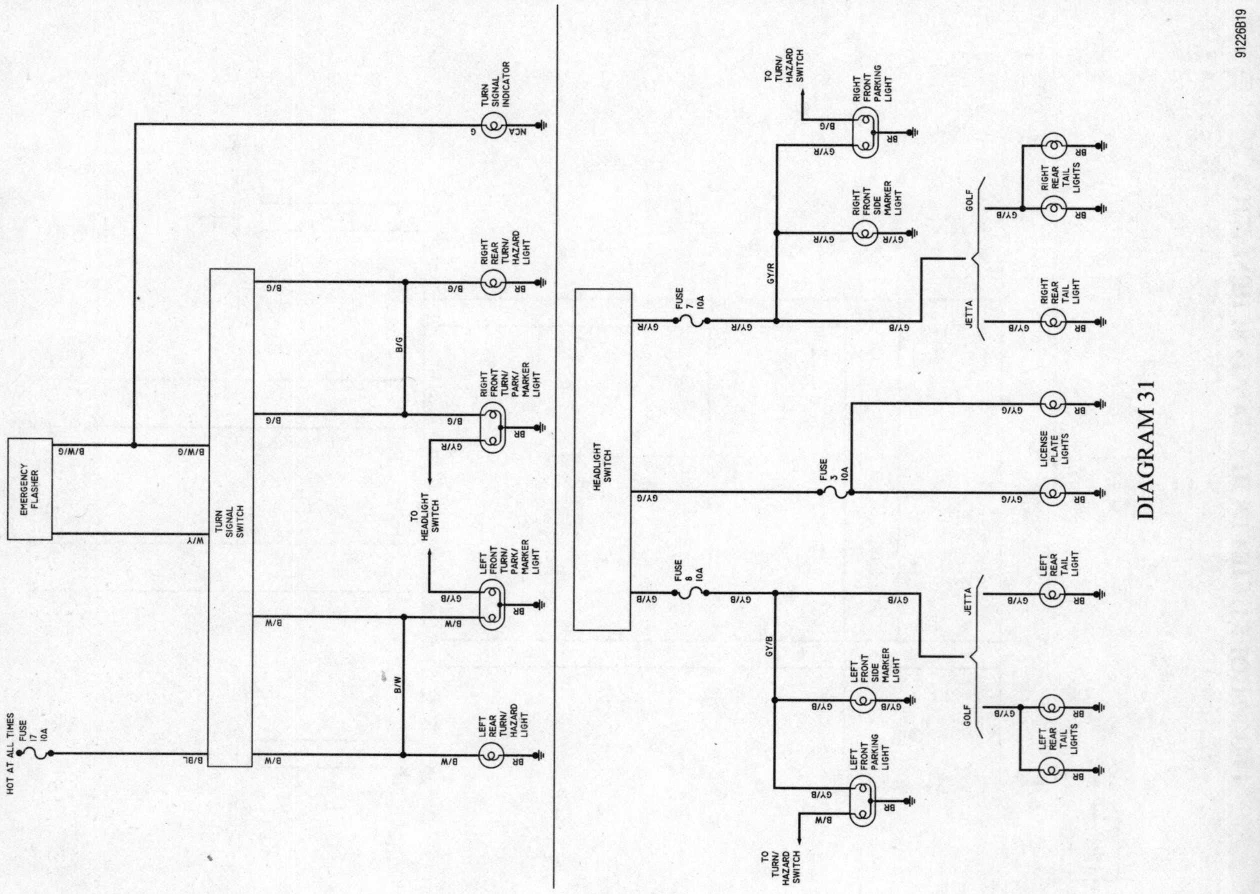

DIAGRAM 31

91226B21

1993-99 GOLF III/JETTA III/GTI (CANADA) CHASSIS SCHEMATICS

w/ DRL

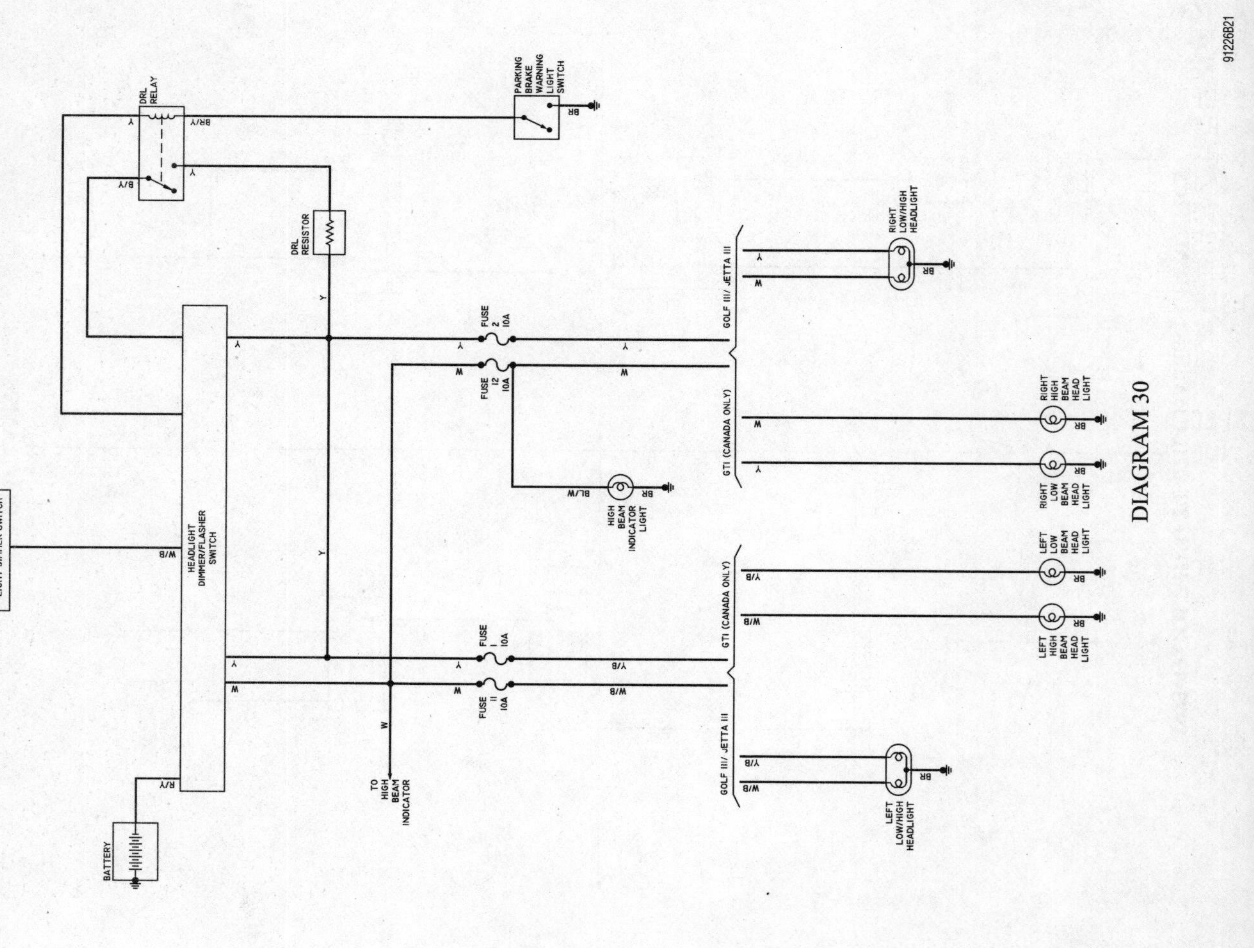

DIAGRAM 30

7
DRIVE TRAIN

MANUAL TRANSAXLE

Understanding the Manual Transaxle

Because of the way an internal combustion engine breathes, it can produce torque, or twisting force, only within a narrow speed range. Most modern, overhead valve pushrod engines must turn at about 2500 rpm to produce their peak torque. By 4500 rpm they are producing so little torque that continued increases in engine speed produce no power increases. The torque peak on overhead camshaft engines is generally much higher, but much narrower.

The manual transaxle and clutch are employed to vary the relationship between engine speed and the speed of the wheels so that adequate engine power can be produced under all circumstances. The clutch allows engine torque to be applied to the transaxle input shaft gradually, due to mechanical slippage. Consequently, the vehicle may be started smoothly from a full stop. The transaxle changes the ratio between the rotating speeds of the engine and the wheels by the use of gears. The gear ratios allow full engine power to be applied to the wheels during acceleration at low speeds and at highway/passing speeds.

In a front wheel drive transaxle, power is usually transmitted from the input shaft to a mainshaft or output shaft located slightly beneath and to the side of the input shaft. The gears of the mainshaft mesh with gears on the input shaft, allowing power to be carried from one to the other. All forward gears are in constant mesh and are free from rotating with the shaft unless the synchronizer and clutch is engaged. Shifting from one gear to the next causes one of the gears to be freed from rotating with the shaft and locks another to it. Gears are locked and unlocked by internal dog clutches which slide between the center of the gear and the shaft. The forward gears employ synchronizers; friction members which smoothly bring gear and shaft to the same speed before the toothed dog clutches are engaged.

Back-up Light Switch

REMOVAL & INSTALLATION

Cabriolet

On the Cabriolet, the back-up light switch is mounted in one of three positions: screwed into the front face of the transaxle beside the oil filler plug, screwed into the top of the transaxle case to the left of the shift linkage, or mounted as a microswitch on top of the transaxle with a lever that is activated by the external shift linkage.

Fox

The Fox back-up light switch is screwed into the rear of the transaxle housing. Simply unscrew it from the housing to remove or replace.

1990—92 Golf and Jetta

The back-up light switch includes the fifth gear switch used by the up-shift light. It is mounted to the selector shaft housing on top of the transaxle, secured with 2 bolts and sealed with an O-ring.

1. Make sure the transaxle is in neutral.
2. Disconnect the wiring and remove the bolts to remove the switch. Be careful not to loose the O-ring or bolt bushings.
3. Fit the bushings and O-ring onto the switch and install it onto the transaxle. Tighten the bolts to 7 ft. lbs. (10 Nm) and connect the wiring.

1995—99 Cabrio, 1993–99 Golf and Jetta

1. Remove the negative battery cable.
2. Remove the electrical connector.
3. Unscrew the switch using a wrench to break it loose.
4. Remove the back up light switch from the housing.
5. Keep the O-ring.
To install:
6. Installation is the reverse of removal.

ADJUSTMENT

The back up lights cannot be adjusted.

Manual Transaxle Assembly

REMOVAL & INSTALLATION

Cabriolet

➡**If equipped with electronically theft-protected radio, obtain the security code before disconnecting the battery.**

1. Remove the battery.
2. Detach the backup light switch connector and the speedometer cable from the transaxle. Plug the speedometer cable hole.
3. Turn the crankshaft to align the timing marks to TDC.
4. To disconnect the shift linkage, pry open the ball joint ends and remove both selector rods. Remove the pin, disconnect the relay rod and put the pin back in the hole on the rod for safe keeping.
5. Raise and safely support the vehicle and remove the front wheels. Connect the engine sling tool VW–10–222A or equivalent, to the loop in the cylinder head and just take the weight of the engine off the mounts. Do not try to support the engine from below.
6. Remove the drain plug and drain the oil from the transaxle.
7. Detach the clutch cable from the linkage and remove it from the transaxle case.
8. Remove the starter and front engine mount. On 16 valve engines, remove the engine damper.
9. Remove the small cover behind the right halfshaft flange and remove the clutch cover plate.
10. Disconnect the halfshafts from the drive flanges and hang them up with wire. Do not let them hang by the outer CV-joint or the joint may come apart.
11. Remove the long center bolt from the left side transaxle mount.
12. Remove the entire rear mount assembly from the body and differential housing.
13. Lower the engine hoist enough to let the left mount free of the body and remove the mount from the transaxle.
14. Place a support jack under the transaxle, remove all the transaxle-to-engine bolts and carefully pry the transaxle away from the engine. Lower the transaxle from under the vehicle.
To install:
15. Coat the input shaft lightly with molybdenum grease and carefully fit the transaxle onto the engine. If necessary, put the transaxle in any gear and turn an output flange to align the input shaft spline with the clutch spline.
16. Install the engine-to-transaxle bolts and tighten to 55 ft. lbs. (75 Nm).
17. When installing the mounts to the transaxle, tighten the bolts to 33 ft. lbs. (45 Nm). Install but do not tighten the bolts that go into the rubber mounts.
18. Install the starter and front mount.
19. With all mounts installed and the transaxle safely in the vehicle, allow some slack in the lifting equipment. With the vehicle safely supported, shake the engine/transaxle as a unit to settle it in the mounts. Tighten all mounting bolts, starting at the rear and working forward. Tighten the rubber mount bolts to 25 ft. lbs. (35 Nm). Tighten the front mount bolts to 38 ft. lbs. (52 Nm).
20. Install the halfshafts and tighten the bolts to 33 ft. lbs. (45 Nm). Install the clutch cover plates.
21. Connect the shift linkage and clutch cable and adjust as required.
22. Complete the remaining installation and refill the transaxle with oil.

Fox With 4-Speed Transaxle

1. Disconnect the negative battery cable.
2. Disconnect the exhaust pipe from the manifold and its bracket on the transaxle.
3. Remove the square-headed bolt on the shift linkage. Later models have a hex head bolt.
4. Press the shift linkage coupling off.
5. Disconnect the clutch cable.
6. Disconnect the speedometer cable.
7. Detach the halfshafts from the transaxle.
8. Remove the starter.
9. Remove the inspection plate.

10. Remove the engine-to-transaxle bolts.
11. Remove the transaxle crossmember.
12. Support the transaxle with a jack.
13. Pry the transaxle out from the engine.
14. Lift the transaxle out of the car with an assistant.

To install:

15. Connect the transaxle to the engine. Tighten the bolts to 40 ft. lbs. (55 Nm).
16. Install the transaxle crossmember. Do not fully tighten the bolts until the transaxle is aligned and fully installed in the vehicle. On models with the rubber core rear transaxle mount, the rubber core must be centered in its housing.
17. Install the starter and inspection plate.
18. Install the axle shafts. Tighten the bolts to 33 ft. lbs. (45 Nm).
19. Connect the speedometer and clutch cables.
20. Connect the shift linkage.
21. Connect the exhaust pipe to the manifold.
22. If necessary, refill the transaxle. Refer to Section 1 for procedures.
23. Adjust the clutch.
24. Connect the negative battery cable.

Fox With 5-Speed Transaxle

1. Disconnect the negative battery cable.
2. Remove the upper engine-to-transaxle bolts.
3. Disconnect the clutch cable from the clutch lever and route the cable off to the side and out of the way.
4. Disconnect the speedometer cable from the transaxle.
5. Disconnect the exhaust pipe from the manifold and its bracket on the transaxle.
6. Remove the engine stop bolts from the block.
7. Disconnect the front exhaust pipe from the catalytic converter.
8. Unbolt the exhaust pipe support from the transaxle.
9. Unbolt the axleshafts from the transaxle flanges. Tie the shafts up and out of the way.
10. Unplug the back-up switch wire.
11. Unbolt and remove the cover plate.
12. Remove the starter.
13. Remove the bolt from the shift rod coupling and pry the linkage from the coupling.
14. Pull the shift rod coupling from the shift rod.
15. Support the transaxle with a jack or support tool 2071 and raise the transaxle slightly.
16. Remove the transaxle support bar bolts and pivot the support to the rear. Remove the support bar mount.
17. Remove the lower engine/transaxle bolts.
18. Using a large prybar, separate the transaxle from the engine and lower it from the vehicle using the jack.

To install:

19. Make sure the mainshaft splines are clean, then lightly lubricate them with molybdenum disulfide grease or spray.
20. Raise the transaxle onto the engine and install the lower engine/transaxle bolts. Tighten the bolts to 40 ft. lbs. (55 Nm).
21. Install the mounts and mounting support brackets. Tighten the transaxle mounting fasteners to the following specifications:
    a. Subframe support-to-body—40 ft. lbs. (55 Nm).
    b. Mount-to-bracket—18 ft. lbs. (25 Nm).
    c. Mount-to-body—80 ft. lbs. (108 Nm).
    d. Front bracket-to-transaxle —40 ft. lbs. (55 Nm).

➥**Make sure the engine/transaxle mounts are aligned and free of tension before tightening the fasteners. All the mount rubber cores should be centered in the mount.**

22. Connect the shift rod coupling to the shift rod.
23. Connect the shift rod linkage to the shift rod coupling. Tighten the shift rod bolt to 14 ft. lbs. (19 Nm).
24. Install the starter. Tighten the starter mounting bolts to 14 ft. lbs. (19 Nm).
25. Install the cover plate and tighten the bolts to 7 ft. lbs. (10 Nm). Make sure the cover plate is properly seated.
26. Plug in the back-up switch wire.
27. Connect the axleshaft to the transaxle. Tighten the flange bolts to 30 ft. lbs. (40 Nm).

28. Attach the exhaust pipe support to the transaxle.
29. Connect the front exhaust pipe to the catalytic converter.
30. Install the engine stop bolts and tighten them to 18 ft. lbs. (25 Nm).
31. Connect the exhaust pipe to the bracket and manifold. Tighten the manifold nuts to 22 ft. lbs. (30 Nm).
32. Connect the speedometer and clutch cables.
33. Install the upper engine/transaxle bolts. Tighten the bolts to 40 ft. lbs. (55 Nm).
34. Connect the negative battery cable.

1990–92 Golf and Jetta

➥**If equipped with electronically theft-protected radio, obtain the security code before disconnecting the battery.**

1. Remove the battery.
2. Detach the backup light switch connector and the speedometer cable from the transaxle; plug the speedometer cable hole.
3. Remove the upper engine-to-transaxle bolts.
4. Remove the 3 right side engine mount bolts, between the engine and firewall.
5. To disconnect the shift linkage, pry open the ball joint ends and remove the shift and relay shaft rods.
6. Remove the center bolt from the left transaxle mount.
7. Raise and safely support the vehicle and remove the front wheels. Connect the engine sling tool VW–10–222A or equivalent, to the loop in the cylinder head and just take the weight of the engine off the mounts. On the 16 valve engine, the idle stabilizer valve must be removed to attach the tool. Do not try to support the engine from below.
8. Remove the drain plug and drain the oil from the transaxle.
9. Remove the left inner fender liner.
10. Disconnect the halfshafts from the inner drive flanges and hang them from the body.
11. Remove the clutch cover plate and the small plate behind the right halfshaft flange.
12. Remove the starter and front engine mount.
13. Disconnect the clutch cable and remove it from the transaxle housing.
14. Place a jack under the transaxle and remove the last bolts holding it to the engine. Remove the remaining transaxle mount bolts and mounts.
15. Carefully pry the transaxle away from the engine and lower it from the vehicle.

To install:

16. Coat the input shaft lightly with molybdenum grease and carefully fit the transaxle in place. If necessary, put the transaxle in any gear and turn an output flange to align the input shaft spline with the clutch spline.
17. Install the engine-to-transaxle bolts and tighten to 55 ft. lbs. (75 Nm).
18. When installing the mounts to the transaxle, tighten the rear bracket-to-engine bolts and the transaxle support bolts to 18 ft. lbs. (25 Nm). Tighten the left bracket-to-transaxle bolts to 25 ft. lbs. (35 Nm) and the remaining mounting bolts to 44 ft. lbs. (60 Nm). Install but do not tighten the bolts that go into the rubber mounts.
19. Install the starter and front mount.
20. With all mounts installed and the transaxle safely in the vehicle, allow some slack in the lifting equipment. With the vehicle safely supported, shake the engine/transaxle as a unit to settle it in the mounts. Tighten all mounting bolts, starting at the rear and working forward. Tighten the bolts that go into the rubber mounts to 44 ft. lbs. (60 Nm).
21. Install the halfshafts and tighten the bolts to 33 ft. lbs. (45 Nm). Install the clutch cover plates.
22. Connect the shift linkage and clutch cable and adjust as required.
23. Install the inner fender and complete the remaining installation. Refill the transaxle with oil.

1995–99 Cabrio, 1993–99 Golf and Jetta

♦ **See Figures 1 thru 9**

1. Raise and support the vehicle.
2. Detach the negative battery cable.
3. The removal of the front body clip, radiator, cooling fans, and the hook and lock mechanism is not required but will greatly increase the accessibility of the transaxle.

Fig. 1 Location of upper transaxle bolts

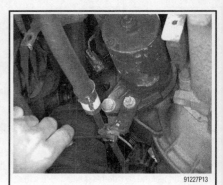

Fig. 2 Mark the exact location of each bolt. There will be bolts of different size, thread pitch, and design

Fig. 3 Detaching the bracket from the starter

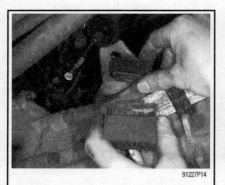

Fig. 4 Remove the clutch cable from the bottom of the cable (transmission side)

Fig. 5 Disconnecting the shifter weight from the transmission by pulling the cotter pin and lifting up

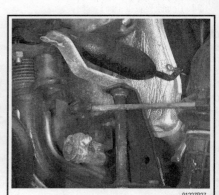

Fig. 6 Location of the shift weight

Fig. 7 Remove all wiring harnesses from the transmission

Fig. 8 View of the rear motor mount support bracket

Fig. 9 Manual transmission input shaft

4. Remove all electrical wiring from the transaxle.
5. Remove all ground straps from the transaxle housing.
6. Support the transmission.
7. Detach the gearshift selector rods/cables.
8. Remove the support bracket from the rear of the transaxle assembly.
9. Remove the clutch shield plate.
10. Detach the drive axles at the transmission, tie the drive axles up and out of the way.
11. Position the steering wheel to full lock left.
12. Remove all but two of the transmission bellhousing bolts.
13. Remove the front engine mounting crossmember.
14. Remove the remaining bell housing bolts and then pull the transaxle from the engine.
To install:
15. Installation is the reverse of removal.

Gear Case, Input Shaft and Pinion Shaft

DISASSEMBLY

▶ **See Figures 10, 11 and 12**

➡The 5th gear synchronizer bolt and all circlips should be replaced any time they are removed. The 3rd gear circlip is used to adjust end play and comes in different thickness. The input shaft used with 8 valve engines is different from 16 valve engines and they cannot be interchanged.

1. Mount the transaxle assembly in a holding fixture.
2. Mount a bar with a bolt and spacer across the bellhousing to support the mainshaft.

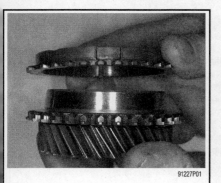

Fig. 10 View of a synchronizer blocking
ring and gear assembly

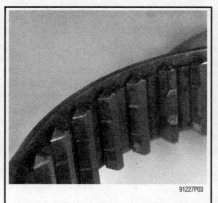

Fig. 11 Inspect all gears for chipped teeth

Fig. 12 Synchronizer sleeve engaged with
third gear

3. Remove the cap from the drive flange and discard it.

4. The left drive flange must be removed to disassemble the case. If the differential is to be removed, both drive flanges must be removed. There is a strong spring pushing the drive flange out against the circlip. If the special removal tool is not available:

• Locate a heavy bar that fits across the flange but leaves room around the side to access the circlip. Drill a 0.470 inch (12mm) hole through the center.

• Locate a long bolt or threaded rod that fits the M10 threads in the center of the output shaft.

• Use the bar and bolt to draw the flange down against the spring just enough to unload the circlip.

• Remove the circlip, then remove the bolt to remove the output flange.

➡The left and right drive flanges are different. Label them for proper
assembly and keep them together with the tapered rings.

5. Remove the end cover and gasket. DO NOT remove the selector rod that has the small spring on the end. The selector assembly will fall apart inside the transaxle.

6. Remove the back-up light switch.

7. Remove the selector shaft detent plungers. Remove the cover, spring and selector shaft.

8. Use a screwdriver to move both front selector forks to engage 5th and reverse at the same time. This will lock the gear train so it cannot turn.

9. Remove the bolt from the center of the 5th gear synchro assembly. The bolt is very tight and is held in with thread locking compound. Make sure the transaxle is securely supported.

10. Pry the locking plate up and remove it. Unscrew the selector tube to remove the shift fork and synchro as an assembly. The tube does not move up or down, the shift fork will move up the tube. Be careful not to remove the selector rod.

11. Remove the circlip from 5th gear. On the 16 valve engine, 5th gear is secured with a plate. It may be necessary to use a puller to remove 5th gear.

12. Remove the reverse shaft fixing bolt from the side of the case.

13. Use an M6 12 point socket to remove the 4 bolts holding the input shaft bearing retainer to the rear of the case.

14. Remove the bolts holding the case halves together.

15. Secure a puller to the rear cover bolt holes so the bolt contacts the input shaft. Carefully press the housing off the rear bearing and lift the housing away from the transaxle. There may be a shim on top of the bearing.

16. To remove the shift forks, lift the selector rod slightly and remove the shift forks as an assembly.

17. To remove the input shaft, remove the 4th gear circlip. Lift out 4th gear and the input shaft together.

18. To remove the pinion shaft, the gears must be removed first. Remove the 3rd gear circlip and lift 3rd gear, 2nd gear, the bearings and the synchro assembly off the shaft. Be sure to place them on the bench in order, facing the same way, to ease correct assembly.

19. Remove the reverse gear and shaft.

20. Use a puller to remove the 1st gear and the 1st/2nd synchro together.

21. Remove the bolts to remove the bearing plate and the pinion shaft.

22. Third and 4th gear synchronizer must be pressed off the pinion shaft.

23. Before disassembling the synchronizers, measure the wear at dimension

a with a feeler gauge. If the gap is 0.020 inches (0.5mm) or less, the synchronizer ring must be replaced.

24. The bearings can be removed from the shafts and the case with the appropriate pullers. If bearings are removed, they should be replaced. Pay attention to any shims or spacers and make sure they are labeled for correct installation.

ASSEMBLY

1. If the transaxle case, ring gear or the side bearings are replaced, adjust differential side bearing pre-load before assembling the transaxle.

2. If none of these items is being replaced, go to Step 6. If new bearings are being installed, heat the bearing to about 212°F (100°C) and press it onto the shaft until it is fully seated. Be sure to replace the race in the housing.

3. Install a 0.65mm (0.025 inch) shim into the housing and temporarily install the bearing outer race. If this shim is not on hand, a thicker shim may be used but it must be small enough to allow some pinion shaft end play.

4. Set the pinion shaft into place. Do not oil the bearings or turn the shaft. Fit the outer race onto the smaller bearing, install the bearing plate and tighten the bolts to 30 ft. lbs. (40 Nm).

5. Attach a dial indicator to the case and measure the end play of the shaft. Be careful not to turn the shaft or the bearings will settle and cause an incorrect reading.

6. The correct bearing shim size is obtained by adding the end-play measurement, the starting shim and a bearing pre-load of 0.20mm (0.008 inches). For example:

• Starting shim: 0.65mm (0.025 inches)
• End play: 0.30mm (0.012 inches)
• Pre-load: 0.20mm (0.008 inches)
• Correct shim: 1.15mm (0.045 inches)

7. Shims are available in sizes from 0.65mm–1.40mm (0.025–0.055 in). Install the correct shim and oil the bearings before installing the pinion shaft.

8. Install the bearing plate and tighten the bolts to 30 ft. lbs. (40 Nm). When the bearing pre-load is correct, it should require 5–13 inch lbs. to turn the shaft with new bearings or at least 3 inch lbs. with used bearings.

9. Install the 1st gear thrust washer with the shoulder facing the bearing plate.

10. If the synchronizer was disassembled:

• The original first gear synchronizer ring has a space with 3 teeth missing. The replacement ring has a full set of teeth and dimension **a** will be 0.042–0.066 inches (1.1–1.7mm).

• When assembling the 1st/2nd gear synchronizer, the groove in the hub must face first gear. The groove may be on the face or the edge of the teeth.

• The bent tab on the end of the key retainer spring must fit into one of the keys.

11. Install the needle bearing. The sychronizer hub should be heated to about 250°F (120°C) and must be pressed onto the shaft. Align the synchro ring grooves with the keys.

12. Install the reverse gear shaft and the gear.

13. If the 2nd gear needle bearing was removed, the race must be pressed or driven onto the shaft. Install the bearing, synchronizer assembly and 2nd and 3rd gears.

14. Install the 3rd gear circlip and make sure there is no gear end play. If the gear moves on the shaft or if the circlip cannot be installed, there are circlips available in thickness from 0.098–0.118 inches (2.5–3.0mm).

15. When assembling the input shaft, the new third gear synchronizer ring dimension **A** is 0.045–0.068 inches (1.15–1.75mm). The groove in the outer teeth must be towards fourth gear, the chamfer on the splines must be towards third gear.

16. If the input shaft has not been disassembled, remove the ball bearing with a puller that contacts only the inner race.

17. Install the input shaft assembly.

18. Install 4th gear and the circlip onto the pinion shaft.

19. Install the original ball bearing shim and press the bearing into the case. The wide shoulder on the inner race faces 4th gear.

20. Install the bearing retainer plate. Apply a thread locking compound to the bolts and tighten them to 11 ft. lbs. (15 Nm).

21. Install the shift fork assembly.

22. Temporarily install the bolt into the reverse gear shaft. Turn the shaft so the bolt is evenly spaced between the case bolt holes, then remove the bolt.

23. Install a new gasket or apply a silicone sealer to the gear carrier.

24. Make sure the input shaft is supported at the bell housing. Slip the case onto the carrier and carefully drive the inner race of the ball bearing onto the input shaft.

25. Install a new gasket and start the bolt into the reverse gear shaft.

26. Install the case bolts and tighten them to 18 ft. lbs. (25 Nm). Tighten the reverse shaft bolt to 18 ft. lbs. (25 Nm).

27. Install the drive flange with a new circlip.

28. Heat 5th gear to about 212°F (100°C) and install it onto the shaft. Install the thrust washer and circlip.

29. Fit the sychronizer assembly onto the shaft and thread the tube up through the fork. The tube should project 0.197 inches (5.0mm) above the fork. Don't install the locking plate yet.

30. Turn the input shaft at the input end and operate the shift forks to make sure the gears engage. DO NOT remove the shift rod from the tube or the fork assembly will fall apart inside the transaxle.

31. Shift the transaxle into 5th and reverse at the same time to lock it.

32. Apply a thread locking compound to a new synchronizer hub bolt, install the bolt and tighten it to 111 ft. lbs. (150 Nm).

33. Install the selector shaft assembly, spring and cap. Tighten the cap to 37 ft. lbs. (50 Nm).

34. Turn the input shaft while moving the selector shaft in and out, left and right to check engagement of all the gears.

35. Before installing the shift tube locking plate, check the gear alignment:
   - Pull the selector shaft out and turn to the left to select 5th gear.
   - Lift slightly on the shift fork to take up any free play in the sleeve.
   - Measure the overlap of the sleeve on 5th gear. The sleeve must be 0.039 inches (1.0mm) down over the gear. Adjust the sleeve position with the selector tube.

36. Slip 2 wrenches under the fork and press a new locking plate onto the tube.

37. Install the clutch pushrod.

38. Use a new gasket and install the end cover. Tighten the bolts to 18 ft. lbs. (25 Nm).

Shift Linkage

REMOVAL & INSTALLATION

If the shift linkage has never been disconnected, adjustment may not be necessary. Check the condition of the engine/transaxle mounts and make sure the linkage fasteners are secure. If the linkage feels spongy or if it is difficult to put the transaxle into first or reverse, check the condition of the main rod bushing. This is a plastic bearing protected by a rubber boot just behind the shift rod clamp. On Cabriolet, there is a rubber boot around the bushing. Peel back the boot and make sure the nuts and bolts are still secure. If the bushing is broken or worn, it should be replaced. Lightly lubricate the bearing with a light silicone grease and fit the boot into place. Try shifting gears again before deciding to adjust the linkage.

Cabriolet

1. Remove the shift lever knob and the shifter boot.

2. There are 2 holes in the lever bearing plate that should be aligned with the holes in the mounting flange on the body. If necessary, loosen the bolts and move the bearing plate to align the holes.

3. If shifting is still spongy, put the transaxle in neutral and loosen the clamp on the shifter rod. Make sure the rod moves easily in the clamp.

4. Remove the boot protecting the bottom of the shift lever assembly.

5. Move the shift lever so the shift finger is centered in the lock-out plate.

6. Move the lever so the finger is ⁹⁄₁₆ inch (15mm) from the plate, then tighten the clamp. If shifting is still difficult, reduce dimension A to ½ inch (13mm).

Fox

4 SPEED TRANSMISSION

➡**A Volkswagon alignment tool is needed to properly complete this job. This tool is available at your local VW dealer. Ask for tool number (T03 014 000 34 ZEL).**

1. Park the car on a level surface.
2. Set the parking brake.
3. Place the transmission in neutral.
4. Remove the shift rod clamp bolt.
5. Remove the shift lever boot.
6. Align the shift lever housing centering holes with the shift lever bearing housing.
7. Hold the shift lever against the contacts at its left stop. Tighten the upper nut.
8. Align the shift lever toward third gear.
9. Put the transmission in neutral and position the shift finger so that it is aligned with the shift rod.
10. Tighten the clamping rod nut to 87 inch lbs. (10 Nm).
11. Run the shifter through the all of the gears to ensure smooth engagement in all directions.
12. Installation of the remaining components is the reverse of removal.

5 SPEED TRANSMISSION

➡**A Volkswagon alignment tool is needed to properly complete this job. This tool is available at your local VW dealer. Ask for tool number (T03 057 000 34 ZEL).**

1. Park the car on a level surface.
2. Set the parking brake.
3. Place the transmission in neutral.
4. Remove the shift rod clamp bolt.
5. Remove the shift lever boot.
6. Align the shift lever housing centering holes with the shift lever bearing housing.
7. Install the VW special tool number (T03 057 000 34 ZEL).
8. Position the shifter so that it is against its right stop. Tighten the upper nut.
9. Push the shifter towards third and forth gear.
10. Place the transmission in neutral.
11. Align the shift finger with the shift rod.
12. Tighten the clamping bolt to 87 inch lbs. (10 Nm).

1990–92 Golf and Jetta

A special alignment tool is made for adjusting the side-to-side position of the shift lever. On vehicles made after January 1991, the shift lever is equipped with an eccentric for fine adjustment.

1. Make sure the vehicle is on level ground and place the transaxle into neutral.

2. Under the vehicle, loosen the clamp on the shifter rod. Make sure the shifter lever moves freely on the shifter rod.

3. Remove the shifter knob and the boot.

4. Position the gauge alignment tool VW–3104 on the shifting mechanism

(lock it in place). Tighten the clamp bolt to 19 ft. lbs. (25 Nm) and remove the tool.

5. When the shifter is in first gear, dimension **a** should be 0.040–0.060 inches (1–1.5mm) and the gears must engage smoothly when the engine is running.

6. If there is an eccentric adjustment, it can be used to make a fine adjustment of dimension **A** with the shifter in first gear.

1995–99 Cabrio, 1993–99 Golf and Jetta

1. Remove the knob from the know and the boot from the shifter. This will allow you access to the adjustment collar.

2. To remove slop from the shifter, select first gear.

3. The clearance between the shift lever adjustment collar tab and the side of the lever housing should be no greater than 1⁄16 of an inch.

4. If the clearance is greater than 1⁄16 of an inch, loosen the adjusting collar and rotate the collar until the proper clearance is achieved.

5. Tighten the clamping bolt and then install the shifter boot and knob.

Halfshafts

REMOVAL & INSTALLATION

Cabriolet

▶ See Figures 13 thru 19

⁑ WARNING

When loosening or tightening an axle nut, make sure the vehicle is on the ground. The amount of torque required could cause the vehicle to fall off jackstands.

➡ **When removing the right axle shaft, you must detach the exhaust pipe from the manifold and the transaxle bracket. Be sure to buy a new exhaust flange gasket.**

1. With the vehicle on the ground, remove the front axle nut.
2. Disconnect the negative battery cable.
3. Raise and safely support vehicle and remove the front wheels.
4. Remove the ball joint clamping bolt and push the control arm down, away from the ball joint.
5. If necessary, carefully loosen the halfshaft in the hub using a brass drift and hammer.
6. Remove the socket head bolts from the transaxle drive flange.

Fig. 13 Using a 12 point bit to remove the bolts from the inner constant velocity (CV) joint

Fig. 14 Remove the front axle nut with the vehicle on the ground

Fig. 15 Removing the ball joint clamping bolt

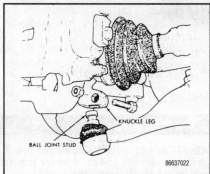

Fig. 16 Push the control arm down, away from the ball joint, after removing the clamping bolt

Fig. 17 If necessary, carefully loosen the halfshaft in the hub using a brass drift and hammer

Fig. 18 Removing the socket head bolts from the drive flange

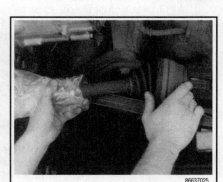

Fig. 19 The halfshafts can be wrapped in plastic to prevent damage to the boots and joints

7. Remove the halfshaft from the drive flange and support it below the flange. Do not let it hang by the outer CV-joint, or the joint may fall apart.

8. Remove the assembly from the vehicle.

To install:

9. Fit the halfshaft to the drive flange and install the bolts. It is not necessary to tighten them yet.

10. Apply a thread locking compound to the outer ¼ inch of the spline. Slip the spline through the hub and loosely install a new axle nut.

11. Assemble the ball joint and tighten the nut and bolt to 37 ft. lbs. (50 Nm).

12. Install the wheel and hold it to keep the axle from turning. Tighten the drive flange bolts to 33 ft. lbs. (45 Nm).

13. With the vehicle on the ground, tighten the axle nut to 195 ft. lbs. (265 Nm) on Golf and Jetta, or 175 ft. lbs. (240 Nm) on other models.

14. Connect the negative battery cable.

Fox

> ### ✳✳ WARNING
>
> **When loosening or tightening an axle nut, make sure the vehicle is on the ground. The amount of torque required could cause the vehicle to fall off jackstands.**

➡**When removing the right axle shaft, you must detach the exhaust pipe from the manifold and the transaxle bracket. Be sure to buy a new exhaust flange gasket.**

1. With the car on the ground, remove the front axle nut.

➡**If necessary, use a long breaker bar with a length of pipe as an extension.**

2. Disconnect the negative battery cable.

3. Raise and support the front of the vehicle.

4. Remove the socket head bolts retaining the axle shaft to the transaxle.

5. Pull the transaxle side of the driveshaft out and up and place it on the top of the transaxle.

6. Pull the axle shaft from the steering knuckle.

To install:

7. Installation is the reverse of removal. Tighten the axle shaft flange bolts to 33 ft. lbs. (45 Nm). The axle nut should be tightened to 145 ft. lbs. (198 Nm) for M18 nuts, or 170 ft. lbs. (231 Nm) for M20 nuts.

1990–92 Golf and Jetta

> ### ✳✳ WARNING
>
> **When loosening or tightening an axle nut, make sure the vehicle is on the ground. The amount of torque required could cause the vehicle to fall off jackstands.**

The torque required to loosen the front axle nut is high enough to make the vehicle fall off of jack stands. Make sure the vehicle is on the ground when loosening or tightening the front axle nut.

1. With the vehicle on the ground, remove the front axle nut.

2. Raise and safely support vehicle and remove the front wheels.

3. Remove the ball joint clamping bolt and push the control arm down, away from the ball joint.

4. Remove the socket head bolts from the transaxle drive flange.

5. Remove the halfshaft from the drive flange and support it below the flange. Do not let it hang by the outer CV-joint or the joint may fall apart.

6. Push the halfshaft out of the hub. A wheel puller may be required.

To install:

7. Fit the halfshaft to the drive flange and install the bolts. It is not necessary to tighten them yet.

8. Apply a thread locking compound to the outer ¼inch of the spline. Slip the spline through the hub and loosely install a new axle nut.

9. Assemble the ball joint and tighten the nut and bolt to 37 ft. lbs. (50 Nm).

10. Install the wheel and hold it to keep the axle from turning. Tighten the drive flange bolts to 33 ft. lbs. (45 Nm).

11. With the vehicle on the ground, tighten the axle nut to 175 ft. lbs. (240 Nm) or Cabriolet or 195 ft. lbs. (265 Nm) on Golf and Jetta.

1995–99 Cabrio, 1993–99 Golf and Jetta

Three suspension systems offered on the A3 platform. A base suspension, plus suspension, and triple roller joint type. An easy way to determine which suspension you have is to note the type of nuts used to fasten the inner Constant Velocity joint to the inner transaxle drive flange. On the base suspension a standard six point hex nut was used. The plus suspension had twelve point self-locking nut. Triple-roller joint style systems are used on vehicles with a four cylinder power plant and an automatic transmission.

BASE SUSPENSION

> ### ✳✳ WARNING
>
> **When loosening or tightening an axle nut, make sure the vehicle is on the ground. The amount of torque required could cause the vehicle to fall off jackstands.**

1. Pry off the dust caps and loosen the axle nut. Do not remove the nut at this point.

2. Raise and support the vehicle on jack stands.

3. Matchmark the ball joints position in the control arm and then remove the ball joints mounting bolts.

4. Remove the bolts that hold the inner Constant Velocity (CV) joint to the transaxle drive flange.

5. Remove the axle shaft nut from the drive shaft.

6. Pull the drive shaft out of the wheel hub.

To install:

7. Installation is the reverse of removal.

8. Tighten the outer CV joint to wheel hub bolt to 195 ft. lbs. (265 Nm).

9. Tighten the ball joint to control arm bolts to 26 ft. lbs. (35 Nm).

10. Tighten the inner CV joint to drive flange bolts to 33 ft. lbs. (45 Nm).

PLUS SUSPENSION

> ### ✳✳ WARNING
>
> **When loosening or tightening an axle nut, make sure the vehicle is on the ground. The amount of torque required could cause the vehicle to fall off jackstands.**

1. Pry off the dust caps and loosen the axle nut. Do not remove the nut at this point.

2. Raise and support the vehicle on jack stands.

3. Matchmark the ball joints position in the control arm and then remove the ball joints mounting bolts.

4. Remove the bolts that hold the inner Constant Velocity (CV) joint to the transaxle drive flange. This will require a 12 point socket.

5. Remove the axle shaft nut from the drive shaft.

6. Pull the drive shaft out of the wheel hub.

➡**You may have to press the halfshaft out of the hub.**

> ### ✳✳ WARNING
>
> **Cover all exposed joints to avoid contamination from entering the joint which will lead to joint failure.**

To install:

➡**Two types of hubs were used on this system. The standard (non-modified) hub used a thread sealer such as Loctite®. Later a modified hub was installed with a stronger hub nut and modified splines. This hub does not require a thread sealant. Please note the following torque specifications below.**

7. Tighten the outer CV joint to wheel hub bolt to 148 ft. lbs. (200 Nm) on vehicles with a modified hub.

8. Tighten the outer CV joint to wheel hub bolt to 66 ft. lbs. (90 Nm) on vehicles with a modified hub.

9. Tighten the ball joint to control arm bolts to 26 ft. lbs. (35 Nm).
10. Tighten the inner CV joint to drive flange bolts to 33 ft. lbs. (45 Nm).

TRIPLE ROLLER JOINT

❊❊❊ WARNING

When loosening or tightening an axle nut, make sure the vehicle is on the ground. The amount of torque required could cause the vehicle to fall off jackstands.

1. Pry off the dust caps and loosen the axle nut. Do not remove the nut at this point.
2. Install an engine support brace across the top of the engine.
3. Remove the bolt from the rear transaxle mount.
4. Fully support the engine and transaxle with the engine hoist.
5. Raise and support the vehicle on jack stands.
6. Matchmark the ball joints position in the control arm and then remove the ball joints mounting bolts.
7. Remove the bolts that hold the inner Constant Velocity (CV) joint to the transaxle drive flange. This will require a 12 point socket.
8. Remove the axle shaft nut from the spindle.
9. Push the engine/transaxle assembly forward and re-support it.
10. Remove the axle from the car by positioning the hub out and slightly to the left.

To install:

11. Installation is the reverse of removal.
12. Tighten the ball joint to control arm bolts to 26 ft. lbs. (35 Nm).
13. Tighten the CV joint to drive flange bolts to 33 ft. lbs. (45 Nm).
14. Outer CV joint to wheel hub bolt to 195 ft. lbs. (265 Nm).

CV-JOINT AND BOOT OVERHAUL

The constant velocity joints (CV-joints) can be disassembled for cleaning and inspection but they cannot be repaired. All parts are machined to a matched tolerance and the entire CV-joint must be replaced as a unit. On Golf and Jetta, the CV-joints are different on the left and right sides and cannot be interchanged.

1. Raise and safely support the vehicle and remove the halfshaft.
2. Pry open and remove the boot clamps with a pair of wire cutters.
3. With the halfshaft securely clamped in a vise, the outer CV-joint can be removed by sharply rapping out on the joint with a plastic hammer. The joint will snap off of the circlip and slide off the axle.
4. To remove the inner joint, remove the circlip from the center and slide the joint off the axle.
5. Both boots can be removed after removing the CV-joint

To install:

6. Always replace both circlips and make sure the CV-joint is clean before installation. Wrap a piece of black electrical tape around the shaft splines and slip the inner clamp and the boot onto the shaft.
7. Remove the tape and install the dished washer with the concave side out so it acts as a spring pushing the CV-joint out. On the outer joint, install the thrust washer and a new circlip.
8. To install the outer joint, place it onto the spline and carefully tap straight in on the end with a plastic hammer. The joint will click into place over the circlip.
9. To install the inner joint, slide it onto the spline and push in enough to allow the circlip to fit into the groove in the axle shaft.
10. Pack the CV-joint with special CV-joint grease. DO NOT use any other type of grease.
11. Pack any remaining grease into the boot and install the clamps on the outer boot.

CLUTCH

▶ See Figure 20

Fig. 20 View of a typical VW clutch

❊❊❊ CAUTION

The clutch driven disc may contain asbestos, which has been determined to be a cancer causing agent. Never clean clutch surfaces with compressed air! Avoid inhaling any dust from any clutch surface! When cleaning clutch surfaces, use a commercially available brake cleaning fluid.

Understanding the Clutch

❊❊❊ CAUTION

The clutch driven disc may contain asbestos, which has been determined to be a cancer causing agent. Never clean clutch surfaces with compressed air! Avoid inhaling any dust from any clutch surface! When cleaning clutch surfaces, use a commercially available brake cleaning fluid.

The purpose of the clutch is to disconnect and connect engine power at the transaxle. A vehicle at rest requires a lot of engine torque to get all that weight moving. An internal combustion engine does not develop a high starting torque (unlike steam engines) so it must be allowed to operate without any load until it builds up enough torque to move the vehicle. Torque increases with engine rpm. The clutch allows the engine to build up torque by physically disconnecting the engine from the transaxle, relieving the engine of any load or resistance.

The transfer of engine power to the transaxle (the load) must be smooth and gradual; if it weren't, drive line components would wear out or break quickly. This gradual power transfer is made possible by gradually releasing the clutch pedal. The clutch disc and pressure plate are the connecting link between the engine and transaxle. When the clutch pedal is released, the disc and plate contact each other (the clutch is engaged) physically joining the engine and transaxle. When the pedal is pushed inward, the disc and plate separate (the clutch is disengaged) disconnecting the engine from the transaxle.

Most clutches utilize a single plate, dry friction disc with a diaphragm-style spring pressure plate. The clutch disc has a splined hub which attaches the disc to the input shaft. The disc has friction material where it contacts the flywheel and pressure plate. Torsion springs on the disc help absorb engine torque pulses. The pressure plate applies pressure to the clutch disc, holding it tight against the surface of the flywheel. The clutch operating mechanism consists of a release bearing, fork and cylinder assembly.

The release fork and actuating linkage transfer pedal motion to the release bearing. In the engaged position (pedal released) the diaphragm spring holds the pressure plate against the clutch disc, so engine torque is transmitted to the input shaft. When the clutch pedal is depressed, the release bearing pushes the diaphragm spring center toward the flywheel. The diaphragm spring pivots the fulcrum, relieving the load on the pressure plate. Steel spring straps riveted to the clutch cover lift the pressure plate from the clutch disc, disengaging the engine drive from the transaxle and enabling the gears to be changed.

The clutch is operating properly if:

1. It will stall the engine when released with the vehicle held stationary.

2. The shift lever can be moved freely between 1st and reverse gears when the vehicle is stationary and the clutch disengaged.

Driven Disc and Pressure Plate

REMOVAL & INSTALLATION

▶ **See Figures 21 thru 29**

The clutch driven disc contains asbestos, which has been determined to be a cancer causing agent. Never clean clutch surfaces with compressed air! Avoid inhaling any dust from any clutch surface! When cleaning clutch surfaces, use a commercially available brake cleaning fluid.

This type of clutch is similar to a motorcycle clutch. The pressure plate is bolted to the crankshaft and the flywheel bolted to the pressure plate. The clutch release lever and bearing are in the left end of the transaxle. The clutch is actuated by a release rod which passes through a hollow transaxle shaft. The throwout bearing is in the transaxle and lubricated with transaxle oil.

➡**A special tool VW 547 is required to center the clutch disc.**

1. Remove the transaxle.
2. Attach a toothed flywheel locking device and gradually loosen the flywheel to pressure plate bolts one or two turns at a time in a crisscross pattern to prevent distortion.
3. Remove the flywheel and the clutch disc.
4. Use a small pry bar to remove the release plate retaining ring. Remove the release plate.
5. Lock the pressure plate in place and unbolt it from the crankshaft. Loosen the bolts one or two turns at a time in a crisscross pattern to prevent distortion.

Fig. 21 Remove the bolts from the fly-wheel

Fig. 22 Clutch friction plate

Fig. 23 Flywheel, clutch friction plate (clutch disc), and pressure plate

Fig. 24 Close up of the clutch disc. Notice the criss-cross fiber re-enforcement in the disc's friction surface. This clutch design reduces clatter upon engagement

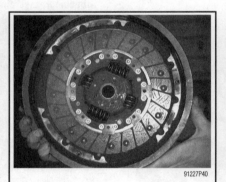

Fig. 25 Clutch disc positioned inside the flywheel

Fig. 26 Release plate and spring clip

Fig. 27 Squeeze the spring clip to remove it from the release plate

Fig. 28 Pressure plate to crankshaft bolts

Fig. 29 Match the dowel pin with the edge of the pressure plate

To install:

6. Use new bolts to attach the pressure plate to the crankshaft. Use a thread locking compound and tighten the bolts in a diagonal pattern to 22 ft. lbs. (30 Nm) plus ¼ of a turn.

7. LIGHTLY lubricate the clutch disc splines, release plate contact surface, and pushrod socket with multipurpose grease. Install the release plate, retaining ring, and clutch disc.

8. Use special tool VW 547 or equivalent to center the clutch disc.

9. Install the flywheel, tightening the bolts one or two turns at a time in a crisscross pattern to prevent distortion. Tighten the bolts to 15 ft. lbs. (20 Nm).

10. Install the transaxle.

ADJUSTMENTS

All VW models are equipped with a self-adjusting clutch cable. The VR-6 has a hydraulic clutch which is also self-adjusting.

Master Cylinder

REMOVAL & INSTALLATION

▶ **See Figure 30**

1. Remove the negative battery cable.
2. Detach the brake line from the master cylinder.
3. Cap off the open line.
4. Detach and cap off the supply line at the master cylinder.
5. Disconnect the relay plate from the left retainer.
6. Detach the pedal cluster protective plate.
7. Detach the master cylinder push rod from the pedal cluster.
8. Remove the mounting bracket support.
9. Remove the master cylinder.

To install:

10. Installation is the reverse of removal.
11. Do not forget to install the retainer on the master cylinder push rod.
12. Engage the retainer by depressing the clutch pedal
13. Thoroughly bleed the clutch master cylinder

Slave Cylinder

REMOVAL & INSTALLATION

1. Disconnect the negative battery cable.
2. Raise and safely support the vehicle.
3. Disconnect the hydraulic line fitting(s) for the clutch slave cylinder.

Fig. 30 View of the brake/clutch master cylinder

91229P01

4. From inside the transaxles bellhousing, remove the 3 clutch slave cylinder retaining bolts and remove the clutch slave cylinder.
5. Remove the clutch slave cylinder.

To install:

6. Installation is the reverse of removal.
7. Reconnect the negative battery cable.
8. Bleed the hydraulic clutch system, if required.
9. Check for proper clutch operation.

HYDRAULIC SYSTEM BLEEDING

1. Disconnect the negative battery cable.
2. Clean the top of the brake master cylinder fluid reservoir before opening it.
3. Be sure that there is adequate fluid in the clutch master cylinder fluid reservoir before attempting to bleed the system.
4. Check the fluid level throughout the bleeding procedure.
5. Connect a hose to the bleeder valve fitting on the clutch slave cylinder.
6. Submerge the other end of the hose into a container of clean brake fluid.
7. Push the clutch pedal down while opening the bleeder on the clutch slave cylinder.
8. Watch for air bubbles escaping from the hydraulic system.
9. Close the bleeder before releasing the clutch pedal.
10. Repeat the procedure until no more air bubbles are seen.
11. Reinstall the rubber inspection cover to the bell housing.
12. Top off the clutch master cylinder fluid reservoir and install the diaphragm and cap securely.
13. Reconnect the negative battery cable.
14. Check the clutch for proper operation.

AUTOMATIC TRANSAXLE

Fluid Pan

REMOVAL & INSTALLATION

1. If equipped, remove the drain plug and let the fluid drain into a pan. If the pan has no drain plug, loosen the pan bolts until a corner of the pan can be lowered to drain the fluid.
2. Remove the pan bolts and take off the pan.
3. Discard the old gasket and clean the pan out. Be very careful not to get any threads or lint from rags into the pan.
4. The manufacturer recommends that the filter needn't be replaced unless the fluid is very dirty and burnt smelling. When replacing the strainer be careful, the specified torque for the strainer screws is only 24 inch lbs. (3 Nm).
5. Replace the pan with a new gasket and tighten the bolts, in a criss-cross pattern, to 15 ft. lbs. (20 Nm).
6. Using a long necked funnel, pour in 2.5 qts. (2.3L) of Dexron®II automatic transaxle fluid through the dipstick tube. Start the engine and shift through all the transaxle ranges with the car stationary. Check the level on the dipstick with the lever in Neutral. It should be up to the lower end of the dipstick. The difference between marks is 1 pint (0.23L). Add fluid as necessary, drive the car until it is warmed up and recheck the level.

Understanding the Automatic Transaxle

The automatic transaxle allows engine torque and power to be transmitted to the front wheels within a narrow range of engine operating speeds. It will allow the engine to turn fast enough to produce plenty of power and torque at very low speeds, while keeping it at a sensible rpm at high vehicle speeds (and it does this job without driver assistance). The transaxle uses a light fluid as the medium for the transmission of power. This fluid also works in the operation of various hydraulic control circuits and as a lubricant. Because the transaxle fluid performs all of these functions, trouble within the unit can easily travel from one part to another. For this reason, and because of the complexity and unusual operating principles of the transaxle, a very sound understanding of the basic principles of operation will simplify troubleshooting.

Neutral Safety Switch / Back-up Light Switch

The combination neutral start and backup light switch is mounted inside the shifter housing. The starter should operate in Park or Neutral only. Adjust the switch by moving it on its mounts. The back-up lights should only come on when the shift selector is in the Reverse position.

Automatic Transaxle Assembly

REMOVAL & INSTALLATION

Cabriolet

1. Disconnect both battery cables.
2. Withdraw the speedometer drive gear, then plug the hole in the transaxle.
3. With the vehicle on the ground, remove the front axle nuts.
4. Raise and safely support the vehicle, then remove the front wheels. Connect the engine sling tool VW–10–222A or equivalent sling, to the cylinder head and just take the weight of the engine off the mounts. On 16-valve engines, the idle stabilizer valve must be removed to attach the tool. Do not try to support the engine from below.
5. Remove the driver's side rear transaxle mount and support bracket.
6. On Golf and Jetta, remove the front mount bolts from the transaxle and from the body and remove the mount as a complete assembly.
7. Remove the selector and accelerator cables from the transaxle lever but leave them attached to the bracket. Remove the bracket assembly to save the adjustment.
8. Remove the halfshafts.
9. Remove the heat shield and brackets and remove the starter. On Cabriolet, the front mount comes off with the starter.
10. Remove the bellhousing lower cover and turn the engine as needed to remove the torque converter-to-flywheel bolts.
11. Remove the remaining transaxle mounts and, on Golf and Jetta, the subframe bolts and allow the subframe to hang free.
12. Support the transaxle with a jack and remove the remaining engine-to-transaxle bolts. Be careful to secure the torque converter so it does not fall out of the transaxle.
13. Carefully lower the transaxle from the vehicle.
To install:
14. When reinstalling, make sure the torque converter is fully seated on the pump shaft splines. The converter should be recessed into the bell housing and turn by hand. Keep checking that it still turns while drawing the engine and transaxle together with the bolts.
15. Install the engine-to-transaxle bolts and tighten to 55 ft. lbs. (75 Nm).
16. Install all mount and subframe bolts before tightening any of them. Tighten the bolts starting at the rear and work forward. Tighten the smaller bolts to 25 ft. lbs. (34 Nm) and the larger bolts to 58 ft. lbs. (80 Nm). Remove the lifting equipment when all mounts are installed.
17. Install the torque converter-to-flywheel bolts and tighten them to 26 ft. lbs. (35 Nm).
18. Install the starter and tighten the bolts to 14 ft. lbs. (20 Nm). Install heat shields.
19. Make sure the halfshaft splines are clean and apply a thread locking compound to the splines before sliding it into the hub. Connect the halfshafts to the drive flanges and tighten the bolts to 33 ft. lbs. (45 Nm). Install new axle nuts, but do not fully tighten them until the vehicle is on the ground.
20. If removed, fit the ball joints to the control arm and tighten the clamping bolt to 37 ft. lbs. (50 Nm).
21. Connect and adjust the shift linkage as required.
22. When assembly is complete and the vehicle is on its wheels, tighten the axle nuts to 195 ft. lbs. (265 Nm).
23. Unplug the hole in the transaxle, and insert the speedometer drive gear.
24. Connect the battery cables.

1990–92 Golf and Jetta

1. If equipped with electronically theft-protected radio, obtain the security code before disconnecting the battery.
2. Disconnect the battery and the speedometer drive and plug the hole in the transaxle.

3. On Golf and Jetta, with the vehicle on the ground, remove the front axle nuts.

➡**When loosening or tightening an axle nut, make sure the vehicle is on the ground. Axle nut torque is high enough that loosen it with the vehicle on jack stands may cause the vehicle to fall.**

4. Raise and safely support the vehicle and remove the front wheels. Connect the engine sling tool VW–10–222A or equivalent, to the cylinder head and just take the weight of the engine off the mounts. On 16 valve engine, the idle stabilizer valve must be removed to attach the tool. Do not try to support the engine from below.
5. Remove the driver's side rear transaxle mount and support bracket.
6. On Golf and Jetta, remove the front mount bolts from the transaxle and from the body and remove the mount as a complete assembly.
7. Remove the selector and accelerator cables from the transaxle lever but leave them attached to the bracket. Remove the bracket assembly to save the adjustment.
8. Remove the halfshafts.
9. Remove the heat shield and brackets and remove the starter. On Cabriolet, the front mount comes off with the starter.
10. Remove the bellhousing lower cover and turn the engine as needed to remove the torque converter-to-flywheel bolts.
11. Remove the remaining transaxle mounts and, on Golf and Jetta, the subframe bolts and allow the subframe to hang free.
12. Support the transaxle with a jack and remove the remaining engine-to-transaxle bolts. Be careful to secure the torque converter so it does not fall out of the transaxle.
13. Carefully lower the transaxle from the vehicle.
To install:
14. When reinstalling, make sure the torque converter is fully seated on the pump shaft splines. The converter should be recessed into the bell housing and turn by hand. Keep checking that it still turns while drawing the engine and transaxle together with the bolts.
15. Install the engine-to-transaxle bolts and tighten to 55 ft. lbs. (75 Nm).
16. Install all mount and subframe bolts before tightening any on them. Tighten the bolts starting at the rear and work forward. Tighten the smaller bolts to 25 ft. lbs. (34 Nm) and the larger bolts to 58 ft. lbs. (80 Nm). Remove the lifting equipment when all mounts are installed.
17. Install the torque converter–to–flywheel bolts and tighten them to 26 ft. lbs. (35 Nm).
18. Install the starter and tighten the bolts to 14 ft. lbs. (20 Nm). Install the heat shields.
19. Make sure the halfshaft splines are clean and apply a thread locking compound to the splines before sliding it into the hub. Connect the halfshafts to the drive flanges and tighten the bolts to 33 ft. lbs. (45 Nm). Install new axle nuts but do not fully tighten them until the vehicle is on the ground.
20. If removed, fit the ball joints to the control arm and tighten the clamping bolt to 37 ft. lbs. (50 Nm).
21. Connect and adjust the shift linkage as required.
22. When assembly is complete and the vehicle is on its wheels, tighten the axle nuts to 195 ft. lbs. (265 Nm) on Golf and Jetta or 175 ft. lbs. (240 Nm) on Cabriolet.

1995–99 Cabrio, 1993–99 Golf and Jetta

1. Disconnect the battery cables.
2. Remove the battery.
3. Remove all electrical connections and vacuum lines from the transaxle.
4. On 6 cylinder models remove the multi-function transaxle range switch.
5. Position the selector lever to the Park position.
6. Detach the selector lever cable.
7. Remove the selector lever cover. Remove the selector lever cable circlip. Remove the cable.
8. Support the engine from the top with the appropriate brace.
9. Remove the power steering hose support bracket.
10. On vehicles equipped with the VR-6, remove the electrical connector from the cooling fan.
11. Remove the bolt from the front engine mount.
12. Detach the mount from the engine block by removing the mounting bolts.
13. Remove the coolant recovery tank.

14. Completely remove the left rear engine mount.
15. Remove the transmission mounting bolts at the top only.
16. Remove the protective shield from the automatic transmission fluid (ATF) pan.
17. On VR-6 engines, remove the right side accessory drive belt shield.
18. Remove the torque converter mounting nuts.
19. Remove the vibration damper from the 6 cylinder engine.
20. Detach the drive axles from the transaxle.
21. Support the right side axle.
22. Remove the left front wheel.
23. Position the steering wheel to full right lock.
24. Matchmark the position of the ball joint in relation to the lower control arm.
25. Remove the ball joint mounting bolts.
26. Pull the ball joint from the control arm.

➡**The left hand drive axle must be removed if the vehicle is equipped triple-roller type CV joints.**

27. Support the transmission from the under side using a special transmission jack or the proper jack adapter.
28. Remove the bolts from the lower engine/transmission mounting bolts.
29. Pivot the engine forward using a suitable jack/support.
30. Pull the engine from the transmission.
31. Lower the engine with the support jack.
32. Lower the transaxle. You may have to re-position the transaxle several times to ease removal.

➡**Be sure to secure the torque converter to the transaxle.**

To install:
33. Install the transaxle assemble in the reverse order of removal. Tighten the fasteners to the following specifications.
34. The front engine mount should be secured at a tighten of 44 ft. lbs. (60 Nm).
35. When installing the drive axle to the transaxle flange tighten the bolts to 33 ft. lbs. (45 Nm).
36. The torque converter to flex plate (drive plate) should be tightened to 44 ft. lbs. (60 Nm).
37. After installing the left motor mount, tighten the mounting bolt(s) to 44 ft. lbs. (60 Nm).

38. Ball joint to control arm nut(s) should be tightened to 26 ft. lbs. (35 Nm).

Halfshafts

REMOVAL & INSTALLATION

▶ **See Figure 13**

➡**The torque required to loosen the front axle nut is high enough to make the vehicle fall off of jack stands. Make sure the vehicle is on the ground when loosening or tightening the front axle nut.**

1. With the vehicle on the ground, remove the front axle nut.
2. Raise and safely support vehicle and remove the front wheels.
3. Remove the ball joint clamping bolt and push the control arm down, away from the ball joint.
4. Remove the socket head bolts from the transaxle drive flange.
5. Remove the halfshaft from the drive flange and support it below the flange. Do not let it hang by the outer CV-joint or the joint may fall apart.
6. Push the halfshaft out of the hub. A wheel puller may be required.

To install:
7. Fit the halfshaft to the drive flange and install the bolts. It is not necessary to tighten them yet.
8. Apply a thread locking compound to the outer ¼ inch of the spline. Slip the spline through the hub and loosely install a new axle nut.
9. Assemble the ball joint and tighten the nut and bolt to 37 ft. lbs. (50 Nm).
10. Install the wheel and hold it to keep the axle from turning. Tighten the drive flange bolts to 33 ft. lbs. (45 Nm).
11. With the vehicle on the ground, tighten the axle nut to 175 ft. lbs. (240 Nm) or Cabriolet or 195 ft. lbs. (265 Nm) on Golf and Jetta

CV-JOINT AND BOOT OVERHAUL

Refer to the procedure for CV-joint overhaul under manual transaxle in this section.

TORQUE SPECIFICATIONS

Component	English Specifications	Metric Specifications
Axle hub nuts		
Cabriolet	170 ft. lbs.	230 Nm
Cabrio	195 ft. lbs.	265 Nm
Fox	170 ft. lbs.	230 Nm
Axle shaft to transaxle bolt		
Cabriolet	32 ft. lbs.	43 Nm
Cabrio	32 ft. lbs.	43 Nm
1993-99 Golf		
Balance weight mount bolt		
Cabrio	22 ft. lbs.	30 Nm
1993-99 Golf	22 ft. lbs.	30 Nm
Clutch cover-plate bolt		
Cabriolet	15 ft. lbs.	20 Nm
1990-92 Golf	15 ft. lbs.	20 Nm
Clutch master cylinder mounting bolt		
Cabrio	18 ft. lbs.	25 Nm
1993-99 Golf	18 ft. lbs.	25 Nm
Drive shaft flange		
Cabriolet	32 ft. lbs.	43 Nm
1990-92 Golf	32 ft.lbs.	43 Nm
Drive shaft to transaxle		
Fox	33 ft. lbs.	45 Nm
Engine mount to subframe		
Cabrio	37 ft. lbs.	50 Nm
1993-99 Golf	37 ft. lbs.	50 Nm
Engine bracket bolt		
1993-99 Golf (right)	44 ft. lbs.	60 Nm
Flywheel bolt(s)		
Cabriolet	15 ft. lbs.	20 Nm
Cabrio	44 ft. lbs.①	60 Nm①
1990-92 Golf	44 ft. lbs.①	60 Nm①
Gear shift cable bolt		
All	18 ft. lbs.	25 Nm
Pressure plate bolt		
Cabriolet	22 ft. lbs.①	30 Nm①
Cabrio		
Cable style clutch	22 ft. lbs.①	30 Nm①
Hydraulic clutch	15 ft. lbs.	20 Nm
Fox	20 ft. lbs.	25 Nm
1990-92 Golf	22 ft. lbs.①	30 Nm①

91227T01

TORQUE SPECIFICATIONS

Component	English Specifications	Metric Specifications
Starter bolt		
Cabriolet	44 ft. lbs.	60 Nm
Cabrio		
Cable style clutch	44 ft. lbs.	60 Nm
Hydraulic clutch	18 ft. lbs.	25 Nm
1990-92 Golf	44 ft. lbs.	60 Nm
Transaxle to engine bolt		
Cabriolet	55 ft. lbs.	75 Nm
Cabrio		
Cable style clutch	26 ft. lbs.	35 Nm
Hydraulic clutch	18 ft. lbs.	25 Nm
Fox	40 ft. lbs.	55 Nm
1990-92 Golf	55 ft. lbs.	75 Nm
Transaxle		
1993-99 Golf (front mount)	44 ft. lbs.	60 Nm

① Turn an additional 90 degrees

91227T02

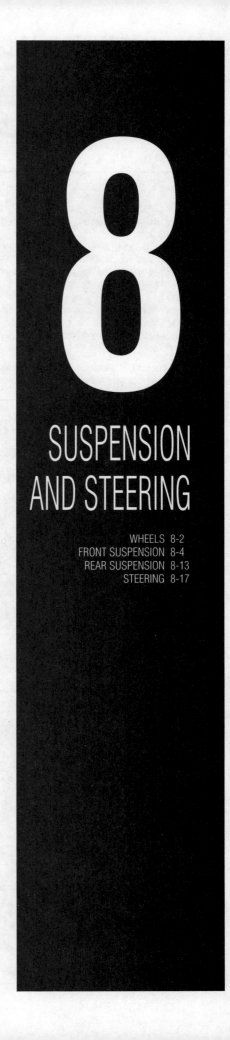

8

SUSPENSION AND STEERING

WHEELS

Wheels

REMOVAL & INSTALLATION

▶ **See Figures 1, 2 and 3**

1. Park the vehicle on a level surface.
2. Remove the jack, tire iron and, if necessary, the spare tire from their storage compartments.
3. Check the owner's manual or refer to Section 1 of this manual for the jacking points on your vehicle. Then, place the jack in the proper position.
4. If equipped with lug nut trim caps, remove them by either unscrewing or pulling them off the lug nuts, as appropriate. Consult the owner's manual, if necessary.
5. If equipped with a wheel cover or hub cap, insert the tapered end of the tire iron in the groove and pry off the cover.
6. Apply the parking brake and block the diagonally opposite wheel with a wheel chock or two.

➡**Wheel chocks may be purchased at your local auto parts store, or a block of wood cut into wedges may be used. If possible, keep one or**

Fig. 1 Break the lug bolts/nuts free while the vehicle is on the ground. Do not completely remove the lug bolts/nuts until the wheel is off the ground

Fig. 2 Once the vehicle is off the ground, remove the lugs

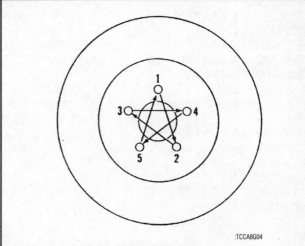

Fig. 3 Typical wheel lug tightening sequence

two of the chocks in your tire storage compartment, in case any of the tires has to be removed on the side of the road.

7. If equipped with an automatic transmission/transaxle, place the selector lever in **P** or Park; with a manual transmission/transaxle, place the shifter in Reverse.
8. With the tires still on the ground, use the tire iron/wrench to break the lug nuts loose.

➡**If a nut is stuck, never use heat to loosen it or damage to the wheel and bearings may occur. If the nuts are seized, one or two heavy hammer blows directly on the end of the bolt usually loosens the rust. Be careful, as continued pounding will likely damage the brake drum or rotor.**

9. Using the jack, raise the vehicle until the tire is clear of the ground. Support the vehicle safely using jackstands.
10. Remove the lug nuts, then remove the tire and wheel assembly.@INSTALL:To install:
11. Make sure the wheel and hub mating surfaces, as well as the wheel lug studs, are clean and free of all foreign material. Always remove rust from the wheel mounting surface and the brake rotor or drum. Failure to do so may cause the lug nuts to loosen in service.
12. Install the tire and wheel assembly and hand-tighten the lug nuts.
13. Using the tire wrench, tighten all the lug nuts, in a crisscross pattern, until they are snug.
14. Raise the vehicle and withdraw the jackstand, then lower the vehicle.
15. Using a torque wrench, tighten the lug nuts in a crisscross pattern to 81 ft. lbs. (110 Nm). Check your owner's manual or refer to Section 1 of this manual for the proper tightening sequence.

❋❋ WARNING

Do not overtighten the lug nuts, as this may cause the wheel studs to stretch or the brake disc (rotor) to warp.

16. If so equipped, install the wheel cover or hub cap. Make sure the valve stem protrudes through the proper opening before tapping the wheel cover into position.
17. If equipped, install the lug nut trim caps by pushing them or screwing them on, as applicable.
18. Remove the jack from under the vehicle, and place the jack and tire iron/wrench in their storage compartments. Remove the wheel chock(s).
19. If you have removed a flat or damaged tire, place it in the storage compartment of the vehicle and take it to your local repair station to have it fixed or replaced as soon as possible.

INSPECTION

Inspect the tires for lacerations, puncture marks, nails and other sharp objects. Repair or replace as necessary. Also check the tires for treadwear and air pressure as outlined in Check the wheel assemblies for dents, cracks, rust and metal fatigue. Repair or replace as necessary.

Wheel Lug Studs

REMOVAL & INSTALLATION

With Disc Brakes

▶ See Figures 4, 5 and 6

1. Raise and support the appropriate end of the vehicle safely using jackstands, then remove the wheel.
2. Remove the brake pads and caliper. Support the caliper aside using wire or a coat hanger. For details, please refer to Section 9 of this manual.
3. Remove the outer wheel bearing and lift off the rotor. For details on wheel bearing removal, installation and adjustment, please refer to Section 1 of this manual.
4. Properly support the rotor using press bars, then drive the stud out using an arbor press.

➡️If a press is not available, CAREFULLY drive the old stud out using a blunt drift. MAKE SURE the rotor is properly and evenly supported or it may be damaged.

To install:

5. Clean the stud hole with a wire brush and start the new stud with a hammer and drift pin. Do not use any lubricant or thread sealer.
6. Finish installing the stud with the press.

➡️If a press is not available, start the lug stud through the bore in the hub, then position about 4 flat washers over the stud and thread the lug nut. Hold the hub/rotor while tightening the lug nut, and the stud should be drawn into position. MAKE SURE THE STUD IS FULLY SEATED, then remove the lug nut and washers.

7. Install the rotor and adjust the wheel bearings.
8. Install the brake caliper and pads.
9. Install the wheel, then remove the jackstands and carefully lower the vehicle.
10. Tighten the lug nuts to the proper torque.

With Drum Brakes

▶ See Figures 7, 8 and 9

1. Raise the vehicle and safely support it with jackstands, then remove the wheel.
2. Remove the brake drum.
3. If necessary to provide clearance, remove the brake shoes, as outlined in Section 9 of this manual.
4. Using a large C-clamp and socket, press the stud from the axle flange.
5. Coat the serrated part of the stud with liquid soap and place it into the hole.

To install:

6. Position about 4 flat washers over the stud and thread the lug nut. Hold the flange while tightening the lug nut, and the stud should be drawn into position. MAKE SURE THE STUD IS FULLY SEATED, then remove the lug nut and washers.
7. If applicable, install the brake shoes.
8. Install the brake drum.
9. Install the wheel, then remove the jackstands and carefully lower the vehicle.
10. Tighten the lug nuts to the proper torque.

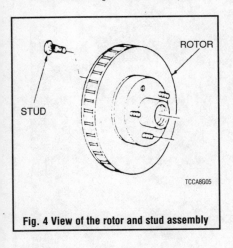

Fig. 4 View of the rotor and stud assembly

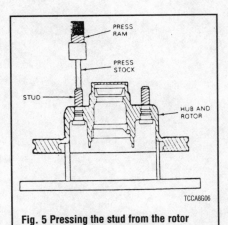

Fig. 5 Pressing the stud from the rotor

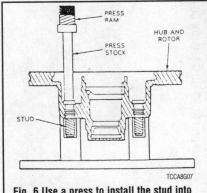

Fig. 6 Use a press to install the stud into the rotor

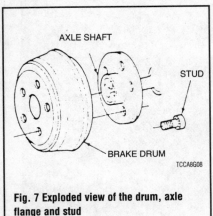

Fig. 7 Exploded view of the drum, axle flange and stud

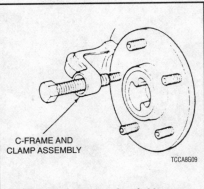

Fig. 8 Use a C-clamp and socket to press out the stud

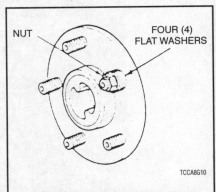

Fig. 9 Force the stud onto the axle flange using washers and a lug nut

FRONT SUSPENSION

COMMON FRONT SUSPENSION COMPONENT LOCATIONS

1. Outer tie rod end
2. Tie rod
3. Strut and spring assembly
4. Sway bar mounting bushing
5. Sway bar
6. Sway bar end link
7. Lower control arm
8. Lower control arm bushing

Coil Springs

REMOVAL & INSTALLATION

▶ **See Figures 10 thru 21**

1. Remove the strut from the vehicle.
2. Clamp the Spring Compressor VAG 1752/2 or equivalent in a vise.
3. Install the strut into the spring compressor.
4. Pry off the mounting bolt cap.
5. Compress the coil spring and remove the self-locking nut from the piston rod.
6. Matchmark the position of the spring retainer and spring mount.
7. Remove the spring seat and related components noting the order of removal.
8. Remove the strut from the spring compressor.

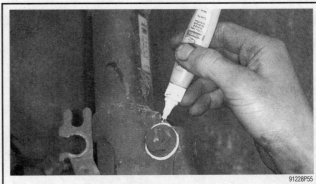
Fig. 10 Matchmark the position of the strut to the spindle-knuckle before removal

Fig. 11 A typical strut type coil spring compressor

Fig. 12 Exploded view of strut assembly

Fig. 13 Install the strut rod boot as shown

Fig. 14 Install the spring

Fig. 15 The base of the spring must be seated against the bottom of the strut assembly

Fig. 16 Do not forget to install all of the necessary washers

Fig. 17 Next put on the spring retainer

Fig. 18 Turn the spring retainer to properly seat it on the spring

Fig. 19 Mate the strut bearing with the spring retainer

91228P53

Fig. 20 Insert the spring plate retaining nut

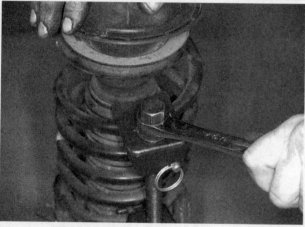

91228P54

Fig. 21 Once the spring is securely fastened on the strut and the upper spring plate retaining nut is tightened to 30 ft. lbs. (41 Nm), slowly and carefully remove the spring compressor

9. Release the tension on the coil spring, and remove the spring out of the compressor.

To install:

10. Install the new spring into the compressor.
11. Compress the spring and insert the strut through the spring.
12. Install the spring seat and related components in the reverse order as they were removed and aligning the matchmarks.
13. Install a new self-locking nut.
14. Reinstall the mounting bolt cap.
15. Release the spring compressor and install the strut into the vehicle.

Struts

REMOVAL & INSTALLATION

Fox

1. Disconnect the negative battery cable.
2. With the car on the ground, remove the front axle nut.
3. Loosen the wheel bolts.
4. Raise and support the front of the car. Use jackstands. Remove the wheels.
5. Remove the brake caliper from the strut and hang it with wire. Detach the brake line clips from the strut.
6. At the tie rod end, remove the cotter pin, back off the castellated nut, and pull the tie rod end from the strut with a puller.
7. Loosen the stabilizer bar bushings and detach the end from the strut being removed.

8. Remove the ball joint from the strut.
9. Pull the axle driveshaft from the strut.
10. Remove the upper strut-to-fender retaining nuts located under the engine hood.
11. Pull the strut assembly down and out of the car.

To install:

12. Installation is the reverse of removal. Observe the following torque specifications:

- Axle nut—145 ft. lbs. (195 Nm) for M18 nuts or 175 ft. lbs. (238 Nm) for M20 nuts
- Ball joint-to-strut nut—25 ft. lbs. (34 Nm) for M8 nuts or 36 ft. lbs. (49 Nm) for M10 nuts
- Caliper-to-strut bolts—44 ft. lbs. (60 Nm)
- Stabilizer-to-control arm bolts: 7 ft. lbs. (10 Nm).

1990–94 Cabriolet, 1990–92 Golf and Jetta

The upper strut-to-steering knuckle bolt may have an eccentric washer for adjusting wheel camber. Use a wire brush to clean the area and use a cold chisel to mark a fine line on the washer and the strut together. This matchmark may be enough to preserve the front wheel camber adjustment. It will at least be accurate enough to allow driving the vehicle to a shop for a proper front wheel alignment. If there is no eccentric washer, a new bolt and eccentric washer can be substituted. The parts are available through the dealer.

A special tool is required to remove the upper strut nut on Golf and Jetta. If necessary, it can be made by cutting away part of a 22mm socket.

1. Raise and safely support the vehicle and remove the front wheels.
2. Detach the brake line from the strut and remove the caliper. DO NOT let the caliper hang by the hydraulic line, hang it from the body with wire.
3. Clean and matchmark the position of the strut–to steering knuckle bolt.
4. Remove the bolts and push the steering knuckle down away from the strut. Support the knuckle so it is not hanging on the outer CV-joint.
5. On Cabriolet, remove the nuts holding the rubber strut bearing to the body and lower the strut from the vehicle.
6. On Golf and Jetta, use a hex wrench to hold the shock absorber rod and use the cut-away socket to remove the upper nut. Lower the strut from the vehicle.

To install:

7. Place the strut into the fender and install the nuts. On Cabriolet, tighten the 3 nuts to 14 ft. lbs. (20 Nm). On Golf and Jetta, install a new center nut and tighten it to 44 ft. lbs. (60 Nm).
8. Fit the knuckle into the strut and install the bolts. Make sure the matchmarks are aligned and install the nuts.
9. On Golf and Jetta, the strut–to–knuckle bolts are 2 different wrench sizes. Tighten the 19mm bolts to 70 ft. lbs. (95 Nm) and the 18mm bolts to 59 ft. lbs. (80 Nm).
10. On Cabriolet, tighten the strut–to–knuckle bolts to 70 ft. lbs. (95 Nm).
11. Install the brake caliper and tighten the bolts to 44 ft. lbs. (60 Nm).
12. Install the wheel and align the front wheels.

1995–99 Cabrio, 1993–99 Golf and Jetta

♦ **See Figures 22 thru 28**

The upper strut-to-steering knuckle bolt may have an eccentric washer for adjusting wheel camber. Use a wire brush to clean the area and use a cold chisel to mark a fine line on the washer and the strut together. This matchmark may be enough to preserve the front wheel camber adjustment. It will at least be accurate enough to allow driving the vehicle until a proper front wheel alignment can be performed. If there is no eccentric washer, a new bolt and eccentric washer can be substituted. The parts are available through the dealer.

A special tool is required to remove the upper strut nut. If necessary, it can be made by cutting away part of a 22mm socket.

1. Raise and safely support the vehicle and remove the front wheels.
2. If equipped, disconnect the ABS wheel speed sensor.
3. Detach the brake line from the strut and remove the caliper. DO NOT let the caliper hang by the hydraulic line, hang it from the body with wire.
4. Clean and matchmark the position of the strut-to-steering knuckle bolt.
5. Remove the bolts and push the steering knuckle down away from the strut. Support the knuckle so it is not hanging on the outer CV-joint.
6. Use a hex wrench to hold the shock absorber rod and use the cut away socket to remove the upper nut. Lower the strut from the vehicle.

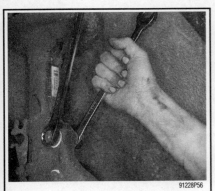

Fig. 22 Two closed end wrenches are needed to loosen the strut to knuckle bolts

Fig. 23 Note the location of the strut to knuckle bolts

Fig. 24 Pull the knuckle far enough away from the strut to allow removal of the strut

Fig. 25 Remove the strut mounting plate cap

Fig. 26 A socket and an allen key may be needed to remove the strut mounting nut

Fig. 27 Strut mounting plate and nut

Fig. 28 Remove the strut assembly from the vehicle

To install:

7. Place the strut into the fender and install the nuts. Install a new center nut and tighten it to 44 ft. lbs. (60 Nm).

8. On the Cabrio, Golf, and Jetta fit the knuckle into the strut and install the bolts. Be sure the matchmarks are aligned and install the nuts.

➡**On the Cabrio, Golf, and Jetta the strut-to-knuckle bolts are 2 different wrench sizes. Tighten the bolts to 70 ft. lbs. (95 Nm).**

9. Install the brake caliper and tighten the bolts to 44 ft. lbs. (60 Nm).

10. Install the wheel and align the front wheels.

OVERHAUL

Some special tools are required to disassemble the strut. First is a good quality spring compressor, usually available at larger parts stores. Also a special socket is needed to remove the upper strut nut. If necessary, it can be made by cutting away part of a 22mm socket. The same tool is required to remove the strut from Golf and Jetta.

⁕ CAUTION

The coil spring is very strong and under considerable pressure. If the correct tools and techniques are not available, do not attempt this job. Improper handling of coil springs can cause serious or fatal injury.

1. Remove the strut.

2. Anchor the strut in a vise so it cannot move and attach the spring compressor.

3. Compress the spring and remove the center nut at the top of the strut assembly. Remove the upper spring seat and spring. With the spring still in the compressor, place it where it will not be disturbed. The springs are color coded. When replacing, make sure both replacement springs have the same color code.

4. Use a pipe wrench to remove the threaded collar from the top of the strut. Remove the strut from the vice and pour the fluid into a drain pan.

5. Remove the strut rod and discard all the internal parts.

To install:

6. The new insert is probably a gas pressure shock absorber. Pour about 2 oz. of the old hydraulic oil into the strut and install the new insert. The fluid will help dissipate heat and extend the life of the insert.

7. Install the threaded collar and tighten it to 30 ft. lbs. (40 Nm).

8. Fit the spring into place, install the upper seat and start the nut onto the rod. It may be easier to tighten the nut before removing the spring compressor. Tighten the nut to 44 ft. lbs. (60 Nm) and carefully remove the spring compressor.

Lower Ball Joint

INSPECTION

1. To check the ball joint, raise and safely support the vehicle. Let the front wheels hang free.

2. Insert a prybar between the control arm and the ball joint clamping bolt. Be careful to not damage the ball joint boot.

3. Measure the play between the bottom of the ball joint and the clamping bolt with a caliper. Total must not exceed 0.100 inch (2.5mm).

REMOVAL & INSTALLATION

Fox

1. Disconnect the negative battery cable.
2. Jack up the front of the vehicle and support it on jackstands.
3. Matchmark the ball joint-to-control arm position on the Dasher, Fox and Quantum.
4. Remove the retaining bolt and nut from the hub (wheel bearing housing).
5. Pry the lower control arm and ball joint down and out of the strut.
6. Remove the two ball joint-to-lower control arm retaining nuts and bolts on the Fox .
7. Remove the ball joint assembly.

To install:

8. Install the ball joint in the reverse order of removal. If no parts were installed other than the ball joint, align the matchmarks made earlier. No camber adjustment is necessary if this is done. Pull the ball joint into alignment with pliers. Observe the following torque's:
   • Control arm-to-ball joint bolts—47 ft. lbs. (65 Nm)
   • Strut-to-ball joint bolt—25 ft. lbs. (34 Nm) for M8 bolts or 36 ft. lbs. (48 Nm) for M10 bolts
9. On the Golf, Rabbit, Jetta and Scirocco, bolt the new ball joint in place (bolts are provided with the replacement ball joint), and tighten them to 18 ft. lbs. (25 Nm). Tighten the retaining bolt holding the ball joint to the hub to 21 ft. lbs. (28 Nm).

1990–94 Cabriolet, 1990–92 Golf and Jetta

1. Raise and safely support the vehicle, allowing the front wheels to hang. Remove the front wheels.

2. Remove the ball joint clamping bolt.
3. Pry the lower control arm down to remove the ball joint from the steering knuckle.
4. Remove the ball joint–to–lower control arm retaining nuts and bolts or drill out the rivets with a ¼ inch (6mm) drill. Remove the ball joint.
5. Install the new ball joint in the reverse order of removal. If no parts were installed other than the ball joint, no camber adjustment is necessary. Tighten the 2 control arm-to-ball joint bolts to 18 ft. lbs. (25 Nm) and the ball joint clamping bolt to 37 ft. lbs. (50 Nm).

1995–99 Cabrio, 1993–99 Golf and Jetta

▶ **See Figures 29 thru 36**

1. Raise and safely support the vehicle, allowing the front wheels to hang. Remove the front wheels.
2. Remove the ball joint clamping bolt.
3. Pry the lower control arm down to remove the ball joint from the steering knuckle.

Fig. 29 Remove the ball joint nut

Fig. 30 Use a brass drift to remove the pinch nut if it is stuck

Fig. 31 View of ball joint pinch nut and bolt

Fig. 32 Remove the ball joint to lower control arm bolts

Fig. 33 You may need to spread the knuckle-hub assemble to remove the ball joint

Fig. 34 When using a fork style ball joint separator be careful not to tear the boot on the ball joint

Fig. 35 A short pry tool may be all that is needed to separate the ball joint from the knuckle

Fig. 36 View of ball joint and lower control arm

Fig. 37 Removal of the sway bar endlink attaching nut

Fig. 38 Sway bar link nut, washer, and bushing

4. Remove the ball joint-to-lower control arm retaining nuts and bolts or drill out the rivets with a ¼ inch (6mm) drill. Remove the ball joint.

To install:

5. Install the new ball joint in the reverse order of removal. If no parts were installed other than the ball joint, no camber adjustment is necessary. Tighten the two control arm-to-ball joint bolts to 18 ft. lbs. (25 Nm) and the ball joint clamping bolt to 37 ft. lbs. (50 Nm).

Sway Bar

REMOVAL & INSTALLATION

▶ **See Figures 37, 38 and 39**

1. Disconnect the negative battery cable.
2. Raise the front of the vehicle and support it with jackstands. Remove the front wheels.
3. Remove the bolts/nuts securing the outer ends of the sway bar, then remove the bolts/nuts securing the brackets.
4. Remove the sway bar.

To install:

5. Position the sway bar in the vehicle.
6. Install the bolts/nuts securing the brackets. Tighten them until just snug (they will be fully tightened later).
7. Install the bolts/nuts securing the outer ends of the sway bar. Tighten until just snug (they will be fully tightened later).

➡**On Golf and Jetta models, the collars of the washers face away from the bushings. The conical side of the bushings face the washers.**

8. Install the wheels, then lower the vehicle.
9. Bounce the vehicle several times and allow the vehicle to stabilize.
10. On Jetta and Golf models, tighten the bolts/nuts to 18 ft. lbs. (25 Nm). On other models, tighten the bolts/nuts to 15 ft. lbs. (20 Nm).
11. Connect the battery cable.

Fig. 39 Lift up on the sway bar and slide the end link off the end of the bar

Lower Control Arm

REMOVAL & INSTALLATION

▶ **See Figure 40**

Fox

1. Disconnect the negative battery cable.
2. Raise the vehicle and support it on jackstands. Remove the wheels.
3. Remove the nut and bolt attaching the ball joint to the hub (wheel bearing housing), then pry the joint down and out of the hub.
4. Remove the stabilizer bar.
5. Detach the control arm mounting bolts from the frame.
6. Remove the bolts securing the control arm, then remove the arm.

To install:

7. Installation is the reverse of removal. Observe the following torque's:
   - Fox control arm-to-subframe bolts—50 ft. lbs. (37 Nm).
   - Fox ball joint-to-hub bolt—25 ft. lbs. (34 Nm) for M8 nuts or 36 ft. lbs. (49 Nm) for M10 nuts.
   - Stabilizer bar link rods—18 ft. lbs. (25 Nm).
   - Stabilizer bar bushing clamp bolts—32 ft. lbs. (43 Nm).

1990–94 Cabriolet, 1990–92 Golf and Jetta

When removing the driver's side control arm on Golf and Jetta equipped with an automatic transaxle, it may be necessary to lift the engine/transaxle. First support the engine from above or below. Remove the front left engine mounting nut and bolt, remove the rear mount and raise the engine to expose the front control arm bolt.

1. Raise and safely support the vehicle and remove the wheels.
2. Remove the ball joint clamping bolt and pry the control arm down.
3. Remove the rubber bushings to unfasten the stabilizer bar.
4. Remove the control arm mounting bolts and remove the control arm.

To install:

5. Installation is the reverse of removal. Tighten the following components:
   - Cabriolet control arm bushing bolts—50 ft. lbs. (68 Nm).

Fig. 40 Removal of the lower control arm

- Golf and Jetta front bushing bolts—96 ft. lbs. (130 Nm), rear bolts—59 ft. lbs. (80 Nm).
- Stabilizer bar link rods—18 ft. lbs. (25 Nm).
- Stabilizer bar bushing clamp bolts—32 ft. lbs. (43 Nm).
- Ball joint clamping bolt—37 ft. lbs. (50 Nm).

BUSHING REPLACEMENT

1. Remove the control arm.
2. Position the control arm on a press. Carefully push the bushing out of the control arm using the press.

To install:

3. Lightly lubricate, then position the bushing on the control arm. On Golf and Jetta models, align one arrow with the dimple on the control arm (the kidney shaped opening in the bushing must face the center of the vehicle when the control arm is installed).
4. Carefully press the bushing into the control arm.
5. Install the control arm.

1995–99 Cabrio, 1993–99 Golf and Jetta

1. Chock the rear wheels and then lift the vehicle supporting it on jack stands.
2. Remove the front wheel.
3. Base suspension models require the removal of the connecting link to the control arm.
4. Plus suspension models require the removal of the nut that attaches the stabilizer bar to the control arm.
5. Separate the link from the arm.
6. Matchmark the correct installed position of the ball joint into the control arm.
7. Remove the ball joint.
8. Remove the pivot bolt from the control arm.
9. Remove the rear control arm mounting bolt.
10. Pull the rear control arm from the vehicle.

To install:

11. Install the control arm and slide the ball joint into it.
12. Push the control arm pivot bolt through the control arm. Also install the rear mounting bolt. Tighten the pivot bolt to 37 ft. lbs. (50Nm) and then turn it another 90°. The rear mounting bolt is to be tightened to 52 ft. lbs. (70Nm) and then turn it 90°.
13. Align the ball joint retaining plate on top of the control arm then install the ball joint bolts. Tighten the bolts to 26 ft. lbs. (35Nm).
14. Install the connecting links.
15. Install the wheel and tire. Tighten the lug nuts to 81 ft. lbs. (110Nm).

Steering Knuckle and Spindle

REMOVAL & INSTALLATION

Fox

✳✳ CAUTION

The torque required to loosen the front axle nut is high enough to make the vehicle fall off of jackstands. Make sure the vehicle is on the ground when loosening or tightening the front axle nut.

1. Disconnect the negative battery cable.
2. With the vehicle on the ground, remove the front axle nut.
3. Raise the vehicle and support with jackstands.
4. Remove the front wheels.
5. Mark the knuckle-to-strut housing for installation alignment.
6. Remove the brake caliper and hang it from the frame using a piece of wire. DO NOT allow the caliper to hang from the brake hose.
7. Remove the tie rod nut and cotter pin. Disconnect the tie rod using a separator.
8. Disconnect the lower control arm from the knuckle.
9. Remove the two strut-to-knuckle bolts.
10. Slide the axle shaft out of the bearing and remove the knuckle.

To install:

11. Install the knuckle onto the vehicle and slide the axle shaft into the bearing.

12. Reconnect the lower ball joint, tie rod end, strut and caliper.
13. Tighten the axle nut. On Fox tighten the M18 nut to 145 ft. lbs. (197 Nm) and the M20 nut to 170 ft. lbs. (231 Nm). On Golf and Jetta tighten to 195 ft. lbs. (265 Nm). On other models, tighten to 173 ft. lbs. (235 Nm).
14. Install the tire and lower the vehicle.
15. Connect the battery cable.

1990–94 Cabriolet, 1990–92 Golf and Jetta

✳✳ CAUTION

The torque required to loosen the front axle nut is high enough to make the vehicle fall off of jack stands. Make sure the vehicle is on the ground when loosening or tightening the front axle nut.

1. With the vehicle on the ground, remove the front axle nut.
2. Raise and safely support the vehicle and remove the front wheels.
3. Detach the brake line from the strut and remove the caliper. Do not let the caliper hang by the hydraulic line, hang it from the body with wire.
4. Remove the caliper carrier and brake rotor.
5. Remove the cotter pin and nut and press out the tie rod end. A small puller is required.
6. Remove the ball joint clamp bolt and push the control arm down to disengage the ball joint.
7. Front wheel camber is set with eccentric washers on the bolts holding the bearing housing to the strut. Clean and mark the position of these washers so they can be reinstalled in the same position.
8. Remove the bolts and take the knuckle and bearing housing off the strut.

To install:

9. Fit the knuckle to the strut and install the bolts. Align the marks and tighten the nuts to 70 ft. lbs. (95 Nm).
10. Make sure the axle splines are clean and apply a bead of thread locking compound to the outer portion. Slid the axle into the hub and install a new axle nut. Do not tighten it yet.
11. Fit the lower ball joint in place and install the clamp bolt. Tighten it to 37 ft. lbs. (50 Nm).
12. Connect the tie rod and tighten the nut to 26 ft. lbs. (35 Nm), then tighten as required to install a new cotter pin.
13. Install the brake disc and caliper. Tighten the carrier bolts to 92 ft. lbs. (125 Nm) and the caliper guide bolts to 18 ft. lbs. (25 Nm). Secure the brake line in place.
14. With the wheel installed and the vehicle on the ground, tighten the axle nut to 175 ft. lbs. (237 Nm) on Cabriolet or 195 ft. lbs. (265 Nm) on Golf and Jetta.

1995–99 Cabrio, 1993–99 Golf and Jetta

▶ **See Figures 41, 42 and 43**

1. Detach the negative battery cable.
2. Remove the wheel cover and or center cap.
3. While the vehicle is still on the ground, loosen the drive axle (halfshaft) retaining nut.

✳✳ CAUTION

Do not remove the drive axle retaining nut if the vehicle is up on jackstands. A significant amount of torque is needed to remove this nut and may cause the vehicle to fall off the stands.

4. Crack the lug nuts loose at this time.
5. Lift and then support the vehicle with jackstands.
6. Remove the front wheel and tire assembly.
7. Remove the driveaxle (halfshaft) retaining nut and its washer.
8. Detach the Antilock Brake System (ABS) sensor.
9. Remove the brake disc from the hub.
10. Detach the caliper from the hub assembly.
11. Hang the caliper from a piece of mechanics wire.

✳✳ WARNING

Do not allow the caliper to hang from the brake hose. This will lead to premature hose failure.

Fig. 41 The halfshaft must be removed from the knuckle-spindle. If it is stuck, use a brass drift and lightly tap it through the knuckle-spindle

Fig. 42 View of axle shaft nut and washer

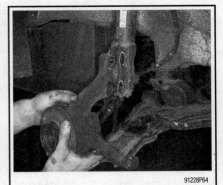

Fig. 43 Removal of the knuckle-spindle assembly

12. Remove the tie rod end nut.
13. Use a tie rod end separator to pull the tie rod end from the steering knuckle.
14. Matchmark the balljoint and then remove the retaining bolts.
15. Matchmark the position of the strut to steering knuckle bolt and then remove the necessary nuts and bolts.
16. Free the steering knuckle from the strut by pulling it out. This is a great time to remove the splined axle shaft from the spindle. If the axle halfshaft is lodged in the spindle use a brass drift and hammer to knock it through the spindle.

☀☀ WARNING

Use caution not to damage the threads on the halfshaft when knocking the it through the spindle.

➡**If tapping on the axle shaft ceases to loosen it, use a puller to press it out of the hub.**

17. Once the halfshaft is removed from the spindle, support it so that it does not pull the inner joint out of the socket.

To install:

➡**Replace all self locking nuts that have been removed from the suspension. Nuts of this design were created with a one time use in mind. They will not stay tight if reused.**

18. Clean and then engage the drive axle (halfshaft) splines with the spindle. Install the nut and use it to pull the driveshaft back into the spindle.
19. Install the steering knuckle with the strut.
20. Align the balljoint with the control arm.
21. Install the control arm to balljoint fasteners.
22. Align the ball joint with the matchmarks that were made and then tighten the fasteners.
23. Install the tie-rod end into the steering knuckle and install the nut. Tighten the nut to 26 ft. lbs. (35Nm).
24. Install the brake discs and then the calipers. If applicable, install the ABS wheel sensor.
25. Tighten the drive axle retaining nut to 66 ft. lbs. (89 Nm).
26. Install the tire and tighten the lug nuts to 81 ft. lbs. (109 Nm).

Front Wheel Bearings

ADJUSTMENT

The front wheel bearings are sealed, no adjustment is necessary or possible.

REMOVAL & INSTALLATION

1990–94 Cabriolet, 1990–93 Fox, 1990–92 Golf and Jetta

WITHOUT ANTI-LOCK BRAKES (ABS)

➡**The hub and bearing are pressed into the knuckle and the bearing cannot be reused once the hub has been removed.**

Without Anti-Lock Brakes (ABS)

1. Disconnect the negative battery cable.
2. With the vehicle on the ground, remove the front axle nut. Raise and safely support the vehicle.
3. Remove the steering knuckle.
4. To remove the hub, support the knuckle assembly in an arbor press with the hub facing down.
5. Use a proper size arbor that will fit through the bearing and press the hub out.
6. If the inner bearing race stayed on the hub, clamp the hub in a vise and use a bearing puller to remove it.
7. On the knuckle, remove the splash shield and internal snap-rings from the bearing housing.
8. With the knuckle in the same pressing position, press the bearing out.
9. Clean the bearing housing and hub with a wire brush, then inspect all parts. Replace parts that have been distorted or discolored from heat. If the hub is not absolutely perfect where it contacts the inner bearing race, the new bearing will fail quickly.

To install:
10. The new bearing is pressed in from the hub side. Install the snap-ring and support the steering knuckle on the press.
11. Using the old bearing as a press tool, drive the new bearing into the housing up against the snap-ring. Make sure the press tool contacts only the outer race of the bearing.
12. Install the outer snap-ring and splash shield.
13. Support the inner race on the press and drive the hub into the bearing. Make sure the inner race is supported or the bearing will fail quickly.
14. Install the steering knuckle, then carefully lower the vehicle. BE SURE to tighten the axle nut correctly before allowing the vehicle to roll.
15. Connect the battery cable.

WITH ANTI-LOCK BRAKES (ABS)

1. Disconnect the negative battery cable.
2. With the vehicle on the ground, remove the front axle nut. Raise and safely support the vehicle.
3. Remove the steering knuckle.
4. Clamp the upper knuckle-to-strut bolt boss in a vice.
5. Install the special press tool onto the hub (as shown in the illustration) and press the hub out of the bearing.
6. If the inner bearing race stayed on the hub, clamp the hub in a vise and use a bearing puller to remove it.
7. On the knuckle, remove the splash shield and internal snap-rings from the bearing housing.
8. After removing the snap-ring, the same press tool can be used to push the bearing out of the knuckle.
9. Clean the bearing housing and hub with a wire brush, then inspect all parts. Replace parts that have been distorted or discolored from heat. If the hub is not absolutely perfect where it contacts the inner bearing race, the new bearing will fail quickly.

To install:
10. The new bearing is pressed in from the hub side using a regular arbor press. Install the snap-ring and support the steering knuckle on the press.

11. Using the old bearing as a press tool, drive the new bearing into the housing up against the snap-ring. Make sure the press tool contacts only the outer race of the bearing.

12. Install the outer snap-ring and splash shield. If removed, install the speed sensor rotor onto the hub.

13. Support the inner race on the press and drive the hub into the bearing. Make sure the inner race is supported or the bearing fail quickly.

14. Install the steering knuckle and carefully lower the vehicle. BE SURE to tighten the axle nut correctly before allowing the vehicle to roll.

15. Connect the battery cable.

1995–99 Cabrio, 1993–99 Golf and Jetta

➡ **The hub and bearing are pressed into the knuckle and the bearing cannot be reused once the hub has been removed.**

1. With the vehicle on the ground, remove the front axle nut.
2. Raise and safely support the vehicle and remove the steering knuckle.
3. Clamp the upper knuckle-to-strut bolt boss in a vice.
4. Install the special press tool onto the hub as shown and press the hub out of the bearing.
5. If the inner bearing race stayed on the hub, clamp the hub in a vise and use a bearing puller to remove it.
6. On the knuckle, remove the splash shield and internal snap-rings from the bearing housing.
7. After removing the snap-ring, the same press tool can be used to push the bearing out of the knuckle.
8. Clean the bearing housing and hub with a wire brush and inspect all parts. Replace parts that have been distorted or discolored from heat. If the hub is not absolutely prefect where it contacts the inner bearing race, the new bearing will fail quickly.

To install:

9. The new bearing is pressed in from the hub side using a regular arbor press. Install the snap-ring and support the steering knuckle on the press.
10. Using the old bearing as a press tool, press the new bearing into the housing up against the snap-ring. Be sure the press tool contacts only the outer race of the bearing.
11. Install the outer snap-ring and splash shield. If removed, install the speed sensor rotor onto the hub.
12. Support the inner race on the press and press the hub into the bearing. Be sure the inner race is supported or the bearing fail quickly.
13. Install the steering knuckle and be sure to tighten the axle nut correctly before allowing the vehicle to roll.

Wheel Alignment

If the tires are worn unevenly, if the vehicle is not stable on the highway or if the handling seems uneven in spirited driving, the wheel alignment should be checked. If an alignment problem is suspected, first check for improper tire inflation and other possible causes. These can be worn suspension or steering components, accident damage or even unmatched tires. If any worn or damaged components are found, they must be replaced before the wheels can be properly aligned. Wheel alignment requires very expensive equipment and involves minute adjustments which must be accurate; it should only be performed by a trained technician. Take your vehicle to a properly equipped shop.

Following is a description of the alignment angles which are adjustable on most vehicles and how they affect vehicle handling. Although these angles can apply to both the front and rear wheels, usually only the front suspension is adjustable.

CASTER

♦ **See Figure 44**

Looking at a vehicle from the side, caster angle describes the steering axis rather than a wheel angle. The steering knuckle is attached to a control arm or strut at the top and a control arm at the bottom. The wheel pivots around the line between these points to steer the vehicle. When the upper point is tilted back, this is described as positive caster. Having a positive caster tends to make the wheels self-centering, increasing directional stability. Excessive positive caster makes the wheels hard to steer, while an uneven caster will cause a pull to one side. Overloading the vehicle or sagging rear springs will affect caster, as will raising the rear of the vehicle. If the rear of the vehicle is lower than normal, the caster becomes more positive.

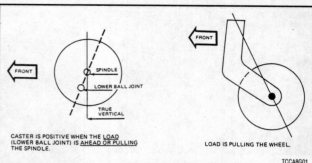

Fig. 44 Caster affects straight-line stability. Caster wheels used on shopping carts, for example, employ positive caster

CAMBER

♦ **See Figure 45**

Looking from the front of the vehicle, camber is the inward or outward tilt of the top of wheels. When the tops of the wheels are tilted in, this is negative camber; if they are tilted out, it is positive. In a turn, a slight amount of negative camber helps maximize contact of the tire with the road. However, too much negative camber compromises straight-line stability, increases bump steer and torque steer.

TOE

♦ **See Figure 46**

Looking down at the wheels from above the vehicle, toe angle is the distance between the front of the wheels, relative to the distance between the back of the wheels. If the wheels are closer at the front, they are said to be toed-in or to have negative toe. A small amount of negative toe enhances directional stability and provides a smoother ride on the highway.

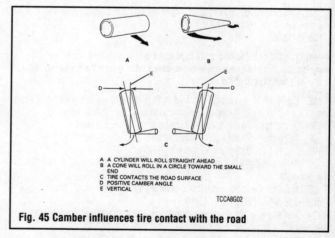

Fig. 45 Camber influences tire contact with the road

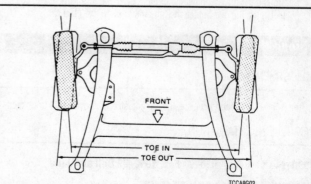

Fig. 46 With toe-in, the distance between the wheels is closer at the front than at the rear

REAR SUSPENSION

COMMON REAR SUSPENSION COMPONENT LOCATIONS

1. Coil springs
2. Spindle
3. Lower strut bushing
4. Strut
5. Rear axle mounting bolt
6. Rear axle

Coil Springs

REMOVAL & INSTALLATION

Please consult the coil spring procedure listed under front suspension section of this chapter.

Struts

REMOVAL & INSTALLATION

❊❊ WARNING

Do not remove both suspension struts at the same time or the axle beam will be hanging on the brake lines.

1. On Cabrio, Golf, and Jetta, perform the following:
   a. Working inside the vehicle, remove the cap from the top shock mount and remove the top nut, washer and rubber bushings.
   b. Remove the second nut.
   c. Slowly lift the vehicle and safely support it. Do not place supports under the axle beam.
2. Unbolt the strut from the axle and carefully remove the strut and spring from the vehicle. It may be necessary to press the axle down slightly.
   To install:
3. Install the shock on the axle assembly. Do not tighten the nut until the vehicle is on the floor at normal riding height.
4. On the Cabrio, Golf, and Jetta, perform the following:
   a. Install the upper end of the strut to the body.
   b. Tighten the lower nut to 11 ft. lbs. (15 Nm) and the upper nut to 18 ft. lbs. (25 Nm).
   c. Install the wheel and lower the vehicle to the floor.
   d. Tighten the lower strut mounting nut to 52 ft. lbs. (70 Nm).

OVERHAUL

Some special tools are required to disassemble the strut. First is a good quality spring compressor, usually available at larger parts stores. Also a special socket is needed to remove the upper strut nut. If necessary, it can be made by cutting away part of a 22mm socket. The same tool is required to remove the strut from the 1990–92 Golf and Jetta.

❊❊ CAUTION

The coil spring is very strong and under considerable pressure. If the correct tools and techniques are not available, do not attempt this job. Improper handling of coil springs can cause serious or fatal injury.

1. Remove the strut.
2. Anchor the strut in a vise so it cannot move and attach the spring compressor.
3. Compress the spring and remove the center nut at the top of the strut assembly. Remove the upper spring seat and spring. With the spring still in the compressor, place it where it will not be disturbed. The springs are color coded. When replacing, make sure both replacement springs have the same color code.
4. Use a pipe wrench to remove the threaded collar from the top of the strut. Remove the strut from the vice and pour the fluid into a drain pan.
5. Remove the strut rod and discard all the internal parts.
   To install:
6. The new insert is probably a gas pressure shock absorber. Pour about 2 oz. of the old hydraulic oil into the strut and install the new insert. The fluid will help dissipate heat and extend the life of the insert.
7. Install the threaded collar and tighten it to 30 ft. lbs. (40 Nm).
8. Fit the spring into place, install the upper seat and start the nut onto the rod. It may be easier to tighten the nut before removing the spring compressor. Tighten the nut to 44 ft. lbs. (60 Nm) and carefully remove the spring compressor.

Semi-Independent Rear Axle

REMOVAL & INSTALLATION

1. Disconnect the negative battery cable.
2. Raise and safely support the vehicle and remove the rear wheels.
3. On 1993–99 Golf and Jetta vehicles, disconnect the parking brake cables at the lever.
4. Remove the rear brake caliper or drum.
5. Disconnect the brake line and remove the caliper or back plate (with brakes attached) from the vehicle.
6. Disconnect the other end of the brake line and unclip the brake line and parking brake cable from the axle.
7. If equipped, unhook the brake pressure regulator spring from the bracket.
8. Support one side of the axle beam so it does not fall and remove the lower shock mount bolts from both sides.
9. Unless that is the part being repaired, avoid removing the axle bushing brackets. Removing these will mean aligning the rear bushings upon reassembly.
10. Remove the bolt from the center of each bushing and lower the axle from the vehicle.
    To install:
If the axle beam mounting brackets were removed from the axle beam, the brackets must be aligned. Position them so that they are at 12° to the axle beam. Then tighten the pivot nuts.
11. Install the axle but do not tighten the bushing bolts yet. They should be tightened with the vehicle on the ground to properly align the bushings.
12. Install the brakes, connect the hydraulic lines and bleed the brakes.
13. With the vehicle on the ground, tighten the right side axle bushing bolt first, then pry the left side bushing slightly towards the center of the vehicle and tighten the left side.
14. Tighten the axle bushing bolts to 44 ft. lbs. (60 Nm) and the lower shock mount bolts to 52 ft. lbs. (70 Nm).

Sway Bar

REMOVAL & INSTALLATION

The A2 (1990–92 Golf and Jetta) and A3 (1993–99 Golf and Jetta /1995–99 Cabriolet) chassis may have been equipped with a rear sway bar from the factory, although it is not removable because it is an integral part of the rear axle.

Rear Wheel Bearings

ADJUSTMENT

1990–94 Cabriolet, 1990–93 Fox, 1990–92 Golf, and Jetta

1. Raise and support the vehicle safely.
2. Remove the grease cap.
3. Remove the cotter pin and the locking nut.
4. While turning the wheel, so the wheel bearing does not jam, tighten the adjusting nut firmly.
5. Back the nut off slightly. The nut is properly adjusted when it is possible to pry the thrust washer side to side with some drag by using finger pressure on the tool.
6. Install the locking nut and a new cotter pin. When installing the cap, be sure it is securely in place.

1995–99 Cabrio, 1993–99 Golf and Jetta

♦ See Figures 47 thru 65

1. Raise and safely support the vehicle. Remove the rear wheels.
2. On drum brakes, insert a small prytool through a wheel bolt hole and push up on the adjusting wedge to slacken the rear brake adjustment.
3. On disc brakes, remove the caliper.

Fig. 47 A chisel with a sharp edge can be used to remove the dust cap

Fig. 48 Remove the dust cap

Fig. 49 Remove the cotter pin

Fig. 50 Use pliers to hold the end of a stuck cotter pin and then lightly tap the pliers with a hammer to remove the pin

Fig. 51 Remove the locking cap

Fig. 52 Most VW's have a 24 mm nut holding the rotor on the spindle

Fig. 53 Remove the nut holding the rotor on the spindle

Fig. 54 Remove the thrust washer

Fig. 55 View of the outer wheel bearing

Fig. 56 Remove the brake rotor

Fig. 57 Inner wheel seal and bearing

Fig. 58 Once the wheel bearing is thoroughly packed with grease it can be installed into the rotor

Fig. 59 The location of the race in the rotor

Fig. 60 Drive the race out of the rotor using a punch and moderate size hammer

Fig. 61 View of the race removed from the rotor

Fig. 62 Use a bearing and race driver to re-install the race. This tool can be found at most auto parts suppliers

Fig. 63 Work fresh wheel bearing grease into the bearing as shown

Fig. 64 Commercially available tools such as this one make bearing packing easier

Fig. 65 Install the seal using an appropriate driver

5. Remove the brake drum or rotor and pry out the inner seal to remove the inner bearing.

6. Clean all the grease off the bearings using solvent. If the bearings appear worn or damaged, they must be replaced.

7. To remove the bearing races, support the drum or rotor and carefully drive the race out with a long drift pin. They can also be removed on a press.

To install:

8. Carefully press the new race into the drum or rotor. The old race can be used as a press tool but be sure it does not become stuck in the hub.

9. Pack the inner bearing with clean wheel bearing grease and fit it into the inner race. Press a new axle seal into place by hand.

10. Lightly coat the stub axle with grease and install the drum or rotor. Be careful not to damage the axle seal.

11. Pack the outer bearing and install the bearing, thrust washer and nut.

12. To adjust the bearing pre-load:

    a. Begin tightening the nut while turning the drum or rotor.

    b. Tighten the wheel axle nut to 87 inch lbs. (10 Nm).

    c. When the nut is snug, try to move the thrust washer with a screwdriver.

    d. Back the nut off until the thrust washer can be moved without prying or twisting the screwdriver.

13. Without turning the nut, install the locking ring so a new cotter pin can be installed through the hold in the stub axle. Bend the cotter pin.

14. Pack some grease into the cap and install it.

4. Remove the grease cap, cotter pin, locking ring, axle nut and thrust washer. Carefully remove the bearing and put all these parts where they will stay clean.

STEERING

✳✳ CAUTION

The Supplemental Inflatable Restraint (SIR) system must be disarmed before performing service around SIR system components or SIR system wiring. Failure to do so may cause accidental deployment of the air bag, resulting in unnecessary SIR system repairs and/or personal injury.

Steering Wheel

REMOVAL & INSTALLATION

1990–94 Cabriolet, 1990–93 Fox, 1990–92 Golf and Jetta

1. Grasp the center cover pad and pull it from the wheel.
2. Loosen and remove the steering shaft nut, then the washer.
3. Matchmark the steering wheel position in relation to the steering shaft so that when you install it, the wheel is perfectly level when the tires are straight ahead.
4. Pull the steering wheel off the shaft. You may need a puller to perform this operation. Under no circumstances should you bang on the shaft to try to free the wheel, or you may damage the collapsible steering column.
5. Disconnect the horn wire.
6. Replace the wheel in the reverse order of removal. On the Fox with the tires straight ahead, the canceling lug on the steering wheel must point to the right and the turn signal lever must be in the neutral position. Tighten the steering shaft nut to 36 ft. lbs. (48 Nm).

1995–99 Cabrio, 1993–99 Golf and Jetta

1. Remove the negative battery cable.
2. Center the steering wheel.
3. Remove the air bag mounting screws from rear of the steering wheel.
4. Carefully remove the air bag from the steering wheel.
5. Matchmark the steering wheel and the column. Remove the hex nut and remove the steering wheel.

To install:

6. The steering wheel and its components can be installed in the reverse order of removal.

➡**See the air bag removal and installation sections in this book to ensure safe installation.**

Turn Signal (Combination) Switch

REMOVAL & INSTALLATION

1990–94 Cabriolet, 1990–93 Fox, 1990–92 Golf and Jetta

1. Disconnect the battery ground cable.
2. Remove the steering wheel.

➡**On Cabriolet with an air bag, remove the spiral spring assembly.**

3. Remove the switch retaining screws.
4. Pry the switch housing off the column.
5. Disconnect the electrical plugs at the back of the switch.
6. Remove the switch housing.
7. Install in the reverse order of removal.

1995–99 Cabrio, 1993–99 Golf and Jetta

1. Remove the negative battery cable.
2. Center the steering wheel.
3. Remove the air bag. As always follow all safety precautions.
4. Remove the screws holding the steering column trim.
5. Detach the steering column trim covers.

6. Remove fasteners that are holding the switches to the column.
7. Pull the switches away from the steering column and remove the wiring.
To install:
8. Installation of the steering column switches is the reverse of the removal procedure.

Ignition Switch

REMOVAL & INSTALLATION

The ignition switch is located at the bottom of the ignition key cylinder body. To remove the ignition switch, first remove the ignition lock cylinder.

Ignition Lock Cylinder

REMOVAL & INSTALLATION

1990–94 Cabriolet, 1990–93 Fox, 1990–92 Golf and Jetta

▶ **See Figure 66**

1. Disconnect the negative battery cable.
2. Remove the steering wheel, then remove the steering column covers.
3. Remove the turn signal and wiper switches.
4. Disconnect the ignition switch wiring.
5. On some models, the hole in the lock body for removing the ignition lock cylinder was not drilled by Volkswagen. To make the hole, use the following measurements in conjunction with the illustrations. Drill the hole where "a" and "b" intersect on the lock body. The hole should be drilled 0.19 inch (3mm) deep
6. Remove the lock cylinder by pushing a small drill bit or piece of wire into the hole and pulling the cylinder out. It might be easier to insert the ignition key, turn it to the right a little and pull on it.

To install:

7. Insert the lock cylinder into the housing with the key in the cylinder.
8. While gently turning the key side-to-side, press the cylinder in to the stop. It should click into place.
9. Temporarily fit the steering wheel onto the splines, then make sure the column locks and unlocks smoothly.
10. Install the switches, column covers, wiring and the steering wheel.
11. Connect the battery cable.

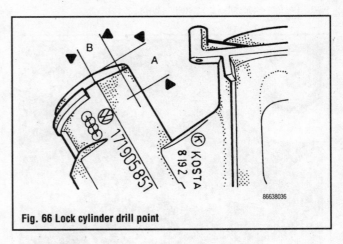

Fig. 66 Lock cylinder drill point

1995–99 Cabrio, 1993–99 Golf and Jetta

1. Disconnect the negative battery cable.
2. Center the steering wheel.
3. Remove the air bag.

4. Remove the steering column switches.

5. If the vehicle is equipped with an automatic transmission, detach the shift lock cable from the lock cylinder housing.

6. Remove the adapter sleeve from the steering column.

7. Remove the spring and horn contact ring from the steering column assembly.

8. Detach the sheer bolt.

9. Insert the ignition key and unlock the cylinder, then detach the wiring connectors.

10. Once all wiring has been detached, slide the housing off the steering column.

11. Mark and drill the lock cylinder as shown and described in the above procedure.

12. Compress the stop spring and pull the lock cylinder out of the steering column housing.

13. Put the new lock cylinder into the steering lock housing.

14. Insert the key into the lock cylinder.

15. While you gently turn the key, insert the lock cylinder fully into the housing.

16. The rest of the installation procedure is the reverse of removal.

➡**Always use a new shear pin when installing the lock cylinder.**

Steering Linkage

REMOVAL & INSTALLATION

◆ **See Figure 67**

Tie Rod Ends

FOX

➡**On manual steering and TRW power steering gear, only the right side tie rod end is removable. The left tie rod must be replaced if the end joint is worn. On all vehicles, the front wheels must be aligned after steering gear repairs.**

1. Disconnect the negative battery cable.

2. Raise the front of the car, then support it with jackstands. Remove the front wheels.

3. Disconnect the outer end of the steering tie rod from the steering knuckle by removing the cotter pin and nut, then pressing out the tie rod end.

➡**A small puller or tie rod separator is required to free the tie rod end.**

4. Under the hood, pry off the lock plate and remove the mounting bolts from both tie rod inner ends.

5. Pry the tie rod out of the mounting pivot and remove.

91228P24

Fig. 67 Use a tie rod end removal tool to pop it loose from the knuckle

To install:

6. If you are replacing an adjustable tie rod, adjust the new tie rod to the same length.

7. Install the tie rod on the mounting pivot. Tighten the pivot bolts to 40 ft. lbs. (54 Nm). Install a new lock plate.

8. Connect the tie rod to the steering knuckle. Tighten the tie rod-to-steering knuckle nut to 22 ft. lbs. (30 Nm). Install a new cotter pin.

9. Install the front wheels, then lower the vehicle. Have the alignment (toe) checked.

10. Connect the battery cable.

1990–94 Cabriolet, 1990–92 Golf and Jetta

➡**This procedure may throw the vehicles wheel alignment (specifically the toe angle) out of specification. A wheel alignment is recommended upon completion of the following steps.**

1. Raise and safely support the vehicle on jack stands and center the steering wheel.

➡**On manual steering and TRW power steering gear, only the right side tie rod end is removable. The left tie rod must be replaced if the end joint is worn. On all vehicles, the front wheels must be aligned after steering gear repairs.**

2. Remove the cotter pin and use a ball joint press to disconnect the tie rod end from the steering knuckle. If a ball joint press is not available:
   • Loosen but do not remove the nut from the tie rod end.
   • Place a floor jack under the tie rod as close to the end as possible and raise it just enough to put pressure on the tie rod end. Do not lift the suspension.
   • Where the tie rod end fits into the steering knuckle, rap sharply with a hammer directly on the end of the steering knuckle boss. The tie rod end should jump out of the tapered hole in the boss.

3. Mark or measure the length of the right tie rod so it can be installed with the correct toe adjustment.

4. On the right side tie rod, hold the rod with a wrench and loosen the lock nut. Count the number of turns required to remove the tie rod end.

5. To remove the left tie rod, disconnect the rubber boot from the end of the steering rack and turn the steering wheel all the way to the right.

6. Loosen the lock nut and unscrew the tie rod from the steering rack.

To install:

7. Installation is the reverse of removal. Make sure each tie rod is the original length before tightening the lock nuts.

8. After inserting the tie rod end into the steering knuckle, tighten the nut to 26 ft. lbs. (35 Nm) and tighten as required to install a new cotter pin.

1995–99 Cabrio, 1993–99 Golf and Jetta

➡**This procedure may throw the vehicles wheel alignment (specifically the toe angle) out of specification. A wheel alignment is recommended upon completion of the following steps.**

1. Engage the parking brake.

2. Raise and safely support the vehicle on jack stands and center the steering wheel.

➡**Do not lift the suspension.**

3. Remove the front wheel(s).

4. Hold the tie-rod end and loosen the jam nut a half turn.

5. Loosen and remove the nut from the tie rod end that attaches it to the steering knuckle.

6. Use a ball joint / tie-rod end separator to pull the tie-rod end from the steering knuckle.

7. Count and record the number of turns that are required to remove the tie-rod end from the rod itself. This will allow you to position the new tie-rod end close to the original mark, thus keeping the vehicles alignment close to specification.

To install:

➡**A new tie-rod end retaining nut is required any time the nut has been removed.**

8. Clean the tie-rod end threads as well as those on the tie-rod.

9. Install a new tie-rod end onto the tie-rod and thread it to the correct number of threads.

10. Tighten the jam nut to 26 ft. lbs. (35 Nm).

11. Install the tie-rod end into the spindle.

12. Install the lock-nut and tighten to 37 ft. lbs. (50 Nm).

13. Install the tire and wheel assembly. Tighten the lug nuts to 81 ft. lbs. (110 Nm).

14. Lower the vehicle and test the steering.

15. Check to ensure all components have been reinstalled and tightened to the proper setting.

16. Have the vehicles alignment checked by and authorized repair facility.

Manual Steering Gear

ADJUSTMENTS

The adjusting screw is on the rack housing and adjusts pinion gear-to-rack clearance. Turning the screw clockwise tightens the clearance. Turn the adjusting screw no more than 20 degrees and test drive the vehicle after each adjustment. If the adjustment does not improve steering response or feel, return the screw to its original position and look for worn or damaged steering or suspension parts.

REMOVAL & INSTALLATION

1990–94 Cabriolet, 1990–92 Golf and Jetta

1. Raise and safely support the vehicle on jack stands and remove the ignition key to lock the steering wheel.

2. Remove the bolt from the steering shaft universal joint. Matchmark the universal joint to the pinion shaft.

3. Disconnect the tie rod ends from the steering knuckles.

4. Remove the mount nuts to remove the steering rack as an assembly.

5. Installation is the reverse of removal. Fit the pinion shaft into the universal joint while fitting the steering gear into place on the body.

6. Tighten the steering gear mount nuts and the universal joint bolt to 22 ft. lbs. (30 Nm).

7. After inserting the tie rod ends into the steering knuckle, tighten the nut to 26 ft. lbs. (35 Nm) and tighten as required to install a new cotter pin.

Fox

1. Disconnect the negative battery cable.

2. Pry off the lock plate and remove both tie rod mounting bolts from the steering rack (inside the engine compartment). Carefully pry the tie rods out of the mounting pivot.

3. Remove the lower instrument panel trim.

4. Remove the shaft clamp bolt. Pry off the clip, then drive the shaft toward the inside of the car with a brass drift.

5. Remove the steering rack mounting bolts.

6. Turn the wheels all the way to the right and remove the steering rack through the opening in the right wheel housing.

To install:

7. Position the rack in the vehicle. Tighten the mounting bolts to 15 ft. lbs. (19 Nm).

8. Temporarily install the tie rod mounting pivot to the rack with both mounting bolts. Remove one bolt, install the tie rod, and reinstall the bolt. Do the same on the other tie rod. Tighten the pivot bolts to 40 ft. lbs. (54 Nm). Make sure to install a new lock plate.

9. Install the clip, then tighten the clamp bolt. Install the lower instrument panel trim.

10. Connect the battery cable.

OVERHAUL

The steering rack and pinion assembly is not designed to be rebuilt and service parts are not available.

Power Steering Gear (rack and pinion where applicable)

ADJUSTMENT

1990–94 Cabriolet, 1990–93 Fox, 1990–92 Golf and Jetta

ZF STEERING GEAR

1. This job requires 2 people. With the vehicle on the ground and the wheels straight ahead, turn the steering wheel back and forth about 30° with the engine not running.

2. If the steering feels loose or makes noise, have an assistant turn the adjusting bolt clockwise until the noise stops. The noise may not stop completely so do not continue tightening the adjustment.

TRW STEERING GEAR

1. Remove the steering gear from the vehicle.

2. Loosen the lock nut and use the special pin wrench to turn the adjuster until the rack can be moved by hand without binding or excessive free play.

3. Install the steering gear.

REMOVAL & INSTALLATION

Fox

▶ See Figure 68

1. Disconnect the negative battery cable.

2. Pry off the lock plate and remove both tie rod mounting bolts from steering rack (inside the engine compartment). Carefully pry the tie rods out of the mounting pivot.

3. Remove the lower instrument panel trim.

4. Remove the shaft clamp bolt. Pry off the clip, then drive the shaft toward the inside of the car with a brass drift.

5. Disconnect the power steering hoses. Place a pan under the steering rack to catch any fluid.

6. Remove the steering rack mounting bolts.

7. Turn the wheels all the way to the right and remove the steering rack through the opening in the right wheel housing.

To install:

8. Position the rack in the vehicle. Tighten the mounting bolts to 15 ft. lbs. (19 Nm).

9. Temporarily install the tie rod mounting pivot to the rack with both mounting bolts. Remove one bolt, install the tie rod, and reinstall the bolt. Do the same on the other tie rod. Tighten the pivot bolts to 40 ft. lbs. (54 Nm). Make sure to install a new lock plate.

10. Install the clip, then tighten the clamp bolt. Install the lower instrument panel trim.

11. Connect the power steering lines, then refill the fluid reservoir.

12. Connect the battery cable and properly bleed the power steering system as described in this section.

1990–94 Cabriolet, 1990–92 Golf and Jetta

1. Raise and safely support the vehicle on jack stands and remove the ignition key to lock the steering wheel.

2. Place a catch pan under the power steering gear to catch the fluid.

3. Disconnect the suction hose and the pressure lines and drain the fluid into the catch pan (discard the fluid).

4. Remove the bolt from the steering shaft universal joint. Matchmark the universal joint to the pinion shaft.

5. Disconnect the tie rod ends from the steering knuckles.

6. Remove the mount nuts to remove the steering rack as an assembly.

To install:

7. Fit the pinion shaft into the universal joint while fitting the steering gear into place on the body.

8. Tighten the steering gear mount nuts and the universal joint bolt to 22 ft. lbs. (30 Nm).

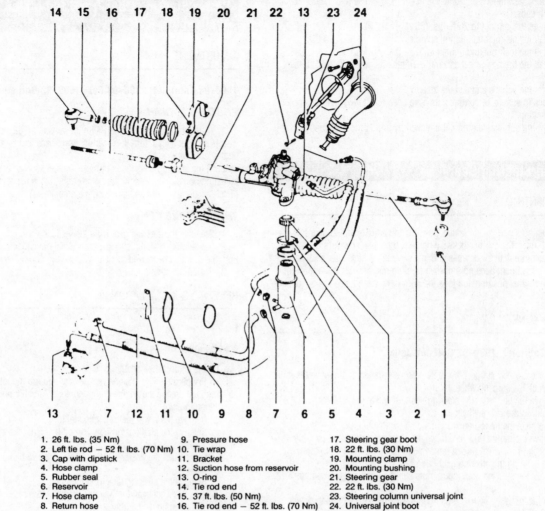

1. 26 ft. lbs. (35 Nm)
2. Left tie rod — 52 ft. lbs. (70 Nm)
3. Cap with dipstick
4. Hose clamp
5. Rubber seal
6. Reservoir
7. Hose clamp
8. Return hose
9. Pressure hose
10. Tie wrap
11. Bracket
12. Suction hose from reservoir
13. O-ring
14. Tie rod end
15. 37 ft. lbs. (50 Nm)
16. Tie rod end — 52 ft. lbs. (70 Nm)
17. Steering gear boot
18. 22 ft. lbs. (30 Nm)
19. Mounting clamp
20. Mounting bushing
21. Steering gear
22. 22 ft. lbs. (30 Nm)
23. Steering column universal joint
24. Universal joint boot

86638044

Fig. 68 Power steering rack assembly exploded view

9. After inserting the tie rod ends into the steering knuckle, tighten the nut to 26 ft. lbs. (35 Nm) and tighten as required to install a new cotter pin.

10. Connect the hydraulic lines, refill the fluid reservoir and bleed the system as described later.

1995–99 Cabrio, 1993–99 Golf and Jetta

1. Raise and safely support the vehicle.
2. Remove both front wheels and disengage both tie rod ends.
3. Remove the low pressure (suction) hose from the pump and drain the system into a catch pan. Properly discard the fluid.
4. At the steering column, remove the boot clamp, push the boot towards the body and remove the clamp bolt from the universal joint.
5. On Cabrio models, remove the exhaust manifold and shift linkage bracket.
6. Remove the rack mounting clamp nuts and remove the clamps.
7. At this point on some vehicles, the rack cannot be removed from the body. Support the engine/transaxle and remove the subframe bolts to allow the rack to move towards the rear. On Cabrio models, remove the transaxle mount and bracket.
8. Disconnect the power steering hydraulic lines and remove the rack toward the right.

To install:
9. Be sure the mounting bushings are in good condition. Fit the rack assembly into place and tighten the clamp nuts to 22 ft. lbs. (32 Nm)

10. Install any subframe bolts that were removed.
11. Connect the hydraulic lines and install the steering column universal joint bolt.
12. Fill the system with new fluid and run the engine to check for leaks and bleed the system.

Power Steering Pump

REMOVAL & INSTALLATION

♦ See Figure 69

1990–94 Cabriolet, 1990–93 Fox, 1990–92 Golf and Jetta

1. Place a catch pan under the power steering pump to catch the fluid.
2. Remove the suction hose and the pressure line from the pump, then drain the fluid into the catch pan (discard the fluid).
3. Loosen the tensioning bolt at the front of the tensioning bracket and remove the drive belt from the pump pulley.
4. Remove the pump mounting bolts and lift the pump from the vehicle.

To install:
5. To install, reverse the removal procedures. Tighten the mounting bolts to 15 ft. lbs. (20 Nm) and adjust the drive belt. Fill the reservoir with approved power steering fluid and bleed the system.

Fig. 69 Remove the power steering pump once all fasteners and lines have been removed

1995–99 Cabrio, 1993–99 Golf and Jetta

1. Disconnect the negative battery cable.
2. Remove the power steering V-belt.
3. Detach the hoses from the power steering pump and cover the ends of the hoses with a plastic bag to prevent dirt from entering.
4. Remove the fasteners from the adjusting bracket. Then remove the bracket from the assembly.

5. Disconnect the pivot bracket and the pump by removing the bolts.
6. Pull the bracket and pump away from the engine as an assembly.

To install:

7. Install the pump and the brackets as an assembly to the engine block.
8. Install the adjusting bracket to the engine block and power steering pump.

➡**There is no need to tighten the pivot bracket bolts at this time. They must be loose to allow an adjustment later in this procedure.**

9. Attach the pump adjusting bracket.
10. Install the lower power steering hose.
11. Fill the reservoir with power steering fluid.
12. To bleed the power steering pump, rotate the pump pulley by hand.

✳✳ WARNING

Severe damage will occur if the pump is not bled before the engine is started.

13. Install the pressure hose.
14. Install the V-belt.
15. Fill the pump reservoir to the proper mark.
16. Connect the negative battery cable.

BLEEDING

1. Fill the reservoir to the MAX level mark with approved power steering fluid.
2. With the engine idling, turn the wheels from the right to the left side as far as possible, several times.
3. Refill the reservoir to the MAX level and repeat the procedure until the level does not change.

TORQUE SPECIFICATIONS

Component	English Specifications	Metric Specifications
Air bag retaining screws	89 inch lbs.	10 Nm
Front Suspension		
Ball joint-to-steering knuckle	41 ft. lbs.	55 Nm
Control arm rear mounting bolt	125 ft. lbs.	170 Nm
Control arm front mounting bolt	90 ft. lbs.	125 Nm
Hub and bearing assembly-to-steering knuckle bolts	70 ft. lbs.	95 Nm
Knuckle-to-strut bolts	133 ft. lbs.	180 Nm
Strut		
Strut dampener shaft retaining nut	52 ft. lbs.	70 Nm
Strut-to-body mounting bolts/nuts	18-20 ft. lbs.	25-27 Nm
Subframe mounting bolts	96 ft. lbs.	130 Nm
Sway bar-to-subframe bolts	49 ft. lbs.	66 Nm
Sway bar links-to-sway bar	13 ft. lbs.	17 Nm
Tie-rod end-to-steering knuckle nuts	44 ft. lbs.	60 Nm
Wheel hub retaining nut	185 ft. lbs.	260 Nm
Power rack and pinion		
Inner tie rod-to-rack and pinion	74 ft. lbs.	100 Nm
Intermediate steering shaft upper pinch bolt	30 ft. lbs.	41 Nm
Outer tie rod jam nut	50 ft. lbs.	68 Nm
Rack-to-subframe retaining bolts	89 ft. lbs.	120 Nm
Steering shaft-to-rack and pinion flange lower pinch bolt	30 ft. lbs.	41 Nm
Power steering pump		
Hose fittings	20 ft. lbs.	27 Nm
Pump retaining bolts	22 ft. lbs.	30 Nm
Rear suspension		
Coil-over shocks		
Coil-over shock-to-body mounting bolts	21 ft. lbs.	28 Nm
Coil-over shock-to-body mounting nut	15 ft. lbs.	20 Nm
Lower mount bolt	125 ft. lbs.	170 Nm
Control arm/axle		
Mounting bolts	52 ft. lbs. ①	72 Nm ①
Brake line bracket mounting bolts	97 inch lbs.	11 Nm
Wheel hub mounting bolts	44 ft. lbs.	60 Nm
Steering wheel center nut	30 ft. lbs.	41 Nm
Wheel lug nuts	100 ft. lbs.	140 Nm

① Rotate an additional 120°

91228C01

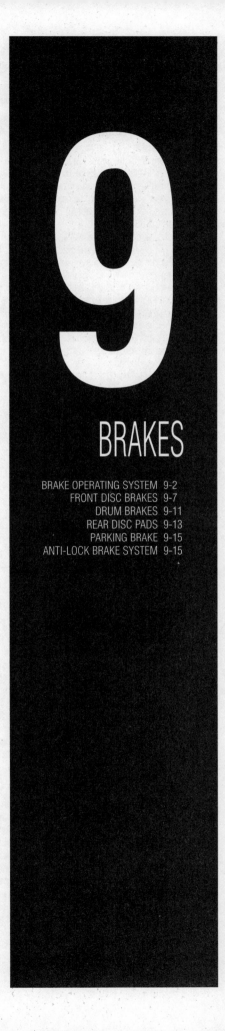

9

BRAKES

BRAKE OPERATING SYSTEM

Basic Operating Principles

Hydraulic systems are used to actuate the brakes of all modern automobiles. The system transports the power required to force the frictional surfaces of the braking system together from the pedal to the individual brake units at each wheel. A hydraulic system is used for two reasons.

First, fluid under pressure can be carried to all parts of an automobile by small pipes and flexible hoses without taking up a significant amount of room or posing routing problems.

Second, a great mechanical advantage can be given to the brake pedal end of the system, and the foot pressure required to actuate the brakes can be reduced by making the surface area of the master cylinder pistons smaller than that of any of the pistons in the wheel cylinders or calipers.

The master cylinder consists of a fluid reservoir along with a double cylinder and piston assembly. Double type master cylinders are designed to separate the front and rear braking systems hydraulically in case of a leak. The master cylinder coverts mechanical motion from the pedal into hydraulic pressure within the lines. This pressure is translated back into mechanical motion at the wheels by either the wheel cylinder (drum brakes) or the caliper (disc brakes).

Steel lines carry the brake fluid to a point on the vehicle's frame near each of the vehicle's wheels. The fluid is then carried to the calipers and wheel cylinders by flexible tubes in order to allow for suspension and steering movements.

In drum brake systems, each wheel cylinder contains two pistons, one at either end, which push outward in opposite directions and force the brake shoe into contact with the drum.

In disc brake systems, the cylinders are part of the calipers. At least one cylinder in each caliper is used to force the brake pads against the disc.

All pistons employ some type of seal, usually made of rubber, to minimize fluid leakage. A rubber dust boot seals the outer end of the cylinder against dust and dirt. The boot fits around the outer end of the piston on disc brake calipers, and around the brake actuating rod on wheel cylinders.

The hydraulic system operates as follows: When at rest, the entire system, from the piston(s) in the master cylinder to those in the wheel cylinders or calipers, is full of brake fluid. Upon application of the brake pedal, fluid trapped in front of the master cylinder piston(s) is forced through the lines to the wheel cylinders. Here, it forces the pistons outward, in the case of drum brakes, and inward toward the disc, in the case of disc brakes. The motion of the pistons is opposed by return springs mounted outside the cylinders in drum brakes, and by spring seals, in disc brakes.

Upon release of the brake pedal, a spring located inside the master cylinder immediately returns the master cylinder pistons to the normal position. The pistons contain check valves and the master cylinder has compensating ports drilled in it. These are uncovered as the pistons reach their normal position. The piston check valves allow fluid to flow toward the wheel cylinders or calipers as the pistons withdraw. Then, as the return springs force the brake pads or shoes into the released position, the excess fluid reservoir through the compensating ports. It is during the time the pedal is in the released position that any fluid that has leaked out of the system will be replaced through the compensating ports.

Dual circuit master cylinders employ two pistons, located one behind the other, in the same cylinder. The primary piston is actuated directly by mechanical linkage from the brake pedal through the power booster. The secondary piston is actuated by fluid trapped between the two pistons. If a leak develops in front of the secondary piston, it moves forward until it bottoms against the front of the master cylinder, and the fluid trapped between the pistons will operate the rear brakes. If the rear brakes develop a leak, the primary piston will move forward until direct contact with the secondary piston takes place, and it will force the secondary piston to actuate the front brakes. In either case, the brake pedal moves farther when the brakes are applied, and less braking power is available.

All dual circuit systems use a switch to warn the driver when only half of the brake system is operational. This switch is usually located in a valve body which is mounted on the firewall or the frame below the master cylinder. A hydraulic piston receives pressure from both circuits, each circuit's pressure being applied to one end of the piston. When the pressures are in balance, the piston remains stationary. When one circuit has a leak, however, the greater pressure in that circuit during application of the brakes will push the piston to one side, closing the switch and activating the brake warning light.

In disc brake systems, this valve body also contains a metering valve and, in some cases, a proportioning valve. The metering valve keeps pressure from traveling to the disc brakes on the front wheels until the brake shoes on the rear wheels have contacted the drums, ensuring that the front brakes will never be used alone. The proportioning valve controls the pressure to the rear brakes to lessen the chance of rear wheel lock-up during very hard braking.

Warning lights may be tested by depressing the brake pedal and holding it while opening one of the wheel cylinder bleeder screws. If this does not cause the light to go on, substitute a new lamp, make continuity checks, and, finally, replace the switch as necessary.

The hydraulic system may be checked for leaks by applying pressure to the pedal gradually and steadily. If the pedal sinks very slowly to the floor, the system has a leak. This is not to be confused with a springy or spongy feel due to the compression of air within the lines. If the system leaks, there will be a gradual change in the position of the pedal with a constant pressure.

Check for leaks along all lines and at wheel cylinders. If no external leaks are apparent, the problem is inside the master cylinder.

DISC BRAKES

Instead of the traditional expanding brakes that press outward against a circular drum, disc brake systems utilize a disc (rotor) with brake pads positioned on either side of it. An easily-seen analogy is the hand brake arrangement on a bicycle. The pads squeeze onto the rim of the bike wheel, slowing its motion. Automobile disc brakes use the identical principle but apply the braking effort to a separate disc instead of the wheel.

The disc (rotor) is a casting, usually equipped with cooling fins between the two braking surfaces. This enables air to circulate between the braking surfaces making them less sensitive to heat buildup and more resistant to fade. Dirt and water do not drastically affect braking action since contaminants are thrown off by the centrifugal action of the rotor or scraped off the by the pads. Also, the equal clamping action of the two brake pads tends to ensure uniform, straight line stops. Disc brakes are inherently self-adjusting. There are three general types of disc brake:

- Fixed caliper.
- Floating caliper.
- Sliding caliper.

The fixed caliper design uses two pistons mounted on either side of the rotor (in each side of the caliper). The caliper is mounted rigidly and does not move.

The sliding and floating designs are quite similar. In fact, these two types are often lumped together. In both designs, the pad on the inside of the rotor is moved into contact with the rotor by hydraulic force. The caliper, which is not held in a fixed position, moves slightly, bringing the outside pad into contact with the rotor. There are various methods of attaching floating calipers. Some pivot at the bottom or top, and some slide on mounting bolts. In any event, the end result is the same.

DRUM BRAKES

Drum brakes employ two brake shoes mounted on a stationary backing plate. These shoes are positioned inside a circular drum which rotates with the wheel assembly. The shoes are held in place by springs. This allows them to slide toward the drums (when they are applied) while keeping the linings and drums in alignment. The shoes are actuated by a wheel cylinder which is mounted at the top of the backing plate. When the brakes are applied, hydraulic pressure forces the wheel cylinder's actuating links outward. Since these links bear directly against the top of the brake shoes, the tops of the shoes are then forced against the inner side of the drum. This action forces the bottoms of the two shoes to contact the brake drum by rotating the entire assembly slightly (known as servo action). When pressure within the wheel cylinder is relaxed, return springs pull the shoes back away from the drum.

Most modern drum brakes are designed to self-adjust themselves during application when the vehicle is moving in reverse. This motion causes both shoes to rotate very slightly with the drum, rocking an adjusting lever, thereby causing rotation of the adjusting screw. Some drum brake systems are designed to self-adjust during application whenever the brakes are applied. This on-board adjustment system reduces the need for maintenance adjustments and keeps both the brake function and pedal feel satisfactory.

Troubleshooting the Brake System

Problem	Cause	Solution
Low brake pedal (excessive pedal travel required for braking action.)	• Excessive clearance between rear linings and drums caused by inoperative automatic adjusters • Worn rear brakelining • Bent, distorted brakeshoes, front or rear • Air in hydraulic system	• Make 10 to 15 alternate forward and reverse brake stops to adjust brakes. If brake pedal does not come up, repair or replace adjuster parts as necessary. • Inspect and replace lining if worn beyond minimum thickness specification. • Replace brakeshoes in axle sets • Remove air from system. Refer to Brake Bleeding.
Low brake pedal (pedal may go to floor with steady pressure applied.)	• Fluid leak in hydraulic system • Air in hydraulic system • Incorrect or non-recommended brake fluid (fluid evaporates at below normal temp). • Master cylinder piston seals worn, or master cylinder bore is scored, worn or corroded	• Fill master cylinder to fill line; have helper apply brakes and check calipers, wheel cylinders, differential valve tubes, hoses and fittings for leaks. Repair or replace as necessary. • Remove air from system. Refer to Brake Bleeding. • Flush hydraulic system with clean brake fluid. Refill with correct-type fluid. • Repair or replace master cylinder
Low brake pedal goes to floor on first application—o.k. on subsequent applications.)	• Disc brake pads sticking on abutment surfaces of anchor plate. Caused by a build-up of dirt, rust, or corrosion on abutment surfaces	• Clean abutment surfaces
Fading brake pedal (pedal height decreases with steady pressure applied.)	• Fluid leak in hydraulic system • Master cylinder piston seals worn, or master cylinder bore is scored, worn or corroded	• Fill master cylinder reservoirs to fill mark, have helper apply brakes, check calipers, wheel cylinders, differential valve, tubes, hoses, and fittings for fluid leaks. Repair or replace parts as necessary. • Repair or replace master cylinder
Decreasing brake pedal travel (pedal travel required for braking action decreases and may be accompanied by a hard pedal.)	• Caliper or wheel cylinder pistons sticking or seized • Master cylinder compensator ports blocked (preventing fluid return to reservoirs) or pistons sticking or seized in master cylinder bore • Power brake unit binding internally	• Repair or replace the calipers, or wheel cylinders • Repair or replace the master cylinder • Test unit according to the following procedure: (a) Shift transmission into neutral and start engine (b) Increase engine speed to 1500 rpm, close throttle and fully depress brake pedal (c) Slow release brake pedal and stop engine (d) Have helper remove vacuum check valve and hose from power unit. Observe for backward movement of brake pedal. (e) If the pedal moves backward, the power unit has an internal bind—replace power unit

TCCA9C01

Troubleshooting the Brake System (cont.)

Problem	Cause	Solution
Spongy brake pedal (pedal has abnormally soft, springy, spongy feel when depressed.)	• Air in hydraulic system • Brakeshoes bent or distorted • Brakelining not yet seated with drums and rotors • Rear drum brakes not properly adjusted	• Remove air from system. Refer to Brake Bleeding. • Replace brakeshoes • Burnish brakes • Adjust brakes
Hard brake pedal (excessive pedal pressure required to stop vehicle. May be accompanied by brake fade.)	• Loose or leaking power brake unit vacuum hose • Incorrect or poor quality brakelining • Bent, broken, distorted brakeshoes • Calipers binding or dragging on mounting pins. Rear brakeshoes dragging on support plate. • Caliper, wheel cylinder, or master cylinder pistons sticking or seized • Power brake unit vacuum check valve malfunction	• Tighten connections or replace leaking hose • Replace with lining in axle sets • Replace brakeshoes • Replace mounting pins and bushings. Clean rust or burrs from rear brake support plate ledges and lubricate ledges with molydisulfide grease. NOTE: If ledges are deeply grooved or scored, do not attempt to sand or grind them smooth—replace support plate. • Repair or replace parts as necessary • Test valve according to the following procedure: (a) Start engine, increase engine speed to 1500 rpm, close throttle and immediately stop engine (b) Wait at least 90 seconds then depress brake pedal (c) If brakes are not vacuum assisted for 2 or more applications, check valve is faulty
	• Power brake unit has internal bind • Master cylinder compensator ports (at bottom of reservoirs) blocked by dirt, scale, rust, or have small burrs (blocked ports prevent fluid return to reservoirs). • Brake hoses, tubes, fittings clogged or restricted • Brake fluid contaminated with improper fluids (motor oil, transmission fluid, causing rubber components to swell and stick in bores • Low engine vacuum	• Test unit according to the following procedure. (a) With engine stopped, apply brakes several times to exhaust all vacuum in system (b) Shift transmission into neutral, depress brake pedal and start engine (c) If pedal height decreases with foot pressure and less pressure is required to hold pedal in applied position, power unit vacuum system is operating normally. Test power unit. If power unit exhibits a bind condition, replace the power unit. • Repair or replace master cylinder CAUTION: Do not attempt to clean blocked ports with wire, pencils, or similar implements. Use compressed air only. • Use compressed air to check or unclog ports. Replace any damaged parts. • Replace all rubber components, combination valve and hoses. Flush entire brake system with DOT 3 brake fluid or equivalent. • Adjust or repair engine

TCCA9C02

Troubleshooting the Brake System (cont.)

Problem	Cause	Solution
Grabbing brakes (severe reaction to brake pedal pressure.)	• Brakelining(s) contaminated by grease or brake fluid	• Determine and correct cause of contamination and replace brakeshoes in axle sets
	• Parking brake cables incorrectly adjusted or seized	• Adjust cables. Replace seized cables.
	• Incorrect brakelining or lining loose on brakeshoes	• Replace brakeshoes in axle sets
	• Caliper anchor plate bolts loose	• Tighten bolts
	• Rear brakeshoes binding on support plate ledges	• Clean and lubricate ledges. Replace support plate(s) if ledges are deeply grooved. Do not attempt to smooth ledges by grinding.
	• Incorrect or missing power brake reaction disc	• Install correct disc
	• Rear brake support plates loose	• Tighten mounting bolts
Dragging brakes (slow or incomplete release of brakes)	• Brake pedal binding at pivot	• Loosen and lubricate
	• Power brake unit has internal bind	• Inspect for internal bind. Replace unit if internal bind exists.
	• Parking brake cables incorrrectly adjusted or seized	• Adjust cables. Replace seized cables.
	• Rear brakeshoe return springs weak or broken	• Replace return springs. Replace brakeshoe if necessary in axle sets.
	• Automatic adjusters malfunctioning	• Repair or replace adjuster parts as required
	• Caliper, wheel cylinder or master cylinder pistons sticking or seized	• Repair or replace parts as necessary
	• Master cylinder compensating ports blocked (fluid does not return to reservoirs).	• Use compressed air to clear ports. Do not use wire, pencils, or similar objects to open blocked ports.
Vehicle moves to one side when brakes are applied	• Incorrect front tire pressure	• Inflate to recommended cold (reduced load) inflation pressure
	• Worn or damaged wheel bearings	• Replace worn or damaged bearings
	• Brakelining on one side contaminated	• Determine and correct cause of contamination and replace brakelining in axle sets
	• Brakeshoes on one side bent, distorted, or lining loose on shoe	• Replace brakeshoes in axle sets
	• Support plate bent or loose on one side	• Tighten or replace support plate
	• Brakelining not yet seated with drums or rotors	• Burnish brakelining
	• Caliper anchor plate loose on one side	• Tighten anchor plate bolts
	• Caliper piston sticking or seized	• Repair or replace caliper
	• Brakelinings water soaked	• Drive vehicle with brakes lightly applied to dry linings
	• Loose suspension component attaching or mounting bolts	• Tighten suspension bolts. Replace worn suspension components.
	• Brake combination valve failure	• Replace combination valve
Chatter or shudder when brakes are applied (pedal pulsation and roughness may also occur.)	• Brakeshoes distorted, bent, contaminated, or worn	• Replace brakeshoes in axle sets
	• Caliper anchor plate or support plate loose	• Tighten mounting bolts
	• Excessive thickness variation of rotor(s)	• Refinish or replace rotors in axle sets

POWER BOOSTERS

Virtually all modern vehicles use a vacuum assisted power brake system to multiply the braking force and reduce pedal effort. Since vacuum is always available when the engine is operating, the system is simple and efficient. A vacuum diaphragm is located on the front of the master cylinder and assists the driver in applying the brakes, reducing both the effort and travel he must put into moving the brake pedal.

The vacuum diaphragm housing is normally connected to the intake manifold by a vacuum hose. A check valve is placed at the point where the hose enters the diaphragm housing, so that during periods of low manifold vacuum brakes assist will not be lost.

Depressing the brake pedal closes off the vacuum source and allows atmospheric pressure to enter on one side of the diaphragm. This causes the master cylinder pistons to move and apply the brakes. When the brake pedal is released, vacuum is applied to both sides of the diaphragm and springs return the diaphragm and master cylinder pistons to the released position.

If the vacuum supply fails, the brake pedal rod will contact the end of the master cylinder actuator rod and the system will apply the brakes without any power assistance. The driver will notice that much higher pedal effort is needed to stop the car and that the pedal feels harder than usual.

Vacuum Leak Test

1. Operate the engine at idle without touching the brake pedal for at least one minute.
2. Turn off the engine and wait one minute.
3. Test for the presence of assist vacuum by depressing the brake pedal and releasing it several times. If vacuum is present in the system, light application will produce less and less pedal travel. If there is no vacuum, air is leaking into the system.

System Operation Test

1. With the engine **OFF**, pump the brake pedal until the supply vacuum is entirely gone.
2. Put light, steady pressure on the brake pedal.
3. Start the engine and let it idle. If the system is operating correctly, the brake pedal should fall toward the floor if the constant pressure is maintained.

Power brake systems may be tested for hydraulic leaks just as ordinary systems are tested.

❈❈ WARNING

Clean, high quality brake fluid is essential to the safe and proper operation of the brake system. You should always buy the highest quality brake fluid that is available. If the brake fluid becomes contaminated, drain and flush the system, then refill the master cylinder with new fluid. Never reuse any brake fluid. Any brake fluid that is removed from the system should be discarded.

Brake Light Switch

REMOVAL & INSTALLATION

1. Disconnect the negative battery cable.
2. Unplug the connector on the brake light switch.
3. Rotate the switch 90° counterclockwise and pull outward to remove it.

To install:
4. Place the switch into place and rotate it 90° clockwise.
5. Attach the connector to the brake light switch.
6. Connect the negative battery cable.

Master Cylinder

REMOVAL & INSTALLATION

▶ **See Figures 1, 2 and 3**

Standard (Non-ABS) Brakes

1. To prevent brake fluid from spilling out and damaging the paint, place a protective cover over the fender.
2. Detach the negative battery cable.
3. Remove the master cylinder cap and remove as much fluid as possible.
4. Disconnect and cap the brake lines to keep dirt out.
5. Disconnect the wiring from any switches that may be screwed into the master cylinder.
6. Remove the two master cylinder mounting nuts and pull the master cylinder away from the booster.
7. The reservoir is held into the master cylinder by a press fit into rubber sealing plugs and can easily be pulled off. To reinstall, moisten the plugs with brake fluid and press it on.

❈❈ WARNING

Do not depress the brake pedal while the master cylinder is removed.

To install:
8. Position the master cylinder and reservoir assembly onto the studs and install the washers and nuts. Tighten the nuts to 15 ft. lbs. (20 Nm).
9. Remove the plugs and connect the brake lines.
10. Bleed the brake system.
11. Install all remaining components in the reverse order of removal.

Antilock Brakes (ABS)

1. Bleeding of the antilock brake system requires the use of a scan tool when ever the brake master cylinder reservoir runs dry. Therefore the removal of a defective master cylinder, on vehicles with ABS, should be performed by a professional repair facility.

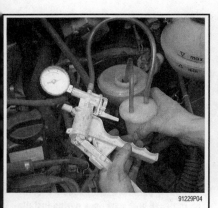
91229P04
Fig. 1 Siphon out the brake fluid

91229P03
Fig. 2 Remove the brake lines

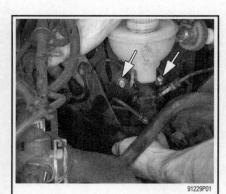
91229P01
Fig. 3 Remove the two master cylinder mounting bolts

Power Brake Booster

REMOVAL & INSTALLATION

▶ **See Figure 4**

1. Remove the master cylinder from the booster.
2. At the pedals, remove the clevis pin on the end of the booster pushrod by unclipping it and pulling it from the clevis.
3. Disconnect the vacuum hose from the booster.
4. Unbolt the booster; remove the 2 nuts under the dashboard or the 4 nuts holding the booster to its bracket. Remove the booster.

To install:

5. Installation is the reverse of removal. Install the master cylinder and bleed the system.

Brake Pressure Regulator

REMOVAL & INSTALLATION

▶ **See Figure 5**

The brake pressure regulator is located at the rear axle, usually on the drivers side. It controls the amount of pressure the rear brakes receive to help prevent premature lockup. It is a weight sensitive device which increases the pressure as the amount of force applied to it increases. Hence more braking force is allowed only if the vehicle is heavily weighed down.

1. Release the pressure from the braking system.
2. Remove the negative battery cable
3. Detach any wiring harnesses from the regulator
4. Remove the bolts that hold the regulator to the under carriage
5. Remove the brake pressure regulator

Brake Hoses and Lines

Metal lines and rubber brake hoses should be checked frequently for leaks and external damage. Metal lines are particularly prone to crushing and kinking under the vehicle. Any such deformation can restrict the proper flow of fluid and therefore impair braking at the wheels. Rubber hoses should be checked for cracking or scraping; such damage can create a weak spot in the hose and it could fail under pressure.

Any time the lines are removed or disconnected, extreme cleanliness must be observed. Clean all joints and connections before disassembly (use a stiff bristle brush and clean brake fluid); be sure to plug the lines and ports as soon as they are opened. New lines and hoses should be flushed clean with brake fluid before installation to remove any contamination.

REMOVAL & INSTALLATION

▶ **See Figures 6 thru 11**

1. Disconnect the negative battery cable.
2. Raise and safely support the vehicle on jackstands.
3. Remove any wheel and tire assemblies necessary for access to the particular line you are removing.
4. Thoroughly clean the surrounding area at the joints to be disconnected.
5. Place a suitable catch pan under the joint to be disconnected.
6. Using two wrenches (one to hold the joint and one to turn the fitting), disconnect the hose or line to be replaced.
7. Disconnect the other end of the line or hose, moving the drain pan if necessary. Always use a back-up wrench to avoid damaging the fitting.
8. Disconnect any retaining clips or brackets holding the line and remove the line from the vehicle.

➡**If the brake system is to remain open for more time than it takes to swap lines, tape or plug each remaining clip and port to keep contaminants out and fluid in.**

Fig. 4 The master cylinder is bolted to the brake booster

Fig. 5 View of the brake pressure regulator

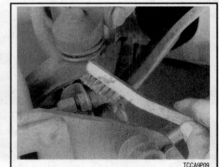

Fig. 6 Use a brush to clean the fittings of any debris

Fig. 7 Use a flare nut wrench to loosen the fitting

Fig. 8 Once loosened, unscrew the brake line by hand

Fig. 9 Any gaskets/crush washers should be replaced with new ones during installation

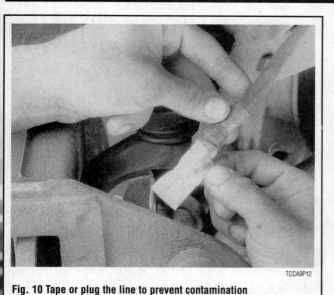

Fig. 10 Tape or plug the line to prevent contamination

Fig. 11 Upon reinstallation, always start threading the fitting by hand

To install:

9. Install the new line or hose, starting with the end farthest from the master cylinder. Connect the other end, then confirm that both fittings are correctly threaded and turn smoothly using finger pressure. Make sure the new line will not rub against any other part. Brake lines must be at least 1/2 in. (13mm) from the steering column and other moving parts. Any protective shielding or insulators must be reinstalled in the original location.

☀☀ WARNING

Make sure the hose is NOT kinked or touching any part of the frame or suspension after installation. These conditions may cause the hose to fail prematurely.

10. Using two wrenches as before, tighten each fitting.
11. Install any retaining clips or brackets on the lines.
12. If removed, install the wheel and tire assemblies, then carefully lower the vehicle to the ground.
13. Refill the brake master cylinder reservoir with clean, fresh brake fluid, meeting DOT 3 specifications. Properly bleed the brake system.
14. Connect the negative battery cable.

Bleeding The Brake System

➡ **If your vehicle is equipped with ABS, and you have allowed the master cylinder to run dry, a scan tool will be needed to successfully bleed all of the air out of the ABS valve body. It is recommended that this bleeding procedure be done by a authorized repair facility.**

When any part of the hydraulic system has been disconnected for repair or replacement, air may get into the lines and cause spongy pedal action (because air can be compressed and brake fluid cannot). To correct this condition, it is necessary to bleed the hydraulic system so to be sure all air is purged.

When bleeding the brake system, bleed one brake cylinder at a time, beginning at the cylinder with the longest hydraulic line (farthest from the master cylinder) first. ALWAYS Keep the master cylinder reservoir filled with brake fluid during the bleeding operation. Never use brake fluid that has been drained from the hydraulic system, no matter how clean it is.

➡ **Use only new DOT 3 or 4 brake fluid in all Volkswagen vehicles. Do not use silicone (DOT 5) fluid. Even the smallest traces can cause severe corrosion to the hydraulic system. All brake fluids are corrosive to paint.**

The primary and secondary hydraulic brake systems are separate and are bled independently. During the bleeding operation, do not allow the reservoir to run dry. Keep the master cylinder reservoir filled with brake fluid.

1. Clean all dirt from around the master cylinder fill cap, remove the cap and fill the master cylinder with brake fluid until the level is within 1/4 in. (6mm) of the top edge of the reservoir.
2. Clean the bleeder screws at all 4 wheels. The bleeder screws are located on the back of the brake backing plate (drum brakes) and on the top of the brake calipers (disc brakes).
3. Attach a length of rubber hose over the bleeder screw and place the other end of the hose in a glass jar, submerged in brake fluid.
4. Open the bleeder screw 1/2–3/4 turn. Have an assistant slowly `depress the brake pedal.
5. Close the bleeder screw and tell your assistant to allow the brake pedal to return slowly. Continue this process to purge all air from the system.
6. When bubbles cease to appear at the end of the bleeder hose, close the bleeder screw and remove the hose. Tighten the bleeder screw to the proper torque:
7. Check the master cylinder fluid level and add fluid accordingly. Do this after bleeding each wheel.
8. Repeat the bleeding operation at the remaining 3 wheels, ending with the one closet to the master cylinder.
9. Fill the master cylinder reservoir to the proper level.

FRONT DISC BRAKES

Brake Pads

REMOVAL & INSTALLATION

Caliper with Guide Pins

The ABS hydraulic modulator is capable of self-pressurizing and can generate pressures above 3000 psi. any time the ignition switch is turned ON. Relieve the system pressure before testing or repairing the hydraulic system. Improper repair or test procedures can cause serious or fatal injury.

1. Raise and safely support the vehicle on jackstands and remove the front wheels.
2. If the brake fluid reservoir level is near the maximum line, siphon some brake fluid from the reservoir to prevent overflowing when the piston is retracted into the cylinder bore.
3. Hold the lower guide pin with an open wrench and remove the bolt securing the caliper to the guide pin. Do not remove the top bolt.
4. Pivot the caliper up on the upper guide pin and slide the pads straight out to remove them.

To install:

5. Place the old pad against the piston and use a C-clamp to push the pis-

ton all the way into the bore. If the rubber boot is split, if there is fluid leaking from the caliper or if the piston will not move in the bore, the caliper must be rebuilt or replaced.

6. Fit the new pads into the carrier and pivot the caliper into place.

7. The original bolts are micro-encapsulated with a thread locking compound. Install a new bolt or clean the old bolt and apply a thread locking compound.

8. When tightening the bolt, be sure to use a back-up wrench to hold the guide pin. Tighten the bolt to 26 ft. lbs. (35 Nm).

9. Pump the brake pedal several times until the pedal is firm, then add new brake fluid as required.

Caliper with Sleeves and Bushings

▶ **See Figures 12 thru 17**

1. Raise and safely support the vehicle on jackstands and remove the front wheels.

2. If the brake fluid reservoir level is near the maximum line, siphon some brake fluid from the reservoir to prevent overflowing when the piston is pushed into the cylinder bore.

3. Put a large C-clamp around the caliper so it contacts the caliper body and the outer brake pad. Tighten the clamp to push the piston into the bore. Remove the clamp and push the caliper in and out to make sure the sleeves and bushings move freely.

4. With a 6mm Allen socket, remove the 2 bolts holding the caliper to the carrier. Push the caliper up and pivot the bottom of the caliper out of the carrier.

5. Hang the caliper from the front spring with a piece of wire. DO NOT let the caliper hang by the hydraulic line.

6. Remove the anti-rattle springs and the pads from the carrier and note their location.

To install:

7. Fit the anti-rattle springs into place and slide the new pads onto the carrier. The tang should be towards the inner pad.

8. Fit the caliper into place at the top and push up so it can be pivoted into

place at the bottom. The tabs on the anti-rattle springs should be pushing against the inside of the caliper.

9. Make sure the caliper mounting bolts are clean. Install the bolts and tighten them to 18 ft. lbs. (25 Nm).

10. Pump the brake pedal several times until the pedal is firm, then add new brake fluid as required.

INSPECTION

The brake pad wear limit is 0.080 inches (2mm). If the pads show signs of heat cracks or if they are worn unevenly, check the caliper for a sticking piston or guides. Check the caliper for signs of fluid leakage or damage to the dust seal. Also check the rotor for signs of heat cracks or discoloration. The minimum allowed thickness of solid brake rotors is 0.393 inches (10mm). Maximum allowed run-out is 0.002 inches (0.06mm). The minimum allowed thickness of vented brake rotors is 0.708 inches (18mm). Maximum allowed run-out is 0.002 inches (0.06mm).

Brake Caliper

REMOVAL & INSTALLATION

▶ **See Figures 18, 19 and 20**

The ABS hydraulic modulator is capable of self-pressurizing and can generate pressures above 3000 psi. any time the ignition switch is turned ON. Relieve the system pressure before testing or repairing the hydraulic system. Make sure the ignition switch stays **OFF** and pump the brake pedal 25–35 times to relieve the system pressure. Improper repair or test procedures can cause serious or fatal injury.

1. Raise and safely support the vehicle on jackstands and remove the wheels.

2. Loosen the hydraulic line at the caliper, then remove the caliper from the carrier. With guide pin calipers, be sure to hold the pin with a back-up wrench

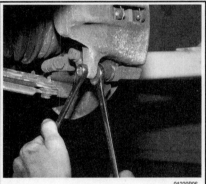

91229P06

Fig. 12 Loosen the caliper mounting bolts

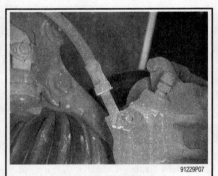

91229P07

Fig. 13 Use caution around the brake hoses. Do not nick, crimp, or twist the exterior rubber case of the hose

91229P08

Fig. 14 Note the position of each bolt removed

91229P09

Fig. 15 Pivot the caliper up and then pull it out to remove

91229P10

Fig. 16 Slide the pads out of the caliper

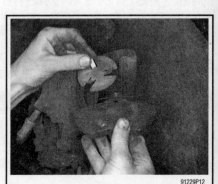

91229P12

Fig. 17 Always reinstall a shim. This thin piece of metal is essential to quiet brake operation

Fig. 18 Once the mounting hardware has been removed, pull the caliper away from the rotor

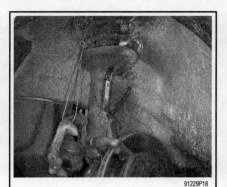

Fig. 19 Never let the caliper hang by the brake hose. Use wire to hang it as shown

Fig. 20 Lube the guide bolts with a synthetic disc brake caliper grease

when removing the caliper bolts. On cars with solid front rotors, remove the brake caliper to wheel bearing housing bolts.

3. Remove the caliper from the hydraulic line and cap the line to prevent fluid leakage.

4. Remove the brake pad wear sensor if equipped.

5. The carrier can be removed by removing the 2 bolts.

To install:

6. If removed, install the carrier. On standard brakes, tighten the carrier bolts to 52 ft. lbs. (70 Nm). On ABS brakes, tighten the carrier bolts to 92 ft. lbs. (125 Nm).

7. Thread the caliper onto the hydraulic line and hand-tighten it. Fit the caliper into place on the carrier.

8. On calipers with guide pins, tighten the bolts to 25 ft. lbs. (35 Nm). On calipers with sleeves and bushings, tighten the bolts to 18 ft. lbs. (25 Nm).

9. Tighten the hydraulic line and bleed the brakes.

OVERHAUL

▶ **See Figures 21 thru 28**

➡ **Some vehicles may be equipped dual piston calipers. The procedure to overhaul the caliper is essentially the same with the exception of multiple pistons, O-rings and dust boots.**

1. Remove the caliper from the vehicle and place on a clean workbench.

✳✳ CAUTION

NEVER place your fingers in front of the pistons in an attempt to catch or protect the pistons when applying compressed air. This could result in personal injury!

Fig. 21 For some types of calipers, use compressed air to drive the piston out of the caliper, but make sure to keep your fingers clear

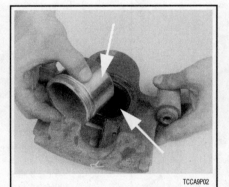

Fig. 22 Withdraw the piston from the caliper bore

Fig. 23 On some vehicles, you must remove the anti-rattle clip

Fig. 24 Use a prytool to carefully pry around the edge of the boot . . .

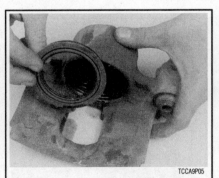

Fig. 25 . . . then remove the boot from the caliper housing, taking care not to score or damage the bore

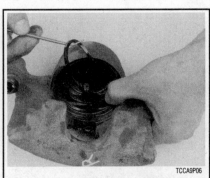

Fig. 26 Use extreme caution when removing the piston seal; DO NOT scratch the caliper bore

➡Depending upon the vehicle, there are two different ways to remove the piston from the caliper. Refer to the brake pad replacement procedure to make sure you have the correct procedure for your vehicle.

2. The first method is as follows:
a. Stuff a shop towel or a block of wood into the caliper to catch the piston.
b. Remove the caliper piston using compressed air applied into the caliper inlet hole. Inspect the piston for scoring, nicks, corrosion and/or

Fig. 27 Use the proper size driving tool and a mallet to properly seal the boots in the caliper housing

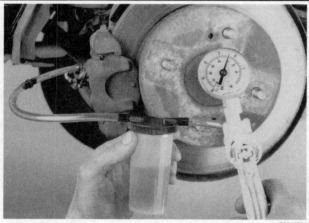

Fig. 28 There are tools, such as this Mighty-Vac, available to assist in proper brake system bleeding

worn or damaged chrome plating. The piston must be replaced if any of these conditions are found.

3. For the second method, you must rotate the piston to retract it from the caliper.
4. If equipped, remove the anti-rattle clip.
5. Use a prytool to remove the caliper boot, being careful not to scratch the housing bore.
6. Remove the piston seals from the groove in the caliper bore.
7. Carefully loosen the brake bleeder valve cap and valve from the caliper housing.
8. Inspect the caliper bores, pistons and mounting threads for scoring or excessive wear.
9. Use crocus cloth to polish out light corrosion from the piston and bore.
10. Clean all parts with denatured alcohol and dry with compressed air.
To assemble:
11. Lubricate and install the bleeder valve and cap.
12. Install the new seals into the caliper bore grooves, making sure they are not twisted.
13. Lubricate the piston bore.
14. Install the pistons and boots into the bores of the calipers and push to the bottom of the bores.
15. Use a suitable driving tool to seat the boots in the housing.
16. Install the caliper in the vehicle.
17. Install the wheel and tire assembly, then carefully lower the vehicle.
18. Properly bleed the brake system.

Brake Rotor

REMOVAL & INSTALLATION

▶ **See Figures 29, 30 and 31**

1. Raise and safely support vehicle and remove the wheel.
2. Remove the brake caliper, pads and the pad carrier.
3. With the wheel removed, the rotor is held in place only with a countersunk screw threaded into the hub. Remove the screw and slide the rotor off.
To install:
4. Install the rotor screw, clean the screw threads with a wire brush and install the screw. Tighten the screw to 15 ft. lbs. (20 Nm).
5. Reinstall the caliper and pump the brake pedal several times to bring the pads into adjustment. Road test the vehicle.

INSPECTION

Brake rotors may be checked for lateral run-out while installed on the car. This check will require a dial indicator gauge and stand to mount it on the caliper. VW has a special tool for this purpose which mounts the dial indicator to the caliper, but it can also be mounted on the shaft of a C-clamp attached to the outside of the caliper.

1. Remove the wheel and reinstall the wheel bolts (tightened to 65 ft. lbs.) to retain the rotor to the hub.

Fig. 29 Loosen the brake pad carrier mounting bolts

Fig. 30 Observe the location and size of each mounting bolt

Fig. 31 Remove the pad carrier and the brake rotor at the same time

2. Mount the dial indicator securely to the caliper. The gauge stem should touch the rotor about 1/2 inch (13mm) from the outer edge.

3. Rotate the rotor and observe the gauge. Radial run-out (wobble) must not exceed 0.002 inches (0.06mm). A rotor which exceeds this specification must be replaced or refinished.

4. Brake rotors which have excessive radial run-out, sharp ridges, or scor-ing can be refinished. First grinding must be done on both sides of the rotor to prevent squeaking and vibrating. Rotors which have only light grooves and are otherwise acceptable can be used without refinishing. The standard solid rotor is 12mm (0.472 inches) thick. It should not be ground to less than 10.5mm (0.413 inches). The standard vented rotor is 20mm (0.787 inches) thick and should be ground to no less than 18.5mm (0.728 inches).

DRUM BRAKES

Brake Drums

REMOVAL & INSTALLATION

Some brake shoes contain asbestos, which has been determined to be a can-cer causing agent. Never clean the brake surfaces with compressed air! Avoid inhaling any dust from any brake surface! When cleaning brake surfaces, use a commercially available brake cleaning fluid.

1. Raise and safely support vehicle and remove the rear wheels.

2. Insert a small pry tool through a wheel bolt hole and push up on the adjusting wedge to slacken the rear brake adjustment.

3. Remove the grease cap, cotter pin, locking ring, axle nut and thrust washer. Carefully remove the bearing and put all these parts where they will stay clean.

4. Carefully remove the drum by pulling it straight off the hub. If the drum is stuck, rock it side to side and top to bottom as you are pulling on it. If it still does not come off you may need to slacken the shoes some more by turning the adjuster with a spooning tool.

5. Before installing, if any brake dust has fallen onto the axle, wipe off all the grease and apply a coat of new high temperature bearing grease. Install the parts in the reverse order of removal.

➡When tightening the axle nut, the thrust washer must still be movable with a small screw driver. Spin the drum and check that the thrust washer can still be moved.

6. When installing the locking ring, keep trying different positions of the ring on the nut until the cotter pin goes into the hole. Don't turn the nut to align the locking ring with the hole in the axle. Use a new cotter pin.

INSPECTION

1. Check the drum for scoring or warping. Also check for signs of heat cracking or discoloring.

2. The maximum inside diameter after resurfacing must be no more than 7.106 inches (180.5mm).

3. The maximum wear limit is 7.126 inches (181mm).

Brake Shoes

INSPECTION

Check the shoes for contamination from brake fluid or axle grease. The mini-mum allowed lining thickness is 0.098 inches (2.5mm). This can be checked through the inspection plug on the back plate without removing the drum.

REMOVAL & INSTALLATION

1. Raise and safely support the vehicle and remove the rear wheels.

2. Remove the rear brake drum.

3. Remove the spring retainers by holding the pin behind the back plate, push in on the retainer and turn it ¼ turn.

4. Remove the shoes from the back plate by pulling first 1 shoe, then the other against the upper spring and from it's wheel cylinder slot. Detach the parking brake cable from the brake lever. The entire shoe assembly should now be free of the vehicle.

5. Carefully note the position of each spring, as spring shapes and posi-tions have varied from vehicle to vehicle and year to year.

6. Clamp the pushrod that holds the shoes apart at the top in a vise and begin removing the springs. Start with the lower return spring, adjusting wedge spring, upper return spring and then the tensioning spring and adjusting wedge.

7. On most vehicles, the parking brake lever must be removed from the old shoes and reused. When new parts are purchased, don't forget the clip that holds the parking brake lever pin in place.

To install:

8. Check the wheel cylinder for frozen pistons or leaks. If any defects are found, replace the wheel cylinder.

9. Inspect the springs. If the springs are damaged or show signs of over-heating they should be replaced. Indications of overheated springs are discol-oration and distortion.

10. Inspect the brake drum and recondition or replace as necessary.

11. Clean the back plate and lubricate the shoe contact points with a suit-able brake lubricant.

12. With the push rod clamped in a vise, attach the front brake shoe and tensioning spring.

13. Insert the adjusting wedge between the front shoe and pushrod so its lug is pointing toward the backing plate.

14. Remove the parking brake lever from the old shoe and attach it onto the new rear brake shoe.

15. Put the rear brake shoe and parking brake lever assembly onto the pushrod and hook up the spring.

16. Connect the parking brake cable to the lever and place the whole assembly onto the backing plate.

17. Install the hold-down springs.

18. Install the upper and lower return springs.

19. Install the adjusting wedge spring.

20. Center the brake shoes on the backing plate, making sure the adjusting wedge is fully released (all the way up) before installing the drum.

21. Install the drum and wheel assembly.

22. Apply the brake pedal a few times to bring the brake shoe into adjust-ment.

23. If the wheel cylinder was replaced, bleed the system.

24. Road test the vehicle.

ADJUSTMENTS

The drum brakes are self-adjusting and require a manual adjustment only after the brake shoes have been replaced, or when the length of the adjusting screw has been changed while performing some other service operation, as, for example, when taking off brake drums.

To adjust the brakes, perform the procedures that follow:

Drum Installed

1. Raise and support the rear of the vehicle on jackstands.

2. Remove the rubber plug from the adjusting slot. On some VW models you may have to knock out a tab in the drum to access the adjuster.

✲✲✲ CAUTION

Brake shoes may contain asbestos, which has been determined to be a cancer causing agent. Never clean the brake surfaces with compressed air! Avoid inhaling any dust from any brake surface! When cleaning brake surfaces, use a commercially available brake cleaning fluid.

3. Insert a brake adjusting spoon into the slot and engage the lowest pos-sible tooth on the starwheel. Move the end of the brake spoon downward to move the starwheel upward and expand the adjusting screw. Repeat this opera-tion until the brakes lock the wheels.

4. Insert a small screwdriver or piece of firm wire (coat hanger wire) into the

adjusting slot and push the automatic adjusting lever out and free of the star-wheel on the adjusting screw and hold it there.

5. Engage the topmost tooth possible on the starwheel with the brake adjusting spoon. Move the end of the adjusting spoon upward to move the adjusting screw starwheel downward and contact the adjusting screw. Back off the adjusting screw starwheel until the wheel spins freely with a minimum of drag. Keep track of the number of turns that the starwheel is backed off, or the number of strokes taken with the brake adjusting spoon.

6. Repeat this operation for the other side. When backing off the brakes on the other side, the starwheel adjuster must be backed off the same number of turns to prevent side-to-side brake pull.

7. Remove the jackstands and lower the vehicle.

8. After the brakes are adjusted make several stops while backing the vehicle up, to equalize the brakes at both of the wheels. Road test the vehicle.

Drum Removed

✳✳ CAUTION

Brake shoes may contain asbestos, which has been determined to be a cancer causing agent. Never clean the brake surfaces with compressed air! Avoid inhaling any dust from any brake surface! When cleaning brake surfaces, use a commercially available brake cleaning fluid.

1. Make sure that the shoe-to-contact pad areas are clean and properly lubricated.

2. Using an inside caliper check the inside diameter of the drum. Measure across the diameter of the assembled brake shoes, at their widest point.

3. Turn the adjusting screw so that the diameter of the shoes is 0.030 in. (0.76mm) less than the brake drum inner diameter.

4. Install the drum.

Wheel Cylinders

REMOVAL & INSTALLATION

1. Raise and safely support the vehicle and remove the wheel, drum and brake shoes.

2. Loosen the brake line on the rear of the cylinder but do not pull the line away from the cylinder or it may bend.

3. Remove the bolts and lock-washers that attach the wheel cylinder to the backing plate and remove the cylinder.

4. Position the new wheel cylinder on the backing plate and install the cylinder attaching bolts and lock-washers. Tighten to 8 ft. lbs. (10 Nm).

5. Attach the brake line.

6. Install the brakes and bleed the system.

7. Road test the vehicle.

OVERHAUL

▶ **See Figures 32 thru 41**

Wheel cylinder overhaul kits may be available, but often at little or no savings over a reconditioned wheel cylinder. It often makes sense with these components to substitute a new or reconditioned part instead of attempting an overhaul.

If no replacement is available, or you would prefer to overhaul your wheel cylinders, the following procedure may be used. When rebuilding and installing wheel cylinders, avoid getting any contaminants into the system. Always use clean, new, high quality brake fluid. If dirty or improper fluid has been used, it will be necessary to drain the entire system, flush the system with proper brake fluid, replace all rubber components, then refill and bleed the system.

TCCA9P13

Fig. 32 Remove the outer boots from the wheel cylinder

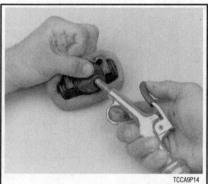

TCCA9P14

Fig. 33 Compressed air can be used to remove the pistons and seals

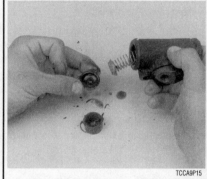

TCCA9P15

Fig. 34 Remove the pistons, cup seals and spring from the cylinder

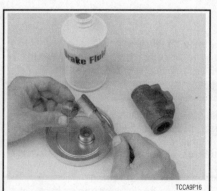

TCCA9P16

Fig. 35 Use brake fluid and a soft brush to clean the pistons . . .

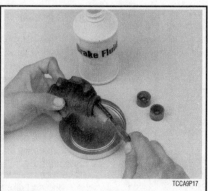

TCCA9P17

Fig. 36 . . . and the bore of the wheel cylinder

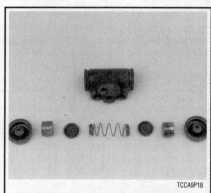

TCCA9P18

Fig. 37 Once cleaned and inspected, the wheel cylinder is ready for assembly

Fig. 38 Lubricate the cup seals with brake fluid

Fig. 39 Install the spring, then the cup seals in the bore

Fig. 40 Lightly lubricate the pistons, then install them

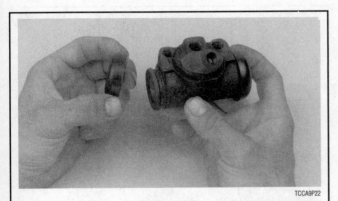

Fig. 41 The boots can now be installed over the wheel cylinder ends

1. Remove the wheel cylinder from the vehicle and place on a clean workbench.

2. First remove and discard the old rubber boots, then withdraw the pistons. Piston cylinders are equipped with seals and a spring assembly, all located behind the pistons in the cylinder bore.

3. Remove the remaining inner components, seals and spring assembly. Compressed air may be useful in removing these components. If no compressed air is available, be VERY careful not to score the wheel cylinder bore when removing parts from it. Discard all components for which replacements were supplied in the rebuild kit.

4. Wash the cylinder and metal parts in denatured alcohol or clean brake fluid.

✳✳ WARNING

Never use a mineral-based solvent such as gasoline, kerosene or paint thinner for cleaning purposes. These solvents will swell rubber components and quickly deteriorate them.

5. Allow the parts to air dry or use compressed air. Do not use rags for cleaning, since lint will remain in the cylinder bore.

6. Inspect the piston and replace it if it shows scratches.

7. Lubricate the cylinder bore and seals using clean brake fluid.

8. Position the spring assembly.

9. Install the inner seals, then the pistons.

10. Insert the new boots into the counter-bores by hand. Do not lubricate the boots.

11. Install the wheel cylinder.

REAR DISC BRAKES

Brake Pads

ADJUSTMENT

➡**Parking brake adjustment is only necessary after replacing brake pads or other brake components. If the parking brake does not hold the vehicle, the rear calipers and brake pads must be removed for inspection.**

1. Raise and safely support the rear of the vehicle on jackstands and remove the rear wheels.

2. With the parking brake handle down and the brake fully released, firmly apply the brake pedal once.

3. Pull the parking brake lever up 2–3 clicks. If the rear wheels cannot be turned by hand, no adjustment is required.

4. If adjustment is required, loosen the locknuts and the adjusting nuts to just relieve the tension on the cables.

5. Hold the release button on the handle and move the handle up and down 3 or more times to seat the cables and make sure they move freely, then leave the handle down.

6. Tighten the cable adjusting nuts evenly until the actuating levers on the calipers just move off their stops. The gap must be less than 0.059 inch (1.5mm).

7. To check for correct adjustment:

a. At the first click, the rotors should turn by hand with some drag.

b. At the second click, the rotors should be difficult to turn.

c. At the third click, it should not be possible to turn the rotors by hand.

d. When the brake handle is released, the rotors should turn freely.

REMOVAL & INSTALLATION

▶ **See Figures 42, 43 and 44**

Some brake pads contain asbestos, which has been determined to be a cancer causing agent. Never clean the brake surfaces with compressed air! Avoid inhaling any dust from any brake surface! When cleaning brake surfaces, use a commercially available brake cleaning fluid.

1. Raise and safely support the vehicle and remove the rear wheels.

2. Remove a sufficient quantity of brake fluid from the master cylinder reservoir to prevent it from over flowing when installing the pads. This is necessary as the caliper piston must be forced into the cylinder bore to provide sufficient clearance to install new pads.

3. Remove the parking brake cable clip from the caliper. Disconnect the parking brake cable.

4. Hold the guide pin with a back-up wrench and remove the upper mounting bolt from the brake caliper.

5. Swing the caliper downward and remove the brake pads.

6. Check the rotor for scoring and resurface or replace as necessary. Check the caliper for fluid leaks or a damaged dust seal. If any damage is found, the caliper will require overhauling or replacement.

Fig. 42 Once the caliper is supported, slide the pads out of the rotor

Fig. 43 Lube the guide bolts with a synthetic caliper grease

Fig. 44 Always inspect the anti rattle clips for damage

To install:

7. Retract the piston into the housing by rotating the piston clockwise.

8. Carefully clean the anchor plate and install the new brake pads onto the pad carrier.

9. Install the caliper to the pad carrier using a new self locking bolt or a thread locking compound and tighten to 26 ft. lbs. (35 Nm).

10. Attach the hand brake cable to the caliper. It may be necessary to back off the adjustment nuts at the hand brake handle.

11. Fill the reservoir with brake fluid and pump the brake pedal about 40 times with the engine off to set the piston. Setting the piston with the power assist could cause the piston to jam.

12. Check the parking brake operation, adjust the cable if necessary.

13. Road test the vehicle.

INSPECTION

- The brake pad wear limit is 0.080 inch (2mm).
- If the pads show signs of heat cracks or if they are worn unevenly, check the caliper for a sticking piston or guides.
- Check the caliper for signs of fluid leakage or damage to the dust seal.
- Check the rotor for signs of heat cracks or discoloration.
- Minimum allowed thickness of solid brake rotors is 0.393 inches (10mm). Maximum allowed run-out is 0.002 inch (0.06mm).

Brake Caliper

REMOVAL & INSTALLATION

▶ See Figures 45 and 46

The ABS hydraulic modulator is capable of self-pressurizing and can generate pressures above 3000 psi. any time the ignition switch is turned ON. Relieve the system pressure before testing or repairing the hydraulic system. Improper repair or test procedures can cause serious or fatal injury.

1. If equipped with ABS, make sure the ignition switch stays **OFF** and pump the brake pedal 25–35 times to relieve the system pressure.

2. Raise and safely support the vehicle on jackstands and remove the wheels.

3. Disconnect the parking brake cable.

4. Loosen the hydraulic line.

5. Use a back-up wrench to hold the guide pins and remove the caliper bolts.

6. Lift the caliper off the carrier and unscrew it from the hydraulic line.

7. The installation is the reverse of removal.

➡Use new caliper mount bolts or clean the old bolts and apply a thread locking compound. Tighten the bolts to 26 ft. lbs. (35 Nm).

8. Bleed the brakes.

Fig. 45 Use two wrenches, one to hold the caliper guide bolt sleeve from spinning and the other to remove the guide bolt itself

Fig. 46 Use a length of wire to hang the caliper. Never let the caliper hang from the brake hose

PARKING BRAKE

Cables

REMOVAL & INSTALLATION

Rear Drum Brakes

1. Block the front wheels and release the hand brake.
2. Raise and safely support the rear of the vehicle.
3. Remove the rear brake shoes.
4. Remove the brake cable assembly from the back plates.
5. Remove the cable adjusting nuts at the handle and detach the cable guides from the floor pan.
6. Pull the cables out from under the vehicle.
7. Installation is the reverse of removal. Adjust the parking brake and road test the vehicle.

Disc Brakes

1. Raise and safely support the vehicle.
2. Release the parking brake. It may be necessary to unscrew the adjusting nuts to provide slack in the brake cable.
3. At each rear wheel brake caliper, remove the spring clip retaining the parking brake cable to the caliper.
4. Lift the cable from the caliper mount and disengage it from the parking brake lever.
5. Pull the cables out from under the vehicle.
6. Installation is the reverse of removal.
7. Adjust the parking brake as described at the beginning of this section.

ADJUSTMENT

➡**Refer to the brake shoe/pad adjustment procedure in this section.**

ANTI-LOCK BRAKE SYSTEM

General Information

Anti-lock Brake Systems (ABS) are designed to prevent locked-wheel skidding during hard braking or during braking on slippery surfaces. The front wheels of a vehicle cannot apply steering force if they are locked and sliding; the vehicle will continue in the previous direction of travel. The 4 wheel ABS system used on Volkswagen vehicles holds the wheels just below the point of locking, thereby allowing some steering response and preventing the rear of the vehicle from sliding sideways.

There are conditions for which the ABS system provides no benefit. Hydroplaning is possible when the tires ride on a film of water, losing contact with the paved surface. This renders the vehicle totally uncontrollable until road contact is regained. Extreme steering maneuvers at high speed or cornering beyond the limits of tire adhesion can result in skidding which is independent of vehicle braking. For this reason, the system is named anti-lock rather than anti-skid. Wheel spin during acceleration on slippery surfaces may also fool the system into detecting a system failure and entering the fail-safe mode.

Under normal conditions, the ABS system functions in the same manner as a standard brake system and is transparent to the operator. The system is a combination of electrical and hydraulic components, working together to control the flow of brake fluid to the wheels when necessary.

The Electronic Control Unit (ECU) is the electronic brain of the system, receiving and interpreting signals from the wheel speed sensors. The unit will enter anti-lock mode when it senses impending wheel lock at any wheel and immediately control the brake line pressures to the affected wheel(s) by issuing output signals to the hydraulic modulator assembly.

The hydraulic modulator contains solenoids which react to the signals from the ECU. Each solenoid controls brake fluid pressure to one wheel. The solenoids allow brake line pressure to build according to brake pedal pressure, hold (isolating the system from the pedal and maintaining current pressure) or decrease by isolating the pedal circuit and bleeding some fluid from the line.

The decisions regarding these functions are made very rapidly and each solenoid can be cycled up to 10 times per second. Volkswagen employs a 3-channel control system. The front wheels are controlled separately; the rears are controlled together, based on the signal of the wheel with the greatest locking tendency.

The operator may feel a pulsing in the brake pedal and/or hear popping or clicking noises when the system engages. These sensations are due to the valves cycling and the pressures being changed rapidly within the brake system. While completely normal and not a sign of system failure, these sensations can be disconcerting to an operator unfamiliar with the system.

Although the ABS system prevents wheel lock-up under hard braking, as brake pressure increases, wheel slip is allowed to increase as well. This slip will result in some tire chirp during ABS operation. The sound should not be interpreted as lock-up but rather as an indication of the system holding the wheel(s) just outside the locking point. Additionally, the final few feet of an ABS-engaged stop may be completed with the wheels locked; the system is inoperative below approximately 3 mph.

When the ignition is ON and vehicle speed is over 3 mph (5 kph), the ECU monitors the function of the system. Should a fault be noted, such a loss of signal from a sensor, the ABS system is immediately disabled by the ECU. The ANTI-LOCK dashboard warning lamp is illuminated to inform the operator. When the ABS system is disabled, the vehicle retains normal braking capacity without the benefits of anti-lock.

Testing

Vehicles with anti-lock brake systems (ABS) have an electronic fault memory and an indicator light on the instrument panel. When the engine is first started, the light will go on to indicate the system is pressurizing and performing a self diagnostic check. After the system is at full pressure, the light will go out. If it remains lit, there is a fault in the system. The fault memory can only be accessed with the VW tester VAG 1551 or VAG 1598, or equivalent. If this diagnostic equipment is not available, most of the system can still be tested with a volt/ohmmeter. Service to the system is quite limited. Most components cannot be repaired, only replaced.

Before diagnosing an apparent ABS problem, make absolutely certain that the normal braking system is in correct working order. Many common brake problems (dragging parking brake, seepage, etc.) will affect the ABS system. A visual check of specific system components may reveal problems creating an apparent ABS malfunction. Performing this inspection may reveal a simple failure, thus eliminating extended diagnostic time.

1. Inspect the tire pressures; they must be approximately equal for the system to operate correctly.
2. Inspect the wheels and tires on the vehicle. They must be of the same size and type to generate accurate speed signals.
3. Inspect the brake fluid level in the reservoir.
4. Inspect brake lines, hoses, master cylinder assembly, and brake calipers for leakage.
5. Visually check brake lines and hoses for excessive wear, heat damage, punctures, contact with other parts, missing clips or holders, blockage or crimping.
6. Check the calipers for rust or corrosion. Check for proper sliding action if applicable.
7. Check the calipers for freedom of motion during application and release.
8. Inspect the wheel speed sensors for proper mounting and connections.
9. Inspect the sensor wheels for broken teeth or poor mounting.
10. Certain driver induced faults, such as not releasing the parking brake fully, spinning the wheels under acceleration, sliding due to excessive cornering speed or driving on extremely rough surfaces may fool the system and trigger the dash warning light. These induced faults are not system failures but examples of vehicle performance outside the parameters of the control unit.
11. Many system shut-downs are due to loss of sensor signals to or from the controller. The most common cause is not a failed sensor but a loose, corroded or dirty connector. Check harness and component connectors carefully.
12. Check for correct battery voltage and inspect the condition of all ABS fuses.

SYSTEM TESTING

1. Make sure the ignition switch is **OFF** and unplug the control unit connector. The control unit is in the right rear of the trunk.
2. Use a volt/ohmmeter and the following charts to test the system. Start at the beginning and work all the way towards the end before removing any components.
3. After repairs, make sure the warning light on the instrument panel operates properly. It should light when the ignition is first turned **ON**, then go out after the vehicle starts moving. If not, the system is still not repaired.

The hydraulic modulator is capable of self-pressurizing and can generate pressures above 3000 psi. any time the ignition switch is turned ON. Relieve the system pressure before testing or repairing the hydraulic system. Improper repair or test procedures can cause serious or fatal injury.

Relieving Anti-lock Brake System Pressure

With the ignition switch **OFF**, pump the brake pedal 25–35 times to depressurize the system. The system will recharge itself via the electric pump as soon as the ignition is turned **ON**. Disconnect the pump or the battery to prevent unintended pressurization. The system can then be serviced and bled normally.

REMOVAL & INSTALLATION

Modulator Assembly

1. Turn the ignition **OFF** and depress the brake pedal 25–35 times to depressurize the modulator assembly. Disconnect the pump or battery to prevent unintended pressurization.
2. Inside the vehicle near the right tail light, locate and disconnect the ABS control unit and the ground connection.
3. Remove the brake fluid from the reservoir with a suction pump.
4. Disconnect the brake lines from the modulator assembly and protect the connections from contamination with suitable plugs.
5. Working inside the vehicle, remove the left shelf under the dash to gain access to the brake pedal linkage. Remove the clevis bolt and disconnect the pedal.
6. Remove the locknuts and remove the pressure modulator.
7. Installation is the reverse of removal. Use new locknuts and tighten to 18 ft. lbs. (25 Nm). Refill the reservoir with new brake fluid and bleed the system.

Wheel Speed Sensor

REMOVAL & INSTALLATION

1. Raise and safely support the vehicle.
2. Remove the wheel and unbolt the sensor from the steering knuckle or stub axle.
3. The rotor portion of the sensor assembly is secured to the inside of the wheel hub. To remove the front rotor, the hub must be pressed out of the front wheel bearing.
4. On the rear wheels, the sensor is pressed into the brake rotor. To remove it:
   - Remove the wheel bearing and the brake rotor.
   - Insert a drift pin through the wheel bolt holes and gently tap the speed sensor rotor out a little bit at each hole, much like removing an inner wheel bearing race.

To install:

5. When reinstalling, use a suitable sleeve to drive the speed sensor rotor into the brake rotor evenly. When the cover ring is installed, the distance from the ring to the splash shield should be 0.375 inch (9.5mm).
6. When reinstalling the sensor, use a dry lubricant on the sides of the sensor and tighten the bolt to 7 ft. lbs. (10 Nm).

Control Valve

REMOVAL & INSTALLATION

1. Make sure the ignition switch is **OFF** and remove the right luggage compartment panel.

2. Remove the control unit and disconnect the wiring.
3. Installation is the reverse of removal. Make sure the warning light on the instrument panel goes out when the vehicle speed is above 3 mph.

Anti-lock Brake Impulse Rotor

REMOVAL & INSTALLATION

➡**Before beginning this procedure, check the availibility of the necessary parts. VW does not sell the impulse sensor ring alone. It is sold only as part of the brake rotor. This component is also know as the wheel speed sensor.**

1. Raise and support the vehicle.
2. Remove the wheel and remove the sensor from the steering knuckle.
3. The rotor is pressed into the rear of the brake rotor or on some models it is located on the outer constant velocity joint.
4. On the rear wheels the sensor is located in the brake rotor.
5. Remove the rear sensor by removing the wheel bearing and then the brake rotor.
6. Insert a drift pin through the wheel bolt holes and gently tap the sensor ring to remove it.
7. Installation is the reverse of removal.

Bleeding (ABS System)

Bleeding may be performed using either a pressure bleeder or the manual method. In either case an assistant will be required to depress the brake pedal. Extreme cleanliness must be observed at all times. If using the manual method, the fluid reservoir must be filled to the upper edge before bleeding begins. Do not allow the fluid level to drop below the MIN mark at any time. Do not reuse fluid released during bleeding.

Front Brakes

1. Turn the ignition switch OFF.
2. Relieve the brake system pressure.
3. If using pressure bleeder equipment, connect it to the brake fluid reservoir and switch it on.
4. Connect a tight-fitting vinyl hose to the bleeder port of the caliper. If using pressure bleeding equipment, begin at the left front caliper. If using the manual method, begin on either side. Immerse the other end of the hose in a container of clean brake fluid.

➡**Use of a cap or cover on the container is recommended. The brake fluid may bleed with enough force to splash out of an open container.**

5. Open the bleeder screw.
6. Have an assistant depress the brake pedal slowly until the fluid flows without bubbles.
7. Close the bleeder screw before the pedal is released.
8. Remove the vinyl tube from the caliper. Inspect and top off the fluid supply in the reservoir if necessary.
9. Repeat the procedure at the opposite wheel.

Rear Brakes

1. Turn the ignition switch OFF.
2. Relieve the brake system pressure.
3. If using pressure bleeder equipment, connect it to the brake fluid reservoir and switch it on.
4. Connect a tight-fitting vinyl hose to the bleeder port of either caliper. Immerse the other end of the hose in a container of clean brake fluid.

✳✳ CAUTION

Use of a cap or cover on the container is recommended. The brake fluid may bleed with enough force to splash out of an open container.

5. Open the bleeder screw. Have an assistant turn the ignition switch **ON**.
6. Press the lever of the proportioning valve towards the axle until brake fluid flows out without bubbles. Release the lever and close the bleeder screw.

Running time of the ABS pump must not exceed 120 seconds at any one time. If this time is approached or exceeded, a minimum of 10 minutes cooling time is required before proceeding. Do not allow the fluid level to fall below the MIN line at any time.

7. Switch the ignition **OFF** while transferring equipment. Remove the vinyl tube from the caliper. Inspect and top off the fluid supply in the reservoir if necessary.

8. Repeat the procedure at the opposite wheel.

9. Once both rear calipers are bled and the service equipment removed, switch the ignition **ON** until the pump shuts off.

10. Fill the brake fluid reservoir to the MAX line.

BRAKE SPECIFICATIONS

All measurements in inches unless noted

Year	Model		Brake Disc Original Thickness	Brake Disc Minimum Thickness	Brake Disc Maximum Run-out	Drum Diameter Original Inside Diameter	Drum Diameter Maximum Machine Diameter	Minimum Lining Thickness ①	Brake Caliper Bracket Bolts (ft. lbs.)	Brake Caliper Mounting Bolts (ft. lbs.)
1990	Cabriolet	F	0.787	0.709	0.002	—	—	0.276	51	18
		R	—	—	—	7.087	7.106	0.098	—	—
	Fox	F	0.472	0.393	0.002	—	—	0.276	48	30
		R	—	—	—	7.087	7.106	0.098	—	—
	Fox Wagon	F	0.472	0.393	0.002	—	—	0.276	48	30
		R	—	—	—	7.874	7.894	0.098	—	—
	Golf w/solid rotor	F	0.472	0.393	0.002	—	—	0.276	51	18
		R	—	—	—	7.087	7.106	0.098	—	—
	Golf w/vented rotor	F	0.787	0.709	0.002	—	—	0.276	51	18
		R	—	—	—	7.087	7.106	0.098	—	—
	Jetta w/solid rotor	F	0.472	0.393	0.002	—	—	0.276	51	18
		R	—	—	—	7.087	7.106	0.098	—	—
	Jetta w/vented rotor	F	0.787	0.709	0.002	—	—	0.276	51	18
		R	—	—	—	7.087	7.106	0.098	—	—
	Jetta w/ABS	F	0.787	0.709	0.002	—	—	0.276	51	18
		R	0.472	0.393	0.002	—	—	0.276	48	26
1991	Cabriolet	F	0.787	0.709	0.002	—	—	0.276	51	18
		R	—	—	—	7.087	7.106	0.098	—	—
	Fox	F	0.472	0.393	0.002	—	—	0.276	48	30
		R	—	—	—	7.087	7.106	0.098	—	—
	Golf w/solid rotor	F	0.472	0.393	0.002	—	—	0.276	51	18
		R	—	—	—	7.087	7.106	0.098	—	—
	Golf w/vented rotor	F	0.787	0.709	0.002	—	—	0.276	51	18
		R	—	—	—	7.087	7.106	0.098	—	—
	Jetta w/solid rotor	F	0.472	0.393	0.002	—	—	0.276	51	18
		R	—	—	—	7.087	7.106	0.098	—	—
	Jetta w/vented rotor	F	0.787	0.709	0.002	—	—	0.276	51	18
		R	—	—	—	7.087	7.106	0.098	—	—
	Jetta w/ABS	F	0.787	0.709	0.002	—	—	0.276	51	18
		R	0.472	0.393	0.002	—	—	0.276	48	26
1992	Cabriolet	F	0.787	0.709	0.002	—	—	0.276	51	18
		R	—	—	—	7.087	7.106	0.098	—	—
	Fox	F	0.472	0.393	0.002	—	—	0.276	48	30
		R	—	—	—	7.087	7.106	0.098	—	—
	Golf w/solid rotor	F	0.472	0.393	0.002	—	—	0.276	51	18
		R	—	—	—	7.087	7.106	0.098	—	—
	Golf w/vented rotor	F	0.787	0.709	0.002	—	—	0.276	51	18
		R	—	—	—	7.087	7.106	0.098	—	—
	Jetta w/solid rotor	F	0.472	0.393	0.002	—	—	0.276	51	18
		R	—	—	—	7.087	7.106	0.098	—	—

91229C01

BRAKE SPECIFICATIONS
All measurements in inches unless noted

Year	Model		Brake Disc Original Thickness	Brake Disc Minimum Thickness	Brake Disc Maximum Run-out	Drum Diameter Original Inside Diameter	Drum Diameter Maximum Machine Diameter	Minimum Lining Thickness ①	Brake Caliper Bracket Bolts (ft. lbs.)	Brake Caliper Mounting Bolts (ft. lbs.)
1992 cont'd	Jetta w/vented rotor	F	0.787	0.709	0.002	—	—	0.276	51	18
		R	—	—	—	7.087	7.106	0.098	—	—
	Jetta w/ABS	F	0.787	0.709	0.002	—	—	0.276	51	18
		R	0.472	0.393	0.002	—	—	0.276	48	26
1993	Cabriolet	F	0.472	0.393	0.002	—	—	0.276	51	18
		R	—	—	—	7.874	7.894	0.098	—	—
	Cabriolet w/Plus susp.	F	0.787	0.709	0.002	—	—	0.276	92	26
		R	0.394	0.319	0.002	—	—	0.276	41	26
	Golf	F	0.472	0.393	0.002	—	—	0.276	51	18
		R	—	—	—	7.874	7.894	0.098	—	—
	Golf w/Plus susp.	F	0.787	0.709	0.002	—	—	0.276	92	26
		R	0.394	0.319	0.002	—	—	0.276	41	26
	Jetta	F	0.472	0.393	0.002	—	—	0.276	51	18
		R	—	—	—	7.874	7.894	0.098	—	—
	Jetta w/Plus susp.	F	0.787	0.709	0.002	—	—	0.276	92	26
		R	0.394	0.319	0.002	—	—	0.276	41	26
	Golf	F	0.472	0.393	0.002	—	—	0.276	51	18
		R	—	—	—	7.874	7.894	0.098	—	—
1994	Golf	F	0.787	0.709	0.002	—	—	0.276	92	26
		R	0.394	0.319	0.002	—	—	0.276	41	26
	Golf w/Plus susp.	F	0.787	0.709	0.002	—	—	0.276	92	26
		R	0.866	0.787	0.002	—	—	0.276	92	26
	Jetta	F	0.394	0.319	0.002	—	—	0.276	41	26
	w/V6	R	0.787	0.709	0.002	7.874	7.894	0.098	51	18
	Cabriolet	F	0.787	0.709	0.002	—	—	0.276	92	26
		R	—	—	—	7.874	7.894	0.098	—	—
	Cabriolet w/rear disc	F	0.787	0.709	0.002	—	—	0.276	92	26
		R	0.394	0.319	0.002	—	—	0.276	41	26
	Golf	F	0.787	0.709	0.002	—	—	0.276	92	26
		R	—	—	—	7.874	7.894	0.098	—	—
	Golf w/rear disc	F	0.787	0.709	0.002	—	—	0.276	92	26
		R	0.394	0.319	0.002	—	—	0.276	41	26
	Jetta	F	0.787	0.709	0.002	—	—	0.276	92	26
	w/rear disc	R	0.394	0.319	0.002	—	—	0.098	92	26
	Jetta w/V6	F	0.866	0.787	0.002	—	—	0.276	92	26
		R	0.394	0.319	0.002	—	—	0.276	41	26

91229C02

BRAKE SPECIFICATIONS
All measurements in inches unless noted

Year	Model		Brake Disc Original Thickness	Brake Disc Minimum Thickness	Brake Disc Maximum Run-out	Drum Diameter Original Inside Diameter	Drum Diameter Maximum Machine Diameter	Minimum Lining Thickness ①	Brake Caliper Bracket Bolts (ft. lbs.)	Brake Caliper Mounting Bolts (ft. lbs.)
1995	Cabrio	F	0.787	0.709	0.002	—	—	0.276	92	26
		R	—	—	—	7.874	7.894	0.098	—	—
	Cabrio w/rear disc	F	0.787	0.709	0.002	—	—	0.276	92	26
		R	0.394	0.319	0.002	—	—	0.276	41	26
	Golf	F	0.787	0.709	—	7.874	7.894	0.098	92	26
		R	—	—	—	—	—	0.276	—	—
	Golf w/rear disc	F	0.787	0.709	0.002	—	—	0.276	92	26
		R	0.394	0.319	0.002	—	—	0.276	41	26
	Golf w/V6	F	0.866	0.787	0.002	—	—	0.276	92	26
		R	0.394	0.319	0.002	—	—	0.276	41	26
	Jetta	F	0.787	0.709	0.002	7.874	7.894	0.276	92	26
		R	—	—	—	—	—	0.098	—	—
	Jetta w/rear disc	F	0.787	0.709	0.002	—	—	0.276	92	26
		R	0.394	0.319	0.002	—	—	0.276	41	26
	Jetta w/V6	F	0.866	0.787	0.002	—	—	0.276	92	26
		R	0.394	0.319	0.002	—	—	0.276	41	26
1996	Cabrio	F	0.787	0.709	—	7.874	7.894	0.276	92	26
		R	—	—	—	—	—	0.098	—	—
	Cabrio w/rear disc	F	0.787	0.709	0.002	—	—	0.276	92	26
		R	0.394	0.319	0.002	—	—	0.276	41	26
	Golf	F	0.787	0.709	0.002	7.874	7.894	0.276	92	26
		R	—	—	—	—	—	0.098	—	—
	Golf w/rear disc	F	0.787	0.709	0.002	—	—	0.276	92	26
		R	0.394	0.319	0.002	—	—	0.276	41	26
	Golf w/V6	F	0.866	0.787	0.002	—	—	0.276	92	26
		R	0.394	0.319	0.002	—	—	0.276	41	26
	GTI	F	0.787	0.709	0.002	—	—	0.276	92	26
		R	0.394	0.319	0.002	—	—	0.276	41	26
	GTI w/V6	F	0.866	0.787	0.002	—	—	0.276	92	26
		R	0.394	0.319	0.002	—	—	0.276	41	26
	Jetta	F	0.787	0.709	0.002	7.874	7.894	0.276	92	26
		R	—	—	—	—	—	0.098	—	—
	Jetta w/rear disc	F	0.787	0.709	0.002	—	—	0.276	92	26
		R	0.394	0.319	0.002	—	—	0.276	41	26
	Jetta w/V6	F	0.866	0.787	0.002	—	—	0.276	92	26
		R	0.394	0.319	0.002	—	—	0.276	41	26
1997	Cabrio	F	0.787	0.709	—	7.874	7.894	0.276	92	26
		R	—	—	—	—	—	0.098	—	—
	Cabrio w/rear disc	F	0.787	0.709	0.002	—	—	0.276	92	26
		R	0.394	0.319	0.002	—	—	0.276	41	26

91229C03

BRAKE SPECIFICATIONS
All measurements in inches unless noted

Year	Model		Brake Disc Original Thickness	Brake Disc Minimum Thickness	Brake Disc Maximum Run-out	Drum Diameter Original Inside Diameter	Drum Diameter Maximum Machine Diameter	Minimum Lining Thickness ①	Brake Caliper Bracket Bolts (ft. lbs.)	Brake Caliper Mounting Bolts (ft. lbs.)
1997 cont'd	Golf	F	0.787	0.709	0.002	—	—	0.276	92	26
		R	—	—	—	7.874	7.894	0.098	—	—
	Golf w/rear disc	F	0.787	0.709	0.002	—	—	0.276	92	26
		R	0.394	0.319	0.002	—	—	0.276	41	26
	Golf w/V6	F	0.866	0.787	0.002	—	—	0.276	92	26
		R	0.394	0.319	0.002	—	—	0.276	41	26
	GTI	F	0.787	0.709	0.002	—	—	0.276	92	26
		R	0.394	0.319	0.002	—	—	0.276	41	26
	GTI w/V6	F	0.866	0.787	0.002	—	—	0.276	92	26
		R	0.394	0.319	0.002	—	—	0.276	41	26
	Jetta	F	0.787	0.709	0.002	—	—	0.276	92	26
		R	—	—	—	7.874	7.894	0.098	—	—
	Jetta w/rear disc	F	0.787	0.709	0.002	—	—	0.276	92	26
		R	0.394	0.319	0.002	—	—	0.276	41	26
	Jetta w/V6	F	0.866	0.787	0.002	—	—	0.276	92	26
		R	0.394	0.319	0.002	—	—	0.276	41	26
1998	Cabrio	F	0.787	0.709	0.002	—	—	0.276	92	26
		R	—	—	—	7.874	7.894	0.098	—	—
	Cabrio w/rear disc	F	0.787	0.709	0.002	—	—	0.276	92	26
		R	0.394	0.319	0.002	—	—	0.276	41	26
	Golf	F	0.787	0.709	0.002	—	—	0.276	92	26
		R	—	—	—	7.874	7.894	0.098	—	—
	Golf w/rear disc	F	0.787	0.709	0.002	—	—	0.276	92	26
		R	0.394	0.319	0.002	—	—	0.276	41	26
	Golf w/V6	F	0.866	0.787	0.002	—	—	0.276	92	26
		R	0.394	0.319	0.002	—	—	0.276	41	26
	Jetta	F	0.787	0.709	0.002	—	—	0.276	92	26
		R	—	—	—	7.874	7.894	0.098	—	—
	Jetta w/rear disc	F	0.787	0.709	0.002	—	—	0.276	92	26
		R	0.394	0.319	0.002	—	—	0.276	41	26
	Jetta w/V6	F	0.866	0.787	0.002	—	—	0.276	92	26
		R	0.394	0.319	0.002	—	—	0.276	41	26
1999	Cabrio	F	0.787	0.709	0.002	—	—	0.276	92	26
		R	—	—	—	7.874	7.894	0.098	—	—
	Cabrio w/rear disc	F	0.787	0.709	0.002	—	—	0.276	92	26
		R	0.394	0.319	0.002	—	—	0.276	41	26
	Golf	F	0.787	0.709	0.002	—	—	0.276	92	26
		R	—	—	—	7.874	7.894	0.098	—	—
	Golf w/rear disc	F	0.787	0.709	0.002	—	—	0.276	92	26
		R	0.394	0.319	0.002	—	—	0.276	41	26
	Golf w/V6	F	0.866	0.787	0.002	—	—	0.276	92	26
		R	0.394	0.319	0.002	—	—	0.276	41	26

91229C04

BRAKE SPECIFICATIONS
All measurements in inches unless noted

| Year | Model | | Brake Disc | | | Drum Diameter | | Minimum Lining Thickness ① | Brake Caliper | |
			Original Thickness	Minimum Thickness	Maximum Run-out	Original Inside Diameter	Maximum Machine Diameter		Bracket Bolts (ft. lbs.)	Mounting Bolts (ft. lbs.)
1999 cont'd	Jetta	F	0.787	0.709	0.002	—	—	0.276	92	26
		R	—	—	—	7.874	7.894	0.098	—	—
	Jetta w/rear disc	F	0.787	0.709	0.002	—	—	0.276	92	26
		R	0.394	0.319	0.002	—	—	0.276	41	26
	Jetta w/V6	F	0.866	0.787	0.002	—	—	0.276	92	26
		R	0.394	0.319	0.002	—	—	0.276	41	26

F - Front
R - Rear

① Disc pad measurements include metal backing plate

91229C05

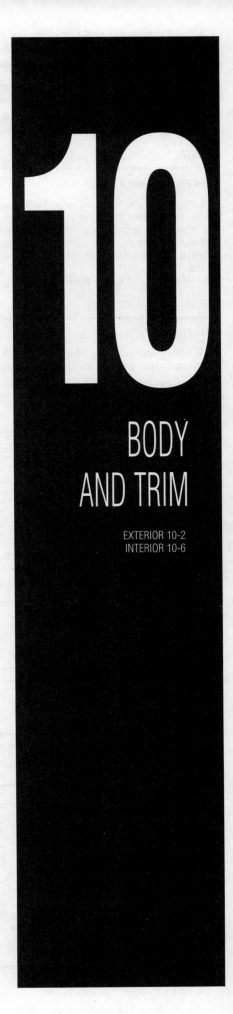

10

BODY
AND TRIM

EXTERIOR

Doors

REMOVAL & INSTALLATION

♦ See Figures 1 and 2

1. Open the door and support it securely with a floor jack or blocks. Remove the door check strap sleeve and remove the door check strap.
2. If necessary, remove the door panel to disconnect the wiring for speakers, electric windows, electric mirrors and the air line for power door locks.
3. Have an assistant steady the door and remove the hinge bolts to remove the door.
4. Installation is the reverse of removal.

ADJUSTMENT & ALIGNMENT

♦ See Figure 3

1. When checking door alignment, look carefully at each seam between the door and body. The gap should be even all the way around the door. Pay partic-ular attention to the door seams at the corners farthest from the hinges; this is the area where errors will be most evident. Additionally, the door should push against the weather-strip when latched to seal out wind and water. The contact should be even all the way around and the stripping should be about half com-pressed. The position of the door can be adjusted in three dimensions: fore and aft, up and down, in and out. The primary adjusting points are the hinge-to-body bolts.

2. Apply tape to the fender and door edges to protect the paint. Two layers of common masking tape works well.
3. Loosen the bolts just enough to allow the hinge to move. With the help of an assistant, position the door up and down as required and snug the bolts.
4. Inspect the door seams carefully and repeat the adjustment until cor-rectly aligned.
5. Inspect the front door seal and determine how much it is being crushed. If there is little or no contact in this area, or if the door is recessed into the body at the front when closed, loosen the hinge-to-door bolts and adjust the door in or out as needed. Don't worry about the latch yet.
6. Make sure the door moves smoothly on the hinges without binding. When the door fits the opening correctly, tighten the bolts.
7. To adjust the latch, loosen the large cross-point screw holding the striker on the door jam on the body. These bolts will be very tight; an impact screwdriver is the best tool for this job. Make sure you are using the proper size bit.
8. With the bolts just loose enough to allow the striker to move if neces-sary, hold the outer door handle in the released position and close the door. The striker will move into the correct location to match the door latch. Open the door and tighten the mounting bolts. The striker may be adjusted towards or away from the center of the car, thereby tightening or loosening the door fit. The striker can be moved up and down to compensate for door position, but if the door is correctly mounted at the hinges this should not be neces-sary.

➡Do not attempt to correct height variations (sag) by adjusting the striker.

9. After the striker bolts have been tightened, open and close the door sev-eral times. Observe the motion of the door as it engages the striker; it should continue its straight-in motion and not deflect up or down as it hits the striker.
10. Check the feel of the latch during opening and closing. It must be smooth and linear, without any trace of grinding or binding during engagement and release. It may be necessary to repeat the striker adjustment several times (and possibly re-adjust the hinges) before the correct door-to-body fit is achieved.

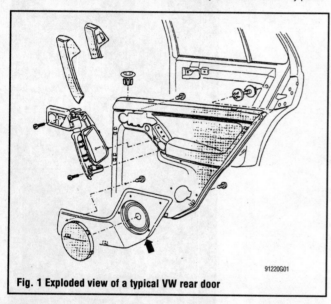

91220G01

Fig. 1 Exploded view of a typical VW rear door

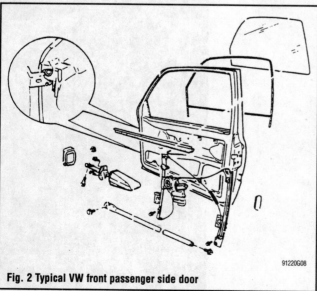

91220G08

Fig. 2 Typical VW front passenger side door

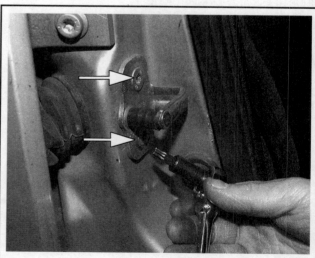

91220P50

Fig. 3 Removal of the door striker may require a Torx style driver

Hood Struts

REMOVAL & INSTALLATION

▶ **See Figures 4, 5, 6 and 7**

1. Support the hood with a prop rod.
2. Remove the spring clip from each end of the hood strut.
3. Pull the base of the hood strut away from the stud on the hood.
4. Replace the hood strut as a unit.

✳ CAUTION

Never puncture the hood strut. This unit contains a high pressure gas that may cause bodily harm if released.

5. Installation is the reverse of removal.

Hood

REMOVAL & INSTALLATION

▶ **See Figures 8, 9 and 10**

1. Raise the hood and support it securely.
2. Cover the painted areas of the body to protect the finish from being damaged. Scribe the hood hinge-to-hood locations for installation.
3. Remove the hood struts if applicable.
4. While an assistant holds the hood, remove the hinge-to-hood retaining bolts.
5. Remove the hood from the vehicle.
6. Installation is the reverse of removal. Align the hood with the scribe marks and tighten the bolts to 15 ft. lbs. (20 Nm).

ALIGNMENT

Loosen the hinge to hood attaching bolts and move the hood from side to side until there is an equal amount of clearance on both sides of the hood and fender. Tighten the hood bolts.

Tailgate, Hatch or Trunk Lid

REMOVAL & INSTALLATION

▶ **See Figure 11**

Rear Hatch

1. Open the rear hatch fully and support it in place.
2. Carefully remove the trim fasteners with a flat screwdriver and remove the trim.
3. Disconnect the wiring and any tubing.
4. Remove the ball studs from both the upper and lower ends of the struts and remove them.

➡**Never disassemble the support strut, as it is filled with high pressure gas. Do not turn the piston rod and the cylinder when the piston rod is extended. When discarding the strut, drill a 2–3mm (0.08–0.12 inch) hole in the bottom of the damper or use a hack saw to release the gas. Make sure to protect yourself against any metal particles that may be thrown into the air by the compressed gas during drilling.**

5. Remove the rear hatch hinge bolts and remove the rear hatch.
6. Installation is the reverse of the removal procedure.

Trunk Lid

1. Open and support the trunk lid securely.
2. If necessary, remove the inner panel to disconnect any wiring or tubing.

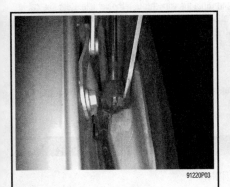

Fig. 4 Using a pry tool, pull the locking clip away from the base of the hood strut

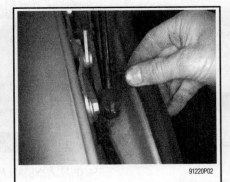

Fig. 5 View of the locking clip

Fig. 6 Pull at the base of the hood strut to remove it

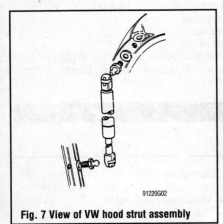

Fig. 7 View of VW hood strut assembly

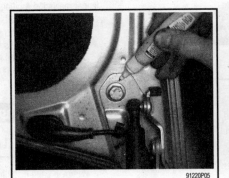

Fig. 8 Matchmark the location of the hood bolts to the hood

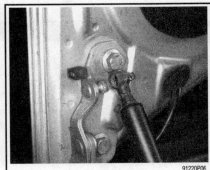

Fig. 9 Remove the hood struts

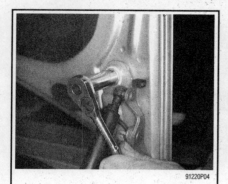

Fig. 10 Remove the hood hinge retaining bolts

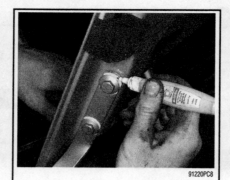

Fig. 11 Matchmark the position of the trunk lid

Fig. 12 Once all of the clips have been released, gently pull the grille away from the vehicle

3. Mark the position of the trunk lid hinge in relation to the trunk lid.
4. With an assistant, remove the two bolts attaching the hinge to the trunk lid. Remove the trunk lid from the vehicle.
5. Installation is the reverse of removal. Align the scribe marks and tighten the bolts to 18 ft. lbs. (25 Nm).

ALIGNMENT

Rear Hatch

1. To align the front-to-rear position of the hatch, loosen the hinge attaching bolts on both the hatch and the body.
2. Position the hatch so the gap is even all the way around the hatch.
3. To adjust the hatch closing position, loosen both the lock and striker bolts.

Trunk Lid

To make the front-to-rear or side-to-side adjustment, loosen the trunk lid attaching bolts and move the trunk lid as necessary. Tighten the trunk lid attaching bolts. To make the up-and-down adjustment, loosen the hinge-to-hinge support attaching bolts and raise or lower the hinge as necessary. The trunk lid is at the correct height when it is flush with the trunk deck.

Grille

REMOVAL & INSTALLATION

▶ **See Figures 12, 13 and 14**

1. Unclip the radiator grille at the lock carrier and remove upward.

➡**Check the rubber supports for damage. Replace any damaged clips as needed.**

2. Installation is the reverse of the removal procedure.

Outside Mirrors

REMOVAL & INSTALLATION

▶ **See Figures 15, 16, 17, 18 and 19**

1. On manual remote control mirrors, unscrew the adjusting knob.
2. On electric remote mirrors, carefully pry the control out of the door and disconnect the wiring.
3. Remove the inside door panel.
4. Remove the cable control lock-nut or disconnect the wiring and remove the screws to remove the mirror from the door.
5. Installation is the reverse of removal.

Antenna

REPLACEMENT

Fender Mount

1. Disconnect the negative battery cable.
2. Remove the radio and the instrument cluster.
3. Remove the drip tray above the firewall under the hood and pull the antenna cable from the foam tube. Note the routing for installation.
4. Remove the rubber grommet and unclip the antenna cable from the water tray.
5. Remove the inner wheelhouse liner.
6. Remove the mast retainer nut from the top of the fender.
7. Pull the assembly downward into the inner wheelhouse and remove the lower mounting bracket.
8. Install the antenna and route the wire through the vehicle. Keep the cable away from the heater control cables.
9. Tighten the mast nut.

Roof Mount

1. Remove the radio.
2. Remove the headliner.
3. Remove the antenna.
4. Installation is the reverse of removal.

Fenders

REMOVAL & INSTALLATION

▶ **See Figures 20 and 21**

1. Use a heat gun and razor blade to soften and cut the PVC bead where the fender meets the A pillar. Be careful not to use too much heat.
2. Remove the front bumper cover.
3. Remove the inner wheel well.
4. Remove the bolts to remove the fender.
5. Installation is the reverse of removal. Be sure the zinc foil plates are in place at the bolt holes on the body. These prevent corrosion between the metal body parts.

Convertible Tops

REMOVAL & INSTALLATION

Removing and installing the convertible top from the frame requires special tools and adhesives and also requires cutting the top fabric. The job is best left to a well equipped body shop with convertible top experience. The procedure

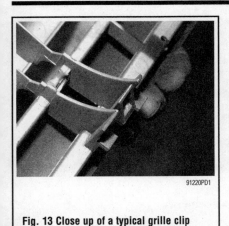

Fig. 13 Close up of a typical grille clip

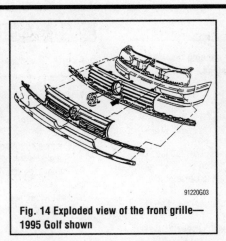

Fig. 14 Exploded view of the front grille—
1995 Golf shown

Fig. 15 Remove the interior cover

Fig. 16 Pull back the insulation

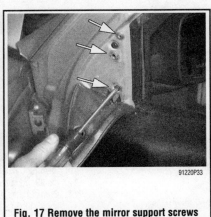

Fig. 17 Remove the mirror support screws

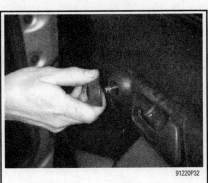

Fig. 18 Remove the mirror adjustment knob

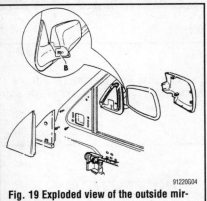

Fig. 19 Exploded view of the outside mirror assembly

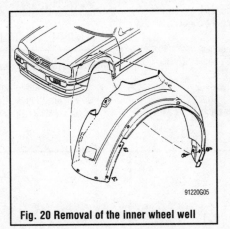

Fig. 20 Removal of the inner wheel well

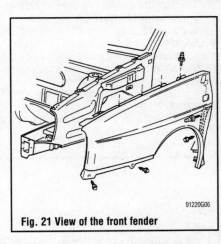

Fig. 21 View of the front fender

described here is for removing the top and frame together as an assembly. Installation requires two people.

1. Open the top to release the tension but don't fold it back yet.

2. Bend open the metal tabs under the luggage compartment lining and pull the headliner off the tabs.

3. Pull the rear window defogger wiring out of the window seal.

4. Remove the window frame hinges and pull the cover off.

5. Remove the trim pieces at the rear corner of the rear windows.

6. On manual tops, remove the bolt to release the tension on the gas pressurized strut. Remove the clip at the other end and remove the strut.

7. If equipped with a power top, disconnect the cylinder from the top frame.

8. Disconnect the tensioning wire from its anchor on each side. A 4mm open end wrench can be used to prevent the wire from twisting.

9. Peel the top cover and tensioning wire out of the channels on the sides, then out of the rear channel.

10. Remove the headliner at the rear corners and remove the belt fastening bracket.

11. Remove the trim pieces covering the main bearing hinge. Remove the three bolts on each side and remove the top as an assembly.

To install:

12. .Fit the top into place and start all the main bearing hinge bolts. When they are all started, tighten them.

13. Attach the belt at the rear corners.

14. Secure the tensioning wire to the anchors at each side and have a helper and top cover into the channel with a wooden drift.

15. Carefully align the beading and drive that into place with the drift.

16. Install the gas strut and try closing the top to make sure it fits properly and operates smoothly.

17. Install the rear window frame.

18. Attach the headliner and install the remaining trim pieces.

MOTOR REPLACEMENT

➡ **The top can be operated by hand if necessary by opening the valve on the pump. Turn the valve counterclockwise until it stops.**

1. Disconnect the negative battery cable.
2. Unclip and remove the left side luggage trim panel.
3. Disconnect the motor wiring.
4. Loosen the filler plug to relieve the pressure. Have a rag handy to catch any fluid that may spill.
5. Disconnect the hydraulic fittings that are accessible. Make sure the fittings are clean before disconnecting them and cover them with plastic or paper to keep dirt out. Do not use rags because the lint is enough to cause problems with the hydraulic system.
6. Remove the mount bolts and remove the pump and disconnect the remaining hydraulic fittings.
7. Installation is the reverse of removal. Fill and bleed the hydraulic system.

INTERIOR

Instrument Panel and Pad

REMOVAL & INSTALLATION

♦ **See Figures 22 and 23**

On Cabriolet with an air bag, disconnect the negative battery cable and wait at least 20 minutes for the back-up power supply to discharge. Make sure no one is in the vehicle when connecting the battery. Unintended deployment of the air bag can cause serious or fatal injury.

1. Disconnect the negative battery cable.
2. Remove the gear shift knob and boot and remove the center console.
3. Remove the steering wheel.
4. Remove the knee bar from below the dashboard.
5. Remove the steering column support bracket and lower the column.
6. Pull the knobs off the heater controls and remove the control assembly and the radio.
7. Remove the headlight switch and switch blanks to gain access to the screws. Remove the instrument cluster and trim panel around the cluster.
8. Remove the glove compartment.
9. At the firewall, remove the plastic tray and remove the 2 nuts holding the top of the dashboard.
10. .Remove the main fuse panel and disconnect the plugs at the back. Disconnect the ground wires.

Power Sunroof

REMOVAL & INSTALLATION

1. Open the sunroof halfway and remove the steel clips at the front edge using a plastic wedge tool.
2. Close the sunroof and push the interior panel back all the way.
3. Remove both front guides from the outer panel.
4. Slide the springs at the rear guide in towards the center.
5. Remove the screws and remove the rear support plates in towards center.
6. Lift the sunroof cover out.
7. Installation is the reverse of removal.

11. Disconnect any remaining wiring from the dashboard and remove the 4 last screws; 1 at each end and 1 at each end of the instrument cluster area. Remove the dashboard.
To install:
12. Fit the dashboard into place and start all 4 screws, then tighten them.
13. Install the fuse panel and connect the wiring.
14. Secure the steering column into place.
15. Install the switches and instrument cluster.
16. Install the heater controls and radio.
17. Install the console and connect all wiring.
18. Connect the battery to test the electrical system.
19. Install the steering wheel, knee bar and all remaining components.

Console

REMOVAL & INSTALLATION

♦ **See Figures 24 thru 30**

1. Disconnect the negative battery cable. If equipped with SRS, wrap the cable in insulated tape, then wait at least 60 seconds before continuing to allow the SRS system time to disable.

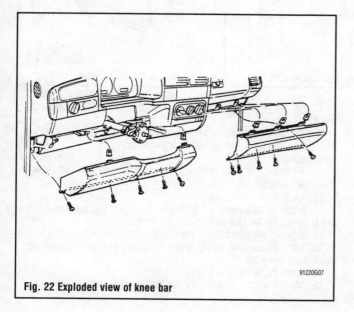

91220G07

Fig. 22 Exploded view of knee bar

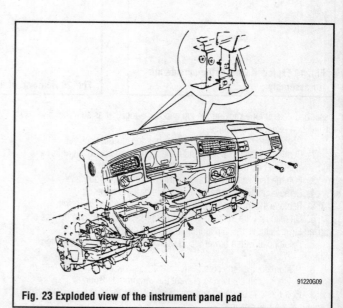

91220G09

Fig. 23 Exploded view of the instrument panel pad

Fig. 24 Unscrew the shift knob from the shaft

Fig. 25 Detach the cup holder from the console

Fig. 26 Remove the fasteners as shown

Fig. 27 Remove the decorative screw covers to gain access to the attaching screws on the sides of the console

Fig. 28 Location of the lower console mounting screws

Fig. 29 Detach the parking brake button end cap

Fig. 30 Remove the console from the vehicle by sliding it over the parking brake lever as shown

✺✺ CAUTION

If equipped with SRS, be careful not to let the console bump against the SRS-ECU during removal and installation.

2. If equipped, remove the rear floor console.
3. If necessary, remove the ashtray and cup holder assemblies.
4. If equipped, remove the carpet inserts from the floor console assembly.

5. On manual transaxle equipped models, remove the manual transaxle shifter knob.
6. On some models, remove the transaxle shift lever trim plate.
7. Remove the screw plugs in the side covers. Remove the retainer screws and the side covers from the vehicle.
8. Remove the front mounting screw cover from the floor console.
9. Label and detach the electrical wire harness connections for the floor console.
10. Remove the retaining screws and the floor console from the vehicle.
To install:
11. Install the floor console in position in the vehicle and secure with the retaining screws.
12. The installation is the reverse of removal.

Door Panels

REMOVAL & INSTALLATION

▶ See Figures 31, 32, 33 and 34

1. Remove the window regulator handle.
2. Remove the arm rest.
3. Remove the door lock knob.
4. Remove the inner door handle cover.
5. Using a flat screwdriver, gently separate the door trim panel clips from the door.
6. Lift the panel to remove it and disconnect the speaker or mirror wires as required.
7. Installation is the reverse of removal. Make sure the sheet of plastic behind the panel is properly sealed against the metal to keep drafts out of the interior.

Fig. 31 Removing the panel from the passenger side door—Jetta

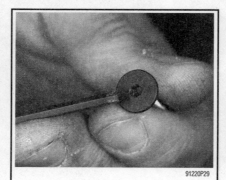

Fig. 32 Many interior panels are held in place using hex head screws

Fig. 33 Removing the door lock knob

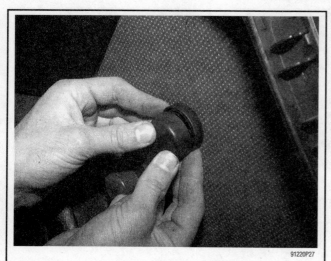

Fig. 34 Press up on the inside clip to release the door handle on a Jetta A3

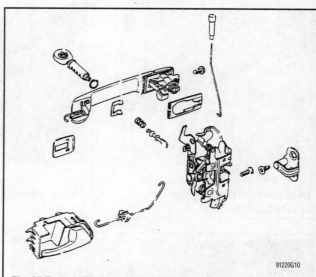

Fig. 35 Typical VW door lock assembly

Manual Door Locks

REMOVAL & INSTALLATION

Manual Door Locks

▶ See Figure 35

1. Remove the door panel.
2. Disconnect the linkage and remove the screws to remove the lock from the door.
3. When installing, hold lever A at a 90 degree angle and secure it with a screwdriver.
4. Insert the rod through the hole in the door and connect the lock linkage.
5. Remove the screwdriver, install the screws and connect the latch linkage.

Power Locking System

TESTING

The heart of the pneumatic central locking system is the bi-pressure pump mounted in the luggage compartment. The pump runs both ways to provide vacuum or pressure as required for locking or unlocking. There are lock actuators at each door, the rear hatch or trunk and at the fuel filler door. The master actuator at the driver's door includes the switch that activates the pump. In normal operation, the pump runs for about 2 seconds and will build enough

pressure or vacuum to operate all locks and activate an internal shut-off switch. If the pump runs for more than 5 seconds, a leak in the system is preventing shut-off switch operation and an automatic shut-off will occur in about 35 seconds. If the pump does not run at all, the problem is most likely electrical.

1. Open the luggage compartment and remove the left side interior trim. Unhook the strap, remove the pump cover and pull the pump out of the housing.
2. Install a small clamp on the hose before the first branching tee and turn the key in the driver's door lock. If the pump does not run at all, go to Step 7.
3. If the pump runs for more than 5 seconds, the shut-off switch inside is faulty and the pump must be replaced. If the pump stops in less than 5 seconds, the pump is good and there is a leak somewhere in the system.
4. Move the clamp to the upper branch of the tee and turn the driver's door lock again. If the pump runs too long, the leak is at the left rear door actuator or the hose.
5. If the pump stops in less than 5 seconds, move the clamp to the next hose junction at the right rear of the luggage compartment and test again. The hose that branches to the right supplies the fuel filler door and trunk or hatch actuator. The hose branching down supplies the right door actuators.
6. Continue moving the clamp towards the actuators until the pump does not stop within 5 seconds. This means the clamp is now past the leak and the previous section of hose or actuator is leaking.
7. If the pump does not run at all, disconnect the wiring and connect a voltmeter or test light to the center and right terminals on the connector. There should be 12 volts when the driver's door is unlocked.
8. Move the tester to the center and left terminals. There should be 12 volts when the driver's door is locked.

9. If the voltages appear as specified, the pump is faulty and must be replaced. If there is no voltage in either or both tests, the lock switch, wiring or fuse is faulty. The switch is part of the master actuator and cannot be replaced separately.

REMOVAL & INSTALLATION

1. To replace the pump, remove the left luggage compartment interior panel and remove the pump cover and the pump. Test the new pump before completing the installation.
2. To replace the actuator, remove the door panel. Follow the hose to the actuator and disconnect the hose and the linkage at the actuator. On the driver's door, disconnect the wiring.
3. Remove the screws and remove the actuator. Connect the hose to the new actuator and test the system before installing it.

Hatch/Trunk Lock

REMOVAL & INSTALLATION

▶ **See Figures 36, 37 and 38**

1. Open the hatch and remove the lock mounting bolts.
2. Lower the lock assembly to gain access to the
3. Pull the lock mechanism from the tailgate

Fig. 36 Removing the latch from the tailgate

Door Glass and Regulator

REMOVAL & INSTALLATION

▶ **See Figure 39**

Fox, Golf and Jetta

1. Lower the window glass and remove the door panel.
2. Carefully peel off the door screen so that it can be reused.
3. Raise the window enough to reach the regulator bolts, hold the glass underneath and unbolt the glass from the regulator.
4. To remove the glass, raise the glass by hand and tilt it as necessary to remove it from the track.
5. To remove the regulator, lower the glass carefully to the bottom of the door and remove the bolts to remove the regulator.
6. Installation is the reverse of removal. Tighten all bolts to 61 inch. lbs. (7 Nm).

Cabriolet

1. Lower the window glass and remove the door panel.
2. Carefully peel off the door screen so that it can be reused.
3. Raise the window enough to reach the regulator bolts, remove the bolts and lift the glass straight out.
4. To remove the regulator, remove the seven screws attaching the window regulator to the door and one screw from the winder.
5. Installation is the reverse of removal.
6. Lubricate the sliding bracket on the regulator.

Electric Window Motor

REMOVAL & INSTALLATION

1. Remove the door panel.
2. Carefully peel off the door screen so that it can be reused.
3. Unbolt the window from the regulator and carefully lower it to the bottom of the door.
4. Disconnect the wiring and remove the motor mounting bolts.
5. Remove the 3 guide rail bolts and lower the motor and guide rail assembly out the bottom of the door.
6. Installation is the reverse of removal.

➡ **The upper cable must be below the guide rail mounting bracket.**

Fig. 37 Remove the bolts from the lock

Fig. 38 Pull the lock from the tailgate

Fig. 39 View of inner door frame and window regulator assembly

Windshield and Fixed Glass

REMOVAL & INSTALLATION

If your windshield, or other fixed window, is cracked or chipped, you may decide to replace it with a new one yourself. However, there are two main reasons why replacement windshields and other window glass should be installed only by a professional automotive glass technician: safety and cost.

The most important reason a professional should install automotive glass is for safety. The glass in the vehicle, especially the windshield, is designed with safety in mind in case of a collision. The windshield is specially manufactured from two panes of specially-tempered glass with a thin layer of transparent plastic between them. This construction allows the glass to "give" in the event that a part of your body hits the windshield during the collision, and prevents the glass from shattering, which could cause lacerations, blinding and other harm to passengers of the vehicle. The other fixed windows are designed to be tempered so that if they break during a collision, they shatter in such a way that there are no large pointed glass pieces. The professional automotive glass technician knows how to install the glass in a vehicle so that it will function optimally during a collision. Without the proper experience, knowledge and tools, installing a piece of automotive glass yourself could lead to additional harm if an accident should ever occur.

Cost is also a factor when deciding to install automotive glass yourself. Performing this could cost you much more than a professional may charge for the same job. Since the windshield is designed to break under stress, an often life saving characteristic, windshields tend to break VERY easily when an inexperienced person attempts to install one. Do-it-yourselfers buying two, three or even four windshields from a salvage yard because they have broken them during installation are common stories. Also, since the automotive glass is designed to prevent the outside elements from entering your vehicle, improper installation can lead to water and air leaks. Annoying whining noises at highway speeds from air leaks or inside body panel rusting from water leaks can add to your stress level and subtract from your wallet. After buying two or three windshields, installing them and ending up with a leak that produces a noise while driving and water damage during rainstorms, the cost of having a professional

do it correctly the first time may be much more alluring. We here at Chilton, therefore, advise that you have a professional automotive glass technician service any broken glass on your vehicle.

WINDSHIELD CHIP REPAIR

▶ **See Figures 40 thru 54**

➡**Check with your state and local authorities on the laws for state safety inspection. Some states or municipalities may not allow chip repair as a viable option for correcting stone damage to your windshield.**

Although severely cracked or damaged windshields must be replaced, there is something that you can do to prolong or even prevent the need for replacement of a chipped windshield. There are many companies which offer windshield chip repair products, such as Loctite's® Bullseye windshield repair kit. These kits usually consist of a syringe, pedestal and a sealing adhesive. The syringe is mounted on the pedestal and is used to create a vacuum which pulls the plastic layer against the glass. This helps make the chip transparent. The adhesive is then injected which seals the chip and helps to prevent further stress cracks from developing. Refer to the sequence of photos to get a general idea of what windshield chip repair involves.

➡**Always follow the specific manufacturer's instructions.**

Inside Rear View Mirror

REPLACEMENT

Twist off style (glass mount)

1. Remove the negative battery cable on models equipped with a map light in the mirror assembly.

Fig. 40 Small chips on your windshield can be fixed with an aftermarket repair kit, such as the one from Loctite

Fig. 41 To repair a chip, clean the windshield with glass cleaner and dry it completely

Fig. 42 Remove the center from the adhesive disc and peel off the backing from one side of the disc . . .

Fig. 43 . . . then press it on the windshield so that the chip is centered in the hole

Fig. 44 Be sure that the tab points upward on the windshield

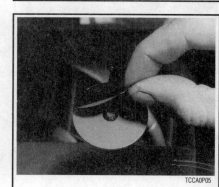

Fig. 45 Peel the backing off the exposed side of the adhesive disc . . .

Fig. 46 . . . then position the plastic pedestal on the adhesive disc, ensuring that the tabs are aligned

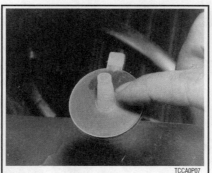

Fig. 47 Press the pedestal firmly on the adhesive disc to create an adequate seal . . .

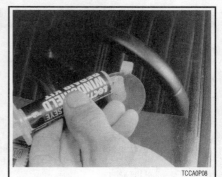

Fig. 48 . . . then install the applicator syringe nipple in the pedestal's hole

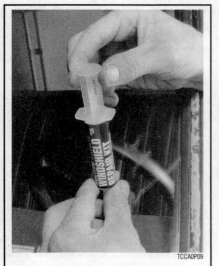

Fig. 49 Hold the syringe with one hand while pulling the plunger back with the other hand

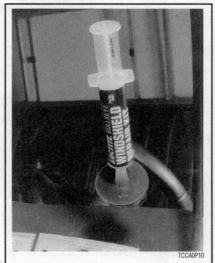

Fig. 50 After applying the solution, allow the entire assembly to sit until it has set completely

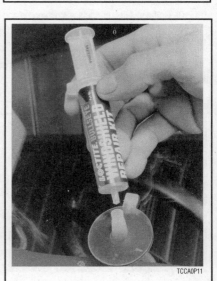

Fig. 51 After the solution has set, remove the syringe from the pedestal . . .

Fig. 52 . . . then peel the pedestal off of the adhesive disc . . .

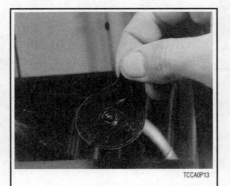

Fig. 53 . . . and peel the adhesive disc off of the windshield

Fig. 54 The chip will still be slightly visible, but it should be filled with the hardened solution

2. Detach any wiring from the mirror assembly.
3. Firmly grasp the base of the rear view mirror and twist it counterclockwise about a quarter to half turn.
4. Remove the mirror assembly from the window.
5. Installation is the reverse of removal.

Machine Screw type

1. Carefully pry the cover (not all models have a cover plate) off using a suitable flat blade screw driver.
2. Remove the rubber damper from the mirror stalk.
3. Remove the machine screw from the base.
4. Remove the mirror assembly.
5. Installation is in reverse order of removal.

Seats

REMOVAL & INSTALLATION

▶ **See Figures 55, 56, 57 and 58**

Front Seats

1. Slide the seat forward to the stop and remove the track cover beside the tunnel.
2. Remove the acorn nut, washer and bolt at the front of the center seat rail.
3. Pull the seat release handle and push the seat back and out of the tracks. Lift the seat out of the vehicle.
4. Installation is the reverse of removal.

Rear Seat

1. On Golf and Jetta, lift the seat cushion up and pull forward to remove it.
2. On Cabriolet, remove the two screws at the front of the seat cushion and pull forward and up.
3. Release the seat backrest and fold forward.
4. Release the locking lug in the mounting and pull the backrest out of the mounting.
5. Installation is the reverse of removal.

Fig. 55 Removing the seat from the front track

Fig. 56 Remove the plastic cover from the rear edge of the seat track

Fig. 57 Remove the fasteners from the rear seat. This may require the use of a hex key

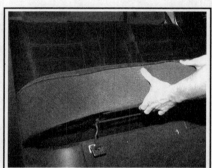

Fig. 58 Once all the bolts have been removed, lift the rear seat out

TORQUE SPECIFICATIONS

Components	English Specifications	Metric Specifications
Doors		
Hinge-to-door bolts/nuts	27 ft. lbs.	36 Nm
Hinge-to-body bolts/nuts	17 ft. lbs.	23 Nm
Door striker bolt(s)		
Unitized bolt/striker	7 ft. lbs.	9 Nm
Striker-to-body bolts	6 ft. lbs	8 Nm
Hood		
Hinge-to-hood bolts/nuts	7 ft. lbs.	9 Nm
Hinge-to-body bolts/nuts	6 ft. lbs.	8 Nm
Latch-to-hood bolts	9 ft. lbs.	12 Nm
Trunk		
Hinge-to-trunk bolts	7 ft. lbs.	9 Nm
Latch-to-trunk bolts	9 ft. lbs.	12 Nm
Fender		
Fender-to-body bolts	7 ft. lbs.	9 Nm
Fender-to-support bolts	5 ft. lbs.	7 Nm

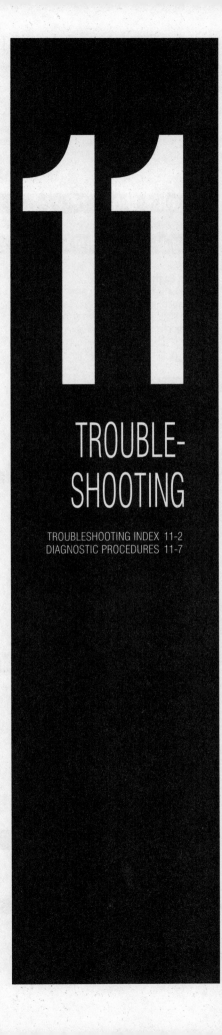

11

TROUBLE-
SHOOTING

Condition	Section/Item Number

The following troubleshooting charts are divided into 7 sections covering engine, drive train, brakes, wheels/tires/steering/suspension, electrical accessories, instruments and gauges, and climate control. The first portion (or index) consists of a list of symptoms, along with section and item numbers. After selecting the appropriate condition, refer to the corresponding diagnostic procedure in the second portion's specified location.

INDEX

SECTION 1. ENGINE

A. Engine Starting Problems

Gasoline Engines

Engine turns over, but will not start	1-A, 1
Engine does not turn over when attempting to start	1-A, 2
Engine stalls immediately when started	1-A, 3
Starter motor spins, but does not engage	1-A, 4
Engine is difficult to start when cold	1-A, 5
Engine is difficult to start when hot	1-A, 6

Diesel Engines

Engine turns over but won't start	1-A, 1
Engine does not turn over when attempting to start	1-A, 2
Engine stalls after starting	1-A, 3
Starter motor spins, but does not engage	1-A, 4
Engine is difficult to start	1-A, 5

B. Engine Running Conditions

Gasoline Engines

Engine runs poorly, hesitates	1-B, 1
Engine lacks power	1-B, 2
Engine has poor fuel economy	1-B, 3
Engine runs on (diesels) when turned off	1-B, 4
Engine knocks and pings during heavy acceleration, and on steep hills	1-B, 5
Engine accelerates but vehicle does not gain speed	1-B, 6

Diesel Engines

Engine runs poorly	1-B, 1
Engine lacks power	1-B, 2

C. Engine Noises, Odors and Vibrations

Engine makes a knocking or pinging noise when accelerating	1-C, 1
Starter motor grinds when used	1-C, 2
Engine makes a screeching noise	1-C, 3
Engine makes a growling noise	1-C, 4
Engine makes a ticking or tapping noise	1-C, 5
Engine makes a heavy knocking noise	1-C, 6
Vehicle has a fuel odor when driven	1-C, 7
Vehicle has a rotten egg odor when driven	1-C, 8
Vehicle has a sweet odor when driven	1-C, 9
Engine vibrates when idling	1-C, 10
Engine vibrates during acceleration	1-C, 11

D. Engine Electrical System

Battery goes dead while driving	1-D, 1
Battery goes dead overnight	1-D, 2

E. Engine Cooling System

Engine overheats	1-E, 1
Engine loses coolant	1-E, 2
Engine temperature remains cold when driving	1-E, 3
Engine runs hot	1-E, 4

Condition	Section/Item Number

SECTION 1. ENGINE (continued)

F. Engine Exhaust System

Exhaust rattles at idle speed	1-F, 1
Exhaust system vibrates when driving	1-F, 2
Exhaust system seems too low	1-F, 3
Exhaust seems loud	1-F, 4

SECTION 2. DRIVE TRAIN

A. Automatic Transmission

Transmission shifts erratically	2-A, 1
Transmission will not engage	2-A, 2
Transmission will not downshift during heavy acceleration	2-A, 3

B. Manual Transmission

Transmission grinds going into forward gears while driving	2-B, 1; 2-C, 2
Transmission jumps out of gear	2-B, 2
Transmission difficult to shift	2-B, 3; 2-C, 2
Transmission leaks fluid	2-B, 4

C. Clutch

Clutch slips on hills or during sudden acceleration	2-C, 1
Clutch will not disengage, difficult to shift	2-C, 2
Clutch is noisy when the clutch pedal is pressed	2-C, 3
Clutch pedal extremely difficult to press	2-C, 4
Clutch pedal remains down when pressed	2-C, 5
Clutch chatters when engaging	2-C, 6

D. Differential and Final Drive

Differential makes a low pitched rumbling noise	2-D, 1
Differential makes a howling noise	2-D, 2

E. Transfer Assembly

All Wheel and Four Wheel Drive Vehicles

Leaks fluid from seals or vent after being driven	2-E, 1
Makes excessive noise while driving	2-E, 2
Jumps out of gear	2-E, 3

F. Driveshaft

Rear Wheel, All Wheel and Four Wheel Drive Vehicles

Clunking noise from center of vehicle shifting from forward to reverse	2-F, 1
Excessive vibration from center of vehicle when accelerating	2-F, 2

G. Axles

All Wheel and Four Wheel Drive Vehicles

Front or rear wheel makes a clicking noise	2-G, 1
Front or Rear wheel vibrates with increased speed	2-G, 2

Front Wheel Drive Vehicles

Front wheel makes a clicking noise	2-G, 3
Rear wheel makes a clicking noise	2-G, 4

Condition	Section/Item Number

SECTION 2. DRIVE TRAIN (continued)

Rear Wheel Drive Vehicles

Front or rear wheel makes a clicking noise	2-G, 5
Rear wheel shudders or vibrates	2-G, 6

H. Other Drive Train Conditions

Burning odor from center of vehicle when accelerating	2-H, 1; 2-C, 1; 3-A, 9
Engine accelerates, but vehicle does not gain speed	2-H, 2; 2-C, 1; 3-A, 9

SECTION 3. BRAKE SYSTEM

Brakes pedal pulsates or shimmies when pressed	3-A, 1
Brakes make a squealing noise	3-A, 2
Brakes make a grinding noise	3-A, 3
Vehicle pulls to one side during braking	3-A, 4
Brake pedal feels spongy or has excessive brake pedal travel	3-A, 5
Brake pedal feel is firm, but brakes lack sufficient stopping power or fade	3-A, 6
Vehicle has excessive front end dive or locks rear brakes too easily	3-A, 7
Brake pedal goes to floor when pressed and will not pump up	3-A, 8
Brakes make a burning odor	3-A, 9

SECTION 4. WHEELS, TIRES, STEERING AND SUSPENSION

A. Wheels and Wheel Bearings

All Wheel and Four Wheel Drive Vehicles

Front wheel or wheel bearing loose	4-A, 1
Rear wheel or wheel bearing loose	4-A, 2

Front Wheel Drive Vehicles

Front wheel or wheel bearing loose	4-A, 1
Rear wheel or wheel bearing loose	4-A, 2

Rear Wheel Drive Vehicles

Front wheel or wheel bearing loose	4-A, 1
Rear wheel or wheel bearing loose	4-A, 2

B. Tires

Tires worn on inside tread	4-B, 1
Tires worn on outside tread	4-B, 2
Tires worn unevenly	4-B, 3

C. Steering

Excessive play in steering wheel	4-C, 1
Steering wheel shakes at cruising speeds	4-C, 2
Steering wheel shakes when braking	3-A, 1
Steering wheel becomes stiff when turned	4-C, 4

D. Suspension

Vehicle pulls to one side	4-D, 1
Vehicle is very bouncy over bumps	4-D, 2
Vehicle seems to lean excessively in turns	4-D, 3
Vehicle ride quality seems excessively harsh	4-D, 4
Vehicle seems low or leans to one side	4-D, 5

Condition	Section/Item Number

SECTION 4. WHEELS, TIRES, STEERING AND SUSPENSION (continued)

E. Driving Noises and Vibrations

Noises

Vehicle makes a clicking noise when driven	4-E, 1
Vehicle makes a clunking or knocking noise over bumps	4-E, 2
Vehicle makes a low pitched rumbling noise when driven	4-E, 3
Vehicle makes a squeaking noise over bumps	4-E, 4

Vibrations

Vehicle vibrates when driven	4-E, 5

SECTION 5. ELECTRICAL ACCESSORIES

A. Headlights

One headlight only works on high or low beam	5-A, 1
Headlight does not work on high or low beam	5-A, 2
Headlight(s) very dim	5-A, 3

B. Tail, Running and Side Marker Lights

Tail light, running light or side marker light inoperative	5-B, 1
Tail light, running light or side marker light works intermittently	5-B, 2
Tail light, running light or side marker light very dim	5-B, 3

C. Interior Lights

Interior light inoperative	5-C, 1
Interior light works intermittently	5-C, 2
Interior light very dim	5-C, 3

D. Brake Lights

One brake light inoperative	5-D, 1
Both brake lights inoperative	5-D, 2
One or both brake lights very dim	5-D, 3

E. Warning Lights

Ignition, Battery and Alternator Warning Lights, Check Engine Light, Anti-Lock Braking System (ABS) Light, Brake Warning Light, Oil Pressure Warning Light, and Parking Brake Warning Light

Warning light(s) remains on after the engine is started	5-E, 1
Warning light(s) flickers on and off when driving	5-E, 2
Warning light(s) inoperative with ignition on, and engine not started	5-E, 3

F. Turn Signal and 4-Way Hazard Lights

Turn signals or hazard lights come on, but do not flash	5-F, 1
Turn signals or hazard lights do not function on either side	5-F, 2
Turn signals or hazard lights only work on one side	5-F, 3
One signal light does not work	5-F, 4
Turn signals flash too slowly	5-F, 5
Turn signals flash too fast	5-F, 6
Four-way hazard flasher indicator light inoperative	5-F, 7
Turn signal indicator light(s) do not work in either direction	5-F, 8
One turn signal indicator light does not work	5-F, 9

Condition	Section/Item Number

SECTION 5. ELECTRICAL ACCESSORIES (continued)

G. Horn

Horn does not operate	5-G, 1
Horn has an unusual tone	5-G, 2

H. Windshield Wipers

Windshield wipers do not operate	5-H, 1
Windshield wiper motor makes a humming noise, gets hot or blows fuses	5-H, 2
Windshield wiper motor operates but one or both wipers fail to move	5-H, 3
Windshield wipers will not park	5-H, 4

SECTION 6. INSTRUMENTS AND GAUGES

A. Speedometer (Cable Operated)

Speedometer does not work	6-A, 1
Speedometer needle fluctuates when driving at steady speeds	6-A, 2
Speedometer works intermittently	6-A, 3

B. Speedometer (Electronically Operated)

Speedometer does not work	6-B, 1
Speedometer works intermittently	6-B, 2

C. Fuel, Temperature and Oil Pressure Gauges

Gauge does not register	6-C, 1
Gauge operates erratically	6-C, 2
Gauge operates fully pegged	6-C, 3

SECTION 7. CLIMATE CONTROL

A. Air Conditioner

No air coming from air conditioner vents	7-A, 1
Air conditioner blows warm air	7-A, 2
Water collects on the interior floor when the air conditioner is used	7-A, 3
Air conditioner has a moldy odor when used	7-A, 4

B. Heater

Blower motor does not operate	7-B, 1
Heater blows cool air	7-B, 2
Heater steams the windshield when used	7-B, 3

DIAGNOSTIC PROCEDURES

1. ENGINE

1-A. Engine Starting Problems

Gasoline Engines

1. Engine turns over, but will not start

a. Check fuel level in fuel tank, add fuel if empty.

b. Check battery condition and state of charge. If voltage and load test below specification, charge or replace battery.

c. Check battery terminal and cable condition and tightness. Clean terminals and replace damaged, worn or corroded cables.

d. Check fuel delivery system. If fuel is not reaching the fuel injectors, check for a loose electrical connector or defective fuse, relay or fuel pump and replace as necessary.

e. Engine may have excessive wear or mechanical damage such as low cylinder cranking pressure, a broken camshaft drive system, insufficient valve clearance or bent valves.

f. Check for fuel contamination such as water in the fuel. During winter months, the water may freeze and cause a fuel restriction. Adding a fuel additive may help, however the fuel system may require draining and purging with fresh fuel.

g. Check for ignition system failure. Check for loose or shorted wires or damaged ignition system components. Check the spark plugs for excessive wear or incorrect electrode gap. If the problem is worse in wet weather, check for shorts between the spark plugs and the ignition coils.

h. Check the engine management system for a failed sensor or control module.

2. Engine does not turn over when attempting to start

a. Check the battery state of charge and condition. If the dash lights are not visible or very dim when turning the ignition key on, the battery has either failed internally or discharged, the battery cables are loose, excessively corroded or damaged, or the alternator has failed or internally shorted, discharging the battery. Charge or replace the battery, clean or replace the battery cables, and check the alternator output.

b. Check the operation of the neutral safety switch. On automatic transmission vehicles, try starting the vehicle in both Park and Neutral. On manual transmission vehicles, depress the clutch pedal and attempt to start. On some vehicles, these switches can be adjusted. Make sure the switches or wire connectors are not loose or damaged. Replace or adjust the switches as necessary.

c. Check the starter motor, starter solenoid or relay, and starter motor cables and wires. Check the ground from the engine to the chassis. Make sure the wires are not loose, damaged, or corroded. If battery voltage is present at the starter relay, try using a remote starter to start the vehicle for test purposes only. Replace any damaged or corroded cables, in addition to replacing any failed components.

d. Check the engine for seizure. If the engine has not been started for a long period of time, internal parts such as the rings may have rusted to the cylinder walls. The engine may have suffered internal damage, or could be hydro-locked from ingesting water. Remove the spark plugs and carefully attempt to rotate the engine using a suitable breaker bar and socket on the crankshaft pulley. If the engine is resistant to moving, or moves slightly and then binds, do not force the engine any further before determining the problem.

3. Engine stalls immediately when started

a. Check the ignition switch condition and operation. The electrical contacts in the run position may be worn or damaged. Try restarting the engine with all electrical accessories in the off position. Sometimes turning the key on an off will help in emergency situations, however once the switch has shown signs of failure, it should be replaced as soon as possible.

b. Check for loose, corroded, damaged or shorted wires for the ignition system and repair or replace.

c. Check for manifold vacuum leaks or vacuum hose leakage and repair or replace parts as necessary.

d. Measure the fuel pump delivery volume and pressure. Low fuel pump pressure can also be noticed as a lack of power when accelerating. Make sure the fuel pump lines are not restricted. The fuel pump output is not adjustable and requires fuel pump replacement to repair.

e. Check the engine fuel and ignition management system. Inspect the sensor wiring and electrical connectors. A dirty, loose or damaged sensor or control module wire can simulate a failed component.

f. Check the exhaust system for internal restrictions.

4. Starter motor spins, but does not engage

a. Check the starter motor for a seized or binding pinion gear.

b. Remove the flywheel inspection plate and check for a damaged ring gear.

5. Engine is difficult to start when cold

a. Check the battery condition, battery state of charge and starter motor current draw. Replace the battery if marginal and the starter motor if the current draw is beyond specification.

b. Check the battery cable condition. Clean the battery terminals and replace corroded or damaged cables.

c. Check the fuel system for proper operation. A fuel pump with insufficient fuel pressure or clogged injectors should be replaced.

d. Check the engine's tune-up status. Note the tune-up specifications and check for items such as severely worn spark plugs; adjust or replace as needed. On vehicles with manually adjusted valve clearances, check for tight valves and adjust to specification.

e. Check for a failed coolant temperature sensor, and replace if out of specification.

f. Check the operation of the engine management systems for fuel and ignition; repair or replace failed components as necessary.

6. Engine is difficult to start when hot

a. Check the air filter and air intake system. Replace the air filter if it is dirty or contaminated. Check the fresh air intake system for restrictions or blockage.

b. Check for loose or deteriorated engine grounds and clean, tighten or replace as needed.

c. Check for needed maintenance. Inspect tune-up and service related items such as spark plugs and engine oil condition, and check the operation of the engine fuel and ignition management system.

Diesel Engines

1. Engine turns over but won't start

a. Check engine starting procedure and restart engine.

b. Check the glow plug operation and repair or replace as necessary.

c. Check for air in the fuel system or fuel filter and bleed the air as necessary.

d. Check the fuel delivery system and repair or replace as necessary.

e. Check fuel level and add fuel as needed.

f. Check fuel quality. If the fuel is contaminated, drain and flush the fuel tank.

g. Check engine compression. If compression is below specification, the engine may need to be renewed or replaced.

h. Check the injection pump timing and set to specification.

i. Check the injection pump condition and replace as necessary.

j. Check the fuel nozzle operation and condition or replace as necess-ary.

2. Engine does not turn over when attempting to start

a. Check the battery state of charge and condition. If the dash lights are not visible or very dim when turning the ignition key on, the battery has either failed internally or discharged, the battery cables are loose, excessively corroded or damaged, or the alternator has failed or internally shorted, discharging the battery. Charge or replace the battery, clean or replace the battery cables, and check the alternator output.

b. Check the operation of the neutral safety switch. On automatic transmission vehicles, try starting the vehicle in both Park and Neutral. On manual transmission vehicles, depress the clutch pedal and attempt to start. On some vehicles, these switches can be adjusted. Make sure the switches or wire connectors are not loose or damaged. Replace or adjust the switches as necessary.

c. Check the starter motor, starter solenoid or relay, and starter motor cables and wires. Check the ground from the engine to the chassis. Make sure the wires are not loose, damaged, or corroded. If battery voltage is present at the starter relay, try using a remote starter to start the vehicle for test purposes only. Replace any damaged or corroded cables, in addition to replacing any failed components.

d. Check the engine for seizure. If the engine has not been started for a long period of time, internal parts such as the rings may have rusted to the cylinder walls. The engine may have suffered internal damage, or could be hydro-locked from ingesting water. Remove the injectors and carefully attempt to rotate the engine

using a suitable breaker bar and socket on the crankshaft pulley. If the engine is resistant to moving, or moves slightly and then binds, do not force the engine any further before determining the cause of the problem.

3. Engine stalls after starting

a. Check for a restriction in the fuel return line or the return line check valve and repair as necessary.

b. Check the glow plug operation for turning the glow plugs off too soon and repair as necessary.

c. Check for incorrect injection pump timing and reset to specification.

d. Test the engine fuel pump and replace if the output is below specification.

e. Check for contaminated or incorrect fuel. Completely flush the fuel system and replace with fresh fuel.

f. Test the engine's compression for low compression. If below specification, mechanical repairs are necessary to repair.

g. Check for air in the fuel. Check fuel tank fuel and fill as needed.

h. Check for a failed injection pump. Replace the pump, making sure to properly set the pump timing.

4. Starter motor spins, but does not engage

a. Check the starter motor for a seized or binding pinion gear.

b. Remove the flywheel inspection plate and check for a damaged ring gear.

1-B. Engine Running Conditions

Gasoline Engines

1. Engine runs poorly, hesitates

a. Check the engine ignition system operation and adjust if possible, or replace defective parts.

b. Check for restricted fuel injectors and replace as necessary.

c. Check the fuel pump output and delivery. Inspect fuel lines for restrictions. If the fuel pump pressure is below specification, replace the fuel pump.

d. Check the operation of the engine management system and repair as necessary.

2. Engine lacks power

a. Check the engine's tune-up status. Note the tune-up specifications and check for items such as severely worn spark plugs; adjust or replace as needed. On vehicles with manually adjusted valve clearances, check for tight valves and adjust to specification.

b. Check the air filter and air intake system. Replace the air filter if it is dirty or contaminated. Check the fresh air intake system for restrictions or blockage.

c. Check the operation of the engine fuel and ignition management systems. Check the sensor operation and wiring. Check for low fuel pump pressure and repair or replace components as necessary.

d. Check the throttle linkage adjustments. Check to make sure the linkage is fully opening the throttle. Replace any worn or defective bushings or linkages.

e. Check for a restricted exhaust system. Check for bent or crimped exhaust pipes, or internally restricted mufflers or catalytic converters. Compare inlet and outlet temperatures for the converter or muffler. If the inlet is hot, but outlet cold, the component is restricted.

f. Check for a loose or defective knock sensor. A loose, improperly torqued or defective knock sensor will decrease spark advance and reduce power. Replace defective knock sensors and install using the recommended torque specification.

g. Check for engine mechanical conditions such as low compression, worn piston rings, worn valves, worn camshafts and related parts. An engine which has severe mechanical wear, or has suffered internal mechanical damage must be rebuilt or replaced to restore lost power.

h. Check the engine oil level for being overfilled. Adjust the engine's oil level, or change the engine oil and filter, and top off to the correct level.

i. Check for an intake manifold or vacuum hose leak. Replace leaking gaskets or worn vacuum hoses.

j. Check for dragging brakes and replace or repair as necessary.

k. Check tire air pressure and tire wear. Adjust the pressure to the recommended settings. Check the tire wear for possible alignment problems causing increased rolling resistance, decreased acceleration and increased fuel usage.

l. Check the octane rating of the fuel used during refilling, and use a higher octane rated fuel.

3. Poor fuel economy

a. Inspect the air filter and check for any air restrictions going into the air filter housing. Replace the air filter if it is dirty or contaminated.

b. Check the engine for tune-up and related adjustments. Replace worn ignition parts, check the engine ignition timing and fuel mixture, and set to specifications if possible.

c. Check the tire size, tire wear, alignment and tire pressure. Large tires create more rolling resistance, smaller tires require more engine speed to maintain a vehicle's road speed. Excessive tire wear can be caused by incorrect tire pressure, incorrect wheel alignment or a suspension problem. All of these conditions create increased rolling resistance, causing the engine to work harder to accelerate and maintain a vehicle's speed.

d. Inspect the brakes for binding or excessive drag. A sticking brake caliper, overly adjusted brake shoe, broken brake shoe return spring, or binding parking brake cable or linkage can create a significant drag, brake wear and loss of fuel economy. Check the brake system operation and repair as necessary.

4. Engine runs on (diesels) when turned off

a. Check for idle speed set too high and readjust to specification.

b. Check the operation of the idle control valve, and replace if defective.

c. Check the ignition timing and adjust to recommended settings. Check for defective sensors or related components and replace if defective.

d. Check for a vacuum leak at the intake manifold or vacuum hose and replace defective gaskets or hoses.

e. Check the engine for excessive carbon build-up in the combus-

tion chamber. Use a recommended decarbonizing fuel additive or disassemble the cylinder head to remove the carbon.

f. Check the operation of the engine fuel management system and replace defective sensors or control units.

g. Check the engine operating temperature for overheating and repair as necessary.

5. Engine knocks and pings during heavy acceleration, and on steep hills

a. Check the octane rating of the fuel used during refilling, and use a higher octane rated fuel.

b. Check the ignition timing and adjust to recommended settings. Check for defective sensors or related components and replace if defective.

c. Check the engine for excessive carbon build-up in the combustion chamber. Use a recommended decarbonizing fuel additive or disassemble the cylinder head to remove the carbon.

d. Check the spark plugs for the correct type, electrode gap and heat range. Replace worn or damaged spark plugs. For severe or continuous high speed use, install a spark plug that is one heat range colder.

e. Check the operation of the engine fuel management system and replace defective sensors or control units.

f. Check for a restricted exhaust system. Check for bent or crimped exhaust pipes, or internally restricted mufflers or catalytic converters. Compare inlet and outlet temperatures for the converter or muffler. If the inlet is hot, but outlet cold, the component is restricted.

6. Engine accelerates, but vehicle does not gain speed

a. On manual transmission vehicles, check for causes of a slipping clutch. Refer to the clutch troubleshooting section for additional information.

b. On automatic transmission vehicles, check for a slipping transmission. Check the transmission fluid level and condition. If the fluid level is too high, adjust to the correct level. If the fluid level is low, top off using the recommended fluid type. If the fluid exhibits a burning odor, the transmission has been slipping internally. Changing the fluid and filter may help temporarily, however in this situation a transmission may require overhauling to ensure long-term reliability.

Diesel Engines

1. Engine runs poorly

a. Check the injection pump timing and adjust to specification.

b. Check for air in the fuel lines or leaks, and bleed the air from the fuel system.

c. Check the fuel filter, fuel feed and return lines for a restriction and repair as necessary.

d. Check the fuel for contamination, drain and flush the fuel tank and replenish with fresh fuel.

2. Engine lacks power

a. Inspect the air intake system and air filter for restrictions and, if necessary, replace the air filter.

b. Verify the injection pump timing and reset if out of specification.

c. Check the exhaust for an internal restriction and replace failed parts.

d. Check for a restricted fuel filter and, if restricted, replace the filter.

e. Inspect the fuel filler cap vent . When removing the filler cap, listen for excessive hissing noises indicating a blockage in the fuel filler cap vents. If the filler cap vents are blocked, replace the cap.

f. Check the fuel system for restrictions and repair as necessary.

g. Check for low engine compression and inspect for external leakage at the glow plugs or nozzles. If no external leakage is noted, repair or replace the engine.

ENGINE PERFORMANCE TROUBLESHOOTING HINTS

When troubleshooting an engine running or performance condition, the mechanical condition of the engine should be determined *before* lengthy troubleshooting procedures are performed.

The engine fuel management systems in fuel injected vehicles rely on electronic sensors to provide information to the engine control unit for precise fuel metering. Unlike carburetors, which use the incoming air speed to draw fuel through the fuel metering jets in order to provide a proper fuel-to-air ratio, a fuel injection system provides a specific amount of fuel which is introduced by the fuel injectors into the intake manifold or intake port, based on the information provided by electronic sensors.

The sensors monitor the engine's operating temperature, ambient temperature and the amount of air entering the engine, engine speed and throttle position to provide information to the engine control unit, which, in turn, operates the fuel injectors by electrical pulses. The sensors provide information to the engine control unit using low voltage electrical signals. As a result, an unplugged sensor or a poor electrical contact could cause a poor running condition similar to a failed sensor.

When troubleshooting a fuel related engine condition on fuel injected vehicles, carefully inspect the wiring and electrical connectors to the related components. Make sure the electrical connectors are fully connected, clean and not physically damaged. If necessary, clean the electrical contacts using electrical contact cleaner. The use of cleaning agents not specifically designed for electrical contacts should not be used, as they could leave a surface film or damage the insulation of the wiring.

The engine electrical system provides the necessary electrical power to operate the vehicle's electrical accessories, electronic control units and sensors. Because engine management systems are sensitive to voltage changes, an alternator which over or undercharges could cause engine running problems or component failure. Most alternators utilize internal voltage regulators which cannot be adjusted and must be replaced individually or as a unit with the alternator.

Ignition systems may be controlled by, or linked to, the engine fuel management system. Similar to the fuel injection system, these ignition systems rely on electronic sensors for information to determine the optimum ignition timing for a given engine speed and load. Some ignition systems no longer allow the ignition timing to be adjusted. Feedback from low voltage electrical sensors provide information to the control unit to determine the amount of ignition advance. On these systems, if a failure occurs the failed component must be replaced. Before replacing suspected failed electrical components, carefully inspect the wiring and electrical connectors to the related components. Make sure the electrical connectors are fully connected, clean and not physically damaged. If necessary, clean the electrical contacts using electrical contact cleaner. The use of cleaning agents not specifically designed for electrical contacts should be avoided, as they could leave a surface film or damage the insulation of the wiring.

1-C. Engine Noises, Odors and Vibrations

1. Engine makes a knocking or pinging noise when accelerating

a. Check the octane rating of the fuel being used. Depending on the type of driving or driving conditions, it may be necessary to use a higher octane fuel.

b. Verify the ignition system settings and operation. Improperly adjusted ignition timing or a failed component, such as a knock sensor, may cause the ignition timing to advance excessively or prematurely. Check the ignition system operation and adjust, or replace components as needed.

c. Check the spark plug gap, heat range and condition. If the vehicle is operated in severe operating conditions or at continuous high speeds, use a colder heat range spark plug. Adjust the spark plug gap to the manufacturer's recommended specification and replace worn or damaged spark plugs.

2. Starter motor grinds when used

a. Examine the starter pinion gear and the engine ring gear for damage, and replace damaged parts.

b. Check the starter mounting bolts and housing. If the housing is cracked or damaged replace the starter motor and check the mounting bolts for tightness.

3. Engine makes a screeching noise

a. Check the accessory drive belts for looseness and adjust as necessary.

b. Check the accessory drive belt tensioners for seizing or excessive bearing noises and replace if loose, binding, or excessively noisy.

c. Check for a seizing water pump. The pump may not be leaking; however, the bearing may be faulty or the impeller loose and jammed. Replace the water pump.

4. Engine makes a growling noise

a. Check for a loose or failing water pump. Replace the pump and engine coolant.

b. Check the accessory drive belt tensioners for excessive bearing noises and replace if loose or excessively noisy.

5. Engine makes a ticking or tapping noise

a. On vehicles with hydraulic lash adjusters, check for low or dirty engine oil and top off or replace the engine oil and filter.

b. On vehicles with hydraulic lash adjusters, check for collapsed lifters and replace failed components.

c. On vehicles with hydraulic lash adjusters, check for low oil pressure caused by a restricted oil filter, worn engine oil pump, or oil pressure relief valve.

d. On vehicles with manually adjusted valves, check for excessive valve clearance or worn valve train parts. Adjust the valves to specification or replace worn and defective parts.

e. Check for a loose or improperly tensioned timing belt or timing chain and adjust or replace parts as necessary.

f. Check for a bent or sticking exhaust or intake valve. Remove the engine cylinder head to access and replace.

6. Engine makes a heavy knocking noise

a. Check for a loose crankshaft pulley or flywheel; replace and torque the mounting bolt(s) to specification.

b. Check for a bent connecting rod caused by a hydro-lock condition. Engine disassembly is necessary to inspect for damaged and needed replacement parts.

c. Check for excessive engine rod bearing wear or damage. This condition is also associated with low engine oil pressure and will require engine disassembly to inspect for damaged and needed replacement parts.

7. Vehicle has a fuel odor when driven

a. Check the fuel gauge level. If the fuel gauge registers full, it is possible that the odor is caused by being filled beyond capacity, or some spillage occurred during refueling. The odor should clear after driving an hour, or twenty miles, allowing the vapor canister to purge.

b. Check the fuel filler cap for looseness or seepage. Check the cap tightness and, if loose, properly secure. If seepage is noted, replace the filler cap.

c. Check for loose hose clamps, cracked or damaged fuel delivery and return lines, or leaking components or seals, and replace or repair as necessary.

d. Check the vehicle's fuel economy. If fuel consumption has increased due to a failed component, or if the fuel is not properly ignited due to an ignition related failure, the catalytic converter may become contaminated. This condition may also trigger the check engine warning light. Check the spark plugs for a dark, rich condition or verify the condition by testing the vehicle's emissions. Replace fuel fouled spark plugs, and test and replace failed components as necessary.

8. Vehicle has a rotten egg odor when driven

a. Check for a leaking intake gasket or vacuum leak causing a lean running condition. A lean mixture may result in increased exhaust temperatures, causing the catalytic converter to run hotter than normal. This condition may also trigger the check engine warning light. Check and repair the vacuum leaks as necessary.

b. Check the vehicle's alternator and battery condition. If the alternator is overcharging, the battery electrolyte can be boiled from the battery, and the battery casing may begin to crack, swell or bulge, damaging or shorting the battery internally. If this has occurred, neutralize the battery mounting area with a suitable baking soda and water mixture or equivalent, and replace the alternator or voltage regulator. Inspect, service, and load test the battery, and replace if necessary.

9. Vehicle has a sweet odor when driven

a. Check for an engine coolant leak caused by a seeping radiator cap, loose hose clamp, weeping cooling system seal, gasket or cooling system hose and replace or repair as needed.

b. Check for a coolant leak from the radiator, coolant reservoir, heater control valve or under the dashboard from the heater core, and replace the failed part as necessary.

c. Check the engine's exhaust for white smoke in addition to a sweet odor. The presence of white, steamy smoke with a sweet odor indicates coolant leaking into the combustion chamber. Possible causes include a failed head gasket, cracked engine block or cylinder head. Other symptoms of this condition include a white paste build-up on the inside of the oil filler cap, and softened, deformed or bulging radiator hoses.

10. Engine vibrates when idling

a. Check for loose, collapsed, or damaged engine or transmission mounts and repair or replace as necessary.

b. Check for loose or damaged engine covers or shields and secure or replace as necessary.

11. Engine vibrates during acceleration

a. Check for missing, loose or damaged exhaust system hangers and mounts; replace or repair as necessary.

b. Check the exhaust system routing and fit for adequate clearance or potential rubbing; repair or adjust as necessary.

1-D. Engine Electrical System

1. Battery goes dead while driving

a. Check the battery condition. Replace the battery if the battery will not hold a charge or fails a battery load test. If the battery loses fluid while driving, check for an overcharging condition. If the alternator is overcharging, replace the alternator or voltage regulator. (A voltage regulator is typically built into the alternator, necessitating alternator replacement or overhaul.)

b. Check the battery cable condition. Clean or replace corroded cables and clean the battery terminals.

c. Check the alternator and voltage regulator operation. If the charging system is over or undercharging, replace the alternator or voltage regulator, or both.

d. Inspect the wiring and wire connectors at the alternator for looseness, a missing ground or defective terminal, and repair as necessary.

e. Inspect the alternator drive belt tension, tensioners and condition. Properly tension the drive belt, replace weak or broken tensioners, and replace the drive belt if worn or cracked.

2. Battery goes dead overnight

a. Check the battery condition. Replace the battery if the battery will not hold a charge or fails a battery load test.

b. Check for a voltage draw, such as a trunk light, interior light or glove box light staying on. Check light switch position and operation, and replace if defective.

c. Check the alternator for an internally failed diode, and replace the alternator if defective.

1-E. Engine Cooling System

1. Engine overheats

a. Check the coolant level. Set the heater temperature to full hot and check for internal air pockets, bleed the cooling system and inspect for leakage. Top off the cooling system with the correct coolant mixture.

b. Pressure test the cooling system and radiator cap for leaks. Check for seepage caused by loose hose clamps, failed coolant hoses, and cooling system components such as the heater control valve, heater core, radiator, radiator cap, and water pump. Replace defective parts and fill the cooling system with the recommended coolant mixture.

c. On vehicles with electrically controlled cooling fans, check the cooling fan operation. Check for blown fuses or defective fan motors, temperature sensors and relays, and replace failed components.

d. Check for a coolant leak caused by a failed head gasket, or a porous water jacket casting in the cylinder head or engine block. Replace defective parts as necessary.

e. Check for an internally restricted radiator. Flush the radiator or replace if the blockage is too severe for flushing.

f. Check for a damaged water pump. If coolant circulation is poor, check for a loose water pump impeller. If the impeller is loose, replace the water pump.

2. Engine loses coolant

a. Pressure test the cooling system and radiator cap for leaks. Check for seepage caused by loose hose clamps, failed coolant hoses, and cooling system components such as the heater control valve, heater core, radiator, radiator cap, and water pump. Replace defective parts and fill the cooling system with the recommended coolant mixture.

b. Check for a coolant leak caused by a failed head gasket, or a porous water jacket casting in the cylinder head or engine block. Replace defective parts as necessary.

3. Engine temperature remains cold when driving

a. Check the thermostat operation. Replace the thermostat if it sticks in the open position.

b. On vehicles with electrically controlled cooling fans, check the cooling fan operation. Check for defective temperature sensors and stuck relays, and replace failed components.

c. Check temperature gauge operation if equipped to verify proper operation of the gauge. Check the sensors and wiring for defects, and repair or replace defective components.

4. Engine runs hot

a. Check for an internally restricted radiator. Flush the radiator or replace if the blockage is too severe for flushing.

b. Check for a loose or slipping water pump drive belt. Inspect the drive belt condition. Replace the belt if brittle, cracked or damaged. Check the pulley condition and properly tension the belt.

c. Check the cooling fan operation. Replace defective fan motors, sensors or relays as necessary.

d. Check temperature gauge operation if equipped to verify proper operation of the gauge. Check the sensors and wiring for defects, and repair or replace defective components.

e. Check the coolant level. Set the heater temperature to full hot, check for internal air pockets, bleed the cooling system and inspect for leakage. Top off the cooling system with the correct coolant mixture. Once the engine is cool, recheck the fluid level and top off as needed.

NOTE: The engine cooling system can also be affected by an engine's mechanical condition. A failed head gasket or a porous casting in the engine block or cylinder head could cause a loss of coolant and result in engine overheating.

Some cooling systems rely on electrically driven cooling fans to cool the radiator and use electrical temperature sensors and relays to operate the cooling fan. When diagnosing these systems, check for blown fuses, damaged wires and verify that the electrical connections are fully connected, clean and not physically damaged. If necessary, clean the electrical contacts using electrical contact cleaner. The use of cleaning agents not specifically designed for electrical contacts could leave a film or damage the insulation of the wiring.

1-F. Engine Exhaust System

1. Exhaust rattles at idle speed

a. Check the engine and transmission mounts and replace mounts showing signs of damage or wear.

b. Check the exhaust hangers, brackets and mounts. Replace broken, missing or damaged mounts.

c. Check for internal damage to mufflers and catalytic converters. The broken pieces from the defective component may travel in the direction of the exhaust flow and collect and/or create a blockage in a component other than the one which failed, causing engine running and stalling problems. Another symptom of a restricted exhaust is low engine manifold vacuum. Remove the exhaust system and carefully remove any loose or broken pieces, then replace any failed or damaged parts as necessary.

d. Check the exhaust system clearance, routing and alignment. If the exhaust is making contact with the vehicle in any manner, loosen and reposition the exhaust system.

2. Exhaust system vibrates when driving

a. Check the exhaust hangers, brackets and mounts. Replace broken, missing or damaged mounts.

b. Check the exhaust system clearance, routing and alignment. If the exhaust is making contact with the vehicle in any manner, check for bent or damaged components and replace, then loosen and reposition the exhaust system.

c. Check for internal damage to mufflers and catalytic converters. The broken pieces from the defective component may travel in the direction of the exhaust flow and collect and/or create a blockage in a component other than the one which failed, causing engine running and stalling problems. Another symptom of a restricted exhaust is low engine manifold vacuum. Remove the exhaust system and carefully remove any loose or broken pieces, then replace any failed or damaged parts as necessary.

3. Exhaust system hangs too low

a. Check the exhaust hangers, brackets and mounts. Replace broken, missing or damaged mounts.

b. Check the exhaust routing and alignment. Check and replace bent or damaged components. If the exhaust is not routed properly, loosen and reposition the exhaust system.

4. Exhaust sounds loud

a. Check the system for looseness and leaks. Check the exhaust pipes, clamps, flange bolts and manifold fasteners for tightness. Check and replace any failed gaskets.

b. Check and replace exhaust silencers that have a loss of efficiency due to internally broken baffles or worn packing material.

c. Check for missing mufflers and silencers that have been replaced with straight pipes or with non-original equipment silencers.

NOTE: Exhaust system rattles, vibration and proper alignment should not be overlooked. Excessive vibration caused by collapsed engine mounts, damaged or missing exhaust hangers and misalignment may cause surface cracks and broken welds, creating exhaust leaks or internal damage to exhaust components such as the catalytic converter, creating a restriction to exhaust flow and loss of power.

2. DRIVE TRAIN

2-A. Automatic Transmission

1. Transmission shifts erratically

a. Check and if not within the recommended range, add or remove transmission fluid to obtain the correct fluid level. Always use the recommended fluid type when adding transmission fluid.

b. Check the fluid level condition. If the fluid has become contaminated, fatigued from excessive heat or exhibits a burning odor, change the transmission fluid and filter using the recommended type and amount of fluid. A fluid which exhibits a burning odor indicates that the transmission has been slipping internally and may require future repairs.

c. Check for an improperly installed transmission filter, or missing filter gasket, and repair as necessary.

d. Check for loose or leaking gaskets, pressure lines and fittings, and repair or replace as necessary.

e. Check for loose or disconnected shift and throttle linkages or vacuum hoses, and repair as necessary.

2. Transmission will not engage

a. Check the shift linkage for looseness, wear and proper adjustment, and repair as necessary.

b. Check for a loss of transmission fluid and top off as needed with the recommended fluid.

c. If the transmission does not engage with the shift linkage correctly installed and the proper fluid level, internal damage has likely occurred, requiring transmission removal and disassembly.

3. Transmission will not downshift during heavy acceleration

a. On computer controlled transmissions, check for failed sensors or control units and repair or replace defective components.

b. On vehicles with kickdown linkages or vacuum servos, check for proper linkage adjustment or leaking vacuum hoses or servo units.

NOTE: Many automatic transmissions use an electronic control module, electrical sensors and solenoids to control transmission shifting. When troubleshooting a vehicle with this type of system, be sure the electrical connectors are fully connected, clean and not physically damaged. If necessary, clean the electrical contacts using electrical contact cleaner. The use of cleaning agents not specifically designed for electrical contacts could leave a film or damage the insulation of the wiring.

2-B. Manual Transmission

1. Transmission grinds going into forward gears while driving

a. Check the clutch release system. On clutches with a mechanical or cable linkage, check the adjustment. Adjust the clutch pedal to have 1 inch (25mm) of free-play at the pedal.

b. If the clutch release system is hydraulically operated, check the fluid level and, if low, top off using the recommended type and amount of fluid.

c. Synchronizers worn. Remove transmission and replace synchronizers.

d. Synchronizer sliding sleeve worn. Remove transmission and replace sliding sleeve.

e. Gear engagement dogs worn or damaged. Remove transmission and replace gear.

2. Transmission jumps out of gear

a. Shift shaft detent springs worn. Replace shift detent springs.

b. Synchronizer sliding sleeve worn. Remove transmission and replace sliding sleeve.

c. Gear engagement dogs worn or damaged. Remove transmission and replace gear.

d. Crankshaft thrust bearings worn. Remove engine and crankshaft, and repair as necessary.

3. Transmission difficult to shift

a. Verify the clutch adjustment and, if not properly adjusted, adjust to specification.

b. Synchronizers worn. Remove transmission and replace synchronizers.

c. Pilot bearing seized. Remove transmission and replace pilot bearing.

d. Shift linkage or bushing seized. Disassemble the shift linkage, replace worn or damaged bushings, lubricate and reinstall.

4. Transmission leaks fluid

a. Check the fluid level for an overfilled condition. Adjust the fluid level to specification.

b. Check for a restricted transmission vent or breather tube. Clear the blockage as necessary and check the fluid level. If necessary, top off with the recommended lubricant.

c. Check for a porous casting, leaking seal or gasket. Replace defective parts and top off the fluid level with the recommended lubricant.

2-C. Clutch

1. Clutch slips on hills or during sudden acceleration

a. Check for insufficient clutch pedal free-play. Adjust clutch linkage or cable to allow about 1 inch (25mm) of pedal free-play.

b. Clutch disc worn or severely damaged. Remove engine or transmission and replace clutch disc.

c. Clutch pressure plate is weak. Remove engine or transmission and replace the clutch pressure plate and clutch disc.

d. Clutch pressure plate and/or flywheel incorrectly machined. If the clutch system has been recently replaced and rebuilt, or refurbished parts have been used, it is possible that the machined surfaces decreased the clutch clamping force. Replace defective parts with new replacement parts.

2. Clutch will not disengage, difficult to shift

a. Check the clutch release mechanism. Check for stretched cables, worn linkages or failed clutch hydraulics and replace defective parts. On hydraulically operated clutch release mechanisms, check for air in the hydraulic system and bleed as necessary.

b. Check for a broken, cracked or fatigued clutch release arm or release arm pivot. Replace defective parts and properly lubricate upon assembly.

c. Check for a damaged clutch hub damper or damper spring. The broken parts tend to become lodged between the clutch disc and the pressure plate. Disassemble clutch system and replace failed parts.

d. Check for a seized clutch pilot bearing. Disassemble the clutch assembly and replace the defective parts.

e. Check for a defective clutch disc. Check for warpage or lining thicknesses larger than original equipment.

3. Clutch is noisy when the clutch pedal is pressed

a. Check the clutch pedal stop and pedal free-play adjustment for excessive movement and adjust as necessary.

b. Check for a worn or damaged release bearing. If the noise ceases when the pedal is released, the release bearing should be replaced.

c. Check the engine crankshaft axial play. If the crankshaft thrust bearings are worn or damaged, the crankshaft will move when pressing the clutch pedal. The engine must be disassembled to replace the crankshaft thrust bearings.

4. Clutch pedal extremely difficult to press

a. Check the clutch pedal pivots and linkages for binding. Clean and lubricate linkages.

b. On cable actuated clutch systems, check the cable routing and condition. Replace kinked, frayed, damaged or corroded cables and check cable routing to avoid sharp bends. Check the engine ground strap for poor conductivity. If the ground strap is marginal, the engine could try to ground itself via the clutch cable, causing premature failure.

c. On mechanical linkage clutches, check the linkage for binding or misalignment. Lubricate pivots or linkages and repair as necessary.

d. Check the release bearing guide tube and release fork for a lack of lubrication. Install a smooth coating of high temperature grease to allow smooth movement of the release bearing over the guide tube.

5. Clutch pedal remains down when pressed

a. On mechanical linkage or cable actuated clutches, check for a loose or disconnected link.

b. On hydraulically actuated clutches, check the fluid level and check for a hydraulic leak at the clutch slave or master cylinder, or hydraulic line. Replace failed parts and bleed clutch hydraulic system. If no leakage is noted, the clutch master cylinder may have failed internally. Replace the clutch master cylinder and bleed the clutch hydraulic system.

6. Clutch chatters when engaging

a. Check the engine flywheel for warpage or surface variations and replace or repair as necessary.

b. Check for a warped clutch disc or damaged clutch damper hub. Remove the clutch disc and replace.

c. Check for a loose or damaged clutch pressure plate and replace defective components.

NOTE: The clutch is actuated either by a mechanical linkage, cable or a clutch hydraulic system. The mechanical linkage and cable systems may require the clutch pedal free-play to be adjusted as the clutch disc wears. A hydraulic clutch system automatically adjusts as the clutch wears and, with the exception of the clutch pedal height, no adjustment is possible.

2-D. Differential and Final Drive

1. Differential makes a low pitched rumbling noise

a. Check fluid level type and amount. Replace the fluid with the recommended type and amount of lubricant.

b. Check the differential bearings for wear or damage. Remove the bearings, inspect the drive and driven gears for wear or damage, and replace components as necessary.

2. Differential makes a howling noise

a. Check fluid level type and amount. Replace the fluid with the recommended type and amount of lubricant.

b. Check the differential drive and driven gears for wear or damage, and replace components as necessary.

2-E. Transfer Assembly

All Wheel and Four Wheel Drive Vehicles

1. Leaks fluid from seals or vent after being driven
a. Fluid level overfilled. Check and adjust transfer case fluid level.
b. Check for a restricted breather or breather tube, clear and check the fluid level and top off as needed.
c. Check seal condition and replace worn, damaged, or defective seals. Check the fluid level and top off as necessary.

2. Makes excessive noise while driving
a. Check the fluid for the correct type of lubricant. Drain and refill using the recommended type and amount of lubricant.
b. Check the fluid level. Top off the fluid using the recommended type and amount of lubricant.
c. If the fluid level and type of lubricant meet specifications, check for internal wear or damage. Remove assembly and disassemble to inspect for worn, damaged, or defective components.

3. Jumps out of gear
a. Stop vehicle and make sure the unit is fully engaged.
b. Check for worn, loose or an improperly adjusted linkage. Replace and/or adjust linkage as necessary.
c. Check for internal wear or damage. Remove assembly and disassemble to inspect for worn, damaged, or defective components.

2-F. Driveshaft

Rear Wheel, All Wheel and Four Wheel Drive Vehicles

1. Clunking noise from center of vehicle shifting from forward to reverse
a. Worn universal joint. Remove driveshaft and replace universal joint.

2. Excessive vibration from center of vehicle when accelerating
a. Worn universal joint. Remove driveshaft and replace universal joint.
b. Driveshaft misaligned. Check for collapsed or damaged engine and transmission mounts, and replace as necessary.
c. Driveshaft bent or out of balance. Replace damaged components and reinstall.
d. Driveshaft out of balance. Remove the driveshaft and have it balanced by a competent professional, or replace the driveshaft assembly.

NOTE: Most driveshafts are linked together by universal joints; however, some manufacturers use Constant Velocity (CV) joints or rubber flex couplers.

2-G. Axles

All Wheel and Four Wheel Drive Vehicles

1. Front or rear wheel makes a clicking noise
a. Check for debris such as a pebble, nail or glass in the tire or tire tread. Carefully remove the debris. Small rocks and pebbles rarely cause a puncture; however, a sharp object should be removed carefully at a facility capable of performing tire repairs.
b. Check for a loose, damaged or worn Constant Velocity (CV) joint and replace if defective.

2. Front or rear wheel vibrates with increased speed
a. Check for a bent rim and replace, if damaged.
b. Check the tires for balance or internal damage and replace if defective.
c. Check for a loose, worn or damaged wheel bearing and replace if defective.
d. Check for a loose, damaged or worn Constant Velocity (CV) joint and replace if defective.

Front Wheel Drive Vehicles

3. Front wheel makes a clicking noise
a. Check for debris such as a pebble, nail or glass in the tire or tire tread. Carefully remove the debris. Small rocks and pebbles rarely cause a puncture; however, a sharp object should be removed carefully at a facility capable of performing tire repairs.
b. Check for a loose, damaged or worn Constant Velocity (CV) joint and replace if defective.

4. Rear wheel makes a clicking noise
a. Check for debris such as a pebble, nail or glass in the tire or tire tread. Carefully remove the debris. Small rocks and pebbles rarely cause a puncture; however, a sharp object should be removed carefully at a facility capable of performing tire repairs.

Rear Wheel Drive Vehicles

5. Front or rear wheel makes a clicking noise
a. Check for debris such as a pebble, nail or glass in the tire or tire tread. Carefully remove the debris. Small rocks and pebbles rarely cause a puncture; however, a sharp object should be removed carefully at a facility capable of performing tire repairs.

6. Rear wheel shudders or vibrates
a. Check for a bent rear wheel or axle assembly and replace defective components.
b. Check for a loose, damaged or worn rear wheel bearing and replace as necessary.

2-H. Other Drive Train Conditions

1. Burning odor from center of vehicle when accelerating
a. Check for a seizing brake hydraulic component such as a brake caliper. Check the caliper piston for surface damage such as rust, and measure for out-of-round wear and caliper-to-piston clearance. For additional information on brake related odors, refer to section 3-A, condition number 9.
b. On vehicles with a manual transmission, check for a slipping clutch. For possible causes and additional information, refer to section 2-C, condition number 1.

c. On vehicles with an automatic transmission, check the fluid level and condition. Top off or change the fluid and filter using the recommended replacement parts, lubricant type and amount. If the odor persists, transmission removal and disassembly will be necessary.

2. Engine accelerates, but vehicle does not gain speed

a. On vehicles with a manual transmission, check for a slipping or damaged clutch. For possible causes and additional information refer to section 2-C, condition number 1.

b. On vehicles with an automatic transmission, check the fluid level and condition. Top off or change the fluid and filter using the recommended replacement parts, lubricant type and amount. If the slipping continues, transmission removal and disassembly will be necessary.

3. BRAKE SYSTEM

3-A. Brake System Troubleshooting

1. Brake pedal pulsates or shimmies when pressed

a. Check wheel lug nut torque and tighten evenly to specification.

b. Check the brake rotor for trueness and thickness variations. Replace the rotor if it is too thin, warped, or if the thickness varies beyond specification. Some rotors can be machined; consult the manufacturer's specifications and recommendations before using a machined brake rotor.

c. Check the brake caliper or caliper bracket mounting bolt torque and inspect for looseness. Torque the mounting bolts and inspect for wear or any looseness, including worn mounting brackets, bushings and sliding pins.

d. Check the wheel bearing for looseness. If the bearing is loose, adjust if possible, otherwise replace the bearing.

2. Brakes make a squealing noise

a. Check the brake rotor for the presence of a ridge on the outer edge; if present, remove the ridge or replace the brake rotor and brake pads.

b. Check for debris in the brake lining material, clean and reinstall.

c. Check the brake linings for wear and replace the brake linings if wear is approaching the lining wear limit.

d. Check the brake linings for glazing. Inspect the brake drum or rotor surface and replace, along with the brake linings, if the surface is not smooth or even.

e. Check the brake pad or shoe mounting areas for a lack of lubricant or the presence of surface rust. Clean and lubricate with a recommended high temperature brake grease.

3. Brakes make a grinding noise

a. Check the brake linings and brake surface areas for severe wear or damage. Replace worn or damaged parts.

b. Check for a seized or partially seized brake causing premature or uneven brake wear, excessive heat and brake rotor or drum damage. Replace defective parts and inspect the wheel bearing condition, which could have been damaged due to excessive heat.

4. Vehicle pulls to one side during braking

a. Check for air in the brake hydraulic system. Inspect the brake hydraulic seals, fluid lines and related components for fluid leaks. Remove the air from the brake system by bleeding the brakes. Be sure to use fresh brake fluid that meets the manufacturer's recommended standards.

b. Check for an internally restricted flexible brake hydraulic hose. Replace the hose and flush the brake system.

c. Check for a seizing brake hydraulic component such as a brake caliper. Check the caliper piston for surface damage such as rust, and measure for out-of-round wear and caliper-to-piston clearance. Overhaul or replace failed parts and flush the brake system.

d. Check the vehicle's alignment and inspect for suspension wear. Replace worn bushings, ball joints and set alignment to the manufacturer's specifications.

e. If the brake system uses drum brakes front or rear, check the brake adjustment. Inspect for seized adjusters and clean or replace, then properly adjust.

5. Brake pedal feels spongy or has excessive travel

a. Check the brake fluid level and condition. If the fluid is contaminated or has not been flushed every two years, clean the master cylinder reservoir, and bleed and flush the brakes using fresh brake fluid that meets the manufacturer's recommended standards.

b. Check for a weak or damaged flexible brake hydraulic hose. Replace the hose and flush the brake system.

c. If the brake system uses drum brakes front or rear, check the brake adjustment. Inspect for seized adjusters and clean or replace, then properly adjust.

6. Brake pedal feel is firm, but brakes lack sufficient stopping power or fade

a. Check the operation of the brake booster and brake booster check valve. Replace worn or failed parts.

b. Check brake linings and brake surface areas for glazing and replace worn or damaged parts.

c. Check for seized hydraulic parts and linkages, and clean or replace as needed.

7. Vehicle has excessive front end dive or locks rear brakes too easily

a. Check for worn, failed or seized brake proportioning valve and replace the valve.

b. Check for a seized, disconnected or missing spring or linkage for the brake proportioning valve. Replace missing parts or repair as necessary.

8. Brake pedal goes to floor when pressed and will not pump up

a. Check the brake hydraulic fluid level and inspect the fluid lines and seals for leakage. Repair or replace leaking components, then bleed and flush the brake system using fresh brake fluid that meets the manufacturer's recommended standards.

b. Check the brake fluid level. Inspect the brake fluid level and brake hydraulic seals. If the fluid level is ok, and the brake hydraulic system is free of hydraulic leaks, replace the brake master cylinder, then bleed and flush the brake system using fresh brake fluid that meets the manufacturer's recommended standards.

9. Brakes produce a burning odor

a. Check for a seizing brake hydraulic component such as a brake caliper. Check the caliper piston for surface damage such as rust, and measure for out-of-round wear and caliper-to-piston clearance. Overhaul or replace failed parts and flush the brake system.

b. Check for an internally restricted flexible brake hydraulic hose. Replace the hose and flush the brake system.

c. Check the parking brake release mechanism, seized linkage or cable, and repair as necessary.

BRAKE PERFORMANCE TROUBLESHOOTING HINTS

Brake vibrations or pulsation can often be diagnosed on a safe and careful test drive. A brake vibration which is felt through the brake pedal while braking, but not felt in the steering wheel, is most likely caused by brake surface variations in the rear brakes. If both the brake pedal and steering wheel vibrate during braking, a surface variation in the front brakes, or both front and rear brakes, is very likely.

A brake pedal that pumps up with repeated use can be caused by air in the brake hydraulic system or, if the vehicle is equipped with rear drum brakes, the brake adjusters may be seized or out of adjustment. A quick test for brake adjustment on vehicles with rear drum brakes is to pump the brake pedal several times with the vehicle's engine not running and the parking brake released. Pump the brake pedal several times and continue to apply pressure to the brake pedal. With pressure being applied to the brake pedal, engage the parking brake. Release the brake pedal and quickly press the brake pedal again. If the brake pedal pumped up, the rear brakes are in need of adjustment. Do not compensate for the rear brake adjustment by adjusting the parking brake, this will cause premature brake lining wear.

To test a vacuum brake booster, pump the brake pedal several times with the vehicle's engine off. Apply pressure to the brake pedal and then start the engine. The brake pedal should move downward about one inch (25mm).

4. WHEELS, TIRES, STEERING AND SUSPENSION

4-A. Wheels and Wheel Bearings

1. Front wheel or wheel bearing loose

All Wheel and Four Wheel Drive Vehicles

a. Torque lug nuts and axle nuts to specification and recheck for looseness.

b. Wheel bearing worn or damaged. Replace wheel bearing.

Front Wheel Drive Vehicles

a. Torque lug nuts and axle nuts to specification and recheck for looseness.

b. Wheel bearing worn or damaged. Replace wheel bearing.

c. Wheel bearing out of adjustment. Adjust wheel bearing to specification; if still loose, replace.

Rear Wheel Drive Vehicles

a. Wheel bearing out of adjustment. Adjust wheel bearing to specification; if still loose, replace.

b. Torque lug nuts to specification and recheck for looseness.

c. Wheel bearing worn or damaged. Replace wheel bearing.

2. Rear wheel or wheel bearing loose

All Wheel and Four Wheel Drive Vehicles

a. Torque lug nuts and axle nuts to specification and recheck for looseness.

b. Wheel bearing worn or damaged. Replace wheel bearing.

Front Wheel Drive Vehicles

a. Wheel bearing out of adjustment. Adjust wheel bearing to specification; if still loose, replace.

b. Torque lug nuts to specification and recheck for looseness.

c. Wheel bearing worn or damaged. Replace wheel bearing.

Rear Wheel Drive Vehicles

a. Torque lug nuts to specification and recheck for looseness.

b. Wheel bearing worn or damaged. Replace wheel bearing.

4-B. Tires

1. Tires worn on inside tread

a. Check alignment for a toed-out condition. Check and set tire pressures and properly adjust the toe.

b. Check for worn, damaged or defective suspension components. Replace defective parts and adjust the alignment.

2. Tires worn on outside tread

a. Check alignment for a toed-in condition. Check and set tire pressures and properly adjust the toe.

b. Check for worn, damaged or defective suspension components. Replace defective parts and adjust the alignment.

3. Tires worn unevenly

a. Check the tire pressure and tire balance. Replace worn or defective tires and check the alignment; adjust if necessary.

b. Check for worn shock absorbers. Replaced failed components, worn or defective tires and check the alignment; adjust if necessary.

c. Check the alignment settings. Check and set tire pressures and properly adjust the alignment to specification.

d. Check for worn, damaged or defective suspension components. Replace defective parts and adjust the alignment to specification.

4-C. Steering

1. Excessive play in steering wheel
a. Check the steering gear free-play adjustment and properly adjust to remove excessive play.
b. Check the steering linkage for worn, damaged or defective parts. Replace failed components and perform a front end alignment.
c. Check for a worn, damaged, or defective steering box, replace the steering gear and check the front end alignment.

2. Steering wheel shakes at cruising speeds
a. Check for a bent front wheel. Replace a damaged wheel and check the tire for possible internal damage.
b. Check for an unevenly worn front tire. Replace the tire, adjust tire pressure and balance.
c. Check the front tires for hidden internal damage. Tires which have encountered large pot holes or suffered other hard blows may have sustained internal damage and should be replaced immediately.
d. Check the front tires for an out-of-balance condition. Remove, spin balance and reinstall. Torque all the wheel bolts or lug nuts to the recommended specification.
e. Check for a loose wheel bearing. If possible, adjust the bearing, or replace the bearing if it is a non-adjustable bearing.

3. Steering wheel shakes when braking
a. Refer to section 3-A, condition number 1.

4. Steering wheel becomes stiff when turned
a. Check the steering wheel free-play adjustment and reset as needed.
b. Check for a damaged steering gear assembly. Replace the steering gear and perform a front end alignment.
c. Check for damaged or seized suspension components. Replace defective components and perform a front end alignment.

4-D. Suspension

1. Vehicle pulls to one side
a. Tire pressure uneven. Adjust tire pressure to recommended settings.
b. Tires worn unevenly. Replace tires and check alignment settings.
c. Alignment out of specification. Align front end and check thrust angle.
d. Check for a dragging brake and repair or replace as necessary.

2. Vehicle is very bouncy over bumps
a. Check for worn or leaking shock absorbers or strut assemblies and replace as necessary.
b. Check for seized shock absorbers or strut assemblies and replace as necessary.

NOTE: When one shock fails, it is recommended to replace front or rear units as pairs.

3. Vehicle leans excessively in turns
a. Check for worn or leaking shock absorbers or strut assemblies and replace as necessary.
b. Check for missing, damaged, or worn stabilizer links or bushings, and replace or install as necessary.

4. Vehicle ride quality seems excessively harsh
a. Check for seized shock absorbers or strut assemblies and replace as necessary.
b. Check for excessively high tire pressures and adjust pressures to vehicle recommendations.

5. Vehicle seems low or leans to one side
a. Check for a damaged, broken or weak spring. Replace defective parts and check for a needed alignment.
b. Check for seized shock absorbers or strut assemblies and replace as necessary.
c. Check for worn or leaking shock absorbers or strut assemblies and replace as necessary.

4-E. Driving Noises and Vibrations

Noises

1. Vehicle makes a clicking noises when driven
a. Check the noise to see if it varies with road speed. Verify if the noise is present when coasting or with steering or throttle input. If the clicking noise frequency changes with road speed and is not affected by steering or throttle input, check the tire treads for a stone, piece of glass, nail or another hard object imbedded into the tire or tire tread. Stones rarely cause a tire puncture and are easily removed. Other objects may create an air leak when removed. Consider having these objects removed immediately at a facility equipped to repair tire punctures.
b. If the clicking noise varies with throttle input and steering, check for a worn Constant Velocity (CV-joint) joint, universal (U- joint) or flex joint.

2. Vehicle makes a clunking or knocking noise over bumps
a. A clunking noise over bumps is most often caused by excessive movement or clearance in a suspension component. Check the suspension for soft, cracked, damaged or worn bushings. Replace the bushings and check the vehicle's alignment.
b. Check for loose suspension mounting bolts. Check the tightness on subframe bolts, pivot bolts and suspension mounting bolts, and torque to specification.
c. Check the vehicle for a loose wheel bearing. Some wheel bearings can be adjusted for looseness, while others must be replaced if loose. Adjust or replace the bearings as recommended by the manufacturer.
d. Check the door latch adjustment. If the door is slightly loose, or the latch adjustment is not centered, the door assembly may create noises over bumps and rough surfaces. Properly adjust the door latches to secure the door.

3. Vehicle makes a low pitched rumbling noise when driven

a. A low pitched rumbling noise is usually caused by a drive train related bearing and is most often associated with a wheel bearing which has been damaged or worn. The damage can be caused by excessive brake temperatures or physical contact with a pot hole or curb. Sometimes the noise will vary when turning. Left hand turns increase the load on the vehicle's right side, and right turns load the left side. A failed front wheel bearing may also cause a slight steering wheel vibration when turning. A bearing which exhibits noise must be replaced.

b. Check the tire condition and balance. An internally damaged tire may cause failure symptoms similar to failed suspension parts. For diagnostic purposes, try a known good set of tires and replace defective tires.

4. Vehicle makes a squeaking noise over bumps

a. Check the vehicle's ball joints for wear, damaged or leaking boots. Replace a ball joint if it is loose, the boot is damaged and leaking, or the ball joint is binding. When replacing suspension parts, check the vehicle for alignment.

b. Check for seized or deteriorated bushings. Replace bushings that are worn or damaged and check the vehicle for alignment.

c. Check for the presence of sway bar or stabilizer bar bushings which wrap around the bar. Inspect the condition of the bushings and replace if worn or damaged. Remove the bushing bracket and apply a thin layer of suspension grease to the area where the bushings wrap around the bar and reinstall the bushing brackets.

Vibrations

5. Vehicle vibrates when driven

a. Check the road surface. Roads which have rough or uneven surfaces may cause unusual vibrations.

b. Check the tire condition and balance. An internally damaged tire may cause failure symptoms similar to failed suspension parts. For diagnostic purposes, try a known good set of tires and replace defective tires immediately.

c. Check for a worn Constant Velocity (CV-joint) joint, universal (U- joint) or flex joint and replace if loose, damaged or binding.

d. Check for a loose, bent, or out-of-balance axle or drive shaft. Replace damaged or failed components.

NOTE: Diagnosing failures related to wheels, tires, steering and the suspension system can often times be accomplished with a careful and thorough test drive. Bearing noises are isolated by noting whether the noises or symptoms vary when turning left or right, or occur while driving a straight line. During a left hand turn, the vehicle's weight shifts to the right, placing more force on the right side bearings, such that if a right side wheel bearing is worn or damaged, the noise or vibration should increase during light-to-heavy acceleration. Conversely, on right hand turns, the vehicle tends to lean to the left, loading the left side bearings.

Knocking noises in the suspension when the vehicle is driven over rough roads, railroad tracks and speed bumps indicate worn suspension components such as bushings, ball joints or tie rod ends, or a worn steering system.

5. ELECTRICAL ACCESSORIES

5-A. Headlights

1. One headlight only works on high or low beam

a. Check for battery voltage at headlight electrical connector. If battery voltage is present, replace the headlight assembly or bulb if available separately. If battery voltage is not present, refer to the headlight wiring diagram to troubleshoot.

2. Headlight does not work on high or low beam

a. Check for battery voltage and ground at headlight electrical connector. If battery voltage is present, check the headlight connector ground terminal for a proper ground. If battery voltage and ground are present at the headlight connector, replace the headlight assembly or bulb if available separately. If battery voltage or ground is not present, refer to the headlight wiring diagram to troubleshoot.

b. Check the headlight switch operation. Replace the switch if the switch is defective or operates intermittently.

3. Headlight(s) very dim

a. Check for battery voltage and ground at headlight electrical connector. If battery voltage is present, trace the ground circuit for the headlamp electrical connector, then clean and repair as necessary.

If the voltage at the headlight electrical connector is significantly less than the voltage at the battery, refer to the headlight wiring diagram to troubleshoot and locate the voltage drop.

5-B. Tail, Running and Side Marker Lights

1. Tail light, running light or side marker light inoperative

a. Check for battery voltage and ground at light's electrical connector. If battery voltage is present, check the bulb socket and electrical connector ground terminal for a proper ground. If battery voltage and ground are present at the light connector, but not in the socket, clean the socket and the ground terminal connector. If battery voltage and ground are present in the bulb socket, replace the bulb. If battery voltage or ground is not present, refer to the wiring diagram to troubleshoot for an open circuit.

b. Check the light switch operation and replace if necessary.

2. Tail light, running light or side marker light works intermittently

a. Check the bulb for a damaged filament, and replace if damaged.

b. Check the bulb and bulb socket for corrosion, and clean or replace the bulb and socket.

c. Check for loose, damaged or corroded wires and electrical terminals, and repair as necessary.
d. Check the light switch operation and replace if necessary.

3. Tail light, running light or side marker light very dim

a. Check the bulb and bulb socket for corrosion and clean or replace the bulb and socket.
b. Check for low voltage at the bulb socket positive terminal or a poor ground. If voltage is low, or the ground marginal, trace the wiring to, and check for loose, damaged or corroded wires and electrical terminals; repair as necessary.
c. Check the light switch operation and replace if necessary.

5-C. Interior Lights

1. Interior light inoperative

a. Verify the interior light switch location and position(s), and set the switch in the correct position.
b. Check for battery voltage and ground at the interior light bulb socket. If battery voltage and ground are present, replace the bulb. If voltage is not present, check the interior light fuse for battery voltage. If the fuse is missing, replace the fuse. If the fuse has blown, or if battery voltage is present, refer to the wiring diagram to troubleshoot the cause for an open or shorted circuit. If ground is not present, check the door switch contacts and clean or repair as necessary.

2. Interior light works intermittently

a. Check the bulb for a damaged filament, and replace if damaged.
b. Check the bulb and bulb socket for corrosion, and clean or replace the bulb and socket.
c. Check for loose, damaged or corroded wires and electrical terminals; repair as necessary.
d. Check the door and light switch operation, and replace if necessary.

3. Interior light very dim

a. Check the bulb and bulb socket for corrosion, and clean or replace the bulb and socket.
b. Check for low voltage at the bulb socket positive terminal or a poor ground. If voltage is low, or the ground marginal, trace the wiring to, and check for loose, damaged or corroded wires and electrical terminals; repair as necessary.
c. Check the door and light switch operation, and replace if necessary.

5-D. Brake Lights

1. One brake light inoperative

a. Press the brake pedal and check for battery voltage and ground at the brake light bulb socket. If present, replace the bulb. If either battery voltage or ground is not present, refer to the wiring diagram to troubleshoot.

2. Both brake lights inoperative

a. Press the brake pedal and check for battery voltage and ground at the brake light bulb socket. If present, replace both bulbs. If

battery voltage is not present, check the brake light switch adjustment and adjust as necessary. If the brake light switch is properly adjusted, and battery voltage or the ground is not present at the bulb sockets, or at the bulb electrical connector with the brake pedal pressed, refer to the wiring diagram to troubleshoot the cause of an open circuit.

3. One or both brake lights very dim

a. Press the brake pedal and measure the voltage at the brake light bulb socket. If the measured voltage is close to the battery voltage, check for a poor ground caused by a loose, damaged, or corroded wire, terminal, bulb or bulb socket. If the ground is bolted to a painted surface, it may be necessary to remove the electrical connector and clean the mounting surface, so the connector mounts on bare metal. If battery voltage is low, check for a poor connection caused by either a faulty brake light switch, a loose, damaged, or corroded wire, terminal or electrical connector. Refer to the wiring diagram to troubleshoot the cause of a voltage drop.

5-E. Warning Lights

1. Warning light(s) stay on when the engine is started

Ignition, Battery or Alternator Warning Light

a. Check the alternator output and voltage regulator operation, and replace as necessary.
b. Check the warning light wiring for a shorted wire.

Check Engine Light

a. Check the engine for routine maintenance and tune-up status. Note the engine tune-up specifications and verify the spark plug, air filter and engine oil condition; replace and/or adjust items as necessary.
b. Check the fuel tank for low fuel level, causing an intermittent lean fuel mixture. Top off fuel tank and reset check engine light.
c. Check for a failed or disconnected engine fuel or ignition component, sensor or control unit and repair or replace as necessary.
d. Check the intake manifold and vacuum hoses for air leaks and repair as necessary.
e. Check the engine's mechanical condition for excessive oil consumption.

Anti-Lock Braking System (ABS) Light

a. Check the wheel sensors and sensor rings for debris, and clean as necessary.
b. Check the brake master cylinder for fluid leakage or seal failure and replace as necessary.
c. Check the ABS control unit, pump and proportioning valves for proper operation; replace as necessary.
d. Check the sensor wiring at the wheel sensors and the ABS control unit for a loose or shorted wire, and repair as necessary.

Brake Warning Light

a. Check the brake fluid level and check for possible leakage from the hydraulic lines and seals. Top off brake fluid and repair leakage as necessary.

b. Check the brake linings for wear and replace as necessary.

c. Check for a loose or shorted brake warning light sensor or wire, and replace or repair as necessary.

Oil Pressure Warning Light

a. Stop the engine immediately. Check the engine oil level and oil filter condition, and top off or change the oil as necessary.

b. Check the oil pressure sensor wire for being shorted to ground. Disconnect the wire from the oil pressure sensor and with the ignition in the ON position, but not running, the oil pressure light should not be working. If the light works with the wire disconnected, check the sensor wire for being shorted to ground. Check the wire routing to make sure the wire is not pinched and check for insulation damage. Repair or replace the wire as necessary and recheck before starting the engine.

c. Remove the oil pan and check for a clogged oil pick-up tube screen.

d. Check the oil pressure sensor operation by substituting a known good sensor.

e. Check the oil filter for internal restrictions or leaks, and replace as necessary.

WARNING: If the engine is operated with oil pressure below the manufacturer's specification, severe (and costly) engine damage could occur. Low oil pressure can be caused by excessive internal wear or damage to the engine bearings, oil pressure relief valve, oil pump or oil pump drive mechanism.

Before starting the engine, check for possible causes of rapid oil loss, such as leaking oil lines or a loose, damaged, restricted, or leaking oil filter or oil pressure sensor. If the engine oil level and condition are acceptable, measure the engine's oil pressure using a pressure gauge, or determine the cause for the oil pressure warning light to function when the engine is running, before operating the engine for an extended period of time. Another symptom of operating an engine with low oil pressure is the presence of severe knocking and tapping noises.

Parking Brake Warning Light

a. Check the brake release mechanism and verify the parking brake has been fully released.

b. Check the parking brake light switch for looseness or misalignment.

c. Check for a damaged switch or a loose or shorted brake light switch wire, and replace or repair as necessary.

2. Warning light(s) flickers on and off when driving

Ignition, Battery or Alternator Warning Light

a. Check the alternator output and voltage regulator operation. An intermittent condition may indicate worn brushes, an internal short, or a defective voltage regulator. Replace the alternator or failed component.

b. Check the warning light wiring for a shorted, pinched or damaged wire and repair as necessary.

Check Engine Light

a. Check the engine for required maintenance and tune-up status. Verify engine tune-up specifications, as well as spark plug, air filter and engine oil condition; replace and/or adjust items as necessary.

b. Check the fuel tank for low fuel level causing an intermittent lean fuel mixture. Top off fuel tank and reset check engine light.

c. Check for an intermittent failure or partially disconnected engine fuel and ignition component, sensor or control unit; repair or replace as necessary.

d. Check the intake manifold and vacuum hoses for air leaks, and repair as necessary.

e. Check the warning light wiring for a shorted, pinched or damaged wire and repair as necessary.

Anti-Lock Braking System (ABS) Light

a. Check the wheel sensors and sensor rings for debris, and clean as necessary.

b. Check the brake master cylinder for fluid leakage or seal failure and replace as necessary.

c. Check the ABS control unit, pump and proportioning valves for proper operation, and replace as necessary.

d. Check the sensor wiring at the wheel sensors and the ABS control unit for a loose or shorted wire and repair as necessary.

Brake Warning Light

a. Check the brake fluid level and check for possible leakage from the hydraulic lines and seals. Top off brake fluid and repair leakage as necessary.

b. Check the brake linings for wear and replace as necessary.

c. Check for a loose or shorted brake warning light sensor or wire, and replace or repair as necessary.

Oil Pressure Warning Light

a. Stop the engine immediately. Check the engine oil level and check for a sudden and rapid oil loss, such as a leaking oil line or oil pressure sensor, and repair or replace as necessary.

b. Check the oil pressure sensor operation by substituting a known good sensor.

c. Check the oil pressure sensor wire for being shorted to ground. Disconnect the wire from the oil pressure sensor and with the ignition in the ON position, but not running, the oil pressure light should not be working. If the light works with the wire disconnected, check the sensor wire for being shorted to ground. Check the wire routing to make sure the wire is not pinched and check for insulation damage. Repair or replace the wire as necessary and recheck before starting the engine.

d. Remove the oil pan and check for a clogged oil pick-up tube screen.

Parking Brake Warning Light

a. Check the brake release mechanism and verify the parking brake has been fully released.

b. Check the parking brake light switch for looseness or misalignment.

c. Check for a damaged switch or a loose or shorted brake light switch wire, and replace or repair as necessary.

3. Warning light(s) inoperative with ignition on, and engine not started

a. Check for a defective bulb by installing a known good bulb.

b. Check for a defective wire using the appropriate wiring diagram(s).

c. Check for a defective sending unit by removing and then grounding the wire at the sending unit. If the light comes on with the ignition on when grounding the wire, replace the sending unit.

5-F. Turn Signal and 4-Way Hazard Lights

1. Turn signals or hazard lights come on, but do not flash

a. Check for a defective flasher unit and replace as necessary.

2. Turn signals or hazard lights do not function on either side

a. Check the fuse and replace, if defective.

b. Check the flasher unit by substituting a known good flasher unit.

c. Check the turn signal electrical system for a defective component, open circuit, short circuit or poor ground.

3. Turn signals or hazard lights only work on one side

a. Check for failed bulbs and replace as necessary.

b. Check for poor grounds in both housings and repair as necessary.

4. One signal light does not work

a. Check for a failed bulb and replace as necessary.

b. Check for corrosion in the bulb socket, and clean and repair as necessary.

c. Check for a poor ground at the bulb socket, and clean and repair as necessary.

5. Turn signals flash too slowly

a. Check signal bulb(s) wattage and replace with lower wattage bulb(s).

6. Turn signals flash too fast

a. Check signal bulb(s) wattage and replace with higher wattage bulb(s).

b. Check for installation of the correct flasher unit and replace if incorrect.

7. Four-way hazard flasher indicator light inoperative

a. Verify that the exterior lights are functioning and, if so, replace indicator bulb.

b. Check the operation of the warning flasher switch and replace if defective.

8. Turn signal indicator light(s) do not work in either direction

a. Verify that the exterior lights are functioning and, if so, replace indicator bulb(s).

b. Check for a defective flasher unit by substituting a known good unit.

9. One turn signal indicator light does not work

a. Check for a defective bulb and replace as necessary.

b. Check for a defective flasher unit by substituting a known good unit.

5-G. Horn

1. Horn does not operate

a. Check for a defective fuse and replace as necessary.

b. Check for battery voltage and ground at horn electrical connections when pressing the horn switch. If voltage is present, replace the horn assembly. If voltage or ground is not present, refer to Chassis Electrical coverage for additional troubleshooting techniques and circuit information.

2. Horn has an unusual tone

a. On single horn systems, replace the horn.

b. On dual horn systems, check the operation of the second horn. Dual horn systems have a high and low pitched horn. Unplug one horn at a time and recheck operation. Replace the horn which does not function.

c. Check for debris or condensation build-up in horn and verify the horn positioning. If the horn has a single opening, adjust the opening downward to allow for adequate drainage and to prevent debris build-up.

5-H. Windshield Wipers

1. Windshield wipers do not operate

a. Check fuse and replace as necessary.

b. Check switch operation and repair or replace as necessary.

c. Check for corroded, loose, disconnected or broken wires and clean or repair as necessary.

d. Check the ground circuit for the wiper switch or motor and repair as necessary.

2. Windshield wiper motor makes a humming noise, gets hot or blows fuses

a. Wiper motor damaged internally; replace the wiper motor.

b. Wiper linkage bent, damaged or seized. Repair or replace wiper linkage as necessary.

3. Windshield wiper motor operates, but one or both wipers fail to move

a. Windshield wiper motor linkage loose or disconnected. Repair or replace linkage as necessary.

b. Windshield wiper arms loose on wiper pivots. Secure wiper arm to pivot or replace both the wiper arm and pivot assembly.

4. Windshield wipers will not park

a. Check the wiper switch operation and verify that the switch properly interrupts the power supplied to the wiper motor.

b. If the wiper switch is functioning properly, the wiper motor parking circuit has failed. Replace the wiper motor assembly. Operate the wiper motor at least one time before installing the arms and blades to ensure correct positioning, then recheck using the highest wiper speed on a wet windshield to make sure the arms and blades do not contact the windshield trim.

6. INSTRUMENTS AND GAUGES

6-A. Speedometer (Cable Operated)

1. Speedometer does not work

a. Check and verify that the speedometer cable is properly seated into the speedometer assembly and the speedometer drive gear.

b. Check the speedometer cable for breakage or rounded-off cable ends where the cable seats into the speedometer drive gear and into the speedometer assembly. If damaged, broken or the cable ends are rounded off, replace the cable.

c. Check speedometer drive gear condition and replace as necessary.

d. Install a known good speedometer to test for proper operation. If the substituted speedometer functions properly, replace the speedometer assembly.

2. Speedometer needle fluctuates when driving at steady speeds.

a. Check speedometer cable routing or sheathing for sharp bends or kinks. Route cable to minimize sharp bends or kinks. If the sheathing has been damaged, replace the cable assembly.

b. Check the speedometer cable for adequate lubrication. Remove the cable, inspect for damage, clean, lubricate and reinstall. If the cable has been damaged, replace the cable.

3. Speedometer works intermittently

a. Check the cable and verify that the cable is fully installed and the fasteners are secure.

b. Check the cable ends for wear and rounding, and replace as necessary.

6-B. Speedometer (Electronically Operated)

1. Speedometer does not work

a. Check the speed sensor pickup and replace as necessary.

b. Check the wiring between the speed sensor and the speedometer for corroded terminals, loose connections or broken wires and clean or repair as necessary.

c. Install a known good speedometer to test for proper operation. If the substituted speedometer functions properly, replace the speedometer assembly.

2. Speedometer works intermittently

a. Check the wiring between the speed sensor and the speedometer for corroded terminals, loose connections or broken wires and clean or repair as necessary.

b. Check the speed sensor pickup and replace as necessary.

6-C. Fuel, Temperature and Oil Pressure Gauges

1. Gauge does not register

a. Check for a missing or blown fuse and replace as necessary.

b. Check for an open circuit in the gauge wiring. Repair wiring as necessary.

c. Gauge sending unit defective. Replace gauge sending unit.

d. Gauge or sending unit improperly installed. Verify installation and wiring, and repair as necessary.

2. Gauge operates erratically

a. Check for loose, shorted, damaged or corroded electrical connections or wiring and repair as necessary.

b. Check gauge sending units and replace as necessary.

3. Gauge operates fully pegged

a. Sending unit-to-gauge wire shorted to ground.

b. Sending unit defective; replace sending unit.

c. Gauge or sending unit not properly grounded.

d. Gauge or sending unit improperly installed. Verify installation and wiring, and repair as necessary.

7. CLIMATE CONTROL

7-A. Air Conditioner

1. No air coming from air conditioner vents

a. Check the air conditioner fuse and replace as necessary.

b. Air conditioner system discharged. Have the system evacuated, charged and leak tested by an MVAC certified technician, utilizing approved recovery/recycling equipment. Repair as necessary.

c. Air conditioner low pressure switch defective. Replace switch.

d. Air conditioner fan resistor pack defective. Replace resistor pack.

e. Loose connection, broken wiring or defective air conditioner relay in air conditioning electrical circuit. Repair wiring or replace relay as necessary.

2. Air conditioner blows warm air

a. Air conditioner system is discharged. Have the system evacuated, charged and leak tested by an MVAC certified technician, utilizing approved recovery/recycling equipment. Repair as necessary.

b. Air conditioner compressor clutch not engaging. Check compressor clutch wiring, electrical connections and compressor clutch, and repair or replace as necessary.

3. Water collects on the interior floor when the air conditioner is used

a. Air conditioner evaporator drain hose is blocked. Clear the drain hose where it exits the passenger compartment.

b. Air conditioner evaporator drain hose is disconnected. Secure the drain hose to the evaporator drainage tray under the dashboard.

4. Air conditioner has a moldy odor when used

a. The air conditioner evaporator drain hose is blocked or partially re-stricted, allowing condensation to build up around the evaporator and drainage tray. Clear the drain hose where it exits the passenger compartment.

7-B. Heater

1. Blower motor does not operate

a. Check blower motor fuse and replace as necessary.
b. Check blower motor wiring for loose, damaged or corroded contacts and repair as necessary.
c. Check blower motor switch and resistor pack for open circuits, and repair or replace as necessary.
d. Check blower motor for internal damage and repair or replace as necessary.

2. Heater blows cool air

a. Check the engine coolant level. If the coolant level is low, top off and bleed the air from the cooling system as necessary and check for coolant leaks.
b. Check engine coolant operating temperature. If coolant temperature is below specification, check for a damaged or stuck thermostat.

c. Check the heater control valve operation. Check the heater control valve cable or vacuum hose for proper installation. Move the heater temperature control from hot to cold several times and verify the operation of the heater control valve. With the engine at normal operating temperature and the heater temperature control in the full hot position, carefully feel the heater hose going into and exiting the control valve. If one heater hose is hot and the other is much cooler, replace the control valve.

3. Heater steams the windshield when used

a. Check for a loose cooling system hose clamp or leaking coolant hose near the engine firewall or under the dash area, and repair as necessary.
b. Check for the existence of a sweet odor and fluid dripping from the heater floor vents, indicating a failed or damaged heater core. Pressure test the cooling system with the heater set to the fully warm position and check for fluid leakage from the floor vents. If leakage is verified, remove and replace the heater core assembly.

NOTE: On some vehicles, the dashboard must be disassembled and removed to access the heater core.

GLOSSARY

AIR/FUEL RATIO: The ratio of air-to-gasoline by weight in the fuel mixture drawn into the engine.

AIR INJECTION: One method of reducing harmful exhaust emissions by injecting air into each of the exhaust ports of an engine. The fresh air entering the hot exhaust manifold causes any remaining fuel to be burned before it can exit the tailpipe.

ALTERNATOR: A device used for converting mechanical energy into electrical energy.

AMMETER: An instrument, calibrated in amperes, used to measure the flow of an electrical current in a circuit. Ammeters are always connected in series with the circuit being tested.

AMPERE: The rate of flow of electrical current present when one volt of electrical pressure is applied against one ohm of electrical resistance.

ANALOG COMPUTER: Any microprocessor that uses similar (analogous) electrical signals to make its calculations.

ARMATURE: A laminated, soft iron core wrapped by a wire that converts electrical energy to mechanical energy as in a motor or relay. When rotated in a magnetic field, it changes mechanical energy into electrical energy as in a generator.

ATMOSPHERIC PRESSURE: The pressure on the Earth's surface caused by the weight of the air in the atmosphere. At sea level, this pressure is 14.7 psi at 32°F (101 kPa at 0°C).

ATOMIZATION: The breaking down of a liquid into a fine mist that can be suspended in air.

AXIAL PLAY: Movement parallel to a shaft or bearing bore.

BACKFIRE: The sudden combustion of gases in the intake or exhaust system that results in a loud explosion.

BACKLASH: The clearance or play between two parts, such as meshed gears.

BACKPRESSURE: Restrictions in the exhaust system that slow the exit of exhaust gases from the combustion chamber.

BAKELITE: A heat resistant, plastic insulator material commonly used in printed circuit boards and transistorized components.

BALL BEARING: A bearing made up of hardened inner and outer races between which hardened steel balls roll.

BALLAST RESISTOR: A resistor in the primary ignition circuit that lowers voltage after the engine is started to reduce wear on ignition components.

BEARING: A friction reducing, supportive device usually located between a stationary part and a moving part.

BIMETAL TEMPERATURE SENSOR: Any sensor or switch made of two dissimilar types of metal that bend when heated or cooled due to the different expansion rates of the alloys. These types of sensors usually function as an on/off switch.

BLOWBY: Combustion gases, composed of water vapor and unburned fuel, that leak past the piston rings into the crankcase during normal engine operation. These gases are removed by the PCV system to prevent the buildup of harmful acids in the crankcase.

BRAKE PAD: A brake shoe and lining assembly used with disc brakes.

BRAKE SHOE: The backing for the brake lining. The term is, however, usually applied to the assembly of the brake backing and lining.

BUSHING: A liner, usually removable, for a bearing; an anti-friction liner used in place of a bearing.

CALIPER: A hydraulically activated device in a disc brake system, which is mounted straddling the brake rotor (disc). The caliper contains at least one piston and two brake pads. Hydraulic pressure on the piston(s) forces the pads against the rotor.

CAMSHAFT: A shaft in the engine on which are the lobes (cams) which operate the valves. The camshaft is driven by the crankshaft, via a belt, chain or gears, at one half the crankshaft speed.

CAPACITOR: A device which stores an electrical charge.

CARBON MONOXIDE (CO): A colorless, odorless gas given off as a normal byproduct of combustion. It is poisonous and extremely dangerous in confined areas, building up slowly to toxic levels without warning if adequate ventilation is not available.

CARBURETOR: A device, usually mounted on the intake manifold of an engine, which mixes the air and fuel in the proper proportion to allow even combustion.

CATALYTIC CONVERTER: A device installed in the exhaust system, like a muffler, that converts harmful byproducts of combustion into carbon dioxide and water vapor by means of a heat-producing chemical reaction.

CENTRIFUGAL ADVANCE: A mechanical method of advancing the spark timing by using flyweights in the distributor that react to centrifugal force generated by the distributor shaft rotation.

CHECK VALVE: Any one-way valve installed to permit the flow of air, fuel or vacuum in one direction only.

CHOKE: A device, usually a moveable valve, placed in the intake path of a carburetor to restrict the flow of air.

CIRCUIT: Any unbroken path through which an electrical current can flow. Also used to describe fuel flow in some instances.

CIRCUIT BREAKER: A switch which protects an electrical circuit from overload by opening the circuit when the current flow exceeds a predetermined level. Some circuit breakers must be reset manually, while most reset automatically.

COIL (IGNITION): A transformer in the ignition circuit which steps up the voltage provided to the spark plugs.

COMBINATION MANIFOLD: An assembly which includes both the intake and exhaust manifolds in one casting.

COMBINATION VALVE: A device used in some fuel systems that routes fuel vapors to a charcoal storage canister instead of venting them into the atmosphere. The valve relieves fuel tank pressure and allows fresh air into the tank as the fuel level drops to prevent a vapor lock situation.

COMPRESSION RATIO: The comparison of the total volume of the cylinder and combustion chamber with the piston at BDC and the piston at TDC.

CONDENSER: 1. An electrical device which acts to store an electrical charge, preventing voltage surges. 2. A radiator-like device in the air conditioning system in which refrigerant gas condenses into a liquid, giving off heat.

CONDUCTOR: Any material through which an electrical current can be transmitted easily.

CONTINUITY: Continuous or complete circuit. Can be checked with an ohmmeter.

COUNTERSHAFT: An intermediate shaft which is rotated by a mainshaft and transmits, in turn, that rotation to a working part.

CRANKCASE: The lower part of an engine in which the crankshaft and related parts operate.

CRANKSHAFT: The main driving shaft of an engine which receives reciprocating motion from the pistons and converts it to rotary motion.

CYLINDER: In an engine, the round hole in the engine block in which the piston(s) ride.

CYLINDER BLOCK: The main structural member of an engine in which is found the cylinders, crankshaft and other principal parts.

CYLINDER HEAD: The detachable portion of the engine, usually fastened to the top of the cylinder block and containing all or most of the combustion chambers. On overhead valve engines, it contains the valves and their operating parts. On overhead cam engines, it contains the camshaft as well.

DEAD CENTER: The extreme top or bottom of the piston stroke.

DETONATION: An unwanted explosion of the air/fuel mixture in the combustion chamber caused by excess heat and compression, advanced timing, or an overly lean mixture. Also referred to as "ping".

DIAPHRAGM: A thin, flexible wall separating two cavities, such as in a vacuum advance unit.

DIESELING: A condition in which hot spots in the combustion chamber cause the engine to run on after the key is turned off.

DIFFERENTIAL: A geared assembly which allows the transmission of motion between drive axles, giving one axle the ability to turn faster than the other.

DIODE: An electrical device that will allow current to flow in one direction only.

DISC BRAKE: A hydraulic braking assembly consisting of a brake disc, or rotor, mounted on an axle, and a caliper assembly containing, usually two brake pads which are activated by hydraulic pressure. The pads are forced against the sides of the disc, creating friction which slows the vehicle.

DISTRIBUTOR: A mechanically driven device on an engine which is responsible for electrically firing the spark plug at a predetermined point of the piston stroke.

DOWEL PIN: A pin, inserted in mating holes in two different parts allowing those parts to maintain a fixed relationship.

DRUM BRAKE: A braking system which consists of two brake shoes and one or two wheel cylinders, mounted on a fixed backing plate, and a brake drum, mounted on an axle, which revolves around the assembly.

DWELL: The rate, measured in degrees of shaft rotation, at which an electrical circuit cycles on and off.

ELECTRONIC CONTROL UNIT (ECU): Ignition module, module, amplifier or igniter. See Module for definition.

ELECTRONIC IGNITION: A system in which the timing and firing of the spark plugs is controlled by an electronic control unit, usually called a module. These systems have no points or condenser.

END-PLAY: The measured amount of axial movement in a shaft.

ENGINE: A device that converts heat into mechanical energy.

EXHAUST MANIFOLD: A set of cast passages or pipes which conduct exhaust gases from the engine.

FEELER GAUGE: A blade, usually metal, or precisely predetermined thickness, used to measure the clearance between two parts.

FIRING ORDER: The order in which combustion occurs in the cylinders of an engine. Also the order in which spark is distributed to the plugs by the distributor.

FLOODING: The presence of too much fuel in the intake manifold and combustion chamber which prevents the air/fuel mixture from firing, thereby causing a no-start situation.

FLYWHEEL: A disc shaped part bolted to the rear end of the crankshaft. Around the outer perimeter is affixed the ring gear. The starter drive engages the ring gear, turning the flywheel, which rotates the crankshaft, imparting the initial starting motion to the engine.

FOOT POUND (ft. lbs. or sometimes, ft.lb.): The amount of energy or work needed to raise an item weighing one pound, a distance of one foot.

FUSE: A protective device in a circuit which prevents circuit overload by breaking the circuit when a specific amperage is present. The device is constructed around a strip or wire of a lower amperage rating than the circuit it is designed to protect. When an amperage higher than that stamped on the fuse is present in the circuit, the strip or wire melts, opening the circuit.

GEAR RATIO: The ratio between the number of teeth on meshing gears.

GENERATOR: A device which converts mechanical energy into electrical energy.

HEAT RANGE: The measure of a spark plug's ability to dissipate heat from its firing end. The higher the heat range, the hotter the plug fires.

HUB: The center part of a wheel or gear.

HYDROCARBON (HC): Any chemical compound made up of hydrogen and carbon. A major pollutant formed by the engine as a byproduct of combustion.

HYDROMETER: An instrument used to measure the specific gravity of a solution.

INCH POUND (inch lbs.; sometimes in.lb. or in. lbs.): One twelfth of a foot pound.

INDUCTION: A means of transferring electrical energy in the form of a magnetic field. Principle used in the ignition coil to increase voltage.

INJECTOR: A device which receives metered fuel under relatively low pressure and is activated to inject the fuel into the engine under relatively high pressure at a predetermined time.

INPUT SHAFT: The shaft to which torque is applied, usually carrying the driving gear or gears.

INTAKE MANIFOLD: A casting of passages or pipes used to conduct air or a fuel/air mixture to the cylinders.

JOURNAL: The bearing surface within which a shaft operates.

KEY: A small block usually fitted in a notch between a shaft and a hub to prevent slippage of the two parts.

MANIFOLD: A casting of passages or set of pipes which connect the cylinders to an inlet or outlet source.

MANIFOLD VACUUM: Low pressure in an engine intake manifold formed just below the throttle plates. Manifold vacuum is highest at idle and drops under acceleration.

MASTER CYLINDER: The primary fluid pressurizing device in a hydraulic system. In automotive use, it is found in brake and hydraulic clutch systems and is pedal activated, either directly or, in a power brake system, through the power booster.

MODULE: Electronic control unit, amplifier or igniter of solid state or integrated design which controls the current flow in the ignition primary circuit based on input from the pick-up coil. When the module opens the primary circuit, high secondary voltage is induced in the coil.

NEEDLE BEARING: A bearing which consists of a number (usually a large number) of long, thin rollers.

OHM: (Ω) The unit used to measure the resistance of conductor-to-electrical flow. One ohm is the amount of resistance that limits current flow to one ampere in a circuit with one volt of pressure.

OHMMETER: An instrument used for measuring the resistance, in ohms, in an electrical circuit.

OUTPUT SHAFT: The shaft which transmits torque from a device, such as a transmission.

OVERDRIVE: A gear assembly which produces more shaft revolutions than that transmitted to it.

OVERHEAD CAMSHAFT (OHC): An engine configuration in which the camshaft is mounted on top of the cylinder head and operates the valve either directly or by means of rocker arms.

OVERHEAD VALVE (OHV): An engine configuration in which all of the valves are located in the cylinder head and the camshaft is located in the cylinder block. The camshaft operates the valves via lifters and pushrods.

OXIDES OF NITROGEN (NOx): Chemical compounds of nitrogen produced as a byproduct of combustion. They combine with hydrocarbons to produce smog.

OXYGEN SENSOR: Use with the feedback system to sense the presence of oxygen in the exhaust gas and signal the computer which can reference the voltage signal to an air/fuel ratio.

PINION: The smaller of two meshing gears.

PISTON RING: An open-ended ring with fits into a groove on the outer diameter of the piston. Its chief function is to form a seal between the piston and cylinder wall. Most automotive pistons have three rings: two for compression sealing; one for oil sealing.

PRELOAD: A predetermined load placed on a bearing during assembly or by adjustment.

PRIMARY CIRCUIT: the low voltage side of the ignition system which consists of the ignition switch, ballast resistor or resistance wire, bypass, coil, electronic control unit and pick-up coil as well as the connecting wires and harnesses.

PRESS FIT: The mating of two parts under pressure, due to the inner diameter of one being smaller than the outer diameter of the other, or vice versa; an interference fit.

RACE: The surface on the inner or outer ring of a bearing on which the balls, needles or rollers move.

REGULATOR: A device which maintains the amperage and/or voltage levels of a circuit at predetermined values.

RELAY: A switch which automatically opens and/or closes a circuit.

RESISTANCE: The opposition to the flow of current through a circuit or electrical device, and is measured in ohms. Resistance is equal to the voltage divided by the amperage.

RESISTOR: A device, usually made of wire, which offers a preset amount of resistance in an electrical circuit.

RING GEAR: The name given to a ring-shaped gear attached to a differential case, or affixed to a flywheel or as part of a planetary gear set.

ROLLER BEARING: A bearing made up of hardened inner and outer races between which hardened steel rollers move.

ROTOR: 1. The disc-shaped part of a disc brake assembly, upon which the brake pads bear; also called, brake disc. 2. The device mounted atop the distributor shaft, which passes current to the distributor cap tower contacts.

SECONDARY CIRCUIT: The high voltage side of the ignition system, usually above 20,000 volts. The secondary includes the ignition coil, coil wire, distributor cap and rotor, spark plug wires and spark plugs.

SENDING UNIT: A mechanical, electrical, hydraulic or electro-magnetic device which transmits information to a gauge.

SENSOR: Any device designed to measure engine operating conditions or ambient pressures and temperatures. Usually electronic in nature and designed to send a voltage signal to an on-board computer, some sensors may operate as a simple on/off switch or they may provide a variable voltage signal (like a potentiometer) as conditions or measured parameters change.

SHIM: Spacers of precise, predetermined thickness used between parts to establish a proper working relationship.

SLAVE CYLINDER: In automotive use, a device in the hydraulic clutch system which is activated by hydraulic force, disengaging the clutch.

SOLENOID: A coil used to produce a magnetic field, the effect of which is to produce work.

SPARK PLUG: A device screwed into the combustion chamber of a spark ignition engine. The basic construction is a conductive core inside of a ceramic insulator, mounted in an outer conductive base. An electrical charge from the spark plug wire travels along the conductive core and jumps a preset air gap to a grounding point or points at the end of the conductive base. The resultant spark ignites the fuel/air mixture in the combustion chamber.

SPLINES: Ridges machined or cast onto the outer diameter of a shaft or inner diameter of a bore to enable parts to mate without rotation.

TACHOMETER: A device used to measure the rotary speed of an engine, shaft, gear, etc., usually in rotations per minute.

THERMOSTAT: A valve, located in the cooling system of an engine, which is closed when cold and opens gradually in response to engine heating, controlling the temperature of the coolant and rate of coolant flow.

TOP DEAD CENTER (TDC): The point at which the piston reaches the top of its travel on the compression stroke.

TORQUE: The twisting force applied to an object.

TORQUE CONVERTER: A turbine used to transmit power from a driving member to a driven member via hydraulic action, providing changes in drive ratio and torque. In automotive use, it links the driveplate at the rear of the engine to the automatic transmission.

TRANSDUCER: A device used to change a force into an electrical signal.

TRANSISTOR: A semi-conductor component which can be actuated by a small voltage to perform an electrical switching function.

TUNE-UP: A regular maintenance function, usually associated with the replacement and adjustment of parts and components in the electrical and fuel systems of a vehicle for the purpose of attaining optimum performance.

TURBOCHARGER: An exhaust driven pump which compresses intake air and forces it into the combustion chambers at higher than atmospheric pressures. The increased air pressure allows more fuel to be burned and results in increased horsepower being produced.

VACUUM ADVANCE: A device which advances the ignition timing in response to increased engine vacuum.

VACUUM GAUGE: An instrument used to measure the presence of vacuum in a chamber.

VALVE: A device which control the pressure, direction of flow or rate of flow of a liquid or gas.

VALVE CLEARANCE: The measured gap between the end of the valve stem and the rocker arm, cam lobe or follower that activates the valve.

VISCOSITY: The rating of a liquid's internal resistance to flow.

VOLTMETER: An instrument used for measuring electrical force in units called volts. Voltmeters are always connected parallel with the circuit being tested.

WHEEL CYLINDER: Found in the automotive drum brake assembly, it is a device, actuated by hydraulic pressure, which, through internal pistons, pushes the brake shoes outward against the drums.

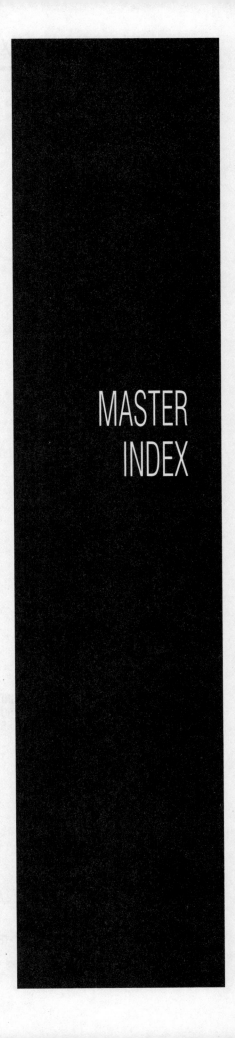

MASTER INDEX

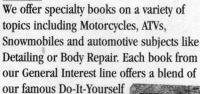

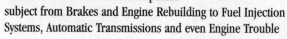